Death in Irish prehistory

Death in Irish prehistory

Gabriel Cooney

Illustrations by Conor McHale

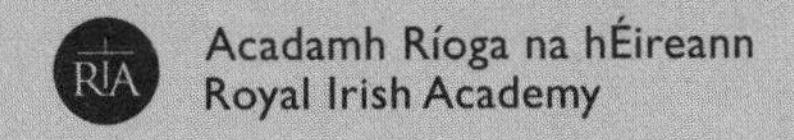

Death in Irish prehistory
First published 2023
Royal Irish Academy, 19 Dawson Street, Dublin 2
ria.ie

ISBN 978-1-80205-009-7 (PB)
ISBN 978-1-80205-010-3 (pdf)
ISBN 978-1-80205-011-0 (epub)

British Library Cataloguing in Publication Data. A CIP catalogue record for this book is available from the British Library.

Edited by Helena King
Book design by Fidelma Slattery
Index by Eileen O'Neill

Printed in Poland by L&C Printing Group

The paper used in this book comes from the wood pulp of sustainably managed forests.

Royal Irish Academy is a member of Publishing Ireland, the Irish book publishers' association

This publication has received support from

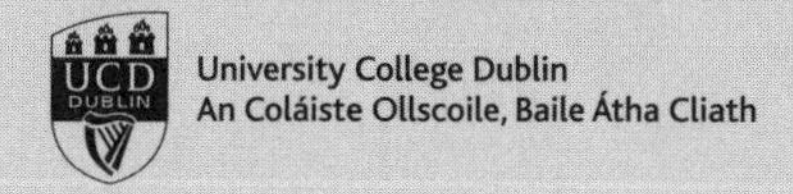

5 4 3 2 1

A note from the publisher
We want to try to offset the environmental impacts of carbon during the production of our books and journals. This year we will plant 45 trees with Easy Treesie. The Easy Treesie—Crann Project organises children to plant trees. Crann—'Trees for Ireland' is a membership-based, non-profit, registered charity (CHY13698) uniting people with a love of trees.

Contents

ACKNOWLEDGEMENTS

I want to start by acknowledging the key role of Conor McHale's illustrations in the book; it has been a pleasure to work with Conor as he responded to ideas and developed the images we have used.

The book has had quite a long history of development, and I am grateful to all the students in UCD who contributed over the years to modules that I taught, and also to numerous colleagues at conferences and seminars for useful discussion and reflection. I am also pleased to acknowledge thc ongoing support and contribution of the UCD School of Archaeology, and I don't think my colleagues will object if I single out Conor McDermott for thanks; Conor supports research and publication in the school in many different ways.

My greatest debt is owed to all the archaeological and osteoarchaeological colleagues whose work is discussed here, and which I hope I have acknowledged appropriately in the book. Any mistakes of interpretation are mine. I am very grateful to Joanna Brück, Neil Carlin, Kerri Cleary, Mark Edmonds, Melanie Giles, Aimée Little, Finola O'Carroll, Aidan O'Sullivan and Graeme Warren for reading earlier drafts of chapters; their comments have significantly improved the text. With regard to photographs, I am very grateful to Ken Williams for the wide range of striking images that he kindly provided; to Muiris O'Sullivan for the photographs from the excavation of the Mound of the Hostages, Tara, and for ongoing discussion; and to Frank Coyne, Ian Doyle, Linda Fibiger, Sally Hayden, Sam Moore, the late Leo Swan and Matthew Von Tersch for photographs they provided. In a similar fashion, I am very grateful to the National Monuments Service, in particular Michael MacDonagh, Ann Lynch and Tony Roche; to the National Museum of Ireland, especially Maeve Sikora, Isabella Mulhall and Clare McNamara; to the Historic Environment Division, Department of Communities, Northern Ireland, specifically Rhonda Robinson, Colin Dunlop and Tony Corey; to Transport Infrastructure Ireland (TII), particularly Rónán Swan, Michael Stanley and Mary Deevy; and to the Discovery Programme, especially John O'Keeffe and Anthony Corns, for assistance. A number of archaeological companies kindly provided images through TII, and in that context I am grateful to Archaeological Consultancy Services (ACS), Archaeological Management Solutions (AMS), Eachtra Archaeological Projects, Colm Flynn Archaeology, Cultural Resources Development Services (CRDS), Headland Archaeology, Valerie J. Keeley Ltd and Margaret Gowen and Co.

As mentioned, the book has been in train for a while, and I am grateful to Nick Maxwell and Colin Ridler for their early support and to Finola O'Carroll, Joanne Gaffrey, Aimée Little and Neil Carlin for discussion and queries at various key times, which inspired me to keep going. In bringing the book to conclusion I have had the pleasure of working with the publications team at the Royal Irish Academy. For this I owe many thanks to Helena King, senior editor; Fidelma Slattery, designer; Ruth Hegarty, managing editor; and Aifric Downey, publication marketing, for doing such a great job, and in such a cheerful and supportive manner.

With the Royal Irish Academy, I am pleased to acknowledge and thank the National Monuments Service, Department of Housing, Local Government and Heritage; the National University of Ireland; Transport Infrastructure Ireland; the College of Social Sciences and Law, University College Dublin; and UCD School of Archaeology for their financial support for the publication.

As ever, my greatest support has been the love of my wife Mary de Courcy and our family, who are a constant reminder that life is to be lived and enjoyed.

Finally, this book is dedicated to inspiring friends
and colleagues who are gone but always remembered:
Vin Davis, Blaze O'Connor and Barry Raftery.

The company of the dead

It's natural that they would feel the cold
much more than we do; but that is partly
what makes them such good company.
They draw closer, rubbing their hands,
and praise the fire: 'That's a fine fire you have down.'

Also, they've no unrealised agendas,
their eager questions no barbed implications.
They're no trouble round the place, their only wish
now to get warmer: apart, that is, from wishing
that they'd kept warmer while they had the chance.

Bernard O'Donoghue in *Outliving* (London: Chatto and Windus, 2003).

1.

Engaging with prehistoric life and death

INTRODUCTION

This is a book about life and death in Ireland over 8,500 years. 'Life' is a word that is in constant use; it is familiar, vital and central to everyday discourse. Archaeologists talk of their task as being to reconstruct life in the past. 'Death' is just as important, however, and recognition of our mortality is central to being human, but talk of death often makes us uncomfortable. In *Quicksand*, Henning Mankell says that 'nobody wants to die, whether they are young or old. Dying is always difficult.'[1] Today it has become the norm to see death as both personal and distant; usually confronted in the case of the demise of family members, friends, or ourselves, or brought into focus by warfare, accidents or events with a high death toll, such as the Covid-19 pandemic. In reality, death is just as constant and central to society as life, and that has been the way over the 10,000 years of definite human presence on the island of Ireland.

In this 10,000-year story, only the most recent 1,500 years are recorded historically, the rest is what is termed 'prehistory', for which we rely on the archaeological record of material remains to inform us. In Ireland, prehistory covers the time from around 8,000 BC—the date for the first definite evidence of human settlement on the island—to about AD 400.[2] The changes associated with the coming of Christianity and the related literary culture around the latter date are seen as marking the beginning of the historic period. Our record of the personal and social lives of people before that are the material remains that have survived over the millennia to be documented as the archaeological record. The most direct record of prehistoric people are their own physical remains, predominantly bones. These provide a material, spiritual and emotional link between the present and the past. Moreover, their discovery confronts us and necessitates inquiry into matters of life and death. The excavation of ancient, or indeed more recent, human burials unsurprisingly generates public interest. One way of understanding this reaction and engagement is to see the excavation of graves and cemeteries as a counter-point to the sense of loss we experience on the death of a loved and missed family member or friend, given that the point of departure is the funeral or burial, most often in a cemetery. In some senses archaeological excavation brings the dead back to life; as human remains are revealed we have contact with people long dead. This also brings our human fascination with death into focus. Joanna Sofaer puts this very well in *The body as material culture*: 'we instinctively recognise their bodies as we recognise our own; they are essentially us'.[3] [FIG. 1.1, PL. 1.A].

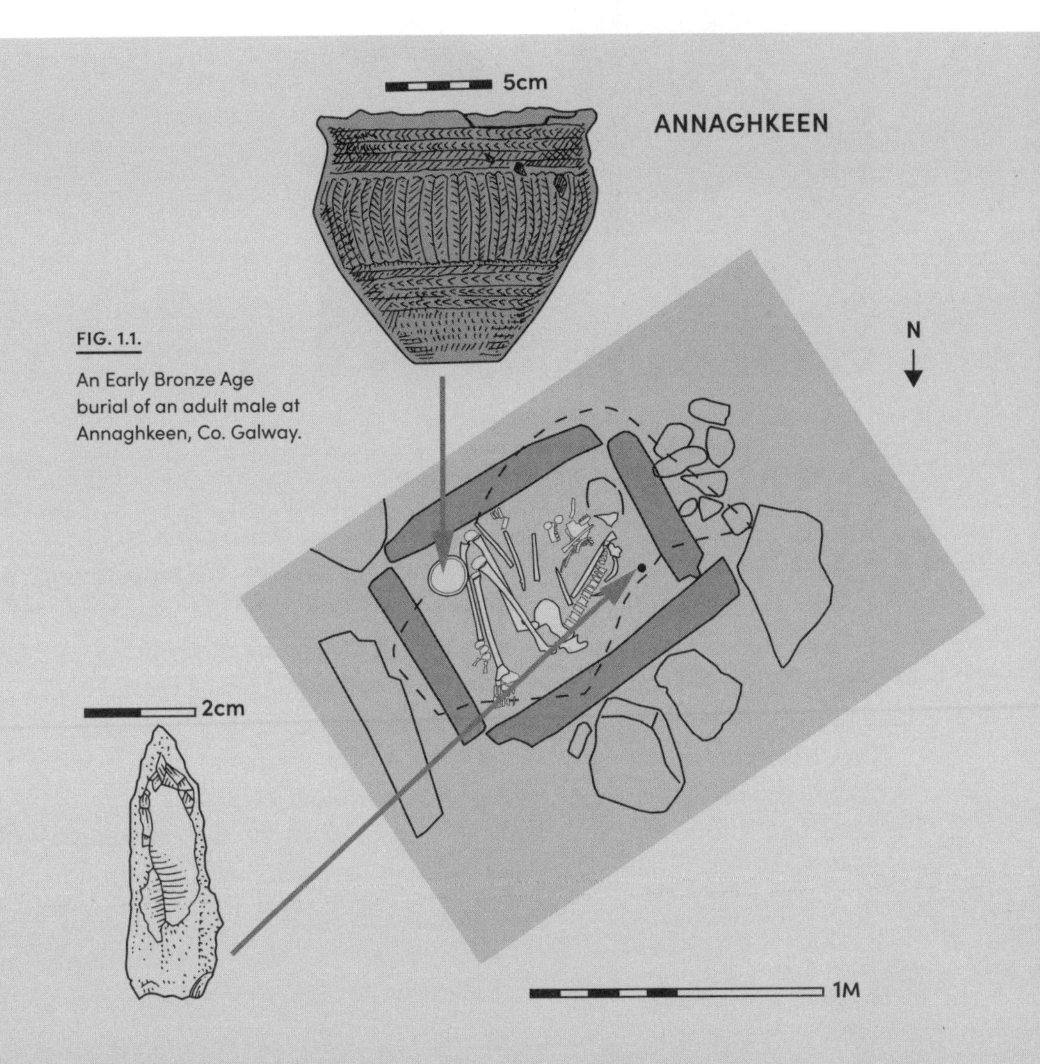

FIG. 1.1.

An Early Bronze Age burial of an adult male at Annaghkeen, Co. Galway.

PL. 1.A.

Archaeologists excavating an Early Bronze Age cist burial at Tevrin, Co. Westmeath in 2019.

BRINGING THE DEAD BACK TO LIFE

Physical evidence of people and of how they were treated in death provides us with important insights on life in the past. The empathy created by this kind of direct, human encounter and the issues it raises prompt the questions archaeologists are most frequently asked. Who lived in Ireland thousands of years ago? Where did these people come from? How did they live and die? What were they like? Did they have religious beliefs?[4] The treatment of people when they died, the complexity of their mortuary rites, their deposition and burial and the character and diversity of the evidence we recover from their graves or other resting places are the central foci of this book. We recover this information through excavation, aided by analytic approaches and collaborative work with colleagues from a range of disciplines. These lines of inquiry provide us with insights—ordinary and extraordinary—into the lives of people whose names we will never know. On the other hand, these insights can provide such a detailed understanding that we may come to know these people as individuals and can recognise and discuss specific incidents or events in their lives. For example, we can detect in skeletal remains what would have been life-changing bone fractures or patterns of daily, repeated physical work that resulted in alterations in bone structure.

As well as acknowledging the importance of these insights and their implications for our ability to talk about personal lives and deaths, we can go further and use this information as a basis for understanding and interpreting societies. The treatment of the dead in prehistory is one of the major sources of evidence we have for past cultural practices and the character of society in many parts of Europe. But with the exception of archaeologists, most people today are probably unaware of the rich and varied evidence we have for the complex ways in which the living responded to death, or how people thought about and constructed formal social relationships with the dead in prehistory.[5] There are a number of reasons for this lack of awareness. In part it is a result of the way we as archaeologists often write about the past. While we recognise the importance of mortuary practices and incorporate them into narratives, we tend to focus on site-, regional- or period-based discussions rather than drawing out the burial record itself as a major theme across time and space in understanding lives and societies.

It is worth contrasting the central place that death is given in the narratives that archaeologists write about the past with the largely marginalised role that death is given in major historical accounts of modern society in Ireland. Social or historical analyses of modern Irish society tend to consider death from the perspective of the personal, family and social impact of specific deaths, or particular kinds of tragic deaths, rather than seeing and examining death as a key, integral, ongoing part of social life, as archaeologists do.[6] When death is discussed in sociological terms it is most often in the context of changing patterns of mortality over time. Is it because we have such a rich documentation of the lives of people today and in the recent historic past that we tend to underplay the wider social significance of mortuary practices, except in the case of tragic deaths, the deaths of public figures and commemorations that have a political context? This general lack of discussion might, at least in part, also reflect what Philippe Ariès described in his analysis of changing historical attitudes to death as the tendency of modern, Western societies to regard death as invisible, deniable, largely hidden away from everyday experience.[7] Death tends to be seen in personal or abstract sociological terms rather than as the major, unifying existential issue facing us all, regardless of belief. **[PLS 1.B AND 1.C]**

In reality, however, we are constantly reminded of the wider social and cultural import of the treatment of the dead in Irish society today. There have been significant changes in mortuary practice in recent years that both reflect and indicate wider social and religious changes. There has been a marked increase in the rate and provision of cremation, for example, but we have also seen a return to popularity of the custom of waking the dead, even if this is often an attenuated version of what was the traditional practice.[8] It is said that one of the culturally distinctive features of Irish life today, in an increasingly globalised and homogenised world, dominated by internationally shared patterns of behaviour, is the way in which death is socially acknowledged. As Thomas Lynch, the poet, writer and undertaker, put it in *Booking passage*, the Irish know what to do when there is a dead body in the room. Funerals are attended by an extended circle of family and friends and are a complex weave of grief, celebration of the life of the deceased and social gathering. It is acknowledged that one of the major social impacts of the Covid-19 pandemic in Ireland was the disruption of this way of marking death. As society in Ireland becomes more culturally diverse, it has

PL. 1.B.

Zen Buddhist cemetery, the temple of Ryosokuin, Kyoto, Japan.

PL. 1.C.

The Erico Production coffin-making workshop in Accra, Ghana.

become more obvious that the rituals and customs by which the death of people is acknowledged and celebrated are deeply embedded in cultural practice. Responses to death in twenty-first century Ireland demonstrate that we see it through a filter of particular religious and social beliefs and traditions. This also explains the mixture of familiarity and shock with which we view images of the funerals and mortuary customs of people who have different belief systems. In recent years we have all too often seen the different ways in which Islamic, Jewish, Christian and other victims of conflicts in Afghanistan, Ethopia, Israel, Palestine, Syria, Ukraine and Yemen are treated in death.[9]

Interpreting mortuary practices as a basis for understanding societies provides us with an opportunity to compare past practices with the treatment of the dead and of death in Ireland today, and to reflect on death as an event and process both in our personal lives and in a wider social context. The rich archaeological and historical record for mortuary practices provides us with the opportunity to better understand people and societies in the past. For early medieval Ireland, the discussion of results from archaeological work brought together by Chris Corlett and Michael Potterton and in the major *Mapping Death* project led by Elizabeth O'Brien are complemented by consideration by Aidan O'Sullivan and colleagues of death and burial as part of their wider discussion of that period. Books by Susan Leigh Fry and Clodagh Tait have provided significant new insights on death and dying in medieval and early modern Ireland.[10] Here, I am taking the discussion of death back in time, to when the earliest human communities settled on the island.

PERCEPTIONS OF PREHISTORY

This notion of tacking or moving between past and present is useful in exploring the ways in which we perceive prehistoric people and times. Understandably, the foci in many discussions are the major monuments that people built, or the objects they used that are now on view in museums. Despite our recognition of the capability of people to build monuments such as Newgrange in the Boyne Valley before 3000 BC, with a deliberate orientation of the entrance towards sunrise at the mid-winter solstice, we are still inclined to view them in a simplistic light and judge them through the lens of our own cultural context. We set prehistoric people apart, as being distant and different, less complex culturally than ourselves. Hence the popularity of portraying them as cave men or women, the continued use of terms such as 'primitive' or 'stone age', and the extraordinary persistence and popularity of the myth that people lived at the same time as dinosaurs. Alternatively, we cast them in our reflection, giving them modern concerns, such as a presumed obsession with the observation of linear time and a scientific approach to life, as reflected in theories about prehistoric astronomical observatories. In reality, people in traditional, small-scale societies had fundamentally different notions of the meaning and marking of time than we do in modern society.[11]

Focusing on how the dead were treated facilitates a different approach, allowing us to engage with how people might have created and understood their cultural worlds, and to attempt to interpret their beliefs about what happened after death and the complex relationships between the living and the dead. **[PL. 1.D]**

Unfortunately, in many wider treatments of the past in Ireland, the first eight thousand years of the social narrative of Irish lives gets short shrift. As Thomas Bartlett blithely asserted in his *Ireland: a history*, 'the archaeological and historical evidence for pre-Christian Ireland unfortunately does not enable us to confidently discern fable from fact'.[12] The absence of a written record is seen as making understanding of the prehistoric past more difficult, more open-ended and fragmented. Of course the archaeological record is fragmentary, but to assume that we can only write historical narratives when we have documents is to privilege what are in themselves often partial and very biased sources. Part of the problem lies with the term 'prehistory' itself, implying as it does a qualitative difference between

PL. 1.D.

Newgrange passage tomb, Brú na Bóinne, Co. Meath, with satellite passage tombs, pit enclosure and Great Stone Circle, from the south-east.

text-based history and a history based on the archaeological record of human material culture. At a global level, the view has been taken that we should talk about deep-time history or deep history, rather than prehistory, and recognise that everything about the human past is history.[13] It is only the sources or archives that we use which vary, depending on time and place. Here, the term prehistory is used advisedly, recognising that it is accepted terminology but noting that it can carry unwarranted connotations of this time and of the people who lived during it as being less important than the era and the people of literate history.

In underplaying our ability to utilise the material culture record to understand Irish prehistory we are missing out on two key aspects of this long period that have wider significance. First, there is its long-term significance for understanding Irish cultural identities and social history. After all, this period takes up over three-quarters of all the time that people have lived on the island. Human presence and impact across the island was widespread and shaped the character of the landscape. Second, the archaeologist's focus on the material record helps us understand the complex ways in which people construct, sustain and change social identities and histories through the active ways in which they use, relate to and engage with the world around them. In short, we define ourselves and others through things, our 'stuff'. This perspective is crucial for interpreting the significance of materiality in specific cultural contexts, both in the past and in present-day society.[14]

Taking up this point, thinking about the links between people and their material surroundings might initially seem distant from our modern lives and lifestyles, often projected as being based on rapidly developing technologies, consumption, shelf-lives, fashions, styles, obsolescence and disposability. In reality, our lives now, as much as the lives of people in the past, are built on relationships with the material world. The nature of these relationships in the past, specifically, are explored by archaeologists, but their reality and complexity are captured by a range of other approaches too, notably poetry. Both archaeologists and poets try to tease out the complex webs of peoples' relationships with stuff. Bjørnar Olsen and colleagues reflect this in the memorable phrase 'we have always been cyborgs'.[15] Eavan Boland, Moya Cannon and Seamus Heaney too have written about objects, illuminating how we can uncover memories, identities and the meaning and depth of human relationships spanning past and present through mundane materials—the everyday bits and pieces that surround us.[16]Archaeologists now routinely use concepts such as entanglement and object biographies to demonstrate how deeply interwoven the lives of people are with the things we use.[17] In the poem 'The lava cameo', Boland writes about a brooch that was a gift to mark the relationship between her grandfather and grandmother, and which also served to indicate her grandmother's social standing.[18] Two generations later it had become a family heirloom, handed on; the poet's tangible link to the past and to her understanding of family history. In 'The company of the dead', Bernard O'Donoghue reminds us that as well as sharing objects once owned by people now dead, the living continue to share the company of the dead themselves. The dead are, as he says, 'good company'. So, we live in the present but carry the past with us.[19] Through the rich array of behaviour, things, times and places associated with the treatment of the dead, therefore, we can portray both a sense of individual lives and deaths and tease out the wider implications of the relationships between the living and dead in societies in Ireland over a span of 8,500 years.

We are talking about a very long period of time; four times longer than the period conventionally described as Irish history. Traditionally, the way archaeologists have discussed and written about prehistory is to divide it into periods, representing and following internationally recognised classifications. These periods are seen to correspond to blocks of time and to significant social and technological patterns of life, and in turn are subdivided into phases. **[FIG. 1.2]**

We often align discussion of major topics, such as the treatment of the dead, along the same lines. Hence, we talk about the Mesolithic (in Ireland this runs from 8000 BC to 4000 BC) as a time when people lived by fishing, gathering and hunting. This was followed by the Neolithic (from 4000 BC to 2450 BC), when the beginnings of farming and the building of monuments are among the main social markers. As the name suggests, the Bronze Age (from 2450 BC to 800 BC) is defined as a time of technological innovation, with the first use of metalworking and a new array of material culture, much of which pertains to the marking of social standing and relationships of people in life and death. The most recent prehistoric period, the Iron Age (from 800 BC to AD 400), might logically be

MESOLITHIC	EARLIER	8000 to 6700 BC
	LATER	6700 to 4000 BC
NEOLITHIC	EARLY	4000 to 3600 BC
	MIDDLE	3600 to 2900 BC
	LATE	2900 to 2450 BC
BRONZE AGE	CHALCOLITHIC	2450 to 2200 BC
	EARLY	2200 to 1600 BC
	MIDDLE	1600 to 1200 BC
	LATE	1200 to 800 BC
IRON AGE	EARLY	800 to 400 BC
	MIDDLE	400 BC to AD 1
	LATE	AD 1 to AD 400

FIG. 1.2.

The major archaeological and chronological periods from 8000 BC to AD 400.

seen as the timespan when we should have most confidence in social interpretation. After all, this is when we are closest to the emergence of text-based history, and it is often regarded as the time when Ireland became Celtic. Technologically, as the name suggests, it is at this time we see the first appearance of the use of iron. As we will see, however, the character of the evidence justifies Barry Raftery's description of the Irish Iron Age as enigmatic.[20]

This four-drawer filing-cabinet approach is useful for the purposes of description and analysis; however, it suffers from being much too neat in dealing with the complexity of cultural life in the past. Consideration of mortuary practices in the archaeological record makes it clear that we should recognise that approach as a modern classificatory device to help us understand what were very different times. The burial record poses questions that force us not just to explore the record within these defined time divisions, but also to think across them. Many locations are used and re-used for human burial over long periods of time. Specific places were perceived across multiple human generations as being appropriate for human burial and/or for the deposition of human bone. For example, at a small cave in Killuragh townland in east Co. Limerick, in a low hill with outcropping limestone, two narrow passages lead into a small chamber, with further passages beyond going further into the hill. Excavation by Jane O'Shaughnessy and Peter Woodman revealed evidence for the placement of human bone either in the cave or outside its entrance at different times over a period of 6,000 years—from the Earlier Mesolithic to the Early Bronze Age. At Kilmahuddrick in west Co. Dublin, excavation of a ring-barrow by Ian Doyle indicated a series of cremation deposits within the area defined by a circular ditch that were dated from before 1000 BC to the last few centuries BC, and there is a strong possibility that activity at the site may have started considerably earlier.[21] **[PL. 1.E]**

It is not necessary in either of these examples, or many others, to argue for any direct continuity of use of, or respect for, the specific locations to recognise that there is something culturally interesting and important in this very strong attachment to place. Why did people repeatedly return to place the dead in such locations? Recognising the time blocks and the accompanying cultural labels that archaeologists use—which tend to dominate the way we think about and discuss the prehistoric past but that can be useful anchor points—can we identify important longer-term patterns of social memories, commemoration and identities that span across the boundaries of those time blocks? The implications of the ongoing veneration, visitation, adaptation and alteration of places

PL. 1.E.

The ring-barrow at Kilmahuddrick, Dublin after excavation, viewed from the west.

that became sacred as burial locations is one of the major themes that run through this book.[22]

Alongside acknowledging the importance of place, we need to think more carefully about concepts of time. Anthropologist Maurice Bloch wrote about the way in which different concepts of time run concurrently through peoples' lives. In the everyday sense of time, which is most often in focus, people tend to be open to change and innovation. Then there is ritual time, relevant to the way in which key individual and social occasions are marked by ceremonies that illustrate and provide an understanding of how the world works.[23] Rituals may be practised and maintained over long periods of time. For example, the basic Christian mode of burial orientation—extended inhumation, with the person on their back in the coffin and grave, and placed so that the head faces east, *That they may face the rising sun* as the title of John McGahern's novel aptly puts it—has remained unaltered since the mid-first millennium AD, despite many changes in other aspects of Christian theology.[24] On the other hand, ritual is also adaptable to changing needs and often draws on previous practices for authority and inspiration. Thus, this classic Christian burial orientation arose in the context of the late Roman practice of east–west inhumation burials. In Ireland, as we will discuss in more detail in a later chapter, Elizabeth O'Brien has demonstrated that there was a transitional period between the fifth and at least the end of the seventh century AD, if not indeed over a significantly longer period, when traditional pre-Christian modes of burial were still practised, despite the island being actively Christianised.[25]

RELIGION AND COSMOLOGY

Anthropological and religious studies indicate that virtually all peoples act, both through specific ceremonies and in their daily lives, according to beliefs in supernatural forces. These beliefs are culturally prescribed, and they constitute cosmologies—ways of explaining the world and the place of people in it.[26] Robert Bellah has identified a range of cultural capacities, such as communal dancing, storytelling and theorising, whose emergence in deep history made religious development possible. Anthropologists make a porous distinction between religions that depend on written texts or scriptures, which have provided the basis for the major religions, such as Judaism, Christianity and Islam, and those in which belief is passed on orally. The latter tend to be local in scale and relevance, flexible in structure and representative of traditional beliefs grounded in intimate knowledge of particular regions. In these smaller scale, orally based religions, the idea and image of the sacred may be seen as being integral to features and objects in the environment rather than as one supreme divinity. The framework of practice also tends to be more flexible, but particular individuals may be ascribed powers of communication with supernatural forces.[27]

Prehistoric religions in Ireland have not been the subject of much recent debate. Ronald Hutton has explored this topic, but primarily in relation to Britain. His conclusion is an important one, in that he recognises the presence of religion and religious practice and places in Britain from the Palaeolithic period onwards.[28] In an important contribution in the Irish context, Dáithi Ó hÓgáin interpreted the character of religion by using early literary sources, which he sees as referring to the oral traditions of later prehistoric societies. He works from this back to earlier periods, drawing on the archaeological record. For example, he considers the megalithic tomb at Newgrange in terms of how it was perceived later in prehistory and early history as the home of deities and the burial place of the kings of Tara and discusses what this perception and mythology represents, both in terms of continuity and transformation of its original role.[29] **[PL. 1.D]**

I would argue that from the very start of human settlement in Ireland, peoples' lives were lived according to religious and cosmological beliefs as they sought to understand the world and universe. These beliefs provided, in Timothy Insoll's terms, an 'overarching framework for (all) other aspects of life'.[30] Religious beliefs may well have been complex and have changed over time. Religion would have informed behaviour and material culture across every aspect of life, including the treatment of the dead and beliefs about the supernatural world. Ritual as reflected in mortuary practice would have focused attention on the relationship between the earthly and spiritual realms. Because of the central and transforming role of death, therefore, the archaeological interpretation of mortuary practices is crucial to understanding prehistoric cosmologies and societies.

The general absence of religion from archaeological narratives about prehistory should be seen not only as a reflection of the difficulty of capturing intangible religious beliefs from the archaeological record, but also as reflective of the perspective of archaeologists. As Insoll points out, archaeologists in western Europe up to recently largely wrote from and within a Christian perspective and therefore underplayed the role of prehistoric religions. Now increasingly, in Ireland and elsewhere, they write from a secular perspective and tend to underplay the significance of religion in the past because of the limited relevance it has in their own lives.[31] This poses a challenge both for our understanding of the role of religion in creating and sustaining social and cultural identities and for our attitudes to prehistoric people. The widespread use of terms such as 'pagan' or 'pre-Christian' Ireland could be read as implying that prehistoric people—unlike the Christianised people of the historic period in Ireland—lacked religion. In writing about the Neolithic period in Ireland, I argued that we should assume that people in that period had religious beliefs, rather than questioning their presence.[32] The issue then is one of interpreting those beliefs. Interestingly, another interplay between past and present is that interpretation of prehistoric sites from a cosmological perspective has become a focus of a range of religious beliefs today—such as 'new age' or Celtic spirituality—and is providing the basis for quite a different approach to and focus on understanding those sites, as discussed by Hutton in relation to Britain.[33]

The particular form that rituals take, the relationships they establish between people, and the way in which people view the supernatural world are shaped by and in turn shape the way that society operates. Thus, society and religion are intimately related and are often seen as standing in symbolic relationship to each other. Rituals are created and carried out to reflect and put beliefs into practice; they may be linked to particular deities or may be carried out at critical times in the year in a foraging or farming cycle. They may also take the form of rites of passage; the social marking and confirmation of the transition of people through major life stages: birth, initiation into adulthood, marriage and death. Death brings the community and the person face to face with the supernatural forces at the core of cosmological and religious belief. It is not surprising then that the marking and celebration of death is a key feature of ritual in many societies. In this context it is also useful to see ritual as encompassing a range of activities; at one end of the spectrum those that are formal, defined and carried out at special places and times—'consecrated actions' as Clifford Geertz termed them—and at the other their echo in daily social etiquette. This helps us to see how actions and relationships established or redefined in the context of formal, religious ritual—such as mortuary practices—can permeate the whole of the social fabric, as they underlie, ripple through and give symbolic meaning to more regular, daily, ritualised acts.[34]

APPROACHING THE ARCHAEOLOGY OF DEATH

Since the formal beginnings of the discipline in the nineteenth century the interpretative frameworks that archaeologists use to discuss the burial record have changed radically.[35] In the eighteenth and nineteenth century, excavation of burial mounds became an increasingly popular antiquarian activity. This was a reflection of the potential of such sites to provide rich artefactual material, feeding a growing demand and fashion for private and institutional collections. The results were seen as providing physical evidence for the ancestors of local populations, often imbued with patriotic or nationalistic overtones and linked to mytho-historical accounts. Hence the publication of the Loughcrew, Co. Meath complex of passage tombs by Eugene Conwell in the 1860s and 1870s focused on the description of the central tomb, Cairn T on Carnbane East, as the burial place of the Ollamh Fodhla, a legendary Irish royal figure. **[PL. 1.F]**

The accumulation of data from the excavation of burials in Ireland and other areas of Europe laid the foundations for the formulation of chronological schemes based on typology and seriation. These schemes were central to the formulation and writing of the first overviews of European prehistory. They also provided the basis for recognising the occurrence of distinctive regional differences in material culture in the major phases of prehistory.[36]

This was the context in which Gordon Childe and other scholars formulated what has come to be called the cultural-historical approach, which dominated archaeological research for much of the twentieth century. It was cultural in the sense that it was based on the premise that similar assemblages of artefacts, burial customs and domestic architecture could be regarded as reflecting the standard behaviour and beliefs of a distinctive culture or people, sometimes with a historic or linguistic identity. Where there was good supporting physical evidence from burials in the form of distinct skeletal forms, particularly the skull or cranium, this culture could be regarded as a race. It was historical in two senses; first, as Liam de Paor eloquently put it, this approach gave primacy to written records. Archaeological remains were regarded

PL. 1.F.

Cairn T, Loughcrew, Co. Meath and the cluster of passage tombs on Carnbane East, at the centre of the Loughcrew cemetery, from the north-east.

as second-best and fragmentary sources of information and, as the focus shifted to issues of intangible culture, such as religious beliefs and social organisation, were regarded as markedly less reliable. It was historical in a second sense of having a primary focus on a historical narrative; describing changes over time. In these narratives the supposed stability of archaeological cultures implied that they would change only as a result of major external influences, such as population movement or the inflow of new ideas and technologies.[37]

This concept was taken to extremes in support of the search for the origins of the Aryans under the influence of Nazi ideology, which also focused on the concept of race as the basis for discrimination against and persecution of people of different religious or cultural beliefs. While this may seem invidious, distasteful and distant from Ireland, we need to be aware, as Catherine Nash has pointed out, of the way in which craniology and the concept of racial differences influenced discussions of people and populations in Ireland well into the mid-twentieth century.[38]

More important in an archaeological context was Childe's concept that a culture could be equated to a people, and that the associated material was a straightforward reflection of normal cultural practices (pots = people). There was a related assumption that one standard mode of burial and mortuary practice would typify a culture. If there were exceptionally richly furnished burials, these represented a social élite. Major changes were brought by movement and by new people. This cultural historical approach to the interpretation of burial data has been deeply influential in archaeological studies in Ireland. It is the basic structure that underpinned how archaeologists approached research, classification and collection of data through excavation and survey up to at least the 1970s. Indeed, it still implicitly informs archaeological practice today.[39] [FIG. 1.3]

An interpretative or paradigm shift occurred in the 1960s and early 1970s, particularly in North America and Britain; it came to be called new or processual archaeology and was aligned strongly with anthropology and concerned with understanding human behaviour.

FIG. 1.3.

A cultural-historical perspective; the Bronze Age chapter headings in Herity and Eogan 1977, illustrated by drawings of relevant pottery styles.

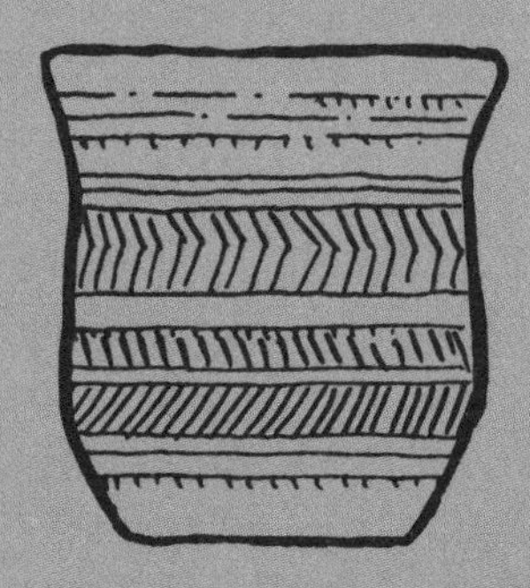

BEAKER PEOPLES

and the Beginnings of a New Society

FOOD VESSEL PEOPLE

Consolidation of the Single Grave Culture

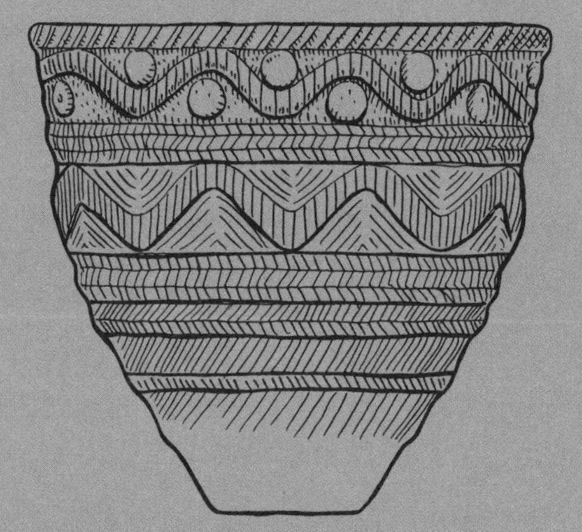

URN PEOPLE

Further Arrivals and New Developments

The term 'processual' describes the concern with understanding the processes by which societies operate and change over time.[40] This approach challenged some of the central tenets of the cultural historical approach. The interpretation of mortuary data became a central focus of and demonstration project for the new processual approach, which was scientific and systematic in tenor. Of critical importance was the view that archaeological material was linked to all aspects of life and society, because of the inter-related nature of the cultural system. This represents a radical shift away from the view that archaeological material has very limited potential to inform us about issues such as social organisation and religion. Through rigorous and comparative analysis and the application of scientific techniques and methodologies it was argued that hypotheses could be made about the nature of human behaviour that created the archaeological record. In turn, these could be tested against that record.

Mortuary data provided a rich data source to test these concepts. An influential observation was that of Lewis Binford, who argued, using a processual approach, that mortuary practice could be seen as a direct reflection of the character of the contemporary, living society. He demonstrated that mortuary practices varied within societies and argued that the extent of that variation reflected the complexity of the particular society. Hence, mortuary practice could be used to reconstruct social complexity. This approach has been influential in a large number of studies of mortuary practice, internationally as well as in Ireland. Perhaps an even more significant legacy has been the concern with more rigorous data collection and the application of statistical methods and scientific techniques (all hallmarks of the processual approach) within the general practice of archaeological fieldwork.[41] **[FIG. 1.4]**

Another turn in archaeological theory since the 1980s embraces a diversity of approaches under the label post-processual and interpretative archaeology. As part of a wider shift in the humanities and social sciences to a post-modern perspective, this reflects a central tenet of post-modernism; namely that data and theory are

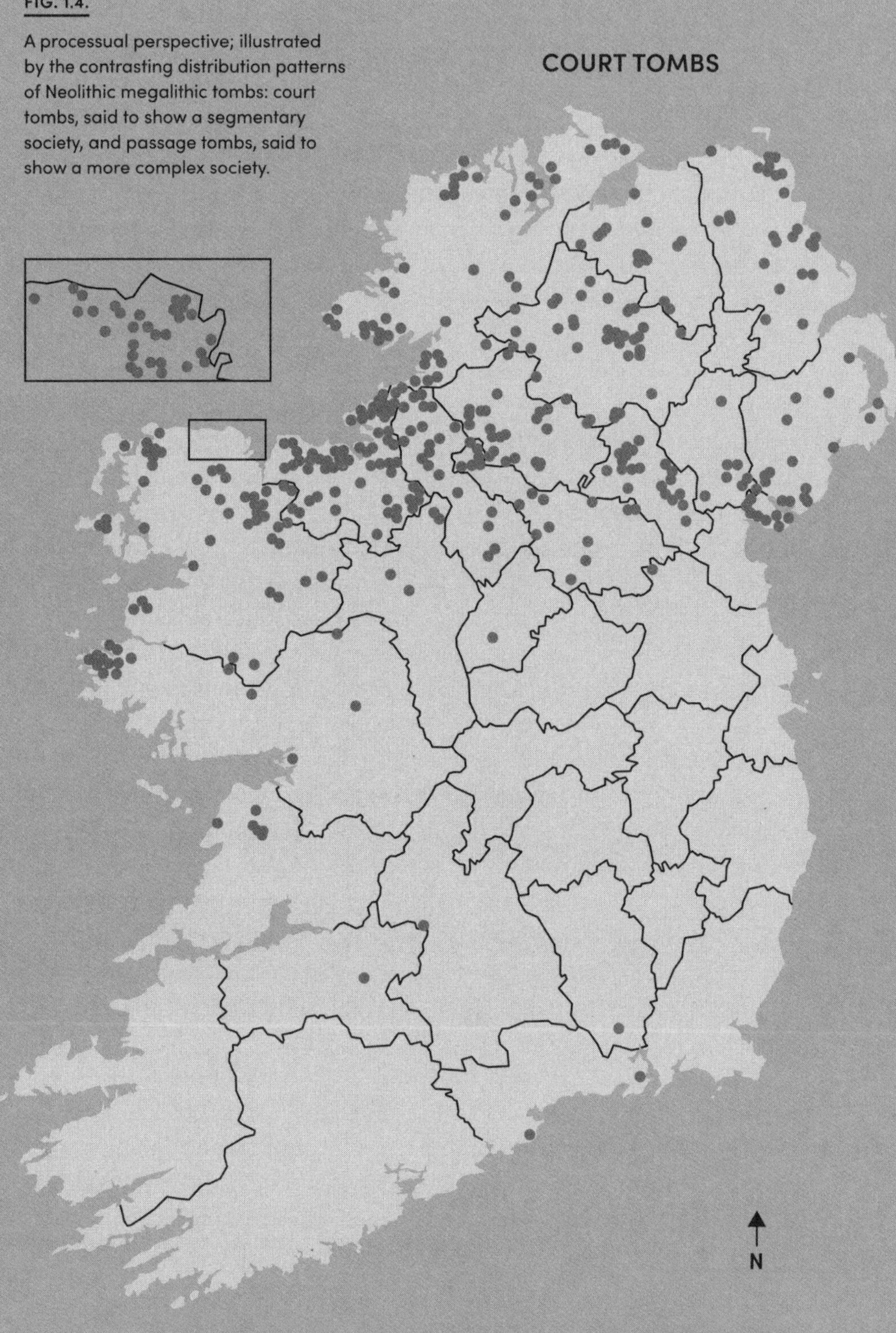

FIG. 1.4.

A processual perspective; illustrated by the contrasting distribution patterns of Neolithic megalithic tombs: court tombs, said to show a segmentary society, and passage tombs, said to show a more complex society.

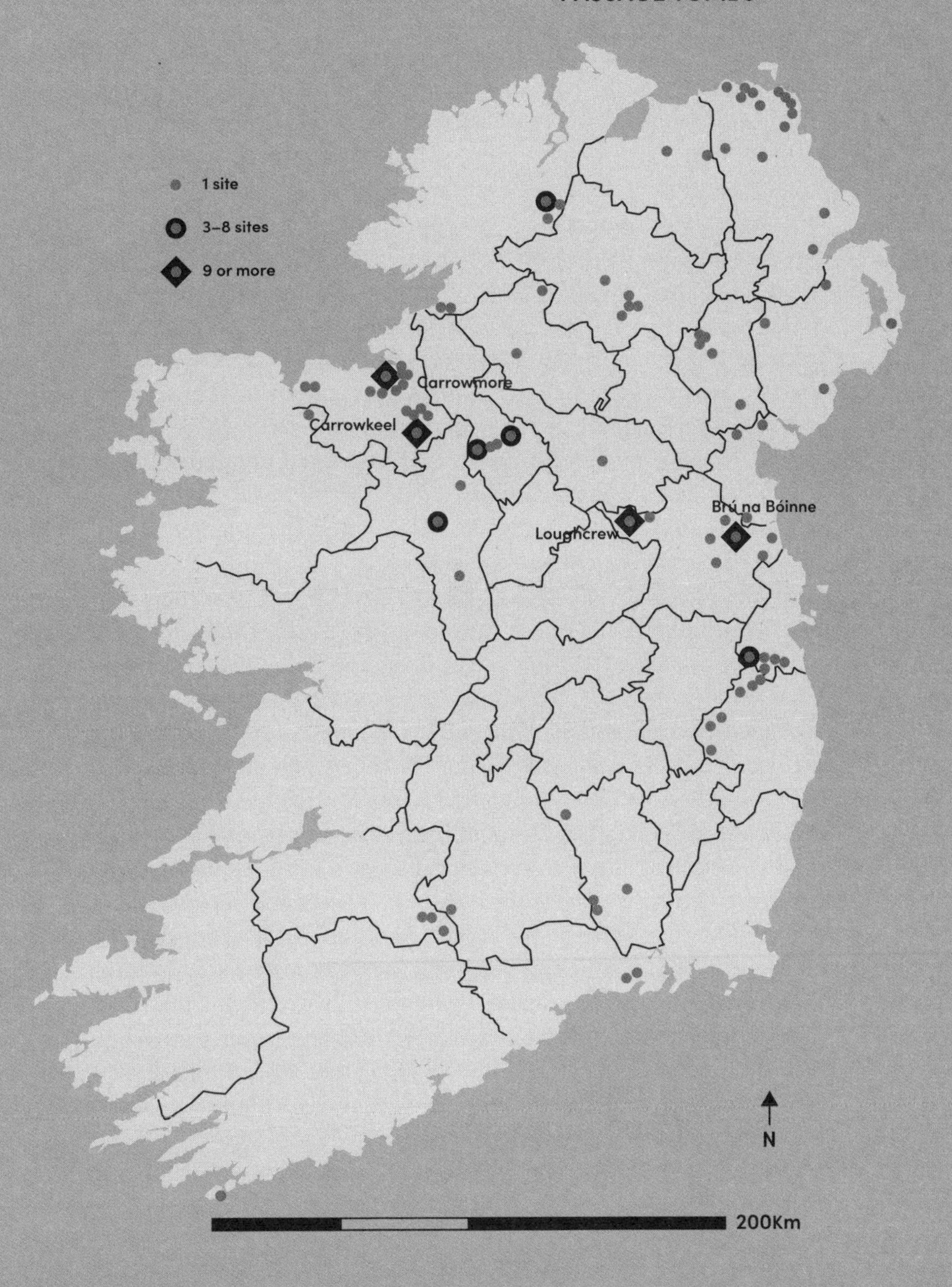
PASSAGE TOMBS
1 site
3–8 sites
9 or more
Carrowmore
Carrowkeel
Loughcrew
Brú na Bóinne
N
200Km

inter-related, hence there is no one 'right' or 'best' way to understand or interpret an issue. Historical disciplines like archaeology have to face the task of understanding the meaning of the record of human activity in the past, and the implication that any reading of the past is influenced by the social context in which the archaeologist is writing. The past is written in the present, a point made above in relation to the attitude of archaeologists to religion.[42]

Interpretative archaeology has opened up an exciting array of research avenues in relation to the archaeology of death. The significance of the material expression of personal and social identities and differences—as defined, for example by gender and age—has emerged as a major theme. There has also been a recognition of the need to explore the complementary balance between 'top–down' concepts of social order and power and the 'bottom–up' role of people as active social agents in creating the fabric of social life. Rather than seeing material culture as a passive reflection of past technologies, we now appreciate that it has an active role and meaning and is crucial in the construction of social life.[43]

In this context it has become clear that we cannot treat mortuary practice simply as creating a mirror-image of life. There are cases in the archaeological record in which there is a deliberate arrangement and distortion of identity at death by the living participants in the mortuary ceremonies, which serves to emphasise the point that the dead don't bury themselves. For instance, the bones of different individuals may be brought together to make it look like one person is represented. Likewise, burial of particular people may have been used as a context either to create or disrupt social cohesion among the living. The treatment of the dead may have varied depending on their age, gender, social status and mode of death. Detailed analyses of deposits of human bone and their contexts have made it clear that in many cases there were complex, drawn-out funerary and mortuary processes, involving a number of stages over protracted periods of time, unlike the relatively rapid funeral and burial processes that we are much more familiar with today. Human bone was

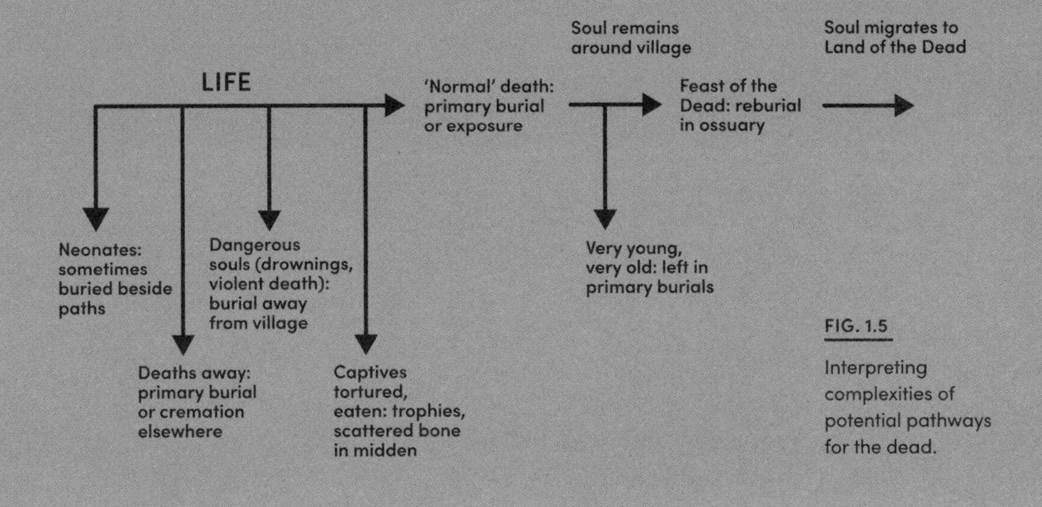

FIG. 1.5

Interpreting complexities of potential pathways for the dead.

frequently utilised and deposited in a range of different contexts. A broad relationship can be drawn and a distinction can be made in this context between burial rites and ancestor or ancestral rites. In the latter cases, the social importance and symbolic value of human bone, and its veneration, are apparent in its use in ceremonies after a person's death. These ceremonies may take place close to where burial occurred, or the human bone may be transferred elsewhere and continue to have an important social relevance and meaning long after the actual death of the person.[44] [FIG. 1.5]

On reflection, when we look again at our own society, there are in fact echoes of this emphasis on the metaphorical and symbolic power of human bone, particularly the skull. It can be seen, for example, in the veneration of the physical remains—what are referred to as primary relics—of Catholic saints, such as the head and other bones of the seventeenth-century archbishop of Armagh and martyr, St Oliver Plunkett, which are on display in St Peter's Catholic Church in Drogheda, Co. Louth. The continuing power of relics is also evidenced by the crowds that turned out to touch the casket containing the bones of St Theresa of Avila and other relics of this saint when they toured Ireland in recent years, and in the ceremonies arranged for the veneration of a relic of St Teresa of Calcutta and its placement in Newry Cathedral in 2017.[45]

Major traditions of archaeological thought have been presented here, and elsewhere, in sequential terms, as representing paradigm shifts. The reality is that current methodologies and interpretations contain elements of all three of the broad approaches outlined above. The classificatory labels that we use to describe material culture are derived from a cultural-historical perspective. Many of the methodological approaches and advances have a background in processual archaeology. Archaeologists now use an interpretative framework to try to understand mortuary practice in the past.[46] Such an interpretative stance recognises that death can tell us about people and the social context of their lives. It is in death that we are offered the opportunity to meet some of the people who inhabited Ireland in prehistory. It is our privilege and responsibility as archaeologists to come face to face with this human and social side of that time, and to reflect on and write about that encounter.

Most people think of archaeology as peeling back layers, 'excavating the past', but this simply demonstrates the metaphorical power of the professional activity that archaeologists are best known for—excavation. In reality, we have to recognise that while it is understood by going back, history is lived and created over the course of time. We have to begin from the bottom up in order to understand the dense accumulation of cultural behaviour that creates the human sense of time and place, which is always influenced by what happened in the past. To take account of the complexity of this lived reality, we explore how practices and places that emerge as culturally important at particular times and in specific contexts took on a longer-term significance and role.

To facilitate discussion and to provide a recognisable framework, this book follows the approach of breaking prehistory into major chronological blocks and moving forward through them over time. As a prelude to each of the time-based chapters (Chapters 3–7) there is a fictional account of a burial or a ceremonial event involving the use of human bone. The aim of these accounts is to provide a different kind of reflective narrative, complementing the

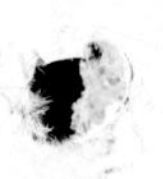

discussion of the archaeological record. To put this discussion into context, Chapter 2 tackles general issues that confront us when we begin to write about people and death in the past. The challenge of writing this kind of prehistory has become both more pressing and more attainable because of the amount of development-led archaeology that began during the economic boom or 'Celtic Tiger' phase of Irish society, from the mid-1990s to the mid-2000s. The amount of archaeological work carried out over and since that time is unprecedented.[47] As a result of that investment we now have access to a very large amount of data, and large-scale and smaller developments and research projects continue to reveal new sites and associated data. **[PL. 1.G]**

Informed by this information, a range of scientific advances and current interpretative approaches, this book takes the opportunity to provide a detailed understanding and narrative of prehistoric death—and life—in Ireland.

PL. 1.G.

The ring-ditch cemetery at Ask, Co. Wexford under excavation, looking south-east towards Ask Hill.

2.

Peopling prehistory

RECOVERING THE PAST

The remains of a substantial number of people who lived at different times in prehistory have survived to the present and become part of the archaeological record. This is primarily because of the care with which they were treated after death.[1] As part of their rigourous research for The People of Prehistoric Ireland project, Eileen Murphy and Barra Ó Donnabháin documented burials from over 1,400 sites.[2] Bearing their research in mind and taking all potential extenuating factors into account, a broad estimate of the number of individuals represented by the human remains that have been recovered, based on the figures from each of the major periods focused on in this book—Mesolithic, Neolithic, Bronze Age and Iron Age—is likely to be in excess of 5,000 people.[3] This figure covers a time-span of more than 8,000 years, so clearly we cannot take this evidence as providing a realistic basis for what the scale of the population actually was at any particular time. For example, from the first 4,000 years of human settlement on the island, we currently have the physical remains of about 10 people.[4]

So how do we explain the gap between the numbers of people represented in the record and actual populations? For a start, archaeological excavation provides details of only a small sample of the places used by prehistoric societies for the formal burial and deposition of human remains. There are many other unexcavated sites visible in the landscape today, such as megalithic tombs or burial mounds, that may contain human bone. Others have been eroded, removed or covered by the sea. In addition, what are referred to as 'flat cemeteries'—so-called because they have no surface definition today—were at times preferred places for burial. The use of land over the millennia for farming, along with other landscape changes, has resulted in the removal of what may have been the visible foci or markers of such cemeteries. Unlike visible, above-ground monuments built to contain or cover human burials, flat cemeteries are difficult to find, and their extent can only be revealed through archaeological survey and excavation. Furthermore, certain types of soils, such as acidic ones, are not conducive to the long-term preservation of bone. Hence in some cases we may find graves, but the inhumed bone placed within them has been totally decomposed, or may only survive as a faint soil shadow. It is clear also that cremation was an important aspect of the treatment of the dead in many traditions of burial in prehistoric Ireland. Estimating the number of actual people represented in cremated or inhumed deposits containing multiple individuals (referred to as commingled) can be a difficult task.[5]

These are some of the reasons why it is difficult to use the known record of human skeletal remains to give any direct indication of the size of prehistoric populations. From the details of the archaeological record that have been assembled and analysed we can, however, begin to think about this issue from the point of view of the living: the people who buried their dead, or placed human bones, in particular places or monuments. Taking this perspective, it becomes clear that depending on their age, gender and social status, for example, the dead were treated in different ways. Some people were treated with particular care; these are the visible dead. The reality is, however, that we simply do not know how the majority of the population was treated at death. For example, we would expect that in the small-scale societies that would have been typical, the birth (fertility) and death (mortality) rates of children or sub-adults would have been high, however, there can be an under-representation of non-adults in the actual burial record.[6] Although a small number of sites with a high proportion of non-adult burials have been found, these are exceptional. It would seem that in prehistory, many children were buried in different ways and in different places than adults; a practice that is known in many societies, past and present.[7] [FIG. 2.1]

On the other hand, we must be cautious about imposing modern assumptions about the social distinction between adults and non-adults based on the osteological record. We know that the notion of 'childhood', for example, is socially constructed and varied.[8] The need for caution in moving from the evidence from the

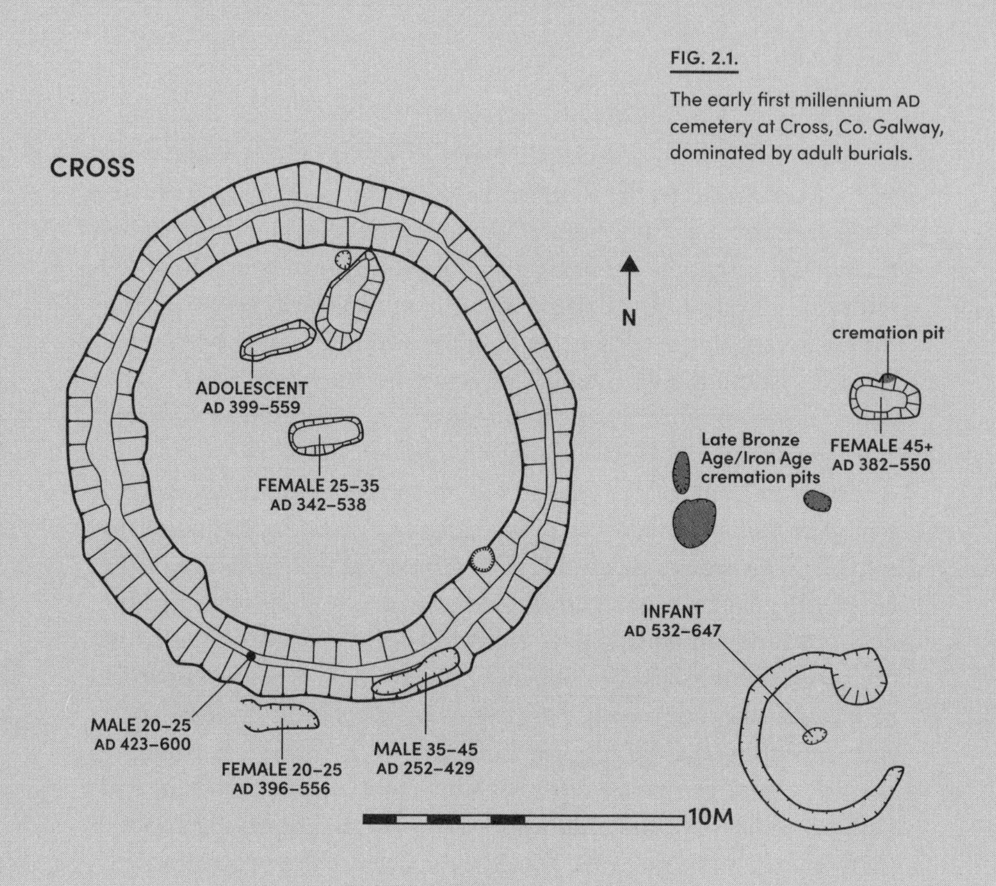

FIG. 2.1.

The early first millennium AD cemetery at Cross, Co. Galway, dominated by adult burials.

skeletal record to social interpretation is even more fraught when it comes to the relationship between sex and gender. It is quite a while since Rosemary Joyce cautioned against archaeologists using any assumed two-sex/two-gender model against the known background of the complexity and variety of ways in which people in human societies construct these differences.[9] Here, care is taken to try to consistently refer to 'sex' when referring to the skeletal record and to 'gender' when talking about social roles and identities of people and the differences between them; and rather than there being two clearly defined sex categories, biological variability is a reality and has to be considered alongside the social construction of gender. Not surprisingly, distinctions regarding the treatment of the dead based on gender are difficult to generalise about. The evidence across the fourth, third and into the second millennium BC, during the Neolithic and the Early Bronze Age, has been interpreted as suggesting that adult males are often more prominent than females in formal burial rites in Ireland. A rough demographic balance between men and women would be expected in contemporary living populations, hence it might appear that in some cases men and women were treated differently. We need to recognise that there are difficulties in determining the sex of adult skeletons; these cannot always be definitively identified as male or female, and there are many cases in which the individual can only be identified as an adult. This can mask patterns in mortuary practice.[10]

Looking at the detail of mortuary practices, it is apparent that differences in terms of the presence of non-adults and adults and gendered differences are important as expressions of social attitudes and beliefs. Nevertheless, while recognising that archaeological estimates are based on a minimum number of individuals (MNI), which could underestimate the actual number of people in a deposit, it is worth reiterating the key point that the remains of only *some* of the deceased members of the contemporary living population were placed in formal burial places and other sites where archaeologists find human bone. It is worth considering an example. The court tomb is one of the styles of megalithic tomb constructed by early farming communities during the fourth millennium BC. There are over 400 such monuments known in Ireland. Estimates of the labour needed to construct such a monument suggest that an average-sized court tomb would have required the input and effort of a group of 25–50 people. In this sense court tombs are the result of communal labour. In excavated court tombs, however, the average number of people represented by inhumed and cremated remains is less than ten; the well-preserved deposits at Parknabinnia, Co. Clare are something of an exception, having at least 20 individuals represented. Some court tombs were in use over substantial periods of time and were subject to continued deposition of human remains.[11] Thus, the people whose remains ended up in such monuments appear to represent a small, selected proportion of the local population over several generations. [PL. 2.A]

PL. 2.A.

Annaghmare, Co. Armagh court tomb.

SOCIAL IDENTITIES AND POPULATION LEVELS

A number of questions arise from these observations. First, why were people accorded different kinds of post-mortem treatment on the basis of criteria such as age and gender? Second, what happened to those—the majority of the living population—whose remains were not selected for deposition in formal places that have been the focus of archaeological work? Third, can we obtain some idea of the overall size of the population on the island of Ireland at various times to assess the demographic context of the human remains that we have in the archaeological record?

Looking at the first issue, anthropological research indicates that age and gender are the two most common bases on which people are treated differently when they die. These have been and continue to be the most widely used axes of social differentiation—in life and death—in societies of varying complexity, from the egalitarian to those with marked social ranking.[12] It is this social differentiation that seems to be reflected in, and marked by, how people are treated in death and other rites of passage. For example, a categorisation of social status describes two types: achieved and ascribed. Achieved status is accorded to an individual on the basis of their prowess and personal qualities. These might be reflected in the way the death of such an individual is marked, but the status of the individual is carried with them into the grave. Social position is tied to personal qualities, hence by definition it cannot be passed on. Ascribed social status on the other hand is trans-generational. In this case social status is conferred on a group—lineage- or kin-based—rather than on the individual. Membership is the key to status. Status is carried on, transmitted across generations; indeed, this attribute is critical to the continuation of the social standing of the group.[13] This is an explanation of why young children can sometimes be treated in a very 'adult-like' way in death. Although, it is worth remembering the discussion of childhood above, and that in other times individuals may have been integral, contributing members of society at a significantly younger age than is the case in modern Western society. The treatment of the dead can become a way of marking, re-marking and remembering the long-term nature of the group, which is important in societies in which authority is seen to be handed on from the past. Mary Helms has argued that the key to understanding the emergence of leading groups in traditional societies is how they establish links with the past, with the ancestors and with the origins of the society in which they exist.[14]

What happens at death is that the place the deceased person held in society is marked and remembered by the living. From this perspective it may be useful to think about identities and status in early societies in terms of the relationships *between* people, animals and things, rather than by projecting discrete, individual identities that we tend to be concerned with in society today. Tim Ingold has argued that there are two ways of constructing identity in small-scale societies. First, there is a sense of genealogical identity. In this case origins provide an understanding of who people think they are. This can be linked with the emergence of notions of ascribed status. Second, there is relational identity, whereby the construction and maintenance of links between persons and things are at the heart of peoples' sense of who and what they are. Helms has pointed out that such societies are always concerned to a greater or lesser extent both with ancestral origins and how the on-going activities of the living, including the treatment of the dead, fit with the past. Relational identities thus provide us with approaches to think about how identities are built around relationships with other people, with things and with the past.[15]

The archaeological evidence offers us opportunities to examine this issue critically. Joanna Brück has eloquently shown how the ways people in Bronze Age Britain were buried and the character and range of objects placed with them can inform us about the web of relationships within which the deceased lived and died. The funerary rite also directly reflects how the participants in the mortuary rituals wished to portray the person in death. [FIG. 2.2][16] Taking

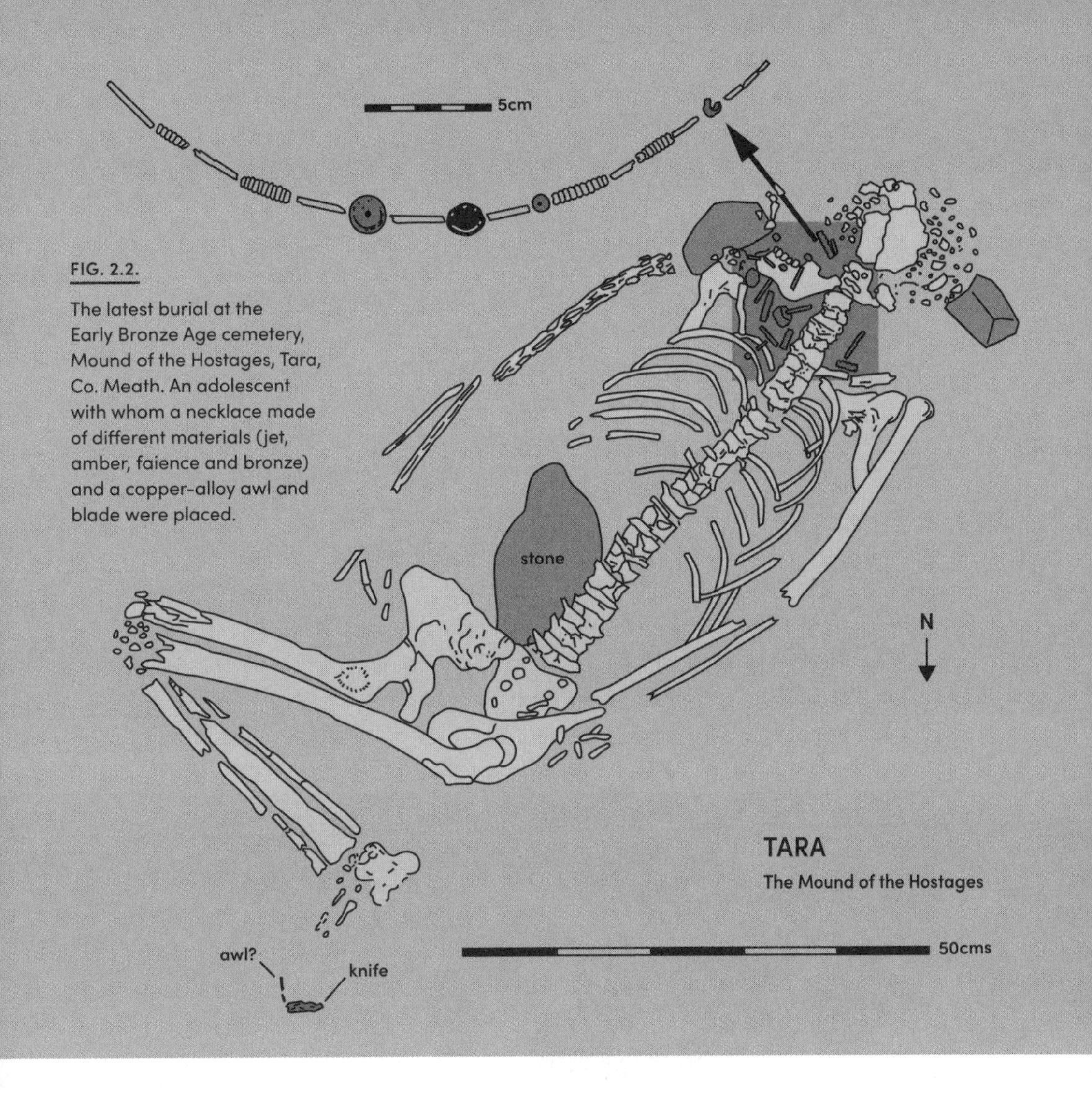

FIG. 2.2.

The latest burial at the Early Bronze Age cemetery, Mound of the Hostages, Tara, Co. Meath. An adolescent with whom a necklace made of different materials (jet, amber, faience and bronze) and a copper-alloy awl and blade were placed.

a different perspective, we may be able to recognise from the skeletal evidence the re-occurrence of physical traits in the bones of different people in a grave or monument. This information can be used to explore the extent to which there were biological and genetic links between people buried close together or placed in the same burial context. In four multiple burials at the third-millennium BC site at Eulau, Germany, which appeared to be the result of a violent event, adults and children faced each other. A direct child–parent genetic relationship was demonstrated in one grave; a wider argument was made that genetic kinship was a focal point of social organisation in Eulau.[17]

What can we say then about the treatment at death of the majority of the living population whose remains were not selected for final deposition in formal burial places? Because their burial was not formally marked or monumentalised this is a difficult question to answer. Customs and practices differ depending on social and cultural contexts and change over time. As suggested in the discussion above, treatment varies depending on the age and gender—and indeed the circumstances of death—of the deceased. Moreover, unless a person was accompanied by diagnostic artefacts when they were buried, or the bones are directly dated as part of an archaeological investigation, it may be difficult to establish when the remains date from. And if further evidence were needed of the complexity

PL. 2.B.

A Balinese Hindu ceremonial placement of cremated bone in the sea, near Goa Lawah, Bali, Indonesia.

of the issue, it can be found in a paper that was intended to inform archaeologists about the variety of mortuary rites that characterise societies across the world, and which has become a classic cautionary tale; Peter Ucko illustrated a wide range of practices that would leave little or no trace for the archaeologist. These include exposure on the ground surface after death; burial in trees or open water; and the scattering of bone after cremation.[18] **[PL. 2.B]**

Given that the known burial record itself is a such a partial representation of early societies, to a large extent reflecting decisions made by communities about the way in which the remains of people would be remembered or forgotten, can we explore the demographic and social context of the burial evidence we have? The importance of addressing this question is that it informs our understanding of the proportion of the population who were given formal treatment at death. Discussion of this subject is based on factors such as the size of the island of Ireland; its ecology; likely population density figures per square kilometre under different subsistence strategies; the scale of, and labour investment in, monuments built at different times; and the potential trajectory of the island's population over the course of prehistory. In an important paper incorporating over 9,000 radiocarbon dates from over 2,600 archaeological sites, Rowan McLaughlin argues that the temporal frequency patterns of these dates—from the Mesolithic to the later medieval/modern period—can be used as a proxy for fluctuating levels of human activity and population in Ireland in the past.[19] **[FIG. 2.3]**

In summary McLaughlin's model suggests a low population for the Mesolithic, numbering 10,000–50,000 people; an Early Neolithic explosion when the population is seen as being in the order of one million; followed by a decrease in the Middle and Late Neolithic. During the Bronze Age he argues there was a population in the order of two million people with some fluctuation, followed by a lull in the Early Iron Age. Population is seen as recovering in the Middle or Developed Iron Age, again up to a million people, and then falling until AD 200. From this point in the Late Iron Age, it

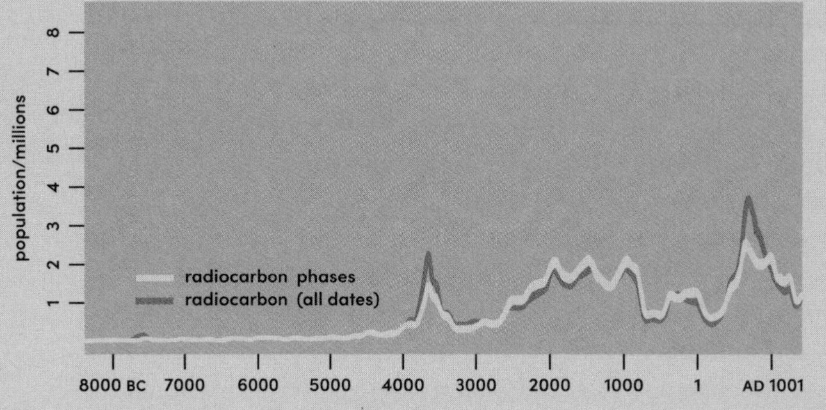

FIG. 2.3.

Kernel density models of archaeological radiocarbon dates from Ireland as a basis for population estimates from 8000 BC to AD 1000.

is argued by McLaughlin that there was strong growth, continuing into the early medieval period and peaking around AD 700, when the island population is assessed at being well over two million.[20]

So, what are we to make of this population model? It certainly demonstrates the value of the large-scale public and private investment in development-led archaeology that has transformed our evidence of the scale and extent of human activity during the prehistoric, early medieval and later periods on the island. In that sense it backs up the perspective offered in Chapter 1 that the extent to which the cultural landscape of the island was shaped in prehistory has not been widely understood. McLaughlin's population figures are significantly higher than those used in previous discussions. On the other hand, the patterns of high and low human activity that he identifies across prehistory have been identified in other studies and by colleagues using a range of approaches incorporating archaeological and palaeoenvironmental indicators to identify social and environmental changes and potential links to climate as a driver of change.[21] One of the key issues is the assumption that the frequency distribution of radiocarbon dates over time directly reflects changes in population and can be used as the basis for population estimates.

There appears to be some elision in the discussion—from talking about growth rates of radiocarbon dates to population growth rates. The main archaeological rationale provided is a discussion of apparent 'boom-and-bust' cycles during the Neolithic period in Europe. It would have been useful to clarify that this reflects a social evolutionary perspective on the past. Recent discussion has suggested that there may well have been cycles of population growth and decrease within the Neolithic in Ireland, with population decreasing in the period after 3400 BC, coinciding with a shift to wetter conditions. At the same time radiocarbon dating indicates that the mega-passage tombs of Knowth and Newgrange, and probably Dowth, may all have been built within the two centuries before 3000 BC, requiring a significant level of population, at least within the wider area of the Boyne Valley in eastern Ireland.[22] The conundrum of how this period of tomb building can be seen as corresponding to a period of low population is not adequately explained by McLaughlin. In this context we might be cautious about the overall approach and the population figures provided. For more on this, see the discussions of particular periods in the relevant chapters below.

Two additional observations provide some sense of lived reality to apply to population estimates. A key social issue was the scale and character of the communities within which people lived. These were the effective social and kin networks within which relationships were formed and maintained. We have indications from the size of monuments constructed at particular times— through the very act of construction itself—that the scale of the broad social polities to which people would have had a sense of belonging and contributing to varied over time. The evidence indicates, however, that we are justified in continuing to describe these communities as small-scale, with face-to-face contact and personal knowledge forming the register of everyday lives.[23] Another way of thinking about the links between people in a population is to consider broad demographic and biological patterns. It is probable that over half the population at any time were children. Hence the effective breeding population, or the people who were parenting children, would have been, by definition, smaller than the total population. This provides us with a better sense of the degree of the biological 'relatedness' of people on the island at different times in the past.[24]

LIFESTYLE AND HEALTH

The issue of how we relate the evidence from the dead of particular periods to the scale and organisation of their contemporary living societies will be a recurring one in the following chapters. What I want to provide here is some impression of the range of information about people and their lifestyles that can be extracted from skeletal material, recognising that detailed analyses have been published for a range of sites.[25] [FIG. 2.4]

Of the small number of human remains from the Mesolithic, the most informative osteoarchaeological account is that by Catryn Power of the human remains found in Peter Woodman's excavation at Ferriter's Cove on the Dingle Peninsula in Co. Kerry. These appear to represent at least one mature male who died in his late twenties or thirties. The radiocarbon date from the bones indicated that this man lived sometime around 4000 BC. The remains consisted of fragments of long bones and teeth. Five of the seven teeth had wear or dental attrition, due to the nature of the diet or the use of the teeth for activities such as gripping. In relation to diet, the level of carbon-13—a stable isotope of carbon—in human skeletal remains is related to the major sources of protein an individual consumed. The isotopic evidence from the Ferriter's Cove remains suggest that this man had relied heavily on coastal and marine food sources during his life. This profile is comparable with Mesolithic populations elsewhere in western Europe and conveys some sense of the everyday life of this early inhabitant of the area we now call the Dingle Peninsula.[26]

Physical remains of considerably more people are known from Neolithic and later contexts, and Power has provided a valuable

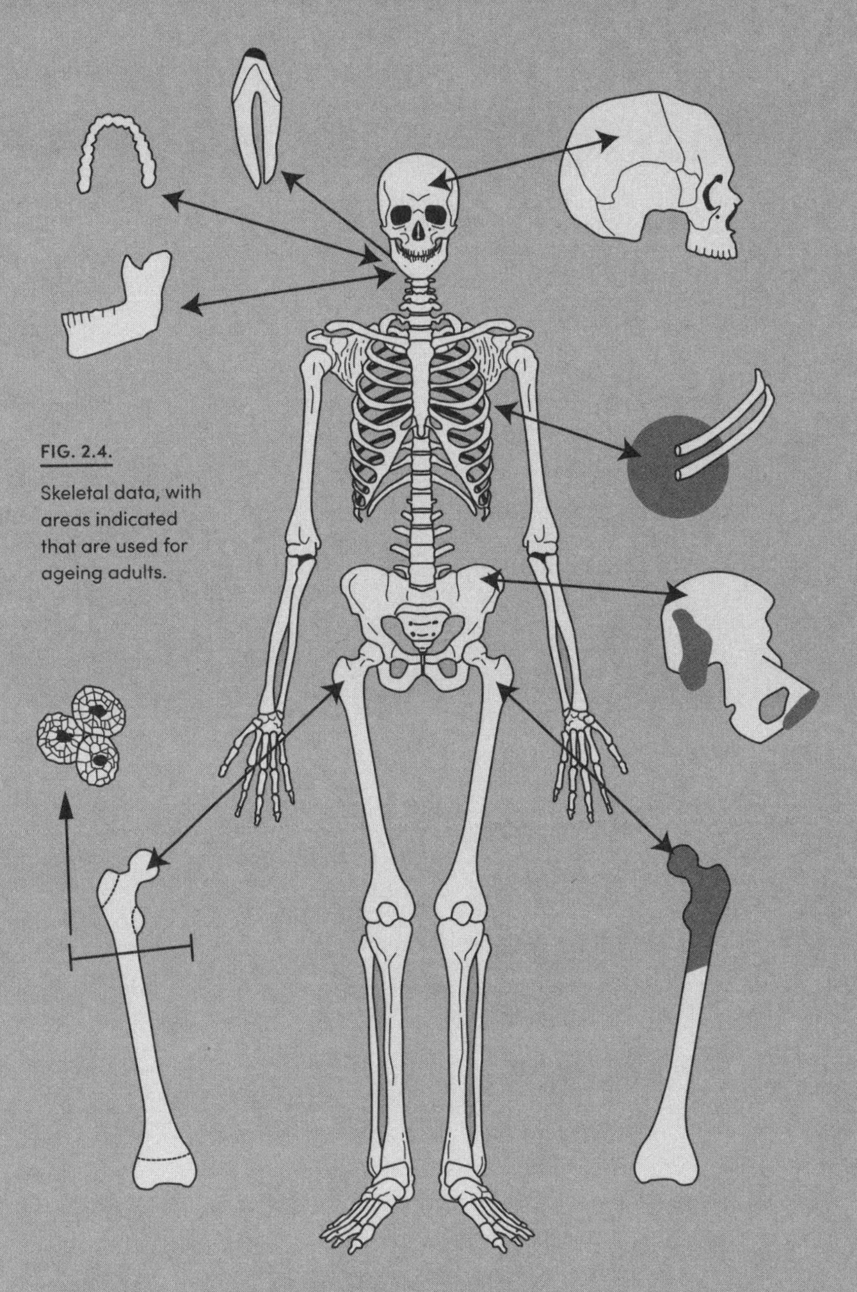

FIG. 2.4.

Skeletal data, with areas indicated that are used for ageing adults.

SKELETAL DATA ARE USED FOR INTERPRETATION OF:

- Mortuary treatment
- Taphonomy
- Sex
- Age-at-death
- Stature and body proportions
- Disease and trauma
- Diet
- Physical exertion
- Stress
- Migration and ancestry

Individual
▼
Population
▼
Inter-Population
▼
Inter-Regional
▼
Diachronic

review of some of these individuals. Representations and descriptions of prehistoric people often suggest that they would have been more muscular but smaller than people today, but it is worth thinking about these descriptions more closely. For example, bone cross-sectional geometry and sites of muscular attachment (entheses) provide markers for different activities. Muscularity and leanness were the result of the wide range of physical activities that would have characterised everyday life. The level of technological aid that prehistoric people had was much lower than what we take for granted today. Hence, there was a much greater need for direct human input and physical labour on tasks, but also consequent impacts and stresses on the body and bones and resultant skeletal adaptation. In terms of stature in the admittedly small sample analysed by Power, the average height of males in the Bronze Age at 170.2cm (5ft 7in) was shorter than the 178cm (5ft 10in) average for men today, but the females, at 165 cm (5ft 5in), were the same average height as women in Ireland today.[27]

Stature is strongly influenced by diet and nutrition. Some analyses indicate that in Europe stature did not significantly change over the course of the Palaeolithic, Mesolithic or Neolithic, although others suggest skeletal changes, including reduced stature, in early farmers. This indicates that we should disabuse ourselves of any idea that the diet and health of early farmers was necessarily better than that of hunter-gatherers. Data from Europe and the Near East suggest the contrary, with increased rates of dental caries among farming populations, due to the higher consumption of carbohydrates, and a higher incidence of palaeopathologies (diseases that leave an impact on human bone and hence can be detected through osteoarchaeological analysis). This pattern is related to the ease with which infectious disease spread as population density, sedentism and close contact with domesticated animals increased. We need to look at this model of health decline carefully, however, and in local and regional contexts.[28]

Whatever about the consequences of agriculture in terms of health, stable isotope analysis indicates that there was a widespread and marked change in diet from around 4000 BC in Atlantic Europe, including Ireland. There was a move towards a much greater reliance on terrestrial sources of food. This change has been linked to a switch to domesticated food sources, particularly cattle and cereal crops. It appears that this pattern of reliance on terrestrial food sources is the dominant one in Ireland from the beginnings of the Neolithic, even when people lived in coastal areas.[29]

Looking at a sample of over two hundred individuals Power's observations suggest that there were some persistent health and dietary patterns in prehistoric human populations in Ireland. Commenting on similar evidence from Britain, Charlotte Roberts and Margaret Cox detailed a picture of people's health between the Neolithic and the Iron Age as one with considerable discomfort as a result of dental problems, rheumatism, arthritis, metabolic disease and broken bones, including from trauma, a comment that could equally be applied to Ireland.[30] Remembering the point made above that the dead visible in the archaeological record were in most cases socially selected, and possibly comprised of leading (and potentially the healthiest) members of the population, it can be suggested that the persistent problems these people endured, such as arthritis and rheumatism, would have been more widespread in the general living population.

One of the most striking features is that in about a quarter of all the Neolithic and Bronze Age people examined by Power, there were stress lines (enamel hypoplasia) in their teeth. This indicates that as children, these people were subject to systemic stresses, such as dietary deficiencies and illness.[31] As mentioned above, in these traditional societies high infant mortality rates would be expected. Therefore many children, sadly, did not survive the stress that we see in the teeth and bones of those who survived into adulthood. **[PL. 2.C]**

The physical difficulties that people would have suffered as a result of bone fractures can be detected in the healing patterns

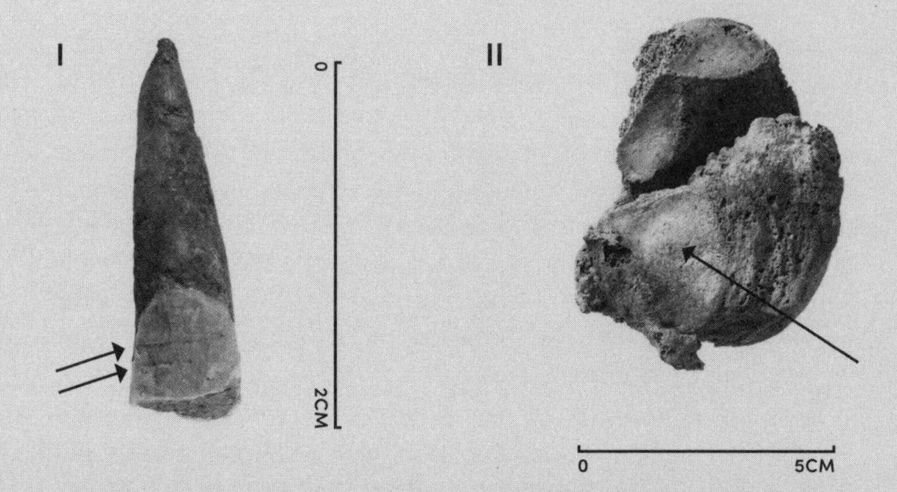

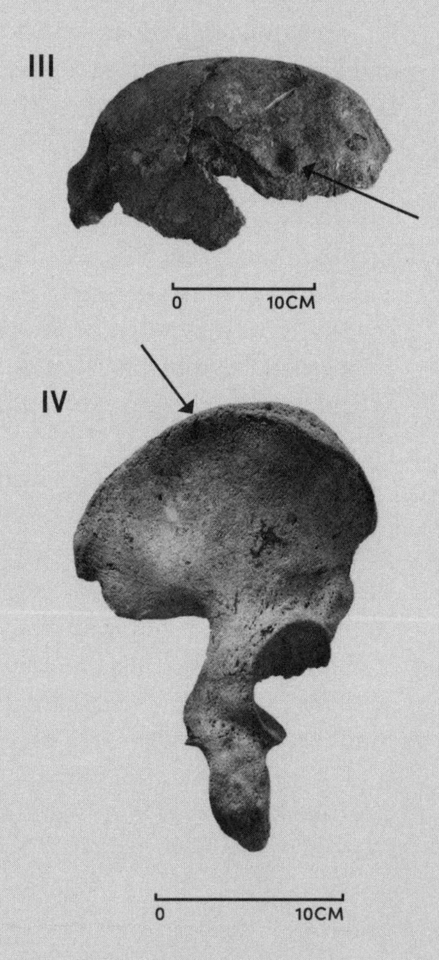

PL. 2.C.

Palaeopathologies in the skeletal assemblage from Poulnabrone, Co. Clare portal tomb. Clockwise from above: I -dental enamel hypoplasia, II -adult left talus (ankle) bone with sheen (eburnation) as a result of abrasion of cartilage, III -depressed fracture to cranium of a younger or middle adult, IV -dorsal view of right hip bone of an adult with embedded tip of projectile point.

visible in the bones of some individuals. In interpreting these patterns, however, we have to be aware of what is referred to as 'the osteological paradox'; the paradox being that the individuals who have skeletal indicators of palaeopathologies are in fact the 'healthy' people, those who lived long enough to develop lesions. There were many who actually may have died from a given disease, as with children who died from dietary deficiencies and illness, without there being any resultant skeletal damage. [PL. 2.CII]

The study of palaeopathologies can help us understand the general health status of prehistoric populations. In the sample examined by Power there were in fact relatively low incidences of pathologies that would suggest infection and iron deficiency anaemia-related conditions. There were hints, however, that these may have been more a problem for people at other specific times in prehistory.[32]

As well as these general indicators of health and nutrition, we can talk about the length of time that people could have expected to live in prehistory. Today in Ireland most women can expect to live into their eighties (average life expectancy is 84) and men into their late seventies (average life expectancy is 80-81).[33] For prehistoric people the reality was different. Having survived childhood, reaching the age of 30 was an expectation that most people could have entertained; this is the pattern we see in the age-at-death statistics, although accurately estimating the age of older adults continues to be an area of contention in bioarchaeology. Some people did live for much longer, such as the man who appears to have been around 60 years old when he died and was placed in the chamber of a monument at Ashley Park, Co. Tipperary sometime around 3600 BC, and the woman from Ballymacaward, Co. Donegal who was a similar age when she was laid to rest in her grave in the fifth to sixth century AD.[34] In all probability these individuals would have outlived all their contemporary age cohort. They would have been regarded as exceptional in terms of their long lives, given the average length of life in local populations.

These demographic realities had consequences for a number of key social parameters relevant to the discussion of relationships and the differentiation between people in communities—such as the definition of the age at which someone was deemed to move from being a non-adult to an adult in social and biological terms—and for how these are reflected in the ways people were treated at death. They must also have influenced the relationships between generations within a family or household unit and the status of older adults. We could expect these elders would have been regarded with veneration and awe, since tradition and knowledge in traditional small-scale societies is seen to come from the living who have died, the ancestors and the past generations. The length of a prehistoric generation is taken here as being between 25 and 30 years.[35]

VIOLENCE AND CONFLICT

From the skeletal record it is apparent that some bone fractures appear to be the result of offensive blows struck against the person. More exceptionally there is evidence that individuals were killed. The nature of violence and war is a notable topic of research and discussion in the archaeological literature, after a period from the 1960s to the 1990s when it was under-emphasised. At that time much of the discussion of earlier prehistory in particular was couched in terms that suggested that conflict did not play a significant role in social life. The change in perspective is perhaps not surprising, given the increasing occurrence of warfare in the modern world since the 1990s. As well as being a sign of the times we live in, as Jean Guilaine and Jean Zammit put it, this interest is also a result of increasing evidence indicating that violence and conflict were recurring aspects of life in prehistoric societies.[36] **[PL. 2.C.III AND IV]**

A graphic example that Detlef Jantzen and colleagues have reported on is what appears to be a Bronze Age battlefield in the Tollense Valley, north-eastern Germany. Here discoveries of bronze

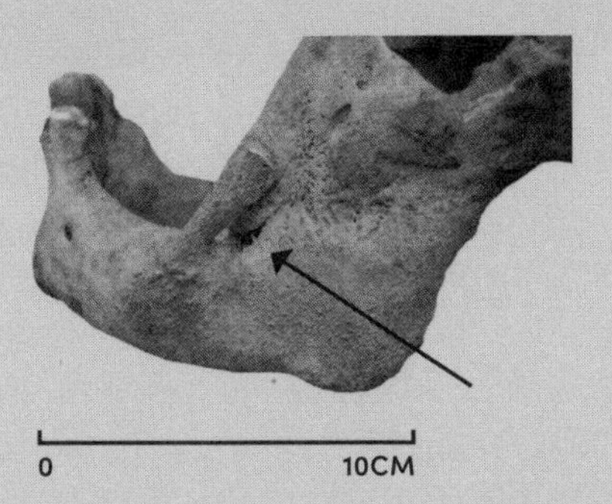

PL. 2.D.

A well-healed, perforating traumatic injury on the left side of the lower mandible of a Neolithic adult female, probably over 25 years old, from Kilgreany Cave, Co. Waterford. Likely to have been caused by horizontal penetration with a sharp object.

and wooden weapons as well as human skeletal remains (of around 140 individuals, with an estimate of the total number of the dead as being more than 700) with traces of violence and trauma, appear to be the remains of a conflict or battle that occurred between 1300 to 1200 BC. The location is a swampy river valley. Individuals were pursued or killed on the spot, or their bodies were thrown in the river.[37] Looking at Ireland in prehistory, we have material evidence for a variety of weapons of conflict, notably when metal technology is introduced but also in stone-using societies, a point amplified by the results of experimental work. From the Mesolithic and Neolithic periods, large numbers of projectile points and stone axeheads have survived. At least some of these could have been effective as weapons as well as tools. From the time of the establishment of farming communities in the early fourth millennium BC, there is also a concern—more evident at some times than others—with defence. This is most clearly expressed in the construction of earthen or stone boundaries, enclosing areas of occupation.[38]

Christopher Knüsel has commented that when archaeologists are examining evidence for actual violence or warfare the answer should be sought in human remains, as wounds not only impact soft tissue but, depending on their severity and extent, will also affect the skeleton.[39] And evidence has survived on human skeletal remains of fractures and trauma caused by weapons. Examples include the man of mature years buried in a monument built for him at Linkardstown, Co. Carlow around 3600 BC, who appears to have been struck on the head with a stone axehead. A woman who was over 25 at the time of her death and was buried in Kilgreany Cave, Co. Waterford around 3600–3350 BC had suffered a traumatic injury to the left side of her lower jaw bone, inflicted by a sharp object, possibly an arrowhead. [PL. 2.D] From later prehistory, around 1000 BC, at Drumman More lake, Co. Armagh, there is the example of a Late Bronze Age socketed knife apparently having been driven into a human cranium.[40] These could be construed as isolated incidents, picked from a record extending over 8,000 years, but in the light of the wealth and diversity of related evidence across Europe, we can accept Helle Vandkilde's view that low-level conflict was endemic in society in Europe during prehistory.[41]

That phrase 'low-level' is important, as it stresses the need to think of violence in this context not so much in terms of organised war in the modern sense but as one element of the mechanisms by which relationships within and between communities were conducted and problems resolved. Anthropological evidence suggests that violence in small-scale societies in modern times has this social character. The action generally consists of display, of skirmishes; the level of fatalities is low and the maintenance or the restoration of honour is important.[42] There are a more restricted number of examples in prehistoric Europe of organised violence, such as the Tollense battle mentioned above. But evidence for such violence does occur at different periods: a number of Linear Pottery (Neolithic) burials and deposits from around 5000 BC, such as those at Talheim and Schöneck-Kilianstadten, Germany and Asparn/Schletz, Austria, and the Early/Middle Bronze Age burial dating to round 1700 BC at Wassenaar, the Netherlands all appear to be the result of clashes in which communities were attacked and massacred.[43] Hence there was the possibility of conflict at a larger, more organised scale. Following wider European trends from around the middle of the second millennium BC there is an

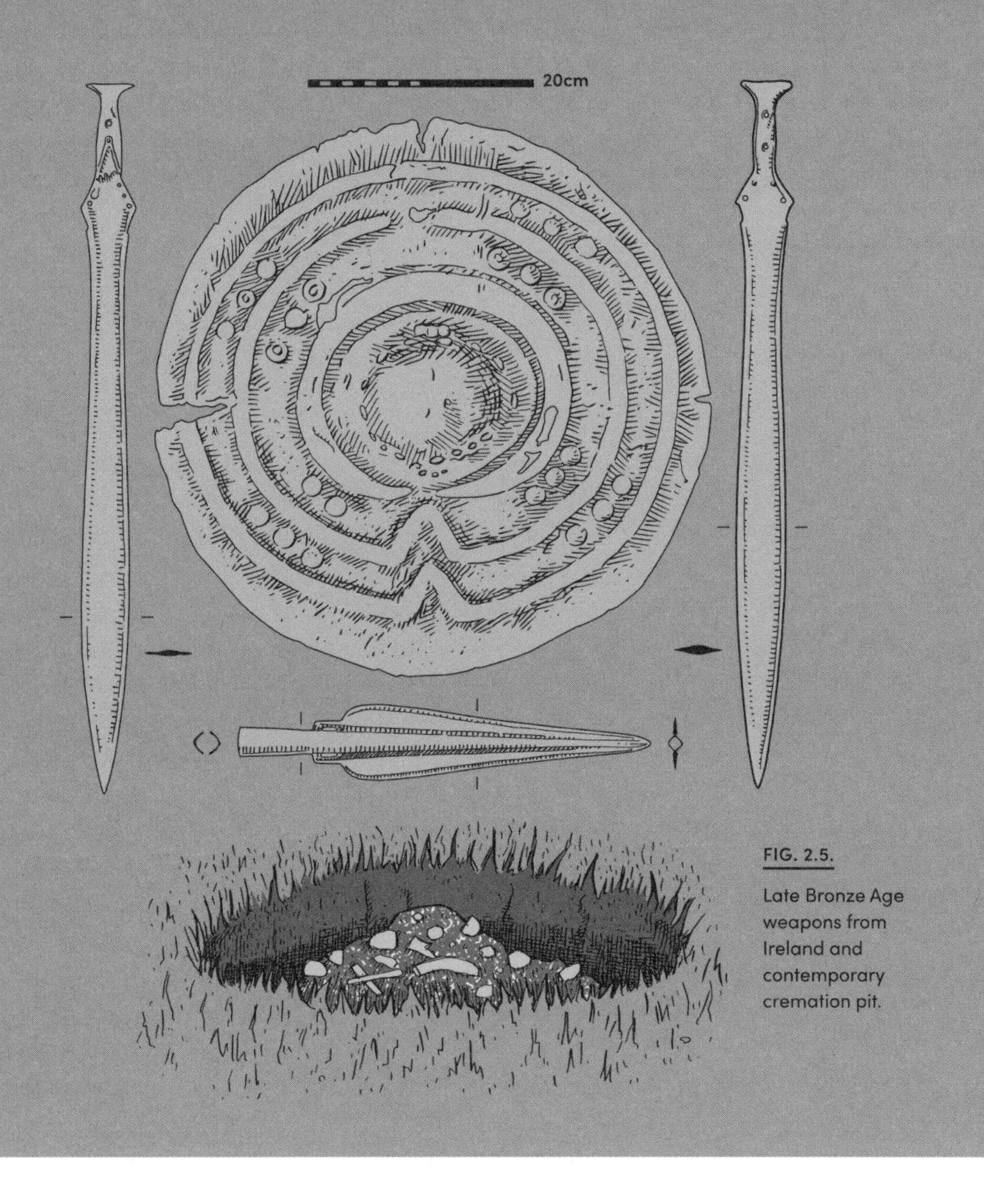

FIG. 2.5.

Late Bronze Age weapons from Ireland and contemporary cremation pit.

increased visibility of bronze weapons in Ireland, and from around 1400 BC the appearance of large, defended hill-top enclosures or hillforts.[44] It is possible to see in this phenomenon and other elements of the archaeological record the emergence of polities who, on occasions, may have been in conflict with each other—occasions when the term warfare might have been justified. This may have been both prompted by and centred on a warrior élite, or the presence of such élites in the service of leaders. In Ireland this is indicated not so much by the burial record but by the type of material found in later prehistoric hoards.[45] Remembering Knüsel's point above, however, a major problem we have is that the burial record for this period is dominated by cremation, therefore there is little direct evidence of whether violent trauma was actually a factor of how people died. [FIG. 2.5]

Violence and conflict may have been related to the issue of cultural identities and the extent to which contemporary groups had different and competing senses of territorial and social identity. This is the kind of scenario that the increasingly regionalised material record in later prehistory may reflect and have contributed to. In writing about earlier prehistoric times, we have perhaps too readily assumed that similarities in the cultural record across the island indicate a common, shared and island-wide sense of cultural identity. Jim Mallory has argued that in the last centuries BC a five-province cosmological principle underpinning both the sense of regional differences discussed above and a form of island-wide consciousness may have emerged.[46] We have to be careful of anachronistically exporting notions of identity constructed by and through the course of Irish history and that are therefore not relevant in earlier times.

IDENTITIES, LANGUAGES AND ANCIENT DNA

In terms of daily life at a time when people's movements were by foot or by boat, the world that people knew intimately and identified would have been a local one—the area that could be reached within a few hours' walk of home. In the case of mobile groups who shifted home regularly, their locality would encompass a wider landscape. It is important that we do not confuse this focus on the local and immediate with any sense of isolation however. People were in touch with other polities and areas in Ireland and abroad;

there was a continuing flow of materials between people and places. As a result of these webs of contacts, objects were exchanged, used and could be lost or deposited at a considerable distance away from where they were produced. Other goods were brought by sea to and from Ireland, providing the physical evidence for ongoing links with Britain and northwest continental Europe.[47]

As noted in Chapter 1, archaeologists are often asked questions about how prehistoric people in Ireland would have seen themselves. What did they look like? What did they call themselves? What language would they have spoken? Would they have had an awareness of living on an island? What sense of kinship and wider social identity did they have? These are important issues, and a multidisciplinary approach to them—directing attention to the particular value of bringing together archaeological, linguistic and genetic evidence—has been a focus of research for over 30 years. More recently, the genomics revolution has seen the sequencing of complete human genomes and the extraction of a[ncient] DNA from people of the past. Of all the scientific techniques for the extraction of information from human remains, aDNA analysis has had the greatest impact in European prehistoric studies — and, linked to the ease with which people today can access genetic information about themselves, the widest public appeal. The relationships between these kinds of evidence are returned to in later chapters, but here some wider contextualisation is offered.[48]

It might be useful to begin by thinking about the sense of place people on the island of Ireland might have had. Recognising the prominence of woodland in the landscape, travel by inland waterways and coastal movement were important. Taking into account the number and wide distribution of hill-top monuments, it is clear that on occasions people viewed the land and the sea from hills and mountains. With this lived experience it seems likely that there would have been a widespread sense and knowledge of living on an island, and the possibility of social networks spanning the island. This should not, however, be taken as necessarily meaning that people would have regarded themselves as sharing a common cultural identity.[49] It is worth remembering that up to the 1970s archaeologists commonly saw distinctive sets of material that they recognised in the archaeological record as the direct material expression of the customs and behaviour of distinctive peoples. Modern labels describing the archaeological material were used to identify different 'cultures'. As changes were recognised in the archaeological material, these were seen as representing the advent of new people.[50] This type of formulation is now widely acknowledged as being over-simplified. We now recognise the degree of fluidity in the ways material culture was actively used by people, the substantial overlaps there are between supposedly discrete cultural assemblages, and the wide range of processes involved in changes in material culture.[51]

The most widely applied cultural distinction is a differentiation between pre-Celtic and Celtic populations in Ireland. It has been argued on the basis of language studies that the Irish language was first introduced into Ireland around 500 BC. This was regarded as being contemporary with archaeological evidence in Continental Europe for people whom Classical writers described as 'keltoi'. Hence a connection was forged between archaeology and language. Ireland was described as becoming 'Celtic' at this time, and technologically this was seen as being represented in the transition from the Bronze Age to the Iron Age. The picture is much more complex than this, however. For a start, one of the interesting features of the archaeological evidence in the middle of the first millennium BC is the lack of significant cultural change; the beginnings of ferrous technology can in fact now be dated to a few hundred years earlier. It is clear that a small number of objects were imported onto the island, and the art style that is most commonly described as Celtic (the La Tène style) was used imaginatively on a range of materials and objects made in Ireland, but the overwhelming signal that we have is of continuity with what had gone before. This makes the notion of language replacement at this time difficult to explain.[52]

Barry Cunliffe and John Koch have argued that the best interpretation of the archaeological and linguistic evidence is that Celtic as an Indo-European language—and the social systems associated with it—originated and developed as a *lingua franca* in the Atlantic Zone of Europe in the period between 5000 BC to 2700 BC, spreading eastwards into middle Europe in the third millennium BC. In the first millennium BC they envisage a breakdown of systems of social contact that had developed in the Atlantic Zone over the previous thousand years or so, leading to the development of distinctive, regional forms of Celtic languages.[53] Not surprisingly this 'Celtic from the west' hypothesis has been strongly contested by proponents of the traditional view that the Celtic language group formed in the northern European Alps in the Iron Age—the 'Celtic from the east' tradition.[54] But it aligns with the arguments of Colin Renfrew, who has suggested that the Indo-European language ancestral to Irish came to the island around about 4000 BC. This is based on the view that the spread of the Indo-European languages across Europe required a major cultural impetus to bring about the extent of language dispersal that was involved, and Renfrew sees the spread of farming as being the prime candidate for this cultural dispersal.[55] In a wide-ranging review of the evidence, Mallory has suggested that the most probable period of the introduction of Irish lies between 1000 BC and the first century BC. He sees this language shift as being potentially linked to the appearance and spread of hillforts and of an élite warrior class before 1000 BC, with the rise of major provincial/royal ritual centres in the first century BC also being a vehicle for language shift and consolidation and for the materialisation of the five-province cosmological principle and identity mentioned above. This also chimes with the 'Celtic from the centre' hypothesis articulated by Patrick Sims-Williams, which argues that Celtic languages spread into Ireland and Britain around 1000 BC.[56] **[FIG. 2.6]**

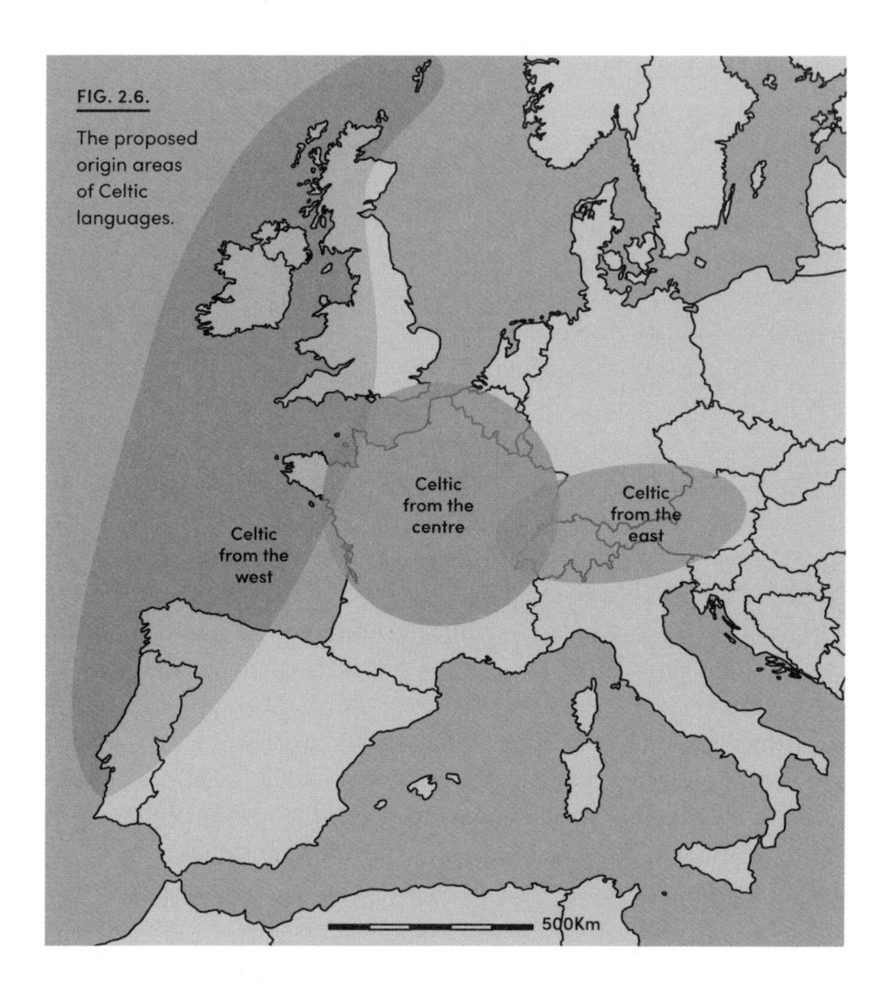

FIG. 2.6.
The proposed origin areas of Celtic languages.

Alongside archaeology and linguistics, it is important to consider the genetic evidence. As far back as the early 1980s Luigi Luca Cavalli Sforza and Albert Ammerman argued that the principal pattern of modern genetic variation in Europe graded from south-east to north-west, in a movement broadly similar to the pattern for the spread of farming over the period from 7000 BC to 4000 BC. This takes us over time and space from the earliest farming-based settlements in Greece—with a background in the beginnings of farming well over a thousand years earlier in the Near East—to the time that we begin to see evidence for farming in north-west Europe, including in Ireland and Britain.[57] More subtle analyses of this modern genetic data suggested up to seven major clusters of genetic similarity or ancestry.[58] From an Irish perspective, it was suggested that an east-to-west genetic differentiation within the modern population of the island might reflect important differences in genetic history. Geneticists argued that in the west of the island there are more people whose genetic ancestry reflects the original inhabitants, back to the first settlement of the island round about 8000 BC, while in the east there is a higher proportion of people whose ancestry indicates the impact of those who came into Ireland at the time of the introduction of farming and during later episodes of population inflow.[59] Mapping different kinds of genetic variation (by analysing Y-chromosome and mitochondrial DNA) provided the basis for distinguishing respectively between male and female inputs into different episodes of population history.[60]

It must be remembered that all this genetic information is modern, and it is based on reconstructing genetic histories from present-day populations. In his overview of the genetic history of the modern Irish population, Mallory carefully assessed how the evidence could be read as supporting two models that are contradictory! Catherine Nash has indicated how complex the network of influences and effects between population genetics and cultural politics has become, both in Ireland and in genealogies of the Irish diaspora. The genetic record in modern populations is a very generalised one; the sum of many generations of genetic change, drift and admixture. As Mallory and Ó Donnabháin argue, it is probable that there were recurring flows of population in and out of Ireland, particularly through the north-east and the south-east, where the geographical configuration of land and sea bring the islands of Ireland and Britain closest together.[61] **[PL. 2.E]** This relationship is a physical reminder that the Irish Sea acts as a centre to the coastlands on either side of it, rather than as an entity separating two

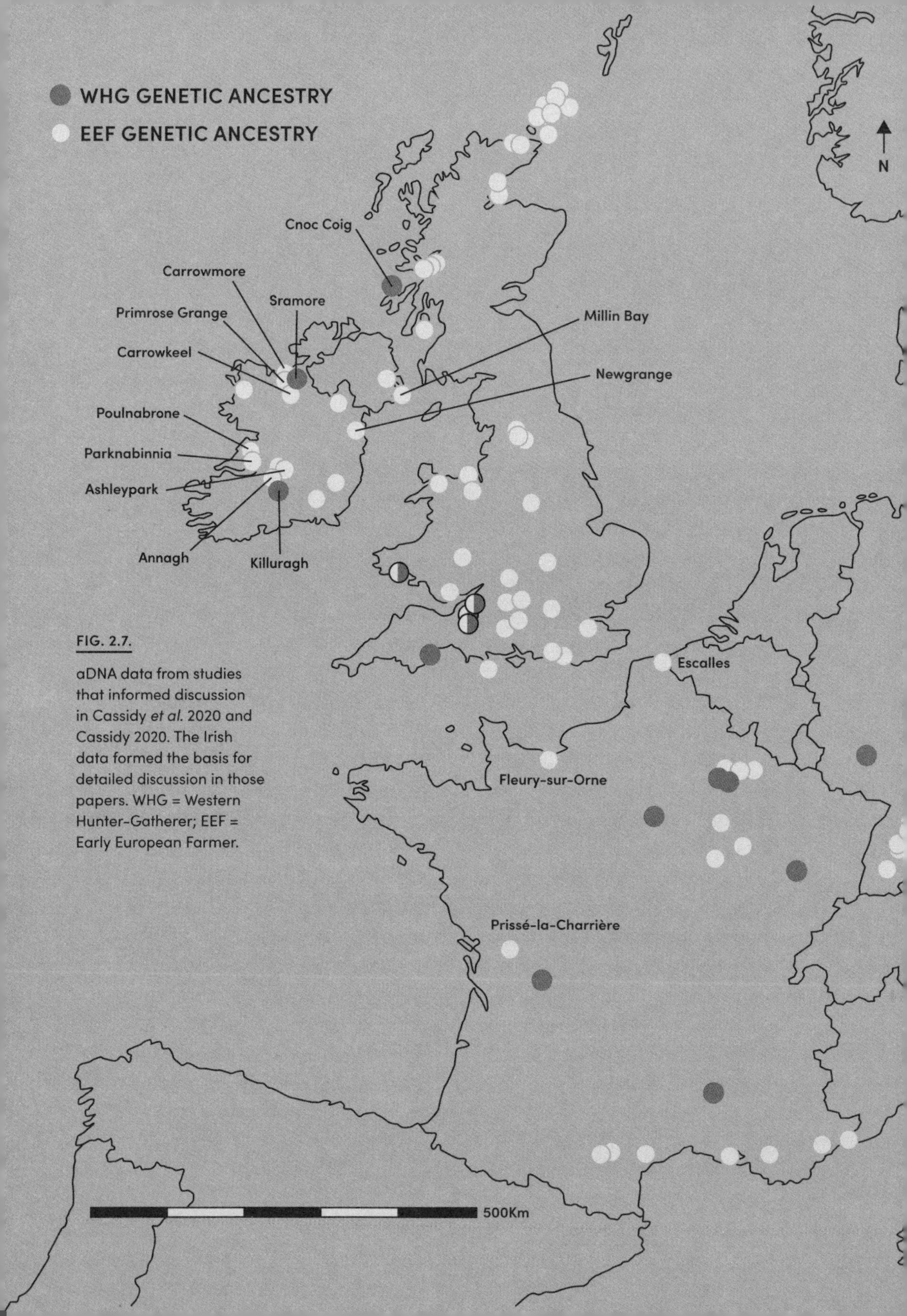

FIG. 2.7.

aDNA data from studies that informed discussion in Cassidy *et al.* 2020 and Cassidy 2020. The Irish data formed the basis for detailed discussion in those papers. WHG = Western Hunter-Gatherer; EEF = Early European Farmer.

large islands. Indeed, it could be argued that the label of Ireland as a 'Celtic' island has inhibited us from accepting the very strong, continued links that existed between people in eastern Ireland and the western littoral of Britain, from the Scilly Isles to the Northern Isles.[62]

PL. 2.E.

Looking across the North Channel to Scotland from the passage tomb at Carnanmore, Co. Antrim.

By contrast, the extraction of aDNA from human remains in the archaeological record provides evidence that is directly relevant to prehistoric people. At a European level this exciting research has provided archaeologists and geneticists with a new and rich set of data, generated considerable public interest, and in some cases resulted in dramatic re-interpretations of the archaeological record.[63] In Ireland, a suite of papers published by Lara Cassidy, Dan Bradley and colleagues have had an important impact on our understanding of Mesolithic, Neolithic and Bronze Age society on the island.[64] **[FIG. 2.7]**

The study of ancient genomes provides new and important information about people's chromosomal sex, appearance, genetic ancestors, biological relationships, health/disease and mobility. Nevertheless, the results of aDNA research are foci of recent and ongoing debate. A key issue is the role of aDNA in the interpretation of the archaeological record. A critical problem is the frequent assumption by archaeologists as well as geneticists that scientific techniques provide more accurate answers to the questions posed to archaeologists than do other kinds of archaeological evidence. Unfortunately, in many aDNA studies genetic or biological identity is frequently conflated with ethnic, cultural or linguistic identities; kinship with biological relatedness. Fuzzy archaeological concepts such as 'cultures' are mis-used as fixed, analytical categories, and there has been a focus on migration—particularly featuring men—as the primary explanation for changes in the genetic record. Maps have been generated suggesting sweeping cultural movements across Europe, which have the potential to feed into discussion about present-day migration.[65] All this is allied to an under-appreciation of the complexity of the archaeological record and a lack of reflection on the uncritical use of concepts embedded in Western society today as the basis for explaining the past. For example, it is clear from anthropological research that ideas of the person, the body, gender and kinship are culturally situated and socially constructed. The focus on migration and population movement brings us back to the cultural–historical fixation with population change as the major driver of social and cultural change. In addition, many of the problems that characterised the application of modern DNA to the past—such as the assumption that biological ancestry underpins our sense of who we really are—continues to inform much aDNA research.[66]

At a broader level it is interesting to consider how useful a 'big picture' view of events—such as that derived from aDNA research focusing on changes in ancestry proportions in populations over time—actually is for understanding the human realities of the past.

We need to complement this research by considering the details and messiness of the contexts of human life and death. Archaeologists, looking at mortuary practices, can point to the actions and behaviour of individual people, people we may not be able to name but whose lives we can come to know. This detailed human record tells us how social and cultural identities were constructed in relation to and in the context of particular places and locales. People's sense of who they were was intimately tied not just to community settings, but also to lives lived at a local scale. Broader cultural concepts and traditions may have been practiced over large areas, but these concepts were put into action in quite different ways through the relationships between people, animals and things in different communities. Patterns of change over time, and the reception of and reaction to new influences, are likely to have been diverse and related to local histories and ecologies.[67]

Not surprisingly then there has been a strong focus in the archaeological literature in recent years arguing that as a counter and complement to big-picture approaches we need to pay more attention to local and regional scales of analysis if we really want to find out what was going on in the past. Isotopic analyses discussing human mobility and diet and the application of aDNA analysis to interpret kinship practices at a detailed, local level have the potential to create links between generalised overviews and the detail of local variability in lifestyles that comes through in the bioarchaeological and archaeological record. This is a key point. Rather than presuming any teleological trend to the working out of deep history, we need to see it as the result of messy, lived-out relationships within social webs that involved humans, non-human others and places, and which were constantly being re-spun by human actions.[68] A critical part of those lives was how the dead were treated. This provides the basis for the narrative that unfolds in the following chapters.

3.

Connecting with the landscape: death in the Mesolithic

Leaving the ancestor

It was an unusual day, with the wind coming in from the sea, whipping up the waves and making the water foam—like it did in a river when it flowed over rocks as it came down from the mountains. Most days, the wind smelled of the land and came through the trees from the direction of where the big river entered the sea. It would be good to get out of the salty wind and the drops of water falling from the darkening grey sky. She turned from the tide and put her back to the wind, walking away from the shore, up the little rise, feeling the sharp edge of shells against her toes, and then down, out of the wind, into the warmth and closeness of the house. They had come back to this place a few days ago, and there was agreement that they had been guided well. There were lots of shellfish waiting to be collected and eaten. The children scouting in the woods had seen the footprints and droppings of the animal that grunted like a person in their sleep, and whose flesh was so different in taste from fish, plants and nuts. Describing for other houses how to get to this spot, they called it the seal hill: when the sea was at its highest against the land, from the sea the soft, low hill looked like a seal asleep on a low rock, partially surrounded by water. They had camped where the hill made a sheltering curve against the winds. So, when the wind had changed direction and started to come in from the sea, they knew that it was a good time to mark their ties to this place.

It was dark inside and she sensed that her child had fallen asleep, warmed by the presence of other people. As usual they had spent the brightest hours of the day outside, working and mending, carving, talking of people and the ways and means of doing and making things. They were looking forward to the time when the days would be longer. Then they would meet other families to celebrate; a couple of them hoped to meet a partner. She was thinking about seeing the house in which she had been born and grown up.

Now that daylight was fading, most of the people were gathered, expectant, waiting for the ceremony to begin. The seal-skin bag that carried their ancestor was placed on the ground in the centre of the house by the fire, surrounded by people. The ceremony began; grandfather telling the story of their origins. Their ancestor, like those of all the families they knew, had come from the sea. In the beginning people and seals all lived together, but then people started to move farther from the sea, getting to know the land and the hills and setting up their own houses. But they were always drawn back to the sea and the water. Tales were told of seals who lived with people and of people who, when out fishing off the coast, had chosen the company of seals and never came back. As grandfather spoke, people sensed the presence of the ancestor.

She looked around and saw that her child was now wide awake. Grandfather was holding the leg bone of the ancestor and telling stories about how it had guided him to the knowledge to see into the land and the sea. Holding the bone helped him to sense when the salmon would come back from the cold water to the north. It told him where the best fruit and berries were. It gave him strength in leading his family, and the good fortune to have so many healthy children in the house. The bone had been passed on over generations, a sacred thing said to be from when people and seals spoke the same words. Now he had decided that the time was right for the ancestor to go back to the sea and the seals. The people had noted the mark of the sea on the land after big storms and tides that were higher than anybody could remember. Grandfather had thought about this for a long time, and now knew that the sea was calling and needed the ancestor.

Earlier in the day they had decided on the right place for the bone—between the house and the sea. Now they were waiting for the right time. Grandfather had gone quiet. He was tapping the bag against the stone axe blade that had come from the river and that came alive in ceremonies, when it could talk. Some people were wondering if they would catch the voices in this wind and rain. Suddenly the noise of the wind dropped and they heard crying from the sea—a calling for the people to return their ancestor to those who needed him most. People were both glad and frightened. They followed grandfather as he went outside, carrying the bag carefully.

Moving to the right, he circled the house three times to help the ancestor say goodbye to the people and to connect him to the place. They came to the spot where they had decided to place the bone, amongst shells, so that it would go back and become part of the flesh of the seal hill. Grandfather looked around, saw the woman and beckoned her little girl to come to him. She could see everyone else looking at her daughter. Somebody whispered that now they knew why the little girl always played at the edge of the land with her feet in the sea, and why grandfather talked to her. The woman wondered what the future held for her daughter. Grandfather took the bone out, placed the girl's right hand and his own on the bone and put it in the ground. As they did, the woman noticed how quiet the night had become and saw that the full moon was casting its white light over them.

PL. 3.A.

The location of Rockmarshall, Co. Louth, from the west. Lighter coloured morainic ridges above lower ground. Approximate location of the middens highlighted.

The small-scale excavations carried out by Frank Mitchell in the 1940s at Rockmarshall, on the southern side of the Cooley Peninsula in Co. Louth,[1] revealed important evidence for the periodic use and occupation by hunter-gatherers during the fifth millennium BC of a low, but locally impressive, natural knoll which formed part of a morainic ridge. At that time the Irish Sea would have lapped against the southern side of the knoll. The main surviving evidence for Later Mesolithic activity was an accumulation of shells—the remains of shellfish collected and eaten by people as part of a range of subsistence activities at the site. As a result of changes in land–sea relationships after the maximum post-glacial rise of sea level, the Rockmarshall knoll is now about 350m inland from the present shore of Dundalk Bay. One of the bone fragments that Mitchell recovered in the excavation, from a tightly packed shell midden, was part of a human femur which was dated from 4710 BC to 4370 BC.[2] This bone and the Rockmarshall location are the context of the fictional account above that forms the backdrop for considering the treatment of the dead during the Mesolithic period in Ireland. [Pl. 3.A]

INTRODUCTION

Rockmarshall was used by people in the last millennium of the Mesolithic period in Ireland, which extended over four thousand years, from 8000 BC to 4000 BC. Graeme Warren has usefully distinguished earlier pioneer and exploration activity and the definite establishment of widespread settlement on the island from around 8000 BC. Recent dating of what may be a butchered bear patella or knee bone from the Alice and Gwendoline Cave, Co. Clare, from between 10,800 BC to 10,500 BC, might indicate a Late Upper Palaeolithic human presence in Ireland, raising the prospect of a significant pushing back of initial human presence on the island. The date of 9080 BC–8400 BC obtained for a brown bear vertebra with cut marks, from the Catacombs Cave, Co. Clare, may represent another example of this pioneer activity.[3]

The human bone from Mitchell's excavations at Rockmarshall is one of the surprisingly few surviving pieces of direct, physical evidence we have of the people who lived in Ireland during the Mesolithic. The population of the island is likely to have been in the low thousands, at most 10,000 at any one time during this period. People lived by highly organised, seasonally varied foraging and fishing. They depended on their knowledge of the largely woodland environment and its fauna and flora for their food, raw materials and way of life, constructing a cultural landscape marked by routine and sacred activities.[4] This foraging lifestyle continued to play a significant role in settlement and social patterns long after the introduction of farming, shortly after 4000 BC.

These first Mesolithic inhabitants of Ireland are likely to have come immediately from adjacent areas of western Britain. This movement was part of the broader repopulation of north-west Europe after the end of the Ice Age, with hunter-gatherers—belonging to a specific genetic cluster termed Western Hunter-Gatherers (WHGs)—moving along Atlantic coasts. The genetic evidence suggests that this re-expansion occurred in a general northerly direction, along the Atlantic seaboard.[5]

Christopher Meiklejohn and colleagues have shown that cemeteries are a notable feature of Mesolithic mortuary practice in Europe throughout the period, and as Paul Pettitt details, they appear towards the end of the Palaeolithic.[6] Cemeteries are areas deliberately defined and used for human burial, continuing in use over several generations. Complex ceremonies surrounding the burial of individuals are known from Mid Upper Palaeolithic human societies, but at that time formal burial appears to have been rare, and the dead were buried in close proximity to where people lived. It is against this background that the use of cemeteries in the final Palaeolithic and in the Mesolithic period can be seen as representing a major social change, even when they occur close to areas of settlement. Pettitt argues that if there is any point in prehistory when an essentially 'modern' approach to burial emerged, this is it.[7] Although limited, the evidence for human remains and burials dating to the Irish Mesolithic is very much in keeping with trends across Europe. It should, however, be noted that Ireland stands in contrast to some areas of western Europe, such as southern Scandinavia, Brittany and Iberia, where there is evidence of large Mesolithic cemeteries and rich individual burials.[8] Similar developments occurred in some other parts of Europe.[9]

The emergence of cemeteries has been taken to indicate the presence and currency of cultural concepts such as descent—indicated by people selecting a location and going back to that place to bury and remember successive generations. The burial of the dead in a defined area also emphasises ideas of social complexity, membership of a group or society and related ideas of inheritance, rights and territoriality being passed on by lineal descent through social memory expressed in the continued use of cemeteries.[10]

Burial in the European Mesolithic shows considerable diversity of practice. Whereas single interments seem to be the dominant burial mode, multiple burials do occur, and there appear to have been complex mortuary ceremonies, with a particular focus on the skull. Both inhumation and cremation were practised. There is evidence that bones or body parts were kept in circulation amongst the living. In Scandinavia, Liv Nilsson Stutz has shown that there are instances of human bones being deliberately removed from graves. Human bone parts, referred to as loose human bone (LHB), often occur on settlement sites, and in some cases these were deliberately deposited. Decorated human bone and artefacts made from human bone also occur.[11] On occasion, domestic dogs were buried with people, and/or in a similar manner to them. In addition, objects made from organic materials, such as red deer antler, were often placed with the dead in graves. The deposition of red ochre (a pigment derived from haematite) in graves and on bodies indicates a concern with material metaphors of blood, vitality, vividness—all indicating an apparent concern with continuing life after death.[12] European Mesolithic cemeteries are one of a number of markers in the archaeological record that indicate social transformations in this period, especially in southern Scandinavia. [FIG. 3.1]

Until very recently, the apparent paucity of the burial record in Ireland was taken as one of a number of indicators that there was a distinctive way of life (and death) on the island during the Mesolithic. Mesolithic foragers in Ireland stand out because of their apparent limited reliance on hunting terrestrial animals. In contrast to the practice in some other areas of Europe, gathering and fishing are assumed to have been the main subsistence activities in Ireland. In addition, by around 6,800 BC to 6,500 BC a distinct lithic technology was developed, involving a shift away from the microlithic tools that continued to be used throughout much of western Europe and providing a basis for distinguishing an Earlier from a Later Mesolithic.[13] It appears that Mesolithic groups in Ireland (and Britain) may also have contrasted with their contemporaries in some parts of Europe by moving, over the course of the period, to a pattern of settlement that became more, rather than less, mobile. This corresponded to a shift away from a way of life that relied on the use of base camps on a more-or-less continual basis through the year as the central feature of the settlement and subsistence pattern.

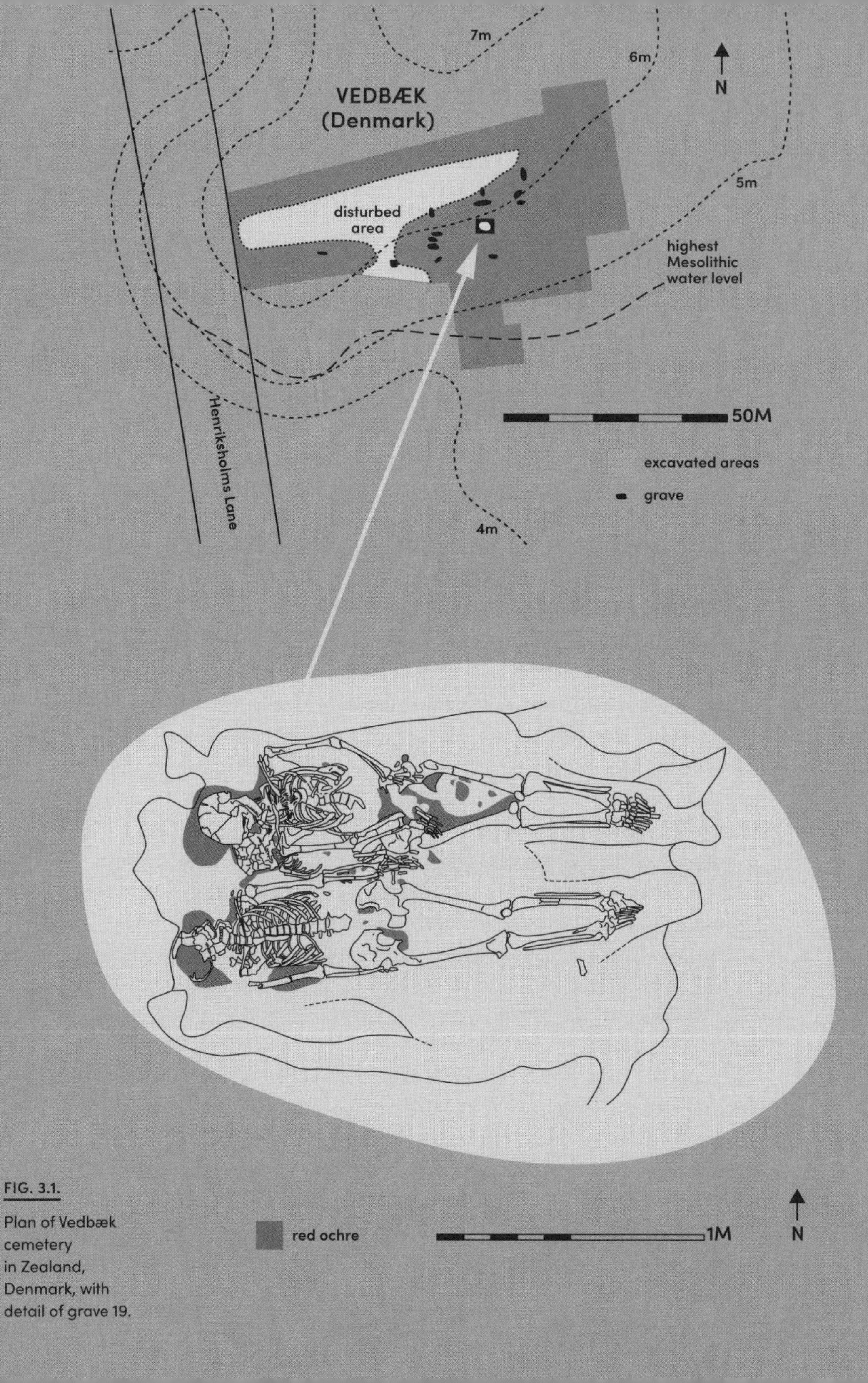

FIG. 3.1.

Plan of Vedbæk cemetery in Zealand, Denmark, with detail of grave 19.

The best example of a base camp found in Ireland is at Mount Sandel in Co. Derry, dating to around 7700 BC, early in the Mesolithic.[14]

As Peter Woodman and Graeme Warren have discussed, some of these distinctive patterns are related to the particular ecological character of the island of Ireland while others are the result of particular ways of life and society developed over time, through and by the activities of people in this island landscape. For example, the limited role of hunting can be directly related to the island's ecology. Most of Ireland was covered by a Late Glacial Maximum Ice Sheet, and the landmass was subsequently defined as an island as a result of rising sea levels since around 14,000 BC in the Late Glacial. This limited re-colonisation by plants and animals resulted in a restricted number of native species of mammal, including mountain hare, bear and wolf, that could have been hunted. Surprisingly there is little evidence for the hunting of seals.[15] The human role in shaping the ecology and landscape of Ireland is indicated by the probability that people introduced wild boar, supplementing their food supplies to facilitate settlement.[16] It is against this background that we can discuss the evidence we have for the treatment of the dead during this period.

DEATH IN THE IRISH MESOLITHIC: BURIAL AND DEPOSITION

As Meiklejohn and Woodman have detailed, the few known remains of people from the Mesolithic period in Ireland come from just nine sites. Most of these finds are the result of archaeological excavation: at Rockmarshall, Co. Louth mentioned above and excavated in the 1940s; Ferriter's Cove on the Dingle Peninsula in Co. Kerry, excavated in the 1980s and 1990s; Killuragh Cave, Co. Limerick, excavated during the 1990s; and Hermitage, Co. Limerick, excavated in 2001.[17] A human tooth was found during excavations at the Port of Larne, Co. Antrim in 1999/2000 of a pit complex dating from between 7300 BC to 6500 BC. Analysis by Marion Dowd (as part of a programme of dating human remains in caves) of human bone discovered by cavers in Sramore Cave, Co. Leitrim, indicated that it dates to the end of the Mesolithic or the beginning of the Neolithic. A pilot project of radiocarbon dating and isotope analysis by Thomas Kador provided a second, similar date from Sramore, and also a new date for remains found at Stoneyisland, Co. Galway in 1929 as a result of turf-cutting. The orginal context would have been open water; the new date suggests the deposition of the remains at Stoneyisland may have taken place before 5000 BC, while the original radiocarbon date from the site would place it at the Mesolithic/Neolithic interface. Excavations on a motorway route at Ballynaclogh, Co. Galway in 2008 recovered two teeth in a context that, like Sramore and Stoneyisland, could be either late Mesolithic or early Neolithic.[18] Finally, as part of a programme of dating the numerous bone points recovered in 1938 by dredging the River Bann at Loughan Island, upstream of rapids known as the Cutts, and of Mount Sandel mentioned above, a portion of a human ulna (the thinner and longer bone in the forearm) was recognised, and this dates from between 6077 BC to 5922 BC.[19] From this summary it is clear that much of what we know about human remains from the Irish Mesolithic comes from work undertaken over the past 20 years. This provides a new perspective on the treatment of the dead, and indeed on the Irish Mesolithic itself. **[FIG. 3.2]**

Hermitage—located on the east bank of the River Shannon overlooking a fording point at the falls of Doonass—is the most significant of Ireland's Mesolithic mortuary sites for a number of reasons. It was excavated by Tracy Collins and Frank Coyne in advance of pipelaying.[20] The earliest burial activity there is dated to well before 7000 BC, which places it early in the Mesolithic period. There are two Mesolithic burial deposits (and probably a third), and surface finds of stone tools indicate possible occupation activity. The oldest burial, dated between 7520 BC to 7210 BC, is the remains of an adult, identified as probably a male. The body had been cremated and

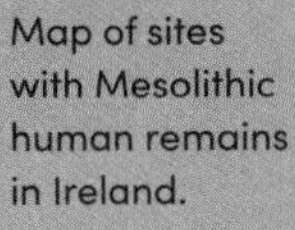

FIG. 3.2.

Map of sites with Mesolithic human remains in Ireland.

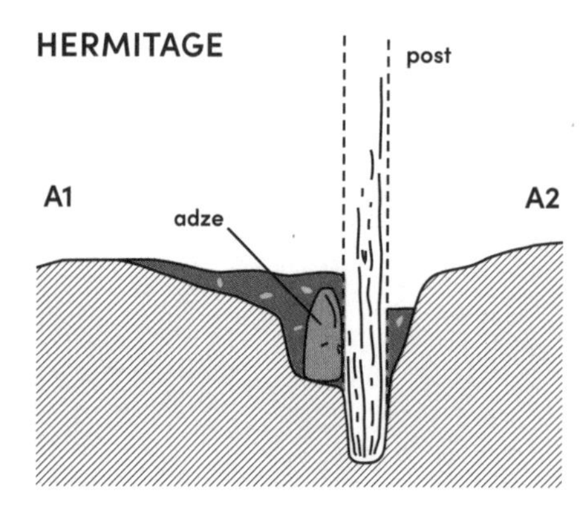

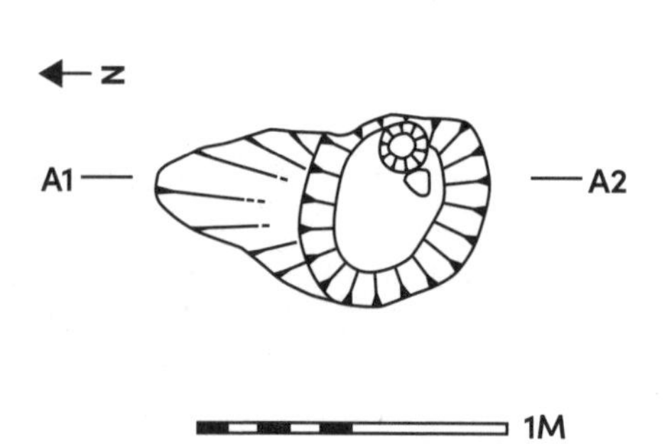

FIG. 3.3.

Hermitage, Co. Limerick, plan and cross-section of the Pit A burial feature.

PL. 3.B.I (Right)

The shale adze found with the Earlier Mesolithic cremation in Pit A at Hermitage, Co. Limerick.

PL. 3.B.II (Opposite)

The location of Hermitage, Co. Limerick on the eastern bank of the River Shannon. Location of cremation pits and associated features highlighted.

then virtually all the burnt bone—almost 2,000 grams (close to the average predicted weight of a cremated adult male)—was collected and placed in a sub-circular pit (Pit A), in a crescent shape apparently around a wooden post. This may have been erected to mark the place of burial, acting as a visible grave marker. A shale adzehead was placed resting against the post, with the blade or cutting edge, which had been deliberately blunted, facing down into the pit and earth. A burnt microlith and a microblade were found within the deposit. The degree of burning of all the objects indicates that they were not with the individual when the cremation took place, but rather were placed in the pit where they came into contact with the hot cremains.[21] [FIG.3.3, PL. 3.B.I, PL. 3.B.II]

About 150m away was a second, larger pit (Pit B) containing burnt bone of an adult who had also been cremated. This was a partial representation (179g) of the remains of the person, with a focus on the cranium, which had been placed in the pit with heat-shattered stone and pieces of baked and burnt clay. The human bone was dated from between 7170 BC to 6830 BC. In the case of these two deposits, similar dates were obtained from charcoal in the pits. There was a third pit (Pit C) to the east, with minute fragments of cremated bone, too small for positive identification. A date from charcoal indicates that the bones were placed there around 6610 BC–6370 BC.[22]

Hermitage is a striking addition to our understanding of the life and death of Mesolithic people in Ireland. Acknowledging the time gap between the dates from the burial deposits, and that Pits A and B are 150m apart, people used this location to bury individuals on up to three occasions over a period of a thousand years. The rite was cremation, contrasting with the evidence for unburnt bone from other Mesolithic sites in Ireland. While inhumation tends to dominate general discussion of Mesolithic burials and deposition of human bone at a European level, the widespread use of cremation has been recognised over the past ten years.[23] In all probability, after their death the bodies of the people buried at Hermitage would have been placed on a pyre for cremation. The evidence indicates that in the case of the individual in Pit A, all the cremated bone was collected from the funeral pyre and then placed carefully in the pit. Cremated bones were placed around the axe and the post, and it seems that the microlith and microblade (which appears to have been broken) were placed on or into the cremated bones. So there was a careful sequence of activity, and the burial was deliberately marked by the living with a timber post. This makes it one of the few ceremonial structures that we can date to the Mesolithic in Ireland or Europe.[24] Against this background we can regard the partial collection—with a focus on the cranium—and placement of cremated bone dated to around 7,000 BC in Pit B as also representing a careful, deliberate act. This focus on ceremony and formality of mortuary practice is a key feature of Hermitage.

Another striking feature in an Irish context is the similarity between the Earlier Mesolithic cremations at Hermitage and those that occur in later prehistoric cemeteries, discussed in subsequent chapters. The placement of objects with the remains of individuals is a feature of these later cemeteries in Ireland (and in Mesolithic cemeteries elsewhere in Europe). The objects from Hermitage indicate that the concept of relationships between people and objects being sustained, or perhaps even created, at death was present from an early stage in the Irish Mesolithic. Certainly the large, carefully manufactured and totally polished adzehead of shale, probably made from a relatively local source, provides further confirmation of the evidence from Earlier Mesolithic occupation sites that people in Ireland, as in Scandinavia, but unlike in many other parts of Europe, were using ground and polished stone adze and axeheads.[25]

In the literature it is argued that there is a strong link between stone axes and early farming communities in the Neolithic period, and it has been demonstrated on the basis of a number of lines of evidence that such objects also had an important symbolic role. The deliberate placement of the Hermitage adze—blade down in a cremation deposit—indicates that such a role may have been established much earlier in Ireland than previously had been thought. The identification of the burial as probably that of an adult male may anticipate the evidence seen in later contexts that the use of stone axeheads appears to have a strong gender association with males.[26] That this may also have been the case in hunter-gatherer societies is indicated by their occurrence with burials in the Scandinavian Mesolithic. It should be noted, however, that the cremation pit burial at Hammelev, southern Jutland in Denmark, dating to 8250 BC, which provides the closest parallel with Hermitage, consists of the deposition of a partial collection of cremated bones—mostly relating to the upper part of an adult, probably female—along with a number of stone tools, including an unpolished flint core axe, which were unburnt, a burnt bone pin and burnt limb bones of a wild cat.[27]

In the hunter-gatherer communities of the Maritime Archaic Tradition in eastern North America (from 3000 BC to 1000 BC) there is a recurring pattern of large, carefully finished ground and polished axeheads, adzeheads and gouges being placed, with other objects, in graves. Interestingly, at the Port Au Choix cemetery in Newfoundland such objects were found more frequently with women than men.[28] Microwear analysis and experimental research by Aimée Little and colleagues suggests that the Hermitage adze was deliberately blunted as part of the funerary rites. Did this action express not just the end of its life, but also symbolise the death of the individual? The adze was certainly closely entangled with the life and death of the deceased. It is possible that it had been used in the working of wood for the pyre and the wooden grave marker, making it a striking example of the intertwined lives of people and things?[29]

Excavation at Hermitage indicates that there may have been contemporary settlement activity in the immediate vicinity. Here we can see a connection with a general concentration of Mesolithic sites in similar riverine locations in Ireland, and perhaps also the deliberate deposition of axeheads in wet locations. Work in Sweden has documented the deliberate placement of human heads on sticks in water at the site of Kanaljorden, Motala, above stone packing which also contained human and animal (brown bear and wild boar) skulls. This suggests, as Richard Chatterton has put it, that water was an important symbolic as well as economic resource during the Mesolithic period.[30] This broad point is emphasised by the locations of the other finds of human bone in Earlier Mesolithic contexts in Ireland. For example, a human molar tooth was found in a pit complex dated between 7300 BC to 6500 BC on a Mesolithic occupation surface buried below several metres of storm beach deposits at Larne, Co. Antrim, on the coast of the Irish Sea. This may be an instance of loose human bone (LHB) in an occupation context. [31] Other examples are the deposits from Killuragh Cave, Co. Limerick, close to and above the River Mulkear, discussed below.

The burials and deposits of human bone in Britain broadly contemporary with Hermitage were also mainly placed in caves. But a recently dated site in south-west Britain that has some affinities with the location of Hermitage is the Early Mesolithic cemetery at Greylake in Somerset. Here the bones of at least five individuals were found in a quarry in 1928, but only dated in 2011. The burials dated between 8540 BC to 8280 BC. At that time the site would have been on an island in a flood plain, now a wetland known as the Somerset Levels, echoing a locational pattern for burials seen more broadly across Europe.[32] Until the dating of the Greylake bones, the human remains from the well-known Aveline's Hole cave site in the Mendip Hills, about 25kms to the north of Greylake, had been regarded as evidence of the earliest British Mesolithic cemetery. Our knowledge about Aveline's Hole has suffered because of its discovery in the late eighteenth century and the wartime loss of excavation records and skeletal material in the twentieth century. The cave is the largest known Mesolithic cemetery in Britain. It is estimated that 50 or more individuals were deposited there, in both articulated burials and as dis-articulated bones. It was used from 8660 BC to 8205 BC, centring on *c.* 8400 BC. Following a gap of nearly 5,000 years there was renewed deposition of human remains, specifically crania, in the Early Neolithic.[33]

Chantal Conneller has pointed out the wider significance of cave sites, such as Aveline's Hole, for human deposition in the Mesolithic. In England and Wales twelve of the fourteen sites with Mesolithic human skeletal material are cave sites. Most of these, while not used for occupation in the Mesolithic, had been visited in earlier, colder times by either Palaeolithic hunter-gatherers or Ice Age mammals. The physical remains of this earlier use would have been encountered by Mesolithic people depositing their dead. This focus on caves suggests—perhaps unlike at Hermitage—a deliberate placement of human remains away and apart from daily life, in special places. This is an unusual pattern in a wider Western European context in which most human remains are found close to or within settlement sites, with the cemeteries located close to the living.[34]

The cave at Killuragh, Co. Limerick, 22km south-east of Hermitage, is sited in a limestone ridge overlooking the Mulkear River to the east. At the cave, two entrances led via two low, narrow passages into a small chamber. Excavations here in the 1990s by Jane O'Shaughnessy and Peter Woodman provided evidence for disarticulated human bone and microliths. Episodic activity included the deposition of bones belonging to individuals dating to 7130 BC –6700 BC and to 7030 BC–6600 BC. This was the first of a number of episodes of use of Killuragh cave for the deposition of human bone and objects, the next being in the Later Mesolithic, 2,000 years later. The Later Mesolithic bones represent at least two individuals dated to around 4700 BC–4450 BC and 4440 BC–4080. A tooth dated to

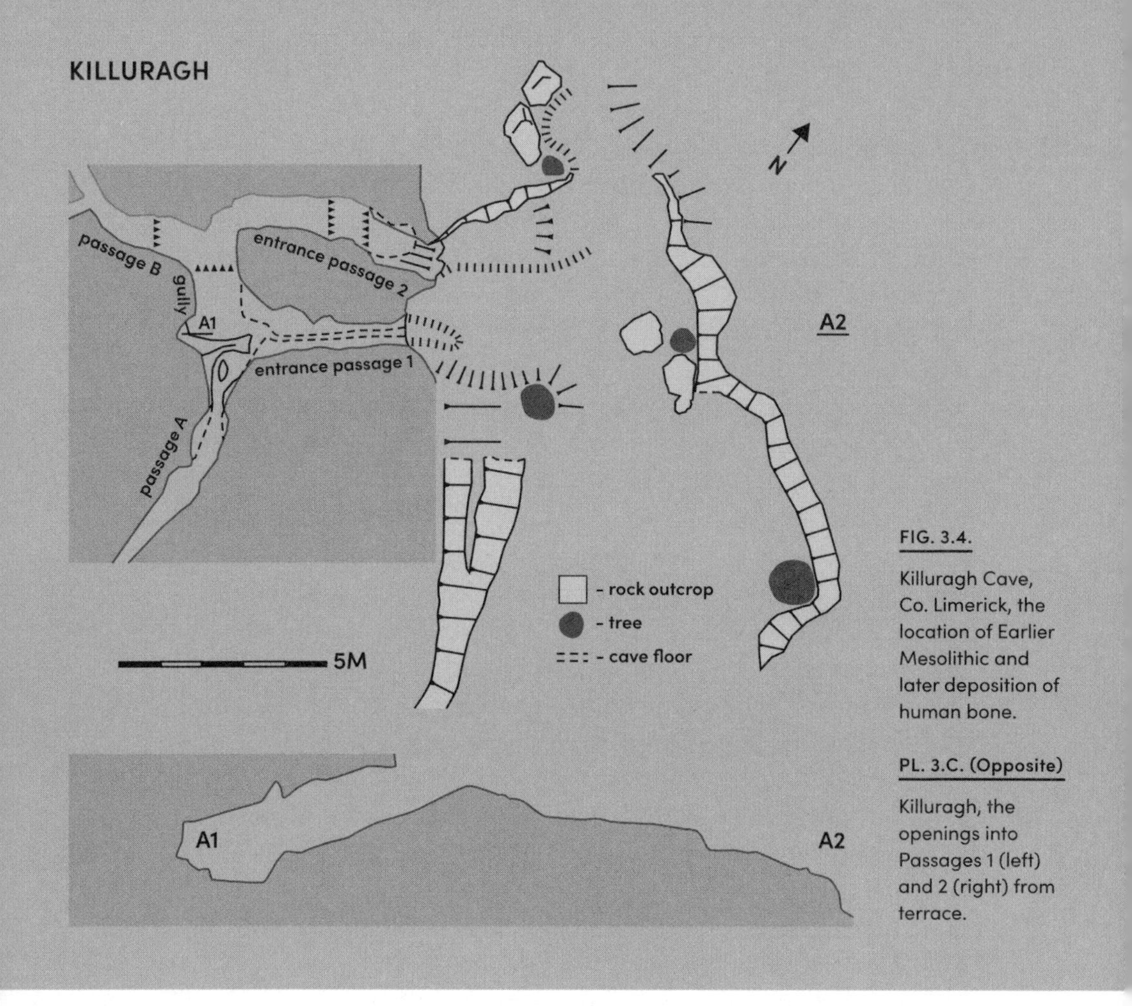

FIG. 3.4.

Killuragh Cave, Co. Limerick, the location of Earlier Mesolithic and later deposition of human bone.

PL. 3.C. (Opposite)

Killuragh, the openings into Passages 1 (left) and 2 (right) from terrace.

4790 BC–4610 BC produced an aDNA signature indicating (along with the individual from Sramore, see below) that the genomes of Irish hunter-gatherers form a distinct cluster within Western Hunter Gatherers in north-west Europe. Several of the Mesolithic human bones and lithics at Killuragh were weathered. This suggests that disarticulated bones had been deliberately placed on the terrace outside the entrance to the cave and were subsequently washed or carried into the cave interior. Analysis of stable isotopes of both the Earlier and Later Mesolithic human bones from Killuragh suggest a land-based diet, and Woodman suggested that the role of

eels and lampreys, giving a freshwater signature, could be important in interpreting the detail of the results of the isotope analysis. The re-use of the cave into the Neolithic and Bronze Age for the deposition of human bone indicates the site's continuing significance. As the excavation report is titled, this was a persistent place, regularly visited and remembered from generation to generation over several millennia.[35] [FIG. 3.4, PL. 3.C]

Dowd has highlighted the importance of three human bones found by cavers about 15m inside the entrance in a tight narrow passage at Sramore Cave, Co. Leitrim. These consist of the fragments of a femur, mandible and humerus that represent one adult, probably male, aged over 20 at death. Dowd has commented that the occurrence of large skeletal elements and representation of different anatomical regions may indicate that a complete body was placed in the cave. Two radiocarbon dates on different bones indicate that the individual died between 4220 BC to 3950 BC. Thomas Kador's project examining the potential of strontium isotope analysis to reveal the movement of early prehistoric individuals suggests that the person may have lived relatively locally to the cave, while the stable isotope analysis indicated that the person's diet was largely based on terrestrial sources, which could have included those from farming activity. The dates from Sramore significantly predate the main Neolithic use of caves—between 3600 BC to 3400 BC—documented by Dowd. They appear to be best interpreted as representing hunter-gatherer depositional activity in this cave in the last centuries of the Mesolithic period; this is supported by the aDNA analysis, which indicates that the human genome of this individual matches the distinct Irish cluster within Western Hunter Gatherers.[36]

The fifth millennium BC dates for human bone at Killuragh and Sramore fit with other Later Mesolithic human remains from Ireland dated to after 5000 BC and with what might be read from the archaeological record as an apparent concentration of evidence for human activity, and treatment of the dead, in this millennium. What is interesting is that Killuragh Cave indicates a long-term, recurring use of a cave site across the Earlier to Later Mesolithic transition and a gap of two millennia.

Kador also obtained data from the individual at Stoneyisland. The articulated skeleton was found face upwards with the arms extended, suggesting that the body of this adult male had been placed in open water, had settled to the bottom of a lake and was subsequently covered by bog. These remains had previously been dated to 4320 BC–3720 BC, making this one of the earliest dated 'bog bodies' from Europe. This would fit in with a practice known across north-west Europe of placing offerings and deposits in bogs and open water. A new radiocarbon date obtained as part of Kador's project dated the Stoneyisland remains from between 5215 BC to 5027 BC. If this is a Later Mesolithic individual, it pushes the practice of deposition of human bodies in open water, and the associated beliefs and rites, well back into the Mesolithic period in Ireland, tying in with wider European Mesolithic practices of placing human and animal parts into open water. Strontium isotope analysis indicated that the man had either spent his early years in an area of Tertiary geology, such as north-east Ireland, or had a highly mobile childhood. The stable isotope analysis indicated that the man consumed a diet rich in freshwater fish. This would be consistent with the location of Stoneyisland close to the north shore of Lough Derg and the Shannon River system, and with the focus on freshwater fish associated with Mesolithic settlement in the Irish midlands.[37]

The first recorded piece of Later Mesolithic human bone in Ireland—and for long time after its discovery in the late 1940s the only Mesolithic human remains known from the island—was that found during the excavations by Frank Mitchell at Rockmarshall and featured in the fictional sketch at the start of this chapter. Mitchell excavated three areas on a morainic ridge running east to west, which during the Later Mesolithic would have been on the Irish Sea coast. At Rockmarshall the ridge resembled an elongated promontory with the sea lapping along its southern side and shallow lagoon-like conditions to the east and west. Among concentrations of shellfish, fish bone, evidence for fires and burning and stone tools in a hollow on the north side of the ridge (midden III), Mitchell recovered the shaft of a human femur, which was in a poor state of preservation. This has been dated to between 4710 BC to 4370 BC. It would appear to be an isolated, loose piece of human bone (LHB). The stable isotope analysis of the bone provided a mixed terrestrial and marine signature, as might be expected from the location of the site, with the indication of terrestrial resources consistent with the person moving between the coast and inland during their life.[38] **[SEE PL. 3.A]**.

The Rockmarshall discovery can be compared with the scattered remains of at least one mature adult in their late 20s or early 30s recovered during the excavations by Woodman and colleagues at Ferriter's Cove on the Dingle Peninsula mentioned in the previous chapter. There, a wave-cut platform had created a shelf-like feature that people returned to on numerous occasions over a prolonged period of time to utilise a range of coastal resources. Their activities

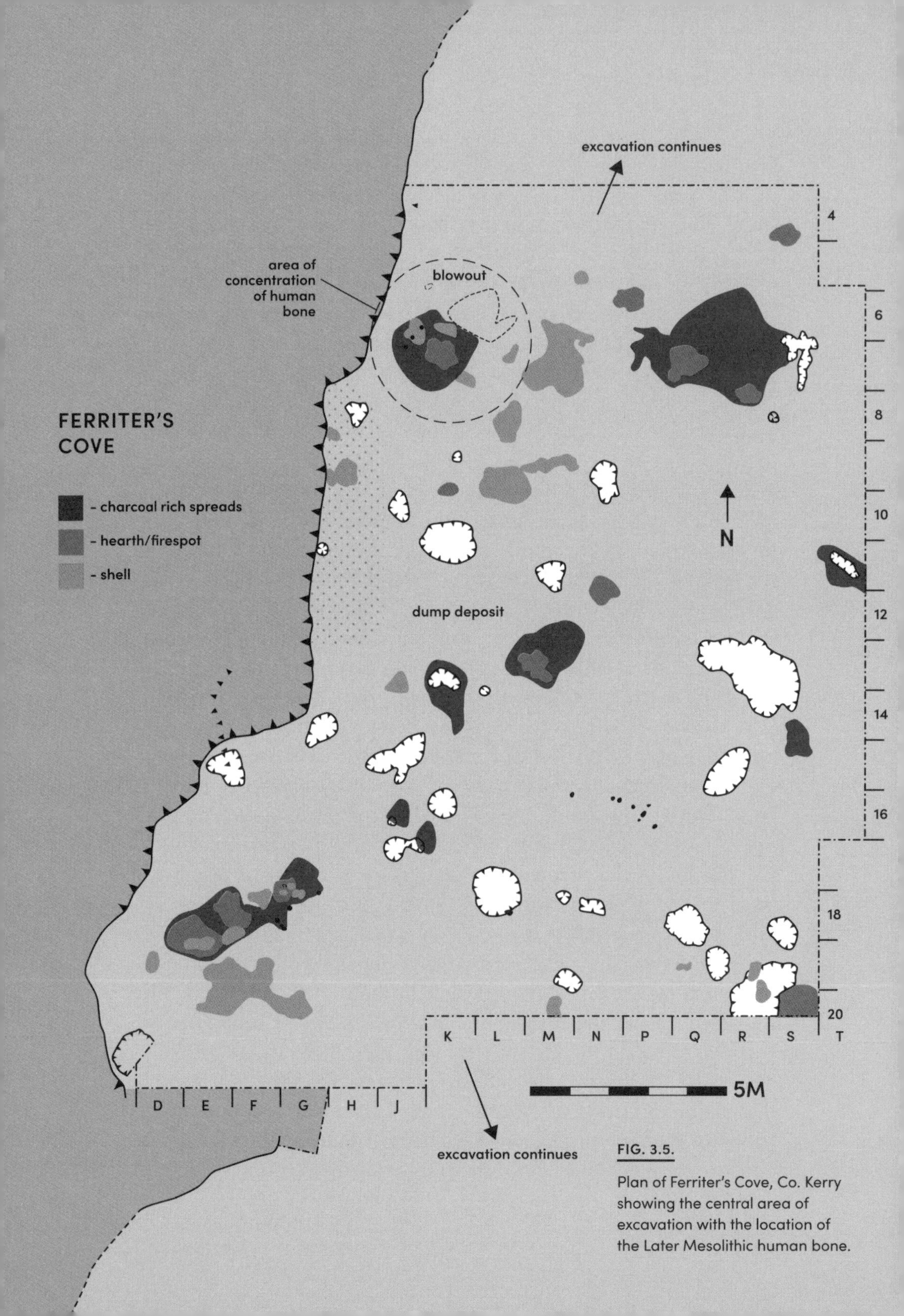

FIG. 3.5.

Plan of Ferriter's Cove, Co. Kerry showing the central area of excavation with the location of the Later Mesolithic human bone.

led to a build-up of deposits and eventually the area that was utilised as a living space became covered in sand. At Ferriter's Cove the human bones came from several locations in the northern and central area of the excavation. Other important evidence was also recovered, including the earliest domesticated cattle bone known from Ireland or Britain. The cattle bone dates to between 4500 BC to 4170 BC. The human remains consisted of several bone fragments, mainly of lower limbs, and teeth, four of which were found close together in the northern area. It is possible that the remains come from more than one person. The human bone was dated to between 4150 BC to 3700 BC. It is clear from the stable isotope analysis that this individual had a diet heavily based on marine resources, consistent with the location and character of the Ferriter's Cove site. In the southern area of the site, a cache or hoard of five shale axeheads, which had been carefully arranged, was placed in a hollow in the sand and covered over.[39] **[FIG 3.5]**

The reasons for the occurrence of human bone at Rockmarshall and Ferriter's Cove, places that were occupied on a seasonal basis in the Later Mesolithic, are the subject of some debate. The episodic reuse of Killuragh cave over the course of the Mesolithic and into later periods, however, suggests that at least in the case of this cave the deliberate deposition of disarticulated human remains was central to what drew people back to the site. The cave at Sramore was also used for deposition, in this case of a body. Both sites echo a wider pattern of deposition in caves seen in southern Britain. Thinking about caves as liminal, sacred or dangerous places may also provide a connection with the location of the man at Stoneyisland in open water. By contrast, at Ferriter's Cove and Rockmarshall (and indeed at Hermitage and Larne in the Early Mesolithic) the occurrence and deposition of human bone seems to be embedded in a wider set of activities, as paralleled for example in the middens on Oronsay in Scotland's Hebrides.[40]

MESOLITHIC COSMOLOGY AND RELIGION

To try to understand the context in which these burials and placements of human bone were occurring, it is important to think about how Mesolithic people might have seen their place in the world. There is an obvious problem in trying to bridge the gap between our lives in the twenty-first century and an entirely different way of life and death in a prehistoric foraging world, in a very different Irish landscape. Nevertheless, an understanding of modern hunting-gathering-fishing societies, and of those recorded in detail in the ethnoarchaeological and anthropological record, offers a potential guide as to how Mesolithic people in Ireland might have viewed their world. In an important review, David Whitley commented that 'the hunter-gatherer cognitive world was varied, quite complex and we should expect that their religious, ritual and symbolic systems would be equally rich, nuanced and variable'. Whitley identified five major points of distinction between hunter-gatherer and Western Judaeo-Christian religious traditions.

Hunter-gatherer religions include animistic beliefs: holding that the world is ensouled or numinous. Arising from the numinous nature of the world, hunter-gatherer religions commonly recognise sacred places on the landscape where rituals take place. Ceremonies, such as burial, can also occur in everyday settings, and there is often no rigid distinction between sacred and profane space. The relationship between myth and ritual varies. Among some hunter-gatherers religious ritual is closely related to origin myths, in others there is no direct linkage. Hunter-gatherer religions are syncretic rather than exclusionary; they maintain a core of belief and practices, with change consisting of the addition or subtraction of other elements over time. Finally, as in many traditional systems, religious knowledge is often carefully controlled, kept secret, restricted and has to be earned. Whitley suggests that most ethnographic hunter-gatherer religions can be seen as part of a spectrum, with shamanism and world-renewal occupying the two poles. Shamans are understood to be ritual specialists who have direct interactions with the spirit world, achieved by entering an altered state of consciousness. The focus of world renewal beliefs are ceremonies intended to renew the earth, ensure the continued availability of resources and the health of people, and to prevent hardship and misfortune. In this context other beings are regarded with respect and trust; for example, the remains of dead animals are treated carefully so that animals will continue to offer themselves to people. The cosmology of northern Boreal hunter-gatherers, as detailed for example by Peter Jordan and Marek Zvelebil, provides a potentially useful comparative context.[41]

In that world the woodland landscape is viewed as permeated with the spirit world. This also affects animals and plants and is reflected in the seasonally varied character of the landscape and resources. People treat other living creatures with respect, and the boundaries between people and animals are viewed as permeable. Humans are seen as capable of changing shape and appearance—'shape-shifting', becoming hybrid beings with animal and human effects. In cosmological terms, in the beginning there would have been ancestors and animals, who may have many shared features. A recurring feature in northern Boreal hunter-gatherer views of the world is to see it in terms of a three-tiered world (sky, earth and underworld) around a sacred axis or *axis mundi*. This can be expressed metaphorically as a tree that links an underworld (in coastal areas seen as the sea), the human world and the upper world (the sky). The tree has its roots in the underworld, is a vital component of the living world and points the way to the sacred world of the past and the ancestors. The shaman, with the ability to communicate and mediate between the human, animal and supernatural worlds, has a key role.[42]

People explain where they have come from through creation myths, which invoke the power of places, animals and things in the local environment. Through myths and rituals, places are remembered and woven into oral traditions. In this way important places are socialised and made an integral, persistent part of the cultural process by which knowledge is passed on. Shamans have a particular gift in recognising the relationships between people, animals and the non-terrestrial world around them. These people can, through performance and ceremony, achieve transformations by entering an altered state of consciousness, marking them as having the special gift of communication with the world of the spirits. During the winter, when longer periods of darkness create the impression of the world closing in, the spirits are believed to be closer and more powerful.[43]

Sacred places are viewed as providing connections between and portals to the different layers of the cosmos. Talking about the archaeology of natural places, Richard Bradley drew attention to the power and role of such places. Water sources—the sea, rivers and lakes—represent the underworld. Places where water bubbles up, or seems to vanish, are entry points to this spirit world. Mountains and hilltops are the closest we can get to the sky. Islands, in particular, are viewed as sacred places because they are literally land set apart, surrounded by water and, when seen from any distance, bringing together land, sea and sky. Recognising that we are using ethnoarchaeological analogy as the basis for archaeological interpretation, we can now go back and discuss the human remains from the Irish Mesolithic in the context of the broad framework of ideas and beliefs this approach provides us to think with.[44]

UNDERSTANDING DEATH IN THE IRISH MESOLITHIC

As noted above, cemeteries are a distinctive feature of the European Mesolithic. It should be emphasised—contrary to the social evolutionary view still seen in the general literature that many of these cemeteries date to late in the Mesolithic—that Meiklejohn and colleagues have shown they extend across the time depth of the period.[45] A cemetery serves a range of potentially different roles: to be a visible reminder of ancestral presences, to demonstrate ownership of local resources, to express the social place of—and differences between—individuals, and as a place linking the worlds of the living and the dead. For the living, the burial and treatment of the dead provide opportunities, as Rick Schulting suggests, 'to create new or emphasise existing social roles, to create and pay debts and to attract and bind followers'. As Liv Nilsson Stutz has discussed, the presence of cemeteries could create persistent nodes in the landscape that were transition places between the living and dead.[46]

The Hermitage cemetery should be considered in this context. Hermitage is exceptional in a European context and stands apart from other Mesolithic cemeteries in terms of the focus on cremation and the dispersed location and very small number of burial deposits. In relation to the latter point, it is important to remember that Hermitage was found as a result of the laying of a pipeline and that only a 10m-wide strip was excavated. Is it possible that the earliest burial excavated at Hermitage, denoted with a timber post, remembered a key individual/ancestor, whose death was also marked by the placement of a specially made adzehead with his cremated remains? With successive generations, the focus may have shifted from remembering personalised, short-lived presences to commemorating more abstract, mythological ancestors who helped explain where people came from and who still had a role in their destiny. The choice of a riverside location for the Hermitage cemetery can also be seen as fitting with the placement of human remains in places that were regarded as sacred, as Hutton put it in *Pagan Britain*, 'places of natural power and ancestral mythology'.[47]

At Killuragh Cave there is evidence for long-term, episodic re-use of the cave for deposition of human bone—from the Earlier Mesolithic into later phases of Irish prehistory. In England and Wales there are a number of examples in addition to Aveline's Hole where caves and rock shelters were used for the placement of human bone. Caves are seen as conduits to the other world, and the presence of human bone would of course have heightened the ancestral associations of those particular places.[48] On the island of Caldey in south Wales, human bone was placed in a number of the limestone caves and fissures in the Mesolithic and later periods. This was a location that had also been occupied in the upper Palaeolithic, but at that time it had been linked to the mainland. At Caldey, the rise in sea-level during the Mesolithic created an island.[49] It is not difficult to imagine how the island might have taken on a particular role for people living in that region. Was it seen as a place from which ancestors came and to which remains of the dead, perhaps particularly those who were esteemed when alive, were brought to join the ancestral world—an island of the dead? In both north-west Europe and north-east America, hunter-gatherer cemeteries were frequently placed in the coastal zone, sometimes on offshore islands that emphasise the interplay of the land and the sea, the living and the dead; 'burial beyond the water' as Zvelebil says.[50] This may be viewed in the context of the belief in present-day small-scale, traditional coastal societies in other parts of the world that on death the spirits of the dead travel to off-shore islands, are reunited with the other spirits and are revitalised.[51]

On the other hand, as Conneller pointed out, the burials at Aveline's Hole (and Gough's Cave in the same area) stand apart from other sites in Britain where isolated human bones have been recovered. The phenomenon of isolated bone could be the result of a number of different processes, one of them being the deliberate deposition of disarticulated human remains. In their examination of the spatial distribution of human bone excavated from the Mesolithic shell midden site of Cnoc Coig on Oronsay in Scotland's Inner Hebrides, Meiklejohn and colleagues were able to distinguish between groups of loose bone and two bone groups—composed of hand and feet bones from at least three people in each case—that had been purposefully deposited, providing clear evidence of deliberate deposition.[52] In one of these bone groups, human hand bones and seal flipper bones were deposited, making a very strong link between humans and seals. There are other examples of deliberate deposition of specific body parts in the European Mesolithic, for example placement of skulls in cave sites in Germany.[53] **[FIG.3.6]**

Conneller and Nilsson Stutz comment on the need to interpret cemeteries in broader frameworks of belief, and in terms of the central place of death, dealing with dead bodies and the transformation of people after death.[54] We could think of the Mesolithic treatment of the dead as centring on three approaches. It could involve the burial of complete bodies (in some cases after cremation); the purposive deposition of selected human bones after the defleshing of the body through burial, excarnation or cremation; and

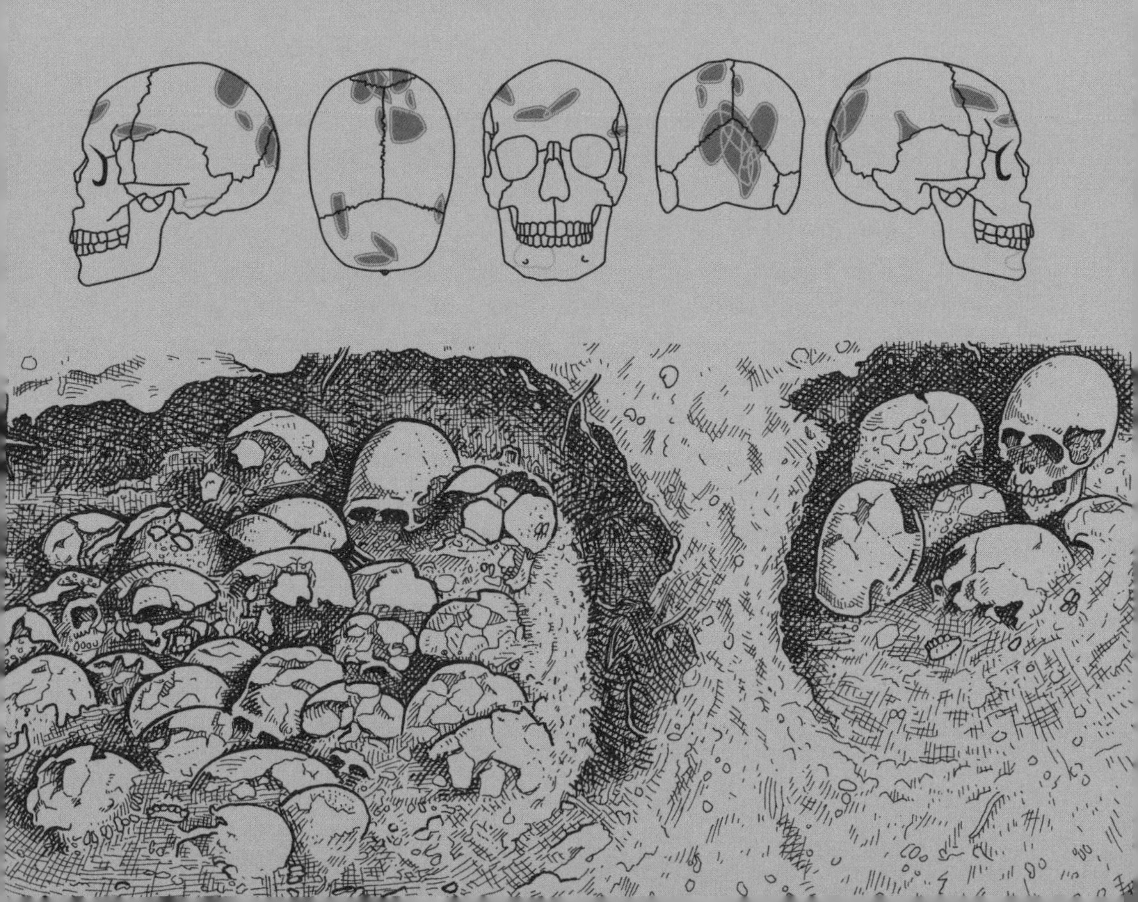

FIG. 3.6.

Ofnet, Bavaria, Germany; skull deposit, with blunt-force trauma indicated on skulls.

finally the wider phenomenon of placement of loose human bone on Mesolithic sites, some of which might represent deliberate deposition. It is useful to bear this variability in mind when looking at the Irish evidence.

It is difficult to argue—given the framework of cosmological belief set out above and the evidence from Hermitage, Killuragh and Sramore—that there was not intentional behaviour behind the placement of bone at these sites. Indeed, the limited evidence that we currently have throws light on wider issues of Mesolithic mortuary practice in Europe, and this wider European evidence can usefully be drawn on when thinking about the nature of life and death in Ireland. Despite the small number of known Mesolithic sites in Ireland, we find all three approaches to the treatment of the dead, emphasising that the evidence is very much in keeping with wider European practices. At Sramore we appear to have the deposition of a complete body, and at Hermitage (Pit A) the deliberate collection and placement of all an individual's bones after cremation. At Hermitage Pit B (after cremation) and Killuragh there was purposive deposition of human body parts in specific contexts. The focus on the cranium at Hermitage Pit B is paralleled in a focus on crania and skulls elsewhere. At sites like Rockmarshall and Ferriter's Cove, the loose human bone could be the result of a number of depositional processes, one of them being deliberate deposition by the living. At Stoneyisland, we appear to have the deliberation deposition of a body in open water. We might see Hermitage, Killuragh, Sramore and Stoneyisland as directly informing our understanding of Mesolithic mortuary practice, with the treatment of the dead at other Irish sites being more ambiguous, but considering the evidence in the context of the framework of cosmological belief set out above there are some significant similarities.

The occurrence of isolated human bone, or scatters, at Rockmarshall, Ferriter's Cove or Larne may look much more casual, but their presence becomes more meaningful when the location and context of these bones and the activities of the living that produced them are explored. Depositing human (and animal) bone at ostensibly places where people were living, eating and sleeping supports the idea that at places like Ferriter's Cove, Rockmarshall and Larne the boundary between the living and the dead may have been porous. Part of the awareness that Mesolithic people had of the richness of the coastal zone in terms of food sources would have been knowledge of the daily pattern of the tide and longer-term tidal patterns. This, after all, is where the land meets the sea. Alongside its rich potential in terms of food procurement, people may have perceived it as where the land ended and the underworld began. In that context it may have been thought appropriate to leave the bodies of the dead to be taken by or to go back to the sea. An alternative is that we are seeing the curation of human bone in these living places in the coastal zone. Conneller has suggested that through disarticulation, post-mortem movement and deposition, the dead were extended across space and continued to be part of the material networks of the living.[55] This is the kind of scenario suggested in the fictional account of an event at Rockmarshall presented above that might explain the isolated human femur there.

Returning to the issue of population, even going for a minimal figure for the living population and a generation span of 25–30 years, multiple thousands of people would have lived and died on the island over the 4,000-year course of the Mesolithic. While most of them, particularly babies and young children, may have been disposed of or buried when they died in ways we cannot hope to recover, the evidence from places like Hermitage and Killuragh suggests that there is potential to find further Irish evidence of Mesolithic burials and deposits of human bone. We need to be careful, however, not to perceive life and death in the Mesolithic as reflecting a prelapsarian Eden, where a low level of population lived in social and ecological harmony, along the lines of the anthropologist Marshall Sahlins's generic view of hunter-gatherers as the 'original affluent society'. Indeed, this is a view that has been put forward for southern Scandinavia by Tilley.[56]

A cautionary, realistic note is provided by evidence for violence on some north European Mesolithic skeletal remains. In the cases of both the group of human skulls deposited in the cave at Ofnet in Germany and crania intentionally placed and displayed in a lake at Kanaljorden in Sweden, there was evidence of blunt-force trauma, suggesting blows to the head resulting in injuries and fractures. One potential source of such violence might have been competition between communities, leading to raiding and warfare. Contact between dispersed households and groups at particular times of the social and foraging year not only brought the potential of interaction and exchange, but also the possibility of conflict—a reality of Mesolithic life and potential cause of death.[57] [SEE FIG. 3.6]

THE LONG-TERM INFLUENCE OF MESOLITHIC BURIAL PRACTICE

Questions about how this period came to an end continue to be a key focus of research. The transition from the Mesolithic to the Neolithic, involving as it does the move from a hunting-gathering lifestyle to one based to a greater or lesser extent on domesticated animal and plant food sources, is seen as marking key changes in European prehistoric societies.[58] One of the points of contrast that has been highlighted is in mortuary practice. In many areas of north-west Europe, including Ireland, the building of monuments by the living in early agriculturally based communities to contain and celebrate selected human remains of members of previous generations is seen as marking a new way of thinking about the world. These monuments are regarded as a material expression of a concern with both the past and the future. Hence the focus tends to be on the *differences* between Mesolithic and later mortuary practice. These differences include the observation that from the Neolithic period onwards, evidence for the treatment of the dead in prehistory is much more visible and often monumentalised.[59]

I want to suggest a different view of the relationship between Mesolithic and later mortuary practices, however: that concepts developed in the Mesolithic about the proper treatment of the remembered dead and their placement in the landscape continued to have social relevance in later times. If we go back to cosmological beliefs, the acknowledgement of the importance of special places that provide a link with the sacred is a feature shared by many religions of widely different scale. The terms 'holy' or 'sacred' are used in relation to mountains, pools/wells, caves/grottoes in many different religious contexts. Hence, we might expect that such places in the Irish landscape—some first recognised, named and perhaps used by people during the Mesolithic—would have had a sacred resonance for later generations. Killuragh Cave provides a striking example: deposition started there in the Earlier Mesolithic and continued episodically over five thousand years, to the Late Bronze Age.

At the moment we simply do not know the extent to which the cultural changes that mark the end of the Mesolithic were the result of new people coming into Ireland. Views on this issue vary and have changed over time. One position taken in the literature has been that all the changes said to be characteristic of the Neolithic could have come about through the networks of contact and exchange that existed between communities in coastal locations in Ireland, Britain and adjacent Continental areas. This would have given access to the new ideas, materials, resources that became available in the centuries around 4000 BC without population movement having been a major factor.[60] A contrary view—widely held as a truism up to the 1970s—was that the changes were of such an order that they implied the presence of a new, migrating population.[61] This view has come back to the fore and is seen as being supported by a range of evidence, including the extent and character of the cultural (including dietary) changes that follow on from the beginning of the Neolithic and the genetic evidence, particularly from aDNA.[62] A middle-ground position is to recognise that substantial numbers of new people may have come onto the island, perhaps moving into areas that were not heavily utilised by indigenous hunter-gatherer-fisher communities, but also mingling with them. Patterns of interaction and exchange between these groups would have developed over time, contributing to the particular character of the Neolithic in different regions.[63]

In this context a continuity of knowledge of sacred places might also be expected, given the background of the syncretic nature of hunter-gatherer cosmology set out above. Or to put it in another way, we could see the use of particular, natural places for burial or deposition of human bone in Ireland as reflecting practice and belief that has its initial roots in the Mesolithic. In this way, the first people to inhabit the land had an enduring influence on the placement of the dead in the landscape.

The early Mesolithic evidence from Hermitage certainly suggests that a burial practice that previously had been seen as typical of the period after 2200 BC in reality had been practised thousands of years earlier. The evidence from Pit A, as we have seen, indicates the cremation of an individual on a pyre and the placement of the burnt bone fragments, as well as pyre residue and objects, in a pit dug for the purpose and then marked by a timber post. Pit B shows the deliberate collection from a pyre and deposition of some cremated bone, particularly the cranium, of another person, some considerable time later. Normally these practices are seen as part of the variety of mortuary rites that emerged with the diversification of the treatment of the dead in the Early Bronze Age,[64] after a long period in the fourth and earlier third millennium when the most common form of evidence we have for the treatment of the dead is for the placement of bones of a number of individuals in megalithic tombs. With the shift in attention away from the communal to a greater deliberate focus on the retention of the identity of the individual in death came the appearance of individual graves, both in cases in which the burial rite was by inhumation and where it followed cremation.

The Neolithic is the period noted for the use of monuments to contain and celebrate the bones of ancestors, but it must be remembered that, as was the case in the Earlier Mesolithic in Ireland, where we have seen evidence of individual cremation, burial and deposition, we also have evidence of individual Neolithic cremations (and inhumations). For example, at the periphery of the complex monument at Millin Bay, Co. Down, dated to the later fourth millennium BC, there are a number of individual adult cremations. In addition, a large, central, stone-lined pit contains a collective deposit dominated by the inhumed bones of adolescents and children.[65] So, another view of the practice of individual cremation is to view it is an element of burial practice that continues from the Earlier Mesolithic into later periods, expressing both the concept of the individual and also—in combination with other practices, such as the complementary use of inhumation—relationships and differences between people in society.

Hermitage itself poses important questions about this continuity. Given the Bronze Age date for another cremation in a pit in the area,[66] are we looking here at a place that in some manner retained a sense of being an appropriate, sacred space set aside for burial over millennia, or is this the result of a random re-use at a much later date of a place where all memory of its earlier use had long gone?

We have evidence that the kinds of sacred places recognised by Mesolithic people retained that status in later times. Caves, for example, were used for burial also in later periods. There seems to be a greater sense of continuity in their use in Ireland than in Britain, where the Mesolithic use of caves appears to cease in the centuries immediately after 6000 BC. As mentioned above, Killuragh Cave has produced evidence of later activity, and Dowd has shown that there were deposits and burials in caves dating to the Neolithic, as at Kilgreany, Co. Waterford and Annagh, Co. Limerick; that caves were used for burial and deposition during the Bronze Age, as at Knockinny Cave, Co. Fermanagh, Glencurran, Co. Clare and

Castlemartyr Cave, Co. Cork; and this practice—although attenuated—continued into the Iron Age. As Dowd has emphasised, what we are seeing is a clear expression of the idea of the cave as a sacred place, providing access to the otherworld, and as an arena in which beliefs about the living and death were both enacted and reinforced.[67]

Nothing might seem more different from the closed, dark, quiet world of a cave than the windy, salty, open environment of the seashore, but this is another context in which we might see beliefs and practice about the treatment and placement of the dead having their roots in Mesolithic times. Like caves, the seashore is an environment where different elements of the world meet, in this case land and sea. This heightens its significance in a cosmological context. It is also an important zone because of its ecological richness. As discussed above, human bone was frequently placed in coastal locations in Ireland and elsewhere. This practice again continues in later periods. Dalkey Island, Co. Dublin is a small, offshore island with a long history of use in the Mesolithic, from 6000 BC, probably on a seasonal, episodic basis. It seems that activity on the island included the deliberate placement of material in pits. It is in this context of the site as a special place that we can consider its use in the Neolithic as a place of burial. Two areas of shell midden were recognised during excavation; at the base of one of these the apparently disarticulated bones of an adult male dating from between 3090 BC to 2620 BC were placed in a crouched position, and a mass of shells were inside the skull. There were clearly a number of stages in the post-mortem treatment of this person.[68] This small, offshore island may have been seen as a place that had a long history and a sacred character that made it appropriate as a burial place.

The use of shell middens continued into the later prehistoric times, and there are indications from places other than at Dalkey that, alongside their formation as a result of the eating of shellfish and other resources, they retained a symbolic significance. During excavations directed by Göran Burenhult at Carrowmore, Co. Sligo in 1981, a shell midden at Culleenamore, on the southern shore of the Knocknarea peninsula, overlooking Ballysadare Bay, was excavated. An unexpected discovery was a circular grave pit cut into the outer edge of the Iron Age midden, in the lowest part of the accumulation of sea-shells and other material. Over the grave there was a further build up of sea-shells—mostly of oyster—and above it were two separate, successive spreads of charcoal, representing hearths used for cooking the oysters The grave, 55cm across and 25cm deep, had been dug to hold the body of a young child, aged one or two years when they died. This might be regarded as the disposal of a child who, not being a full social person, could be buried in a peripheral location, away from the main community focus of burial—wherever that might have been. This interpretation is undermined by the careful burial of the child and the objects left in the grave, which suggest that a strong human connection was felt by the mourners. On excavation a tiny, perforated blue glass bead and a bronze ear-ring were found with the bones. This burial is the inspiration for Una Mannion's poem 'Crouched Burial', which features at the end of the book. **[FIG. 3.7]** [69]

As Sheila Paine pointed out in her work on the role of amulets, in many societies small babies are seen as particularly vulnerable to evil and illness. People did not understand why so many babies died, so amulets were used to ward against death.[70] The most common way for an amulet to be worn is as a pendant around the neck, next to the skin. The glass bead in the Culleenamore burial may well have been strung and put on the child soon after birth, to hold the soul in the body, protecting the infant from ill and ensuring they stayed in the human world. Certain parts of the body need special protection, and the ear is an orifice through which it is often believed spirits could enter the body. The child's ear may have been pierced when they were was a few months old, so that they could be protected by the ear-ring.

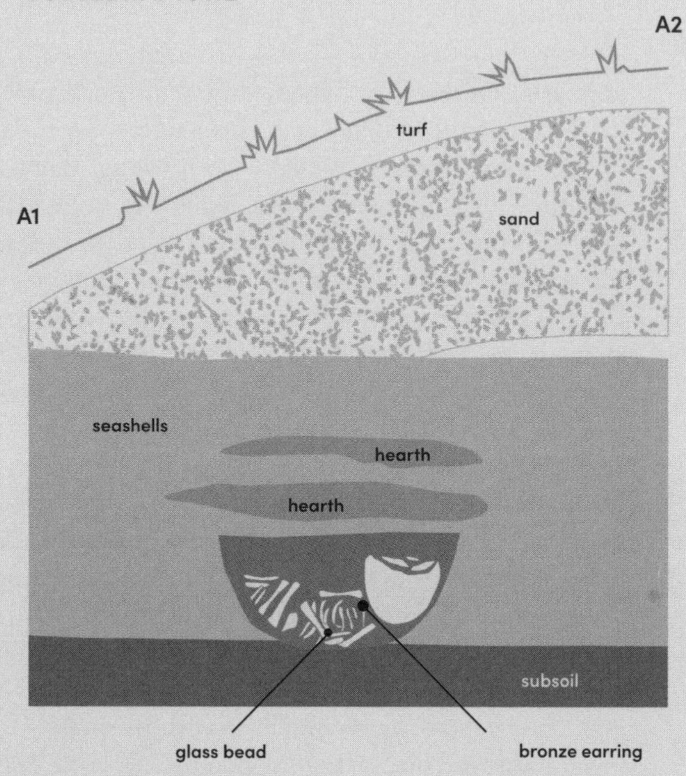

FIG. 3.7.

Culleenamore, Co. Sligo; Iron Age infant burial in a midden.

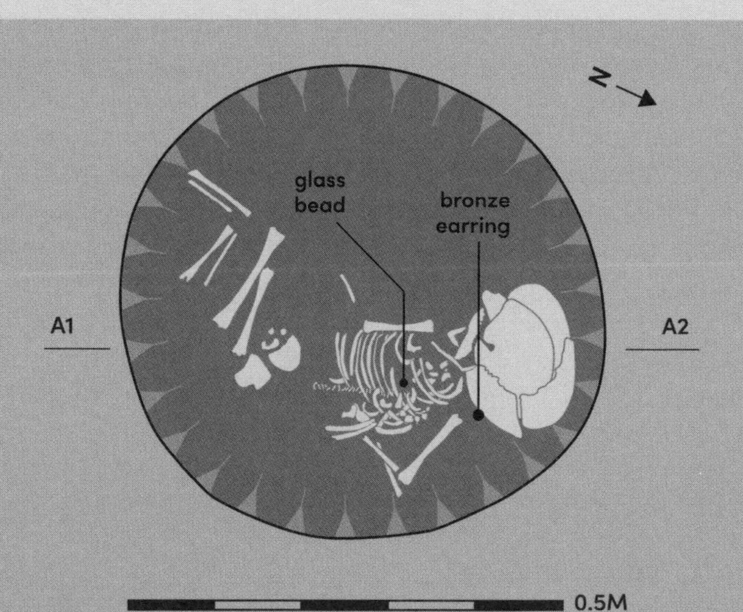

The deposition of individual human bones on Mesolithic sites perhaps anticipates the practice of votive offerings—for example the placement of metalwork in wetlands, sometimes in open water—that become more obvious in the archaeological record in later prehistory.[71] If we bring these two practices together, then we can see that human bone might also have been seen as a very appropriate and powerful votive offering. We have evidence from other parts of Europe, such as southern Scandinavia, that deliberate deposition, and the use of human bone in such deposits, begins in the Mesolithic.[72]

At Stoneyisland in Co. Galway, the body placed in open water sank to the bottom of what was then a lake. The radiocarbon dates indicate that this happened either in the Later Mesolithic or around the time of the Mesolithic–Neolithic transition. The preservation of such bodies created the bog bodies that are such an evocative human feature of later prehistory. What the Stoneyisland body suggests is that people were placed in wetlands as a means of disposing of a body from at least the fifth millennium BC. We don't know whether the Stoneyisland person had died and was then placed in the water or whether disposal in the water was a motive in their death, but we do have a clearer case of the placement of human bone as an offering from Carrigdirty, Co, Limerick. Here, on the Shannon estuary—in what would have been seasonally flooded and seasonally used estuarine wetlands with reedbeds, mudflats and nearby woodland—a human cranial fragment of an adult aged between 25 and 35 years, dating from between 3634 BC to 3370 BC, was found with a scatter of other material, including a stone axehead, chert flakes, woven basketry, swan and cattle bone, and the right clavicle from an adult human.[73] It is interesting to think of this placement of a human cranial fragment as a *memento mori*; as well as being a ceremonial practice associated with later prehistoric societies, it echoes the deposition of cranial remains in the Earlier Mesolithic at Hermitage (Pit B) and in European Mesolithic contexts. The placement of human skulls in wetlands forms part of a wider pattern of deposition of material, particularly metalwork, in these locations.[74] It is also worth drawing attention to the possible similarity between the Carrigdirty deposit and the bones deposited at Ferriter's Cove and Rockmarshall up to a thousand years earlier. One interpretation of the human bone on these latter two sites is that we are seeing the deliberate deposition of individual bones or scattered human remains as at Carrigdirty, but in a dryland, coastal context.

The focus on coastal and low-lying wetland areas that is often seen as a distinctive characteristic of Mesolithic people living in Ireland brings with it the assumption that journeying by inland and coastal waters would have been something ordinary, everyday, at the heart of life. There is physical evidence that this journeying by water must have been a central feature of Mesolithic lives in the possible oak logboat from Lough Neagh at Brookend, Co Tyrone, dating to before 5000 BC.[75] Journeys over water were part of the web of everyday life, but they would also have been inherently dangerous, requiring people to travel over a fluid, changing, powerful and dangerous medium. It may be relevant to see the idea of a journey over water as part of the way in which the dead were perceived as moving from the world of the living to the ancestral world 'beyond the water'. As Crumlin-Pedersen and colleagues have shown, in Scandinavia this was a concept that endured over millennia: from the placement by Mesolithic people of human remains under a logboat in shallows at Møllegabet, off the small island of Dejrø, Denmark, to the Viking ship burials such as at Oseberg in Norway.[76] In Ireland we have no such direct evidence, but the use of coastal locations for burial or deposition, the use of islands and the placement of human remains in wetlands all could be seen to relate to the concept of lives being borne away in or across water. Echoes of this occur in the treatment of the dead at different places, at different times during prehistory, but the idea seems to be there from the Mesolithic. [FIG. 3.8]

There is an interesting tension between this idea of a distance being created between the world and the living and the dead and the

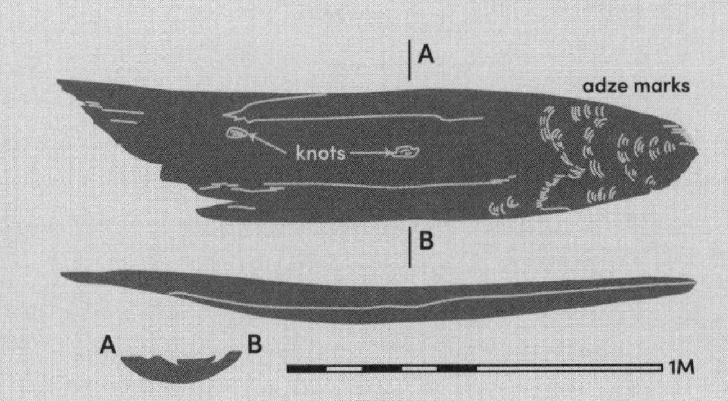

FIG. 3.8.

Lough Neagh, Brookend dugout? (after Fry 1990); the Møllegabet boat burial.

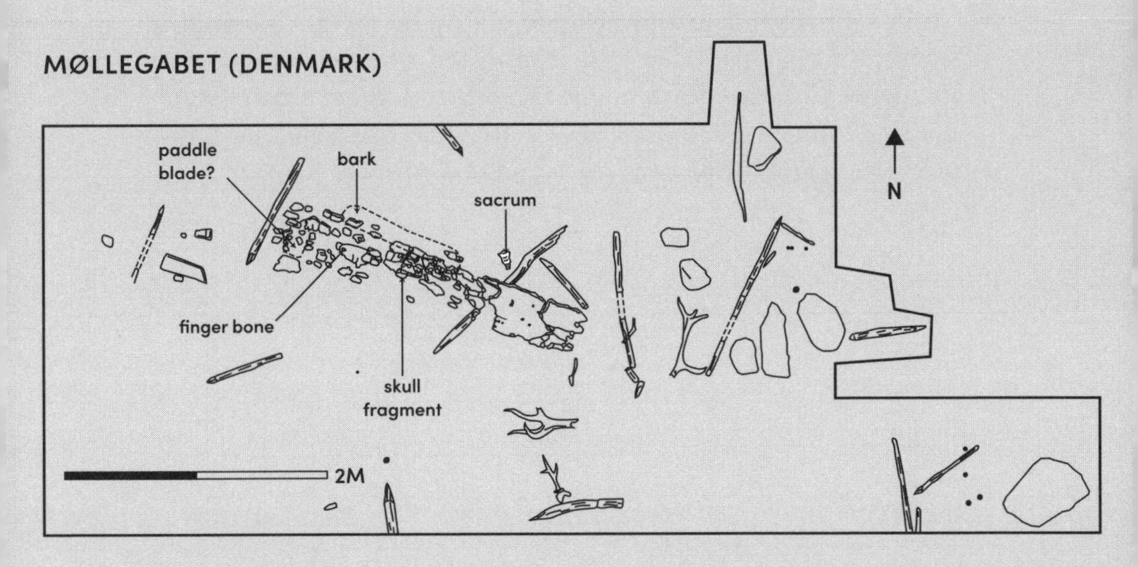

general view that in hunter-gatherer-fisher worlds the landscape is seen as numinous, imbued with the presence of spirits. It is argued that the changing relationship between people and their environment brought about by greater control over their food sources through agriculture and the construction of monuments evoked a changed relationship with the ancestors.[77] In an agricultural world, the ancestors are more likely to have been seen as immemorial, transcendent, attesting to a different sense of time and place. We will return to these ideas in looking at the Neolithic, but it should be borne in mind that the spiritual world of hunter-gatherers could have accommodated both a belief in the continuing presence of the dead and the need of chosen people who had died to depart on a journey to rejoin the spirit world they had come from. Indeed, it could be suggested that the persistence of hunter-gatherer spiritual beliefs amongst farmers might have been as socially significant as the continuity of hunting and gathering itself, which has long been the focus of discussion about the interaction between hunter-gatherers and farmers.[78]

As a final word in this chapter, it may be useful to consider whether during the Mesolithic the sacred quality of water and its connection with death might also relate to the ultimate origin myth and story of Mesolithic people: that they had come across the water, from another place to the island they knew as home.

4.

Making monuments and engaging with the dead

A death in the house

They came from the direction of the sea, and the shadows were lengthening as the sun moved closer to meeting the land and disappearing into the darkness. A boy ran back and forth throwing stones at cattle to keep them away, and a little girl with a long stick walked behind the animals. People approached the upright stones, squeezing through the narrow gap between them, and spread out, turning to the left, close to the upright stones of the court. They made way for newcomers, keeping an eye on the small children who were running around, jumping on stones that had been carefully placed to give a flat floor to the open area of the court. Before they had made the monument many of them were familiar with the place, they knew where the old house had stood, and some of them were related to the house family. It was sad that the great-grandmother had died, but as was the custom this was also a time to celebrate, to remember her spirit and knowledge coming down the generations. The family was looking forward to the next birth and her life being renewed. This house of stone would now be a shrine and the resting place of remembered people from previous generations.

Pointing to the spot, they talked about where the old wooden house had stood. Some said it had been abandoned a few generations ago, when the great-grandmother was young; others thought it was more recently. All agreed that, as was the tradition, the timber house had been burnt to end its life. Particular respect had been given to the posts standing near where the burnt bones of ancestors had been placed in the house, and the stone house for the ancestors was deliberately placed close to that spot. Pits with offerings had been dug about 30 paces apart. Around the pits closest to where the sun set, stones were positioned to stand upright so that the innermost chamber would be close to where the innermost part of the house was said to have been. The stones of the wall marking the edge and outer boundary of the new stone shrine ran over where the old house for the living had stood. The people from the house just across the stream to the south had started to build a new structure for their ancestors over the other pits, closest to where the sun rose. Linked by the court and facing each other, these structures were placed to show how in life these two houses and families were linked and shared people, animals, things, work, food and materials. Now, their ancestors would join and continue to look after them. To show the links between the living and the dead, people had brought materials, carried on their heads and backs, from the floor of their living houses, scattering it inside the stone chambers. Fires had been lit; fires to heat up the chambers and provide a warm place for the dead.

A mother was bending down and talking to a little child who had run to the entrance of the eastern shrine house. She whispered to him that people only went beyond the doorway to carry the ancestors to the other world, or when there was trouble and they needed to talk with the dead. Beside her, someone chuckled and said that with the stone walls of the court all around them, the crowd were like cattle in one of the fields. Silence descended as the people of the house came into the court. They still bore the marks of grief on their faces, in their hair and on their bodies. Surrounded by relations a woman bore the burnt bones of great-grandmother and other ancestors in a pot. It was carried as carefully as if it was great-grandmother's skull itself. The person leading the ceremonies crouched down and went into the shrine house as the sun was setting behind it and the higher land from where some of them had come that day. The children were told what was going on inside: the bones would be placed in a pit that had been dug in the ground and would then be covered with stones. Now the ancestors would really be part of the land. They would be remembered as daily life and time went on: every day when the sun rose again, when people had occasion to walk on the stones in the court, or as they just passed by, herding cattle, reminiscing about the place and its stories.

PL. 4.A.

The central court tomb and rectangular house at Ballyglass, Co. Mayo during excavation. View from the north-east.

At Ballyglass in northwest Mayo there are two megalithic tombs of the court tomb type built by early farmers between 3700 and 3550 BC and sited just 230m apart within a wider cluster of these monuments. They are located to the east of the well-known blanket bog-covered Neolithic field system at Céide Fields. The tombs were excavated by Seán Ó Nualláin as part of a programme of fieldwork conducted by Ruaidhrí de Valera and himself. The tomb known as Ballyglass 1 or Ma. 13 is a central court tomb.[1] An open-air, stone-lined court was entered from the north-east, and two-chambered, roofed galleries opened off the court to the east and west. These galleries were encased within a rectilinear, kerbed cairn. Excavation revealed the presence of a rectangular timber building—a house—under the cairn, just west of and predating the tomb. The house belongs to a widespread tradition of similar buildings dating in Ireland from 3720 to 3620 BC. The timber house appears to have been deliberately demolished, and the south-west part of the kerb of the tomb cairn was placed over the filled-in house foundations. It is possible that the dismantled and covered-over remains of the house were visible before being covered by the cairn. The fictional account above, suggested to have taken place sometime around 3600 BC, shortly after the tomb structure is considered to have been completed, draws on details revealed by the excavation. [See Fig. 4.3].

THE VISIBLE DEAD IN THE NEOLITHIC

The megalithic monuments at Ballyglass referred to in the fictional account above demonstrate the different world constructed by early farming communities in Ireland compared to to that of the hunter-gatherers discussed in the previous chapter. It is often suggested that the terms Mesolithic and Neolithic have so much baggage attached to them that they hinder rather than assist in understanding the changes that happened in Ireland and Britain from around 4000 BC. Part of the problem with the use of the blanket terms Mesolithic and Neolithic is that when we examine the evidence from different regions—for example within the islands of Ireland and Britain—it is clear that there were considerable differences in terms of when and how the transition happened, and of the social interactions that prevailed in the period from 4000 BC to 3500 BC.[2] Traditionally the changes were seen in economic terms—as marking a transition from a hunting-gathering to a farming lifestyle. Then came the recognition that the switch-over in subsistence was more complex and drawn-out in some cases, with wild food supplies continuing to play a significant role in people's lives. This prompted a shift in the focus of discussion in recent years, to consideration of the transition as involving new ideas; new relationships between humans, animals, things and their environment; the building of monuments and the active use of a wider range of materials—notably pottery and stone tools, sometimes obtained from particular sources and specific locations.[3] Monuments to contain the remains of selected individuals were central to the transformation.

For a number of reasons—including the dramatic changes in diet suggested by isotopic analysis, the impact of aDNA studies, and the rise of a cultural evolutionary approach to understanding the development of the European Neolithic—current discussion has seen a return to an emphasis on economic factors. It is now also recognised, however, that the remains of the dead provide direct genetic, dietary and dating evidence for the transition between the

Mesolithic and the Neolithic. Ironically, however, whereas greater focus is being placed on the concept of the body in the Neolithic, and the relationship of the living and the dead, it can be argued that relatively less attention is being paid to death itself and to the character of mortuary practices. The placement of selected human remains in monumental structures is regarded as one of the distinctive features of the Neolithic, not just in Ireland and Britain but throughout Atlantic Europe, from Iberia to Scandinavia. It documents new ways of thinking about the relationship between the living and the physical remains of the dead, and a concern about remembering previous generations.[4] The evidence of how the dead were treated is central to our understanding of the Neolithic. People would have had a familiarity with the presence of the dead, expressed in mortuary rites and in the continued circulation of human bone among the living. While such activity is a point of continuity with the Mesolithic, a striking contrast, however, is the very significant increase in the number of people whose remains have been recovered through archaeological excavations. [PL. 4.B]

In the 1990s Eoin Grogan and I suggested that in excess of 400 individuals dating to the Irish Neolithic were known from excavations. The explosion of archaeological investigations and research in Ireland since then has meant that many more Neolithic sites have now been investigated. While most of these are settlement-related and non-monumental, some have produced important burial evidence, and important assemblages have been published. On current evidence, an estimate that the remains of well over 1,000 Neolithic individuals have been recovered would not be too far off the mark.[5]

Given that the Neolithic lasts 1,500 years compared to the 4,000-year span of the Mesolithic in Ireland, the number of Neolithic remains recovered is significant compared to the very small number of Mesolithic people surviving in the record. People occupied and settled much of the island, lowlands and uplands at one time or another in the Neolithic. Using a generation length of 25–30 years, this gives us a sense of 50–60 human generations living

PL. 4.B.

Poulnabrone portal tomb, Co. Clare.

and dying over the period. Population estimates vary: McLaughlin suggests one million people as the highest level of population during the Neolithic, whereas others suggest that around 100,000–150,000 people may have been living on the island at this time.[6] These estimates help put the archaeological record of Neolithic burials of over 1,000 people in its contemporary social context. Even if burials recovered reached the low thousands, it is striking that such a small proportion of the population is represented by this physical record. As Mandy Jay and Chris Scarre have said in discussing the British Neolithic, we need to recognise that the majority of the Neolithic dead are invisible in the record.[7]

Yet, over a millennium-and-a-half, there is a rich and varied record of mortuary practice. This is documented through the deposition of human remains in specific settings. Megalithic tombs have tended to dominate narratives of the Irish Neolithic, given both their number—over 1,500—and their context as part of a wave of monumentalisation across western Europe from the later fifth millennium BC.[8] Documentation of settlement evidence from development-led excavation programmes since the mid-1990s has provided a more balanced view of the social context of megalithic monuments and a better understanding of the world of the living during the Neolithic.[9]

These monuments appear to have acted as a visible marker and memorial or shrine for the deposits of human remains that they contain. Sometimes, only the bones of one or a very small number of people are present; indeed, no bone may be present. In other cases, the skeletal remains of significant numbers of people have been recovered. The social significance of this is indicated by the number of people who would have actively participated in making these monuments. If the remains from these sites represent only a small proportion of the entire Neolithic population, how do we explain such striking contrasts in the treatment of the dead?

One explanation might be that the sample of known Neolithic megalithic tombs and monuments excavated is small; only about 100 tombs have been scientifically excavated. Nineteenth-century explorations of Neolithic sites do mention the discovery of human bone, but most was either not recovered or has not survived. From the pattern of occurrence of human remains in carefully excavated sites, however, we can be confident that many unexcavated sites will contain the remains of only a small number of individuals. Excavated court tombs, like Ballyglass, have generally produced the remains of between six and ten individuals. In considering the reliability of such figures, we have to bear in mind a number of factors. Most simply, it is possible that some tombs had been cleared out periodically.[10] Another factor to consider is that acidic soils common in western and upland parts of the island where many tombs are located are not conducive to the long-term survival of human bone. Here, cremated bone is more likely to survive than bone that is unburnt. When only cremated bone is found in a site on acidic soil, we cannot assume that inhumed bone was not originally present. Furthermore, the bone of children had been considered more liable to decomposition than the more strongly calcified bone of adults. In an important study of human remains from the earlier Neolithic in southern Britain, however, Martin Smith and Megan Brickley made the observation that in assemblages where the preservation of adult bone was good, the bones of children and infants were as well preserved.[11]

One way of quantifying the extent of potential biases is to consider the results from excavation of sites on calcareous soils, which are conducive to the survival of human bone. On the limestone uplands of the Burren in Co. Clare, the two-chambered court tomb excavated by Carlton Jones at Parknabinnia contained the remains of at least 20 individuals, most of them inhumed, placed there from 3715 BC, with the deposition of human remains continuing until between 2880 BC to 2760 BC. The majority were young adults who died between the ages of 25 to 35 years, but there were bones from some people who had lived past 45.[12] Ann Lynch's excavation of the portal tomb at Poulnabrone on the Burren revealed the presence of the disarticulated remains of a minimum of 36 people: 19 adults and 17 sub-adults. In the commingled remains (primarily unburnt but including some burnt bone) all age categories were represented: from foetus/perinate and neonate/infant to old adult women and men. The initial use of the tomb for burial in the Neolithic is modelled as starting between 3885 BC and 3720 BC, and ending between 3355 BC and 3135 BC. A cranium was deposited under the edge of the cairn in the later third millennium BC, and a neonate was placed in the portico of the tomb in the middle of the second millennium BC.[13] While this evidence might suggest a picture of communal burial, the reality is more complicated; the placement of dead people within both tombs was selective, successive and restricted.

This can be seen by looking at Poulnabrone in more detail. There was a mass of disarticulated bone in the chamber, and some evidence of articulation. Some bones had been scorched and burnt and many were found in cracks or grykes in the limestone. There was an over-representation of hand and feet bones and discrepancies between upper- and lower-body elements. The conclusion of the excavator, Ann Lynch, and Jessica Beckett, the osteoarchaeologist, is that the patterning was the result of successive placement of bodies and the re-arrangement of bone within the tomb, combined with possible removal of some bones and placement of disarticulated bones that came from corpses originally deposited and kept elsewhere. As Barra Ó Donnabháin and Mara Tesorieri put it in their bioarchaeological analysis, the funerary rites 'emphasised the partibility of bodies and were characterised by multi-phased ceremonies involving the socially sanctioned removal of some remains.' The construction of the monument is, in all likelihood, contemporary with the earliest deposition of a body. Rick Schulting, in modelling the dated remains, argued that they could be seen as representing burial activity in a phase that lasted between 390 and 695 years (within the date range given above) or two phases within the date range from 3825 BC to 3000 BC: a first phase that lasted 100–260 years, followed by a gap of 85–255 years, and then a second phase lasting up to 195 years. The human bone comes from individuals from multiple generations over a period of several hundred years, representing long-lived if intermittent deposition of human remains. If there were a single phase of activity, one way of thinking about this is in terms of a person being placed in the tomb every 10–20 years or so.[14] **[FIG. 4.1]**

There are exceptional sites like the Mound of the Hostages (*Duma na nGiall*) passage tomb at Tara, Co. Meath, where a very different picture of mortuary practice emerges. Here, Muiris O'Sullivan estimated that the skeletal remains, dominantly cremated, represent over 200 people. We will return to this question of how distinctly different mortuary practice was in passage tombs in the centuries just before and around 3000 BC. Even in the case of the Mound of the Hostages, where the detailed chronology of the site—based on directly dating cremated and unburnt human bone—suggests that deposition in the Neolithic took place over a period of less than 300

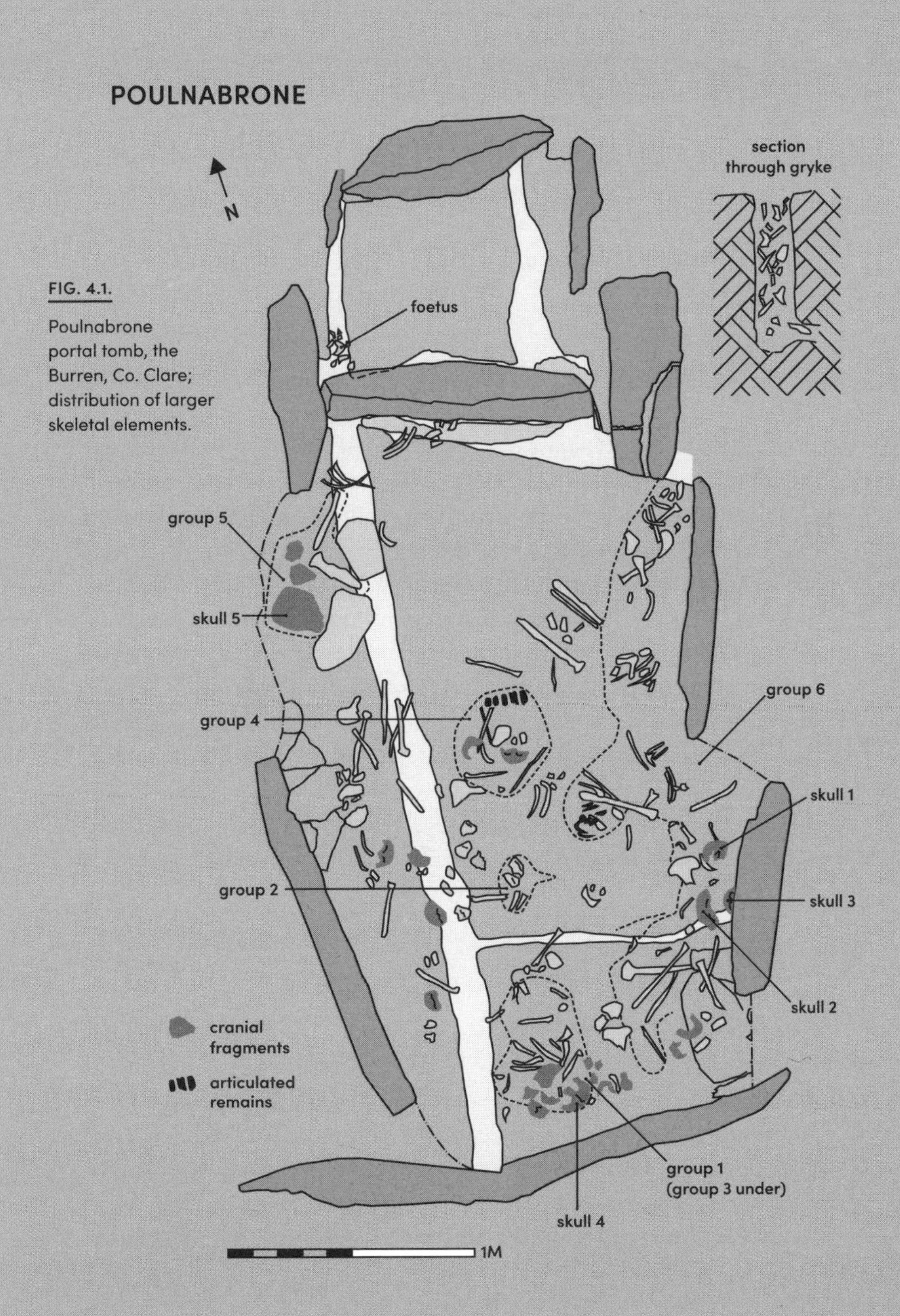

FIG. 4.1.

Poulnabrone portal tomb, the Burren, Co. Clare; distribution of larger skeletal elements.

FIG. 4.2.

Types of megalithic tomb—reconstruction drawings.

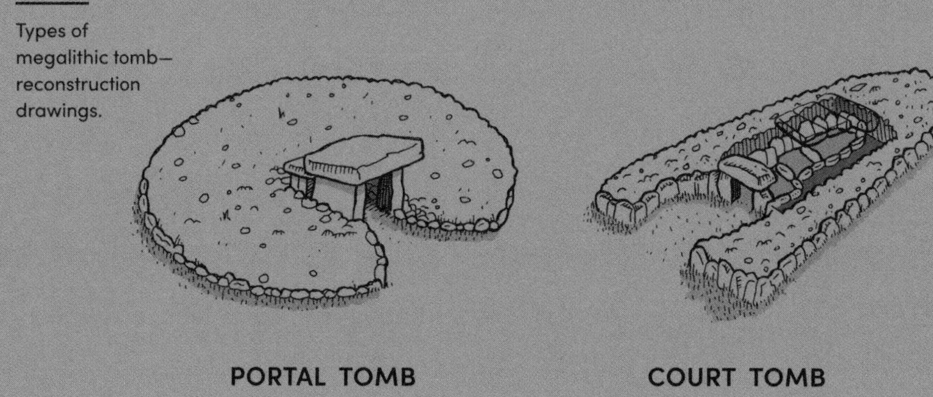

years, and that the deposits were commingled, it still appears that the remains placed within the tomb were those of selected individuals.[15]

What we can see in the treatment of these visible people was a concern, as Smith and Brickley put it, to produce remains that were skeletonised and disarticulated, including through use of burning and cremation.[16] The remains placed in monuments during complex, formal deposition ceremonies represented only a small proportion of the contemporary society. Bearing in mind the caveats expressed above, it would seem that this *selection* of individuals for particular post-mortem treatment and deposition is a key feature in understanding Neolithic society. What was the basis on which it was deemed appropriate for the remains of particular people to be placed in such monuments, and how were the rest of the population treated after death?

PLACING THE DEAD

Before addressing these questions, we should acknowledge that this is a very detached, prosaic way of describing the treatment of the bodies of the dead. We always need to bear in mind the social and emotional impact of human death. As pointed out by Mike Parker Pearson, our dealings with death are characterised by powerful emotions and emotive power play. Returning to our questions, it is useful to discuss the contexts in which we find deposits of human bone.

There are four main types of megalithic tomb, each named after a distinctive architectural feature. Portal, court and passage tombs all date to the fourth millennium BC; the fourth and most numerous type of megalithic tomb—wedge tombs—date from 2450 BC to 2050 BC, in the period known as the Chalcolithic, and these are considered in the next chapter.[17] **[FIG. 4.2]**

Portal tombs are related to court tombs and are part of a long cairn and barrow tradition that occurs across north-west Europe. The dramatic outline of portal tombs is created by the higher front end of the roof stone(s) being carried by two tall portal stones that also define the entrance into the tomb chamber. One strand of research has focused on the raising of these heavy and often dramatic roof-stones, 'stones that float to the sky' as Vicki Cummings and Alasdair Whittle put it, as a defining feature of these monuments. The most important and best-dated portal-tomb mortuary assemblage comes from Poulnabrone, as discussed above. The dating of Poulnabrone makes it the earliest megalithic monument in Ireland; the evidence at the portal tomb of Killaclohane I, Co. Kerry, has been interpreted as suggesting a primary phase of burial there between 3800 BC and 3700 BC. Reflecting on the few dates for human remains from other portal tombs in Ireland and south-west Britain, Tatjana Kytmannow commented that it is not possible to say whether cremation or inhumation was used first; indeed at Poulnabrone as pointed out above there is evidence of deliberate burning of inhumed bone.[18] **[SEE PL. 4.B]**

The defining feature of court tombs is a formal, open-air court of upright stones in front of the entrance to roofed chambers or galleries. Galleries were covered by a stone cairn of elongated shape. Different articulations of court and gallery provide a number of forms of court tomb. [SEE PLS 2.A AND 4.C] The commonest type is a two-chambered gallery entered from an open, horseshoe-shaped court; rarer forms include central court tombs, like the one at Ballyglass. Schulting and colleagues have demonstrated that their first construction and use took place from 3700 BC to 3550 BC.[19] Mortuary practice in these monuments incorporated the use of both inhumation and cremation. As outlined above at Parknabinnia, the character of the bone and the depositional patterns have been interpreted as reflecting primary inhumations disturbed in the course of successive interments. By contrast, at Ballyglass and Tully, Co. Fermanagh the surviving deposits consist of cremated remains.[20] [FIG. 4.3]

PL. 4.C.

Malin More court tomb, Co. Donegal, full court with twin, two-chambered galleries.

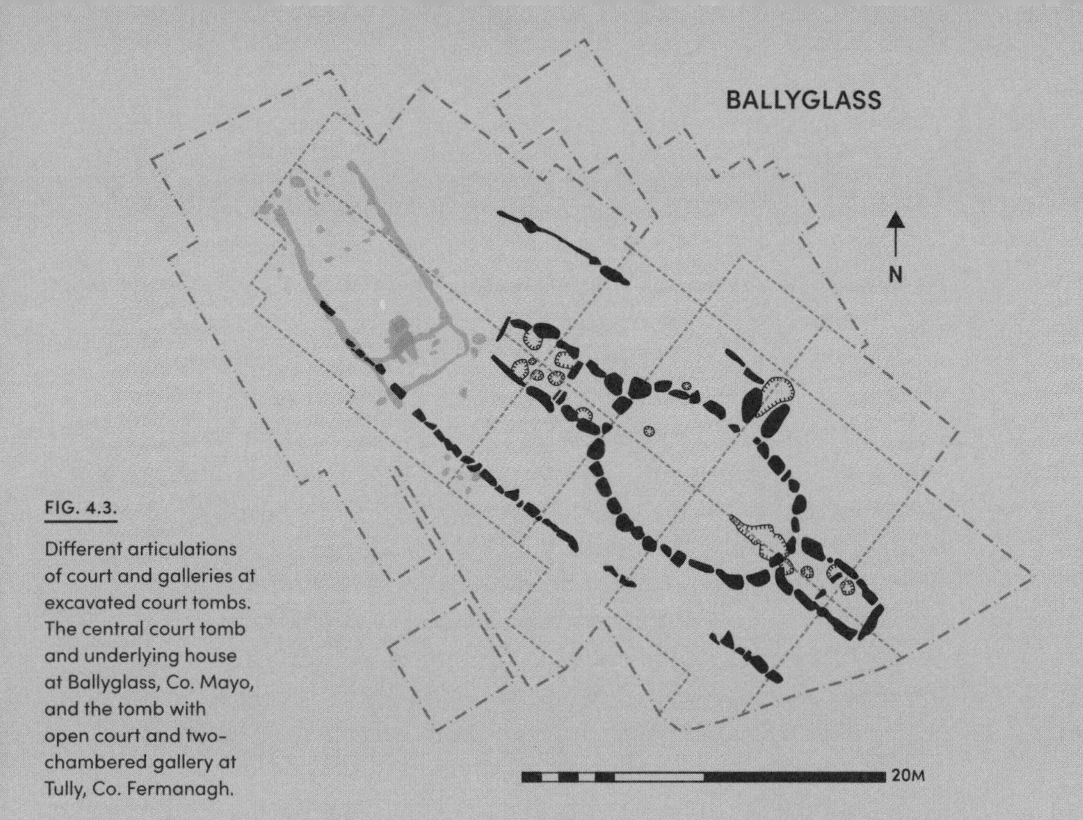

FIG. 4.3.

Different articulations of court and galleries at excavated court tombs. The central court tomb and underlying house at Ballyglass, Co. Mayo, and the tomb with open court and two-chambered gallery at Tully, Co. Fermanagh.

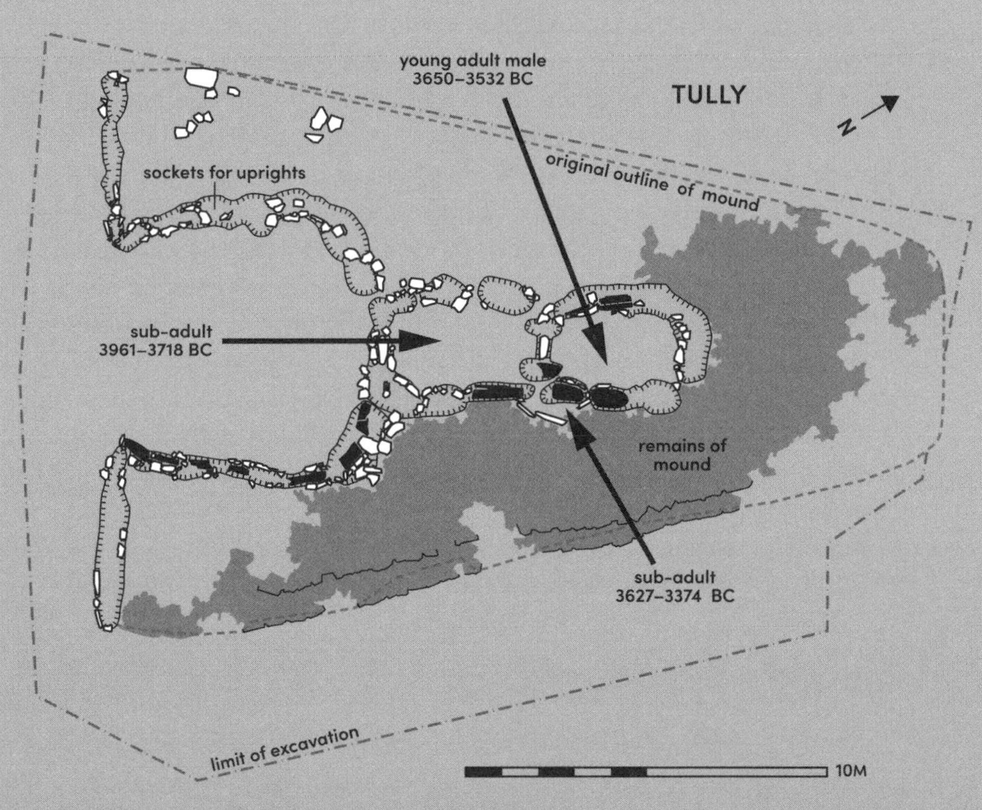

In the second half of the fourth millennium BC there is an increasing diversity of mortuary practice, with a particular focus on use of passage tombs. These are defined by a passage leading to a chamber, whose form varies. The roofed passage and chamber are covered by a round cairn or mound, defined by a ring of kerb-stones at its base. Recent discussions of the dating of passage tombs indicates that their use began before 3600 BC, with more elaborate forms, exemplified in the massive passage tombs of Newgrange, Knowth and Dowth in Brú na Bóinne, dating to the later part of the fourth millennium BC.[21] **[SEE PLS 1.D AND 1.F]** In this tradition, the practice of cremation has traditionally been seen as constituting the major treatment of the body after death. Human remains occur in what are frequently described as communal deposits, consisting of the remains of several individuals. The number of people represented within tombs varies, with some sites, such as the Mound of the Hostages at Tara and the Great Mound at Knowth, producing large assemblages. In reality, there was a complex sequence to the treatment at death of the remains of those placed in passage tombs. The frequent occurrence of unburnt bone in deposits, particularly adult skull and long bones and the bones of young children, suggests that there was a primary stage when soft tissue was allowed or facilitated to decompose. Were individuals cremated at different times and locations and then brought together, or was there a rite of communal cremation? Some young children were not cremated. Passage-tomb mortuary practice indicates that inhumation and cremation were not opposed rites, but were used in combination during a complex, multi-stage post-mortem treatment of the dead, a point returned to below.[22] **[PL. 4.D]**

Linkardstown burials are characterised by the placement of one or more inhumed individuals (either articulated or disarticulated) in a central cist under a cairn covered by a mound, accompanied by a highly decorated, round-based pot. These tombs are located in the southern part of the island and have been interpreted as communal

PL. 4.D.

Mound of the Hostages, Tara, Co. Meath. East end of Cist II after removal of fill, showing skulls and cremated bone spilling from the tomb interior.

memorials to leading individuals. Dating of human bone suggests that Linkardstown burials were in use from before 3600 BC to 3300 BC. These are burials of specific individuals (usually adult males), often accompanied by the deposition of the bones of a child or children, as at Ashley Park, Co. Tipperary. [FIG 4.4] Inhumation and multi-stage mortuary treatment is dominant, as at Poulawack on the Burren. Here, it appears that the disarticulated bones of three adults from well-preserved skeletons, and the bones of an infant, were brought to a cist from another location. While the dominant mortuary rite is inhumation, cremation was practiced. For example, one of two adult burials in the cist at Jerpoint West, Co. Kilkenny had been cremated.[23]

As Dowd has shown, a significant number of caves, all in areas with limestone bedrock, have produced unburnt human bone from

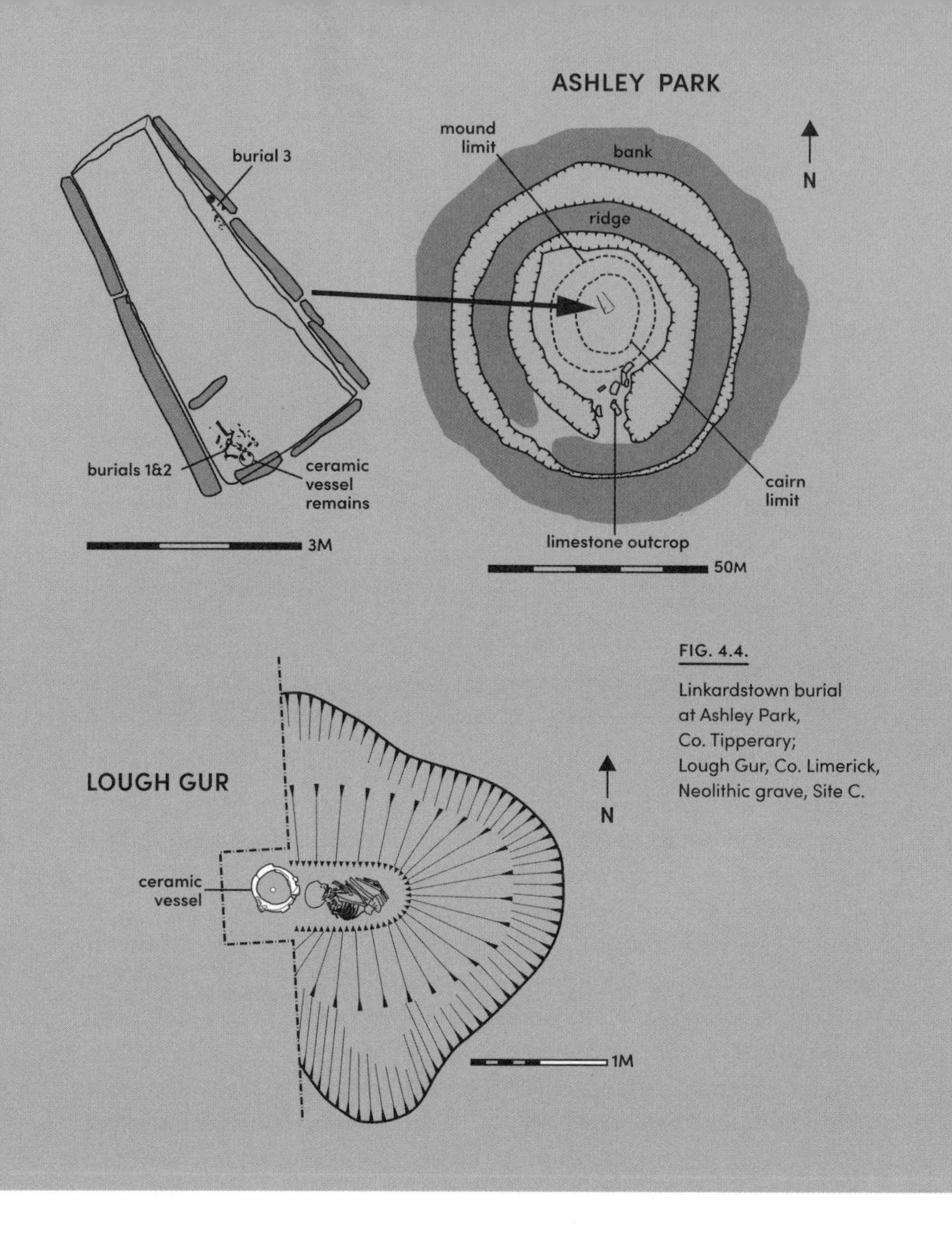

FIG. 4.4.

Linkardstown burial at Ashley Park, Co. Tipperary; Lough Gur, Co. Limerick, Neolithic grave, Site C.

the Neolithic period, with a marked concentration of dates in the period from 3600 to 3400 BC. Human bone is mostly recorded as isolated bones, but the placement of bodies also occurs, as at Annagh, Co. Limerick and Kilgreany, Co. Waterford. Dowd has suggested

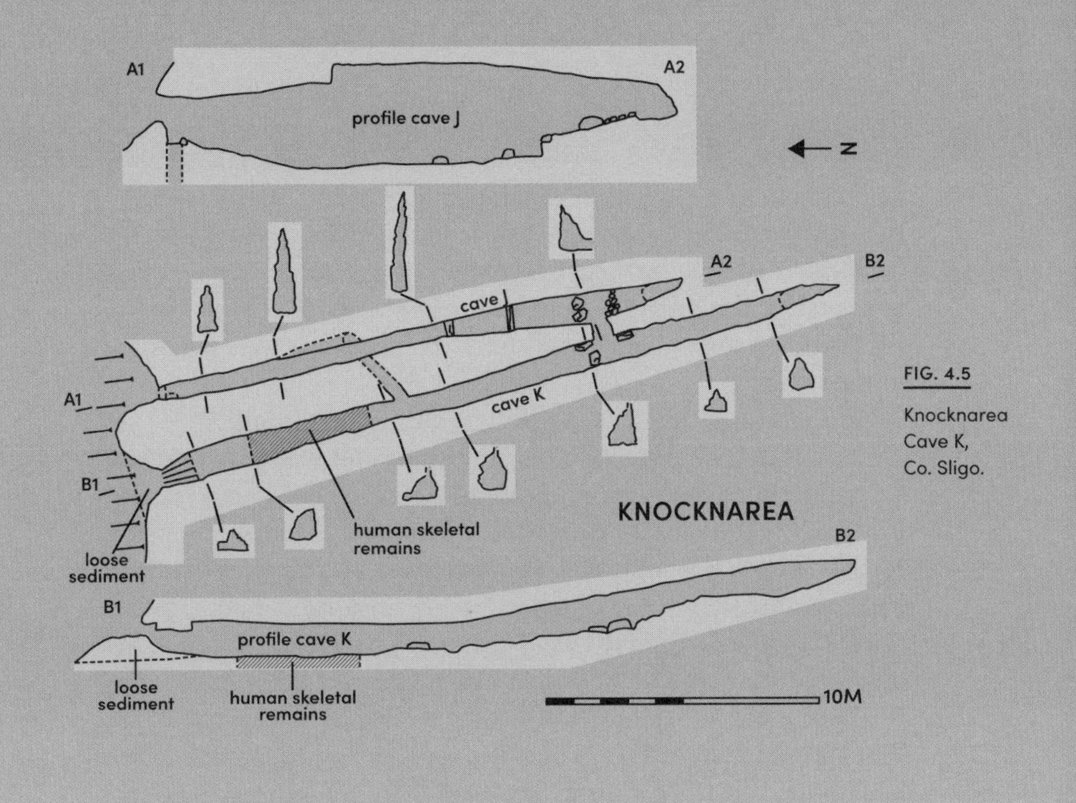

FIG. 4.5

Knocknarea Cave K, Co. Sligo.

that the repeated occurrence of smaller quantities of human bone in caves might indicate two different practices. Bodies placed in caves became skeletonised and then selected bones were removed from the cave, as at Knocknarea, Co. Sligo in the Middle Neolithic; or deliberate, token deposition of disarticulated human bone occurred. [FIG. 4.5] In the talus cave or boulder chamber at Glennamong, Bengorm, Co. Mayo, both of these practices were carried out in the Middle and Late Neolithic.[24] Part of the purpose of building a monument may have been to replicate the notion of a sacred space, such as a cave, that had a special link with the otherworld. The passage element in passage tombs, in its most accentuated form in monuments like Newgrange and Knowth, emphasises the distance and journeying involved in moving from the outside to the space where it is appropriate to place the bones of the dead. In addition, there are places that seem to fall between the two categories—natural place and monument—such as Glennamong, suggesting that the distinction may have been less important and apparent to people in the Neolithic. At Ballycarty, Co. Kerry, a passage tomb was quarried from and built into and on a prominently located limestone reef on the floor of a river valley. Fossils from the limestone were deposited in the tomb.[25]

The mortuary record for the Late Neolithic, from 2900 BC to 2500 BC is not well defined. It is difficult to find definitive evidence for human bone from specific contexts. Cremated bone from features is frequently too small to be positively identified as human. In portal tombs and court tombs, with the exception of a few sites such as Parknabinnia, deposition of bone appears to cease around 3100 BC. There are indications of dynamic change, as Neil Carlin has pointed out, with the use of a new ceramic style—Grooved Ware, originating in Orkney in the far north of Scotland—being incorporated into mortuary practice, such as at the major passage tomb complex of Brú na Bóinne. This is accompanied by a gradual shift in ceremonial foci towards outdoor enclosures of varying size, but again in these enclosures it is difficult to identify human bone.[26] [SEE PL. 1.D]

Most of the contexts outlined above are linked by having a substantial stone component. In other cases, structures made of wood and other materials were used. Such non-megalithic sites may have been an important component in mortuary practice in the Early Neolithic and are well-known in Britain, associated with rectilinear enclosures and sealed by a long, or more occasionally a round, mound. The commonest form consists of two large posts (or a split oak tree-trunk) placed in the ground a few metres apart, with a box-like structure, reminiscent of the form of the chambers of court tombs and portal tombs, built utilising these posts as the gables. Alternatively, the posts may have supported an open-air platform. The structure is sometimes divided by another post placed upright in the centre. The best example in Ireland is Dooey's Cairn (Ballymacaldrack) in Co. Antrim. [FIG. 4.6] Here, such a structure

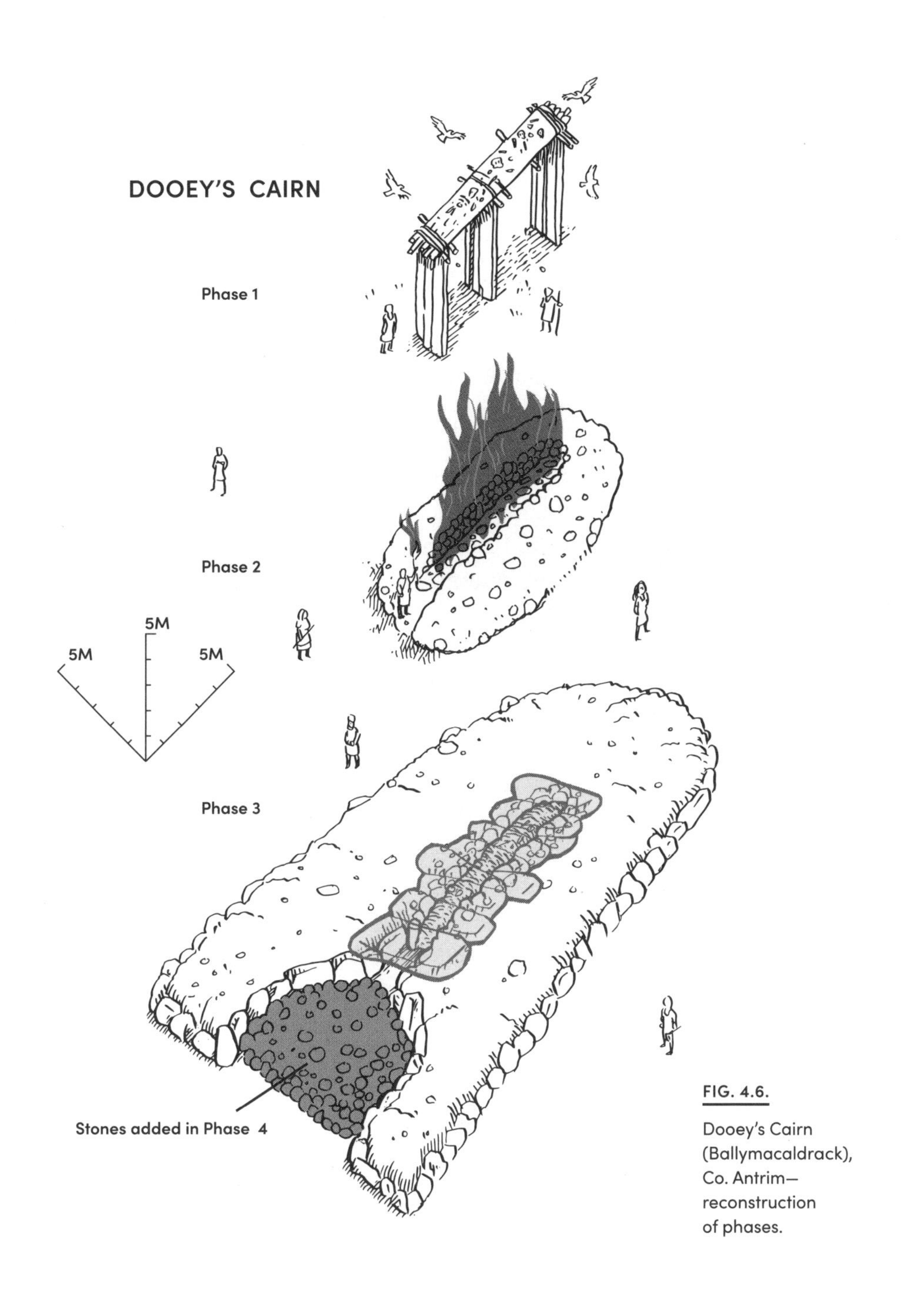

FIG. 4.6.

Dooey's Cairn (Ballymacaldrack), Co. Antrim—reconstruction of phases.

was built and it and the human bones within (or on top) were burnt. It was rebuilt with drystone sidewalls and incorporated as part of a roofed court tomb, a translation of the monument into stone as seen also in Britain, for example in south-west Scotland.[27]

In terms of non-monumental burial, we have examples of bodies in graves dug for that express purpose. At Knockadoon, Lough Gur, Co. Limerick, just upslope from a settlement area, an adolescent was buried and a Neolithic pot similar to those found with Linkardstown burials was placed at her/his head, suggesting a date for the burial between 3600 BC to 3300 BC. [SEE FIG. 4.4] Such unmarked graves may have been a more widespread practice, but are difficult to recognise in the archaeological record. Alternatively, a person may have been cremated and their cremated bones placed in a pit. Placement in pits of both unburnt, disarticulated bone and cremated human and animal bone is a feature particularly of the second half of the fourth millennium BC. It can be related to a wider and consistent appearance of burnt material in pits, as detailed by Jessica Smyth, suggesting that fire and burning had an important role in depositional activity.[28]

This discussion covers the varied post-mortem treatment of selected, visible individuals during the Neolithic. It is very difficult to provide anything other than a very broad outline of how the majority of people were treated at death. Without some dating evidence it is impossible to say how many unmarked inhumations or cremations, a recurrent feature on large-scale excavation projects, might be Neolithic in date. After death people may have been deliberately exposed to the elements and scavenging animals. This practice is known historically from various parts of the world and continues in some areas, as with the sky burials of Nepal and Tibet. Bodies may also have been placed in water. So too may cremated remains; this is a common feature of Hindu mortuary practice today.[29] [SEE PL. 2.B]

WHO WERE THE DISTINGUISHED DEAD OF THE NEOLITHIC?

The remains of the dead placed in monuments include individuals of all ages, from babies to old people, women and men. The adults include women who were young and of child-bearing age, and also of post-menopause middle and old age. There may well have been differences between the social place of women of child-bearing age and those who, more exceptionally in Neolithic times, lived on into post-menopause. The roles of men could also have changed over the course of adulthood. Middle-aged and old adults may have been seen as elders in the community.[30]

Does the differential treatment of people in death reflect social roles and identities? There may have been specific circumstances, such as the manner of death, that prompted a particular response to a death by a community. It has been suggested that placing the remains of the dead in megalithic tombs might have been a way of dealing with difficult people and deaths; that people deemed different, as a result of illness or perceived witchcraft, or a violent death, had to be treated and contained in a special way after death. Recognising that view, the age and gender profiles of people whose remains were placed in tombs suggest they represented important families or kin groups. Following the recognition through archaeological and aDNA analyses of a five-generation family among the individuals buried at a long cairn at Hazleton North, Gloucestershire, Fowler argues that the arrangement of tomb chambers was related to the negotiation of kinship. In this context, human remains can be seen as material expressions, across generations, of ideas of genealogical ancestry and rebirth.[31]

In Neolithic societies the focus on the past can be seen in sequences and episodes of activities at particular places and monuments. These episodes can be short or may span a millennium or more. There seems to have been a concern with maintaining or re-negiotating patterns of life and relationships that could be traced from the past. Key figures in this process were people who had lived in the past—the ancestors. The term ancestor refers either to distant beings involved in the mythic origins of people, or to specific, named persons remembered for living a socially significant life. These two types of ancestors can be combined. James Whitley argued the term has been used in an uncritical way in the study of the Neolithic of Ireland and Britain. Nevertheless, its use is important in understanding the character of society. For example, it has clarified that Neolithic human bone deposits are evidence not just of mortuary practices, but, as importantly, of the active use of human bone in rites and ceremonies. As Andy Jones put it, 'relations of ancestry are produced through continued engagement with the ancestors'.[32]

The significance of ancestors in providing links with the past and sustaining the world into the future has been highlighted by Mary Helms. She presumes that the creation and recognition of ancestors is most directly associated with the familial domain of social life and the house.[33] Belonging to a house is critical to sustaining the success of a group in daily and ceremonial activities and in demonstrating kinship and belonging. In kinship, descent is a key element, but marriage, affinity and alliances (forms of cognatic kinship) are also important, as is the role of places, things and non-human beings. The recently deceased may have a relatively short shelf-life as ancestral beings, and/or over time they may become remembered collectively as creator ancestors.[34]

Over generations, memories of individuals fade but their continued social significance can be remembered and materialised in careful and curated deposits of bone. Talking about the treatment of the dead within Neolithic communities in the Levant, Ian Kuijt distinguished between the direct and personal memory of the now dead when they were alive, and longer-term memory based on reference to the physical remains of the deceased. As detail is forgotten the deceased come to be characterised as remote, anonymous.[35] Agricultural groups were reliant to a greater or lesser extent on domesticated food sources, plants and animals—for both subsistence and their symbolic properties. The critical importance of maintaining and sustaining plants and animals through their life cycles would have encouraged a greater concern with time and continuity, with concepts of fertility, growth and renewal, all linked with daily and seasonal cycles as exemplified in the movement of the sun. In this context, the honoured or remembered dead would have been important in demonstrating the durability of the group and the links between the living and previous generations.[36] Those links could be articulated through the construction and use of tombs.

The challenge was how to create ancestors, convey them safely to an after or other life, and for them to continue to be present and 'alive' to help the living. The dichotomy between the decomposition of a body on death and ancestors as active and immortal presences had to be confronted. There were a number of ways of doing this, such as creating monuments with the intention of both protecting the contained human remains and making them visible in the landscape. Above all, what people seem to have been concerned about in the Neolithic was the direct and material expression of links with the ancestors by cleansing and purification, retention, active use, veneration, careful deposition and division of the physical remains of the dead. This was, to use Paul Connerton's term, an incorporated practice, providing a vital way of remembering the past.[37]

Thinking more widely, in religious systems corporal relics are the physical remains of a venerated person. Part of the power of such relics resides in their treatment compared to the remains of other deceased persons, who are forgotten. As Helms remarks, 'preservation of the bones of those who deserve to be remembered, helps to create that memory and thus tangibly evidences the reality of (house) ancestors'.[38] She stresses the intimate relationship between such bones and notions of fertility. The remains of ancestors materialise a concern with time and ensuring the continuity of resources. They become a key physical resource themselves in helping to maintain natural and human fertility.

The significance of the carefully deposited human bones that survive from the Neolithic is that in most cases they can be read as representing ancestors. By contrast, the bones of thousands of people from multiple generations who did not achieve or retain ancestral significance have not survived, or are not visible because they were not treated with the same degree of ceremony and complexity of use after death. In relation to ancestral bone, specific skeletal elements are seen as highlighting and summarising who a person was and their relationships with the living. These are the skull and long bones. It is not surprising that we see evidence that these body parts were regarded as special and were often treated in different ways after death. The skull or cranium in particular could evoke both directly remembered individuals and those deceased ancestors from previous generations whose memory was now referenced only by their physical remains. Such ancestral bone is powerful, because it can be used for active social and ceremonial intervention in the present.[39] [SEE PL. 4.D]

THE LIVING AND THE DEAD

Today we operate in a social framework where the individuality and bounded nature of a person is assumed. But in reality identities are relational, socially constructed and built on interactions in a familial and wider social sphere with other people, things and non-human beings. This is reflected in the idea of distinct *body worlds*: the totality of bodily experiences, practices and representations that form the heart of specific social and material worlds. The celebration of death—the nexus of living and dead bodies—is an arena in which we might expect to be able to identify a Neolithic body world. The most striking feature of many skeletal assemblages is the evidence they provide for complex and perhaps prolonged mortuary rituals. Mortuary practice was multi-stage, and—at least in some traditions—involved a number of locations. Over time the body was broken down into multiple, smaller constituents. The intention seems to have been to end up with dry bone—burnt or unburnt. Today we tend to see inhumation and cremation as alternative, perhaps opposed, mortuary practices by the living, in the context of the Neolithic, however, concern with breaking down the dead by cremation to produce cremated bone fragments could be seen as a quicker alternative to multi-stage inhumation rites, or indeed may be integrated with them.[40]

In one of the classic anthropological discussions of death, Robert Hertz argued that the meaning of cremation was not to destroy the body of the deceased, but to recreate it and make it capable of entering a new life.[41] More broadly this could be seen as an intent of Neolithic mortuary rituals: insuring the safe translation of the important dead into an ancestral world. This involved the living coming into bodily contact with the remains of the dead, particularly through the reduction of bodies to disarticulated bone. There were important differences in practice between and within different Neolithic mortuary traditions. Furthermore, in the dynamic and active context of ceremonial occasions, different communities would have given a local flavour to the wider frameworks of practice they saw as appropriate.

A widely recurring feature in Irish Neolithic mortuary practice was a distinction between the treatment of infants (birth–3 years), children (3–12 years) and older persons (adolescents and adults). Most discussions of mortuary practice have focused on adults, not surprisingly given their dominance in skeletal remains in formal contexts such as megalithic tombs. Bearing in mind changing social definitions of childhood, however, it is important to consider the sub-adults. In pre-industrial societies mortality would generally be highest among infants and younger children. There is debate about the proportion of deaths accounted for by sub-adults in such societies, with figures ranging from approximately 30% to over 50%.[42] As a generalisation, between 25% and 30% of the individuals in Neolithic burial contexts appear to be sub-adults. From Poulnabrone, Poulawack and Parknabinnia the overall figure given by Beckett is 74% adults and 26% sub-adults. In Tomb 1B East in the Knowth passage tomb complex, the ratio is 65% : 35%.[43]

One of the few Neolithic human bone assemblages dominated by children are the burials found associated with the settlement site of

Knockadoon, Co. Limerick.[44] These are articulated burials—placed in graves or hollows and covered—close to where the living carried out their daily lives. The practice of treating children differently at death and their burial close to the living is a common practice in small-scale, non-Western societies. This is also the case in the archaeological record; for example, on Linear Pottery settlement sites in central and western Europe in the centuries before 5000 BC there are frequent examples of people burying their dead children in the spaces beside and between contemporary longhouses.[45] Anthropologists argue that the difference in status between small children on the one hand and adolescents and adults on the other is that the former are not completely incorporated into society. They are relatively recently arrived and indeed may personify the rebirth of relatives from previous generations. As part of the familial domain, children are a symbol of its fertility and regeneration. In that context it is not surprising they would frequently be buried at the heart of the community.[46]

What about the children placed with adolescents or adults in formal monuments? Do they represent the collective identity of a kin group or community? One explanation is that particular families might have begun to emerge as leading ancestral lineages and children of such lineages may have been treated as quasi- or potential adults, with status ascribed to them because of their family. For example, Jones pointed out that in the Parknabinnia court tomb there are two individuals—a child and an adult—who both have an open metopic suture at the front of the skull. This is an inherited condition, so this child may be related to the adult.[47] In other cases, the remains of children are treated and placed in ways that contrast with and highlight the adults. Small children are sometimes distinguished by being inhumed while adults are cremated, as appears to have been the case in some passage tombs, such as Fourknocks and the Mound of the Hostages at Tara. Muiris O'Sullivan has noted at the latter site that every significant deposit of cremated bone had unburnt children's bones with it. By way of contrasting practice, it should be noted that at the Knowth Tomb 1B East passage tomb

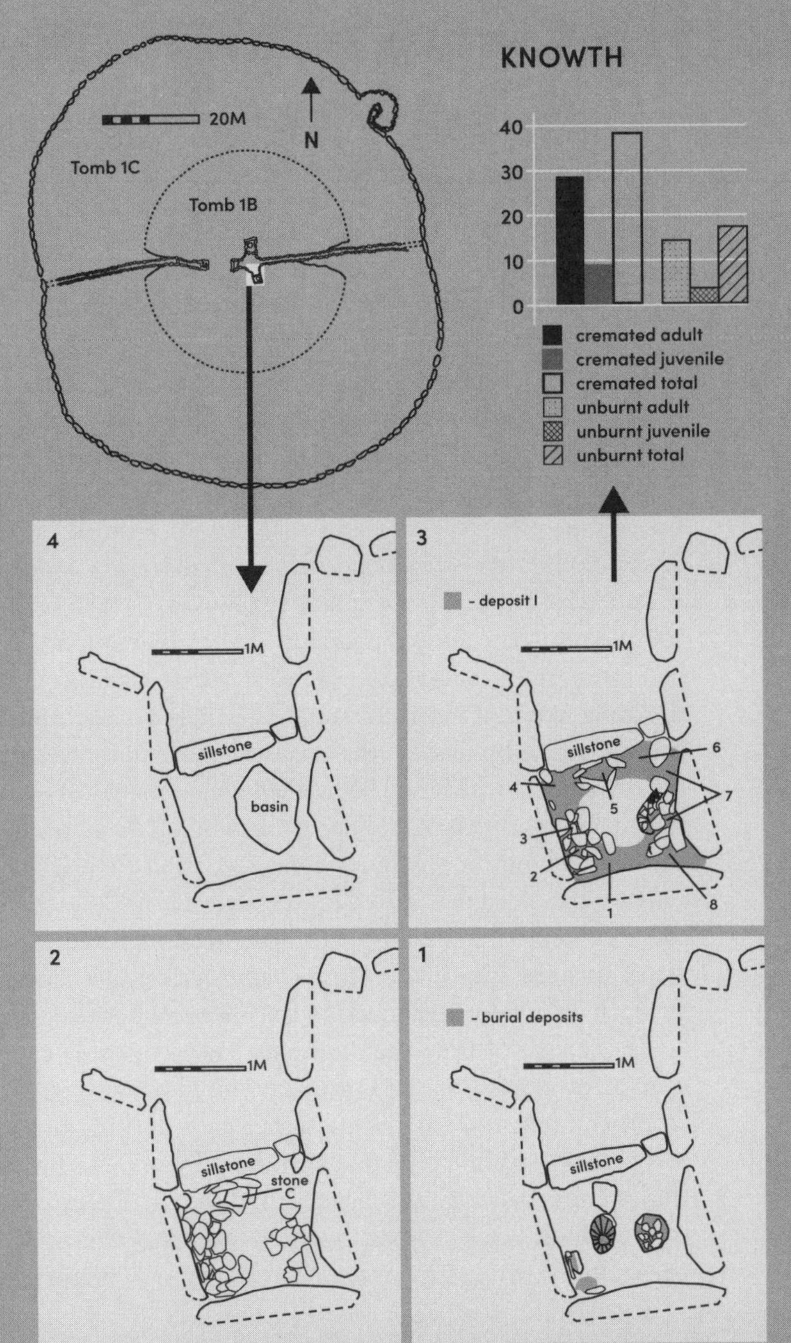

FIG. 4.7.

Sequence of burial deposits in the left-hand recess of Tomb 1B, Great Mound, Knowth, with a graph showing overall pattern of mortuary rite. Depositional sequence begins from bottom-right.

there is the deliberate inclusion of cremated and unburnt bones of infants and children.[48] **[FIG. 4.7]**

Breaking down bodies after death not only facilitated the journey the dead took but also made it easier to actively utilise human bone, along with other objects and materials, in ceremonies and practices expressing the relationships between living people, places, animals and things. We can consider this by considering general sequences or episodes of activities at monumental and related sites where human bone was deposited.

First, a location that may already have been a landmark was chosen—such as a prominent outcrop or boulder—or the construction of the monument made the location special. Then a structure was created, often accompanied or preceded by burning activity. Frequently, pits were dug and material—sometimes involving the bones of children—was deposited in them and/or around the base of structural stones. At Creggandevesky, Co. Tyrone, cremated bone was placed in the socket of one of the jambs marking the entrance to a court tomb gallery, and part of a carinated pot in the socket for the other jamb. At Annaghmare, Co. Armagh court tomb **[SEE PL. 2.A]** activity began by placing the backstone of the tomb structure in a hollow in rock, which had been filled with a matrix of cultural material, including the cremated bones of a child.[49] Next, bodies, disarticulated bone and/or cremated bone and other deposits were placed in the tomb structures. Over time these were added to, and in some cases particular bones appear to have been removed to other locations. At some sites it was deemed appropriate, as a closing episode, to block off any further access to the ancestral bones.

The length of time such episodes and sequences covered could span many generations and several hundred years, as at Poulnabrone. In other cases, such as the passage tombs at Tara and Knowth, it was compressed into a couple of hundred years. The order in which things happened may also have been different. Over time, the form of the monument or shrine in which the bones were held may have been altered, as at Dooey's Cairn. What was important was the continuing or renewed veneration of the ancestral bones and the links between the living and the dead. As time went on these bodily links would have deepened as the cycle of movement from life to death to life was repeated and previous ceremonies remembered. In some instances there may have been distinct phases of deposition, as Michael Connolly suggests on the basis of the pottery assemblage at Killaclohane I portal tomb.

With the ongoing use of tombs, earlier deposits had to be moved to make way for later deposits. At Parknabinnia, the older inhumed deposits appear to be more fragmentary and the later ones more articulated. In other cases, human remains were placed in the structure as bones, not as bodies. So there would have been handling of the dead in other places before they were placed in the monument. This is clear in the case of cremated bone and is also emphasised by the occurrence in passage tombs of deposits consisting of the cremated—and sometimes unburnt—remains of several individuals. Inhumed bone was also introduced into structures, however, as partially articulated, or more commonly as unarticulated, bones.

At the passage tombs Cairns H and K at Carrowkeel, Co. Sligo, Jonny Geber identified cut marks that were made as part of a dismemberment process. Eileen Murphy recognised that bones in the main deposit at Millin Bay, Co. Down, consisting of the inhumed bones of adolescents and adults, were deliberately defleshed. One of these individuals has been dated to between 3500 BC and 3130 BC.[50] Defleshing may have been employed to speed up the process by which impure, soft, decaying tissue could be transformed into the hard, enduring bones of the ancestors. That this transformation of the dead into ancestors also happened more slowly is indicated by differences in the surface appearance of unburnt bones, as in the central cist at Poulawack, suggesting that the bones had been placed somewhere else before deposition. If material was being moved around and being brought into a tomb, the counter-point was removal of material from tombs for veneration and use. Indeed, there are tombs where skulls and long bones are under-represented.[51]

Linkardstown tombs provide the best example of a set of ceremonial actions to establish and celebrate ancestors. Monuments were built to honour particular dead individuals. The events—from construction to sealing off the structure containing human bone—happened over a short period. The bones of small children were sometimes placed with the old males who appear to have been the focus of veneration. At Ashley Park, for example, the remains of a new-born baby appear to be placed as a foundation deposit to mark the creation of the structure by quarrying bedrock. The disarticulated remains of an elderly man placed within the monument are accompanied by the bones of a 2–3-year-old. Cattle bone in the cairn may indicate a funeral feast or may be an analogy with the death of the man.[52] [SEE FIG. 4.4]

Alongside the reality of high infant mortality rates, the nature of such deposits raise the possibility of infanticide. It seems clear that infanticide was widespread in the past and indeed sadly is still practiced in parts of the world today. The reasons for infanticide are culturally determined and may involve beliefs such as that children could be reborn at a more auspicious time.[53] Trying to understand this in a cultural framework, rather than automatically employing our own morality as the context to assess behaviour in the past, might help us understand how it might have been deemed acceptable, even appropriate, for children to accompany venerable ancestors in death.

At some sites there is evidence of the blocking off of access to ancestral deposits—creating a sense of an ancestral world. This involved the creation of physical barriers using blocking material such as stone, the deposition of cultural material such as pottery and animal bone that relates to the ancestors, and the deposition of human bone, perhaps to complete the sense of an ancestral community.[54] [SEE FIG. 4.6] One might argue that this sealing off would reduce the power and place of the ancestors. On the other hand, the monuments in which such bones are placed may come to represent in tradition and memory a more ambiguous ancestral world, open to re-interpretation.[55]

One of the enduring legacies of the Neolithic was the creation of many new special places in the landscape, alongside those already long recognised as important, such as caves, springs, hill- and mountain-tops and islands. Different social, kinship and cosmological traditions are reflected in the architecture of the monuments and their location. These monuments often contain or build on attributes of natural places, and appear to symbolically refer to them. After all, they are in many ways islands of the dead. This image is best expressed by the actual siting of monuments on islands or on mountain-tops. To summarise, there are monuments where ancestral deposits are placed so that the living have a sense of spatial and temporal connection to them, for example in court tombs and portal tombs. Andrew Powell suggested that single-chamber portal

PL. 4.E.

The eastern part of the Carrowkeel, Co. Sligo passage tomb cemetery with four tombs to the right; to the left and above the gorge is another tomb, with settlement area (Mullaghfarna) visible below it.

tombs emphasise the unity of the kin group and its presence in the landscape, with the linear arrangement of chambers in court tombs portraying a stronger sense of lineage stretching from the living to the dead. Tombs like Ballyglass can be seen as reflecting two segments or moieties within a lineage. By contrast, in many passage tombs there is a clear separation between the living and the ancestral world, created by the passage element. A passage can, however, also symbolise access. Are we seeing here a shift from a world view that sees the dead of previous generations as close and immanent, to one focused on an ancestral world regarded as significant but quite different—a place to be journeyed to, with ancestors who were regarded as transcendent.[56] Do these differences reflect changing concepts over the course of the Neolithic, with the development of the passage tomb tradition in the later fourth millennium BC? Or did more complex relationships between the living and the dead develop over time, with different kinds of ancestors in different monuments assisting the living? **[PL. 4.E]**

SOCIAL BODIES

Frequent reference has been made above to local communities and social groups. At the same time, we can see echoes of wider principles and traditions in locally based actions in specific contexts. In recent archaeological discussion there has been a focus on the strength of the record of life and death at a micro-scale and local level being matched by an ability to provide more detailed historical narratives.[57] One of the reasons this is possible is because people shared similar material culture and ways of life as a cultural framework at a regional level. We interpret such frameworks—brought into active engagement with the world as a body world—either by focusing on particular time periods, such as the early Neolithic, or by examining bodily experiences, practices, activities and material within particular cultural traditions, such as the Irish passage tomb tradition.[58]

What were the organisational networks that actively linked communities and helped to underpin a sense of what was the right and proper way to do things, for example in relation to mortuary and ancestral practices? How were key underpinning social principles, such as gender, expressed in Neolithic body worlds—both within communities and across such networks? Some caution is needed in discussing Neolithic social organisation, not least because of the complex relationships between the living and the dead and our reliance on the remains of the dead in social interpretation. Nevertheless, based on the evidence of their engagement with the dead, there are lines of research that indicate how Neolithic people may have lived and related to each other communally and across wider networks. We can consider the degree to which a sense of social cohesion is reflected in the practices of different communities *within* a tradition, and the distinct differences that distinguish *between* traditions. Over time, the ancestral world and its relationship with the living becomes more complex. Ancestors have to support not only the vitality of individual houses/groups, but also the relationship between such groups who, as well as having ancestors and lineages in common, for example through the establishment of marriage links, may be competing for social position. In relation to gender, John Robb and Oliver Harris suggest that how gender was understood in the Neolithic varied depending on the context. There were contexts of action for which gender was not particularly relevant.[59] The question is, can we identify these trends in the archaeological record?

Looking at the south-east Burren during the earlier Neolithic, Carleton Jones suggested we might conceptualise Neolithic society as being structured in a widening series of kinship ties. Social groups remembered and respected their lineages by placing the remains of selected individuals in four court tombs local to settlement areas. Two adjacent tombs could represent two complementary social groups or moieties of a clan or local tribe; hence there might have been two clans in the area. He argues that the ancestral past of the two clans was represented by the deposits in the portal tomb at Poulnabrone to the north and another at Ballycasheen to the south, both on important routeways. These two portal tombs represented the past of the respective clans to the wider world, with the Linkardstown burial at Poulawack being for tribal leaders. This perspective is not inconsistent with the aDNA evidence from Poulnabrone and Parknabinnia, which found evidence for distant kinship in both; the evidence from Primrose Grange court tomb, Co. Sligo, of close biological kin relations among three individuals; and the reality that kinship is not just based on biology, but is worked in and through social relationships.[60]

There has been debate about how social networks might have changed over time. The classic stance has been to see court tombs and passage tombs (see FIG. 1.4), and the activities and the deposits within them, as reflecting two different societies—with a shift from a simpler, segmentary format to a more complex society over the course of the Neolithic.[61] As Richard Bradley has argued, however, we need to start from the premise that people would have imbued the past with meaning, and that this would have been the frame of reference for contemporary life.[62] So, while the dating of developed passage tombs indicates that their main period of use came significantly later than that of court tombs, the landscape of the later fourth millennium BC was invested with the physical and tangible remains of earlier activity—monuments and bones, memories and stories of ancestral beings—all of which had to be accommodated in the contemporary world. [PL. 4.F]

Drawing on Powell's discussion, the contrasts between court tombs and passage tombs could be usefully thought of in terms of what we might respectively call houses for local ancestors and abodes for ancestors whose links to the living stretched over a much wider area. Elements of that wider social affiliation and associated networks are reflected in the prominent hill-top siting of many passage tombs with specific orientations and distant visibility. Indeed, aDNA indicates distant genetic relations between those whose remains were placed in the Carrowmore and Carrowkeel cemeteries, Newgrange and Millin Bay.

PL. 4.F.

Looking south to a court tomb at Clontygora, Co. Armagh, with the passage tomb on Black Mountain, Co. Louth in the background, location indicated by hilltop mast.

We can also consider how different kinds of ancestors might have worked together for the living. For example, aDNA analysis identified a close biological relationship between a person in the Primrose Grange court tomb and one in the Listoghil passage tomb at Carrowmore, about two kilometres apart. Court and portal tombs were highly visible and some continued to be used alongside passage tombs. There are very interesting spatial relationships between these monuments in areas where their distribution overlaps, as in the Cooley and Mourne Mountains. Here, portal tombs are located in low-lying areas and court tombs often on the boundaries between areas likely to have been used more regularly and intensively and upland areas, which would have seen more seasonal use. In this sense, both tomb types symbolise the place of local communities. The hill-top siting of passage tombs, sometimes shrouded in clouds, or covered by snow in winter, suggests a higher world; apart, but visible from a distance.[63] Does this narrative sufficiently consider how such local and wider social worlds would actually have been linked? How would living people have engaged with each other? What were the levels of contact, the networks of relationships, that people shared with each other in daily life, and in dealing with the dead? **[PLS 4.E, 4.F]**

Addressing this problem, Alasdair Whittle drew on models put forward by Nuestupný and Gamble.[64] Evžen Nuestupný couched his approach in terms of communities. Formed of groups of families/households, these communities live in areas where close social ties within groups created relationships of assistance. At a remove from this, but forming an essential framework for each community area, is the world of 'otherness' in which there are shared and understood material and symbolic cultures and beliefs. Beyond this again, is the strange world consisting of unknown people and places, with whom there are occasional contacts. Clive Gamble talks more directly in terms of people. Personal security and a sense of well-being and relatedness is provided by a network of people. The routine of everyday life revolves around an effective network of up to twenty people—relations and friends with familial or residential links. An extended network of 100–400 people can be drawn on if necessary. Shared material culture and symbolic value systems provide the articulation of this network. Beyond this is a global network: the people who might be encountered over a life, defined by being different, 'other', ranging from casual acquaintances to strangers.

Taking a different perspective, Robin Dunbar has argued that a grouping of around 150 people forms a very widely occurring social unit, regardless of the scale of the society itself.[65] He was looking at the significance of language and gossip in informing social order and cohesion, and argues that 150 represents the maximum number of people that we can have a genuine social relationship with, in the sense of knowing who people are and how they relate to us. Dunbar points out that in small-scale societies, this figure also represents the number of living descendants an ancestral couple could have after four generations, or as far back as any living person in the group would remember from personal experience.[66] Relating this to Gamble's extended network provides us with a measure of the scale at which Neolithic people might have actively related to the world of the ancestors.

Wider social worlds are reflected by and in traditions of material culture and the movement of certain objects over considerable distance. For example, in the passage-tomb tradition that reaches its peak in the largest tombs of the complexes in the Boyne Valley, Loughcrew, Carrowkeel and Carrowmore, a very large number of people contributed to the construction of the monuments, sharing a sense of social collectivity and identity. Concepts of clan, community and extended network give us a sense of the scale of social and ancestral life that had the most detailed and immediate meaning for people. In this realm, direct links could be remembered back to particular ancestors. Beyond that the ancestors are more likely to have been seen as a collective, reflecting depth in time of the society as well as the social links between wider networks. Those links might have been expressed by the physical movement of ancestral bones from a local network sphere to this wider social world. Jostling for positions of social influence might be reflected through the prominence given to the location and treatment of ancestral remains.

We can develop the discussion by looking in more detail at the Irish passage tomb tradition.[67] Passage tomb architecture, art and patterns of funerary deposition created a very distinctive place for the dead as, for example, at Fourknocks, Co. Meath. Guillaume Robin suggests that the interplay of these components indicates a symbolic world based on a system of concentric spaces, a central axis that is at once an axis of access and opposition in terms of spatial organisation. In terms of mortuary activity, the primary focus appears to be on creating ancestors through cremation. The special role of the head and long bones of adults and the bones of children were recognised by sometimes leaving them unburnt and depositing them in particular ways. This implies that rather than a body always being cremated, bones may have been burnt sometime after death, or indeed, as suggested by the deposition of unburnt bone in caves, as at Knocknarea, some individuals were not cremated.[68] **[FIGS 4.8, 4.9]**

The tradition starts early in the Neolithic with the construction of small tombs, of simple design, often on hilltops, with the monuments known and visible to the local world. Over the course of the second half of the fourth millennium, from 3500 BC–3000 BC, places of particular importance and veneration emerged, now recognised as passage tomb complexes. Groups of people came to build monuments and place their ancestors within them, expressing their links with the wider social world that they belonged to. It is striking that this social network, involving large numbers of living and dead persons, developed at a time when there was a supposed dip in human activity following the earlier Neolithic; this suggests a need for caution in the use of generalised 'boom and bust' models of population.[69]

At Carrowkeel, isotopic analysis of bones indicates a relatively diverse population, with people coming from different areas within the wider locality. Robert Hensey has argued that the tombs may have been used as places of initiation, marking the beginning of adulthood. At a broader social level, Frank Prendergast has discussed how the distribution pattern of passage tombs can be thought of in terms of the deliberate creation of a large social network of visibility.[70] The deposits within the tombs were deliberately created by the living, who placed the cremated remains of different people together with unburnt bones, including those of infants, and objects, which in some cases were burnt. The treatment of adults is similar for male and female sexed bodies, suggesting that gender was not particularly relevant in this context; this may also be reflected in the abstract nature of passage tomb art, even where anthropomorphic

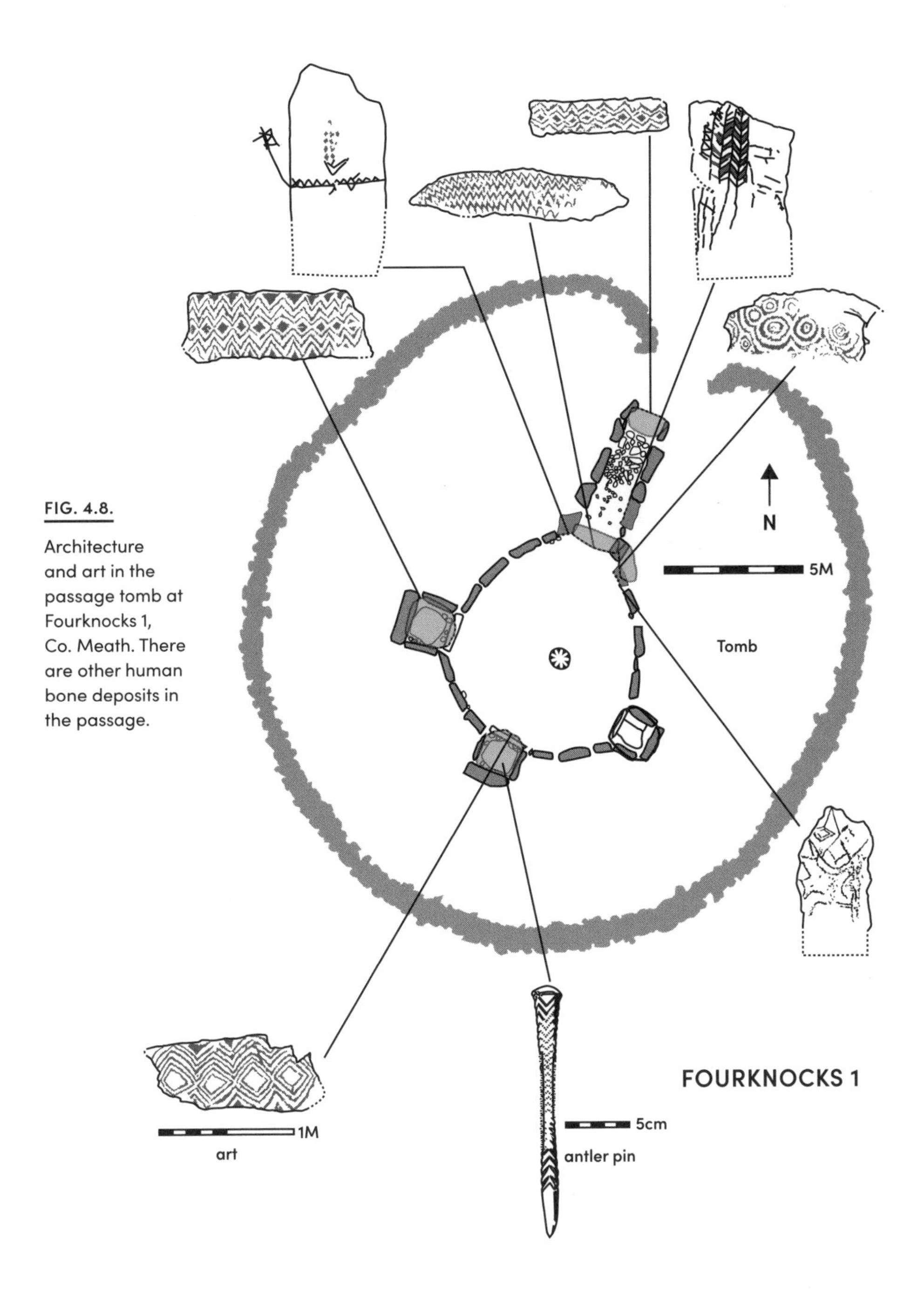

FIG. 4.8.

Architecture and art in the passage tomb at Fourknocks 1, Co. Meath. There are other human bone deposits in the passage.

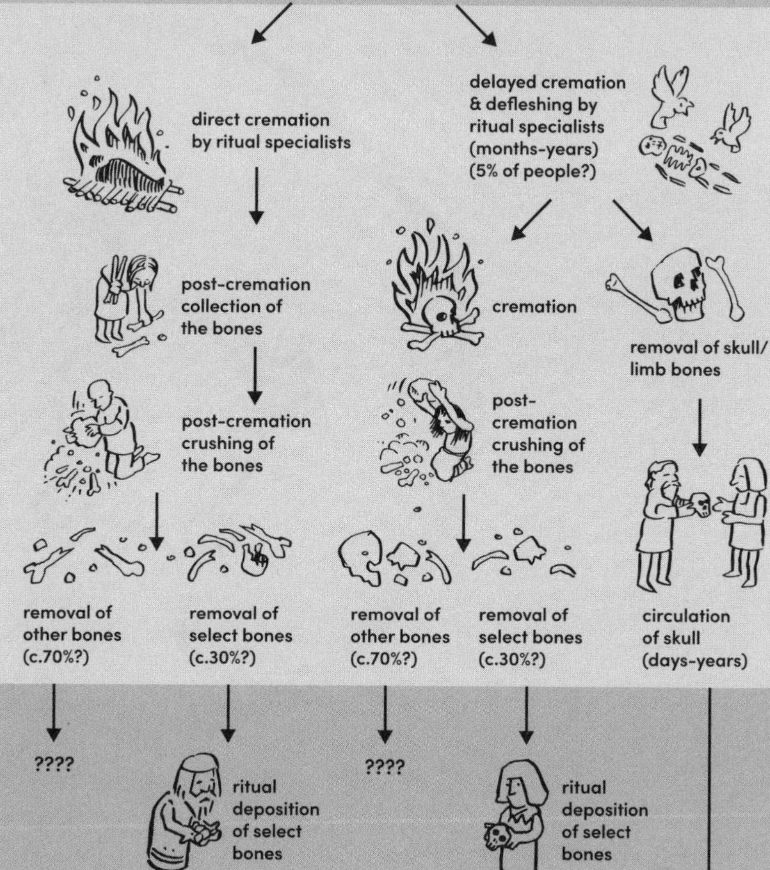

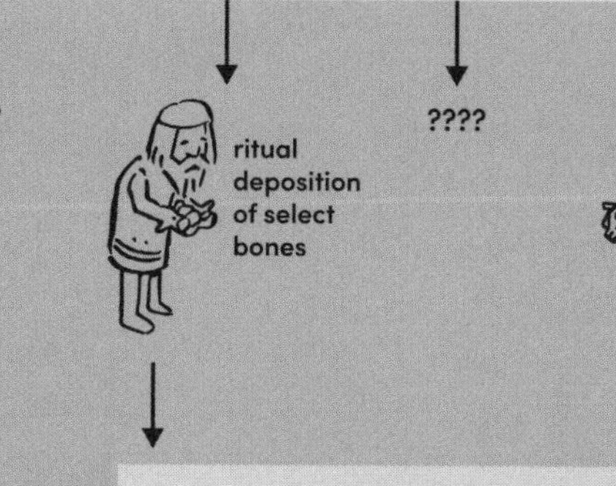

FIG. 4.9.

Conjectural pathways of the Neolithic dead in the developed passage tomb tradition.

designs can be recognised. While aDNA analysis has focused on the recognition of patrilineal descent, maternal ancestry is likely to have been important, and the social construction of kinship to have been complex. The tombs were of increasing size and complexity, evidenced by the large, central sites such as Newgrange, Knowth and Dowth, Cairn T at Loughcrew and Maeve's Cairn on Knocknarea above Carrowmore, which celebrate the potency of ancestral bones and of the monuments themselves to influence life. At Knocknarea, the monuments were enclosed and defined by earthen and stone banks, and the Great Palisade at Newgrange could possibly be contemporary with passage tombs, but is more likely to be later, attesting to the continuing power of this special place. Taking a landscape and skyscape view Prendergast has shown that some tombs are aligned to connect them with other monuments and places and to capture and reflect key turning points in the year, such as the solstices.[71] **[PLS 4.G, 4.H]**

This was an active, evolving tradition of commemoration, which also involved re-working or forgetting the past. At Knowth, decorated stones from a former tomb (or tombs) were placed at key locations in both the eastern and western tombs under the Great Mound. There are echoes and links to other monumental centres in Atlantic Europe in the art and selected objects placed with the dead at Knowth or deposited close to them, emphasising ancestors who stood for a wider world. On the other hand, the distinctive mortuary practices of the Irish passage tomb tradition demonstrates how specific the ancestral world of that tradition was, wrapped by and interwoven with the living, and contrasting with the Orcadian passage tombs, in which large numbers of inhumed remains were placed in monuments. As George Eogan and Elizabeth Shee Twohig put it, these are 'special places for important people'.[72]

But this was not an exclusive tradition, and we find aspects of practices associated with passage tombs in other contexts. Cremation had a long history of use in the Neolithic, and the social impact of the burning of bodies and bones and their treatment after cremation

made it a spectacular technology of rememberance, to use Howard Willams's phrase.[73] The passage-tomb concern with circularity is reflected in Linkardstown tombs. Here, the emphasis is on particular individuals as ancestors. Moreover, the focus on elderly males in Linkardstown tombs suggests that, in this context, gender differences were important. Deposition of Carrowkeel pottery, the ceramic tradition most closely associated with passage tombs, also occurs in court tombs. At Ballynahatty, Co. Down, a small subterranean monument—the 1855 tomb, a version of a passage tomb—contained human skulls and Carrowkeel pots. Carrowkeel pots containing cremated bone were also placed in pits as part of the activities that created the large, open-air ceremonial complex at Ballynahatty at the end of the Neolithic.[74]

PL. 4.G.

Opposite, top: The interior of the passage tomb at Fourknocks, looking from the entrance passage to the back recess.

PL. 4.H.

Oposite, bottom: Loughcrew: looking from Cairn I, Carnbane West to Cairn T, Carnbane East on the skyline. Megalithic art on orthostat on the left.

So, passage tombs demonstrate that wider social networks developed over time, but have we been too inclined to use labels such as 'the Irish passage-tomb tradition' to try to define exclusive social entities? As a generalisation, the local, walked world was what people would have known best. Wider social frameworks existed, however, and people could have travelled considerable distances by water and land. Alongside remembering the dead in a local tomb they could have owed allegiance to broader polities, materialised in the location, construction and use of passage tombs in other regions.

At an emotional, personal level, the death of someone known would have had most impact on peoples' lives. The pain of grief and memories of the dead person would fade, perhaps relieved by a belief that people returned or lived on in another guise. Sadly, there is little trace of most of these people in the archaeological record. What we have are the remains of particular individuals, adults and sub-adults, whose memory and commemoration was socially important. That memory was sustained by contact with ancestral bones.

WHO WERE THEY AND WHAT IS THEIR LEGACY?

On the basis of aDNA it has been suggested that a woman whose cranium was placed in the 1855 monument at Ballynahatty was brown-eyed and had dark-coloured hair, and a similar description has been given for two distantly related men from Glennamong, Bengorm, noting that they were almost certainly intermediate to dark-skinned.[75] Can we build on this kind of specific observation to talk more broadly about what Neolithic people were like? We have some well-preserved skeletal assemblages providing details on peoples' lifestyle and health, now augmented by aDNA and isotopic analysis.

Ó Donnabháin discussed the mostly complete skeletons of three adult males and small portions of two others, also probably adult males, from the cave at Annagh. These date to between 3760 BC to 3120 BC, but it is argued they suggest a short period of use of the cave. Two individuals were over 50 years when they died. The three had a mean stature of 170.2cm (5ft 7in), compared to that of modern Irish males of 178m (5ft 10in). Their teeth reflected generally good dental health, with wear related to a relatively coarse diet and active use of teeth as a tool. Ó Donnabháin commented that the arthritic changes in the non-vertebral joints suggest the men led vigorous, physically active lives. The extent and severity of lesions in the neck and upper back are highly suggestive of transporting heavy loads using the head, neck and upper back, by placing loads directly on the head and carrying weights on the upper back supported by a strap around the forehead. Two of the men had head wounds, which could have been caused by small projectiles such as a sling stone; one had suffered a broken nose and the other a fractured rib. All these injuries are likely the result of interpersonal violence, supporting the view that low-level violence was endemic at this time. The similarity of morphological traits shared by the men at Annagh led Ó Donnabháin to suggest that there was a considerable degree of consanguinity (descent from the same ancestor) among them, although aDNA showed no genetic relationships. In any case, it is

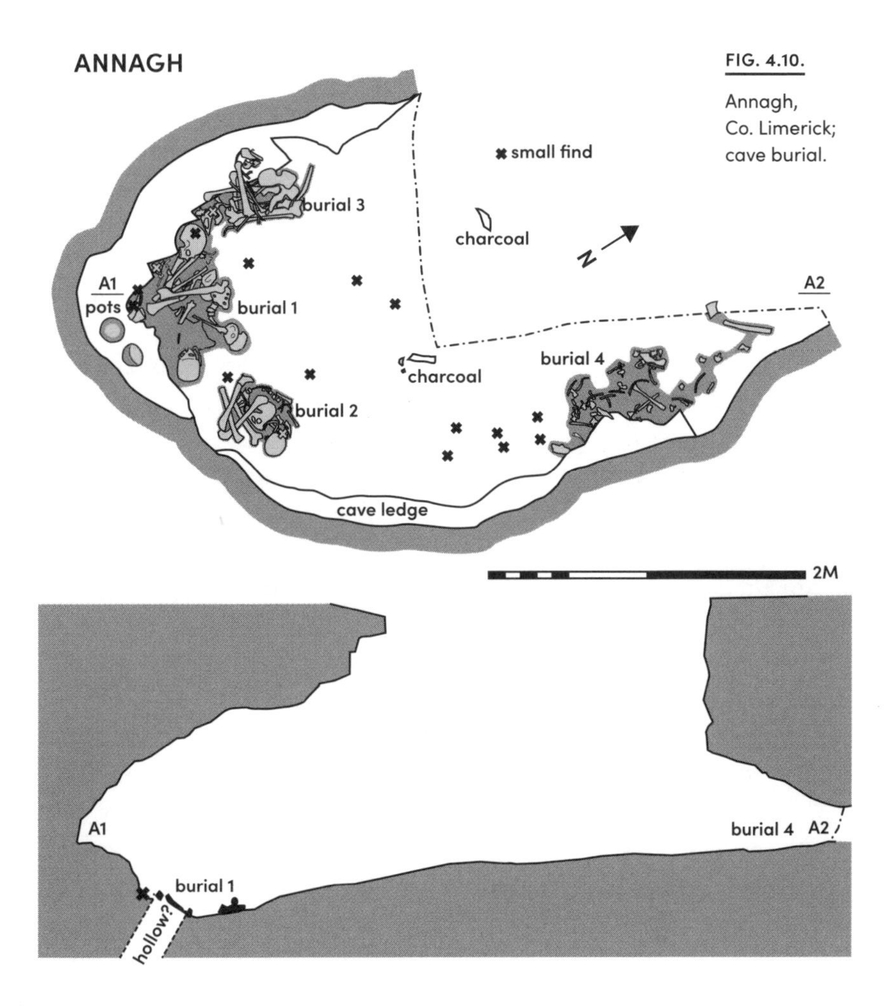

FIG. 4.10.

Annagh, Co. Limerick; cave burial.

hard to disagree with Ó Donnabháin's conclusion that Annagh was an important locus either in the treatment of a community's heroes, or a place reserved for old, venerable men.[76] [FIG. 4.10]

Neolithic life would have revolved around a range of physical activities that had a quotidian basis and were seasonally varied. The physical remains indicate people who were strong and muscular. That kind of life takes its toll, and the common occurrence of arthritis and rheumatism testify to the physical pain that people endured.

We can speculate that such pain was seen as part of the accepted pattern of talk, work and rest. In some cases, teeth indicate shortcomings in diet when people were young. The necessity of a secure food supply would have been one reason people looked to the ancestors to ensure continuing fertility of wild and natural resources.[77]

Competition over resources may have been a factor in the evidence for persistent, low-level endemic violence in European Neolithic societies. A key source of information for violence are skeletal remains from burial contexts. In Britain for example, over 7% of all human crania in such contexts show traumatic injuries. There is a higher prevalence of trauma in males, which suggests that they may have been the main players and instigators of violence. This could have taken the form of individual combat, informal raiding or more organised conflict.[78] In Ireland, alongside evidence from Annagh, there is evidence of trauma at other sites. At Poulnabrone this includes fractures, blunt-force trauma and a weapon wound in the form of the tip of a stone projectile point in an adult hip bone. [SEE PL. 2.C.III AND C.IV]

We cannot be sure what language people used when they communicated and expressed ideas, for example about the relationship of the living and the dead. We can however suggest that, like today, such discussion would have been grounded in the use of metaphors, linking all aspects of peoples' behaviour into their code for living.As noted in Chapter 2, the debate about what language Neolithic people in Ireland spoke really comes down to when Indo-European—a language family that encompasses most languages spoken today between Ireland and India—developed. There are two different hypotheses about the spread of Indo-European languages across Europe. One is that it is associated with the spread of farming from the Near East across Europe, beginning about 7000 BC in Greece, and the second that it happened from between 3000 BC to 2500 BC and is reflected in changes in the archaeological record at that point.[79]

Ancient DNA analysis is a rapidly advancing area of research.[80] However, there are issues with the ways in which genetic research has been used in archaeological interpretation.[81] The spread of the Neolithic across Europe is regarded as primarily the result of Early European Farmers, ultimately from Anatolia, expanding and interacting with local hunter-gatherers (Eastern and Western European hunter-gatherers). The woman from the Ballynahatty 1855 tomb reflects this ancestry. It is argued that the beginning of the Irish Neolithic was the result of a movement of Early European Farmers onto the island—as a replacement population. It appears, however, that there was some genetic input from the Irish Mesolithic population, as reflected, for example, in a later individual from Parknabinnia. This fits with the bigger picture at a European level, of little initial admixture followed by an increase in hunter-gatherer ancestry within the Neolithic population. In the latter stages of the Neolithic at the European level, from around 3000 BC to 2500 BC, a major change in aDNA patterns occurs. This has been argued by David Reich and others to suggest that it was at this time that Indo-European languages spread.[82]

In this context, it might be useful to reflect on the relevance of aDNA for our understanding of lives and deaths in Ireland during the Neolithic. [SEE FIG. 2.7] To date aDNA analysis has been published for about 50 skeletons from a range of mortuary contexts, particularly Poulnabrone, Parknabinnia, Primrose Grange and Carrowkeel. Most of the human remains in specific contexts are genetically unrelated, but it is argued that they suggest an emphasis on patrilineal ancestry.[83] It needs to be emphasised that in many societies, past and present, genetics, blood or biology are neither determining nor necessary factors of relatedness. People make their kin through cultural, including mortuary, practices. The aDNA of unburnt crania from passage-tomb related monuments appear to form a distinct genetic cluster, as Lara Cassidy put it indicating a tangled web of distant genetic relations between individuals in the

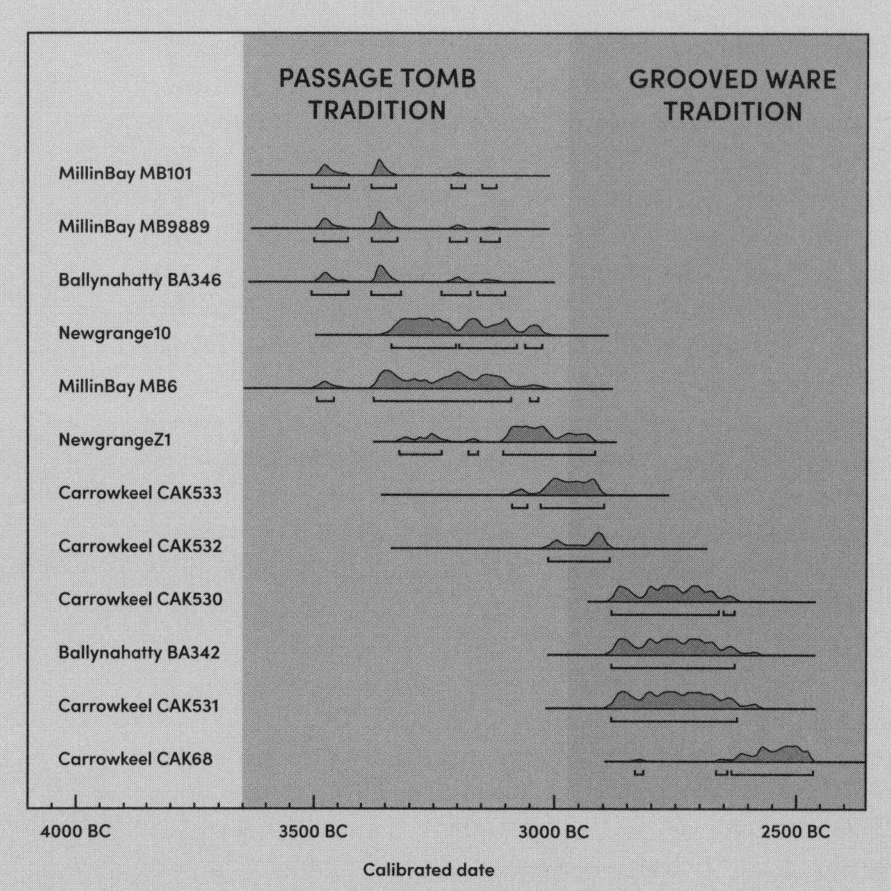

FIG. 4.11.

Cultural continuity of deposition from the Middle into the Late Neolithic in passage tombs indicated by aDNA.

Carrowmore and Carrowkeel cemeteries in Sligo, at Newgrange, Co. Meath and at Millin Bay, Co. Down.[84] This confirms archaeological knowledge that the later, larger passage tombs enabled much-wider scale social connections than those that characterised the earlier Neolithic. Importantly the genetic evidence from Carrowkeel, with deposition continuing down to 2500 BC, indicates that this island-wide shift in social relations went on long after passage tombs were built, but while they continued to be foci of ceremonial activity. This genetic continuity across the transition from the passage tomb to the Grooved Ware tradition is a key discovery for our understanding of the period from 3600 BC to 2600 BC in Ireland and northern Britain.[85] **[FIG. 4.11]**

The most widely cited aDNA data to date has been the genetic signature of a cranium from Newgrange dating from between 3338 BC to 3028 BC, indicating that it belonged to the offspring of full siblings or parent and child. This is presented by Cassidy and colleagues as compelling evidence for the existence of an élite social stratum in the society of the time. This seems quite an interpretative leap based on DNA from one individual and a very restricted use of the anthropological literature on élite incest. Not only are there societies in which incest is deemed socially acceptable at non-élite level, the possibility that incest was actually taboo in passage-tomb society does not appear to have been considered. As discussed above, it has been suggested that one aspect of megalithic tomb mortuary practices may have been dealing with socially 'difficult deaths'. Could this have been such a difficult death?[86] In overall terms the aDNA is consistent with the analysis of the archaeological evidence presented above: one way of making and marking kinship may have been the placement of human remains in megalithic tombs, and we can see significant differences in the way this was done in different mortuary traditions over the course of the Neolithic.[87]

It has been argued here that peoples' sense of themselves and the past would have resided in memories of and respect for the ancestral world. Those memories were not fixed. A standout feature of the material record is evidence that people reconstituted and changed the past through their ceremonial actions. The past was actively invoked to legitimise changes in the present. Monuments that people built became arenas for ceremonial activities and remembrance. These monuments constitute a major physical legacy of the Neolithic; in this sense the period had a significant long-term impact. In later times Neolithic monuments were incorporated into cosmological belief. Then they were regarded as places of deities, linked with the sky and the landscape and key times in the yearly cycle of life and death.[88] Their potency arose from their physical presence, necessitating an explanation in historical and mythic terms, and providing possibilities of active engagement.[89] Monuments fell out of use, others were deliberately altered and sometimes actively defaced in acts of iconoclasm. Evidence of deposition and veneration—when the power of the past appears to have been actively invoked—may be many hundreds of years apart. But the monuments had major impacts on the beliefs of later people.[90]

It has been suggested that we see a major ceremonial change in the later stages of the Neolithic—the centuries after 3000 BC—in the use of large, open-air enclosures or circles. These are built in various areas of Ireland and Britain, constructed at different scales and made from stone, earth and timber; often, however, in long-established sacred places.[91] At Brú na Bóinne, for instance, such enclosures became foci for activity, but with the passage tomb complex in the background. Neil Carlin has pointed to important continuities between such enclosures and the passage tomb tradition, now supported by the aDNA evidence. Ronald Hutton suggests that passage tombs and enclosures demonstrate a concern with circularity, marking a major change from the earlier Neolithic.[92] There also appears to be deliberate referencing to the contemporary domestic world and the use of a specific ceramic type—Grooved Ware—which demonstrates links with the wider world, particularly Orkney.[93] It is said that the use and construction of the enclosures or circles reflected a greater concern with the living and with contemporary society. The ancestral world was still important, and Parker Pearson suggested that this is reflected in the materials that people used: the ancestors celebrated in stone were now part of the land, the activities of the living were carried on in constructions of timber and earth. The connections between the two were created by the movement of people.[94] It is interesting that in Orkney, often seen as the closest parallel for the Boyne Valley in the broader international passage-tomb tradition, passage tombs and enclosures were in contemporary use.[95] Were the social networks established through the construction of passage tombs and related ceremonial activity maintained by a new approach to monuments and things?[96] More dramatic changes in the role of the dead and the pathways that the departed were placed on by the living took place after 2500 BC.

5.

The place of the visible dead in the Chalcolithic and Early Bronze Age

Aligning a death

When he died, late in the day, they placed the corpse in front of the house, protected from general view by the fence; but people could hear and could look over it to see the family mourning. As was the custom, the men of the house washed his body. Kept warm by a fire, his family took it in turns—and as an honour—to hold him, talking to him to help him find his way to the otherworld. They spoke of what he had done and achieved during his life. Someone said it was a good time for him to die and leave all the pain endured towards the end of his life, to celebrate his time on this land and his journey to meet those who had gone before. As a baby he had bound into life; now his family were binding themselves to him as he began his journey to be reborn in the otherworld.

Word of his death spread. The next morning people brought wood for the pyre to the place where cremations took place. They stacked some of the wood in a shape like a grave, other pieces were left to cover the body. At the house, the community waited outside

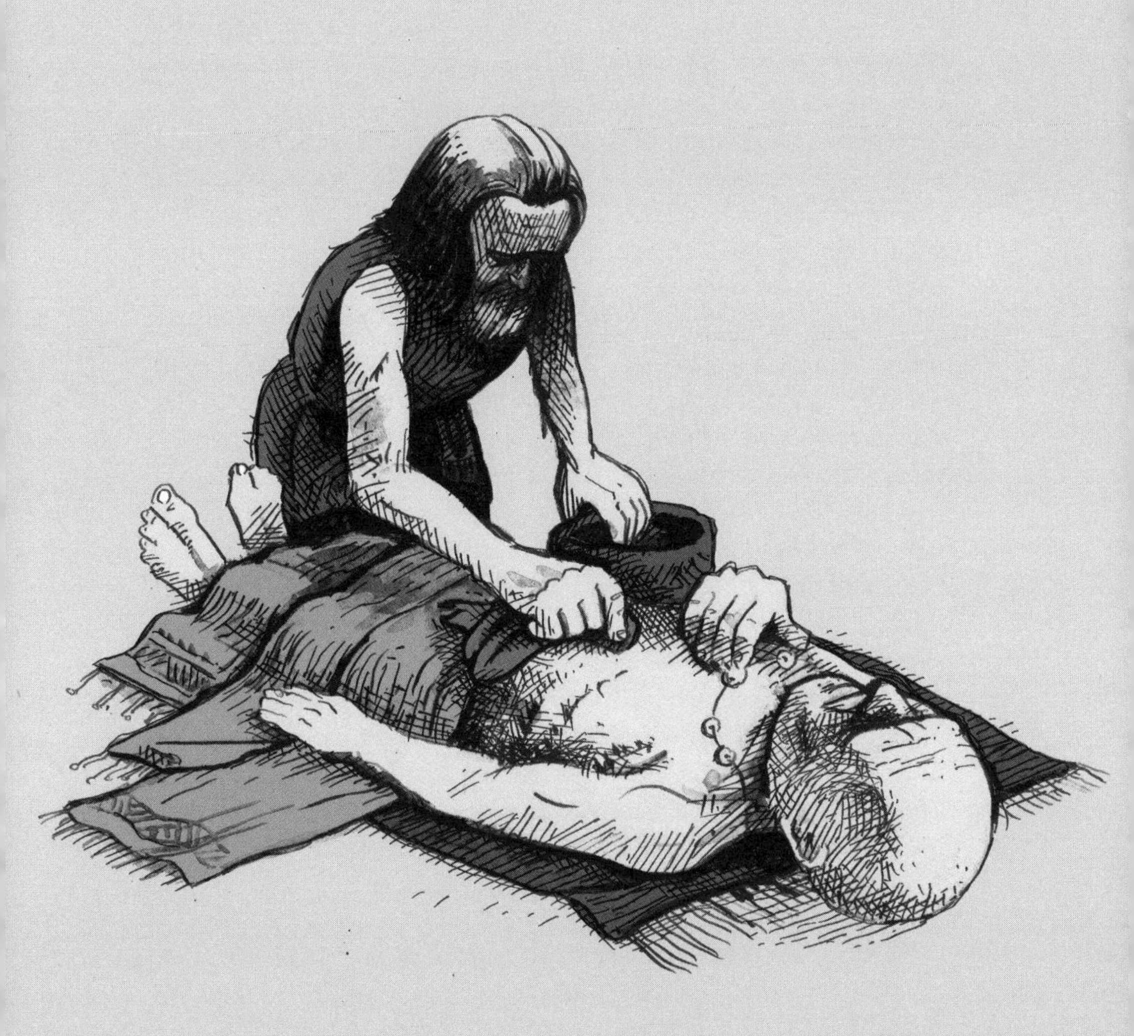

for the procession to begin. People argued about how old he was. Someone said he was older than he seemed; he had worked hard, was very strong even as a boy and had been a true leader during life. He gave wise counsel, even in later years when he was bent and racked with pain in his bones and found it difficult to eat.

The procession made its way from his home to the funeral pyre. The men carried the bier and the women carried offerings. They made lots of noise, chatting and laughing. A couple of times they did a circle, turning to the right, copying the course of the sun and then resuming the route, to confuse the spirit of the deceased in case it tried to find its way back to the house. After he was laid on the wood and blessed with water, his eldest son placed wood over his body and set fire to the pyre at both ends. Everyone stayed as close as they could to the heat of the burning wood and body. His closest relatives had the duty and honour of helping his spirit escape the body more quickly by controlling the pyre, poking it with long sticks and letting the air circulate to burn the flesh more quickly. They raked the edges of the pyre and pushed bones that were not well burnt back into the centre of the fire. The scarlet glow grew brighter in the darkening sky and the air around the pyre shimmered with heat. When the scent indicated that the spirit was free, the flames were put out with water. The pyre was raked and spread out to cool. Shortly afterwards the family bent and gathered bone fragments from the ashes, placing them in two baskets. They tried to put the bones of the head and limbs in one basket.

He had been a leader in life and the community hoped he would continue to give them guidance after his death. His grave had been placed beside the wall of upright stones put up to mark the beginning of the new cemetery. They remembered the dedication ceremony that he had led when relics of an ancestor had been placed in the ground to make it sacred. After his death his own grave had been constructed. Like the cooking pits that held water and were lined with wood, the grave was lined with stones heaved into place.

His remains would be held in this stone room while his spirit journeyed onwards.

As the evening was darker than usual they hurried a little. It was important for his spirit journey that his bones would be in the grave and in water before nightfall. Some of his bones were scattered into the water of the stream nearby. His closest relatives bore most of the larger and heavier bones to the cemetery area. Onlookers peered over the shoulders of his relatives as the fragments of bone were carefully placed on the stone bed of the grave, arranged around a pottery bowl filled with water to sustain him on the next stage of his journey. People were hungry after the long day and were thinking about the food and talk they would have after the ceremony. The capstone was carefully placed over the grave so that it rested on the top of the wall defining the most important place in the cemetery. As they walked away, talking, some of them hoped they might have the honour of this journey at the end of their own lives, and might be placed close to the bones of this man.

Excavation at Grange, Co. Roscommon by Breandán Ó Ríordáin in the 1960s revealed a cemetery mound containing eight cist graves and six pit burials.[1] The mound, about 21m in diameter, was composed of a cairn delimited by a kerb and covered by soil, which extended beyond the kerb. The pit burials were placed after the cists. Six of the cists contained Bowl Food Vessels and human remains. Cremated bone was the main deposit in the cists and the pits. Two of the cists also contained unburnt bone. Three of the pit cremation deposits—one of which (grave 10) included a bronze dagger—were covered by Vase Urns. Grave 10 appears to be one of the latest in the cemetery. Radiocarbon dates indicate that the cemetery was in use from 2200 BC to 1700 BC. One of the cists (grave 8) was placed against a stone alignment of five upright slabs, which formed the eastern part of the kerb. Detailed osteological analysis of the human remains in grave 8 by Barra Ó Donnabháin, his discussion of the treatment of the dead and the features in this area of the site form the basis for the fictional account above.[2] [see Fig. 5.13].

INTRODUCTION: A NEW BODY WORLD?

There were important changes in mortuary practices in European societies in the centuries after 3000 BC, seen as being expressed most clearly in the dominance of single, individual burials. The concept of a person being represented in death is emphasised by the placement of what look like actual or arranged sets of objects and accoutrements with the body; things that someone might have used in life or needed for their life after death. Placed by the living, these items illustrate relationships with the dead. The most common object found is a ceramic container, suggesting the centrality of sustenance for the living continuing to be considered important for the journey to and through the afterlife.[3]

It is argued that these changes demonstrate a shift in concern away from collective ancestors—whose power and place may refer back to an immemorial past—towards more focused genealogies relating to immediate past generations and known individuals.[4] Harris and colleagues have suggested that what emerges is a new kind of relational person. In mortuary practice we see this in 'a complex of material things associated with the singular body and its social relations rather than action on behalf of a larger collectivity'.[5] It is this sense of a distinct Early Bronze Age body world that is suggested in the fictional account above of the post-mortem treatment of the middle-aged to older man at Grange just before 2000 BC. Robb and Harris have argued that a gender system emerges in the European Bronze Age—which persists until the early medieval period—showing an ideal of binary, complementary male and female genders demonstrating persistent, lifelong identities, but also individuals who challenged and subverted this norm.[6]

This focus on the individual in life and death has a major influence on how Chalcolithic (Copper Age) and Bronze Age societies are viewed. The rise of the individual—and in most cases this has been read as meaning 'men'—in death is seen as reflecting a more socially ranked, hierarchical society. It is argued that rank was marked by more elaborate funerary treatment. Burial evidence is seen as mirroring living societies, the objects placed with the dead as representations of personal wealth, obtained through systems of exchange and displayed as part of what has been called a prestige goods economy.[7] Recent aDNA studies have been interpreted as indicating that significant population movements were key to the establishment of this way of life, for example in explaining the widespread distribution of the Beaker Complex across Europe from 2600 BC to 2000 BC.[8] Not surprisingly, when the detail for particular areas, such as Ireland, is examined, this big-picture view of death and the character of social groups during the Chalcolithic and Bronze Age turns out to be overly simplistic.

On the ground over the period considered here, from 2500 BC to 1600 BC, reality was more complicated, varied and localised. Individual burial was practiced in some parts of Ireland from quite early in the Neolithic. In the Chalcolithic period, from 2450 BC to 2000 BC, Beaker pottery—an international style associated with a distinctive set of objects, including copper technology—occurs in a range of burial contexts. The classic single inhumation rite seen as characteristic in other areas, such as Britain, in which a Beaker pot is included with the burial, is absent however.[9] While the most visible aspects of mortuary practice in Early Bronze Age Ireland from 2200 BC are indeed single graves and their occupants, up to one-third of the remains of people that occur in mortuary contexts were placed together. In some cases, persons represented in such deposits were all placed at the same time. In others, it appears there was successive deposition, with graves used for burial on a number of separate occasions.[10] This harks back to the successive, communal deposits that were a feature of the Neolithic. Rather than single burial replacing communal burial, therefore, these two practices were carried on in a complementary manner. Again, those who are visible in the record are persons selected for burial for a range of social reasons. Most of the dead are invisible.

The diversity of mortuary practice at this time is striking. To focus the discussion it is useful to think in terms of two major overlapping, but apparently quite different, traditions of practice [PLS 5.A, 5.B]. In the period to 2000 BC there was a range of mortuary and related depositional practices associated with the use of Beaker pottery. The most visible component of that diversity are wedge tombs. These were constructed and first used in the period from 2450 BC to 2050 BC. As Neil Carlin has put it, this represents a notable re-invention of the megalithic tradition, 500 years after the last passage tombs. Indeed, links with the broader, older megalithic tradition are strong in the Chalcolithic, indicated by the placement of objects and human bone in monuments, some of which may have been over a thousand years old. At the same time, communities building and using wedge tombs deposited Beaker pottery with the dead. Hence wedge tombs provide a key insight into this period of change when Ireland was clearly linked with a wider European world.[11]

The evidence for burial focused on individuals increases markedly after 2200 BC, in Early Bronze Age cemeteries. Their use began when

PL. 5.A.

A wedge tomb at Creevagh, Burren, Co. Clare.

wedge tombs were still being constructed and used; they develop in the centuries around 2000 BC, and in many cases use continues beyond 1600 BC. These cemeteries consist of a varying number of cists and pits—on average about 10 graves. Some don't have a visible marker; these are referred to as flat cemeteries. Where burials are placed in existing monuments or purposely built monuments,the term cairn or mound cemetery is used. It became common to distinguish and mark particular graves, often covering them with a small, round mound or barrow. The material for this barrow could be derived from a ditch, which served to encircle and define the grave. In excess of 600 such cemeteries are now known across the island, with a somewhat restricted occurrence in the south-west. This tradition extends across the Irish Sea into southern Scotland.[12]

PL. 5.B.

Opposite. Drumahoe, Co. Derry; a cist containing an adult male, placed on a surface of white quartz pebbles, with the pelvis of a piglet at his feet and a bronze dagger in a leather sheath across his chest.

The complementarity of the distribution of wedge tombs and cemeteries has long been remarked on, alongside differences in the ceramics found in these contexts. Beaker, a widely occurring international style of pottery, is present in wedge tombs, as well as from a range of other contexts in Ireland. There appears to be a Beaker single burial, albeit without a Beaker pot, at Mell, Co. Louth. Here a sub-rectangular grave aligned east–west contained an inhumation of an adult female (dating 2490 BC–2200 BC), placed on her right side with her head to the west. This has parallels with the placement of women in graves with Beakers in Scotland and Yorkshire.[13] Beaker-associated deposits are also placed in earlier, Neolithic monuments, a practice shared with Beaker users in mainland Atlantic Europe.[14] **[FIG. 5.1]**

The graves in Bronze Age cemeteries feature a range of ceramic styles known as Food Vessels and Urns; these are chronologically successive but overlap in their use and contexts **[FIG. 5.2]**. The use of the earliest style, the Bowl Food Vessel (2160 BC–1920 BC), overlaps with that of Beaker.[15] The Bowl represents a regional development of

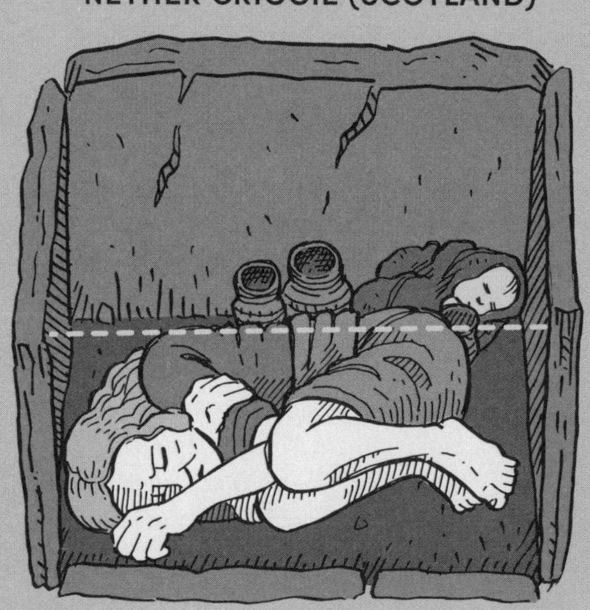

FIG. 5.1.

Chalcolithic burial at Mell, Co. Louth, compared with burial of a young women and infant with three Beakers at Nether Criggie, Dunnottar, Scotland.

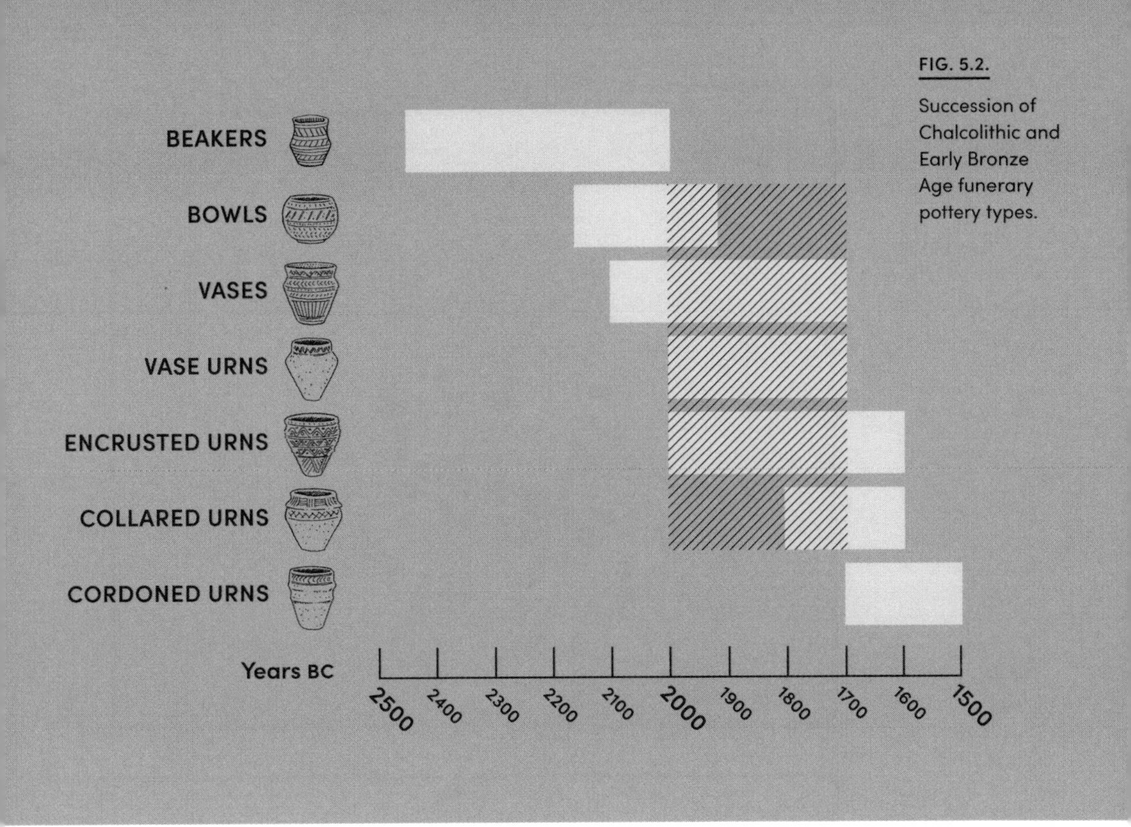

FIG. 5.2.

Succession of Chalcolithic and Early Bronze Age funerary pottery types.

the Beaker phenomenon in Ireland and southern Scotland, replacing a Beaker as an accompaniment in the grave. Bowl burials can be seen as part of a growing regionalisation of burial practice and of the Beaker tradition across Britain and Ireland in the period after 2200 BC.[16]

Up to recently, these archaeological phenomena—wedge tombs and Bronze Age cemeteries—were frequently represented as indicating two different, distinct cultural and ethnic identities. As the origin and use of Bowls indicate, however, the story is much more complicated. There are sites where there is a clear overlap. At Kilmashogue, Co. Dublin a wedge tomb was built and then re-adapted for use as an Early Bronze Age cairn cemetery.[17] [FIG. 5.3]. In both traditions cremation and inhumation were regarded as appropriate post-mortem treatments of the dead, and the remains of individuals as well as grouped deposits occur. There is a strong thread of deposition of

KILMASHOGUE

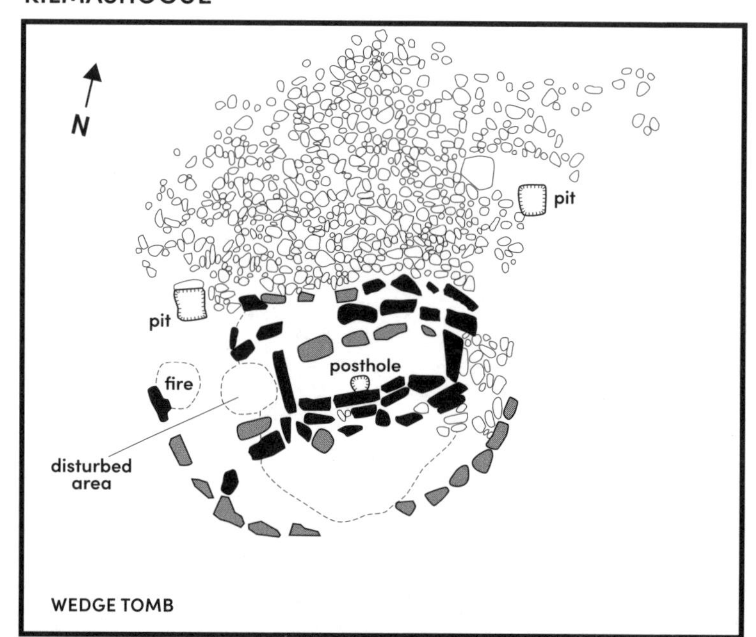

FIG. 5.3.

Kilmashogue, Co. Dublin; wedge tomb and Early Bronze Age cemetery.

human remains not only in new locales, but also in long-established monuments and places. These patterns pose interesting questions about who the visible, distinguished dead were; the choices made regarding different ways of treating the select dead; changes over time; and relationships between the living and the dead.

WEDGE TOMBS—AN OLD AND NEW TRADITION

Why did people in the middle of the third millennium BC suddenly begin to build wedge tombs?[18] There seems to be a focus on their monumental character **[SEE FIG. 4.2, PLS 5.A, 5.C]**. With their covering cairn, these tombs would be visible in the landscape. Wedge tombs are small in scale in many cases, but spaces defined by the tomb chamber(s) created places to which people

PL. 5.C.

The wedge tomb at Labbacallee, Co. Cork from the south-east.

could return to make deposits. At its simplest, the chamber has a box form, wider and higher at the front, with the sides and slab roof narrowing to the back. The covering cairn has a straight façade, narrowing to the back, giving a D- or heel-shape to the monument. There are regional differences in architecture, and the chamber can be elaborated with an access area at the front, a main chamber and a back chamber. Chamber sidewalls can be emphasised by parallel lines of orthostats within the cairn. There is a concentration of wedge tombs in the south-west, in areas like the Burren and the peninsulas of Kerry and Cork, stretching eastwards. Although part of a monumental tradition going back to the early Neolithic, this distribution pattern is—like the tomb form itself—something new; there are relatively few earlier megalithic tombs in the south-west.[19]

In other parts of the island, wedge tombs are often located close to earlier monuments. At Proleek on the Cooley Peninsula, Co. Louth a wedge tomb was placed 80m south-east of a portal tomb; a passage tomb stands on the top of Black Mountain on the skyline to the north. The consistent orientation of wedge tomb entrances towards the west-south-west horizon indicates a particular tradition and set of beliefs. It suggests a strong cosmological concern with the movement of the sun, and a particular focus on the descending or setting sun in late autumn, winter and early spring. Solar symbolism indicates that the tombs and deposits within them could have been powerful metaphors for connections between death and re-birth. As William O'Brien put it, materialising how 'people understood the passing of human life and the journey to the otherworld'.[20] The almost obsessive persistence of building tombs to face south-west might be seen as a prescriptive worldview, but there is a considerable degree of local variation and use of local materials. Tomb location in some instances resembles that of passage tombs: in loose clusters, on hill or ridge tops, sited so that monuments are more visible from certain directions. In other cases, they are placed in more low-key, low-lying locations.

Only 40 of 560-plus wedge tombs have been excavated, in most cases over fifty years ago. Ros Ó Maoldúin's Burren project will provide vital new evidence and perspectives.[21] Currently only 24 of the excavated sites have revealed human bone, with 70–80 individuals represented. There are several reasons why human bone may have been removed, or not survived. Tombs were used and re-used over long periods of time, but the main reason is it appears the amount of bone originally deposited in many tombs was small, involving the remains of a restricted number of individuals.

We can be confident about Beaker-period activity when we have Beaker pottery and mortuary deposits that directly date to this period. Beaker pottery has been found in thirteen wedge tombs, and in nine it has been found directly in association with human bone.[22] The wedge tomb at Largantea, Co. Derry was excavated in the 1930s and re-assessed by Schulting and colleagues in 2008.[23] [FIG. 5.4] There were a number of distinct episodes of deposition of cremated bone, mostly in the main chamber, representing the remains of at least eight people: six adults, a child and an infant. The cremated remains of at least three individuals who died between 2455 BC to 2208 BC were placed in the main chamber with pyre charcoal. This appears to be associated with the use of Beaker pottery. Sherds from four Beaker pots were placed in the entrance chamber with a small amount of cremated bone. Inside the entrance chamber, two almost complete late-style Beakers (post-2250 BC) were placed in a cist-like structure. A date of 2033 BC to 1783 BC from alder charcoal corresponds with the Bowl Food Vessel deposited in the entrance chamber, indicating mortuary activity at this time. A burnt human long bone dated to between 1738 BC and 1505 BC would correlate with the deposition of a Cordoned Urn in the main chamber. The Urn was placed over cremated bone, a burnt bronze razor and a bone toggle—all gathered from a pyre—and an accessory pottery vessel. In the Late Bronze Age, around the turn of the first millennium BC, there was a further phase of activity at the rear of the tomb, with the deposition of flat-bottomed coarse pottery. So, the sequence starts with a communal burial deposit associated with the deposition of Beaker pottery, followed by episodic placement of objects and human remains over a millennium.

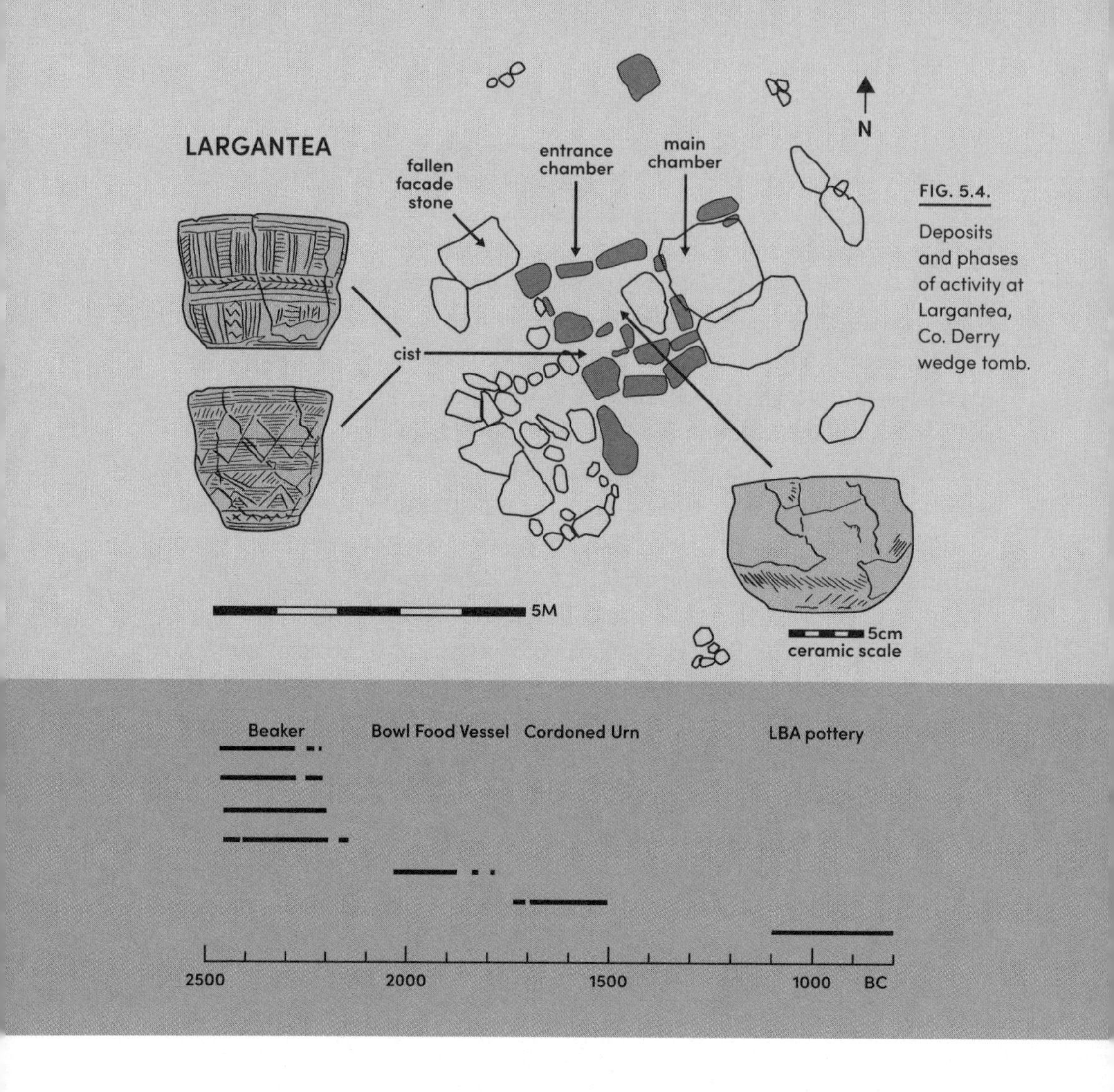

FIG. 5.4. Deposits and phases of activity at Largantea, Co. Derry wedge tomb.

Largantea is one of a number of sites where the initial mortuary phase consisted of a communal deposit, often with Beaker pottery, followed by one or more phases of the placement of individual remains with Food Vessels or under Urns. In some cases there is subsequent funerary activity or other depositional activity.[24] These sites demonstrate clear linkages between the construction and initial use of a wedge tomb and the placement of deposits usually seen as belonging to the separate Early Bronze Age cist and pit-cemetery

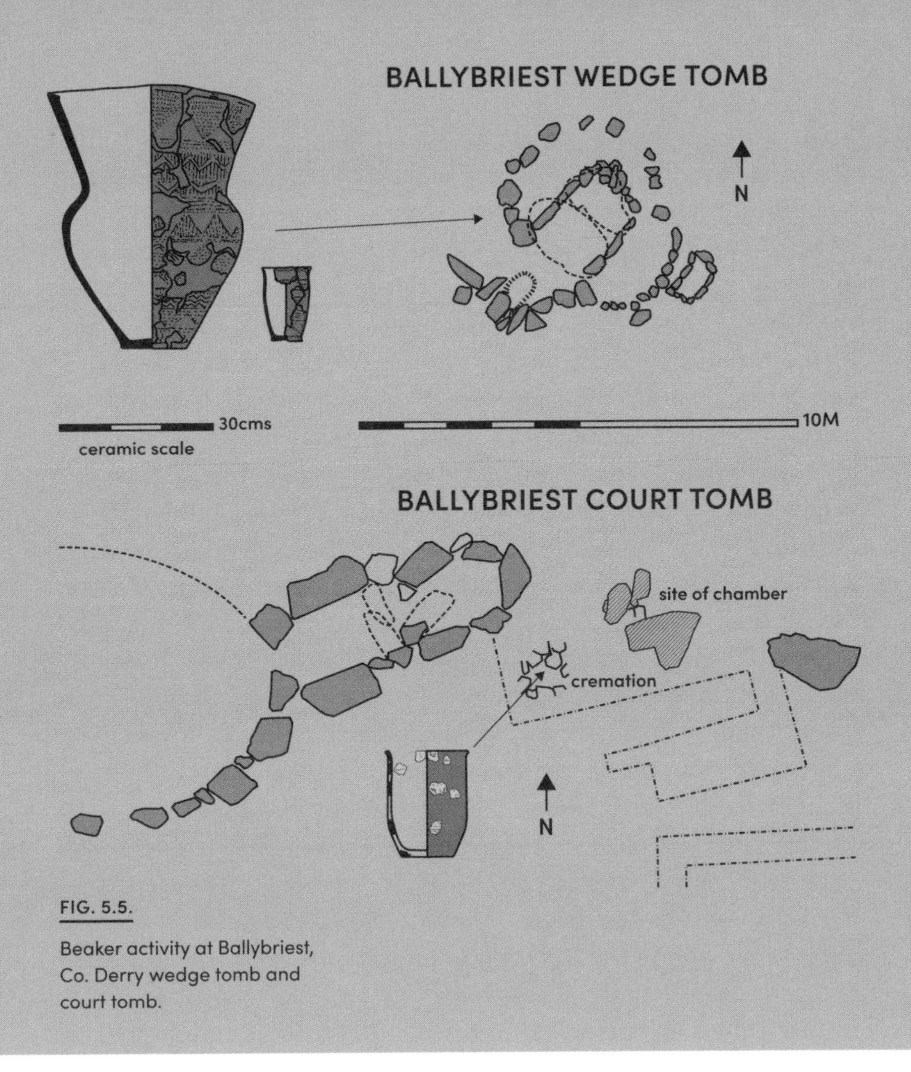

FIG. 5.5.

Beaker activity at Ballybriest, Co. Derry wedge tomb and court tomb.

tradition. As at Largantea, the use of cists to define space is often incorporated into wedge tomb design. Does the shift from a more 'communal' representation of the dead in the Chalcolithic to a greater focus on the individual in the Early Bronze Age indicate changing senses of identities, or are there more complex patterns represented in mortuary treatment?

At Ballybriest, Co. Derry [FIG. 5.5] a large pit was dug and backfilled and then the uprights of a wedge tomb of a simple, one-chambered design were put in place. A sealed deposit in the chamber contained quantities of charcoal, ash and cremated bone, indicating that this material had been gathered at the site of a pyre(s) and deposited in the tomb, along with four late-style Beaker pots, dating to after 2250 BC. The pots were complete when brought to the tomb and then either deliberately smashed or accidentally broken *in situ*. A number of deposits that produced bone may originally have been part of one larger deposit. The small size of much of the cremated bone may suggest it had been pulverized, perhaps to reduce the individuality of the deceased, prior to deposition. There are the remains of at least seven people; including at least one adult male, one adult female, a young child and an infant. The adults probably died in their 20s or 30s. One of these was dated to between 2139 BC and 1830 BC.[25] About 300m to the south-west is a dual court tomb. By the Chalcolithic it had been there for over a millennium. A cist was made in the cairn of the court tomb and the cremated remains of an adult male and sherds of a 'domestic' Beaker pot were placed in it. There is another wedge tomb 100m south of this site.[26]

These deposits suggest a tension or complementarity in Beaker-associated mortuary practice between relational identities that focused on the collective or on an individual; the latter is seen as being at the core of the Beaker body world internationally. There are wedge tombs where the focus seems to have been on the post-mortem treatment of a particular individual. In the large and impressive wedge tomb at Labbacallee, Co. Cork the chamber was divided into a small, inner cist-like compartment and a larger outer chamber.[27] **[FIG. 5.6, PL. 5.C]**. With the exception of her skull, the partially articulated, inhumed remains of a woman were found in the inner compartment, with burnt animal bone and a bone pin. It would appear that, after excarnation, her partially decomposed body—with bones still partially articulated—was placed there. One of the woman's bones was dated from between 2456 BC to 2138 BC. In the inner part of the main chamber, Beaker pottery was placed with disarticulated human and animal bone, in a striking arrangement. A female cranium, without

FIG. 5.6.

The Chalcolithic deposits, focused on an adult female, at Labbacallee, Co. Cork.

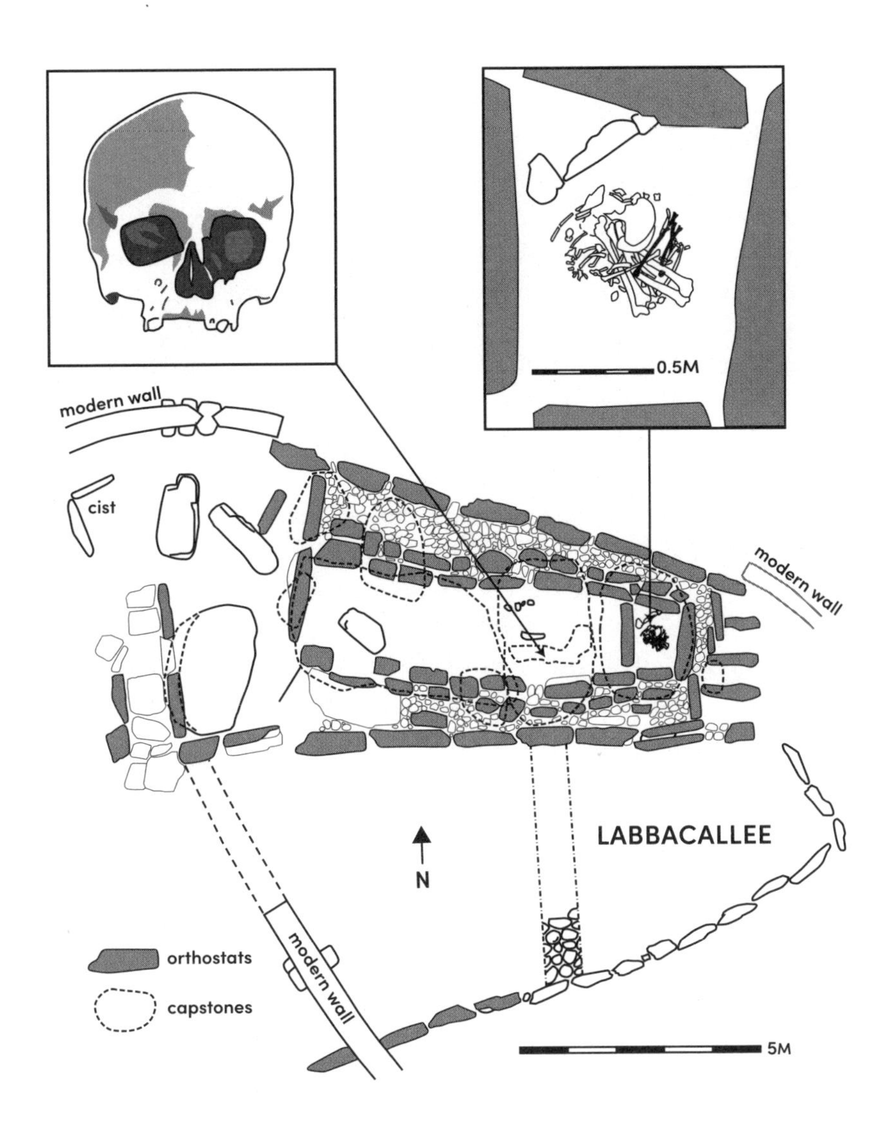

the lower mandible, was set upright between two fragments of the cranium of an adolescent/young adult male, dating to between 2458 BC and 2038 BC. As well as the bones of this young man, there were also those of a child, dating from between 2202 BC to 1776 BC, and a single bone from a neonate/newborn baby.[28] The female cranium was better preserved than the other bones. This, together with its age and sex, strongly suggests that it was that of the woman whose other remains had been placed in the inner compartment.

The woman, young man and child probably died between 2400 BC and 2000 BC. Their deaths could have taken place at intervals during this period, or they could all have occurred over a short window of time, between 2200 BC and 2140 BC.[29] The primary focus was on a particular woman, whose treatment after death involved a number of stages, including the removal of her skull when her body had decomposed and the eventual placement of the rest of her bones in the sealed back compartment of the tomb. The contrast between the treatment of the cranium and the rest of the body is striking. The cranium may have been in circulation and used by the living between its removal from her body and its placement in the tomb. As deposited, it provided a physical connection to other people, as represented by the bones of the young man, child and neonate; the inclusion of animal bone (cattle, sheep and pig), indicates wider social reference. The placement of the partially articulated remains suggests she was being remembered for who she was in life. The tomb was also used during the Early Bronze Age, when at least one cist burial was inserted at the western end, with the bones of an adolescent and two sherds of pottery.[30]

These case studies indicate the range of Beaker-associated mortuary rites in wedge tombs. Remains of adults of both sexes and of juveniles were deposited; either inhumation or cremation rites were used. Beaker sherds occur in other contexts in Ireland, but complete pots were placed in the wedge tombs, mirroring the practice seen in the classic Beaker burial of single inhumations in other regions.[31] In some cases we appear to see a direct association between a Beaker and an individual in a wedge tomb. At Kilhoyle, Co. Derry the excavators observed a very close association of the cremated remains of an adult female and sherds of Beaker on the floor of the main chamber.[32] So, even though the construction and use of wedge tombs harks back to a concept of the communal or collective, there are hints at a focus on the individual that is such a strong element of Beaker mortuary rites elsewhere. The presence of cist-like compartments may demonstrate a concern with defining and individualising particular deposits.

Who were the dead people placed in wedge tombs, and on what basis were they selected by their kin and social group to be treated in this way? William O'Brien's excavations of the Altar and Toormore tombs, on the Mizen Peninsula, Co. Cork, demonstrate the different histories of sites and their local meaning and context.[33] He also discusses the implications of the regional distribution pattern—loose clusters of wedge tombs concentrated in areas with the best settlement potential. O'Brien suggests we see wedge tombs as sacred places, constructed to contain the remains of individuals who, through their achievements in life, gained recognition in death as founding figures for their communities and lineages. The clusters may reflect how families were linked at a local level, over time providing opportunities for the creation and re-working of identities, shared and contested by family-based groups.[34]

In his comprehensive review of the Beaker phenomenon, Carlin takes a somewhat different perspective, arguing that the character of the deposits, including juveniles as well as adults, supports the view that the dead placed in a wedge tomb represent lineages and communities. He focuses on the strong links between wedge tombs and the megalithic tomb tradition, regarding the former as a Beaker-associated and inspired reinvention, enabling the expression of particular social relationships between the living and the dead and the creation of new ancestral spaces. Carlin sees this as part of a wider series of changes in practices and material culture from the middle of the third millennium BC.[35]

The complementarity of the communal and the individual in mortuary deposits in wedge tombs is important to tease out. It might be useful to go back to the idea that a distinct relational personhood or body world was emerging at this time. It is striking how many of the suite of objects associated with the use of Beaker pottery internationally and in Ireland can been seen as symbols of personal identities. As Carlin points out, people in Ireland deliberately kept these symbols separate—putting them in different contexts, such as bogs—and often as hoards.[36] While Beaker-associated objects were put in such contexts and in ways that suggest communal identity, what gives them meaning is that they can be seen to refer to a body identity held constant across different settings. In wedge tombs we can see evidence of practices familiar from the earlier megalithic tomb tradition: burning, fragmentation and careful deposition that is part of the process of making selected dead people into collective ancestors. With wedge tombs, these practices are being carried out by people with a strong sense of the importance of the singular body and its social relations. This becomes clearer over time, as expressed for example in the Bowl burials that were deliberately placed in wedge tombs.[37]

Bearing in mind the number of wedge tombs in Ireland, it is worth thinking about the longer-term importance of these monuments. The history of a specific tomb might help us to understand how transformations of meaning took place over time. The Altar tomb demonstrates phases of use from its construction to the modern period. [FIG. 5.7] Construction involved digging trenches for orthostats, raising orthostats and roofstones, levelling the chamber floor and burying debitage associated with the working of the structural stones. An unburnt tooth dated from between 2316 BC to 1784 BC comes from what appears to be a token deposit of cremated bone of one or more adults. A small pit near the centre of the chamber contained charcoal dated to between 1250 BC and 832 BC, in the Later Bronze Age. Other radiocarbon dates for charcoal indicate activity in the Early Iron Age (from 766 BC to 560 BC). Charcoal from a

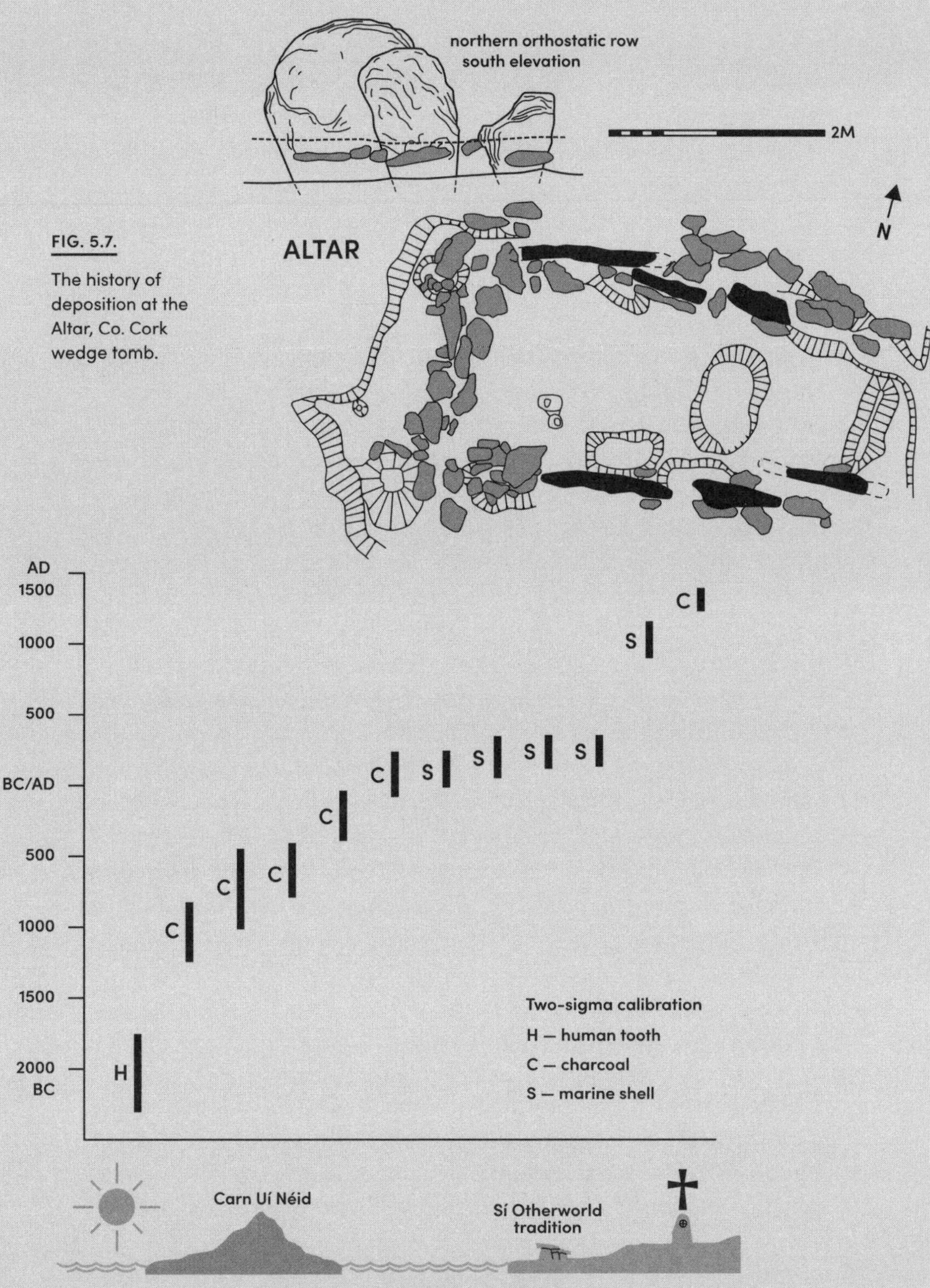

FIG. 5.7.

The history of deposition at the Altar, Co. Cork wedge tomb.

small pit in the south of the chamber was dated to the Middle/Late Iron Age, between 356 BC and AD 68. A smaller pit with shell-rich sediments dated to the Late Iron Age, from AD 124 to AD 224. A stake hole in the tomb entrance area appears to date to the historic period. In later times, fires were lit and stones put into the chamber when land was cleared. According to local tradition, the monument was used as a Penal Mass-rock in the late seventeenth and early eighteenth century.[38]

After its initial construction and use the monument retained significance. On occasions in later prehistory it was thought appropriate to carry out activities there involving the digging of pits and the deposition of shells and other material. Deposition of human bone may have started a sequence of transformations, beginning when the remains of a known individual or individuals was/were represented and held in the tomb. Over time, individual(s) passed out of name to become mythologised, ancestral presences, whose immortality helped to explain origins and guide lives. Myth in this context provides the glue to genealogical and social continuity when, in reality, there would have been changes in how society was organised, at both local and wider levels. O'Brien suggests one reason for the prolonged history of use of Altar is that the entrance of the wedge tomb was deliberately aligned on Mizen Peak, a pyramidal-shaped mountain to the south-west that was a sacred location (*Carn Uí Néid*) in Irish mythology.[39] Wedge tombs became part of landscapes of symbolic meaning, providing a reference point and cosmological basis for local life.

A DIVERSITY OF PRACTICE, 2500 BC–2000 BC

The practice of placing Beaker pottery in Neolithic monuments could be seen as reflecting the pattern evident in the history of Altar: acts making reference to and linking with a distant, mythic past. Carlin has shown that much of the Beaker-associated activity in Ireland involved sherds of Beaker pottery originating from occupation-related contexts. Along with, but in most cases kept separate from, other objects, these sherds were actively used to create, maintain and communicate social values, identities and relationships through deliberate deposition in a range of contexts,[40] many of which strongly echo past practices and traditions. For example, where Late Neolithic timber circles continued in use, Beaker pottery was deposited in the same way as the Grooved Ware it replaced around 2500 BC.

The presence of human bone, usually cremated, with sherds of Beaker pottery in contexts other than the formal Beaker-associated mortuary rites in wedge tombs appears to represent the use of human bone as part of the deposition of a range of materials reflecting shared activities and social ties binding people, places, past and present together.[41] So, what was the role of the post-mortem treatment of the visible dead in this complex social world? How did a very distinctive and widespread tradition of burial and deposition, focused on individuals, appear from shortly after 2200 BC? In approaching these questions, it is important not only to consider human remains with a definite Beaker association, but also to take a broader view of the relevant evidence dating to before 2200 BC. As noted, sherds of Beaker pottery have been found in earlier megalithic tombs, particularly court tombs. Cremated and unburnt bone with dates ranging from 2300 BC to after 2000 BC occurs in other megalithic tombs, sometimes with Bowls, and unburnt and cremated bone is found in caves.[42] One interpretation of this evidence is a shift from the deposition of Beaker pottery to commemorate the past, to the formal deposition of human remains to re-activate and add to the power of such places.

To understand the emergence of the focus on single burials we might also look at the components of the cist and pit cemetery tradition itself. Can we trace the origins of key aspects of this Early Bronze Age cemetery tradition before the emergence of Food Vessels? For example, burials in cists without accompanying pottery are an integral part of that tradition, but they also occur earlier. Kerri Cleary has shown that an adult female inhumation from a cist in a cairn at Killarah, Co. Cavan dates to between 2620 BC and 2470 BC.[43] The site at Ballynacarriga, Co. Cork [FIG. 5.8] provides key insights into the development of the cemetery tradition. Fifty metres south of a Late Neolithic/Chalcolithic focus of activity, where Beaker pottery was placed in pits, the deposition of human remains began before 2200 BC. One cist contained a token amount of cremated bone from an infant and juvenile, the latter dated between 2460 BC to 2206 BC. Charcoal from a pit about 5m to the south-west, with no human remains, was dated to between 2461 BC and 2211 BC. After 2200 BC this locus was developed as a funerary complex. Cremation burials in cists and pits were accompanied by Food Vessels or covered by Encrusted Urns. There appear to have been three foci of activity: one immediately beside the Chalcolithic features and the other two defined by ring ditches.[44] Coolnatullagh, Co. Clare on the Burren is another example of a cemetery beginning in the Chalcolithic. In an area with a dense concentration of wedge tombs,

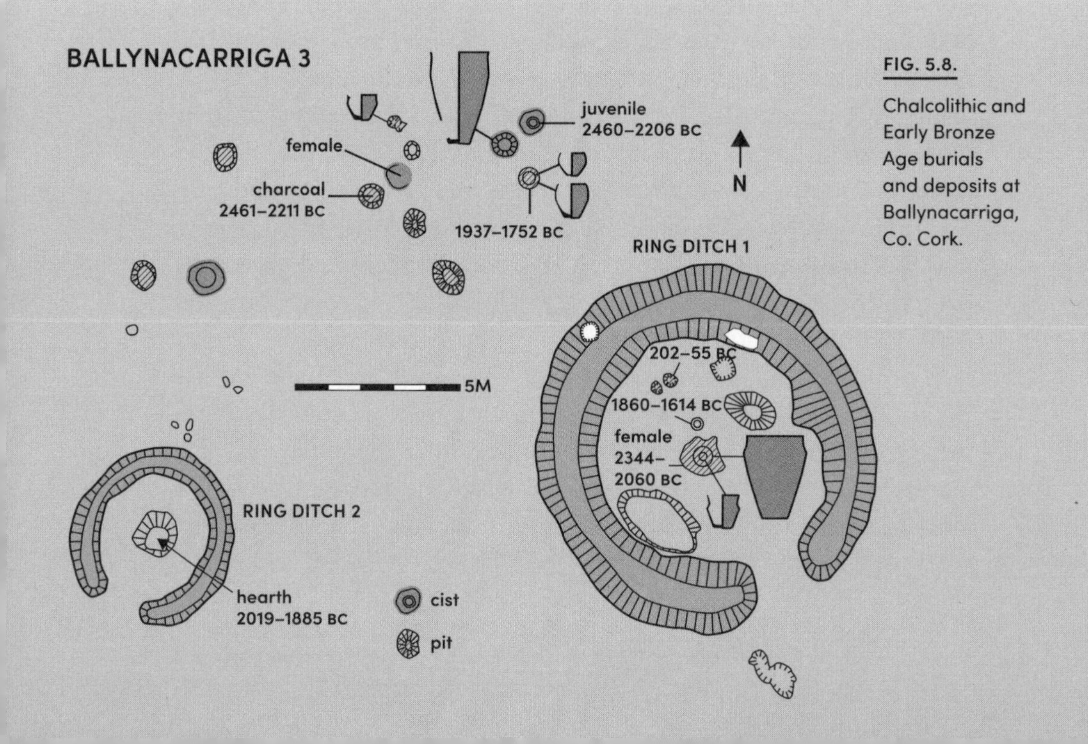

FIG. 5.8.

Chalcolithic and Early Bronze Age burials and deposits at Ballynacarriga, Co. Cork.

a cemetery cairn was constructed at a time when wedge tombs were in vogue. Two small sherds of probable Beaker pottery were found in the cairn. A partially excavated central cist contained the remains of three people: an adult inhumation, a child's scapula and a cremation deposit with cranial and long bones. The adult inhumation dates from between 2460 BC to 2140 BC, pre-dating the widespread use of Food Vessels.[45]

The first phase of the monument at Poulawack, also on the Burren, was a Linkardstown-type burial (cist 8), dated to between 3600 BC and 3300 BC. Anna Brindley and Jan Lanting's review and dating of the 1930s excavation transformed our understanding of this key site.[46] In the later third millennium BC the monument was re-vitalised and expanded with the placement of three cists in the cairn, turning it into a cemetery cairn **[FIG. 5.9]**. Disturbed unburnt bone from an adult and child, in a small cist (4) inserted into the revetment of the cairn dates from between 2498 BC to 2040 BC. Unburnt bone from a child and adolescent in a rectangular cist (5) dates from between 1972 BC to 1682 BC. A large cist (6/6a) east of the Linkardstown cist was divided into two compartments. One part (6) contained the cremated remains of an adult and the unburnt bones of an adolescent (dated to between 2140 BC and 1870 BC) and a child. The other part of the cist (6a) contained the disarticulated remains of an adult male (dated from between 1974 BC to 1686 BC), some cremated bone and a sherd of Beaker pottery. There was mixing of bone between the two compartments, but this may be due to later disturbance. In the deposit in 6/6a we see a range of post-mortem treatments of the dead, no occurrence of Food Vessel pottery but the deposition of what appears to be an antique Beaker sherd.

That Poulawack had continuing importance as an ancestral place is indicated by a third phase of burial activity around 1500 BC. The cairn was enlarged, increased in height and enclosed with a flagstone kerb. Two cists (2 and 3) were placed above and to the east of cist 8. Cist 3 contained the fragmentary remains of the crouched inhumation of a young adult female, dating to between 1610 BC and

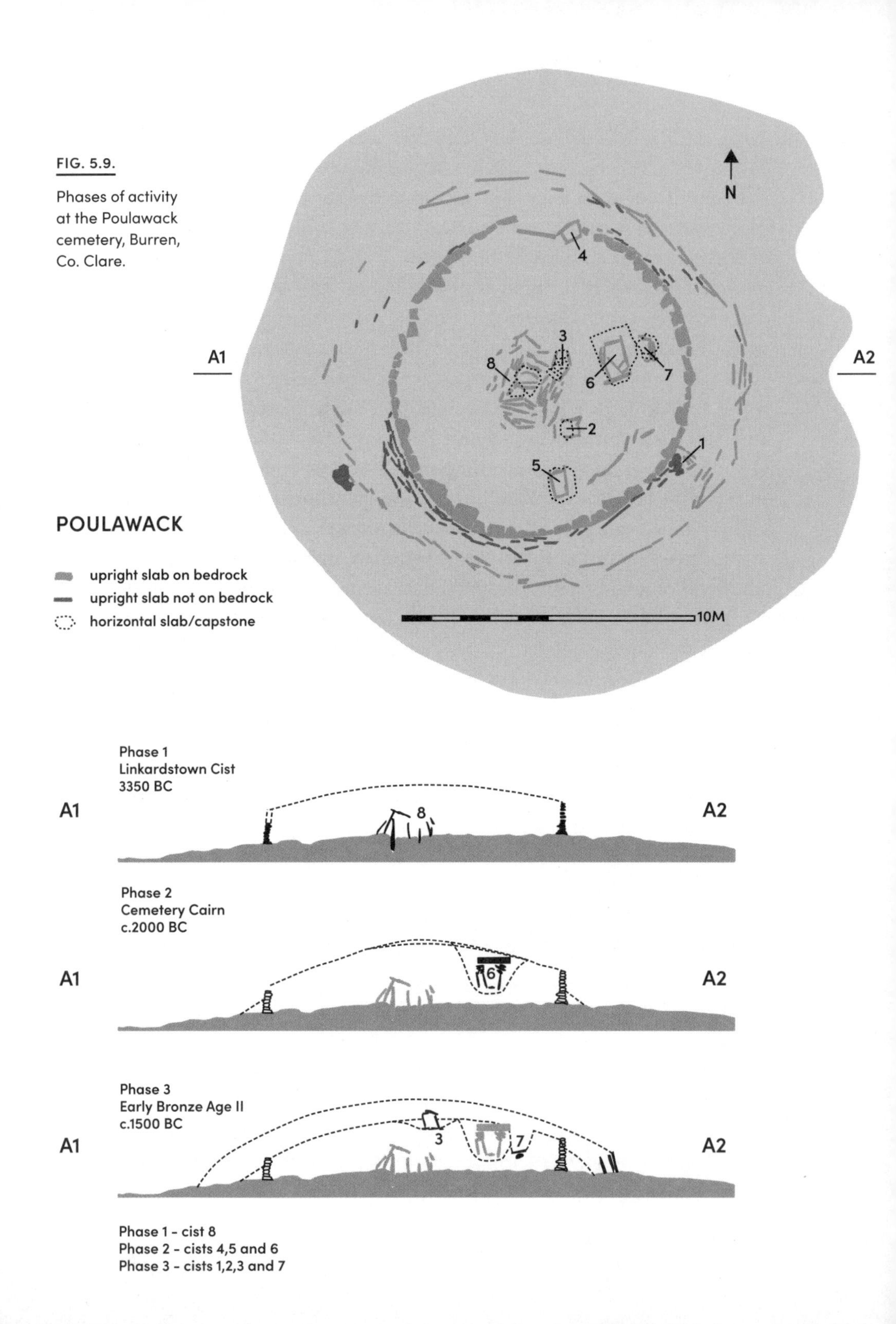

FIG. 5.9.

Phases of activity at the Poulawack cemetery, Burren, Co. Clare.

1432 BC, and cist 2 the cremated bones of an adult female. Cist 7 was placed to the east of cist 6. A partially protected inhumation (1), dating from between 1744 BC to 1452 BC, was placed immediately outside the original revetment.

What can be pulled together from this is that within a diversity of burial practice over the period 2500 BC to 2000 BC we can see the emergence of a cemetery tradition that would continue for at least 500 years, and which would have a key role in the development of mortuary practices over a much longer timespan. Mortuary practices from before 2200 BC clearly had a strong influence.

For example, there are a number of instances, such as at Moneen, Co. Cork, where the central cist resembles a wedge tomb.[47] This fluidity and continuity in practice can also be seen in the curation of the remains of some individuals who died before 2200 BC. Their bones appear to have been kept in circulation and later placed in a cist. At Newtownstewart, Co. Tyrone a segmented cist contained the cremated remains of two people, representing the collection from a pyre of almost all the burnt remains of an adolescent and a middle-/old-aged adult woman. In each case the deposits were accompanied by a Bowl; a burnt, hollow-based arrowhead was placed with the adolescent. [PL. 5.D]. Surprisingly, the radiocarbon dates indicate that the adolescent died between 2475 BC and 2212 BC, while the woman died between 2195 BC and 1951 BC.[48] Based on the dates, it seems improbable that the deaths were contemporary, but the placement of the deposits occurred in a single episode.

Given the wider evidence for curation and mummification of bodies in Bronze Age Britain this should not come as a surprise; indeed, it might also explain some of the early dates of individuals placed in other apparently Early Bronze Age cists and pits.[49] For instance, within ring ditch 1 at Ballynacarriga [SEE FIG. 5.8], the central pit contained an inverted Vase and Encrusted Urn. The latter contained cremated bone from at least three individuals: a young adult female and a midterm *in utero* foetus, with a bone fragment (clavicle) belonging to an older adult. The young pregnant adult

PL. 5.D.

The cremated human bone and Bowl Food Vessels in the segmented cist at Newtownstewart Castle, Co. Tyrone.

female dated from 2344 BC to 2060 BC, so her death would appear to long predate the placement of her cremated remains.[50] If human remains were kept in circulation, so also were sherds of Beaker pottery. Sherds of early style Beakers, dating to before 2200 BC, have been found with Bowls in both wedge tombs and Early Bronze Age burials, so they were deposited after 2200 BC.[51]

It is in this fluid social context, characterised by tension between communal identity and a focus on a body-centred world view, that we can situate the emergence of the cist and pit cemetery tradition. It can be considered an expression of what Stuart Needham calls Beaker fission, or regionalisation of mortuary practice from around 2200 BC in Britain and Ireland.[52] Communities chose to place the remains of selected individuals in what would often become long-lived, episodically used cemeteries. As we have seen, in some cases remains were deposited in places and monuments long-known in the landscape, reflecting the symbolic importance of such loci and giving them a new social relevance. In other instances, new ground and new locations were selected to mark, and became marked by, the graves of the chosen dead.

THE DEVELOPMENT OF EARLY BRONZE AGE CEMETERIES

The traditional interpretation of Earlier Bronze Age burial focused on the burial of individuals. Cemeteries were regarded as being small; single and isolated burials seemed to be common. This reinforced the concept of the dominance of the individual in mortuary practice. The assumption was this reflected the rise of the individual in society, which continues to serve as a broader social model for north-west Europe in the Early Bronze Age. A wealth of new data from large-area excavations, however, allied to a reassessment of existing data, indicates different and more diverse patterns. Yes, isolated individual burials took place and small cemeteries occur, but most burials are in cemeteries varying in size but containing several graves as a minimum, up to one-third of which can contain multiple burials. Some cemeteries contain more than twenty burials and deposits, and one or two exceptional sites like the Mound of the Hostages have more than 40 burials.[53]

We can now place cemeteries in their contemporary social context. In some cases they were located close to the living and to settlement activities. The Early Bronze Age saw an expansion of settlement compared to focal areas of Neolithic activity, and in newly established settlement areas formally marking the burial of particular people might have been important in establishing a sense of place and belonging. Settlement continued in areas of Neolithic activity also, and Early Bronze Age cemeteries frequently have a history of use going back to the early Neolithic. This is not to argue for any direct continuity, but to emphasise that in such areas the landscape was permeated with the past. Against this background there was potential for both unintended but also purposeful use of what might have been perceived as ancient places.[54]

None of the cairns or mounds built to house and cover Early Bronze Age burials remotely approaches the scale of the largest monuments constructed in the latter stages of the Neolithic, but the number of cemetery sites is striking. These were local foci. Cemeteries demonstrate and draw on the local, immediate social ties and networks that bound households and kin groups together, based on shared ideas and values as expressed in behaviour, actions and material culture. A broad repertoire of traditions, practices and materials current over wide areas of Ireland and Britain were utilised by these local social networks. These broader traditions, for example in metalwork and pottery styles, are used by archaeologists to study and define the character of life and death in the Early Bronze Age. But identities, lives and deaths were created and worked through at a local level.[55]

In their cemeteries, we see how the living of the Early Bronze Age practised, over some 600 years—2100 BC to 1600 BC—and about 20 generations, what they considered the appropriate treatment of significant people when they died. In many instances, use of the cemeteries appears to be episodic rather than continuous and encompasses the burial and deposition of human remains, the re-use of some graves, and a general expansion of cemeteries over time. The record is a rich source of information about mortuary practices, and about this period more broadly, because of the range of decisions involved in the post-mortem treatment of human remains. [FIG. 5.10] What was the form of the grave itself, a cist or a pit? Was a body placed in the grave as an inhumation (most frequently in a crouched position) or was it dis-articulated bone (implying initial treatment elsewhere)? Did cremation precede burial, a practice that became more dominant over time? Was the deposit that of an individual or the commingled remains of several individuals? Was it a token

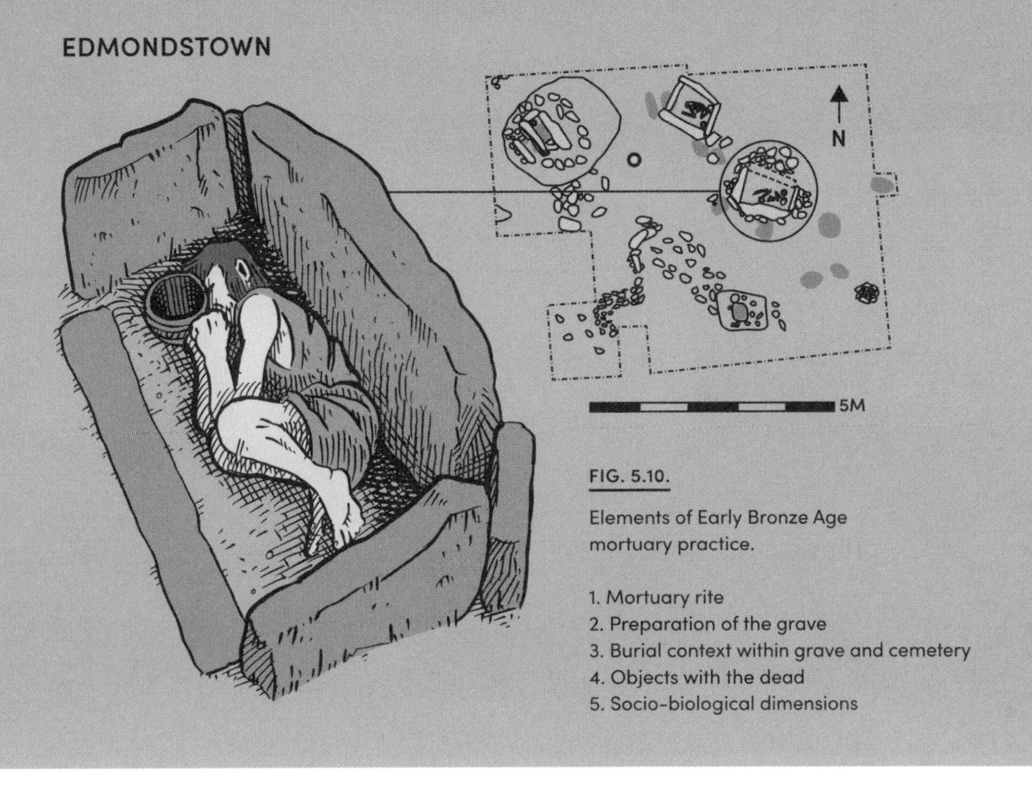

FIG. 5.10.

Elements of Early Bronze Age mortuary practice.

1. Mortuary rite
2. Preparation of the grave
3. Burial context within grave and cemetery
4. Objects with the dead
5. Socio-biological dimensions

deposit or a burial including a token deposit of another individual? How was the burial positioned by the living, were objects or materials placed in the grave? How did these relate to the burial?[56] These variables represent complex webs of ideas, choices and actions. Human remains are a rich source of osteological and biological information, about both individuals and communities.[57] People drew on their social frameworks in active and varied ways to construct their own, specific sense of the world; this is what is reflected in the treatment of the dead.

The most widely studied aspect of this framework of practice is changing pottery styles [FIG. 5.2, PL. 5.E] and the roles they played in mortuary practice.[58] The Bowl (Food Vessel) Tradition can be dated to between around 2160 BC and 1920 BC. Bowl Food Vessels occur in wedge tombs, but Anna Brindley's comment that they emerged in the specific context of a pot to be placed with an individual in

PL. 5.E.

A selection of urns, Vase Food Vessels and Bowl Food Vessels from the Early Bronze Age cemetery at the Mound of the Hostages, Tara, Co. Meath.

the grave seems apposite. The Vase Tradition (Vase Food Vessels, Vase and Encrusted Urns) dates to between 2100 BC and 1600 BC. This tradition shows continuity with Bowls, in that Vase Food Vessels can serve a similar function to Bowls, being placed with an inhumed or cremated burial. There is also a striking change of use, whereby cremated bone is put into Vase or Encrusted Urns, which are then placed mouth down in the grave. This marks a significant move away from crouched inhumation as a mortuary practice. The inversion of urns continues to be the central feature of mortuary practice using Collared Urns, dating from 1800 BC to 1600 BC, and Cordoned Urns, dating to between 1700 BC and 1500 BC. These later urns have an association with bronze razors and faience ornaments, burnt with the body on the pyre and placed in the urn.[59] Using this sequence of dated ceramics and the histories of individual sites, it is clear there was a range of choices available to the living in terms of how they wished to treat individuals on death, particularly during the central 300 years—from 2000 BC to1700 BC—or 10 to 12 generations of the Early Bronze age.

From the beginning, local choices and decisions were made about how particular people would be buried. [FIG. 5.11] In the flat cemetery at Oldtown, Co. Kildare, the body of a middle-aged woman, dated to between 2140 BC and 1920 BC, was arranged in a crouched position in a pit. A layer of fine sand formed the base and stones were placed along the long sides. She was laid on her left side, facing north-east, an upright Bowl Food Vessel beside her head. A quantity of cremated bone of a young adult was placed over her abdominal area and legs. While bones from most parts of the skeleton were represented in this deposit, only some bone from the pyre was placed here. The cremated bone deposit may also contain bones of another, younger person; an adolescent or juvenile. The pit was filled with sand after the burial. The other burials in the cemetery have a similar date.[60]

A short time later at Baggotstown, Co. Limerick, a pit was dug into the ground, a cist constructed of limestone slabs and covered by a mound. It contained the cremated remains of a young or middle-aged adult male and an 8–9-year-old child, two Bowl Food Vessels and a polished, unburnt bone cylinder, with a couple of fragments of animal bone. [FIG. 5.11] The condition of the cremated bone from the two people suggests that they had been cremated separately. Not all the bone was collected from the pyre, but fragments of all major elements of the skeleton were recovered, including the cranium of the child, suggesting considerable care was given to this gathering. A sample of cremated bone provided a date of between 1923 BC to 1695 BC. The form of the Bowls suggests a date of between 1980 BC and 1920 BC.[61]

In some communities a Bowl was placed with a body in the grave, as at Oldtown. The deposit of cremated bone from at least one other person placed across the lower part of this woman's body is closely mirrored in a middle-aged adult male inhumation with

OLDTOWN

bowl

cremation

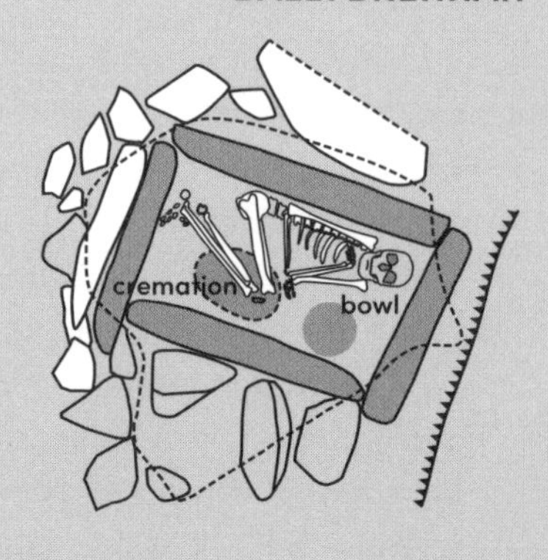

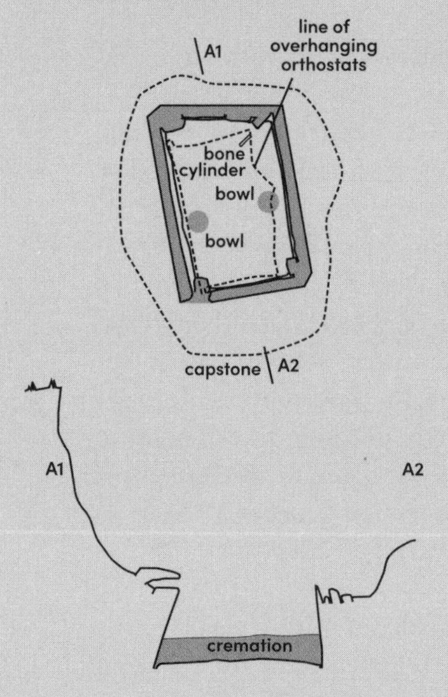

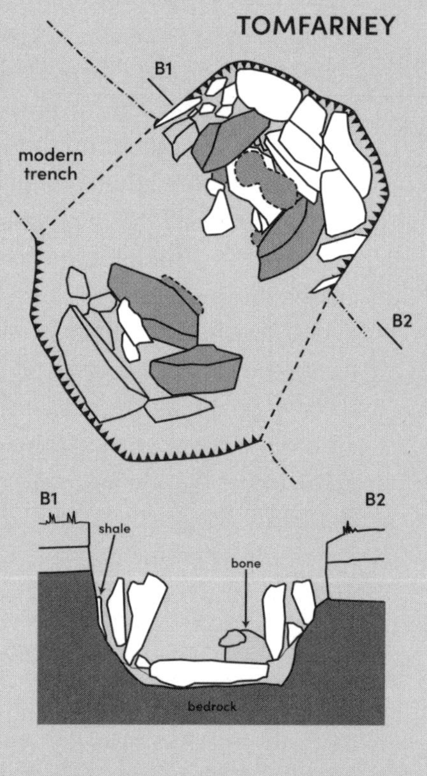

FIG. 5.11.

Early Bronze Age burials at Oldtown, Co. Kildare; Ballybrennan, Co. Westmeath; Baggotstown, Co. Limerick and Tomfarney, Co. Wexford.

cremated bones of an adult male over the knee area, in a cist in the Ballybrennan, Co. Westmeath cemetery. [FIG. 5.11] The focus of the mortuary ritual at Baggotstown that featured cremations of an adult male and child was the careful collection of bone from pyres and its transport to and placement in the grave. While bone from the adult and child were commingled, the two Bowls present suggest recognition that this was a grave for two people.

In terms of physical lifestyle, only a limited amount of information survives in cremated bone. The inhumed bones of the woman from Oldtown provide much more insight. She may have retained memories of food shortages when she was a child, reflected in stress lines in her teeth enamel. A cavity in one of her molars indicates dental discomfort. On the other hand, deposits of teeth calculus suggest a starch-rich food source, such as cereals. Chipping of her lower incisors indicates she habitually used her teeth as a tool. Her knees—particularly the right—indicate osteoarthritis, so she must have suffered from knee pain. That she favoured the use of her right limbs is also indicated by osteoarthritis at the base of the right thumb.

This portrait of a woman from Oldtown is a testament to the character of her own life, but also her kin in the immediate social network in which she lived. These people buried her in what they considered to be an appropriate manner. Rather than our modern concept of a fixity of identity with the physical body of a person, these mortuary practices indicate that selected human bodies were used post-mortem to construct and reflect social ties between the deceased and kinsfolk, animals, things and places. This included placing cremated remains of other persons with inhumations, female and male. At Baggotstown the association between a man and a child was marked or made by mingling their bones. Giving people different post-mortem treatments and then burying them together created linkages and differences between them. Placing objects in the grave, such as pottery vessels, or other materials, such as the bone cylinder in the Baggotstown cist, or animal bone, facilitated the mourners in depicting and demonstrating relationships

PL. 5.F.

The Vase Urn in the cist at the centre of the ring-ditch at Newrath, Co. Kilkenny.

with the dead, providing links between the givers and the deceased that carried on beyond death. The preparation of graves and the placement and presentation of the deceased created visual and material images that stayed with the living and sustained the body image of the deceased. A disturbed cist at Tomfarney, Co. Wexford containing a cremated bone deposit with a date from between 2134 BC to 1947 BC, consisted of the remains of at least seventeen people—twelve adults (at least three male and one female), an adolescent, two children and two infants—along with a perforated stone and a clay bead, providing a contemporary, and very different, communal image of the dead.[62] [FIG. 5.11]

Cemeteries often had a defined spatial extent, setting them apart as distinct places. Just as with the form and organisation of the grave itself, the distribution and position of graves relative to others within a cemetery—alongside the ability to date burials and changing ceramic styles—provides us an opportunity to consider relationships over time represented by the people in different graves.[63]

There does seem to be a marked distinction between a Bowl (Food Vessel) tradition, more focused on inhumation, and a cremation-focused Vase tradition (which includes Vase Food Vessels, Vase Urns and Encrusted Urns), followed by the later Collared and Cordoned

Urns. One key symbolic or representational element linking all types of cinerary urn from 2000 BC to the end of the period is the concept of giving cremated deposits what Howard Williams has usefully referred to as a 'skin'. The cinerary urn appears to signify a body in the grave, re-creating a sense of definition for the person/people inside, whose remains had been fragmented by the cremation process and then gathered together. While the majority of urn burials represent an individual, and hence a straightforward link with a body, examples of multiple individuals in urns suggest complex ideas of the relationship between this notion of an outer skin (pot) and who was contained by it. Furthermore, there are frequent small deposits of both unburnt and cremated bone in and around graves, suggesting that human bone was being used in a variety of ways in addition to being placed as 'burials'.[64] **[PLS 5.E, 5.F]**

With the shift in focus to seeing the burials as a result of complex patterns of practice by the participants in mortuary rituals, consideration of the location and relationships of graves makes it clear that this was not just a case of changing practices over time—a view that has tended to dominate interpretations of graves and cemeteries. Instead, a mortuary tradition, which involved a variety of practices, was utilised to establish different kinds of bonds and ties to the dead. When burying an individual in a cemetery, people actively referenced the communal past through the re-use of graves and the placement of later graves close to earlier ones.[65]

INTERPRETING CEMETERIES: LOCAL AGENCY AND SOCIAL CONTEXT

In a period perceived to be marked by ranking, it is argued that social differentiation is reflected in and reinforced by the ways in which individuals were treated in death. Was this the case? This issue can be addressed by shifting our focus from the grave to the cemetery, thinking about the intentions of mourners as they buried people—in some cases in cemeteries that were in use over many generations. A particular view of Irish Bronze Age society has been suggested by Charles Mount and more recently by Cormac McSparron, drawing on the premise that we can use the burial record as a direct reflection of the nature and organisation of society. It is argued that burial in a cemetery indicates social rank, since only a minority of the population was formally buried. Materials placed with the dead are seen as markers of status, and the way in which the dead were treated as a direct reflection of contemporary society. Mount suggested that society was small-scale and based on patriarchally dominated kin groups. McSparron views Early Bronze Age society as being increasingly socially differentiated, with a proportion of high-ranking individuals (predominantly men) signified by more elaborate funerary treatment.[66]

By contrast, the discussion here focuses on the living in the Early Bronze Age treating the dead in very personalised, active ways, creating images of the dead and their relationships with them. Can we reconcile this approach with a view that Early Bronze Age cemeteries display social differentiation? We should recognise that these perspectives reflect two different interpretative stances. One looks for general patterns of behaviour as the basis for an understanding of the processes underlying social organisation and change over time. Mortuary practice is seen as holding up a mirror to contemporary society. The approach taken here instead envisages people as active social agents, drawing on broad traditions of practice and belief and creating relationships with people, things, animals and places they were close to in life and death. Appropriate actions were undertaken to look after the dead placed in cemeteries, and we should not be surprised if these involved expressions of emotion and grief.[67] The best way to examine the balance between these two views is to look at a number of case studies.

At Newrath, Co. Kilkenny the cremated remains of a middle-aged man, who died between 2020 BC and 1773 BC were placed in a Vase Urn, inverted in a cist, which had tipped slightly to one side.

A sample of human bone from the upper fill of the cist produced a similar date. The cist was constructed in a pit with a central stake-hole. In turn, the cist was centrally placed within a small ring-ditch and covered by a gravel mound. The ditch was partially lined with oak timbers, with a possible entrance on the eastern side. Two exterior post-holes and a feature to the east of them may be associated with funerary rituals. It appears that a significant amount (1450 grams) of cremated bone was carefully collected from the pyre. Burnt cranial fragments from the mound and the fill of the cist match with bones contained in the urn, suggesting that some bone from this individual was deliberately scattered after the urn had been put in the cist. Sherds from a second Vase Urn were found in the mound and basal fill of the ditch. About 30 metres to the south-west was a small cemetery with pit cremations, dating from between 1740 BC to 1500 BC. These contained small amounts of crushed human bone, a rite more commonly seen after 1600 BC. Token deposition of human bone was part of the broadening suite of mortuary practice over the Early Bronze Age.[68] **[FIG. 5.12, PL. 5.F]**.

The focus at Newrath was on the burial of a particular person. By contrast the Grange, Co. Roscommon cemetery was in use over a period of more than 300 hundred years, from before 2100 BC to after 1800 BC.[69] **[FIG. 5.13]** Remains of at least 25 people were placed here, in 14 formal graves and 2 token deposits. This suggests one or two burials per generation. Fourteen of the individuals were adults, nine were juveniles. The ages of the other two people could not be estimated. The adults included young, middle-aged and older individuals. The sex of nine adults could be suggested. All were males or probable males, indicating gender as one rationale for the burial of particular people in the cemetery.

Before the covering cairn was constructed there was a phase of burial when both cremation and inhumation were considered appropriate. For example, a crouched burial of a seven-year-old child was placed in a cist (grave 3) with a Bowl and a pig's hoof. Two Bowls with similar decoration were placed with a large deposit

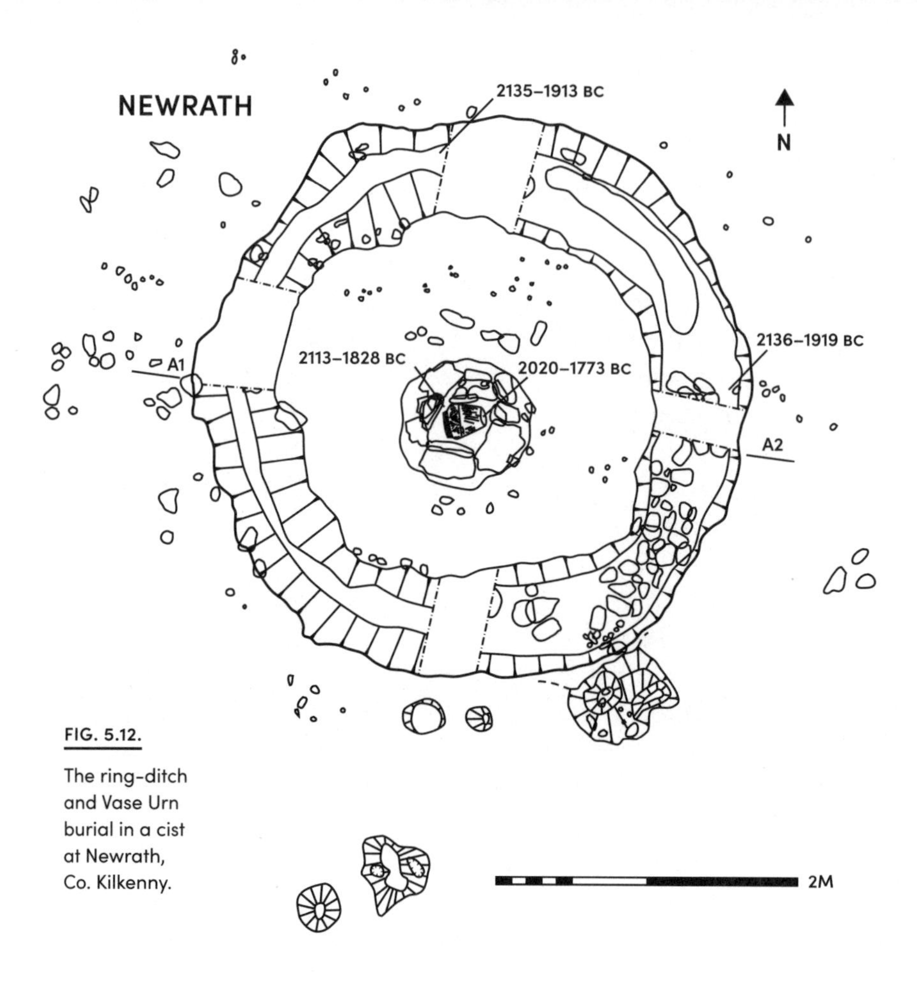

FIG. 5.12.

The ring-ditch and Vase Urn burial in a cist at Newrath, Co. Kilkenny.

of cremated bone in another cist (grave 13). This consisted of the remains of at least four people: an infant, a child and two adults, one of them possibly male. Fragments of burnt animal bone from larger mammals were found, and the few fragments identified came from cattle hooves. Radiocarbon dates from the unburnt bones in two cists (graves 2 and 3) overlap, with the early date of the child in grave 3 (2458 BC–2032 BC) perhaps hinting at curation of the body. The remains in grave 13 were commingled after cremation. Osteological analysis indicated fleshed corpses had been placed on pyres, and there was careful collection of bone from these pyres. Thus, there were variations in the post-mortem treatment of the

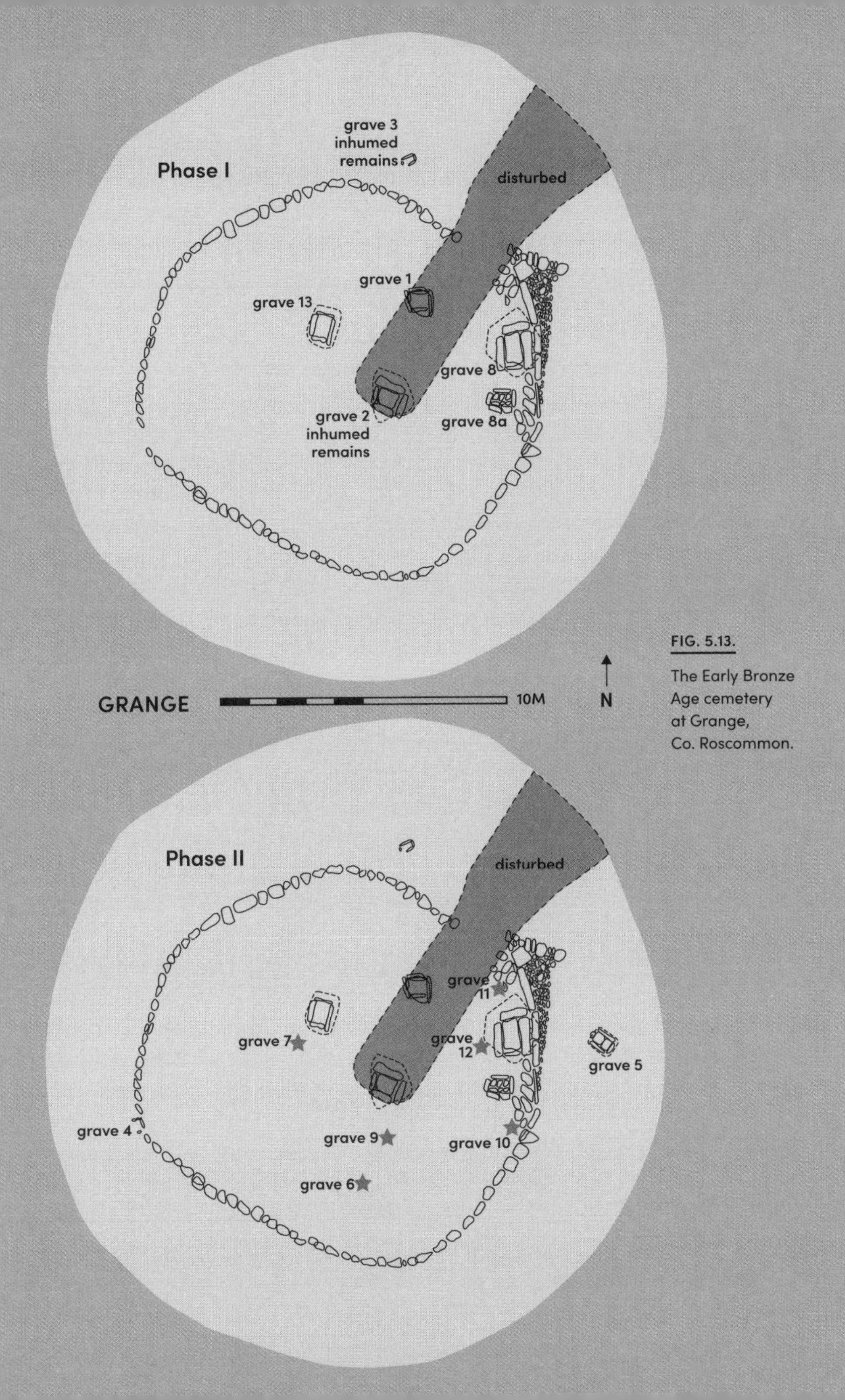

FIG. 5.13.

The Early Bronze Age cemetery at Grange, Co. Roscommon.

dead, with both individual and commingled deposits, but also recurring practices, such as the placement of Bowls and animal hooves.

As the cemetery developed, the eastern area became the focus. As part of the cairn revetment, five large, upright slabs formed an alignment, with a flat slab at its northern end and stone paving to the east. Unburnt child bones and burnt adult bone found within the alignment, and a portion of an unburnt adult cranium found to the west of it, appear to represent foundation deposits. In grave 8a, cremated bone was placed on a stone and then covered by the paved floor of the cist. The rest of the cremated bone deposit was placed in the cist on this floor, with a Bowl. Both deposits represent the same individuals—an adult and a juvenile. In a large cist (grave 8) just to the north, a Bowl was surrounded by a spread of cremated bone, consisting of the remains of a middle-aged or older adult man. This individual is the focus of the fictional scenario at the beginning of this chapter. The capstone of the cist overlay the alignment, suggesting the deliberate interlocking of these structures, which were then encased in the cairn. The remains in the cists (graves 1-3, 8, 8a, 13) represent a complementary focus on individual and commingled deposits.

Sometime after 2000 BC mortuary practice at Grange changed. Cremated remains of individuals were placed in pits (graves 6–7, 9–12), in some cases in Vase Urns, in the mound covering the cairn, and in two cists (graves 4 and 5). The weight of cremated bone deposits found in these graves is in most cases significantly less than in earlier burials. This indicates a shift from the earlier practice whereby all or most of the person's bones were collected and placed in the grave, to now having only a representation of bone from the pyre in the grave—a token deposit. There were complex patterns in the post-cremation treatment of remains; the weathered, cremated bones of an adult (grave 11) and a male adult (grave 12) may have been stored elsewhere before their placement. Pits were placed close to earlier cists, suggesting a deliberate practice of creating physical links with older graves and burial events. The latest dated burial, from 1890 BC to 1700 BC (grave 10), was of a young adult male. All his burnt bones (1,954 grams) and a burnt grooved bronze dagger and its bone pommel were gathered in a Vase Urn and placed in a pit dug into the mantling over the cairn. The dagger had been deliberately twisted—killed?—before being placed, presumably on the body, during the cremation. Grave 10 was located above and south of an earlier cist (grave 8a); this appears to have been the most important long-term focus of activity at the cemetery.

Newrath and Grange appear to support an interpretation of Bronze Age burials reflecting a male-dominated society. Wider comparison, however, indicates varying mortuary practices that were the outcome of local decisions and choices about the treatment of particular dead people. The Keenoge, Co. Meath and Edmondstown, Co. Dublin [FIG. 5.14] cemeteries were in use over much of the course of the Early Bronze Age. In both there are the remains of at least 26/27 people—adults and juveniles—with a small number of cists and a larger number of pits. Pottery is the dominant object placed with the dead, but there are a significant number of individuals, over half of the total in each cemetery, with whom nothing was placed. The remains of adults are dominant. While males occur more frequently, there are a number of adults whose sex could not be definitively identified. Inhumed and cremated remains were placed in graves; over time cremation became the dominant burial rite. In some cases all cremated remains were carefully collected and deposited; in others there was a token representation of the cremated remains of the person.[70]

At Edmondstown the earliest burials are cists dominated by the burial of adult males accompanied by Bowls. These are followed by pit burials in which the cremated remains of children and adults are prominent. The central burial at Keenoge is a crouched inhumation of a woman in a cist accompanied by a Bowl Food Vessel. At Keenoge, the rite of inhumation is strongly associated with women and cremation was not as prominent, which may reflect a particular focus of mortuary activity in the earlier part of the period. At Edmondstown, multiple burial was infrequent; by contrast at Keenoge over two-thirds of the deposits took the form of multiple burials.

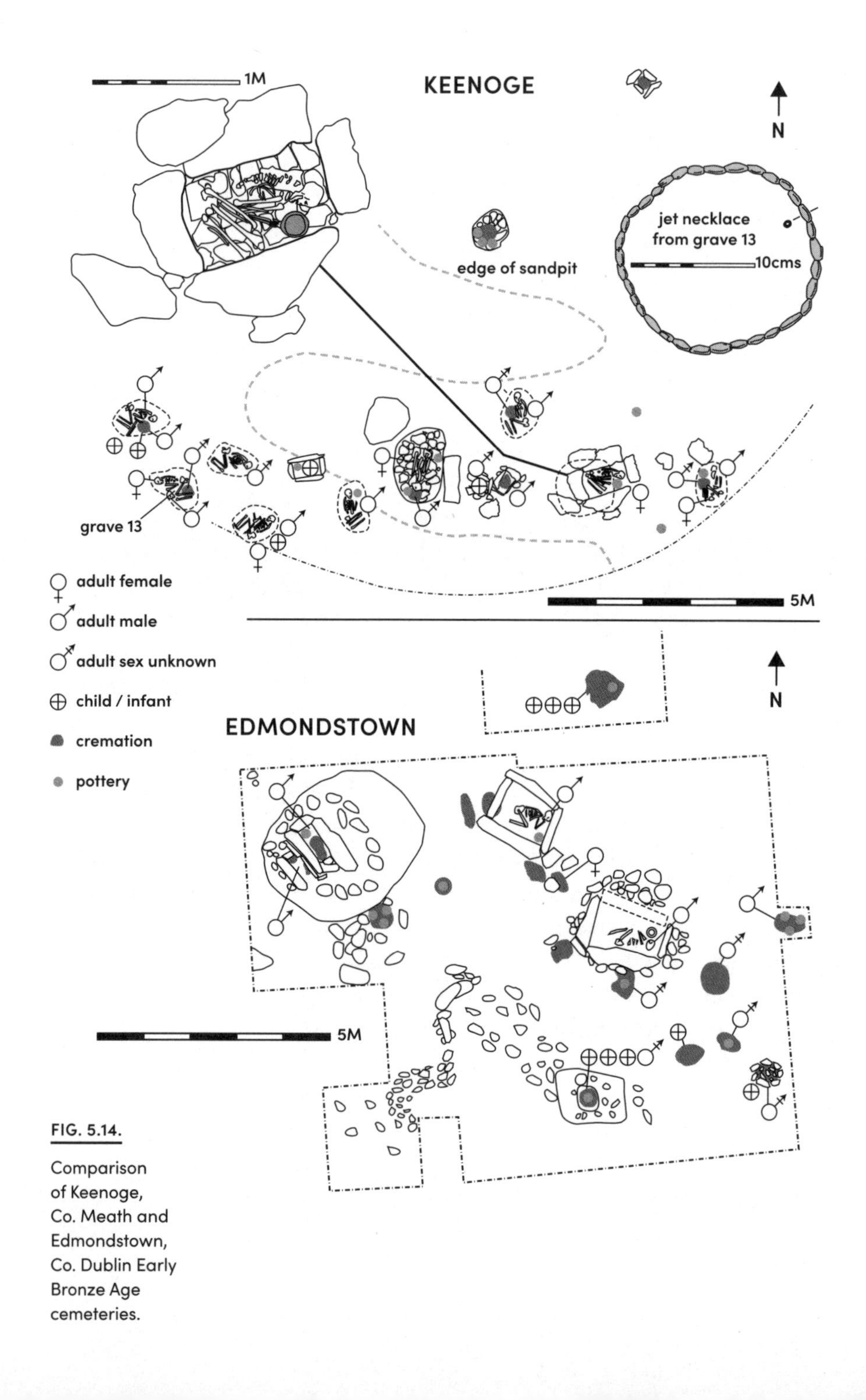

FIG. 5.14.

Comparison of Keenoge, Co. Meath and Edmondstown, Co. Dublin Early Bronze Age cemeteries.

The long history of such sites, and others such as Carn More, Co. Louth where there are distinct phases of activity from 2000 BC to beyond 1600 BC, indicates the selective character of burial, particularly when concentrations of activity at particular times are allowed for. The unidentifiable sex of a significant number of adults makes it difficult to provide a sense of the real gender balance, but the dominance of adults suggest that the juveniles merited placement in cemeteries through their family or lineage links. Indeed, in many cases adult and child remains occur together; at Ballynacarriga 3 for example, there appears to be a particular association of a child placed with a confirmed or likely adult female. There are a small number of cemeteries, such as Fourknocks I, Co. Meath, where children are prominent, but in another Neolithic monument 50m away—Fourknocks II—the Chalcolithic and Early Bronze Age burials were predominantly of adults.[71] It was important to place later burials close to earlier ones, or to re-use existing graves. It may be relevant to think of concentrations within cemeteries representing kin or family areas. Over time, a sense of genealogy and history was created, renewed—or contested—through the burial and placement of particular people close to their ancestral kin.

There are a few exceptionally large sites with more than 30 Early Bronze Age burials, such as the Mound of the Hostages at Tara and the hill-top cemetery mound at Knockast, Co. Westmeath.[72] For the Mound of the Hostages, an extensive series of radiocarbon dates on bone, the sequence of grave and ceramic styles, and analysis of the spatial location of burials provide insights into the development of the cemetery.[73] [FIG. 5.15, PL. 5.G] Activity began between 2220 BC and 2030 BC, and the main use of the cemetery was from 1790 BC to 1605 BC. The earliest burials were in the passage tomb itself, disturbing Neolithic cremation deposits. Crouched burials associated with Bowl Food Vessels were placed in the inner compartment, and a cremation in an Encrusted Urn was placed in the outer compartment. There may have been deliberate blocking of the tomb, as the focus shifted to the over-lying mound. Cremations were associated

TARA, MOUND OF THE HOSTAGES

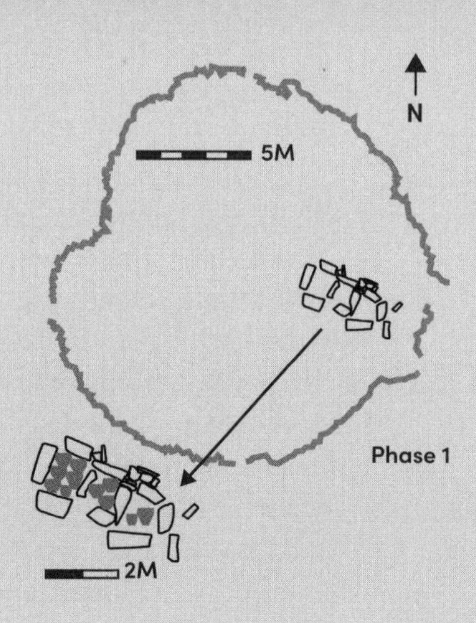

FIG. 5.15.

The Mound of the Hostages, Tara, Co. Meath; interpretative history of the phases of use of Early Bronze Age cemetery.

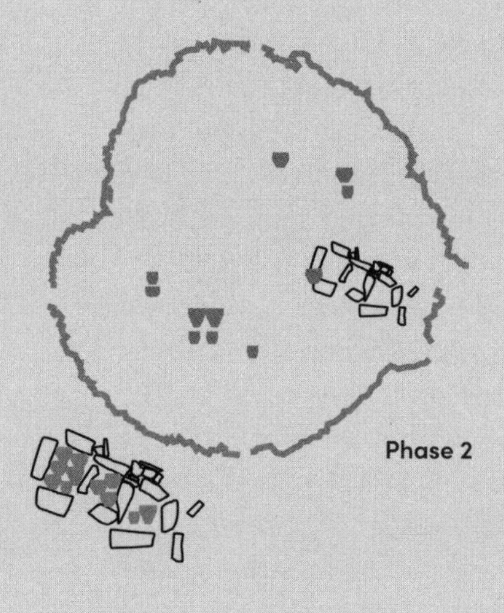

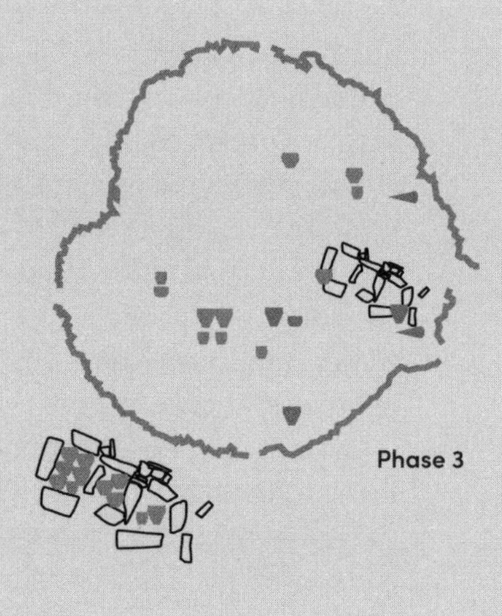

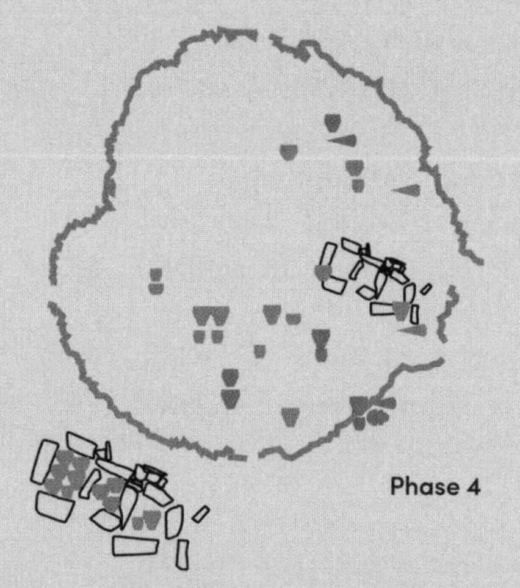

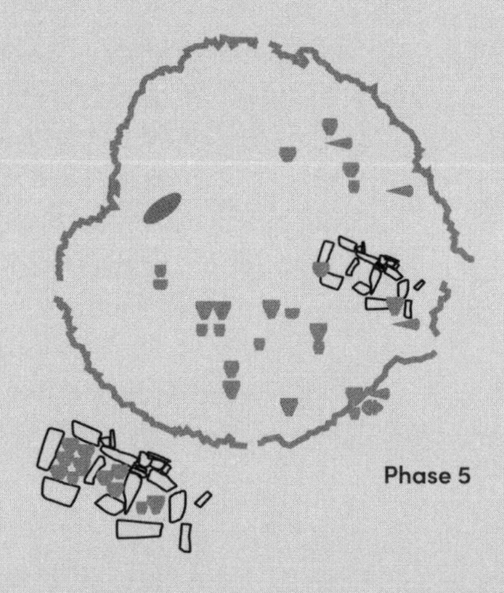

PL. 5.G.

The Mound of the Hostages at Tara, Co. Meath.

with charcoal-filled pits (pyres?) around the mound perimeter. Looking at the burials in the mound (in Encrusted, Vase and Collared Urns) in terms of those dating to before 1900 BC and those that concentrate in the period after that date allows us to see distinct patterning. Burials in the mound are concentrated in groups in the vicinity of the tomb structure, below, and to north and south of it, with an increasing focus on the southern part of the mound. The latest burial, an adolescent, dating to between 1700 BC to 1600 BC and placed after a considerable gap in activity, is very different in character and location from other burials in the mound. This is the crouched inhumation of an adolescent, with a protective slab over the burial. A composite necklace with bone, bronze, faience and jet beads had been placed around the neck, and a copper alloy blade and awl were found at the feet [SEE FIG. 2.2]. This burial is distinctive in terms of the rite used, the objects placed in the grave and its location in the western part of the mound, away from the other burials.[74] Does this use of inhumation, which would have been an anachronistic burial rite for adults and adolescents by this time, deliberately hark back to the beginnings of the cemetery four hundred years earlier, when, in turn, a historical link with the past was created by inserting inhumation burials into the Neolithic passage tomb? This is echoed in the very late use of inhumation at the Poulawack cemetery.

People in Early Bronze Age Ireland lived and died within a social context in which traditions and practices were widely shared and changed over time. Local, immediate, face-to-face encounters with kin and people who were known to each other formed the daily framework in which life and death were faced and understood. What has survived in cemeteries appears to be, in most cases, the material remains of the post-mortem pathways of selected individuals and, in special cases, perhaps as at Tomfarney, the outcome of particular events.

THE CONTEXT AND LEGACY OF CHALCOLITHIC AND EARLY BRONZE AGE BURIALS

The picture presented here of the active, local working out of wider structuring social principles is out of tune with many current interpretations of this period, which are heavily based on aDNA studies and argue that at European level single burial and the spread of Beaker-related material are the ultimate result of a major western migrations of people from the Steppes.[75] While Beaker burials with this distinctive 'Steppe genes' signature have been widely identified in western Europe, the evidence appears to be most dramatic in Britain. It has been suggested that approximately 90% of the indigenous, Neolithic population gene pool in Britain was replaced within a few hundred years.[76] The aDNA from three individuals dating to around 2000 BC in an Early Bronze Age cemetery at Church Bay, Rathlin Island, off the north coast of Ireland have the same 'Steppe genes' signature. Lara Cassidy and colleagues have suggested that people with this gene signature probably came onto the island around 2500 BC, bringing Beaker-related material, and a wave of genomic change, to Ireland. Cassidy and Dan Bradley argue further that the modern populations mostly closely resembling the Rathlin Bronze Age genomes are the Irish, Welsh and Scottish, suggesting some level of continuity from prehistoric times.[77] The sense that this was a key time of change, with long-term demographic and wider impact, is reinforced by the suggestion that the Steppe gene expansion spread Indo-European languages, the forerunners of most modern European languages, with mass migrations providing the necessary mechanism to achieve language change.[78]

The burial record has been pitched into the centre of this debate. Kristian Kristiansen argues that burial rituals are among the most fundamental social institutions because they relate to the transmission of property and power and to cosmology and religion. A radical change in burial rites is seen as indicating alterations in institutions and beliefs. Where such change happens quickly, it signals a social transformation, often under strong external influence.[79] This formulation brings us back to this period being seen as exemplified by the rise of individual (male) burial. When discussed at a very general level, this series of hypotheses might sound plausible, but interpretations have to be nuanced when faced with the complexity and variability of the burial and wider archaeological record. There were strong contacts between Ireland, Atlantic Europe and western and northern Britain during the Chalcolithic and Early Bronze Age, with every possibility of people moving onto and off the island.[80] On the other hand, patterns of continuity of mortuary practices from the Late Neolithic into the Beaker period and from then on into the Early Bronze Age strongly suggest retention of strong trans-generational memories, rather than invented traditions. Incomers fitted into this social context, perhaps in some cases initially as population enclaves. People lived in local worlds but also knew their way around established networks of contact. Exchange with non-local partners may have been more regular than we assume.[81]

PL. 5.H.

The Early Bronze Age 'face mask' cup from Mitchelstown 2, Co. Cork.

There are many instances of genetically diverse populations sharing senses of cultural identity and particular types of material engagement with the world. Genes are what we are made of, culture is how we actively make sense of the world we live in. It seems plausible to think of people in Chalcolithic and Early Bronze Age Ireland—potentially with different backgrounds and origins—developing a particular cultural lifestyle, founded on a distinctive body world focused on relational individuals and expressed in a variety of ways, including the post-mortem treatment of particular people. Glimpses into this world are provided by the anthropomorphic 'face cup', one of a pair, found with a Cordoned Urn at Mitchelstown, Co. Cork, and the pair of ceramic ear-plugs found in a cremation deposit of at least three individuals, two adults and an adolescent/younger adult, in a compartmented cist in the Ballinchalla, Co. Mayo cemetery.[82] [SEE PL. 5.H]

This chapter has outlined the character of the two major traditions of mortuary practice in Ireland in the period 2450 BC–1600 BC. The two traditions could be seen as successive and overlapping, as the Beaker phenomenon became regionalised and diversified. In the wedge tomb tradition, there is a harking back to monumental architecture, which provides a frame for the deposition of human remains and other material. In the cemeteries, the performance of mortuary rituals at graves was central to the post-mortem transformation of particular people. This period was a key transitional point in mortuary practice. Rites and rituals enacted at Early Bronze Age cemeteries, and some of the forms of grave architecture identified there, provide the background of later mortuary practices. In wedge tombs and cist/pit cemeteries there is a strong sense of using and building on the past. Performances and activities created and

materialised local histories and genealogies. In this context, it is relevant to explore how wedge tombs and cemeteries were perceived in a longer time perspective.

Looking at the balance between communal and individual deposits in wedge tombs, William O'Brien concluded that a focus on the burial and commemoration of adult women in some tombs could be seen in the context of a wider pattern of social differentiation.[83] Accepting that this focus on particular women is part of a wider tradition in which either men or women could be commemorated, the trend is worth discussing, as it provides an opportunity to consider the long-term role of monuments such as wedge tombs in the landscape. There is a link between the human remains in a tomb, the local name associated with some of the relevant sites and the tradition of the 'wise woman healer' or *cailleach* in Irish oral tradition. The meaning of Labbacallee is 'the *cailleach*'s bed', and this is a name given to several wedge tombs.[84] Gearoid Ó Crualaoich argues that the *cailleach* represents the archetypal otherworld female, the supernatural female elder. She is the personification of the landscape, associated with fixed locales such as monuments, responsible for forming topographic features and for the power in events such as high tides and thunderstorms. The meaning of the *cailleach* changed over time as traditional beliefs were adapted to a Christian world, but could elements of the *cailleach* owe their initial inspiration to locally important women placed in wedge tombs?[85]

Can we see the transformation over time of a known person with relevance for a local social network into an ancestor, responsible for the origins of the people and the land? The most prominent *cailleach* is the *Cailleach Bhéarra,* associated with the Beara peninsula in south-west Ireland.[86] Beara was a focus for the construction of wedge tombs, and there is a notable concentration of these monuments in this part of the island. Are there elements here reflecting the cosmology of the people who built wedge tombs, which in turn became reflected in the traditions that grew up around them? As the tradition spread from the south-west it may have been transferred to other features, hence perhaps the naming of the passage tomb complex at Loughcrew as *Slievenacailliagh*.[87] **[SEE PL. 1.F]**

As discussed above, O'Brien has explored how the wedge tombs of south-western Ireland were interpreted by later people whose worldview was framed by their own understanding of the past.

Monuments were drawn into an understanding of the landscape that also incorporated natural places in a complex interplay. The later Bronze Age and Iron Age deposits at Altar can be seen in the context of the alignment of the monument on Mizen Peak (*Carn Uí Néid*), a pyramidal peak 13km away to the south-west, seen in oral tradition as the abode of otherworld beings, the *Tuatha Dé Danann*. The wedge tomb was now seen as the abode of the ancestors and a portal to this otherworld. [SEE FIG. 5.7] At *Samhain,* the beginning of winter and a time when the boundaries between the living and the dead are seen as most porous, the sun when seen from Altar sets directly behind Mizen Peak, reflecting the position of the monument as a conduit to the other world.[88]

Turning to the cemeteries, later places of burial are frequently located on or are close to an Early Bronze Age cemetery. At Ballymacaward, Co. Donegal, a cemetery used up to the seventh century AD was focused on an Early Bronze Age cairn containing at least two cists. It appears that later people saw burial close to ancestoral places as important—continuing, renewing or inventing a sense of lineage and history that can be seen in the development of cemeteries during the Early Bronze Age.[89]

In many cemeteries it is possible to identify individuals buried there early in their history of use. They come early in the sequence of activity, effort was expended on them, and they seem to play a significant role in the layout and development of the cemetery. Cist 1 at Edmondstown and grave 6 at Keenoge fit that description well, as indeed do graves 8 and 8a at Grange.[90] Individuals buried in these graves may have become ancestors for their kin and following generations, who remembered and referred to them in burial rites and other rituals. The young adult male in Edmondstown cist 1 either had an unhealed trephination or a circular piece of bone in his skull was removed shortly after death. As one of the few possible early examples of trephination in Ireland, he was a person treated in a special way. Later graves were placed over and around this grave. The woman in Keenoge grave 6 might have been regarded as being very old at death, an honoured elder. Her grave was remembered by being both focal to, but distinguished within, the development of the cemetery.[91] **[SEE FIG. 5.14]**

Tom Booth and colleagues have shown that within British cemeteries there are instances of genetic relationships but also many non-genetically related individuals, indicating that kinship was created and maintained by shared social practices and senses of identity. In Irish cemeteries, males were important, but there is not a clear sense of gender patterning; females were also prominent. The frequent inclusion of children may reflect attempts to ensure the successful reproduction of communities.[92] These complex strands of relationship and memory created a sense of time in which past and present were inter-woven. The inhumed remains of a young female in a pit at the southern end of the cemetery at Keenoge (grave 13), were accompanied by some unburnt bones of an adult male and a few cremated bone fragments. She was buried with a necklace of 40 jet beads around her neck. **[SEE FIG. 5.14]** Some beads were cracked and fractured, and there were inconsistencies in shape and size, suggesting that this may be an heirloom, made up of the remnants of several necklaces, older than the woman it was buried with and either passed on from a previous holder or bestowed on the woman. The same may be said of the composite necklace placed with 'Tara Boy', the final burial at the Mound of the Hostages cemetery. **[SEE FIG. 2.2]** As Joanna Brück has elegantly put it, this kind of object is a visible, material reminder of kinship, 'a stringing together of people across the generations'.[93] The cemeteries had a similar role: the focus on older graves and the re-opening of graves provided opportunities for living kin to create and string together lines of connectivity and descent over time.

How did these traditions emerge? Conventionally, the cemeteries are seen as reflecting a wider north-west European shift to single burial at the beginning of the Bronze Age, while the wedge tombs are viewed as the latest stage in the megalithic tomb tradition in Ireland. Specific site histories demonstrate that the framing of life and death in local, active contexts of meaning was significant. People placing their dead in cists and pits often created a direct, physical link to the past, as seen in the use of wedge tombs, the broader pattern of the placement of Early Bronze Age burials in megalithic tombs, and the adaptation of the cairns and mounds of these monuments as cemetery mounds. In some cases there is no immediate link to past activities before the construction of a wedge tomb or cemetery. In other cases, connections and linkages to the past were deliberately sought: in some parts of the island wedge tombs were frequently placed close to older megalithic tombs. Our division of the past into time periods may hide important traditions and practices of remembrance. The individuals in Neolithic Linkardstown burials are recognised as significant figures, but the use of the mounds over some of these burials as Early Bronze Age cemeteries, as at Poulawack or at Baunogenasraid, Co. Carlow, is seen as a secondary phase, and indeed it is well over a millennium later. But could we consider the Neolithic individuals as mythic, ancestral figures in such cemeteries? In other instances, it appears that there was a more complex attitude to the past, incorporating a degree of iconoclasm. At the Mound of the Hostages at Tara, for instance, Neolithic cremated deposits in the passage tomb were removed to make way for Early Bronze Age burial deposits.[94]

Within these traditions a sense of history was created by the presence of the ancestral dead and the treatment of the dead through rituals that demonstrate shared values. At the start of this period those values were encapsulated and visible in wedge tombs; by the end they had become focused on the mortuary rites and graves of selected individuals. These people came to be rooted in oral narratives, and the places where they were buried continued to have an influence long after the final act of burial.

6.

Tracing lines and courses of history: burial practice in later prehistoric Ireland

A place in history

When the fire had died down at the cremation pyre, bones, charcoal and other material was collected in baskets. The bones were then ground down on stone, to help return them to the earth. People were standing, chatting, close to the entrance to the house, saying that if too much time went by before the young person was brought to the place of the ancestors, their spirit would be unhappy and continue to wander. With the sun high in the sky, cremated bones were placed carefully in a container and carried in a procession that approached the cemetery from the east, passing the mound that marked the edge of the cemetery. It was dry, but the ground underfoot was still wet in places. Some bone was placed on the open water of the lake, to the right of the area of the cemetery, and to the left in the soggy, wetland that flooded in winter. The interweaving of hills, low-lying wetter ground and rivers formed the lie of the land. As the small group walked, an elder pointed to the hills that surrounded the cemetery, to the stones that stood like people on the hill beyond the cemetery to the north-west, and to the mound on a hill to the east. All the hills had stories, and along with the lake and the wet ground

they surrounded the cemetery. A place where people had lived and died for many, many generations.

They walked along the line of the mounds and stopped at the gap in the middle, beside the open ground where the two lines of barrows crossed, and which had been a focus for ceremonies in the past. Someone said that timber posts had marked this important spot. The shadow cast by the sun fell to the north of each mound, making them seem bigger and closer together; appearing to connect them. Now the elder was reciting genealogies, explaining the links between the people within each of the mounds, connecting across them and to the places they came from. Looking to the west, someone said that the small mound there was where the oldest ancestors were, still keeping an eye on the living and the dead.

As the group bearing the bones approached, people waiting stood aside, forming a semi-circle on the far side of the grave. The area had been prepared and a pit had been dug in the ground. They knew in other places the custom was to place bones in the ground directly below the pyre where the bones were burnt. The right words were recited and repeated; bones were placed in the pit; after a pause, a waiting, more bone was placed on top. Someone said that this was to show that the kin groups represented in the person were still with their bones in the grave. As the soil was put over the pit, some of the group felt pangs of memories and loss, alongside relief that the ceremony had been done properly. There was sadness this person who had so much promise had died early in their adult life, but also a sense that because their bones were being placed in this place they would contribute to the continuing life of the kin and community-whose past generations could be traced in the lines of the mounds in the cemetery. Someone called out to the dead, chanting that the fire of the pyre had freed their spirit but there would always be a place for them at the home hearth. The area to the east of the grave was left open. This pointed to the highest ground close by and to the barrow on that hill—the main abode of the spirits, a walk uphill from the cemetery.

As the ground now held bone from a person who had died recently it was dangerous for the living, so most of them retreated and stood in a circle. Kin closest to the deceased dug a ditch around the grave, more or less in the same way as they would start to build a house. But here they were marking a place for the dead. Stones were thrown into the bottom of the ditch. These stones had been brought by different people, so that the person would be surrounded by and reminded of all the wider kin and places they were connected to. They threw more soil up to cover the pit and carefully built it up to show that the space enclosed was now a house for the deceased. They walked away and felt a mixture of loss, rememberance and honour.

PL. 6.A.

The excavation of the barrow cemetery at Ballintaggart, Co. Down.

The barrow cemetery at Ballintaggart, Co. Down was excavated in 2004 by Northern Archaeological Consultancy (NAC) prior to road improvements. The location of the cemetery is described as an isthmus, on a south-facing slope, with the land rising to the north-west, east and south-east, the open water of Lough Brickland to the north-east, and the wetland/ open water of Brown Bog to the south-west. This was a location of activity going back to the Early Neolithic. Radiocarbon dates indicate a maximum period of use for the deposition of human bone between 1628 BC and 766 BC. There are eight barrows and other features on two distinct alignments. Ring barrows 1, 4–7 and a four-post structure were aligned north-west to south-east, perhaps facing towards a dip in the hills to the south-east where the sun rises during mid-winter. The other barrows (3, 2 and 8) and a four-post structure may have been aligned on a large barrow known as Water Hill Fort on Brickland hill over 700m north-east of the cemetery. The account above is based on the features of the Late Bronze Age/ Eary Iron Age barrow 6, one of the latest dated barrows in the Ballintaggart cluster. Here, cremated bones were found in a pit within a ring-ditch, and associated charcoal was dated to between 1018 BC to 766 BC. The 670g of burnt bone represents a single individual, an adolescent or older subadult aged 13–18 years when they died [Fig. 6.7, Pl. 6.A].[1]

FRAGMENTING BODIES, WEAVING PEOPLE TOGETHER

The last chapter focused on the time from 2450 BC to 1600 BC, a transformative period and a nexus of ideas and practices with long-term implications for the next two millennia. The focus here is from 1600 BC to 800 BC, covering the Middle Bronze Age (between 1600 BC and 1200 BC) and the Late Bronze Age, from 1200 BC to 800 BC). The term 'later Bronze Age' is also used below to cover both periods. Chapter 7 covers the time from 800 BC to the mid-first millennium AD, that is from the start of the Iron Age to the beginnings of Christianity and the historic period. There are themes in mortuary practice that continue over the two millennia considered in these chapters.

There is persistence in aspects of mortuary practice and the continued or renewed use of sites after 1600 BC, but in other ways things changed dramatically. Mortuary practice in the Middle and Late Bronze Age has been widely perceived as becoming less visible.[2] It is more useful to think in terms of changing foci of practice. Linda Lynch and Lorna O'Donnell have described this period as being characterised by 'an incredibly intricate and variable physical treatment of the dead'.[3] Cremated bone deposits are the dominant feature of the record. The cremated remains of an individual adult male weigh on average 2,300g and those of an adult female on average 1,600g.[4] Accepting that there is a wide range around these average figures, the amount found in later Bronze Age deposits is nevertheless frequently much less. The representation of an individual by a token quantity of cremated bone was practiced in the Early Bronze Age, as we have seen, but it became more common after 1600 BC. There is a complexity and diversity in the post-cremation treatment of human remains at this time. Selected or token cremation deposits dominate but are complemented on occasion by the careful placement of all the cremated bone of an individual in a grave. Furthermore, in some cases bone appears to have been deliberately pounded and crushed after collection at the pyre, whereas in other cases it was placed in the ground as bone fragments.[5] We don't know how the majority of people were buried or disposed of; once again it is the remains of small numbers of chosen dead who feature in cemeteries and related sites. Comparing later Bronze Age cemeteries to Early Bronze Age ones, there is a greater concentration on adults, and on the representation of single adults in graves.[6]

There is also a move away from what had become the dominant tradition over the course of the Early Bronze Age of covering a cremation with an urn. Cordoned Urns were the form in use at the end of this tradition to around 1500 BC.[7] A domestic variant of this urn type emerged, and plain forms of flat-bottomed, bucket or barrel-shaped vessels developed from this. This pottery became ubiquitous in every-day later Bronze Age contexts, for example on settlement sites, and in contexts suggestive of a more ceremonial purpose, as in placement with the dead. Cremation deposits were in some instances placed in or under pots, or broken pottery sherds were deposited with cremated bone.[8] These changes happen against an apparent background of continuity of focus on kin and community. For example, in a cist at the Carrig, Co. Wicklow cemetery cremations accompanied by Vase Food Vessels on the floor of the cist were followed by two cremations covered by Cordoned Urns placed in pits in the fill of the cist. The grave was opened again for a cremation placed under an inverted Middle Bronze Age urn. This was cut by a narrower pit, with a deposit of cremated bone accompanied by sherds of coarse pottery.[9] Pottery was the main object placed with the dead in the Early Bronze Age; in some cases other artifacts were also deposited. This practice of placing other objects largely ceases, and alongside the continued deposition of pottery unaccompanied cremations became a much more common and widespread feature of the Middle and Late Bronze Age.[10]

A striking feature of the occurrence of cremated human bone in this period is that it was placed not only in cemeteries, but across a wide range of contexts. The deposition of unburnt bone on non-cemetery sites and places is another element of complexity in the treatment of the dead. The range of places linked by the deposition of human bone is striking. [FIG. 6.1] As in the cemeteries, cremated bone is most commonly found in pits, frequently mixed with charcoal and soil, often accompanied by coarse pottery. These patterns are key to understanding the role of these deposits and the wider issue of identity and perception of the human body—the later Bronze Age body world.

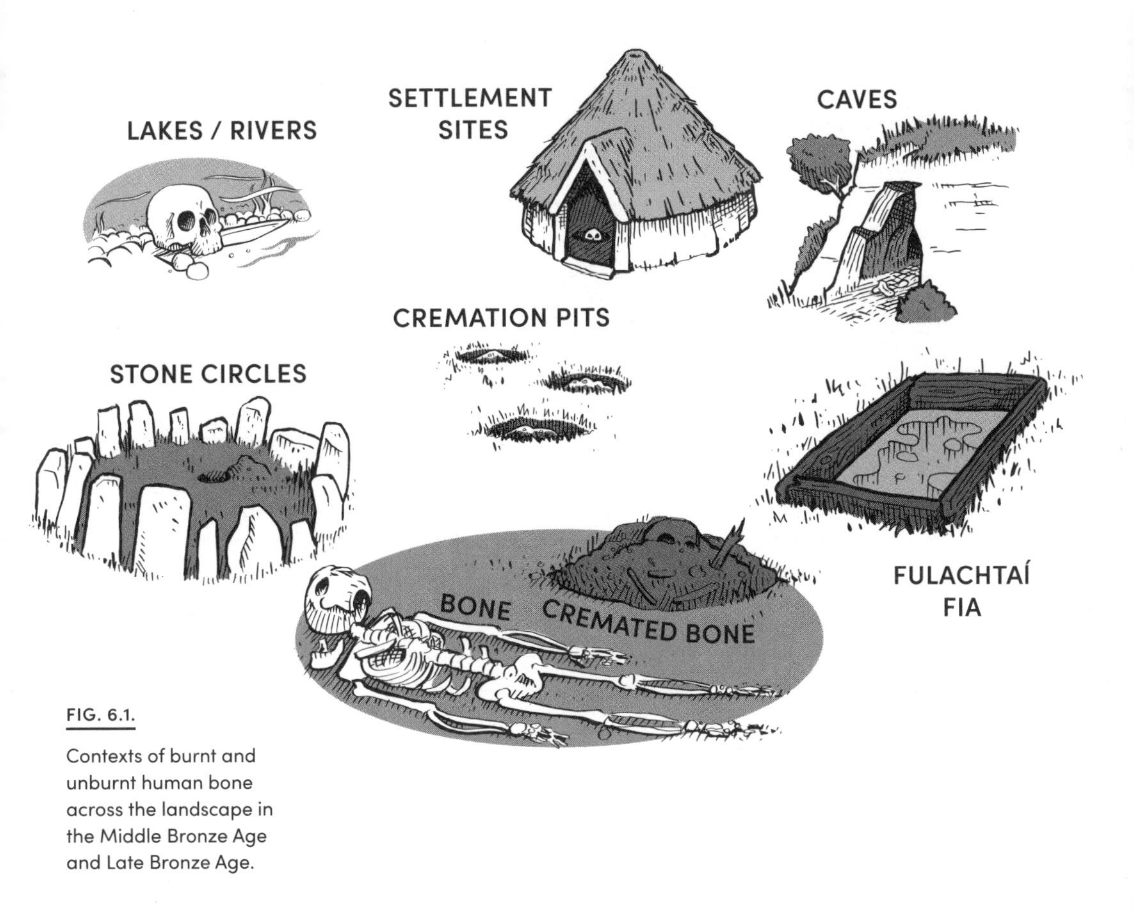

FIG. 6.1.

Contexts of burnt and unburnt human bone across the landscape in the Middle Bronze Age and Late Bronze Age.

House structures and settlements became more visible in the Middle and Late Bronze Age. Small quantities of cremated bone or selected unburnt bones—particularly crania and long bones—are found in some houses, enclosing ditches, associated pits and other features.[11] Mounds of burnt stone or *fulachtaí fia* were an important element of the settlement system, and human skulls have been found associated with a few excavated *fulacht fia* sites. At Inchagreenoge, Co. Limerick, the unburnt skull of an adult male was deposited against the edge of a spring above a spread of burnt stone associated with the use of a timber-lined trough and sealed by a stone capping. A crouched burial of an adult female dating to between 1260 BC to 1020 BC was found within the fill of a *fulacht fia* at Leshemstown, Co. Meath.[12] Bone and bodies were placed in other wet locations, bogs and lakes. Caves were used for occupation, but many were also used for funerary and ceremonial activities, particularly in the Early and Late Bronze Age. There was a preference for the use of deep cave environments. Glencurran Cave, Co. Clare was a focus for deposition for 500–600 years from around 1400 BC. Drystone walling was built to define an area of deposition, and there was at least one child inhumation burial along with deposits of unburnt, disarticulated human bone, particularly clavicles (collar bones); hare bones; and bones of domesticated animals—both newborn and what appear to be meat joints. Sherds of pottery, stone tools, amber and bone beads and perforated shells were also deposited. A hollow stone structure may have been built to mark the end of the use of the cave.[13] Cremation deposits also formed part of the ceremonies and rituals that were conducted at stone circles and related sites, as at Drombeg, Co. Cork.[14]

So, how do we interpret this fragmentation and dispersal of the post-mortem remains of people in different places across the landscape? Perhaps the deposition of human remains marked or added to the cultural significance of such places.[15] The identities of people were created in relational rather than individualistic terms—animals and objects played a key, active role in relational identities and the lives of people, animals and objects were intertwined. Kerri Cleary has suggested that there is a parallel between the deposition of fragmented human remains and fragmented quern stones at settlement sites. We might envisage human bone, therefore, as just part of a wider set of materials that were deployed to mark and make places, and used in other ceremonies. There are indications, however, that the remains of the human dead were of particular cultural significance. Through the dispersal of human bone, different spheres of life and landscape—domestic, ceremonial and mortuary—were brought together.[16]

At first glance this looks like a very different kind of relational identity from that of the Early Bronze Age, which was based on the relationship of material things with defined bodies. It is worth remembering that Early Bronze Age practices emerged from the Beaker period, when there was a tension between expressions of communal and personal identities in mortuary practice and when it was suggested that Beaker-associated objects in different contexts were linked to ideas about the body that held constant across different places in the landscape. After a focus on retaining the bodily identity of some of the visible dead in the Early Bronze Age, it would seem that by the Middle Bronze Age, as Joanna Brück puts it, it had become 'ideologically acceptable to fragment the human body'.[17] Bob Johnston has discussed how the potency of cremated bone was stabilised 'by weaving it into places and the land'.[18] They highlight how in this fragmentation, human remains were woven into the cycle of life by being treated in similar ways to cereals, pots, metalwork and other substances. The 'dead' are fragmented and split up; some are passed on to the next generation of 'bodies' (seed grain, grog in pots, recycled bronze), others are deposited (for example in hoards). Strikingly, both in Ireland and Britain, alongside dispersal and fragmentation there is an emphasis on the definition and deposition of the remains of individuals in Middle Bronze Age cemeteries.[19]

Informed by this widespread deposition of human bone, the focus here is on cemeteries. An important result of recent large-scale, development-led projects has been an enormous increase in the number

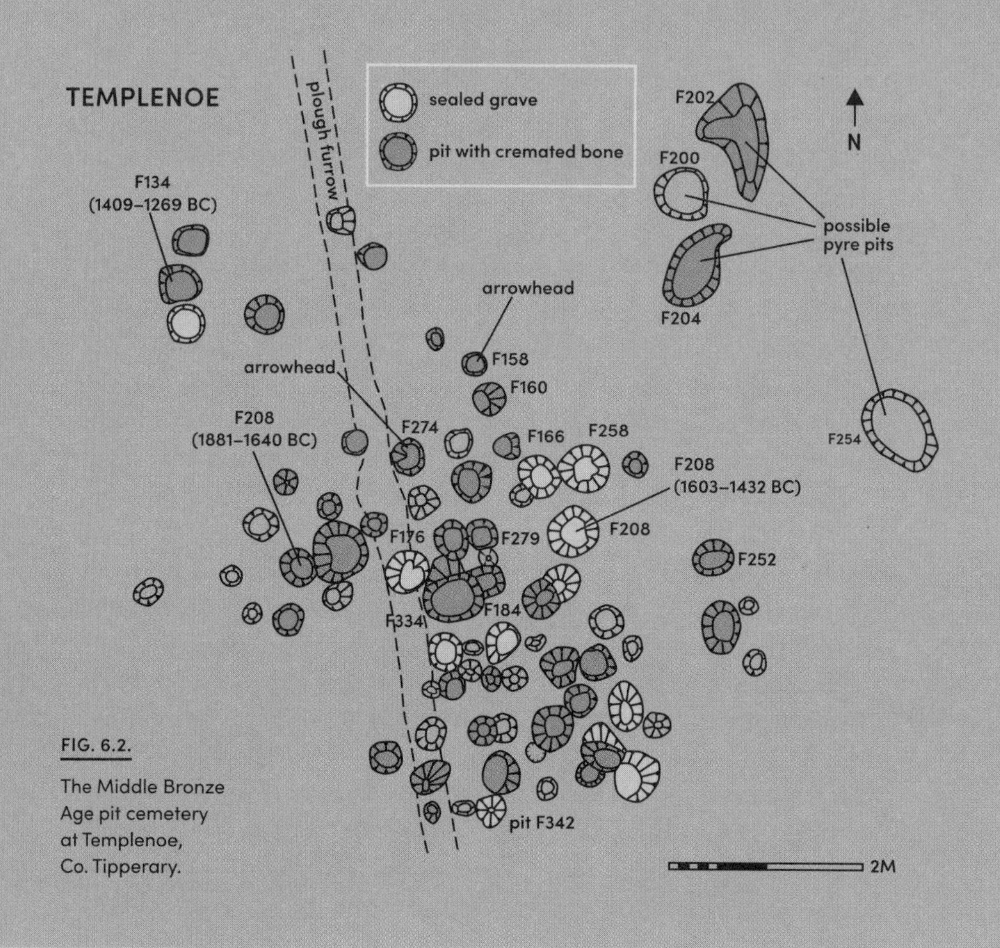

FIG. 6.2.

The Middle Bronze Age pit cemetery at Templenoe, Co. Tipperary.

of later prehistoric cemeteries excavated.[20] Pits containing cremated bone are a very common feature. They do occur as single, isolated features, but more usually form clusters, suggesting they represent specific places: cemeteries, set aside for burial. Cemeteries vary in size, with large examples such as Templenoe, Co. Tipperary and Killoran 10, Lisheen, Co. Tipperary **[FIG. 6.2, PL. 6.B]**, each containing over 70 pits (admittedly not all of them containing cremated bone) in a small area.[21] In some cases, the origin and first use of a cemetery was in the Early Bronze Age. They are again referred to as flat cemeteries as, in many cases, they do not appear to have had any surface definition.

PL. 6.B.

Templenoe, Co. Tipperary pit cemetery from the south.

In other cases, it appears that there may have been wooden upright markers, such as at Manusmore, Co. Clare, or that the cemetery was enclosed, as at Gransha, Co. Londonderry. Many of the sites are on agricultural land; hence, what survives are the lower parts of features cut into the ground, such as pits and ditches.[22] They are often located in low-lying areas, with a preference for south-facing slopes, and were used over considerable periods of time. At Manusmore, for example, there were two multi-period cremation cemeteries 900m apart on a south-facing slope overlooking the course of the River Fergus.[23] The analysis of the cremated remains from such cemeteries provides a rich source of information on and insights into life and death in the later Bronze Age.[24]

Pit cemeteries represent one important dimension of funerary practice. An overlapping and related practice is the enclosure of a single pit or a number of pits within a circular ditch, commonly referred to as a ring-ditch. Thus, we have sites such as Dalystown, Co. Westmeath, where there were seventeen pits. Four of these and a possible pyre site were enclosed by a ditch about 11m in diameter and covered by a low mound [FIG. 6.3]. Deposition of cremated bone may take place in the vicinity of a ring-ditch, rather than inside it, and ring-ditches can occur in clusters with pits, as at Ballybannon 5, Co. Carlow and Ask, Co. Wexford.

Ring-ditches are frequently recorded on aerial photographs. The retention of moisture in ditch fills leads to the enhancement of modern crop growth, resulting in the ditch showing as a darker colour on photographs. Excavation has demonstrated that in many cases ring-ditches were dug not only to enclose an area but also to provide material for a low mound to cover the internal area and/or to form a bank on the outer side of the ditch. This is what is referred to as a round barrow. These occur in considerable numbers as upstanding monuments, with over 2,000 known across the island, and in notable concentrations, both at a regional and cemetery level. They are considerably varied in their form and makeup.[25]

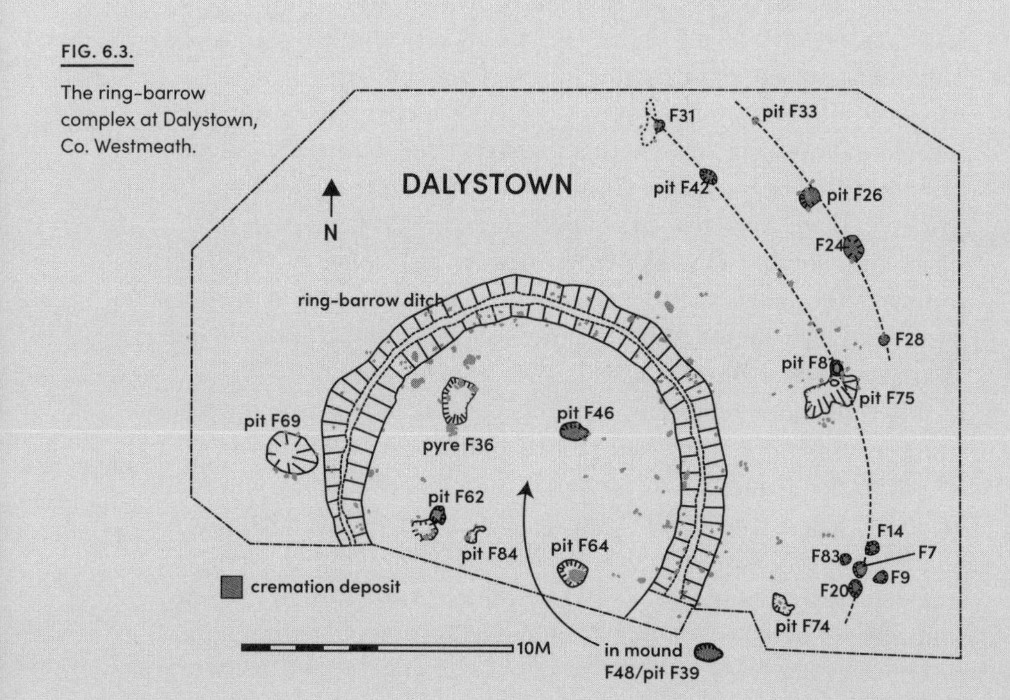

FIG. 6.3.

The ring-barrow complex at Dalystown, Co. Westmeath.

Although already in use, barrows and ring-ditches became a more important and distinctive component of mortuary practice in Ireland from the middle of the second millennium BC until the seventh century AD.[26] Hence, the barrow tradition was an important aspect of the treatment of the dead and of memorialisation, renewal and rememberance over a period of more than two thousand years. Pit cemeteries and ring-ditches/barrows are discussed below as two central, related dimensions of mortuary practice. The former appear to be particularly prominent in the Middle and Late Bronze Age, (from 1600 BC to 800 BC), and continuing into the Iron Age. The latter provide a thread that takes the discussion up to the transformation of worldviews and beliefs that occurred with the impact of Christianisation, and the later stages of that tradition are considered in the next chapter.

FIRE AND THE BODY

The most striking aspect of the Middle and Late Bronze Age mortuary record is the dominance of cremation-based practice and the placement of token deposits of cremated bone in pits. Cremation was practiced in Ireland from the Earlier Mesolithic, but given its prominence, it is appropriate to consider the practice in some detail here. The difficulties of osteological analysis of cremated bone and its archaeological interpretation are significantly increased when dealing with multiple small cremation deposits, compared to the more frequent occurrence in Early Bronze Age contexts of burials containing all the cremated remains of a person. Based on results from carefully excavated and analysed sites, however, we can profile the character of later Bronze Age mortuary practice in some detail—following the treatment of people from their deaths to the cremation, collection and handling of cremated remains, the placement of some of those remains in pits, and subsequent activities.[27] This is done through scientific analysis, but we are recovering the

PL. 6.C.

A Balinese Hindu cremation ceremony at Ulakan, Bali, Indonesia.

PL. 6.D.

The burnt bones in one of the cremation deposits at Templenoe, Co. Tipperary flat cemetery.

material residues of belief systems that underpinned the treatment of the dead, and of practices and rituals that were the behavioural enactment of those beliefs. [PLS 6.C AND 6.D].

The need to tack between analysis and interpretation—between the present and the Bronze Age—is particularly relevant, because much of the reference data used by osteoarchaeologists is drawn from the modern western world, where cremation re-emerged as a practice against a complex backdrop of social change and reform since the nineteenth century. Not surprisingly, the focus in this modern practice of cremation tends to be on technical issues, such as the 'efficiency' of the process.[28] It should be remembered that cremation is the dominant rite in the treatment of the dead in major religions globally, as in Hinduism and Buddhism. In these traditions cremation is central to the frame of life and death and the explanation of the place of people in the world. The spectacle of cremation—the transformation of the body by fire—is a time of celebration as well as grief, and the highlight of ceremonies that often extend over time and space before and after the cremation.[29] This is what we should take as our reference point for understanding the role of cremation in prehistory. The actions of people carrying out mortuary rituals in the Bronze Age may have fragmented and condensed the material traces of the process of cremation, but we can dis-entangle different stages in that process, informed by the study of traditional and modern cremation practices in a range of contexts today.[30]

But we should start with the dead. The majority of cremated bones have the characteristic surface form and fissures associated with the burning of fleshed bodies, and it is generally assumed that the bodies of single individuals were cremated. This would tie in with the greater focus on the remains of single individuals in cremation deposits. In some cases, however, de-fleshed bones, rather than bodies, were cremated. At Dalystown, for instance, two pits contained bone that had been de-fleshed when cremated. This indicates the potential complexity of post-mortem engagements with the dead, suggesting multi-stage treatment of the bodies of some people. It also provides a context in which we can understand how unburnt bone, particularly crania, was in circulation and in some cases formally deposited at this time.[31]

Regarding the pyre itself, that charcoal from the pyre was frequently deposited with cremated bone allows us to identify major tree species used for cremating bodies. Removal of charcoal from pyre sites may be one reason why it has proved difficult to recognise pyres on the ground.[32] Oak was the main wood used; its quality as a fuel would have facilitated the burning of soft tissue and bone. Other species, including alder and pomaceous fruitwood such as apple and cherry, were also utilised. Lynch and O'Donnell suggest that the latter were a deliberate choice—the aroma from fruitwood would help to mask the smell of burning flesh. The minimum temperature required to burn body fats is around 300–500°C; calcination of bone and a resultant white colour occurs when temperatures are above 700°C. The dominance of white, calcined bone in cremation deposits indicates that this degree of heat was frequently achieved. Variation in the colour of the bone—from grey to blue to black—indicates temperature differences, and perhaps also variation in the location of the body within the pyre.[33]

Bodies are likely to have been placed either on top of or within a pyre. It is estimated that a ton of timber, arranged in some form of box-like structure or platform, would have been required for a cremation. It is difficult to clothe the archaeological record with the detail of ceremonial activities that might have surrounded the preparation of the body, or de-fleshed bones, before placement on the pyre, but in at least some instances animals were also put on the pyre and placed with cremated human bone in a pit. Charred wheat and barley that appears to have been placed on or in the pyre has been recovered from several sites, such as Manusmore.[34]

Observation and experimental work indicate it takes about two hours for a human body to burn. Relatively few pyres have been recognised in the archaeological record, but they survive where they have been covered, and hence protected, or where they were built over a pit to aid combustion. At the Templenoe cemetery, four large pits were located to the north-east of the main cluster of pits [SEE FIG. 6.2]. These have been interpreted as possible pyres, positioned adjacent to the cemetery and cleaned out after use. At Newford, Co. Galway a pyre dating from between 1000 BC to 800 BC was placed above a large, rectangular pit, which would have aided an updraft of flames. The pyre had collapsed into the pit and contained only 700g of bone, suggesting other bone had been collected and taken away when the pyre had cooled. Pits nearby contained token amounts of cremated bone. There are instances in which pyres have been protected when covered by a barrow, suggesting a close spatial connection to the placement of the cremated bone. In other instances, a pit to hold cremated bone was dug through a pyre. In Hindu and Buddhist practice the collection of cremated remains from the pyre is as central to the ceremonies as the cremation itself. In later Bronze Age Ireland it was the formative process for the character of the deposits seen in cemeteries and elsewhere.[35]

Osteoarchaeologists gain insight into the practice of collection by thinking in terms of the four anatomical regions of the skeleton (skull, axial or torso, upper limbs and lower limbs). In a typical adult, the bones of the skull weigh some 18% of the total skeleton, the torso bones 23% and the limb bones 59%. In discussion of the burials on the N8 Cashel to Mitchelstown road scheme, with particular reference to Templenoe, Jonny Geber points out that certain bones, such as those from the torso, are fragile, soft and likely to fragment upon cremation; the easiest cremated bones to identify are the skull and teeth.[36] Bearing these factors in mind, the fact that the bones from the skull, and long bones—particularly of the lower body—are consistently present in later Bronze Age cremation deposits from across the island is striking. Commenting on the character of the deposits at the Killoran 10 cemetery, Laureen Buckley suggests the focus was on the collection of the skull and long bones, such as the femur, and that smaller bones may have been ignored. Related to the issue

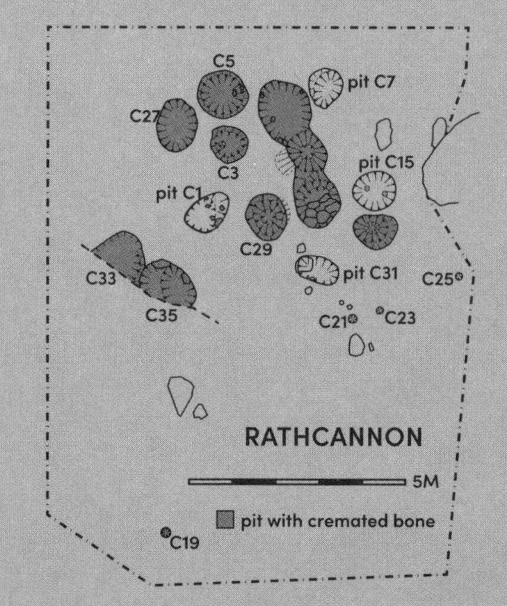

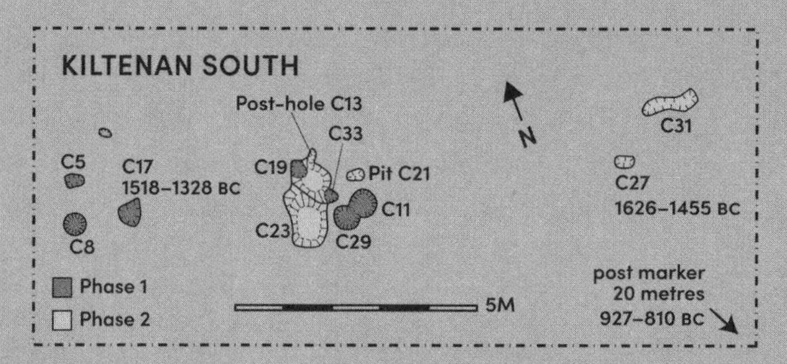

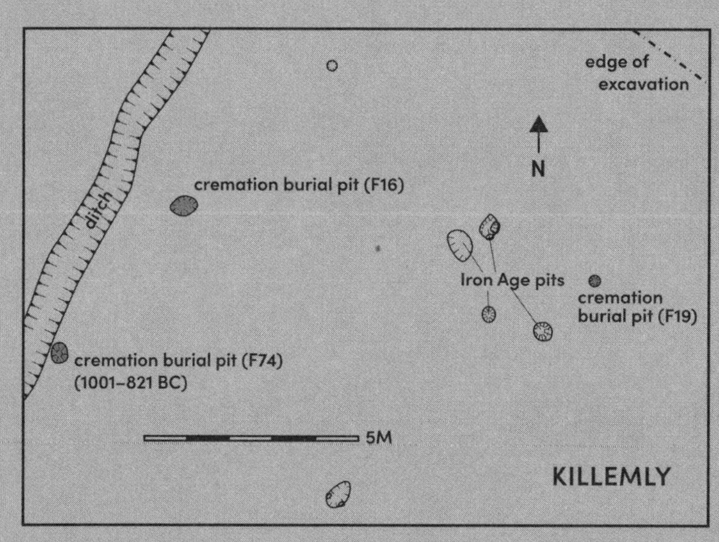

FIG. 6.4.

The Middle Bronze Age cemetery at Rathcannon, Co. Limerick; the Middle and Late Bronze Age cemetery at Kiltenan South, Co. Limerick; and the Late Bronze Age cemetery at Killemly, Co. Tipperary.

of fragmentation is the question of whether there may have been deliberate pounding and crushing of cremated bone. The process of cremation, collecting and placing cremated bone may itself result in fragmentation. However, deliberate pounding or crushing appears in some cases to have been part of the post-collection rites. At Killoran 10 the deposits were highly crushed; at Dalystown it appears that some of the bone was crushed before being deposited, in other cases it was not. At Mitchelstowndown, Co. Limerick, cremated bone was pulverised and used as a paste to line pits into which token deposits of cremated bone were placed. As a contrasting practice, the smoothed edges of cremated bone fractures found at Grey Abbey, Kildare indicate that cremated bone may have been curated and handled for a period after collection and before deposition.[37]

PLACEMENT IN THE GROUND

There is a surprising uniformity to the pits that were dug to hold deposits of cremated bone. They tend to be about 20–50cm in diameter, with a depth of less than 30cm. There are instances of single pits, which can also occur as outliers to clusters of pits. The latter, defined here as pit cemeteries, vary in size: the Late Bronze Age cemetery at Killemly, Co. Tipperary has three pits; the Middle Bronze Age cemeteries at Kiltenan South and Rathcannon, Co. Limerick respectively have eleven (in two phases) and ten pits (with definite cremation deposits); the already mentioned sites at Templenoe and Killoran are much larger [COMPARE FIG. 6.4 WITH FIG. 6.2]. Some cemeteries were in use over considerable periods of time, as at Ballybar Lower 1–3, Co. Carlow, and appear to be linked with contemporary settlement. This is borne out by the extensive distribution of single pits, suggesting close connections between the locales of the living and the dead. As noted above, there are indications that the location of some cemeteries or specific pits within a cemetery were marked by wooden or stone markers.[38]

PL. 6.E.

Middle Bronze Age cremation pits in the Ballaghcullia 3 pit cemetery, under excavation.

In the majority of cases, the bone placed in pits was a partial representation of the burnt human remains that would have been present at a pyre following cremation. [PL. 6.E] Of over 70 deposits on sites along the Gas Pipeline to the West route from Dublin to Limerick, only 12 weighed more than 100g, and most of those were less than 400g. Geber's analysis of the bone from the Templenoe cemetery indicates the complexity of reading and interpreting this kind of record [FIG. 6.2, AND SEE PL. 6.D]. This cemetery contained 74 pits, 57 of which contained cremated bone. In 31 cases this could be definitively identified as human. Other pits contained charcoal and related debris from pyres, but no cremated bone. Radiocarbon dating indicates that the site was in use from before 1800 BC to after 1400 BC. In the central area of the cemetery some earlier pits were cut by later ones. The quantity of bone within pits varied from 1–700g, with the mean being just 80g. That this was intentional is emphasised by the sealing of 12 pits with clay capping, a practice also seen in other cemeteries. A barbed and tanged arrowhead was placed with two of the deposits; two contained cremated animal bone; eight produced charred cereal grains, wild seeds and hazelnut shells. So how many people's remains were deposited? Looking at the cremated remains from 24 pits by age, 20 deposits represented young to middle-aged adults, mostly between 18 and 45 years old with one individual over 50; only 4 deposits represented non-adult remains. The total weight of cremated bone from the cemetery was 8,336g. This is equivalent to the full cremated remains of only three to seven people. Bearing in mind that a person's remains might have been deposited in a number of pits, the age and sex of the individuals that could be identified, and the representation of bone from the four anatomical regions, Geber suggests that the absolute minimum number of individuals is three: a non-adult, an adult female and an adult male! Although the site was in use for some centuries into the Middle Bronze Age, this minimum number could be consistent with one use of each of the possible pyre sites.[39]

In looking at Middle Bronze Age cemeteries in Britain, Edward Caswell and Benjamin Roberts demonstrate that only a minority of people were buried in such cemeteries; this is in total contrast to the view dominant since the 1970s that these were community cemeteries. They assume that each deposit in a pit represents an individual 'burial', thus reaching a minimum figure of over 3,000 individual burials that can be dated to the period.[40] Bearing Geber's approach in mind, if the cremated remains of the same person were fragmented across different pits, the minimum figure for individuals represented in British cemeteries—where over 70% of the deposits where weight is recorded are less than 500g—should probably be reduced. Clearly there is difficulty in establishing from the cremated remains just who and how many people were placed in such cemeteries. Applying the absolute minimum number approach, it could be argued that a very restricted number of people are actually represented by cremation deposits in Middle Bronze Age cemeteries.

By then, representation of individuals by the deposition of all or most of their cremated bones had become less important, but it did happen on occasion, and there is some evidence of an apparent concern that the remains of people are generally not commingled, but kept separate. The dominance of the practice of token deposition, however, supports the suggestion that depositional activity in these cemeteries was just one of the pathways along which the cremated (and unburnt) remains of the dead were taken by the living. The transformation that took place through cremation was important enough for charcoal and other material from the pyre to be treated and placed in pits as if it was, or contained, human bone. Buddhist and Hindu beliefs focus on the concept of cremation facilitating the freeing of the soul or the spirit to continue its journey, with the body returning to its elemental components. Given the range of contexts in which cremated bone was placed in later Bronze Age Ireland, it is tempting to suggest that cremated bone and other materials were fragmented to become a potent way of building a social body—a glue or paste to hold the living together. The focal points of that process were pyres, cemeteries and other places of deposition. To paraphrase Thomas Lynch's observation, cremation made human remains portable, divisible and easier to share among the living.[41]

Activity in pit cemeteries can extend over several hundred years, so the sequence of digging, placing bone and back-filling or sealing pits could have been repeated numerous times. Nevertheless, there are instances where we can see significant changes taking place over time. Dalystown [SEE FIG. 6.3] provides an example; it also represents a site that links the discussion with the consideration of barrows. Here a total of seventeen deposits were found, fifteen of them in pits. The deposits may represent separate individuals, but the total weight of bone is 1,370g, or less than the amount that would represent the complete cremated remains of one individual. Indeed, there was no robust osteological evidence for more than two individuals: an adult and a juvenile.

A number of phases of activity can be identified at Dalystown. The first consists of a possible pyre pit and two cremation pits. These were enclosed by a ditch, and material from the ditch was used to create a low barrow sealing these features. A cremation pit was then inserted into the barrow. The upper fill of the ditch contained cremated bone and charcoal dating to the Late Bronze Age. A number of pits to the east and north-east of the barrow formed two rough arcs and could have been dug and material placed in them at any time during the use of the cemetery. Five pits to the east of the barrow form a distinctive cluster: a central pit with four others carefully positioned around it. This contained a cremation deposit of over 500g, representing an adult whose de-fleshed bones had been cremated. The sides of the pit were fire-reddened and the deposit was sealed by pyre debris. Three of the surrounding pits contained one or two grams of cremated bone and were capped with clay, suggesting a deliberate juxtaposition with the main deposit. The fourth pit, north of the central one, contained almost 300g of the remains of a juvenile (older than 6years) and some worn pottery sherds. The body of the juvenile had not been fully cremated.

Lynch and O'Donnell argue that this pit cluster represents a single, focused ritual, featuring the remains of an adult and juvenile. The other deposit on the site that was identified as being the result of the cremation of de-fleshed bone was the 30g or so of the cremated bones of an adult placed in the pit inserted into the barrow. It is tempting to suggest that this is someone whose remains were fragmented at the site into two pits. Deposition of the cremated remains of this person—marked as being different or special in that cremation occurred a significant time after death—was carried out with ceremony. It may have marked the construction of the barrow, the act by which the cemetery became visible as a monument in the landscape.[42]

BARROWS AS GRAVES AND LANDSCAPE MONUMENTS

In a book on barrows in Britain, Ann Woodward titled two of the chapters 'barrows as graves' and 'barrows as landscape monuments'.[43] This seem apposite in an Irish context where, from the middle of the second millennium BC, there are two linked developments. First, a long-standing practice of defining and marking the graves of particular individuals by placing them within and under a ring-ditch or barrow became increasingly common. Second, over time people located such monuments in relation to others, leading to the development of what are called barrow cemeteries.

We can trace elements of these practices in the Neolithic.[44] Looking more immediately at the Early Bronze Age, one way in which the graves of selected individuals were marked was by covering them with a cairn or mound. In this, monumentality worked at two levels. In the case of cemeteries that have surface definition as mounds or cairns, the monument represents the cemetery, which may have been focused on a central grave. Within other cemeteries, specific graves were monumentalised; the central cist at Keenoge with its covering cairn of stones is an example [SEE FIG. 5.14]. At Corrower, Co. Mayo—a small cemetery mound containing nine graves—two of the burials containing the cremated remains of single adults were covered with small cairns of stone. What happens over the course of the first half of the second millennium BC is that this concept of marking specific graves as monuments becomes a more important element of the funerary rite.[45]

The ring-ditch/barrow concept would have been familiar to people in Ireland as a tradition that was remembered from earlier times and as one that was popular from the Early Bronze Age in areas of Britain linked to Ireland through exchange networks. An immediate Early Bronze Age background may have been provided by a focus on the containment and definition of cremated individuals. In discussing the wider cultural context of the Early Bronze Age burial at Newrath, Co. Kilkenny, where a cist containing the cremation of an adult in a Vase Urn was located at the centre of a small ring-ditch, James Eogan drew attention to a number of other instances where ring-ditches are associated with burials and pottery of the Vase Tradition. In this shift to a greater focus on the containment and marking of the grave of particular individuals, a round barrow became widely used.[46]

Memorialisation of short-term, individual lives provided the basis for longer term histories and traditions, as can be seen at the Kilmahuddrick, Co. Dublin barrow [FIG. 6.5, SEE PL. 1.E]. When excavated, this site appeared as a ring-ditch, over 12m in diameter, but it had been a barrow, and there may have been an outer bank. The ditch was up to 2.5m wide and up to 1.7m deep, narrowing to the base. Limestone blocks exposed by digging the ditch were left *in situ.* Shortly afterwards, stones were placed in the base; among these were what appeared to be a small cist-like structure, but with no evidence of human bone. Fires lit on some of the stones provided a date of between 2398 BC and 2047 BC. The basal silt was dated from between 1208 BC to 935 BC; the lower part of the ditch silted up naturally. At the centre of the enclosed area, the earliest dated feature was a pit containing a heavily crushed cremated bone deposit (200g) of an adult and possibly a juvenile, with a pottery sherd and glass bead. The bone was dated between 992 BC to 822 BC. This deposit was covered and sealed. In turn, the sealing was cut by two features, filled with clay and inclusions of cremated bone. The western feature was filled with two deposits of human cremated bone. The lower represented the remains (700g) of one person, dated to between 1012 BC to 819 BC. The upper was dominated by cremated human skull bone. It is possible that both these deposits represent the same person. The fill of the north-eastern feature contained moderate inclusions of cremated bone.

The back of an unburnt, weathered adult cranium, dated to between 911 BC and 802 BC, was placed on the silted-up surface of the western part of the ditch. Some time after this the ditch was deliberately filled with heat-shattered stone, charcoal and fragments of

FIG. 6.5.

The sequence of activity at the Kilmahuddrick, Co. Dublin ring barrow.

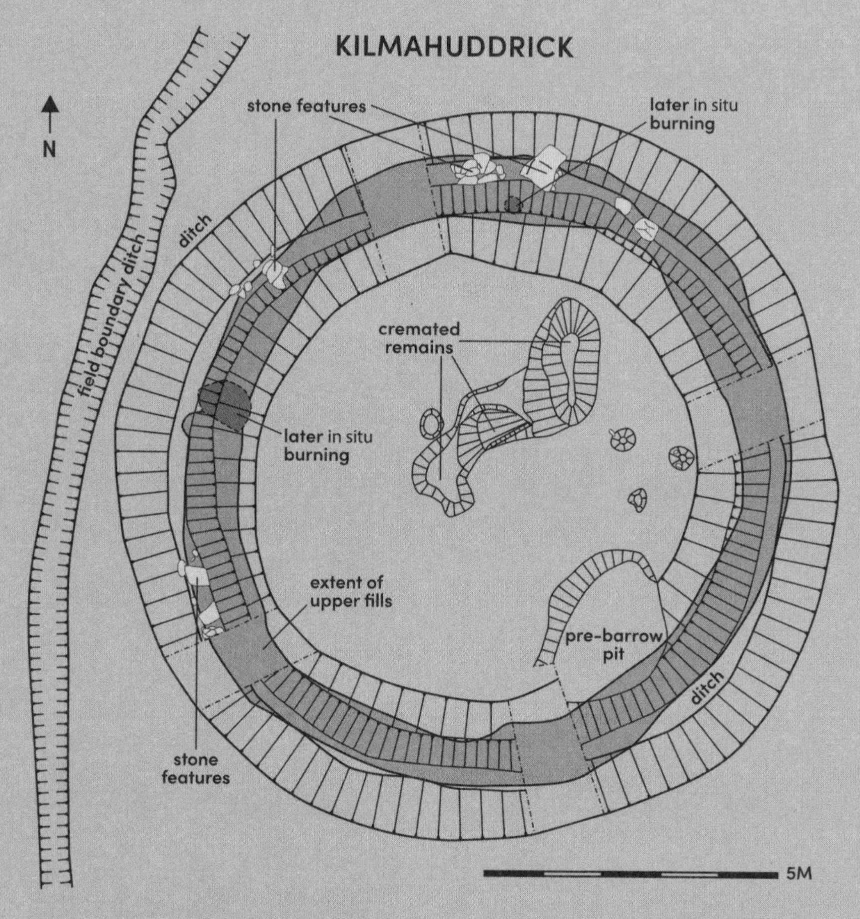

PHASE	SUMMARY	PERIOD
I	Pre-barrow pit.	Early Bronze Age
II	Cutting of ditch. Activity centring on stone features at base of ditch. Initial accumulation of basal silt.	
III	Filling of ditch. Deposition of cremated remains.	Later Bronze Age
IV	Activity related to upper fills of ditch and in situ burning.	Developed Iron Age
V	Cutting of field boundary ditch.	Early Medieval

burnt and unburnt human and animal bone. A sample of the human bone dated from between 373 BC to 111 BC. Around the same time, two spreads of burnt and unburnt bone, both animal and human, were placed outside the ring-ditch. One spread, which also contained a burnt amber bead, was dated to between 393 BC to 192 BC.[47]

What can we make of this complex sequence of activity? There are at least two distinct series of events: from around 1000 BC to 800 BC in the Late Bronze Age, and between 400 BC and 100 BC in the Middle or Developed Iron Age. The earlier dates for activity at the base of the ditch indicate the possibility of a third, earlier phase related to the construction of the monument. The dates after 1000 BC come from the central cremations and the deposition of the cranium in the ditch, placed there sometime after the death of the person and in the longer term after episodes of silting in the ditch and the build-up of a metre of deposit. The deposition of corporal remains of individuals within the barrow and ditch would have given new layers of meaning to the place.[48]

These links and resonances are strongly brought out in the latest activity on the site, dating to the Iron Age. The human and animal bone in the highest level of the ditch fill and in the features to the west of the barrow suggest that the placement of bone was a key element in marking the end of the active presence and use of the barrow in the last centuries BC. There are complex webs of meaning and symbolic action here. Local histories were actively created through this focus on the barrow. As Brück puts it, the construction of barrows and the placement of deposits within them mapped out links or divisions between individuals and broader social groups.[49] Specific individuals were represented in some deposits, but the token and mixed nature of others indicates that human bone was used actively, signalling the continuing engagement of the living with the dead. Given the time intervals and inter-generational gaps between events at Kilmahuddrick, there would have been considerable possibilities for actively deploying the past as an authoritative backdrop for the present.

FOLLOWING LINES, TRACING HISTORIES: BELOW THE SURFACE

PL. 6.F.

LiDAR image of the Hill of Tara, with the barrows showing as both high and low relief features.

Just as the history of specific sites is varied, so is the pattern of spatial distribution of barrows. Isolated, individual barrows occur—as at Kilmahuddrick—but the clustering of barrows into barrow cemeteries is a key development. It was suggested above that the sequence of activity at sites presents a narrative of different local histories. In a complementary manner, can the arrangement of barrows within cemeteries provide information about histories and links between people and groups? Can we see historical identities in these spatial patterns? This point has been made cogently in relation to barrow cemeteries in southern Britain. Woodward pointed out that a number of distinct arrangements can be identified there, including small, nucleated, linear, dispersed and row cemeteries. She suggested that key features are distinct clusters or groupings within cemeteries. The placement of barrows in relation to others appears to demonstrate a concern with the past and the creation of a landscape mnemonic pattern. Monuments could be placed and then recounted as genealogical histories, marking the relationship of descent lines back to a time when mythic lineages were created.[50]

In Ireland there are distinct groups or clusters of barrows. Barrow cemeteries such as those on the Hill of Tara and at Rathcroghan, Co. Roscommon are well known. [PL. 6.F] Large cemeteries of barrows occur in North Munster, for example in Limerick, alongside smaller groups, and there are regional parallels to these Limerick concentrations in Sligo and Roscommon. Richard Bradley has noted an important contrast between the curtailment of barrow-building in southern Britain by 1200 BC and the long continuity of this tradition in Ireland.[51] It is useful here to explore the potential of barrow cemeteries, looking at the evidence from excavations and then the development of cemeteries as monumental complexes.

Derrycraw and Ballintaggart, Co. Down are barrow cemeteries several kilometres apart that were excavated in advance of road

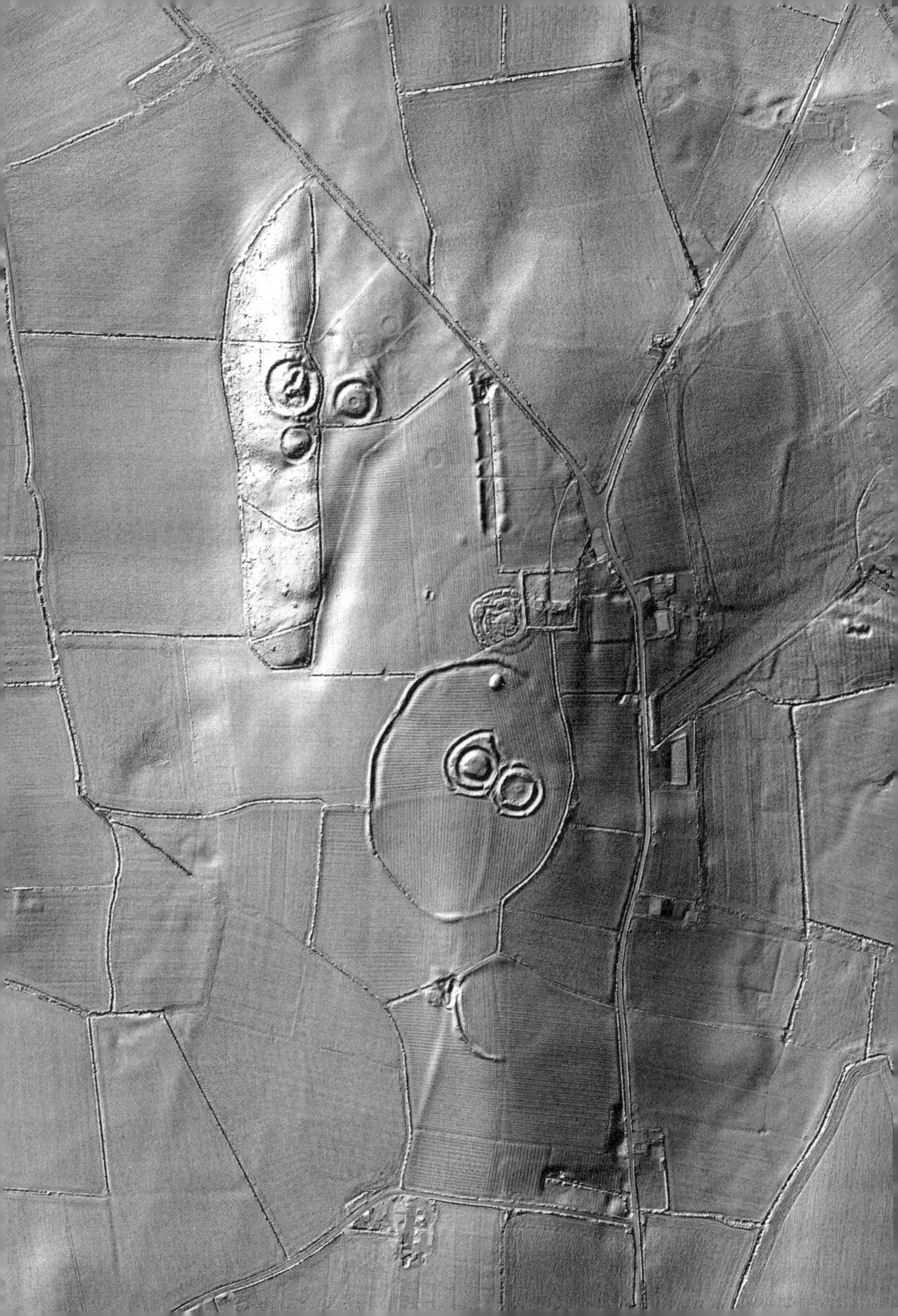

improvements.[52] Both are deliberately located, in dry, slightly elevated areas of inter-drumlin valleys, with wetland prominent in the immediate vicinity and north–south running drumlins forming the skyline. The sites were truncated, hence monuments constructed as low barrows were excavated as ring-ditches. At Derrycraw [FIG. 6.6], against a background of earlier activity, the cemetery may have been in use from before 1600 BC to 1100 BC. An urn burial at the southern end of the cemetery was the earliest mortuary feature, followed by placement of cremation deposits in pits in the cairn, including one in a basket, and then deposits in two of the ring-ditches (3 and 5) close to the cairn. The urn burial was in an upright undecorated Vase Urn, capped with a stone and placed on a shelf in a deeper post-hole, suggesting that the burial had been marked by a post. Almost 1,200g of the cremated bones of a young to middle-aged adult male were contained in the pot. This represents a substantial deposit; in effect a burial, reflecting an Early/Middle Bronze Age transitional phase and contrasting with the token character of the other deposits, each representing an individual, in the cemetery. The most striking deposit in the cairn was the cremated bone of a 13–17-year-old adolescent (270g) in an alder basket placed in a pit. The basket was straight-sided, about 35cm wide and 30cm deep. Two strands of curved wicker may be the remains of handles. The basket, dated to 1628 BC to 1305 BC, was carbonized *in situ*, suggesting that the bones were still hot when placed in it.[53]

Two ring-ditches (1 and 2) are located south of the cairn, and there was little evidence for their use for cremation deposits, which may not have survived. It does appear, however, that ring-ditch 2 was deliberately located in relation to the earlier urn burial. A slot had been dug in the base of the ditch, which may have been designed to hold a wooden palisade; this would have defined the interior, which suggests that it may have been an arena for activity related to the treatment of the dead.[54]

The long-term importance of the locale of the cemetery at Ballintaggart is clear [FIG. 6.7; PL. 6.A]. There were three Early Neolithic

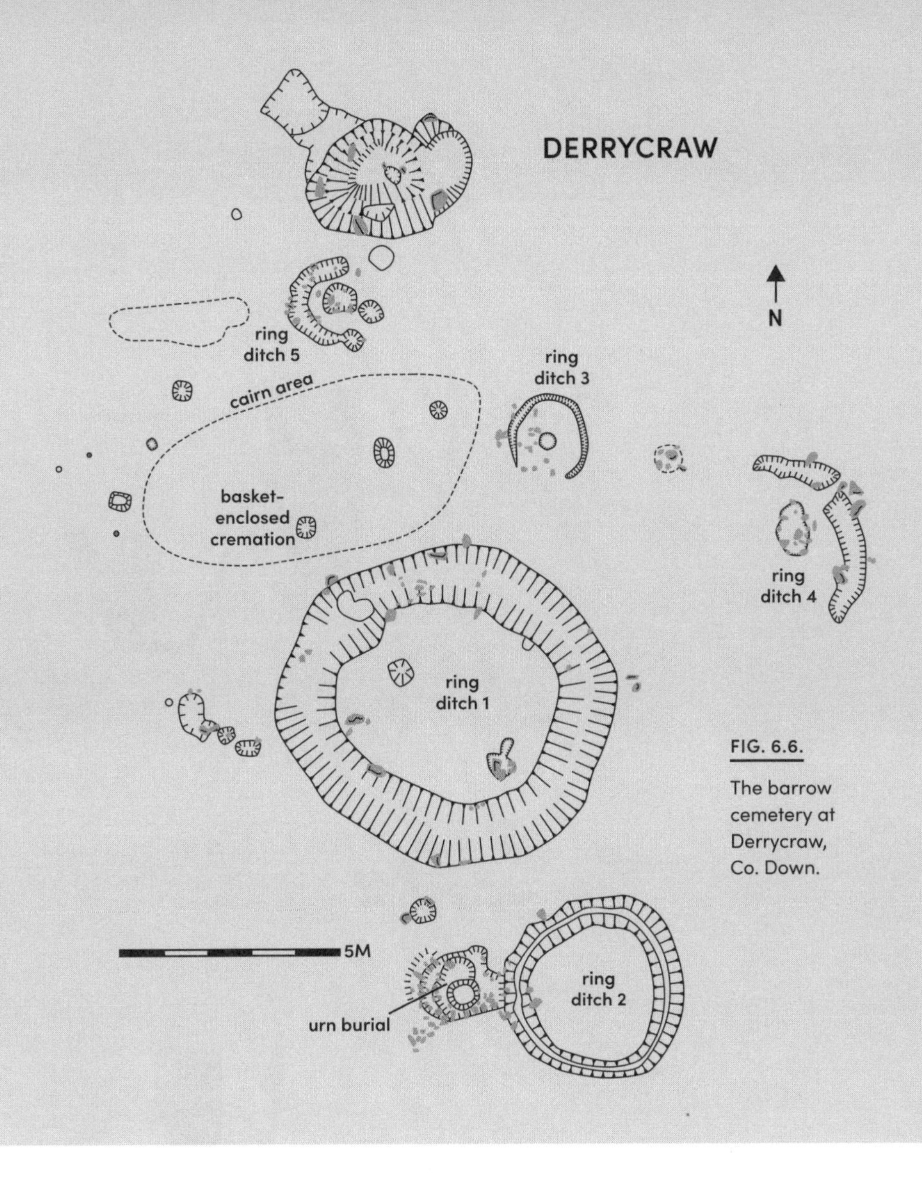

FIG. 6.6.

The barrow cemetery at Derrycraw, Co. Down.

houses to the north-west, with later Neolithic and Early Bronze Age activity to the south-west and north-east.[55] The layout and potential alignments of ring-ditches and other features in the wider landscape are outlined at the start of the chapter as the background to the fictional scenario describing one funerary event at the cemetery. Radiocarbon chronology suggests that the duration of the cemetery

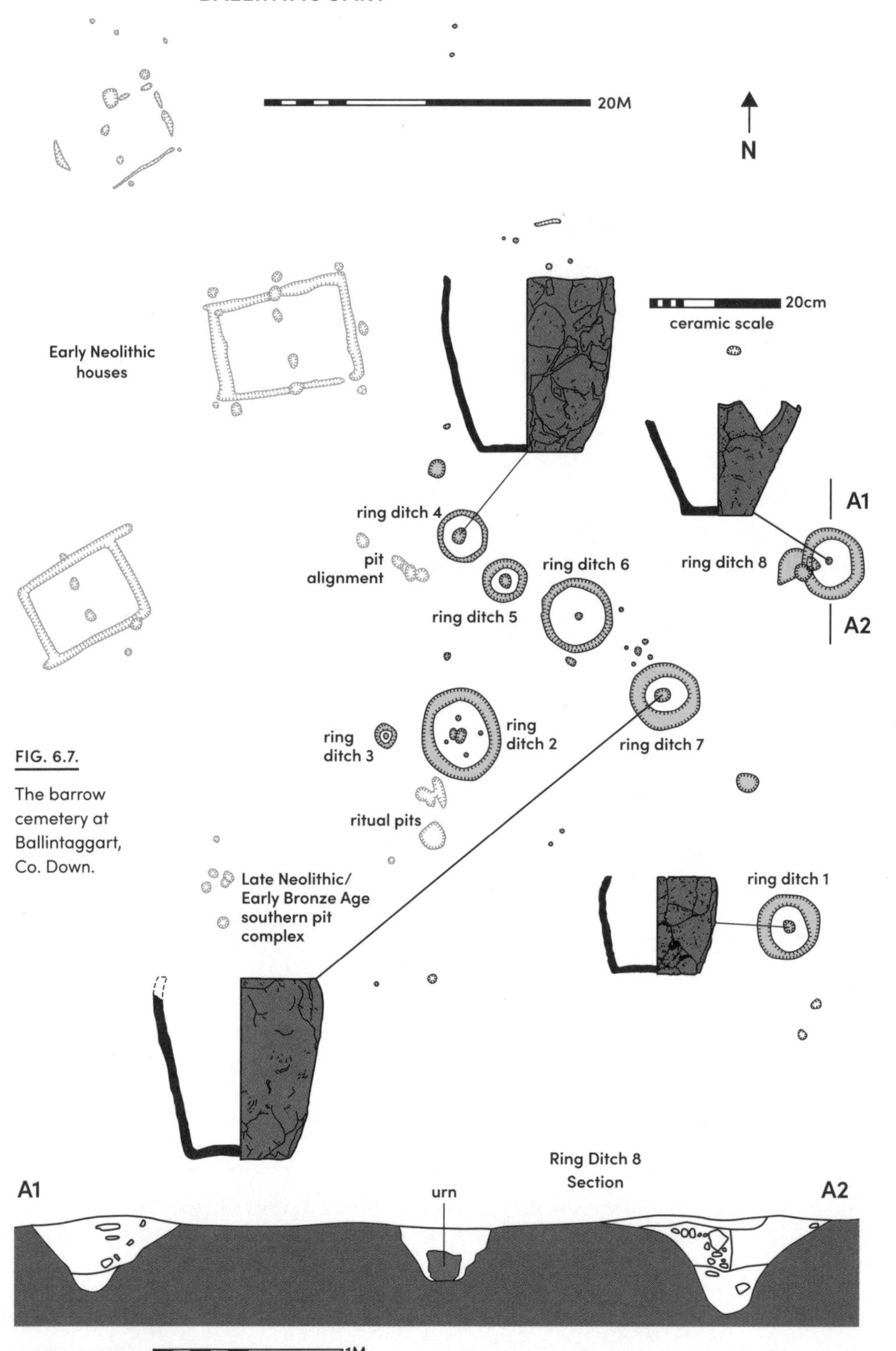

FIG. 6.7.

The barrow cemetery at Ballintaggart, Co. Down.

was from around 1630 BC to 670 BC, with a particular focus of activity between 1300 BC and 800 BC. Ring-ditch 3, situated on the highest location within the cemetery, appears to be significantly earlier than the others; a token cremation deposit (123g, representing a child/adolescent aged 10–15 years, with weathered fragments of a cremated adult cranium and femur) in the pit at the centre was dated between 1628 BC to 1323 BC. The adult bones may have been curated, with a significant gap in time between the adult's cremation and placement of their bone fragments in this deposit. Complex patterns of deposition continue throughout the long use of the cemetery. All the ring-ditches had a central pit with cremation deposits. In some cases these were token deposits, involving an initial deposit followed by a second one; in other cases, the cremated bones represent the burial of an individual within a pot.[56]

We can follow these patterns along one of the major alignment lines within the cemetery, running north-east from ring-ditch 3. There were two episodes of deposition at ring-ditch 2. In the first, 539g of the cremated bones of a middle-aged or older male dating to between 1373 BC and 932 BC were placed with a sherd of pottery in an elongated cist covered with a capstone. Four posts may have formed a free-standing structure around the cist. At some point this was enclosed by a ring-ditch and covered by a barrow. Subsequently, the capstone was removed and placed in the ditch, the central pit was enlarged, and, between 1109 BC and 820 BC, a second cremation deposit (420g) of another middle-aged or older male was placed over the first one. Given the weathered appearance of these bones, it is possible that some time had elapsed between cremation of the individual and the placement of their remains. About 12m north-east of this ring-ditch there was another four-post structure marking a central pit. This had been left as a free-standing structure, with ring-ditches (6 and 7) located to the north-west and south-east. In this pit there were two distinct placements of token deposits of the cremated remains of two young or middle-aged adults; first a female, then a spread of pyre debris, and on top of this a deposit of a male. Twelve metres further north-east, at the eastern edge and lowest part of the cemetery area, there was a deep post-hole and a ramp for a marker post. The marker post can be compared to the one marking the earliest burial at the southern end of the Derrycraw cemetery. There was a burial pit about a metre to the north-east. The post may have marked this burial (8), or, when the decision was made to enclose this pit within a ring-ditch, the post was (or had already been) removed and the post-hole backfilled. The western side of the ring-ditch was dug through this backfill. The burial deposit in the pit confounds perceptions of the dominance of token deposits in the later Bronze Age. It consists of the entire cremated remains, over 1,600g, of a young adult female, dated from between 1190 BC to 927 BC. These had been carefully collected and placed in the truncated base of an urn. The splayed sides of the urn, harking back to the Vase Tradition of the Early Bronze Age, look decidedly antique. Is it possible that this is an antique or heirloom deliberately used to provide an additional veneer or skin of age and authority to the remains of this woman?[57]

What is striking is that there are three other instances of this practice of 'burial' as opposed to token deposition. These burials are each contained with an upright bucket- or barrel-shaped coarse pot, and in the two cases where sex can be identified they are also young or middle-aged females. The location of these burials within the cemetery is interesting; they are on the north-west to south-east axis of the cemetery, in ring-ditch 4 (young adult) at the northern end, ring-ditch 7 at the southern end of the tight group of four barrows, and ring-ditch 1 (young adult female) at the southern end of the cemetery. The character of the burial deposit within ring-ditch 7 also stands out, as it consists of the cremated remains of a young to middle-aged female, a child of between 3 and 6 years old, and a bone fragment from a newborn baby, placed together in the pot. The close similarity of the surface condition of all the cremated bone indicates that these people were cremated together in a single event on a pyre at very low temperature.[58]

Recognising that we are dealing with the post-mortem treatment of selected people, it is hard not to feel a sense of poignancy and be reminded of the grief that such deaths may have brought to the kin of this woman. Considering the dates over the Middle and Late Bronze Age when the cremated remains of these individuals were placed in the ground and their locations within the cemetery, there may be a repeated inter-generational pattern. There is also a deliberate contrast with the contemporary practice of token deposition; differences in burial practice were actively maintained. These burials look like acts of direct remembrance of particular women. Over time they became part of the process by which the memory and standing of past generations could be referred to and drawn on. This is complemented by other approaches to manifesting such wider social references. For example, there is the re-use of pits for deposition, and in some cases bones appear to have been in circulation for a period before being deposited. The cemetery was tied into the wider landscape through the alignments of ring-ditches and other features.[59]

FOLLOWING LINES, TRACING HISTORIES: MONUMENTAL NARRATIVES

Evidence from excavation provides us with detail of the development of individual barrow cemeteries. Consideration of barrows as monuments provides a complementary, broader perspective. Conor Newman provided a useful overview of barrows in the context of the interpretation of the barrow cemetery at Tara. He recognised five basic forms of barrow [FIG. 6.8]: ring-ditches, embanked ring-ditches, ring-barrows, bowl-barrows with outer bank, and bowl-barrows. Newman used trends in dating these types to broadly assign them to different periods. Combining this approach with consideration of the spatial arrangement of barrows provided a framework for considering the development of the Tara cemetery, and a guideline for interpreting the spatial and chronological patterning in other barrow cemeteries [FIG. 6.9, AND SEE PL. 6.F].[60]

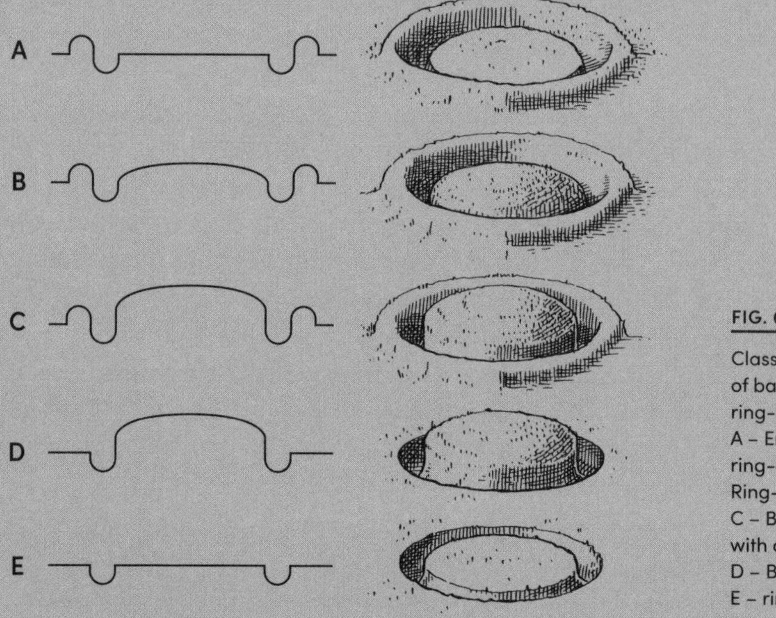

FIG. 6.8.

Classification of barrows and ring-ditches. A – Embanked ring-ditch, B – Ring-barrow, C – Bowl-barrow with outer bank, D – Bowl-barrow, E – ring-ditch.

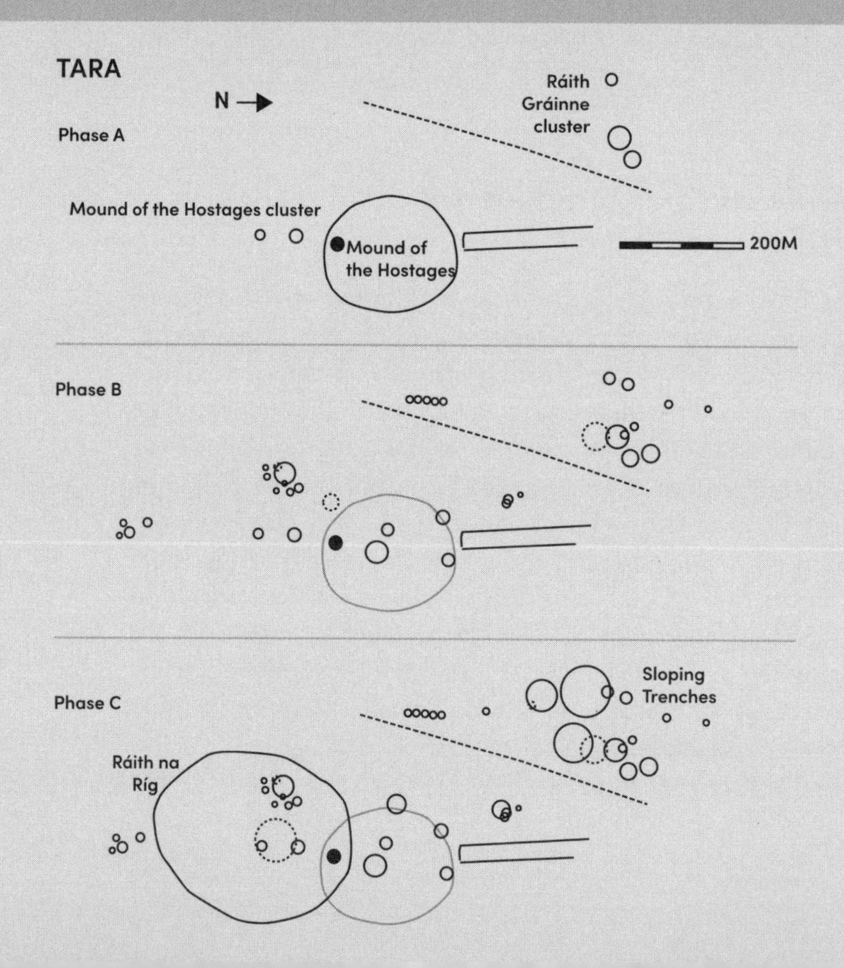

FIG. 6.9.

Hypothetical development of the Hill of Tara, Co. Meath barrow complex in the Bronze Age and into the Iron Age, with two possible clusters indicated.

Neolithic activity at Tara included the construction of the passage tomb known as the Mound of the Hostages. The Mound of the Hostages and the area around it appear to have been a focus of activity in the later Neolithic and into the Bronze Age. A formal entranceway into this area may have been provided by the cursus-like feature known as the Banqueting Hall, although this structure could date as late as the early medieval period. Geophysical survey has demonstrated the presence of a large circular monument—the Ditched Pit Circle—composed of a ditch with posts on either side that respects the southern end of the Banqueting Hall and encloses the Mound of the Hostages. It is in this landscape setting, and thanks to ongoing research, that the broad development of the barrow cemetery can be traced.[61] As we have seen, the Mound of the Hostages was re-used as a cemetery mound in the Early Bronze Age. Against this background it is perhaps not surprising that one of the two small groups of what are postulated to be earliest barrows (phase A) is located to the south of the Mound of the Hostages. The second early group is an east–west line to the west of the north end of the Banqueting Hall, separated from it by a small, dry valley. Over the next millennium, these two clusters—referred to for ease of reference as the Mound of the Hostages cluster and the Ráith Gráinne cluster (after the most prominent barrow in this group)—become larger and more diverse (phase B). In the first century BC the construction of the large enclosure of Ráith na Ríg emphasised the central monuments in the Mound of the Hostages cluster. The Ráith Gráinne cluster was continuing to expand (phase C). In the first millennium AD, some of the barrows were incorporated into the earthworks that were constructed inside and to the north and south of Ráith na Ríg.

The concentrations indicate decisions to place monuments, and the remains and memory of the individuals represented within them, close to and in relation to older and earlier monuments. Barrows were often placed so that they were contiguous with, and overlapped, the central mound of an older barrow incorporated into the bank of a later one. In these cases, the mound of the earlier barrow is kept visible and extends beyond the line of the later barrow. Priority appears to have been placed on preserving and maintaining the central area of earlier barrows. Was this to reference the memory of the individuals represented in them? The most deliberate version of this is seen at Ráith Gráinne itself, where a smaller barrow was placed over the centre of an earlier, larger one. The evidence from excavation of barrows elsewhere suggests that this was a recurrent practice in the Late Bronze Age.[62] Hence, just as people placed deposits or burials under or in individual barrows close to existing foci of activity, so in barrow cemeteries barrows were built close to or to incorporate earlier ones. As barrow cemeteries developed, kin lineage or lineages may have been referenced in the spatial patterns. Episodes of digging pits, placing human bone (often only a token of the cremated remains of the person), digging ditches and placing circular mounds over cremation pits as barrows were remodelled and additions were made to a cluster of barrows, served to reinforce social links.[63]

The barrow complex at Tara provides an understanding of why this became such a pre-eminent sacred place by the end of prehistory. Barrows were located on what was already a sacred hill. A key change in funerary rites and the social role of Tara as a Bronze Age cemetery occurred with the move away from the Mound of the Hostages cemetery mound to the construction of individual barrows. Within the two major clusters of barrows, denser concentrations of barrows occur. A distinctive dip in the ground surface west of Ráith Gráinne provides a clear topographical divide between two such concentrations. To the west of this dip are the Sloping Trenches, which, as the name indicates, involved barrow construction on the steep west-facing slope of the hill, with a line of smaller barrows strung out along the ridge top. Does the elaboration of the cemetery in these clusters reflect tensions, as well as links, between lineages? It certainly seems plausible to think about links between the location of these clusters and the territories of the living. For example, the Sloping Trenches are visible at distance only from the land to the west of Tara. It may well be that the barrow cluster around the Mound of the Hostages hints that this location always had a pre-eminent social position. This would have been reinforced by the enclosure of the central part of the cluster within Ráith na Ríg in the first century BC.[64]

At Slieve Breagh, Co. Meath, the barrow cemetery is on a prominent ridge, with distant views, particularly to the north and south, in an area notable from other barrow cemeteries in similar positions on nearby east-west hills.[65] [FIG. 6.10] The most prominent barrow is a bowl-barrow placed on the highest point of the ridge. The cemetery, dominated by large and small ring-barrows, extends to the east and more extensively to the west of this prominent mound, in two distinct clusters, concentrated in areas of relatively flat ground. Small ring-barrows are located with reference to, and are later than, the large ring-barrows. These large ring-barrows are on the ridgeline and emphasise the linearity of the cemetery. The cemetery became more nucleated with the placement of the small ring-barrows, emphasising the two clusters. Does this arrangement reflect distinct but related lineages? Perhaps as at Tara, the oldest barrow—in this case the bowl-barrow on the highest point of the ridge—represents the foundation of the cemetery?[66]

Tara and Slieve Breagh are examples of hill- or ridge-top cemeteries, a widespread locational pattern for barrow cemeteries. Hilltops were places close to the sky, in contact with the world of the spirits; thus, significant locations for the placement of barrow cemeteries and the formation of ancestral figures. This pattern is complemented by cemeteries in lower-lying, sometimes seasonally wet locations, as at Ballintaggart and Derrycraw. This is particularly the case in North Munster. Eoin Grogan's analysis has shown that there, the barrows tend to be placed on low platforms—or more extensive ridges—along the lower slopes and floors of river valleys, such as the Morningstar River, Co. Limerick. These locations were higher than the surrounding terrain. That effect would have been even more dramatic at times of wet weather and flooding. Spatial analysis suggests that the cemeteries developed around primary sites

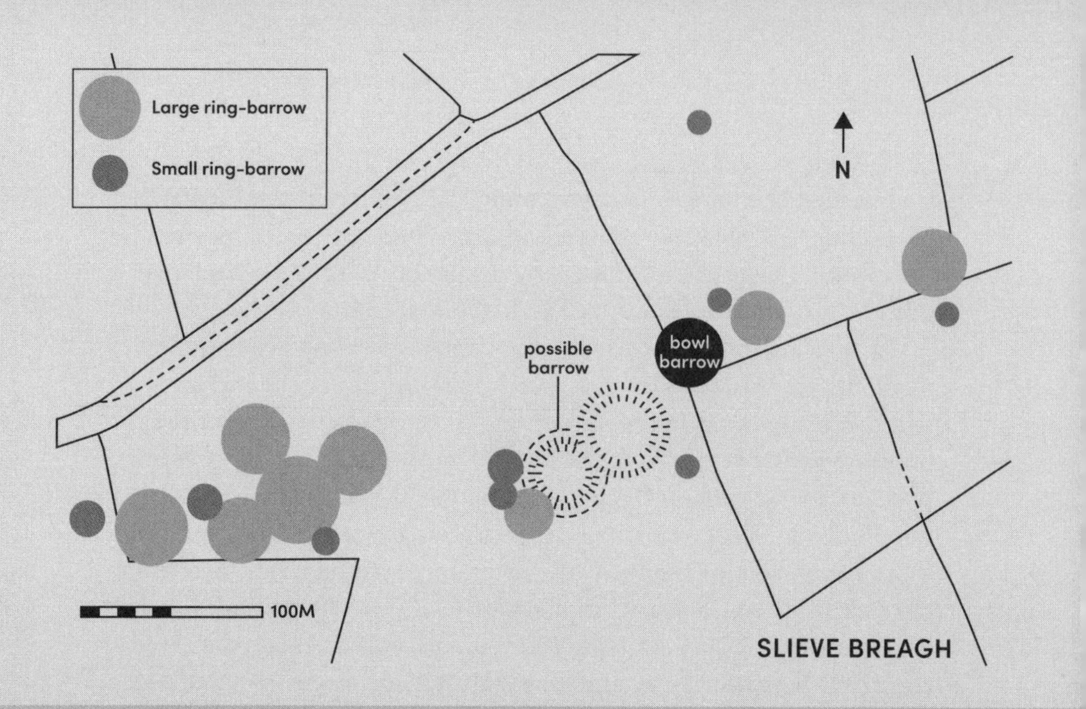

FIG. 6.10. (Above)

The barrow cemetery at Slieve Breagh, Co. Meath.

FIG. 6.11.

The barrow cemetery at Carrowjames, Co. Mayo.

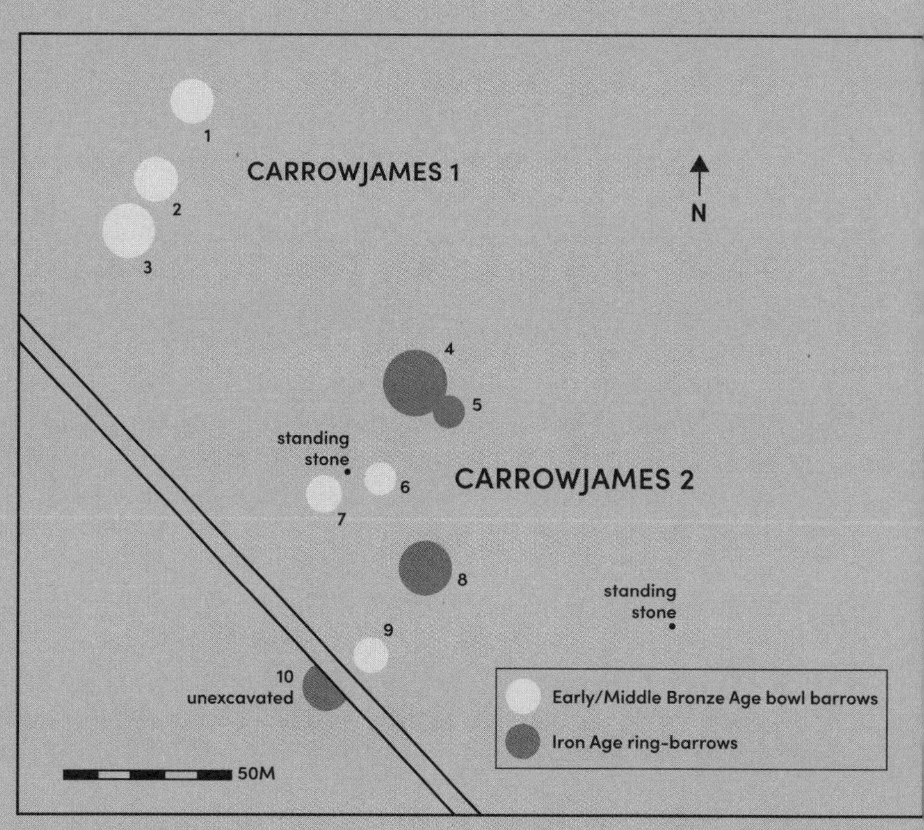

and in the form of distinct clusters, perhaps representing kin groups. The land occupied by such groups, and competition between them, might have been expressed in the location of barrow clusters or cemeteries on opposing sides of streams and rivers.[67]

The cemetery at Carrowjames, Co. Mayo [FIG. 6.11] provides us with the opportunity to explore the development of a low-lying cemetery and to combine monumental and excavation analysis.[68] The barrows were placed on slight, natural rises. Three bowl-barrows (Carrowjames I) were located 90m to the north-west of another group of ring-barrows and bowl-barrows and a couple of associated standing stones. The Carrowjames I barrows (1–3) were of similar construction and size (about 15m in diameter). Each of them had centrally placed burials in pits with other deposits and scatters of cremated bone. In two of the three mounds (2 and 3) the cremated bones of an adult, accompanied by a razor, were contained beneath an inverted Cordoned Urn. In the northernmost mound (1), the cremated bones of an adult and child, accompanied by a razor, were placed in the centrally dug pit and covered by a limestone slab. On the basis of the general dating of Cordoned Urns and razors, these barrows would have been constructed in the period between 1700 BC to 1500 BC. This could have happened over a relatively short period of time, representing the mortuary practice of a particular generation. Alternatively, the linear arrangement may represent the remembrance of individuals and the creation of a sense of kinship within a distinct mortuary tradition through the placement of human remains over a couple of hundred years.

At Carrowjames II to the south-east, the earliest barrows are likely to be the bowl-barrows (6, 7 and 9), about 8m in diameter, all with a central pit. While these sites are difficult to date, they do seem to fit with the dominant pattern that was typical of mortuary activity from around 1600 BC onwards—token deposition of cremated bone and lack of material placed with the dead. To the north and east are ring-barrows (4, 5 and 8, with 10 to the south). Sites 4 and 8 are significantly larger than the others, at over 20m in diameter. Site 8 was of Iron Age date, probably dating to the last few centuries BC. The 25 burial deposits in the interior of Site 8 were clustered around the central area. All were in pits, and in nine cases there were associated artefacts.[69]

Over time at Carrowjames, the eastern cluster became the focus of activity, with Site 8 being late in the development of the cemetery. Site 8 is a cemetery barrow; this is different from the concept of the barrow being the visible marker and reflection of the burial or deposition of the remains of a very small number of specific individuals—which was a dominant theme in the emergence of the barrow tradition. The sequence at Carrowjames is also a reminder that here, and in many other sites over the period 1600 BC to the last few centuries BC, there is a dominant pattern of the token representation of the cremated bones of a person. More exceptionally, most or all the cremated remains of a person were placed in a pit, sometimes contained in a pot. In other cases, it was seen as appropriate to scatter bones on the ground, rather than place them in a pit. Some carefully excavated ring-ditches have revealed no surviving evidence of a central cremation pit, hinting that the focus was on the construction of the monument and the use of the interior. This variety of practices, and the occurrence of human bone much more widely across the landscape, indicates that the post-mortem treatment of human remains facilitated the expression of complex ideas about people and society.

LANDSCAPES OF THE LIVING AND THE DEAD

From the middle of the second millennium BC for a period lasting into the first millennium AD the use of barrows and the development of barrow cemeteries conveyed ideas of memory, memorialisation, renewal and lineage. In some cemeteries a point of origin for the remembrance of particular individual(s) was created through the construction of a prominent barrow. In others, links were established with existing ancestral traditions, as at the Mound of the Hostages,

Tara. As memory of individuals whose remains were placed in barrows faded, ongoing or renewed reference was made to their social importance through the positioning of later barrows. While of longer duration in Ireland, these patterns can also be identified during the Bronze Age elsewhere, such as southern Britain and the southern Netherlands. Paul Garwood, discussing the former, observed that the material and symbolic expression of social links may have facilitated the expression of claims of ancestry that were more fictive than real. In relation to the latter, David Fontijn emphasised how links were established by tradition and tended to by repetition of performances. Kinship relations were re-worked to provide for acknowledgement and inclusion of changing foci of position among the living.[70]

This potential to re-work the past through the actions of the living was facilitated by a focus on the cremation process, including the location and construction of pyres, the cremation itself, the collection and dispersal of cremated bone and pyre material, and the linked acts of formal deposition and related ceremonies, including the construction of barrows. These aspects of the funerary process would have been public, social occasions. The remains of individuals placed in pit and barrow cemeteries were socially selected. In some instances, after cremation people collected all or most of the remains of a person for burial; in most cases, however, there is only a 'token' representation of bone and other material from the pyre in cremation pits. Hence, processes of collection and deposition have to be considered in the context of active choices made by the living in a ceremonial setting. Why were small amounts of bone so frequently placed in what we can too easily and readily refer to as 'graves'? Why was there also the more unusual placement of the entire cremated remains of a person in a pit, sometimes in a pot, as at the Ballintaggart barrow cemetery? What of the token deposits of cremated bone, and unburnt bone, placed in a wide range of other contexts across the landscape? Why were human bones, particularly crania, sometimes kept in circulation long after a person's death or cremation? These issues prompt the wider question of the relationship between mortuary practices and other aspects of the archaeological record. Can we use the later prehistoric mortuary record to inform our understanding of this key period?[71]

Major development-led archaeological projects have dramatically transformed our understanding of later Bronze Age settlement and domestic landscapes, allowing the identification and facilitating the discussion of core areas or micro-landscapes.[72] This provides the basis for more balanced and nuanced interpretations, compared with the traditional archaeological focus on the evidence for non-mortuary ceremony and ritual; notably the production, circulation and deposition of large amounts of metalwork—both as single objects and in hoards—in wetland contexts.[73] Against this background, the significance of the mortuary record has been recognised, but tends to be regarded as puzzling. While other aspects of the evidence have been read as indicating increased social complexity, this is much less evident in the treatment of the dead. Few objects are placed with deposits of cremated bone; those whose remains are placed in cemeteries, or elsewhere, are all treated in similar ways. Where pottery is included, there is no distinction between it and the pottery found on settlement sites. The dead appear to be undistinguished rather than distinguished.[74]

Hence we underplay the significance of the later Bronze Age burial record, particularly when it is compared with the richness and diversity of mortuary practice in the Early Bronze Age. In that period as we have seen, the treatment of the dead appeared to be central to society. The subsequent perceived simplicity is seen to need explanation, through comparison and contrast with other aspects of the material record, focused on the living.[75] Indeed, it could be suggested that the recent discovery of the significance and extent of domestic landscapes, alongside a continuing awareness of the importance of metalwork and the recognition of hillforts as a key component of later Bronze Age landscapes, has heightened this tendency to focus on the living.[76]

Against this background it is worth emphasising key observations central to understanding later Bronze Age mortuary practice. First, it was complex and diverse, as has been discussed above with reference to specific case studies. Second, human bone deposits are not only found in cemeteries, but are fragmented across key places and in a wide range of contexts in the contemporary cultural landscape [SEE FIG. 6.1]. Third, human identity has to be seen as being defined by relationships: to other people, to animals, things and places. With this in mind, it is worth remembering Tim Ingold's point that relationships always have a genealogical aspect; people's sense of who they are is defined with reference to the past, to kin histories—real and mythic. These perspectives provide us with ways of appreciating the key role of the treatment of the visible dead in society, and the complex and subtle interweaving of ideas, things and places that people drew on in incorporating the dead and the past into the affairs of the living.[77]

This interweaving can be seen in the widespread distribution of cremation pits. These occur in clusters as cemeteries—sometimes associated with ring-ditches or barrows, or as single pits, apparently isolated but at least in some cases associated with settlement activity. The frequency and density of these features indicates that we need to re-evaluate our ideas about the place and role of the dead in later prehistoric Ireland. Landscape-based research like that in North Munster or in east County Cork, where concentrations or micro-regions of activity can be recognised, as in the Crusheen area of east Clare, demonstrates that cemeteries were most frequently located in organised landscapes. They were close to special-function sites such as burnt mounds or *fulachtaí fia*, but also in the vicinity of settlement foci and what are likely to have been well-known, habitually used areas at the core of everyday life. Small cemeteries were potentially linked to settlements of a couple of households, with larger ones, particularly of barrows, potentially representing wider communities.[78]

Human bone was placed on settlement sites as well as in cemeteries/other areas specifically focused on mortuary practices. Cleary has shown that deposition both of cremated and inhumed human bone on settlement sites was widespread and deliberately carried out. Cremated bone most commonly occurred as token deposits in pits, but also in post and stake holes, in general deposits or spreads, in the interior of structures and in wall-slots. Inhumed remains were mainly skull fragments, teeth and long bones. In commenting on such practices in southern Britain, Brück drew attention to the metaphorical significance of cremated bone in providing a link between the living and the land, resources, ideas of rebirth and continuity. Such deposits may have been made effective by their positioning within the settlement and their placement at critical times in the life of settlements and the people who lived there.[79]

In bone deposits found on settlements there appears to be a dominance of adults and infants. Keeping the bones of small children with the living may have kept their spirits close to the place they were born. The power of human bone in insuring fertility has been mentioned before, and there appears to be an association between agriculture, cereal growing and death. At Kilmahuddrick, for instance, burnt animal bone was mixed in with human bone in the upper fill of the ditch and in deposits of cremated bone outside it. The occurrence of charred cereal remains with cremation deposits has also been noted. Saddle querns have been found with cremated bone in pits, and Cleary has detailed the parallels in the deposition of human bone and saddle querns in settlement contexts. At Laughanstown, Co. Dublin querns were deliberately deposited in pits, where a representation of human bone might be expected.[80] It is possible that querns were used to crush cremated bone. There could have been metaphorical links between the idea of processing grain to feed the body and the breaking down of bone to free the spirit—and perhaps fertilise the soil.[81]

In considering the variety of evidence for the occurrence of human bone in Middle and Late Bronze Age contexts, one problem is the way we use the term 'burial' to centre and locate the dead in barrows and related sites, such as pit cemeteries, given that in many cases only token deposits are present. Utilising the divisibility and portability of cremated bone, people collected burnt human bone from pyres and placed it in different locations, which may have included cemeteries. Furthermore, the evidence of the cremation of de-fleshed bones at Dalystown demonstrates that in some cases there were a number of stages in the post-mortem treatment of human remains before cremation. In addition, parts of the body were treated differently. The focus on the cranium in many token cremation deposits is complemented by the presence of unburnt skulls and crania, providing supporting evidence for the complex treatment of bodies after death and of the skull's active symbolic role. The placement of parts of human skulls in *fulachtaí fia* or burnt mounds represents deliberate symbolic deposits. This is part of a wider pattern of the deposition of crania in wet places. What of the evidence from Britain indicating curation of human bone for an average of two generations following death? These were people who were still remembered and who signified relationships between the living and the dead. Did deposition of their remains mark a change in their status from 'living' to dead ancestors?[82]

This array of evidence indicates that the presence of the dead permeated all aspects of life in the Middle and Late Bronze Age, perhaps to a greater extent than at any earlier stage in prehistory. People engaged with the physical presence of the dead, purposely dispersed across the landscape, in a wide variety of contexts. In these circumstances a strong sense of connection with the dead, metaphoric links to the life and death of other objects and substances, memorialisation of selected dead people, and mnemonic references to more anonymous ancestors could be regarded as key characteristics of later prehistoric social groups in Ireland. Adults—women and men—and non-adults were treated in death as being socially significant. If people actively participated in the dispersal of human bone across a number of locations after death and cremation, it seems probable that at this point in time the living had a more open sense of what made a person—and a somewhat different view of the body world—than that which prevailed earlier in the Bronze Age.[83] People may have been viewed in terms of relationships with others, places, animals and objects, and of a strong sense of shared, rather than individual, lives. Not all people were regarded as equal, and boundaries and definitions of places were important. Indeed, most people in local populations were excluded from representation in either barrow or pit cemeteries, and the remains of the visible dead were placed in locations that drew attention to boundaries between the living and the dead. Cemeteries can also be interpreted as social arenas in which tensions for social position between leading kin lineages were played out and came into periodic focus.[84]

We need to think more about the partible human body in interpreting other aspects of the archaeological record. The deposition of metalwork has been seen as a key indicator of status differentiation. But if this practice is thought about from a body perspective, it can be argued that it is strongly related to ideas of people—dead and alive. As George Eogan demonstrated, the metalwork itself, as it takes the form of weapons, tools and ornaments, can be seen as relating to human bodies. In this context, Ingold's observation that tools are not just mechanical additions to the body, they extend the whole person, is very apt.[85] On the other hand, relationships between people and things were complex. Fontijn has suggested that potentially conflicting ideas and senses of identities were accommodated by being kept apart, by focusing on different depositional practices in different places. And Brück argues that similarities in the treatment of bodies and objects indicates that the production of things and the construction of the human self were seen as equivalent processes, involving cycles of making, burning, breaking, combination and regeneration. The possession and exchange of objects carried senses of engagement and of the relationships between people. These echoes of human engagement could have been carried by objects as they were placed in the ground. For example, gold neck-ornaments would have had a strong association with the human head. Like human bone, they could have remained symbolically active after deposition. And as Katharina Becker has noted, in some instances they were retrieved for further use, as also were human skulls.[86]

Even if there is no direct link with human remains, the deposition of metalwork revolved around concepts of the body, identities, and the relationships between people in social networks; in that sense metalwork was a form of kinwork. As Anwen Cooper and colleagues point out, objects could have had a 'mortuary' role well away from the deposition of human remains, and the deposition of metalwork and other substances in hoards can be related to mortuary practice in a range of ways. At Tara, two gold torcs were found on the northern side of the Rath of the Synods, within the southern cluster of barrows. In the Late Bronze Age complex at Rathgall, Co. Wicklow excavated by Barry Raftery, there were four cremation deposits in pits within a ring-ditch about 18m in diameter. The central pit had been excavated through a possible funeral pyre. A fragment of a leaf-shaped sword, an incomplete socketed spearhead and a chisel were placed in a pit similar to those containing cremated bone. A link was made here between the deposition of metalwork and of cremated bone, in a manner that suggests that the material was thought of as being related to or like human bone. The occurrence of human skulls in wetland contexts has been referred to above, and it is in this kind of terrain that much metalwork was deposited. More broadly, the concentration of barrow cemeteries and related sites in low-lying, seasonally flooded places like the Morningstar Valley, Co. Limerick, indicates resonances between places that were seen as 'good' and 'right' for the deposition of both human remains and metalwork. Such places would have provided a boundary with, but also a portal and conduit to, the otherworld—connecting the affairs of the living with the supernatural.[87]

What did the world of the living look like in the Middle and late Bronze? It certainly appears that concepts of group identity and scale expanded at this time from a background in the earlier

Bronze Age of a focus on local, small-scale networks of identity and inter-action, and this is reflected in the mortuary record. In detail, however, the social record can be read in quite different ways. On the one hand it has been suggested that this marks a more hierarchical society, with differentiation in a hierarchy of settlements emerging from the Middle Bronze Age onwards, as exemplified in a proposed model of settlement in North Munster, with site clustering representing familial, communal and territorial organisation and with hillforts and hilltop enclosures as the top tier. Whatever about the wider applicability of this regional model, the emergence of hillforts around 1400 BC, with intensification in building and use between 1200 BC and 1000 BC, is seen as reflecting a competitive Late Bronze Age society.[88] On the other hand, Victoria Ginn has shown that in the settlement record, particularly visible in the periods from 1700 BC to 1300 BC and from 1100 BC to 800 BC, evidence for hierarchy—even in a striking example like Corrstown, Co. Antrim, where 74 round houses were placed close together in rows—is not strong. In the case of hillforts, the evidence, including for attacks, could support the idea that these were foci as communal sites of aggregation, rather than the pinnacle of a settlement hierarchy. The metalwork evidence, particularly in terms of its deposition, generally seen as supporting the concept of a competitive, hierarchical society, can also be read as reflecting kin, networks and relations.[89]

What is striking in wider considerations of later Bronze Age society is that there is not more discussion of the relevance of the mortuary record, for example with regard to the potential links between multi-generational houses and cemeteries.[90] As well as complexity and variation of patterns in the settlement, economic and metalwork evidence, there is the widespread occurrence of human remains. There are echoes of the dead across the landscape of the living, supporting ideas of fragmentation and of relationships being used to underpin social cohesion, and at the same time challenging a model of a hierarchical society. There is a deliberate representation of the dead at significant, sacred places. The development of multi-generational barrow cemeteries, in particular, can be seen as reflecting and actively forming part of the emergence of larger-scale social groups, constituted of kin groups represented in clusters within the cemeteries. On hill- and ridge-tops and in low-lying areas, barrow cemeteries are constructed against this cultural backdrop. Within the cemeteries, the placement of graves and barrows could represent patterns of descent; recounted, remembered and re-ordered. The cemeteries provided a sense of material authority, and of legitimacy from the past. In this way they came to represent lines of history.

7.

Reflecting on transitional worlds: switching ancestors

Rings on her toes

Men carried the wrapped body on a bier. They were heading to the largest monument at the eastern end of the burial ground, which some said was the burial place of the person who had first come and cleared the ground here for people to live. They were followed by the village, talking about the sadness of her death for her family, but this was also a time of celebration. It was a wet morning, and the wind was bringing more rain from behind them as they slowly walked up the hill from the houses. It had been decided that rather than burning her body to free her spirit it would be better to allow her to walk after death, as she had in life. Following her journey from the grave she would meet the deceased members of her family and the ancestors.

Then they turned to the west and the children ran along the right side of the group so that the adults would protect them from the rain. All of them knew and respected her family and were glad to be part of the ceremony. Three people headed off to the north, to place offerings in the water hole that provided the village with the best water for drinking and the water that was used in ceremonies, as it was blessed by coming from ancestral grounds.

As they approached the grave they were greeted by the men who had dug it; they had made it so that it would fit her comfortably. Earth from the grave was carefully mounded up beside it. The leading elder had decided on the location. She said it would be good to place the woman on the sunny side of the family enclosure, so she would be connected and conjoined in death to her kin as she had been during her life, and would help to ensure the continuity of the family. The women lined up to take the body from the men, as it was tradition that they would bear her to the grave. Before the procession these women had washed her and dressed her. They remarked how she always liked to plunge into the water after the sweating ceremony and to look well. They had made her ready to be seen by her living relatives for the last time and to greet those who had gone before her after her journey from the grave.

When the rain cleared she was placed in the grave. Everyone gathered around to have a final look. She was laid in the grave on her right side, wearing her best clothes, with sandals carefully placed on her feet. As people felt the wet ground under their feet, they knew she would be dry shod on her journey to the Otherworld. As was the custom they put her head to the north, close to the ancestors in the family enclosure, and placed her hands under her chin with her feet drawn up, as if she were asleep. When she woke, she would be ready to begin her journey in the direction of the setting sun, towards a new life.

To symbolise the start of her journey and her departure from this world, the women threw earth and water over her body. Then the men who had dug the grave quickly pushed the rest of the soil back over it. She was now part of the earth and had begun her journey. On the surface of the grave they placed offerings and then walked back down the hill. The talk was about the pity of her dying the way she did and when she did, and how well the ceremony had been carried out. With luck, she would find the right path, her soul would not come wandering back to upset the living and she would watch over the village like the other ancestors on the hill.

PL. 7.A.I AND 7.A.II

The excavated barrow at Rath, Co. Meath, with the location and details of the crouched burial in the ditch.

At Rath, Co. Meath a complex of Bronze Age and Iron Age features was excavated by Cultural Resources Development Services (CRDS) in advance of a road scheme in 2004. Settlement activity was focused on the lower-lying, south-facing part of the site. North of this, focused on the brow of a hill, was a ring-ditch/barrow cluster. Three ring-ditches on the crest of the hill were broadly aligned north-west to south-east. At the most westerly, originally constructed as a ring barrow, excavation revealed cremated human bone above the basal deposits in the northern half of the ditch, recutting of the ditch, and further episodes of deposition of cremated bone over a long period. A grave for a crouched inhumation was later dug through the fully silted up southern part of the ditch. It held the body of a young adult woman about 157.5cm (5 foot 2 inches) tall. She was placed on her right side, her legs bent, with the ankles drawn up to the thighs, and with her head to the north-west. There were three copper-alloy rings on her toes. Two of these were almost identical spiral-rings, apparently attachments for sandals; a third decorated ring was on the toe next to the little toe of the right foot. The bone was not suitable for dating but parallels in Britain indicate it dates to the Iron Age, probably first century BC–first century AD, and is one of a number of crouched inhumations dating to that time. Isotopic analysis suggests that she lived her life in this locality **[Fig. 7.1, Pls 7.A.I and 7.A.II]**.[1]

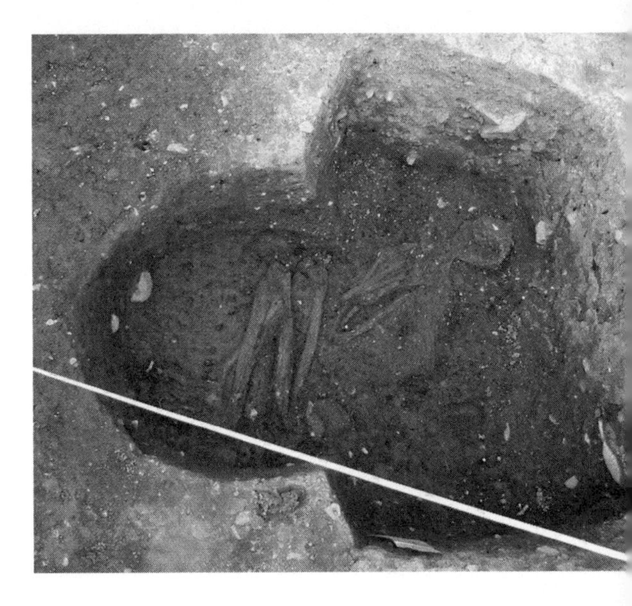

THE MARKING OF THE DEAD IN THE IRON AGE

It was suggested that in the later Bronze Age links could be seen between a growing complexity of society, the treatment of the dead, and the dispersal of their remains across the landscape, complemented by a focus on cemeteries, settlements and the deposition of metalwork and other material as social practices. Current interpretation is that this world altered as a result of climatic deterioration and related social and economic changes after 1000 BC; the relationship between climate and social change is, however, a topic of considerable debate. There is an apparent reduction of activity in the ensuing Early Iron Age (from 800 BC to 400 BC), and more visibility of sites dating to the Developed or Middle (from 400 BC to AD 1) and Late Iron Age (from AD 1 to AD 400). While the overall number of Iron Age sites in Ireland is surprisingly small in comparison to those of the Bronze Age, as has been pointed out by Katharina Becker, and colleagues, large scale, development-led archaeological work has transformed our knowledge of this period.[2]

It is somewhat ironic against this background that the burial record features much more centrally in accounts of the Iron Age than of the later Bronze Age, particularly considering the degree of continuity of mortuary practices and places across the two periods. Indeed, a central feature of the Iron Age is seen as the relationship between the treatment of the dead and wider social, economic and ideological changes that took place from the preceding Bronze Age, during the Iron Age itself and into the early medieval period after AD 400. Burial in the Late Iron Age and early medieval Ireland is the subject of an important monograph by Elizabeth O'Brien. A central theme is what is seen as the 're-emergence' of inhumation as an element of mortuary practice from the second century BC, alongside a continuity of the practice of cremation and a dominance of extended inhumation from around AD 400. Hence the mortuary practice at Rath depicted in the fictional scenario above, with the burial of the woman inserted into the ditch of the ring-barrow with cremation deposits in the ditch itself [FIG. 7.1], has a wider significance in indicating changing social mores about the role of the body after death and how it should be treated.[3]

In the past, the rite of extended inhumation, whereby the person is placed on their back (supine) in the grave with the head to the west, was seen as a direct reflection of the presence of Christianity. It may, however, have been adopted in Ireland before the beginnings of Christianity in the mid-fifth century AD. It might be more useful to think of Christianisation as one of a number of interrelated changes at a time of social flux; what in wider terms would be described as

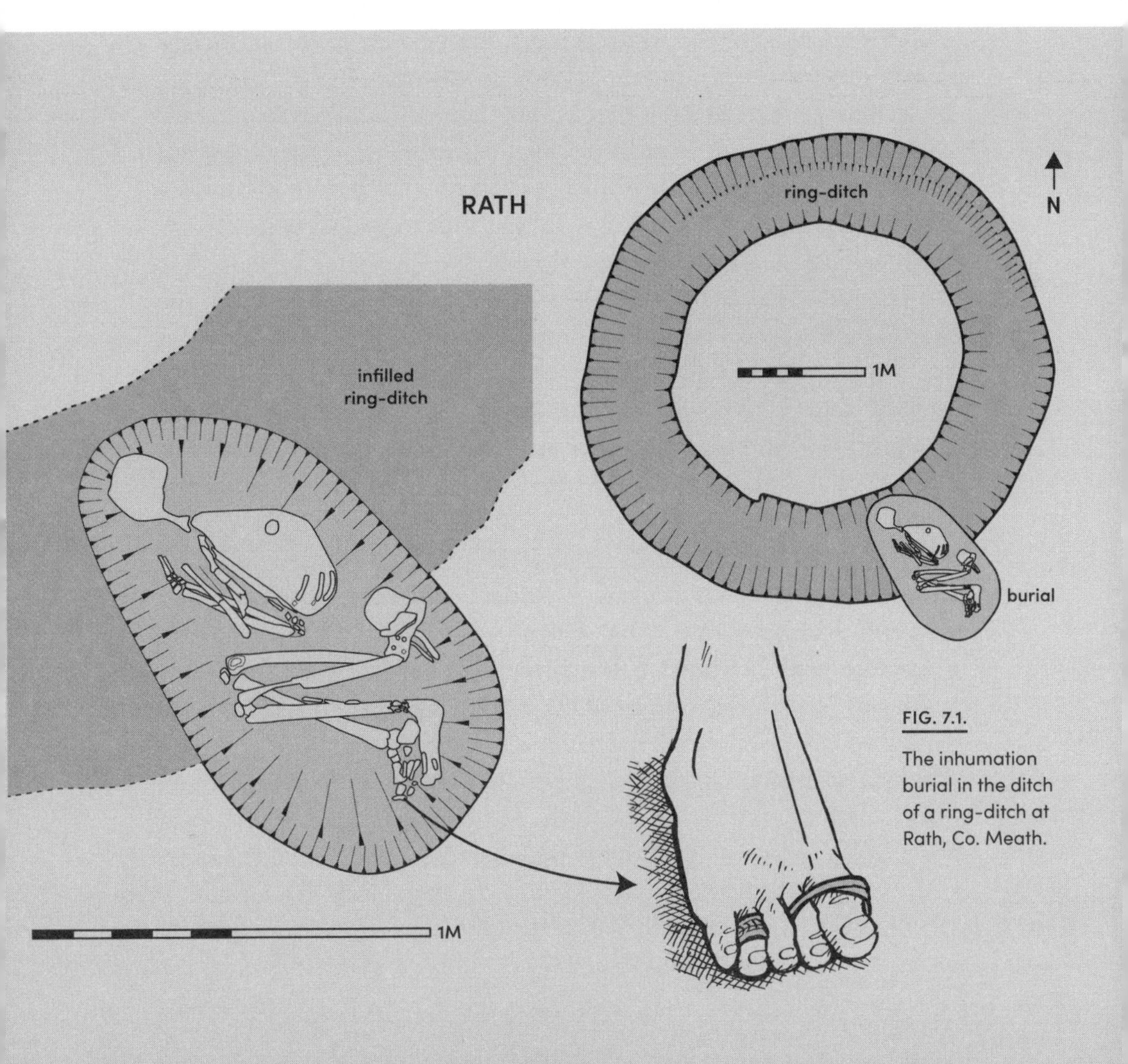

FIG. 7.1.

The inhumation burial in the ditch of a ring-ditch at Rath, Co. Meath.

the shift from late antiquity to the early medieval world.[4] In the centuries after the introduction of Christianity, strong elements of continuity of non-Christian mortuary rites and rituals, including cremation, remain evident. This is demonstrated by the recent recognition of a large number of sites referred to as secular cemeteries, cemetery settlements, settlement/cemeteries or settlement-cemeteries.[5] These refer to family cemeteries where other activities took place. On these sites and in other burials there was a concern to link with long-established, pre-Christian patterns of and places for the treatment of the dead. In some cases, it is possible that the actual burial rite was Christian, with the development of settlement-cemetery sites linked to the wider process of Christianisation of society. There were a variety of unenclosed cemeteries, as well as small ecclesiastical cemeteries, in use at this time. The shift to large-scale, community burial in an ecclesiastical context begins in the eighth century AD. This may have been a gradual process, but importantly it implies the opening up of formal burial rites to wider society.[6]

There has been much discussion of the character of Iron Age society indicated by the archaeological record. Traditionally, the Iron Age was seen as Celtic, hierarchical and tribal; the background for the emergence of the early medieval society recorded in early historic sources. More recently, it is the particularity and ephemeral nature of the evidence—for example for settlement—that has been commented on; the suggestion is that the evidence from the comparatively small number of sites provides a weak basis for the argument for a hierarchical society. Alongside signs of continuity in the location of settlement, mortuary and other activity, there certainly seems to be a break with the Late Bronze Age in socio-economic terms, against a background of environmental change, with evidence of a closing in of the intensively cleared Late Bronze Age landscape. This may have encouraged a greater focus on pastoralism and mobility. In the Developed and Late Iron Age there is evidence of contact with Britain and continental Europe in the form of La Tène and Roman influences and materials, which appear to be both a driver and reflection of social change. Iron was a commonly used technology, but its production may also have been a way of displaying social place. Large-scale communal projects such as the large enclosures at sites like Tara, Emain Macha, Knockaulin, Rathcroghan or the trackway at Corlea are emblematic of regional identities and wider social relations beyond local communities. Part of this complex world is burial and mortuary traditions and customs, and the impact of the Christianisation of society.[7]

The Rath burial can be taken as a pivot point for the discussion of changes in mortuary practice [FIGS 7.1 AND 7.2]. As mentioned in the previous chapter, within a Late Bronze Age hillfort at Rathgall, Co. Wicklow there was an 18m ring-ditch with four deposits of cremated bone and a linked deposition of a metalwork hoard. At the centre of the ring-ditch there was an area reddened by fire with a concentration of stake-holes. This appears to be the site of a pyre. A pit lined with stones was dug through this area, and the cremated bone of an older adult male was placed there. Five metres to the north-east a pit contained a small deposit of the cremated remains of an adult, above possible pyre material, with a pyre site immediately beside it. About 7m to the south-east, was a pit with the bottom deliberately shaped to support the base of a coarse pot. The pot contained the cremated bones of a female. What seemed to be pyre material was placed around the pot. A flat slab was placed directly on top of the pot, and soil and a large stone covered the slab. The hoard was about 3m to the south-west. Another deposit contained slivers of burnt long bone.[8]

We can move forward to consider the evidence for burial at the early medieval cemetery and settlement at Reask, Co. Kerry; what is now referred to as a minor early ecclesiastical site. It incorporates a sequence of burial and habitation from the fifth century AD to the medieval period. The use of the site starts with the construction of a timber round house in the central area. To the east of this was a small cemetery, with domestic structures to the north and south of it, all set within a stone enclosure. In the cemetery area, 42 east–west

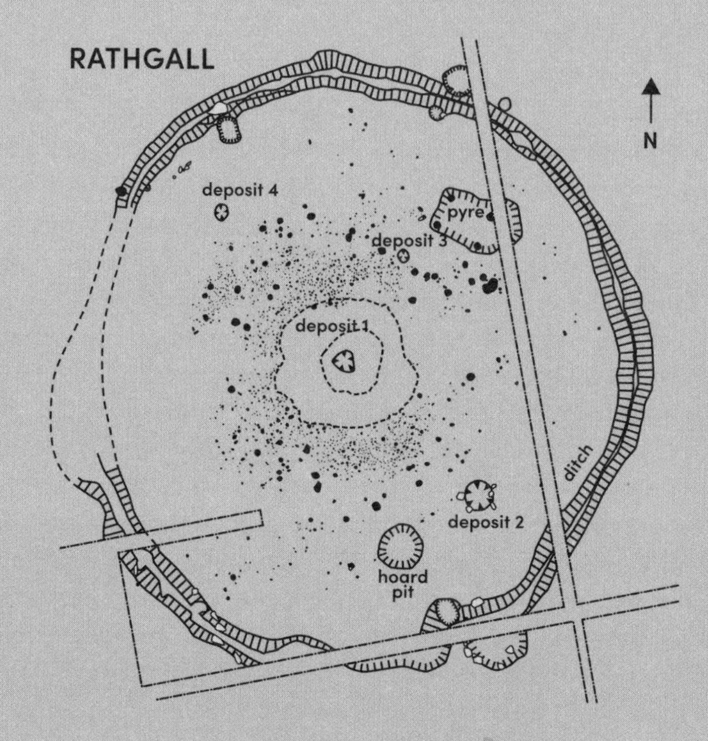

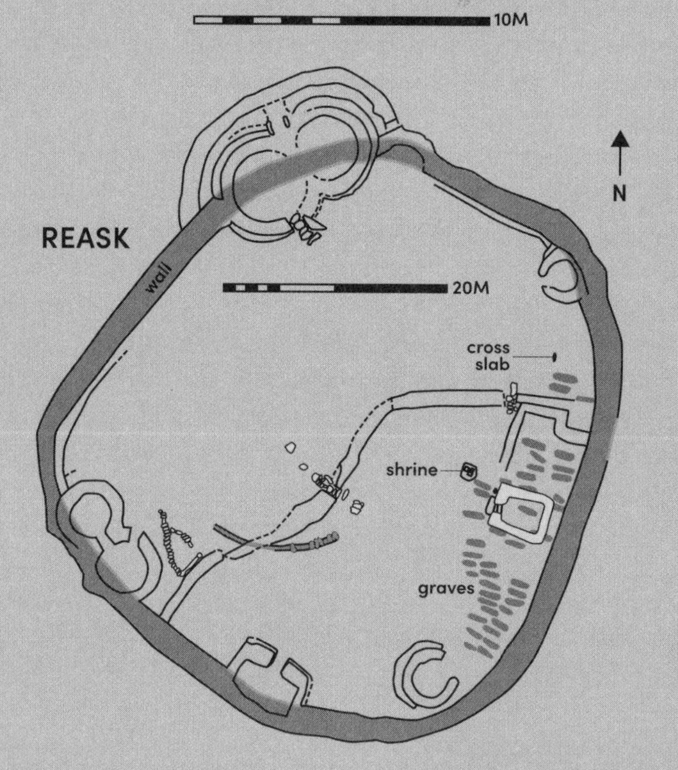

FIG. 7.2.

The Late Bronze Age cremation deposits and hoard in ring-ditch 2 at Rathgall hillfort, Co. Wicklow, and Reask, Co. Kerry early medieval cemetery.

graves were dug, lined with stones and covered with stone lintels laid across the top. Acidic soil conditions meant that no human skeletal remains were found. At the western edge of the cemetery was a feature known as a slab-shrine. This was a square area, about 90cm across, paved with stones and enclosed by slabs. This would have held the disarticulated bones of a person regarded as saintly or holy. It is possible that there was a small timber church or structure just south of this shrine. At the northern end of the cemetery stood a decorated standing stone, inscribed with a cross and the letters DNE (a contraction for *DOMINE* or 'Lord' in Latin) in an early form of Irish script. It was only after this phase that the stone oratory was built, defining the site as monastic in character.[9]

How and why did the transformations in burial practice exemplified in these two sites take place? Were they as dramatic as they appear? There are a number of points to emphasise as a background. First, barrows, ring-ditches and associated practices such as flat cemeteries of pits are a major element of mortuary practice in both the later Bronze Age and Iron Age, as we can see at Rathgall and Rath. Second, significant changes in burial practice took place in pre-Christian times: with an increased visibility of crouched inhumation from the second century BC, as documented by the Rath burial, alongside the continued use of cremation; a subsequent wider use of inhumation as a mortuary rite in the early centuries AD, along with the use of cremation and dominance of inhumation after AD 400. This reinforces the point above about the wider and longer-term context of social fluidity and change in which Christianisation occurred from the fifth century AD on. The context and conduit for these changes was Ireland's position at the edge of the Celtic world and the Roman Empire. There is evidence for continued contact with Britain and the Continent in pre-Roman conquest times, and with Romanised Britain and the wider Roman world in the early centuries AD.[10] Third, the dating of the use of barrows and ring-ditches up to at least the seventh century AD takes us well into the period when Ireland was Christianised. In this period there was a variety of mortuary practices and cemetery forms, some of which are clearly congruent with the new religious ideology and theology, as at Reask. On the other hand, settlement-cemeteries and unenclosed cemeteries—and the continued use of cremation—have a much more ambiguous religious and ideological context.[11]

Much discussion has focused on cremation and inhumation as exclusive mortuary rites in the Iron Age, underplaying evidence for the interplay, diversity and changes over time in their combined and complementary use. The long-established recognition of the role of selected individuals in death continued well into the second half of the first millennium AD. Against this background the syncretic character of early Christianity is evident. As Kevin Whelan put it 'Christianity proved promiscuously permeable to local cultural influences, and there was always diversity within ecclesiastical practice'. This might explain how early Irish Christian saints could on their death become effective ancestral figures.[12]

As well as recognising the Iron Age as a time of flux, both the preceding Late Bronze Age, and the succeeding earliest centuries of the Christian and historic period in Ireland are integral to our understanding of this period. Even longer time-frames and the recognition of different concepts of time and temporalities are also relevant. Barry Raftery graphically described the religious beliefs of the people in Iron Age Ireland and their preoccupation with the supernatural.[13] These beliefs and their rootedness in time and place remind us that people were living in a landscape that had been socialised by human activity for over seven thousand years. Given the blurred lines between gods and mortals and the use of sacred rituals and places, it would not be surprising if echoes of earlier practices in regard to the treatment of the dead and the transformation of some of the dead into ancestors were recurrent, drawn upon and seen as important.[14]

CREMATION IN THE IRON AGE: FORGING IDENTITIES IN DEATH

It is appropriate to begin by considering cremation, which was dominant in the earlier part of the period and continued in use alongside an increasing popularity of inhumation well into the first millennium AD. While the conventional view has been that cremation became much less widely practiced after AD 500, in an important recent contribution Patrick Gleeson and Rowan McLaughlin state that there are more dated cremations for the period AD 400–1200 than for AD 1–400.

We do not know what the range of mortuary treatment was for the majority of the Iron Age population. As in the later Bronze Age, cremated remains predominantly consist of partial or token deposits of people whose post-mortem treatment suggests were regarded as socially significant. Some broad trends can be detected underlying a diversity of mortuary practice. Despite the paucity of deposits dating to the Early Iron Age (from 800 BC to 400 BC) there is a strong sense of continuity with the later Bronze Age. In some cases the deposition of the selected remains of people from later generations continues in places that were long regarded as cemeteries, such as the flat cemetery at Manusmore AR100, Co. Clare. Barrow cemeteries like Carrowjames, Cush, Co. Limerick and Tara continue to expand.[15] At Ballynakelly, Co. Dublin a ring ditch with a pit containing a token cremation on the interior edge of the ditch (both dating to the Middle or Developed Iron Age, between 400 BC and AD 1) was placed on a plateau at the southern edge of a flat cemetery, with cremation pits dating to the later Bronze Age immediately to the north. The ring-ditch/barrow tradition forms the major monumental context for Iron Age cremation deposits, and there is a recurrent trend of constructing such monuments in places and landscapes where there is evidence of earlier, particularly funerary, activity. As Elizabeth O'Brien put it, this created clear links with established ancestors.[16] **[FIG. 7.3]**

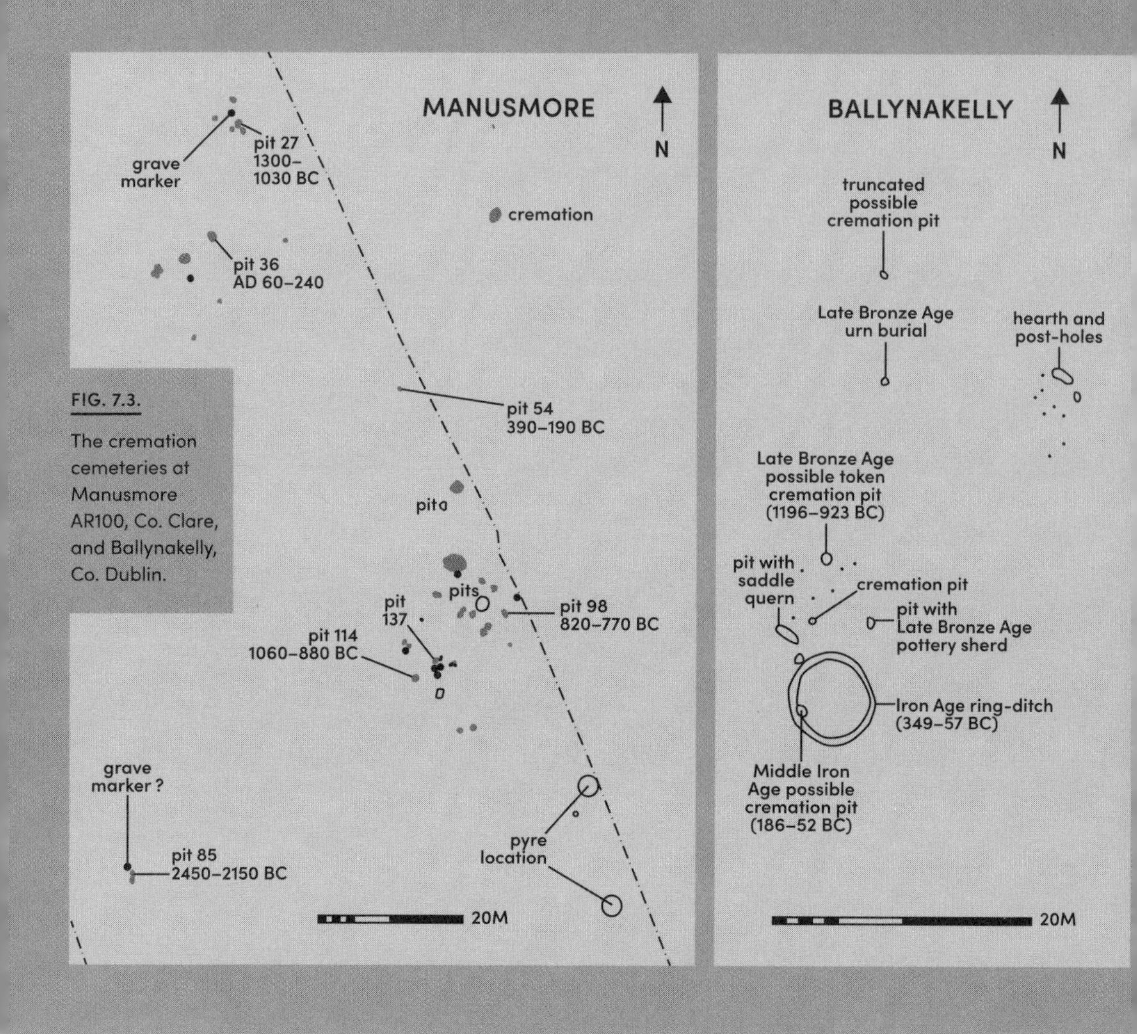

FIG. 7.3.

The cremation cemeteries at Manusmore AR100, Co. Clare, and Ballynakelly, Co. Dublin.

Established practices were used actively, reflecting contemporary needs and the changing ways in which identities and social positions were created and expressed. In some cases the ditches of ring-ditches contained timber planks, enclosing or defining the interior, placed as a burnt lining or representing the remains of pyres. Ring-ditches/barrows were built to create new ritual foci in the landscape, as at Knockcommane, Knockgraffon and Marlhill, Co. Tipperary; Ballinorig West 4 in Co. Kerry; Ballyboy 1 and 2 in Co. Galway. [FIG. 7.4, PL. 7.B] It is notable that the first three of

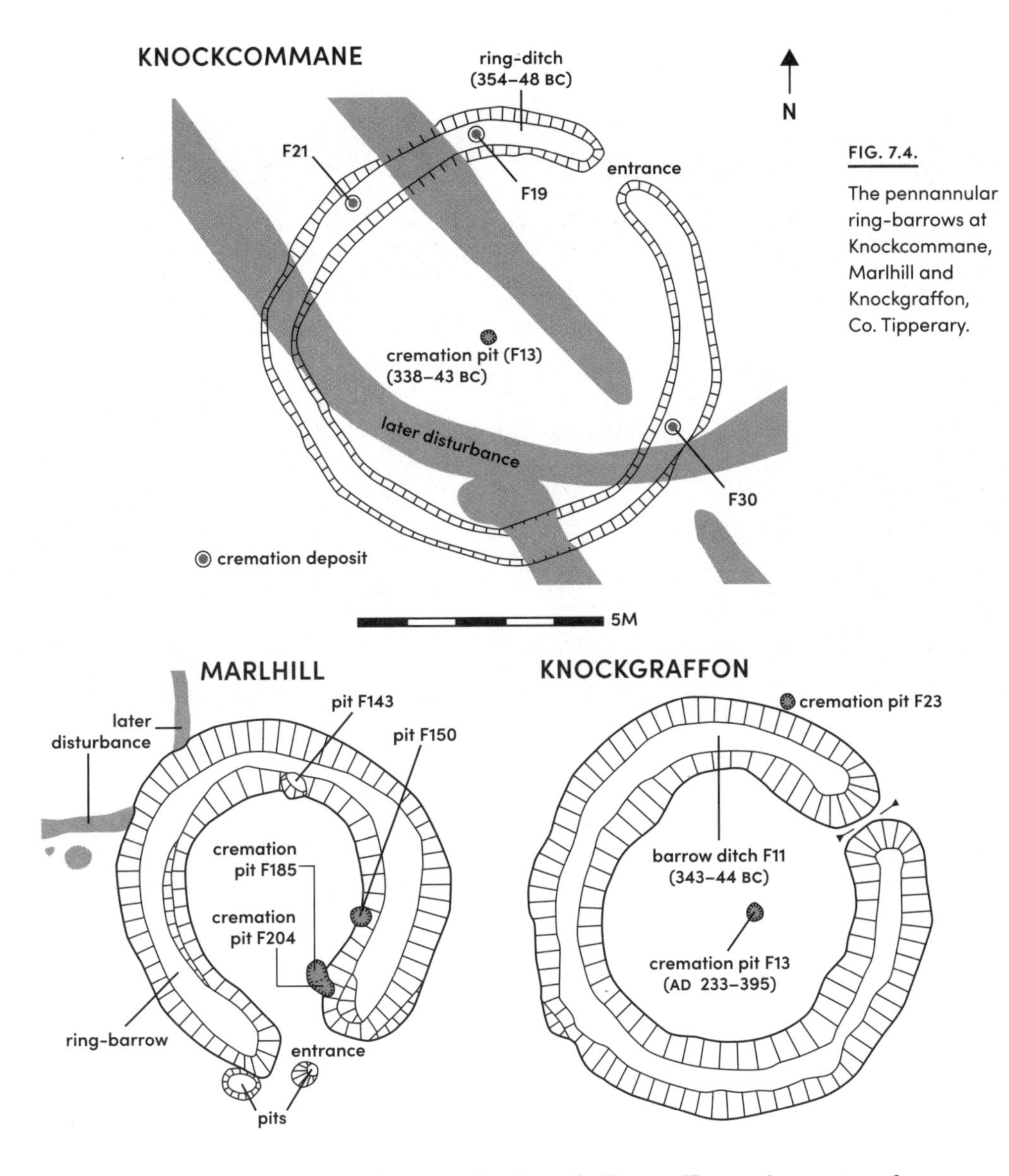

FIG. 7.4.

The pennannular ring-barrows at Knockcommane, Marlhill and Knockgraffon, Co. Tipperary.

these sites are penannular ring-ditches. As James Eogan has pointed out, penannular ring-ditches appear to be a feature of the Iron Age, particularly in the southern part of the island. These were single monuments, with variable histories and periods of use.[17] The complexities of such histories can been seen at a ring-ditch at Ferns Lower, Co. Wexford dating to the Developed Iron Age. Almost

the entire circuit of the ditch had been lined with charred planks, held together with nails. Placed on and into this lining were four cremation deposits. Three of the token deposits incorporated the remains of an adult and juvenile and in one of these—the deposit with the greatest number of objects—the remains of an adult were laid above the sealed remains of a juvenile. In other cases, as at Ballydavis, Co. Laois and Holdenstown 1, Co. Kilkenny ring-ditch/barrow cemeteries were created over the course of the Iron Age and beyond.[18] [FIG. 7.5] Cremation deposits were placed in pits within ring-ditches

PL. 7.B.

Pennannular ring-ditch at Knockcommane, Tipperary from the south-west, with Galtee Mountains in the background.

and under barrows, in pits outside and very frequently in ditches; in the form of foundation deposits, ditch fills and closing deposits.

From the Developed Iron Age on, contact with a wider world, particularly pre-Roman and then Roman Britain, becomes more apparent. At Ferns Lower from this time, the placement of objects with the cremated remains of the dead is prominent. These are personal objects: glass beads, brooches, pins, rings, indications of boxes; either burnt, and hence apparently placed with the corpse in the pyre, or kept separate from the cremation process and placed unburnt with the burnt bone deposit.[19] This signifies an important change in approach to how the living defined the identity and body world of individuals in death. Objects help to negotiate death; they are material traces of relationships and aspects of personhood, they

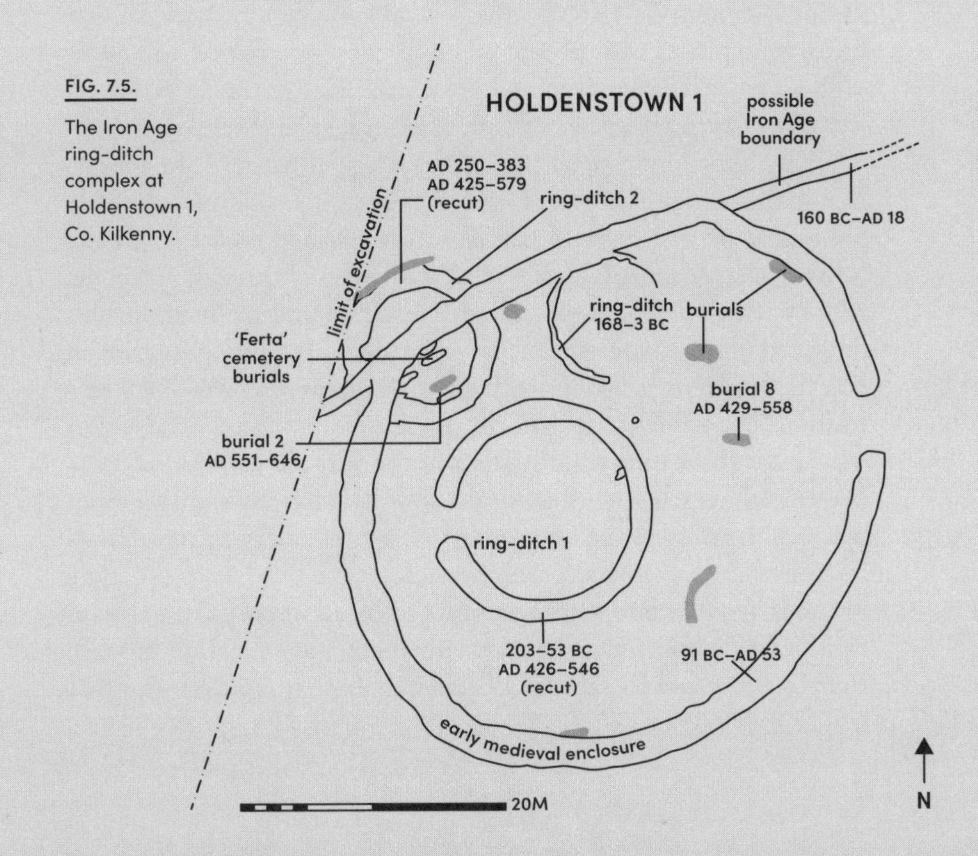

FIG. 7.5.

The Iron Age ring-ditch complex at Holdenstown 1, Co. Kilkenny.

can be heirlooms, gifts, signs of grief or equipment for the afterlife, they allow us to think about the web of social ties and material relations that people create.[20]

At Ballydavis, Co. Laois excavation revealed a cemetery of four ring-ditches and seven furnaces, with pits and post-holes. This association of the working of iron and cremation deposits occurs more widely in the Iron Age. Melanie Giles points out that the significance of ironworking lies in its dual association with transformative power—creative and destructive. It allowed people to use materials in new ways to think about and negotiate the relationships of life and death. At Ballydavis in the ditch of site I there was *in situ* burning and metal-working material. At the centre of this site a cremation deposit, dated to the fourth–first century BC, had been placed in a pit with unburnt objects: a bronze box, a pin or fibula and 80 glass beads. The best parallels for the box come from Yorkshire in north-eastern England in the second century BC. There, similar boxes were placed with people whose bodies were buried, inhumed, with a cart or chariot (such as the female cart burial at Wetwang Slack), in a large pit within and under a rectangular, ditched barrow.[21]

These Yorkshire cart burials and rectangular barrows are a localisation of a wider European burial rite. In turn at Ballydavis, widely held ideas of identity and status were translated and used in the active construction of local social frameworks, through both the rites by which people were treated after death and the relationships indicated by the materials buried with them. As Giles puts it, such objects may have evoked and visibly displayed people's links and relationships within a local world, but also with distant, powerful or what might have been regarded as otherworldly places.[22] At Fore, Co. Westmeath a cremation deposit of an older adult male dating from between the third to the first century BC was placed in a bronze bowl in a pit within an inland promontory fort. The bowl, with a handle in the shape of a bird's head, appears to be an import from Britain or at least demonstrates contact with there. **[FIG 7.6]**. More broadly, Barry Raftery and Elizabeth O'Brien have both made the point that objects found with cremation burials in Ireland in the time spanning the birth of Christ show strong links with Britain. As at Ballydavis, such objects materialised a web of contacts with a wider world.[23]

Proto-Romanisation had been taking place in southern Britain after Caesar's expeditions in the 50s BC, and Britain became fully part of the Roman Empire after the Claudian conquest in AD 43. The coming of the western frontier of the Roman Empire to Britain provided new dimensions to the character of contacts across the Irish Sea. In many parts of Britain inhumation remained the accepted method of burial up to the time of the initial Roman incursions. The shift to cremation in the south-east of Britain starting in the first

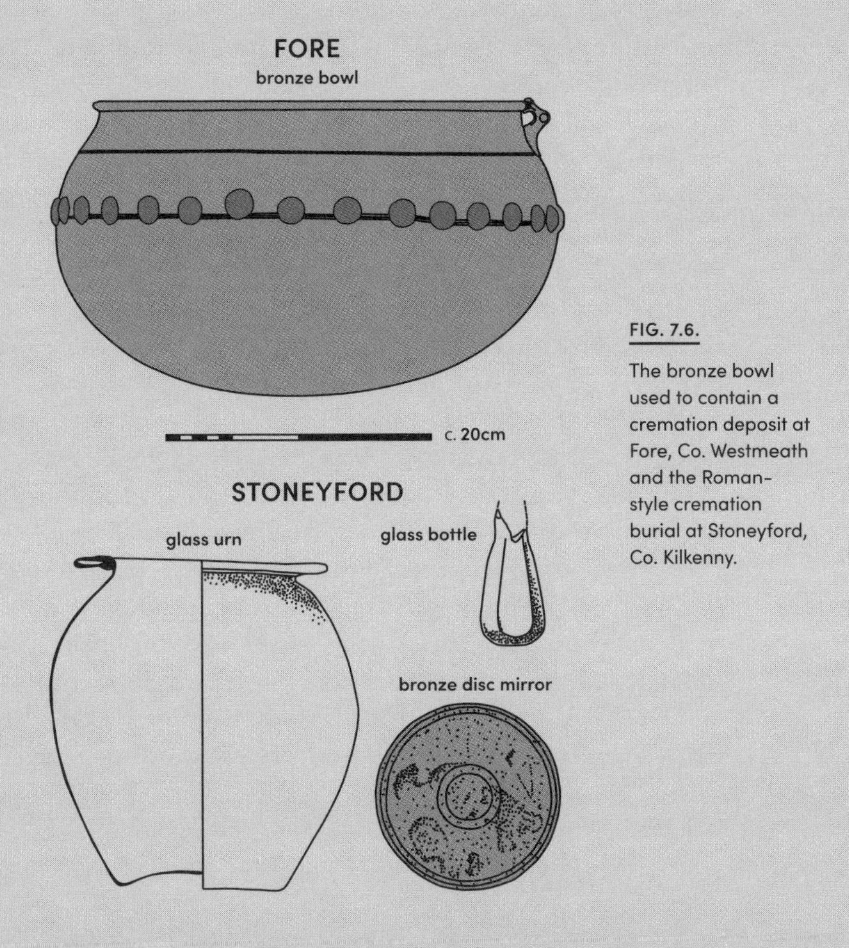

FIG. 7.6.

The bronze bowl used to contain a cremation deposit at Fore, Co. Westmeath and the Roman-style cremation burial at Stoneyford, Co. Kilkenny.

century BC can be seen as indicating contact initially with the edge of the empire, and from the first century AD the direct presence of the Roman army and colonists. Cremation at that time was the standard burial rite in the Roman world.[24] A classic Roman cremation burial dating to the first or early second century AD was found in the nineteenth century at Stoneyford, Co. Kilkenny [FIG. 7.6]. Cremated bones were placed in a glass urn. This was sealed by a bronze disc mirror and accompanied by a small glass bottle. This raises questions both about the particular person buried here and the web of wider social relations in which they lived. The person buried is likely to have been a woman, as indicated by the character of the finds. Was she a person of Roman background who had married into an Irish family with connections to Roman Britain? The fact that the burial rite was Roman in style as well as content suggests an alternative—that the social group in which this person lived and died saw itself as Romanised, carrying out mortuary practice according to contemporary fashion in Britain. As had happened in southern Britain before the Claudian conquest, the process of proto-Romanisation may well have been taking place at this time in eastern Ireland, on the fringes of the empire.[25]

These cremation deposits indicate mortuary rites reflecting the wider context of Iron Age society, but there are also indications of a concern with renewing sacred places imbued with a sense of the past. At Kiltierney, Co. Fermanagh in the last century BC/first century AD, a rock-cut ditch was dug around the base of a passage tomb built three thousand years earlier. The dug material was added to the mound of the passage tomb, in which cremation deposits were placed in small pits. On the outer side of the ditch, scattered deposits of cremated bone were covered by small mounds, which also seem to have been built with material from the ditch. There were 19 mounds in all, each about 3m in diameter and 1m high. Objects were placed with some of the deposits. Further illustrating this link with passage tombs it is worth noting that within the kerb of the megalithic tomb at Grave 26, Carrowmore, Co. Sligo—a monument in the Neolithic passage tomb complex—a ring-ditch with a well-defined entrance produced, in a central grave, the disarticulated, inhumed remains of a young adult female and a foetus or new-born child, along with burnt animal bones. While this could not be dated with certainty, given the extent of related and dated Iron Age activity the excavator argued that it was of the Late Iron Age. At Rathdooney Beg, Co. Sligo a bowl barrow, which appears to be a deliberate scale copy of a Neolithic barrow 20m to the south of it, was constructed between the fourth and second century BC. Cremation had taken place prior to the construction of the barrow, and unburnt human cranial and other bones dated from 370 BC to 50 BC were found in the base of the mound. Immediately west of the bowl barrow and conjoined with it, a ring barrow was constructed. Here, cremation deposits, one dated from between 120 BC to AD 80, were placed in pits in the mound and in the ditch, the latter with iron objects.[26]

This desire to create an active link with long-established sacred places using the remains of the dead can be seen in other practices, such as the deposition of Iron Age material in Neolithic sites; one example being the bone plaques placed in some tombs in the Loughcrew passage tomb complex. The range and richness of Roman finds dating to the early centuries AD deposited in the vicinity of the entrance to Newgrange indicate that, over time, this practice took on a Romanised hue.[27]

In the continued use of barrow cemeteries, and the creation of new cemeteries, the links were to the recent past and were cross-generational. Breaking up and separating sequences of activities in such cemeteries on the basis of a Bronze Age or Iron Age date can mask a real or intended sense of social continuity, the latter in the case where there are chronological gaps in the use of the place. At Ardsallagh, Co. Meath, on a gentle east-facing slope in the valley of the river Boyne, two cemeteries almost a kilometre apart have been discussed by Linda Clarke and Neil Carlin. They were in prominent locations with clear views to the Hill of Tara, 5 km to the south-east. At Ardsallagh 2 [FIG. 7.7, PL. 7.C], a ring-ditch (1), with a diameter of 10.6m was dug in the second century BC–first century AD, based

FIG. 7.7.

The background and development of the ring-ditches at Ardsallagh 2, Co. Meath.

ARDSALLAGH 2

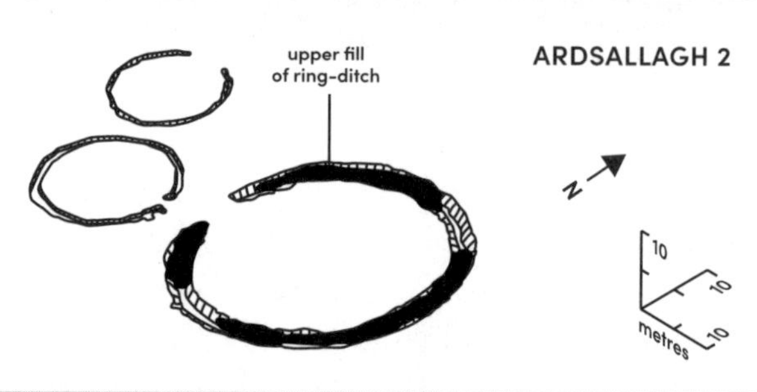

AD 650–770

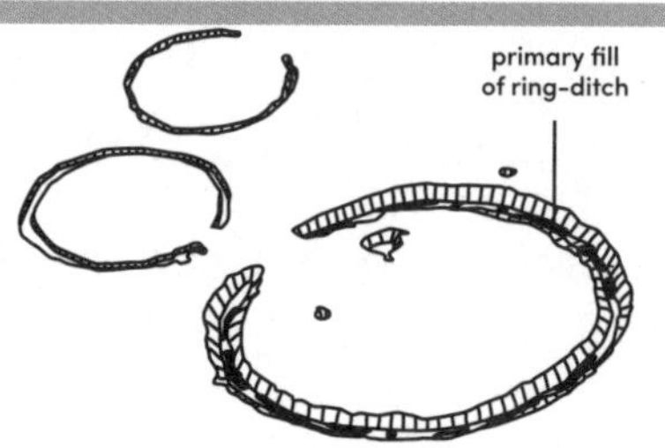

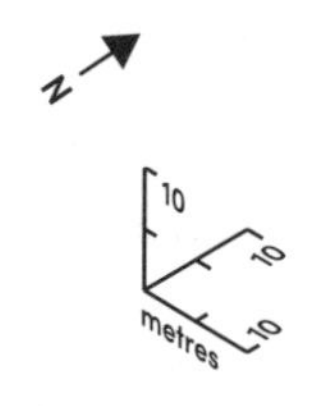

AD 450–640

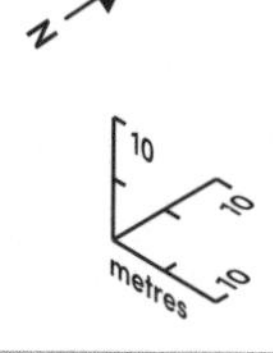

170 BC–AD 50

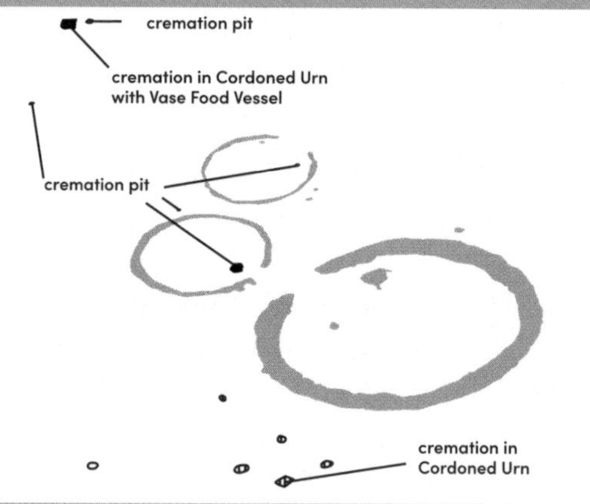

2000–1600 BC

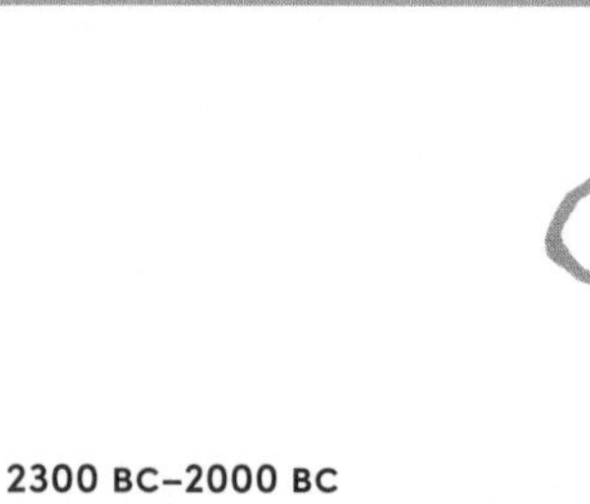

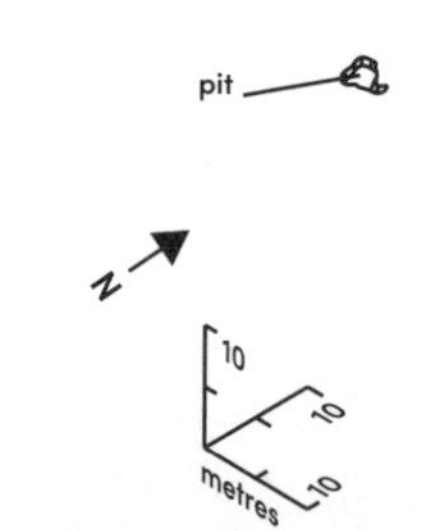

2300 BC–2000 BC

PL. 7.C.

View of Ardsallagh 2, Co. Meath post-excavation, from the east, with the largest ring-ditch in the foreground.

on the dating of the remnants of timber planks in the ditch. The form and similarity of an adjacent ring ditch suggests that it also dates to the Developed Iron Age. The site had been a focus of burial and depositional activity in the Early Bronze Age, with the placement of cremations in urns and isolated cremations in pits. The location of the ring-ditches may represent a deliberate re-use of this location, a point amplified by the fact that the dated ring-ditch was constructed in the immediate vicinity of some earlier cremation pits.[28]

Immediately east of Ring-ditch 1, a much larger ring-ditch, with a diameter of 21m, was constructed at the end of the Iron Age—over 400 years after the smaller ring-ditches. It was built on top of a natural rise that forms the highest point locally. As part of a deliberate backfilling, a ring of stones lined the base. There was one small concentration of clean cremated bone (probably human) above this, and tiny pieces of clean cremated bone (probably human) were scattered in the primary ditch fill, with an animal tooth dating to between AD 450 and AD 640. The in-filled ditch was later re-dug to form a segmented enclosure, with charcoal dating to between AD 650 and AD 770. At Ardsallagh 2, this large ring-ditch appears to have been deliberately placed immediately east and facing ring-ditch 1 as an intentional act and as reference to the past.[29]

The alternative practices of placing a burial deposit immediately under the location of the pyre or separating the location of the pyre from the place of burial were long-established by this time. Two examples in the south-west occur close to areas where there were cremated bone deposits in pits. At Rockfield, Co. Kerry there were circular pyre pits with evidence of intense burning and cremated bone and charcoal. One of these dates from between 780 BC to 380 BC and the other to between 390 BC and 60 BC, indicating continuation of practice over the last millennium BC. At Ballyvelly, Co. Kerry three linear burnt pits were found as part of a complex of features within an area about 12m by 16m, which also included cremation pits, post-holes and linear shallow pits. The linear pits were almost 3m long, about 60cm wide, and just over 20cm deep. They showed signs of intense burning, with charcoal and tiny fragments of burnt bone. The pits are consistent with experimental work on the effectiveness of cremation, which suggests that placing the pyre and body over a pit provides optimal conditions in terms of the speed at which the body will burn. A date from one of the Ballyvelly pits placed its use between the third and fifth century AD.[30]

BURYING BODIES: WHAT WAS THE CONTEXT OF INHUMATION IN THE IRON AGE?

In the first phase of inhumation in the second century BC–first century AD, most inhumations were placed in the grave with the legs in a crouched or flexed position, as was the case with the burial of the woman at Rath. In many areas of Britain, particularly in the south, crouched or flexed inhumation burial, usually with the head to the north, was the predominant rite of burial from the late fourth or third century BC. Hence contact and influences—and possibly the physical presence of people from or with links to Britain—are regarded as the main explanation for this apparent major change in mortuary practice in the Meath–Dublin area of eastern Ireland. It is argued that those buried were people of social prominence who lived and died in a world of contacts across the Irish Sea and perhaps beyond, as indicated by the isotopic evidence for their origins, the novel character of their treatment after death and the objects placed with them in the grave.[31]

O'Brien has stressed that crouched inhumation was very much a minority rite, with the indigenous population continuing to use cremation until after AD 400 when inhumation became more widely practised.[32] Across the Neolithic and Bronze Age there is clear evidence of the use of cremation and inhumation as complementary burial rites; the emphasis in current discussion is on dominant or exclusive burial rites in the Iron Age, with other practices regarded as representing burials outside the norm. Much of this emphasis seems to derive from the perceived significance of changes driven by contact with Britain, the impact of ripples of Romanisation and ideas of indigenous versus intrusive burials.[33] We need to think, however, about the reception and translation of influences and ideas, and potentially people, in specific social contexts in Ireland. We should remember that alongside a continuing history of links with Britain and beyond, there was a long tradition of the complementary use of cremation and inhumation as mortuary rites.

In the context of an apparent initial dominance of cremation, how did what appears to be a very different view of the role of the body after death become socially acceptable to the living as an appropriate treatment for the dead? In the later Bronze Age, token cremation deposits may have reflected and created an image of people as partible, fragmented. The 're-emergence' of inhumation in the second century BC seems to have coincided with an increasing concern with a different representation of people in death. In Iron

Age cremation burials and deposits from the last few centuries BC a trend can be seen towards the re-appearance of objects being placed with the dead. This suggests either that objects were returned to the dead after cremation or that it became important to sustain or re-establish an image of the person as they had been seen at death when placed on the pyre. There is a marked similarity in the character of the objects in such cremations and those placed with crouched inhumations.[34] Was the use of inhumation linked to changing concepts of the person as they faced transformation after death? Almost half of the early crouched inhumations in eastern Ireland were of juveniles or infants, suggesting that inhumation at this time was also an age-specific practice, as noted in earlier periods.[35]

Linked to this point, is it possible that what is described as the *re-introduction* of inhumation in the last couple of centuries BC was actually a widening of the social acceptability of this rite and its increasing archaeological visibility? The evidence from earlier periods in Irish prehistory indicates that rather than regarding particular burial practices as exceptional, deviant or anomalous, and hence decreasing their significance, we need to take a wider view. This is relevant particularly for the Iron Age, a period we know was marked by social change and diversity in mortuary practice.[36] Indeed, until the early medieval period we are still only dealing with the remains of a small proportion of the dead; those whose post-mortem treatment is visible in the archaeological record.

In later prehistory cremation dominates the record, but as already stated inhumation was used for certain individuals or categories of people. The excavations at Dún Aonghasa on the Aran Islands, Co. Galway uncovered the burial of a neonate dating from between 770 BC to 410 BC (and the limb/jaw of a young adult dating to between 170 BC and AD 60). In a shell midden at Culleenamore, Co. Sligo, a circular grave had been cut into the outer edge of an Iron Age midden to hold the body of a young child (one or two years old), buried with a bronze ear-ring and a perforated blue glass bead, the latter found in the chest area [SEE FIG. 3.7]. The objects and general context suggest a date in the last centuries BC or first centuries AD. Both of these child burials are well outside the supposed restricted area in which crouched inhumations generally are seen in the second century BC–first century AD. The Dún Aonghasa burial dates to the Early Iron Age and is further evidence that inhumation may have been a rite used for the burial of young children.[37]

There are other Iron Age inhumed remains outside eastern Ireland, dating from 200 BC to AD 200,[38] but importantly there are also a number of adult inhumations dating from earlier in the first millennium BC, including the crouched male inhumations at Mullamast, Co. Kildare and outside a wedge tomb at Parknabinnia, Co Clare, the latter with evidence of stab wounds to the chest.[39] The disarticulated remains of a middle-aged adult woman dating to between 790 BC and 430 BC were placed in a cave at Robber's Den, Co. Clare.[40] At Derrymaguirk, Co. Roscommon, a grave covered by bog contained the skeletal remains of a young adult woman, dating to between 593 BC and 346 BC, and an infant. The woman was placed as an extended inhumation with her head to the west, in a grave filled with branches and twigs. A block of wood was placed behind her head and a large stone was placed over the pelvic area. The burial was accompanied by bones of sheep/goat and dog, and a red deer antler tine. Because this Early Iron Age burial was later covered by bog, it is usually regarded as a bog body, but the grave was dug into what was then dry land.[41] That it can be linked with broader traditions of burial practice is seen in the parallels with the Leshemstown burial of a woman in a *fulacht fia* dated to between 1260 BC and 1020 BC mentioned in the previous chapter, and to the earliest dated burial forming part of a cemetery at Bettystown (Anchorage), Co. Meath excavated by James Eogan. [FIG 7.8]. There, the focus of activity was from the mid-third to the late seventh century AD. A crouched inhumation of an adult female, located to the west of what would become the focal burial area, however, was dated to between 165 BC and AD 3.[42] This woman, like the Derrymaguirk woman, had a large stone placed on her abdomen. A crouched inhumation of a juvenile nearby is presumed to be contemporary.

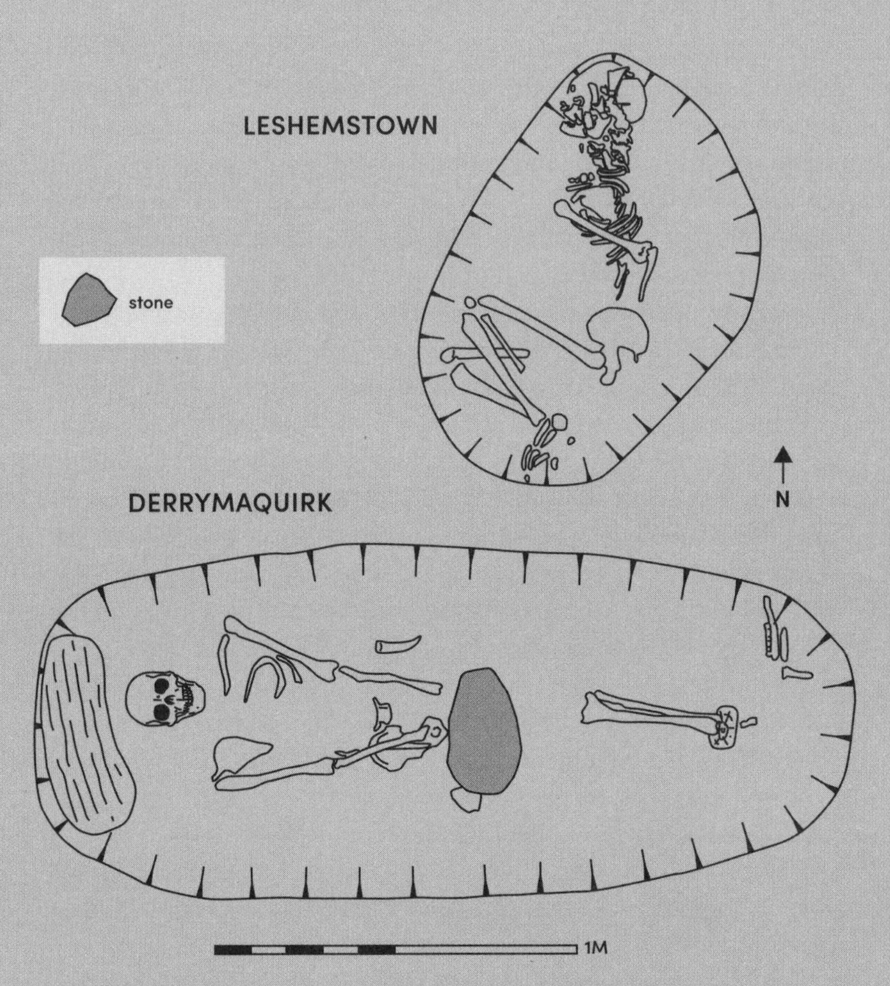

FIG. 7.8.

The Middle/Late Bronze Age inhumation at Leshemstown, Co. Meath; the Early/Developed Iron Age inhumation from Derrymaguirk, Co. Roscommon; the Developed Iron Age inhumation from Bettystown, Co. Meath.

While it is interesting that on the basis of isotope analysis this woman appears to have come from south-east Scotland or Yorkshire or a region in mainland Europe, this is not necessarily reflected in the way in which she was buried. As Jacqueline Cahill Wilson and colleagues have put it, we should be cautious about making a correlation between the likely origin of individuals and the burial rites accorded to them by the living.[43] Indeed, the earliest crouched burial at the Knowth Iron Age cemetery (burial 10) is of a local woman dating to between 175 BC and 50 BC. This particular rite seems as likely to reflect long-established elements and traditions of mortuary practice in Ireland as much as a wider web of contemporary contacts, including the belief that the placement of a large stone may have contained the person within the grave, perhaps reflecting concern with unfinished female lives and procreative power.[44]

BOG BODIES AS INHUMATIONS

If we can see this parallel between what is normally treated as a 'bog body' (Derrymaguirk) in the Early Iron Age and an example of what would be seen as a 'new' burial rite of crouched inhumation from the second century BC (Bettystown) onwards, can a broader consideration of the bog body phenomenon assist in providing us with an understanding of the context and occurrence of these 'early' crouched inhumation burials, and more widely the occurrence of inhumation during the Iron Age? Melanie Giles, in an important discussion of bog bodies, has argued that we need to situate these individuals—who are exceptionally well-preserved in death because of the anaerobic conditions of peat bogs—in their wider social context and the contemporary treatment of the dead. While the disposal of bodies and body parts in bogs goes back to the Mesolithic, it seems particularly apposite to consider the wider significance of this practice in the later Bronze Age and Iron Age because there is an increase in dated interments in bogs in this period in Ireland, Britain and north-west Europe.[45] **[FIG. 7. 9; PL. 7.D]**

The deposition of bog bodies in Ireland spans the duration of the Iron Age. At Gallagh, Co. Galway the body of an adult male was found in a bog at a depth of almost three metres. He was clothed in a leather cape gathered at the neck with a band of willow rods. A pointed wooden post or stake was placed on either side of him, and the dates from his bones span the period from 512 BC to 166 BC. It is very likely that the willow rods were a rope used to strangle him. If that is the case, then his treatment might represent either a sacrifice to the gods or punishment for a crime. His body was placed in a pool or a lake; a liminal, dangerous place because of its close links with the otherworld.[46] Was this a mechanism by the living to ensure the quick movement of the sacrificial victim from their earthly existence, or alternatively to confine the soul and spirit of the person to a state of limbo? Votive offerings or sacrifices appear to be a feature of Iron

PL. 7.D.

The bog body from Clonycavan, Co. Meath.

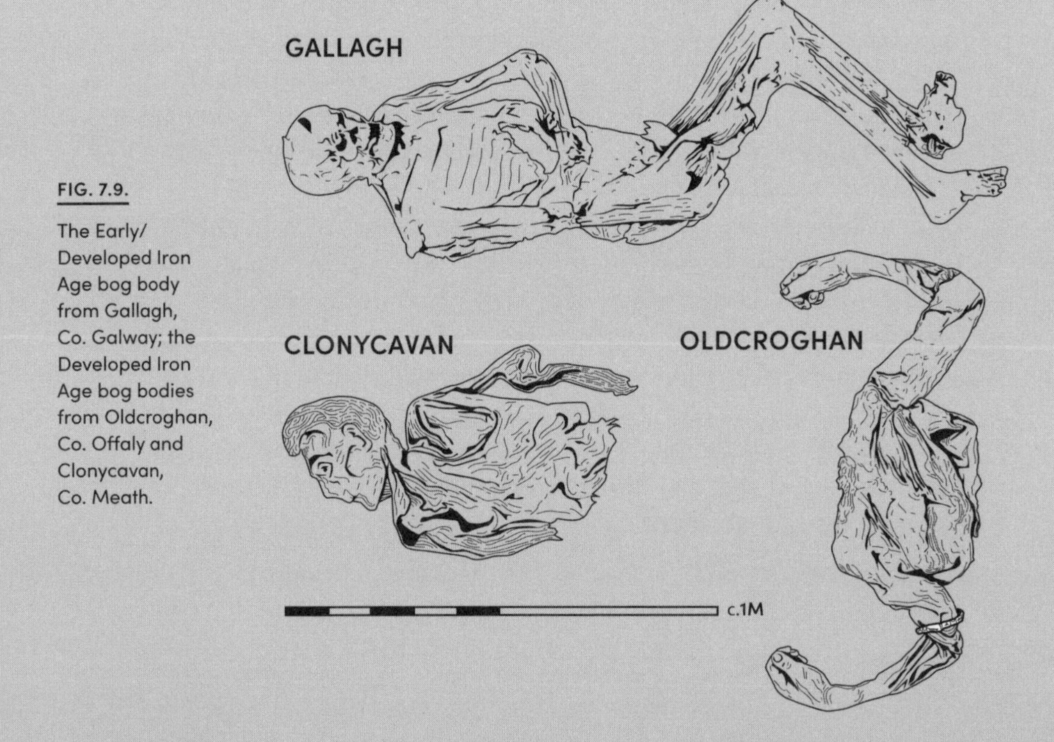

FIG. 7.9.

The Early/Developed Iron Age bog body from Gallagh, Co. Galway; the Developed Iron Age bog bodies from Oldcroghan, Co. Offaly and Clonycavan, Co. Meath.

Age religion, conducted to appease the gods. The people targeted could have been regarded as socially or physically special, those who had transgressed social codes, or were prisoners of wars or hostages.[47]

While there are bog bodies dating to the Early Iron Age, such as Moydrum Man, Co. Meath (753 BC to 409 BC), and others to the Late Iron Age such as Derryvarroge Man, Co. Kildare (between AD 228 to AD 343), the best examples date to the Developed Iron Age.[48] At Oldcroghan, Co. Offaly a man in his early to mid-twenties, standing six feet tall (1.83m), was deposited in a bog pool between 362 BC and 175 BC. He may have been tortured before his demise as his nipples appear to have been partly cut through. He was fatally stabbed in the chest, and a cut on the left arm appears to represent a parry wound, before he was decapitated and dismembered. He was then kept in place by hazel withies inserted through his upper arms. That this treatment was meted out to someone of social standing is indicated not just by his physical stature, which would have been exceptional, but also by other features, such as the care with which his hand nails were treated and an elaborate plaited leather band on his left arm.[49] At Clonycavan, Co. Meath a young adult male, just over five feet (or 1.54m) in height, with a beard and a distinctive hair style, died between 392 BC and 201 BC. [PL. 7.D] We know that in the first century AD the Suebi in Germany prepared their hair carefully before battle, but the hairstyle might also have been part of the rituals, including physical torture, carried out before Clonycavan man was killed by having his skull split open by an axe.[50]

Eamonn Kelly argues that the location of bog bodies and other material in the Iron Age is related to boundaries. His explanation for deposition in these boundary locations—and bogs are suitable wet places to mark the junction between territories—is that these are the material expressions of sovereignty and kingship rituals; demonstrating the link between the earth and the transmission of power from one generation to the next at key territorial locations.[51] In this context the placement of human bodies could either be seen as votive offerings to an earth deity and/or the elimination of potential leaders or rivals at times of social transition. The character and treatment of the males from Oldcroghan and Clonycavan perhaps fit more readily with the second scenario. As Giles has put it, this perspective has the advantage of altering our perception of bog bodies from just victims or social scapegoats to 'powerful, even sacred or semi-divine sovereign kings'.[52] Looking at links between bog bodies and the wider burial record, it is worth emphasising that the individuals represented in burials and deposits are socially selected; barrow cemeteries themselves are often in boundary locations, ditches provide boundaries for individual ring-ditches, and the patterns discussed above regarding the placement of barrows and graves in cemeteries may well echo the transmission of social position over generations. It is against this background that the placement of a middle-aged adult male in a splayed, prone position in the ditch of an enclosure at Carroweighter, Co. Roscommon in the Developed Iron Age might usefully be assessed. As with some of the bog bodies, violence had been meted out to this individual; his right foot had been severed peri-mortem and placed between his legs. The location and character of this burial contrasts with the Early Iron Age deposit of cremated bone of at least one adolescent/young adult above pyre material in a pit at the centre of the enclosure.[53]

The possibility that bog bodies could represent sacrifices to or be material manifestations of deities has been strengthened by the discovery in bogs of what appear to be representations in wood of such deities. [FIG. 7.10, PL. 7.E] Anthropomorphic wooden figurines from Britain and Ireland date from from 3000 BC to 350 BC, and similar figures are known from the wetlands of northern Europe.[54] Some are well-known, such as the figure from Ralaghan, Co. Cavan, made of yew, standing about 1.13m in height and carved between 1253 BC and 829 BC. The legs are slightly flexed, not separated, and at the feet there is a spike or tenon, which would have fitted into a squared wooden pedestal that has not survived. A well-defined pubic area has a central hole, suggesting gender fluidity. While arms are not represented, facial features are detailed.[55] The closest parallel

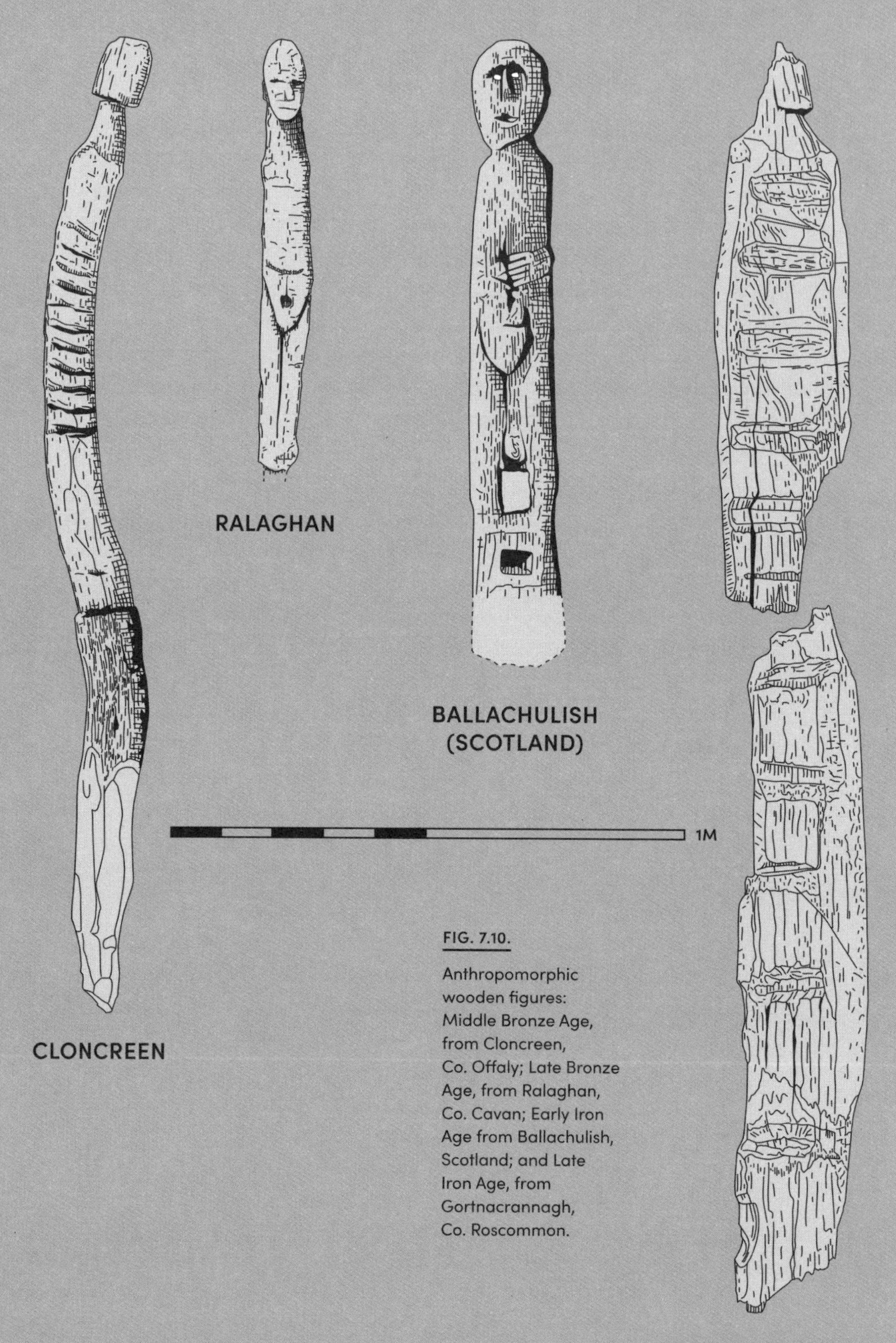

FIG. 7.10.

Anthropomorphic wooden figures: Middle Bronze Age, from Cloncreen, Co. Offaly; Late Bronze Age, from Ralaghan, Co. Cavan; Early Iron Age from Ballachulish, Scotland; and Late Iron Age, from Gortnacrannagh, Co. Roscommon.

PL. 7.E.

The Late Bronze Age wooden figure from Ralaghan, Co. Cavan.

to Ralaghan is the Ballachulish figure from the west coast of Scotland dating to between 791 BC and 411 BC. This figure of oak—which appears to be female—was found face down with wickerwork over it, in a location overlooking Loch Leven.[56]

The trunk of an ash tree, 5m in length, with one end pointed and the other shaped like a head, was laid flat as part of the structure of the wooden trackway at Corlea dated to 148 BC.[57] Recently, a series of figures, carved from alder, have been found at Cloncreen and Ballykean, Co. Offaly, mostly dating to the later Bronze Age. These pieces, up to about 2m in length, are carved in the round to suggest a head at one end and worked to a rough point at the other. The most notable features are notches cut with a bronze axe down the sides of these figurines, defining the torso.[58] They were found in association with brushwood platforms, one on its side directly below a dense layer of brushwood. Similar figures are known from Denmark, several associated with offerings and placed under stones. A figure from Cloncreen dating to around the middle of the second millennium BC displays a concern with distinguishing the upper and lower body. The lower body was left with the bark in place and had a flexed profile, reminiscent of the legs of the Ralaghan figure. The recent discovery at a riverside fen at Gortnacrannagh, Co. Roscommon, of a Late Iron Age notched figure carved of oak suggests that this practice continued. The figure is dated between AD 252 to AD 413; the surviving portion is 2.84m long, with notches along the length. Slight tapering suggests a waist or hips in the middle; the neck and head are damaged. The back is convex and rough. It was found face downwards west of a series of platforms, suggesting deliberate display and decommissioning. The deposition of unburnt human cranial fragments within a trackway appears to be associated with a cluster of animal skulls and artefacts.[59]

Returning to the question of the context of crouched inhumation as a burial rite in the last couple of centuries BC, it is relevant that in wetland areas we can see the practice of the placement of selected individuals in water and the display of the human body in the form of wooden anthropomorphic figures—life-size and larger. That there may have been linkages between these practices is illustrated by the intent to display and venerate the anthromorphic figures as living beings, and convey their 'death', deliberate burial and covering over.

In later prehistoric Ireland, inhumation—whether the burial of bodies or body images—appears to have been restricted to special, unusual people. People who were in some sense both peripheral to society but also of crucial significance and central to it: children; socially élite adult males, seen as related to the gods or as having transgressed social mores; and ancestral, gender-fluid figures. The crouched inhumation burials from the second century BC on may continue a pre-existing tradition of marking the death of special individuals, and could provide an important link to the expansion of the use of inhumation in the early centuries AD. The particular rite of crouched burial in a grave and the objects placed with some burials indicate connections with Britain and farther afield. In addition, elements of this burial rite, the locations and contexts in which people were buried, and links with earlier monuments and graves suggest a concern to integrate past and present. Furthernore, inhumation could have been deliberately used to highlight the social position of individuals. That this mortuary rite took place against a background of some continuity of cosmological or religious belief is indicated by the context in which we find inhumed burials. Given the dynamism of the contemporary social world, considerable variety in practice might be expected, and we find this in the fact that sites already long established as cemeteries or sacred places persist as foci of deposition, and that cremation continued to be practised.

At Tara, the complexity of the treatment of the dead by the living is indicated by Iron Age activity at the adjacent sites of the Rath of the Synods and Ráith na Ríg. [SEE PL. 6.F] Helen Roche's excavation at Ráith na Ríg demonstrated that this large earthwork with external rampart, internal ditch and a timber palisade on the inner bank of the ditch, was constructed in the first century BC. Unburnt human and animal bone appears to have been deliberately deposited in the ditch. These include human cranial bones, possibly of an adolescent male, found close to the base of the ditch accompanied by cattle and sheep bones. The articulated skeleton of an infant, dating to between 42 BC and AD 78, was deliberately deposited with dog bones under sod-like material about a metre above the base of the ditch.[60] Ger Dowling has proposed that these deposits served to intensify and define the symbolic power of the boundary of this enclosure, inserted into the landscape and associated with emerging kingship. It defined the most important zone of the hill, containing the ancient Neolithic passage tomb and one of the major foci of the Bronze Age barrow cemetery.[61] The formal burial of a child echoes the wider occurrence of an age-specific burial rite. The deposit of fragments of a cranium of what may be a young male in the base of the ditch could be seen as a dryland equivalent of a bog body, deposited to mark the creation of a key boundary.

At the Rath of the Synods, a barrow with cremation depositions was remodelled at least once, and a crouched inhumation of an adult on its right side and facing west was placed over the centre of the barrow, apparently disturbing an earlier cremation deposit. To the south-east of this barrow, cremations, crouched inhumations and extended inhumations occur within the multivallate Rath of the Synods enclosure, which is dated to around AD 100 to AD 400, with an assemblage of Roman material focused on glass and pottery drinking vessels. It appears that the inhumation burials by and large post-date the residential enclosure. The character of the Rath of the Synods enclosure, with echoes of the symbolic potency of multiplication seen in both Celtic and Roman contexts, its location just to the north of Ráith na Ríg, the incorporation of an earlier barrow, the exotic and selective range of Romano-British material—and the possibility of the presence of two rectangular shrines—indicate that ritual and ceremonial practice now made reference to and incorporated practices emanating from the Roman world, and more specifically Roman Britain. Irish society, certainly in the east, was clearly being influenced by these wider cultural contacts and influences.[62]

Knowth, Co. Meath was a major centre of Neolithic activity. Unlike Tara it does not seem to have been a focus during the Bronze Age. Its use as an Iron Age cemetery [FIG. 7.11], from the second century BC, appears to represent a deliberate evocation of its status as an ancient, sacred place, chosen, as George Eogan put it, as a 'focus of wider religious significance'.[63] The dated burials centre on the first century AD and all appear to have been flexed or crouched inhumations. Four of the burials were of children and ten were of young adults. The burials were placed on the northern, western and southern side of the Great Mound (Knowth tomb 1) built in the Neolithic to cover two passage tombs. In the early medieval period this would become the focus of considerable settlement (and further burial) activity as the royal site of the rulers of the kingdom of North Brega. The location of the Iron Age burials suggests there was a concern with placing selected individuals close to either the main mound or the small passage tomb mounds, in the shadow of past times.[64]

Eleven of the Knowth burials had grave gifts, such as rings, glass and bone bead necklaces and bracelets. A burial (burials 8/9) that has received particular attention is that dated to between 40 BC and AD 121, of two adult males both around 30 years old, placed on their backs, head to toe, in a north-south orientation. Also placed in the grave, possibly before the bodies were put in, were beads of bone and glass, bone die, gaming pieces, metal rings and smooth stone

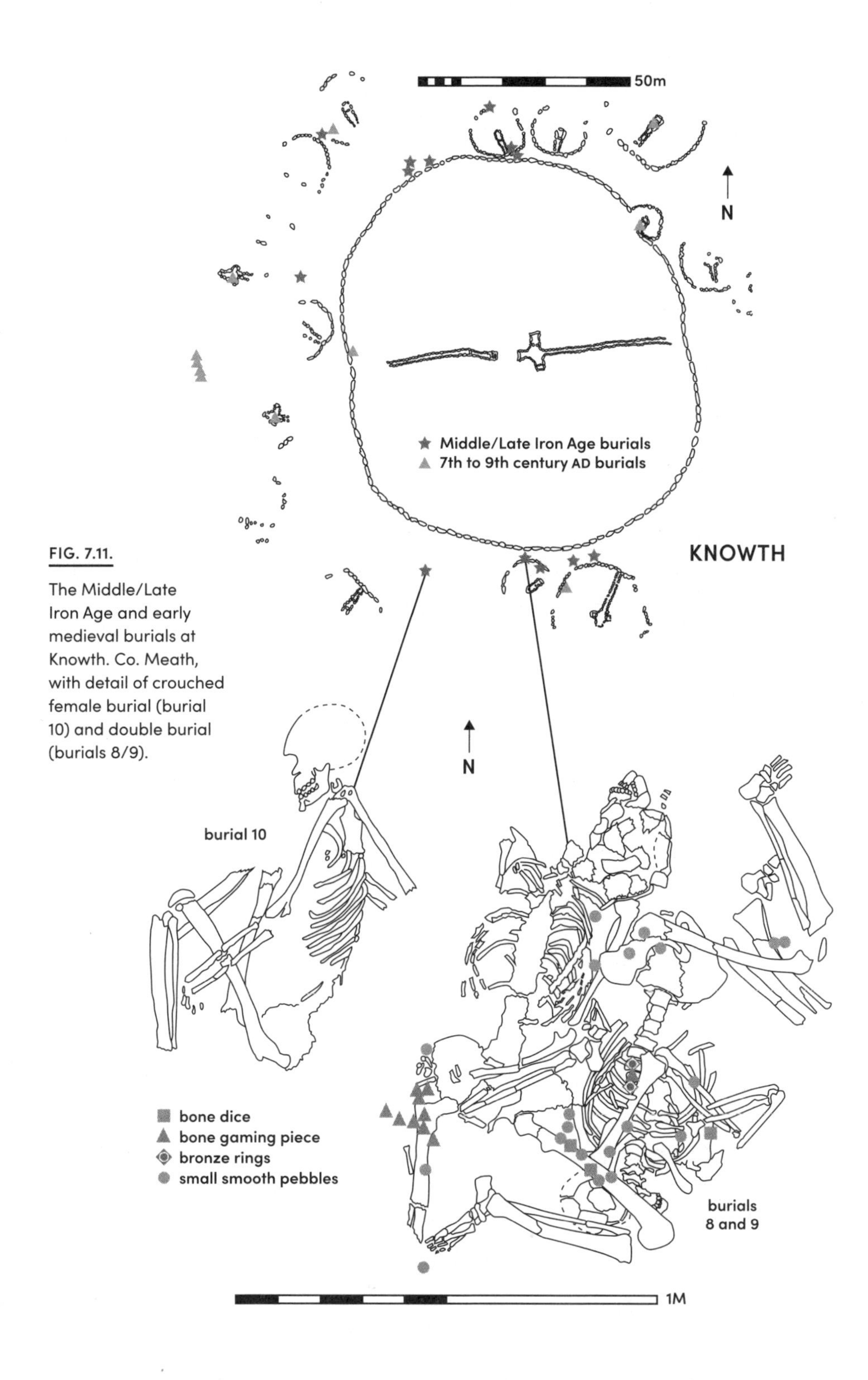

FIG. 7.11.

The Middle/Late Iron Age and early medieval burials at Knowth. Co. Meath, with detail of crouched female burial (burial 10) and double burial (burials 8/9).

pebbles. The men had been decapitated and the heads placed with the bodies. One interpretation of this burial is related to the objects: the bone die and gaming pieces have been read as suggesting the men had transgressed or deviated from social norms. In many societies, however, this kind of material is related to acts of divination rather than recreation. What we may be seeing is the treatment of two individuals who played an important social role. Their violent treatment parallels that meted out to individuals buried in dryland and wetland contexts.[65]

What are we to make of the Iron Age mortuary practices at Knowth? The similarity of some of the objects placed with the dead to those found in a burnt state with cremated deposits elsewhere indicate that cremation and inhumation were practiced at the same time. The burials represent activity over a few hundred years. Combined with the small number of child burials, this suggests socially restricted access to burial. The furnished child burials hint that social status was on a lineage basis. This ties in with the sense of a development of social hierarchy seen in early historic sources. Differentiation is also seen in the presence or absence of material placed with the person in the grave. Isotope analysis suggests that some individuals were local, while others came from either further north in Ireland or from northern Britain.[66] What is clear is that the crouched inhumations of the Middle/Late Iron Age burial phase at Knowth took place in the context of a deliberate evocation of links with the past. Elizabeth O'Brien and Edel Bhreathnach point out this could be attributed to either non-local groups or emerging local dynasties seeking to illustrate or reinforce historical and ancestral connections, as well as the wider connections expressed in the grave goods. The latter can be plausibly linked to other signs of Romanisation in the Boyne area, most immediately to the deposition of Roman objects outside the entrance to Newgrange but also to activity at Tara.[67]

The diversity of the mortuary practices of local social élites at this time can be seen by comparing Knowth with, for example, broadly

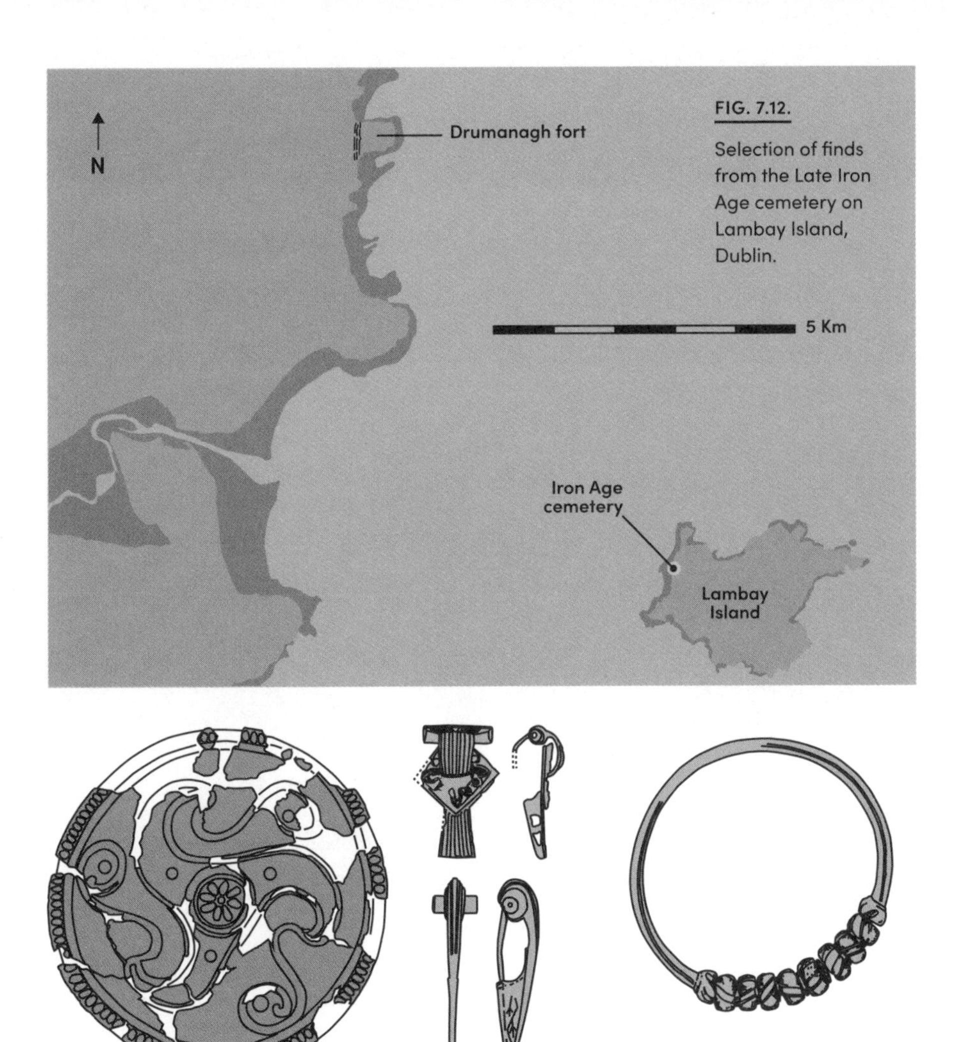

FIG. 7.12.

Selection of finds from the Late Iron Age cemetery on Lambay Island, Dublin.

contemporary activity at the Rathdooney Beg barrows in Sligo or the Roman style cremation burial at Stoneyford in Kilkenny, but particularly with the Late Iron Age cemetery on the island of Lambay, off the coast of Dublin, dating to the first and early second century AD. [FIG. 7.12. PL. 7.F] Here, close to the harbour on the western shore of the island, at least two crouched or flexed burials were found, although there are indications of a greater number of

individuals and burials. The two burials appear to have been in shallow pits. One was, as described by R.A.S. Macalister, accompanied by a 'sword, shield and ornaments' found under 'an iron disc'. Three bronze mounts probably adorned a sword scabbard. Among the ornaments were five Roman fibulae, two bracelets (of jet and bronze) and a beaded, bronze torc. Other finds that have been recognised are two decorated sheet bronze discs and an iron mirror; perhaps the iron disc referred to above. The Lambay burials and grave goods have been discussed as both showing the strength of Roman influences in eastern Ireland at this time and as indicating evidence of people fleeing the empire.[68]

PL. 7.F.

The harbour at Lambay; the Iron Age cemetery is located above the wall at the back of the harbour, left background. The hilltop cairn (Neolithic passage tomb?) of Knockbane is visible on the skyline.

It seems clear that people on Lambay and at Drumanagh, the large promontory fort on the mainland coast immediately north-west of Lambay, had strong links with the Roman world, and this coastal area was a nexus between this internationalised world and social élites in eastern Ireland. There are promontory forts and two ring-ditch clusters on Lambay, indicating a local community who expressed their role and internationalised identity in the way they buried the distinguished dead. They used an inhumation rite that might have a background in the pre-Roman Iron Age in Britain, and that particularly in south-west Britain continued through the Roman period, but that was also a long-established practice in Ireland. The objects placed with the dead demonstrated a mix of technologies and designs coming from Roman (Britain and Gaul), Irish Sea and Irish influences. This is what might be expected, as Cahill Wilson and colleagues put it, 'in the fluid cultural world of Ireland at the edge of empire'.[69]

TRAJECTORIES OF CHANGE IN THE FIRST MILLENNIUM AD; FROM THE IRON AGE TO EARLY MEDIEVAL IRELAND

The Iron Age is regarded as ending at AD 400, with the Christianisation of the island of Ireland seen as marking the establishment of early medieval Ireland.[70] Such a major religious change might be expected to be reflected in mortuary practice. In the fifth to the seventh century AD there is a considerable diversity of graves and cemeteries in use across the island, including burial within Christian consecrated ground. One way of viewing this evidence is to see it as a reflection of the complexities of that conversion process on the ground. It is only after that period that formal Christian cemeteries appear to become the socially acceptable place and mode of burial for the wider population.[71] In the Late Iron Age, from AD 1 to AD 400, there appear to be a smaller number of burials and deposits compared to the preceding Developed Iron Age and the succeeding earliest phase of the early medieval period.[72] The isotopic evidence from human skeletal material and the evidence from material culture, such as imported pottery, indicates that in the Late Iron Age and early medieval periods there was mobility within Ireland and continued contact, including human movement, with late Roman Britain and the wider Roman and post-Roman world; Ireland was a major focus of trade along the Atlantic by the seventh century.[73] So, there are interesting issues to address in assessing the impact of the beginnings of the historic period—and specifically Christian ideology—on approaches to dealing with the dead.

Cremation continued in the Late Iron Age and into the early medieval period.[74] Late Iron Age cremation practices show continuity from earlier in the Iron Age. At the Knockgraffon ring-barrow [FIG. 7.4], analysis of cremated bone in the fill of the ditch identified at least one middle-aged adult, and associated hazel charcoal gave a date of 343–44 BC. A central pit within the ring-ditch produced cremated bone, which could not be definitely identified but seems likely to be human, with a date from associated hazel charcoal of from AD 233 to AD 395. About 2.5km to the south, an unenclosed pit contained a small amount of cremated bone from an old adult, and ash charcoal from the deposit was dated to between AD 40 to AD 350.[75]

Extended inhumation was adopted as the standard Roman rite of burial in the first century AD, and influences from Roman practice appear from the second century AD in Ireland. Burials found at Bray, Co. Wicklow in the nineteenth century were placed east–west, side by side, in graves with a marking stone at the head and foot. The burials were dated to the second century AD by the Roman coins located in the chest area of the skeletons.[76] One significant implication to be drawn from this is that east–west supine burial, often taken as an indicator of Christian burial practice, was being practised in Ireland long before the advent of Christianity. The conventional view is to see these Bray burials as an anomaly to the pattern of a distinct gap between the earlier crouched inhumations and the widespread adoption of extended inhumation after AD 400 in the conversion period, with eventual alignment to Christianising influences.[77] There are, however, sites that supplement the evidence for the adoption of east–west inhumation in a non-Christian context. Extended inhumation burials dating prior to the conversion period were placed into existing ancestral burial places at Carbury Hill. Co, Kildare. Here, at one of the ring barrows (B), there are Iron Age cremations and fifteen extended inhumations, four of which have now been dated. One of these was a male burial dating to between AD 211 and AD 394.[78] This appears to be an early example of the rite of extended inhumation where it seems highly probable that this man was not a Christian.

The end of the Iron Age was a period of major change, spurred by contact with late Roman Britain, crystallised in the Christianising missions of Palladius and Patrick and others in the fifth century. The reception and understanding of innovative ideas, objects and ideology would have differed depending on local community and social contexts. Not surprisingly, when we examine the burial record there is considerable diversity in how extended inhumation was more widely adopted from around about AD 400, and there are a range of contexts in which such burials occur, including apparently open, unbounded cemeteries as well as enclosed ones.[79]

At Cross, Co. Galway [SEE FIG. 2.1] there are Bronze Age cremation deposits, along with an Iron Age one dating from the second century BC to the first century AD. The extended inhumation of a male aged 35–45 years and dating to between AD 252 and AD 429 was placed in a stone-lined grave, disturbed but preserved in the ditch of a ring-ditch. A woman and an adolescent were buried within the ring-ditch, the woman in a central location, and two further female burials were found outside. These four burials dated to between AD 342 and AD 559. A roughly east–west inhumation of a young male dated to between AD 423 and AD 600 was placed between the two ditch fills of the ring ditch. Some disarticulated human remains, animal bones and a few objects also occurred in the ditch fills. The final use of the site was the construction of a small penannular ring ditch to the south-east of the larger one. This contained the burial of an infant dating to between AD 532 and AD 647.[80] While some of the burials might be of Christians, they are buried in a traditional style and place—a *ferta*, an ancestral or kin-group burial ground. The placement of the inhumed remains of a young man in the ditch of the larger ring ditch echoes the placement of cremation deposits at other sites.

At Claristown 2, Co. Meath, an adult male, 35–45 years old, dating from between AD 126 to AD 535, was buried in a stone-lined grave aligned north-east to south-west and covered by a small cairn, on a site where there had been Iron Age domestic activity. The next phase of activity involved the construction of a ring ditch, cut through a sealing layer over the area surrounding the burial, within which the burial was centrally placed, with post-holes arranged in pairs in the ditch. It appears that these posts were taken down. Finally, the ring-ditch was covered by a cairn of stones. The burial and monument became a focus for further burial in the fifth to the seventh century AD, with graves immediately north of the ring-ditch and a smaller group to the south. The Claristown individual appears to represent a pre-Christian style of extended inhumation, interred in a traditional manner in effect creating a *ferta,* which in turn became a focus of burial in the early medieval period.[81]

Enclosed cemeteries provide us with the opportunity to examine how the living deliberately evoked links with the past, or, in keeping with contemporary social transformations, were looking to the future rather than the past. At Ardsallagh 1 [FIG. 7.13], about a kilometre to the north-west of the Ardsallagh 2 ring-ditch cemetery near Tara discussed above, 30 extended inhumations were found in association with a penannular ring-ditch. Activity began in the Late Bronze Age with the deposition of a cremation in a pot. In the last few centuries BC, cremated human remains were placed in pits, located both east and west of the ring-ditch. The ring-ditch itself was constructed in the early centuries of the first millennium AD. In the base of the ditch there was a deposit consisting of the cremated remains of a human cranium, dated between AD 30 and AD 230. In the period

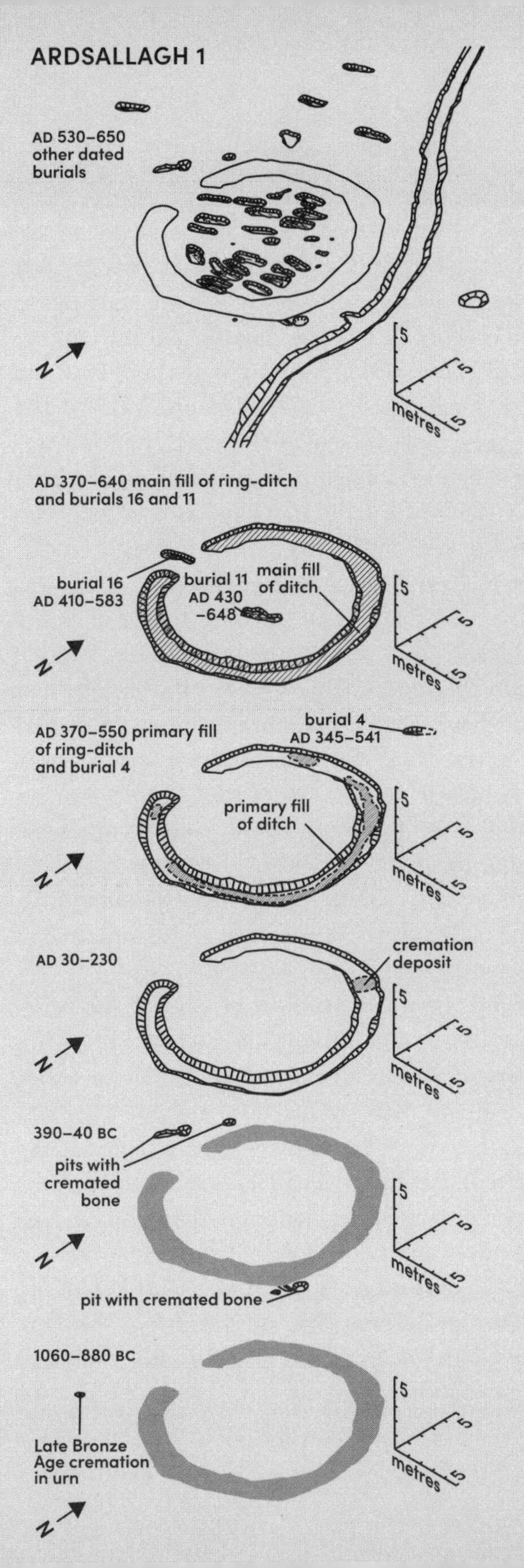

FIG. 7.13.

The background and development of the Late Iron Age ring-ditch at Ardsallagh 1, Co. Meath.

between the fourth and the sixth century AD, a stone layer or setting was placed along the base of the ditch. In turn, this appears to have been deliberately covered by clay and was later re-cut. Two striking features of this sequence are how closely it parallels the activities at the contemporary large ring-ditch at Ardsallagh 2, and the deposition of probable cremated human bone throughout the fills of the ditch, indicating this mortuary practice was still in use. [FIG. 7. 7] The earliest inhumation burials, outside and to the north of the ring-ditch and at the west-facing entrance of the ring-ditch, are broadly contemporary with the filling of the ditch, which dates to between AD 370 and AD 600. The earliest dated burial, from between AD 430 to AD 648, of an adult male and child within the ring-ditch, was off-centre and may have been marked by a post at the head of the grave. The burials nearest the entrance were laid from head to toe in a line that extended into the monument, while in the eastern half of the interior there are clearly defined north–south rows. It would appear that individual graves were respected, and perhaps marked. Albeit there are male burials in important locations, adult females and possible females dominate the burial record; no infants were recovered, suggesting that this may have been a cemetery restricted over generations to a particular cohort of the local population, a point emphasised by the placement of a possible sceptre with one of the burials, dating to between AD 536 and AD 659.[82]

A striking feature from recent excavations of sites of the earliest medieval period has been the recognition of familial or kin group burial grounds set within settlement enclosures. These settlement-cemeteries began in the fifth century AD, with an increased foundation rate in the sixth century. The cemetery tends to be located in the southern or eastern part of the enclosure; is itself often defined by enclosing elements; and can exhibit evidence for links with the prehistoric past or can be a new foundation.[83] While most are located in eastern Ireland, comparison of three cemetery settlements in County Galway in the west indicate their variable site histories.[84] [FIG. 7.14, PL. 7.G] At Treanbaun, a pit dating to the Early Iron Age, from between

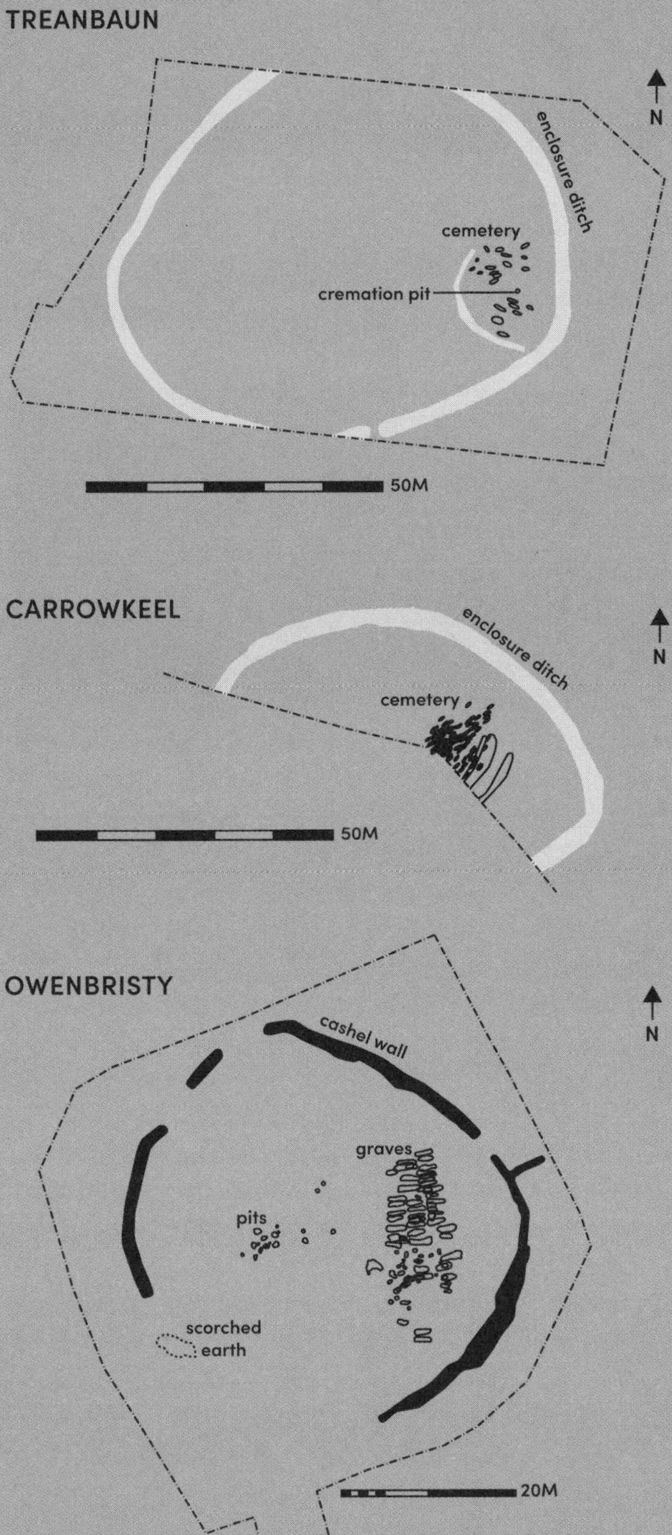

TREANBAUN

N
enclosure ditch
cemetery
cremation pit
50M

CARROWKEEL

N
enclosure ditch
cemetery
50M

OWENBRISTY

N
cashel wall
graves
pits
scorched earth
20M

FIG. 7.14.

Settlement-cemeteries at Treanbaun, Carrowkeel and Owenbristy, Co. Galway.

PL. 7.G.

The settlement-cemetery cashel at Owenbristy, Co. Galway during flood conditions.

750 BC to 390 BC, with a token cremation deposit (human/animal), was centrally placed within a possible ring-ditch. Sometime in the seventh century AD the ring-ditch was truncated on its eastern side by the ditch of a large enclosure. Thirty-one extended inhumation burials were placed in two clusters within the area of the ring-ditch, to the north and south of the centre. The burials date from the late seventh to the early thirteenth century, with a concentration in the period from AD 800 to AD 1000. The demographic profile of the burials, with fifteen adults and sixteen sub-adults, suggests that this was a family cemetery for the occupants of the enclosure.[85]

At the Carrowkeel enclosure—like Treanbaun, on a low ridge within what appears to be an early medieval settlement landscape—a pair of curving ditch segments in the eastern area partially defined a burial area or cemetery, which extended into the unexcavated part of the site. Rather than reflecting or respecting the presence of an older monument, as was the case at Treanbaun, the burial area at Carrowkeel was deliberately defined as a new focus when the larger enclosure was created. In the portion of this burial area that was excavated, there were 132 burials, dating AD 650 to AD 1480, with the main phase of burial being up to AD 1000. In contrast to Treanbaun, the burials are dominated by sub-adults from early in the sequence of placement of burials.[86]

The low-lying site at Owenbristy was a cashel—a circular enclosure defined by a stone wall. Within it, a group of 81 burials was restricted to the east, arranged in three north–south rows, many stone-lined and with lintel slabs. There were 95 individuals, with an almost equal proportion of adults and sub-adults. Interestingly, the main concentration of sub-adult burials was towards the south. The most important time of use for burial was between the mid-sixth and the late tenth century AD. Later in the medieval period the cemetery was reused, mostly for the burial of infants and children. Towards the southern end of the burial area the graves respect a series of pits, which have been interpreted as suggesting a wooden building with an east-west orientation, possibly a church. This, then, is what appears to be an early Christian cemetery and church site.[87]

These three settlement-cemeteries suggest different rationales for the foundation of familial cemeteries from the sixth century AD, related to significant social and economic changes at that time. Significantly, burial continues at these sites well after the conversion period, and only Owenbristy could be seen as a formal Christian cemetery. To reiterate the complexity of this early medieval world, it is useful to discuss one of the 'classic' settlement-cemeteries in eastern Ireland: Raystown, Co. Meath.[88] **[FIG. 7.15]** The enclosed burial area here was at the core of the settlement enclosure. The first burials date from the fourth to the fifth century AD , at a time when the

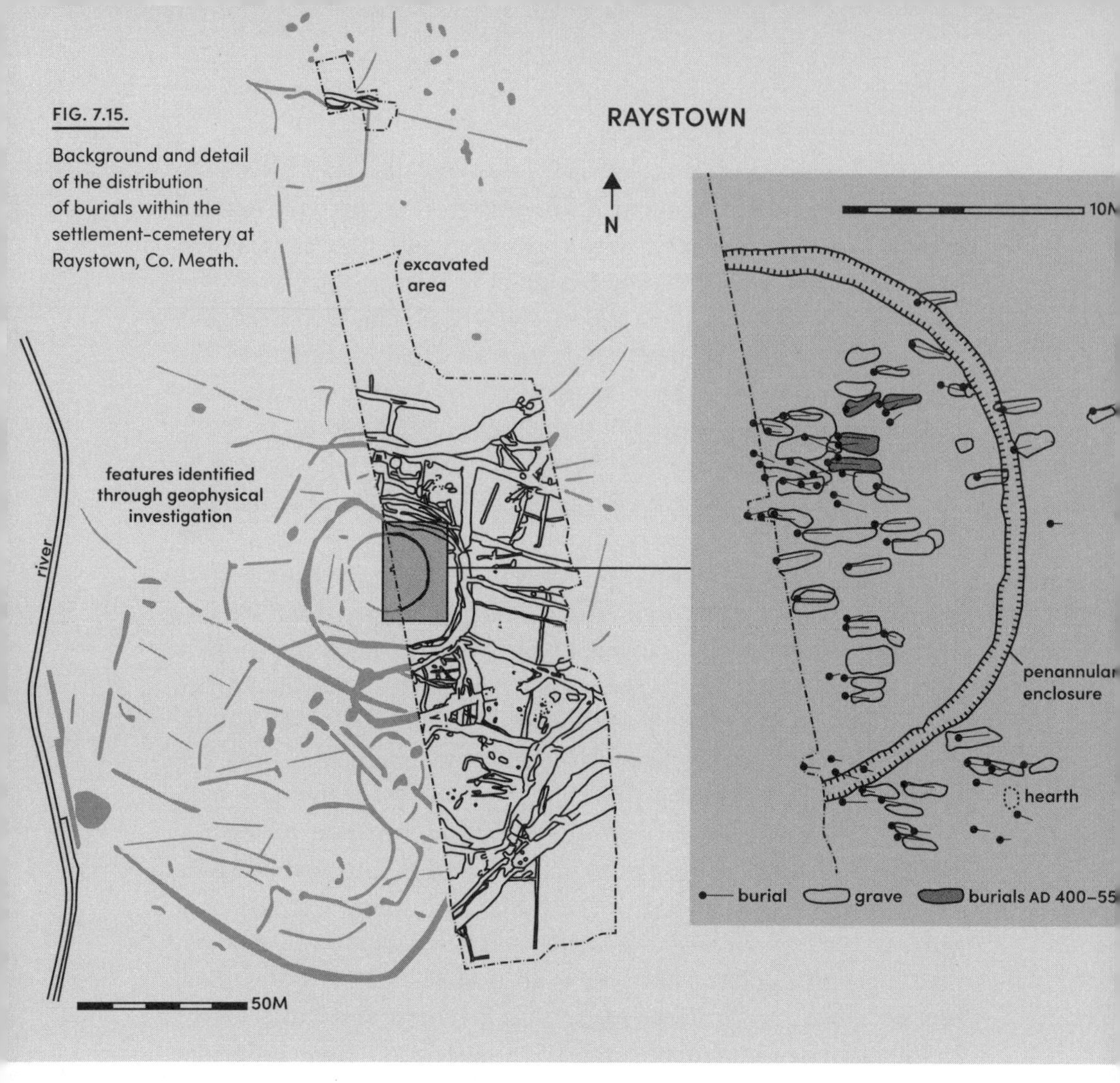

FIG. 7.15.

Background and detail of the distribution of burials within the settlement-cemetery at Raystown, Co. Meath.

earliest churches may have been established in the local territory of southern Brega. A second, outer burial enclosure was added after AD 500. There was no previous burial or ancestral focus at Raystown, and the initiation of a family cemetery seems to have been a key element in the establishment of the site, which continues as a settlement focus up the twelfth century AD. Burial activity continues alongside, and as an integral part of, settlement activities.

The actual settlement evidence from some settlement-cemeteries can be sparse, but we know that Raystown was an important agricultural production centre and residence from its foundation in the fifth century until the Anglo-Norman settlement of the area in the late twelfth century. The presence of mills indicates the importance of crop production and processing, and that Raystown was tied into a wider settlement landscape; a processing centre providing services to other farms within a wider secular or ecclesiastical estate. A total of 93 burials were uncovered at Raystown. It has been estimated that the total burial mortuary population over a period of 500 years may have been in the order of 300–400 people, indicating small numbers of people buried over a long time and multiple generations. Most of the burials took place up to around AD 800, with smaller numbers after that. As Matthew Seaver has noted, adding the outer burial enclosure looks like a deliberate decision, planning for the future expansion (and death) of the community and keeping a boundary between the living and the dead, even if the living and those who had died were close together.[89]

Looking at the earliest activity on the site and considering the first early medieval phases, Raystown exemplifies the scale and complexity of changes taking place in the fifth and sixth century AD. It emphasises the difficulty of placing changes in burial practice solely in the context of a shift to a Christian ideology. The archaeological evidence indicates that rather than Christianisation being an inevitable historical process, it was adopted very slowly and, as Tomás Ó Carragáin has put it, local communities engaged with the new religion on their own terms. As Patrick Gleeson suggests, we need to think about the agency of the living, the dead and their communities in negiotating social lives and worldviews.[90] Non-Christian practices, beliefs and rites which syncretised Christian and non-Christian elements would have been present alongside Christian belief and practice. What we see reflected in and through the burial evidence is the expression and practice of this range of different beliefs.

While Christian communities were already established in Ireland when Palladius was appointed as their first bishop in

431, from his own accounts Patrick, evangelising in the northern half of the country later in the fifth century, seems to have been working in a largely non-Christian environment.[91] The first phase of Christianisation is usually attributed to the influence of contacts with Roman Britain and the prestige associated with the fading Roman Empire, against the background of the status attributed in Ireland to *Romanitas* and possession of Roman material culture since the first century AD.[92] There were many lines of communication with western Britain. Irish settlements were established in Wales and Cornwall. Here memorial stones with Irish ogam inscriptions occur and are frequently found in combination with the more popular Latin inscriptions. Some are Christian in character. People were also moving from Ireland to Britain voluntarily or involuntarily, for example as marriage partners or slaves. Movements of people from Britain may have been the process by which Christians first came to Ireland, but there also appear to have been direct contacts with western France and the Mediterranean, as indicated by material culture and the character of some of the earliest cross-inscribed stones in the south-west of Ireland.[93]

The evidence indicates that the process of Christianisation was gradual, and ultimately its success depended on a significant incorporation of existing religious beliefs and practices. Christianity could be envisaged first as a minority religion, then, as it became more prevalent, as taking a more central role in society, reflected in the number and density of early ecclesiastical sites across the island. It adjusted to local conditions and customs, and in doing so incorporated many local ideas and traditions. Churches were established close to pre-Christian centres. Irish saints, for example Brigid, often appear to be transmogrified versions of old deities. The sacred nature of springs was transformed by their dedication as holy wells. The celebration and marking at special places of key times in the seasonal cycle, which formed the backdrop and rhythm to everyday and ceremonial life in pre-Christian belief, were given a Christian appearance and interpreted in terms of Christian ideology.[94]

This assimilation of pre-Christian practice can be seen in mortuary practice. As we have seen, the burial practice that we take as characteristic of early Christianity—east-west, extended inhumation in graves that were either stone-lined or simply dug and unprotected—appears to have been practiced in Ireland prior to the establishment of Christianity. So, perhaps we need not only to recognise the existence of non-Christian familial cemeteries as discussed above, but also to critically re-assess sites that in the past have been seen as Christian primarily on the basis of this burial rite.[95]

The Christian belief in the literal physical resurrection of the body—that the body would arise again at the Last Judgement—appears to require that the entire body should be buried, or that all parts of the body should be interred together.[96] But as Gleeson and McLaughlin have pointed out, an apparent peak in dated cremations in the seventh and eighth century AD raises new questions and indicates that cremation could have been practiced in a Christian context, as evidenced by the cross-shaped mount found with a cremation deposit at Ask, Co. Wexford.[97] The site of Annaghilla, Co. Tyrone, where cremation deposits were placed from the fifth to the ninth century AD alongside an early medieval inhumation settlement-cemetery, demonstrates that communities were using cremation and inhumation as complementary rites.[98] Gleeson and McLaughlin argue that cremation should be seen as an element of diverse mortuary technologies that remained in use long after conversion and Christianisation.[99] **[FIG. 7.16]**

Not only are inhumation and cremation complementary rites, the continued use of cremation—and excarnation in the form of disarticulated bones—indicates that we have perhaps too readily put mortuary rites into pre-Christian and early Christian categories. As we cannot differentiate between pre-Christian and Christian modes of inhumation burial, in reality there may have been a mixture of people of different faiths buried together or apart. Elizabeth O'Brien's analysis of the historical sources suggests that into the early eighth century, people who were Christians were being buried

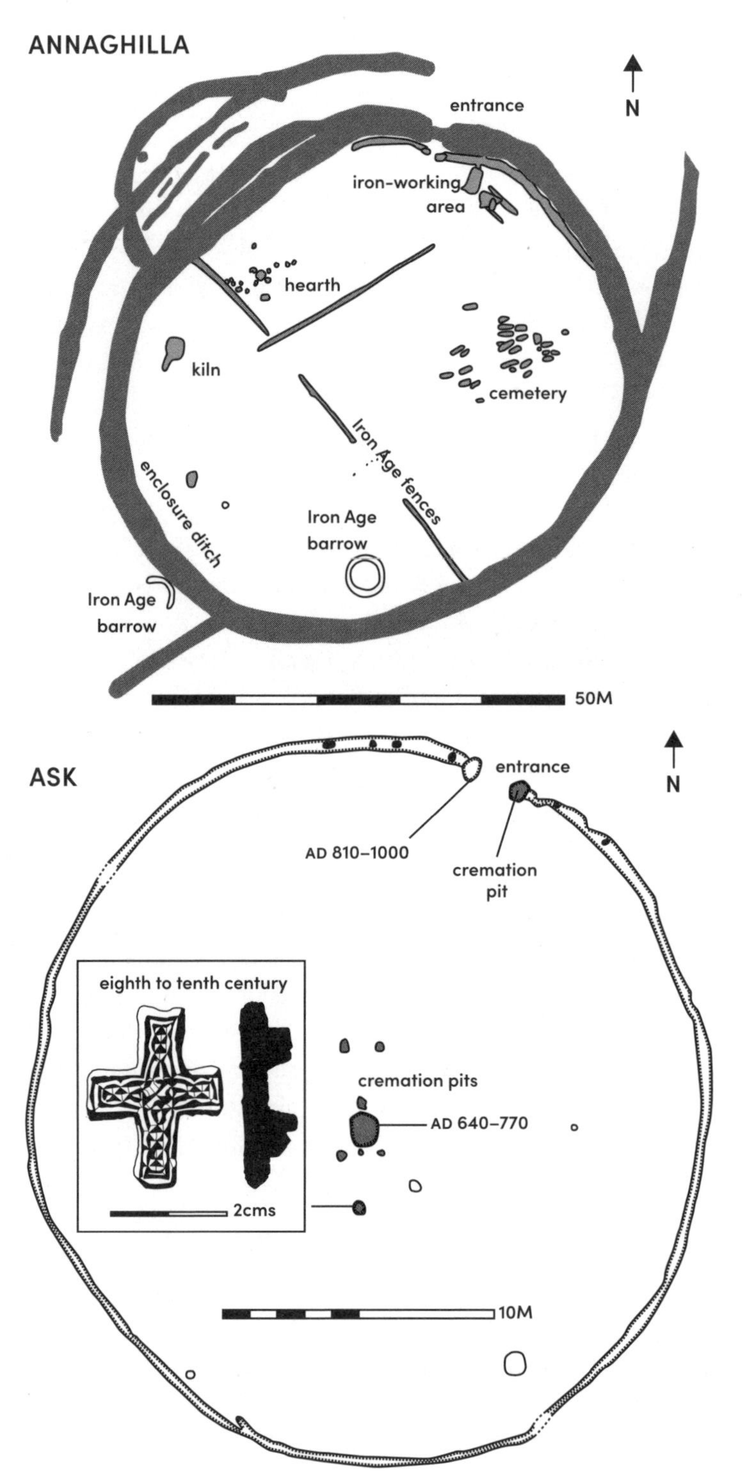

FIG. 7.16.

The cemeteries at Annaghilla, Co. Tyrone, and Ask, Co. Wexford, with detail of a decorated copper-alloy cross-shaped mount from a pit.

alongside people who had different religious beliefs in the small, ditched enclosures referred to as *ferta*, and the family or kin-group cemeteries discussed above.[100] Church tolerance of this position could be seen as a pragmatic recognition of the perhaps tenuous hold of Christianity on much of the population.

With the growing power of the church, however, this practice was increasingly seen as liturgically inappropriate. The term *relic* began to be used by the church authorities for enclosures for burial. It is derived from the Latin, *reliquiae*, referring to the corporal relics of the saints. The burial or reburial of the corporal remains of a saint or holy person within such places provided an alternative focus for burial.[101] Against a background of tradition of burial in sacred places associated with the ancestors—the *ferta*—a move to the *relic* as the place of burial instead would have been socially understood as creating a new sacred focus. Not only were at least some non-ecclesiastical cemeteries abandoned, many small ecclesiastical cemeteries also fell out of use as the focus shifted to burial in community cemeteries at leading local monasteries, where the bones of leading saints were seen as guaranteeing salvation. In the course of the eighth–ninth century, the use of bodily relics of saints was combined with church statutes to identify approved places of burial.[102] Now, non-Christians had to convert to be buried with their kin. We can see this from two perspectives. In the short term it represented the dominance of Christian ideas in burial practice. As Elizabeth O'Brien has put it, 'burial near the bones of a saint become a substitute for burial near the bones of the ancestors'.[103] But viewed in the long term, we might see this as just another shift in the complex, ongoing relationship between the living, the dead and those who had gone before.

Discussing what the burial record can tell of people's beliefs and relationships with Christianity, Ó Carragáin recognised the difficulty of defining an early medieval east–west inhumation as 'pagan' or 'Christian', but argues that we can see Christianisation as having a real, immediate impact on people's understanding of how their world should be ordered, regardless of whether they were Christian or not, as people engaged with the new religion from the fifth century. He suggested that these new ways of engaging with the world can variously be seen in the evidence, from slab and lintelled graves, of a concern with protecting the body until resurrection on Judgement Day; in the manner that burial space and living space were integrated in settlement-cemeteries—in a way they had not been before; and in the new departure in the fifth century of delimiting settlement by a curvilinear enclosure, representing the biblical notion of sanctuary. But Ó Carragáin also recognises the fluidity and hybridity of (mortuary) practices and beliefs and the dialogue between Christian and non-Christian ideas.[104] All of these new departures can just as easily be situated within the milieu of social practices and processes that had been prevalent in Ireland in late pre-Christian times. The adoption of a circular form for both secular and ecclesiastical enclosures in the early medieval period could be seen as a striking endorsement of older traditions. People continued to engage as much with the old as the new. In the turbulent, socially dynamic times of the mid-first millennium AD would it have been evident to people on the ground that Christianity would prevail?

The complexity of the relationship between old and new beliefs is indicated by sites like Johnstown, Co. Meath. Here, a cemetery within a settlement started with the placement of the disarticulated remains of at least three people in a pit, which was covered by a mound in the fourth to the seventh century AD. It did not fall out of use in the eighth century—as might have been expected with the sanction and attraction of burial in ecclesiastical cemeteries—but continued as a burial focus until the fifteenth century. An area south of the enclosure was used as a *cillín* burial ground, for the interment of unbaptised children, up to the beginning of the twentieth century.[105] Here old ways and places continued to have a role in people's lives long after the transition to Christianity. These old ways were effective because, at some level, they continued to have relevance for how people understood death and its place in the immediate social context of their lives.

In 'Saving Grace', John McGahern wrote about the rural perception of the role of the Catholic church in modern Ireland:

> … they saw this version of Roman Catholicism as just another ideological habit they were forced to wear like all the others they had worn since the time of the Druids, observing its compulsory rituals cynically, turning to it only in illness or desperation. Yet none of this is simple … they grew out of a human need. This can be alleviated by material need and scientific advancement, but never abolished. Still sings the ghost, 'What then?'[106]

8.

Postscript:
the living and the dead

Ar scáth a chéile a mhaireann na daoine—
We live in each other's shelter

THE PAST IN THE PRESENT

The father in Valeria Luiselli's haunting novel, *Lost children archive*, about the experience of migrant children in the United States, remarks that '…this whole country is an enormous cemetery … but only some people get proper graves, because most lives don't matter'.[1] All lives matter, but across the span of the first 8,000 years of the settlement of Ireland, we simply do not know how the majority of people were treated at their death and whether they had graves or not. We know how only a minority of the dead were looked after—because their post-mortem treatment mattered to the living and was central to the different social worlds that can be recognised.

The focus of this book is what prehistoric mortuary rites in Ireland tell us about belief and practice in ensuring the dead were treated in an appropriate way. In bringing the book to completion, I was struck by resonances between themes it covers and present-day events and processes. A visit to St Cuthbert of Lindisfarne's shrine in Durham Cathedral just before the Covid-19 pandemic spread in 2020 provided an appreciation of the symbolic power and central position of the bones of the saint in the construction of the medieval cathedral, and of the ongoing importance of the cathedral as a place of prayer, pilgrimage and power, evidenced by its recognition as a World Heritage Site. The continuing power of the bones of the dead is further indicated by the reported removal of the bones of the famed eighteenth-century Russian commander Prince Grigory Potemkin from St Catherine's Cathedral, Kherson, Ukraine in late 2022, when Russian forces retreated from the city.

In Ireland too, the remains of the dead continue to exert influence in society today. Traces of the visible prehistoric dead continue to be revealed, by archaeological (or accidental) discovery. In 2020 a cremation pit cemetery was found beside a Bronze Age settlement

at Ballaghcullia, Co. Roscommon on the route of the N5 road.[2] [PL. 8.A] In regard to more recent history, we have been commemorating the decade between 1912 and 1923, and dealing with the complex manner in which the location and character of the rituals for remembering the dead from the Great War, the 1916 Rising, the War of Independence and the Civil War were shaped by, and in turn themselves shaped, the physical fabric of the landscape of Irish towns and cities. Nuala Johnson's book on the geography of remembrance of the Great War in Ireland is a reminder of this. Eunan O'Halpin and Daithí Ó Corráin recorded the deaths of all who died in the Irish revolution between 1916 and 1921.[3]

PL. 8.A.

Bronze Age settlement at Ballaghcullia, Co. Roscommon, with cremation pit cemetery highlighted on the right, under excavation in 2020.

Death and funerals feature widely in Irish and international fiction, and books about the significance of death as a distinctive element of the culture of contemporary Ireland continue to appear. Furthermore, Irish society is noted for an ability to deal with the dead, as seen in the centrality of the funeral in Irish social life. Curiously, however, the wider social role of death in modern Irish society remains under-examined.[4] Many of us apparently prefer not to have to think about death until it casts its shadow over us in some way. As the title of the novel by Khaled Khalifa about a Syrian family bringing their father to be buried in the ancestral village near Aleppo puts it, *Death is hard work*. It can be seen as macabre, or as a failure of the human body. We tend to assume that medical treatment and technological advances can keep death at bay.[5] The reality, of course, is that we all die.

There were 35,000 deaths in Ireland in 2022, a figure sadly increased over the last few years by fatalities due to Covid-19. The death and funerals of many people are covered by newspapers, television, notably by local radio and social media. As noted above, Irish society is seen as being able to deal with death. Yet there are occasions that give us pause to think about the harsh reality of how particular people are treated in death. A notable example is the discovery of the very high infant mortality rate up to the 1960s, and the treatment of infants' and children's bodies after their death, in mother and baby homes in Ireland.[6]

In the deep past in Ireland there was a diversity of approaches to dealing with these existential issues that might be helpful in reflecting on how we deal with death today. This approach was explored in Samhain, an important collaborative all-island project involving the National Museum of Ireland, Age & Opportunity and Poetry Ireland. It has been developed in a project led by Karina Croucher and colleagues in the UK, which found that archaeology can facilitate discussions and professional practice around death, dying and bereavement by challenging cultural norms, demonstrating and highlighting diversity in death practices. It is the apparent distance of practices in the past that facilitates people today to engage with the experience of death shared by all of us.[7]

Aoife McGrath and Michael Shortall have raised the question of whether the restrictions placed on funerals by public health measures in the face of the Covid-19 pandemic will have a longer-term impact. They note the difficulty of conducting an Irish funeral in those circumstances, of making the time to remember the dead and console the grieving without gathering, touching or sharing. They also note, however, the emergence of new practices: socially distanced guards of honour, lining the roads of the final journey, food left on doorsteps.[8] For an archaeologist this is interesting, as it reflects how changes can occur in rituals and practices and highlights the links between mortuary practice and wider society—something that we focus on and see as a hallmark of societies in the past.

PEOPLE, PLACE AND PRACTICE

Three over-arching themes emerge from the detailed discussion in previous chapters: people, place and practice. It is worth reiterating for a final time that the evidence we have is for the post-mortem treatment of those who, for varying reasons, were regarded as socially significant. This is an interesting parallel with those whose deaths receive wide public notice today—socially prominent individuals, or those whose circumstances of death bring them to broader public and media attention. Tomás Ó Carragáin has suggested that it is only with the emergence of consecrated Christian community cemeteries from the late first millennium AD that the burial places of the majority of the population become visible for the first time.[9] It is true that prior to then particular leading individuals are remembered in death, but it is also the case that the socially significant dead of earlier times represented a range of people—adults, adolescents and children—from kin- or lineage-based groups. The cohort of young adults whose treatment in death is marked in the archaeological record may have been particularly significant. They were no longer dependent on society, but rather society depended on them to provide future generations. If these groups are socially sustained and successful, they become multi-generational in character; on the other hand, as today, their deaths are seen as a particular social as well as family loss.

The project led by Croucher mentioned above was called Continuing Bonds, and it led to discussion of relationships between people and objects as an expression of the relationships between the living and the dead. Reflecting on how simple things can take on special meaning because of their links with the dead is a reminder to us as archaeologists not simply to focus on high-quality 'grave goods' that were placed with the remains of the dead, but to consider how these relationships and links might be expressed in a range of materials, mundane and special, within and beyond the grave, as highlighted by Anwen Cooper and colleagues.[10] More broadly, of course, all the material that archaeologists deal with is, as Louise Erdrich put it, the afterlife of stuff.[11]

This brings us to our second recurring motif: the repetition of burial at particular locations over long periods of time and many generations. In some cases this activity extended over a millennium, and across very different social contexts. Of course, this sense of continuity can mask long periods when burial places may have fallen out of use, or it can take the form of 'invented' traditions—to demonstrate the linkages of new social groups to specific places, land or territory. In either case it is a striking demonstration of the power and attraction of particular places or cemeteries in mortuary practice. Multi-generational usage is one of the defining characteristics of a cemetery—as a social focus, a graveyard, a burial place, a place for the dead to sleep and somewhere they can be contained and remembered. As Thomas Lynch put it, graveyards are 'old arrangements between the living and the living who have died'.[12] Indeed, in rural Ireland today it is still common for people to be buried in graveyards that have been in use since medieval or even early medieval times. So what made particular places ones that would be returned to? What brought about re-use, renewed deposition? Phases of activity may mark specific occasions or social changes and cycles of activity, as has been suggested for megalithic tombs and Early Bronze Age cemeteries, or in some cases may have something to do with places named in oral tradition, in which landscape features are a form of mneomic. Bearing in mind the permeability and adaptability of oral tradition, one example might be the *cailleach* tradition. As discussed in Chapter 5, the *cailleach* represents the archetypal otherworld female, the supernatural female elder and the personification of the landscape. In considering the long-term role of monuments such as wedge tombs, could the focus on particular females seen in some excavated sites; the name Labbacallee (the *cailleach*'s bed) or an equivalent given to some wedge tombs; and the widespread tradition of the wise woman, be an underpinning that provided an incentive to return to such monuments to place the dead?[13]

As has been detailed above, the period 8000 BC to AD 400 is marked by major changes in material culture and mortuary practices. Distinctive elements that mark many of the traditions of prehistoric mortuary practice as apparently different from those of today are that they involved a number of stages, took place over a considerable period of time and were staged in different locations. This is expressed, for example, in the frequency with which disarticulated bones of people are formally deposited. The primary post-mortem treatment of the body—its initial burial—often took place at a location different from where bones were finally deposited. Similarly, it appears that the deposition of cremated remains often occurred somewhere other than the site of the cremation pyre. Burnt bones and other material, including objects placed with the dead on the pyre, were collected after cremation and brought to what was considered a suitable location for deposition. In the communal cremation deposits characteristic of passage tombs during the Neolithic, we see a further complex stage in post-mortem treatment, whereby cremated, and unburnt, remains of different individuals are brought together. While this seems very different to how we deal with the dead today, to paraphrase the McGahern quote at the end of the last chapter, this was a response to a human need in a specific cultural context—to understand what was going to happen next, both to the dead and the living left behind.

Consideration of these themes of people, place and practice suggests that it would be wrong to see patterns in the development of mortuary practice in simple linear, historical terms. The concept of the past was important in prehistoric societies, and the practice of going back, returning to dead people, was key. Going back to human remains for the next stage in their post-mortem treatment, including to bones that may already have been curated, ensured important ancestors continued to circulate and be in active social use long after the biological death of a person. Interestingly, Brück and Booth suggest that in Bronze Age Britain this happened after a couple of generations, while the biographies of these people could still be recounted. As has been stated frequently, we finally die when our name is spoken for the last time.[14] Going back to long-established and long-used places for the deposition of the dead and to practicing the traditions and beliefs that guided these rites provides support for the view that societies had a cyclical view of time, of life, death and rebirth, which would have been closely aligned with foraging and farming lifestyles. These lifestyles were founded on and intimately bound to knowledge of seasonally based growing and breeding patterns in plants and animals. But this view of time also has to allow for forgetting. New technologies, changes in social mores and the impacts of new contacts and people could make tradition and places redundant. Indeed, there may have been contexts and occasions when memories might have been too painful to hold. George Orwell, in *Nineteen Eighty-Four*, coined the phrase 'a memory hole'—a mechanism to ensure that historical documents could be disposed of, to allow for manipulation and rereading of memories of the past.[15] The frequency of the deliberate covering or blocking of mortuary deposits and of monuments that contain such deposits can be read in this way, and as the closing of a chapter. In turn, this could also create a platform on which different active readings of the past could be made.[16]

This process can be seen in the histories of individual sites that have been discussed throughout the book. At any period, there was diversity in mortuary practice, and practices changed over time. Indeed, it could be argued that we have used the term 'burial' too widely to cover what was a range of approaches to the post-mortem treatment of the dead. Nevertheless, the placement of the dead in the earth—or placement of a representation in the form of a deposit of inhumed or cremated bone—was frequently performed against the backdrop of locations and monuments used for that purpose over long periods of time. Mention of the placement of some of the remains of the person in the ground raises the issue of what happened to the rest of the bodies of such individuals after death? At times body parts, particularly crania, were in circulation—in active use by the living. There are repeated instances in which crania were treated in a different way to the rest of the body after death, or ended up in different locations. Barry Raftery made the point that the cult of the head was widespread in all areas of Celtic Europe. The head was seen as the seat of the soul, the essence of human personality and hence could come to represent a deity. This echoes the focus on cranial and skull deposits that can be seen in prehistoric Ireland.[17]

Differentiation in treatment of body parts was an ongoing element of the practice of how and where human remains, and other materials used to express the continuing bonds with the living, were eventually deposited. Although admittedly rare, we have anthropomorphic objects that were used to demonstrate the connections and linkages between the living and the dead, this world and other worlds. Consider the adzehead from the Mesolithic cremation at Hermitage, for instance, placed with a cremation burial of a probable male. [SEE PL. 3.B.I] To paraphrase a Māori expression, though the adze was small, did it equal a man?[18] Similarly, there is the macehead deposited close to human bone deposits in the right-hand recess at the eastern passage tomb under the Great Mound at Knowth, anthropomorphic images in passage tomb art [PL. 8.B], the Bronze Age 'face' cup from Mitchelstown [SEE PL. 5.H], and the wooden figure from Ralaghan [SEE PL. 7.E]. Finally, there are the stone heads of probable Iron Age date, such as the three-faced, gender fluid head from Corleck, Drumeague, Co. Cavan with its Celtic and Roman links [PL. 8.C].

PL. 8.B.

Knowth, Brú na Bóinne, Co. Meath; Tomb 1B West, orthostat 50.

PL. 8.C. (Opposite)

The Late Iron Age head from Corleck Hill, Drumeague, Co. Cavan.

All of this reflects the complex roles of the dead within kin and relational identities in small-scale societies. It also mirrors a belief that after the transition of death, the physical remains and memory of the dead continue to have a social relevance—something that still holds true today. Paul Rosenblatt observed that in most if not all small-scale societies, death is viewed as a transition to some other state. It is understood that the dead will continue to have an impact on and relationship with the living.[19] This is why the treatment of the dead was and is important; they continue to be related to the living. The living would wish to ensure that the shelter and shadows cast by the dead would be benign rather than malevolent.

LOOKING TO THE FUTURE

This book is rooted in an important stage in archaeological research on prehistoric mortuary rites in Ireland. The rich array of evidence that continues to emerge out of major developer-led projects will provide a basis for research long into the future, as will ongoing research projects. Elizabeth O'Brien's book about death in the Iron Age and early medieval period demonstrates the enormous potential of the evidence for the treatment of the dead to contribute to our understanding of the past.[20]

And this is happening at a time when scientific methodologies and approaches are developing in exciting ways. These can be transformative when applied in an integrated, collaborative approach. The study of stable isotopes, for instance, allows us to examine diet and also peoples' biographies—where they lived at different times in their lives—and those of animals associated with them. Such data can be linked with the information available from aDNA, obtained directly from skeletal material, to provide insights into prehistoric people and into the genetic relationships of particular social groups and how these changed over time. The focus of aDNA work has been on looking at changing ancestry over time, but with increased sampling and resolution we are seeing the opportunity to address biological relationships between people in detail. Given the complexity of the social and cultural contexts of the remains of the dead—as reflected in the archaeological record—a theoretically informed approach needs to be adopted if we are to gain the most from the wide range of investigative techniques now available.[21]

Living in the Anthropocene and facing a climate emergency, in which we need to adopt new ways of life, it is important to reflect on how people in the past lived and died, faced and adapted to what in some cases and times were significant environmental changes. Above all, we have to recognise and come to terms with, as Rachel Clarke put it, 'the ubiquitous business of dying'.[22] Sarah Tarlow and Liv Nilsson Stutz remarked that archaeologists have the privilege of coming face to face with dead people from the past, providing possiblities of rewriting those people back into history and reminding us of our shared humanity. Hopefully this book conveys some sense of that shared humanity, in life and death.[23]

Crouched Burial

They move the earth with small trowels and brushes and
all week the seals sing a desolate chorus as if for you.
First a small child's foot
slow sweeps of the brush across your small bones,
your shape in the ditch, taking definition, a slow birth
in the corner of the field by the water's edge.

You are lying on your side
knees pulled into your chest
the thin bones of your arms
holding yourself without your hands
your heavy head bent low towards your small body,
a comma in the earth,
like an ultra sound picture of the earth's womb
where you lay crouched for years.

Beside your ribcage, a single blue glass bead
for your ear a bronze ring,
your grave gifts.
If flowers and herbs cradled your head,
they are dust now.
Someone brought you here
and laid you down with care
your death a secret, your story buried.

In the moon bay
at the edge of earth where they found you
the midden's shells layer time, like growth rings.
Now is our turn on the surface of time
you and your buried bead, prehistory,
before there were written words to remember with.
A sequence of milk teeth along the bone of your jaw and
The buds to permanent teeth spell your age.
You are eighteen months old.

Your bones in the midden are a mystery
Iron Age people did not bury their dead
bodies were left to wind, or wolves or water.
But not you.
Perhaps touching your cold cheek your mother
could not abandon your body to the night
and here, where the land juts out towards the sea and the tide moves,
a place she might find you again,
she brought you.

Una Mannion, Hennessy Literary Awards 2017, Emerging Poetry winner
(*The Irish Times*, 29 March 2017)

NOTES

Chapter 1

[1] Henning Mankell, *Quicksand: what it means to be a human being* (London: Harvill Secker, 2016), 34.
[2] The standard text on Irish prehistory is John Waddell, *The prehistoric archaeology of Ireland* (3rd edn; Dublin: Wordwell, 2022). Gabriel Cooney and Eoin Grogan, *Irish prehistory: a social perspective* (revised edn; Bray: Wordwell, 1999), focus on an interpretative stance on the record. More traditional approaches can be found in Michael Herity and George Eogan, *Ireland in prehistory* (London: Routledge and Kegan Paul, 1977); Peter Harbison, *Pre-Christian Ireland: from the first settlers to the early Celts* (London: Thames and Hudson, 1988) and M. J. O'Kelly, *Early Ireland* (Cambridge: Cambridge University Press, 1989). Laurence Flanagan, *Ancient Ireland: life before the Celts* (London: Gill and Macmillan, 1998), provides a thematic approach. G.F. Mitchell and Michael Ryan, *Reading the Irish landscape* (revised edn, Dublin: Town House, 1997) and papers in James Kelly and Tomás Ó Carragáin (eds), *Climate and society in Ireland: from prehistory to the present* Proceedings of the Royal Irish Academy 120C (Dublin: Royal Irish Academy, 2021) discuss human impact on the Irish landscape.
[3] Joanna Sofaer, *The body as material culture: a theoretical osteoarchaeology* (Cambridge: Cambridge University Press, 2006), 1.
[4] These questions are tackled by, for example, J.P. Mallory, *The origins of the Irish* (London: Thames and Hudson, 2013); and *In search of the Irish Dreamtime: archaeology and early Irish literature* (London: Thames and Hudson, 2015). See also Shane Hegarty, *The Irish (and other foreigners) from the first people to the Poles* (Dublin: Gill and Macmillan, 2009).
[5] Mike Parker Pearson, *The archaeology of death and burial* (Stroud: Sutton, 1996) provides an accessible introduction to the archaeological and anthropological literature on death and burial. See also Nigel Barley, *Dancing on the grave: encounters with death* (London: John Murray, 1996); A.C.G.M. Robben (ed.), *Death, mourning, and burial: a cross-cultural reader* (Oxford: Blackwell, 2004).
[6] Anwen Cooper *et al.*, *Grave goods: objects and death in later prehistoric Britain* (Oxford: Oxbow, 2022), discuss grave goods and death in Britain from 4000 BC to AD 43. For modern Irish society, see, for example, Joe Lee, *Ireland 1912–1985: politics and society* (Cambridge: Cambridge University Press, 1989); Diarmaid Ferriter, *The transformation of Ireland 1890–2000* (London: Profile Books, 2004); Patrick Clancy *et al.* (eds), *Irish society: sociological perspectives* (Dublin: Institute of Public Administration, 1995). Patricia Lysaght, 'Old age, death and mourning', in E.F. Biagini and M.E. Daly (eds), *The Cambridge social history of modern Ireland* (Cambridge: Cambridge University Press, 2017), pp 282–96, provides a valuable discussion of traditional and contemporary death ceremonies in Ireland. William Doherty *Wakes* (Dublin: William Doherty, 2014), documents the wake tradition. Salvador Ryan (ed.), *Death and the Irish: a miscellany* (Dublin: Wordwell, 2016) is a collection of short pieces conveying the complexity of the human relationship with death in Ireland, past and present. See also Lawrence Taylor, 'Bás in Éirinn: cultural constructions of death in Ireland', *Anthropological Quarterly* 62 (4) (1989), 175–87. Bridget English, *Laying out the bones: death and dying in the modern*

Irish novel (Syracuse: Syracuse University Press, 2017), examines the treatment of death in the modern Irish novel.

[7] Philippe Ariès, *Western attitudes towards death from the Middle Ages to the present* (trans. Patricia M. Ranum; Baltimore: Johns Hopkins University Press, 1974); *The hour of our death* (trans. Helen Weaver; New York: Alfred A. Knopf, 1981); and Allan Kellehear, *A social history of dying* (Cambridge: Cambridge University Press, 2007). It should be noted, however, that there is now increasing recognition of the need to approach death as part of life, see, for example, Seamus O'Mahony, *The way we die now* (London: Head of Zeus, 2016); Kathryn Mannix, *With the end in mind: dying, death and wisdom in an age of denial* (London: William Collins, 2017); Rachel Clarke, *Dear life: a doctor's story of love, loss and consolation* (London: Little, Brown, 2020); Kevin Toolis, *Nine rules to conquer death* (London: Oneworld, 2020).

[8] Lysaght, 'Old age, death and mourning' (2017), 287–93. See Toolis, *My father's wake: how the Irish teach us to live, love and die* (London: Weidenfeld and Nicholson, 2017); Lysaght, 'Hospitality at wakes and funerals in Ireland from the seventeenth to the nineteenth century: some evidence from the written record', *Folklore* 113 (2003), 403–26; Doherty, *Wakes* (2014); Maurna Crozier, 'Powerful wakes: perfect hospitality', in C. Curtin and T.M. Wilson (eds), *Ireland from below: social change and local communities* (Galway: Galway University Press, 1987), pp 9–91.

[9] Thomas Lynch, *Booking passage: we Irish and Americans* (London: Jonathan Cape, 2005), 238–41. For the insights his work as an undertaker and writer provides into the complex ways the living deal with the dead, see Lynch, *The undertaking: life studies from the dismal trade* (London: Jonathan Cape, 1997); *Bodies in motion and at rest* (Norton: New York 2000). See also T.G. Long and Thomas Lynch, *The good funeral: death, grief and the community of care* (Louisville, KY: Westminister John Knox Press, 2013). Colin Murray Parkes *et al.*, *Death and bereavement across cultures* (London: Routledge, 1997) demonstrate the diversity and richness of cultural responses to death.

[10] Christiaan Corlett and Michael Potterton (eds), *Death and burial in early medieval Ireland in the light of recent archaeological excavations* (Dublin: Wordwell, 2010); Elizabeth O'Brien, *Mapping death: burial in Late Iron Age and early medieval Ireland* (Dublin: Four Courts Press, 2020); Aidan O'Sullivan *et al.*, *Early Medieval Ireland AD 400–1100: the evidence from archaeological excavations* (Dublin: Royal Irish Academy, 2014); S.L. Fry, *Burial in medieval Ireland 900–1500: a review of the written sources* (Dublin: Four Courts Press, 1999); Clodagh Tait, *Death, burial and commemoration in Ireland, 1550–1650* (Basingstoke, Hamps: Palgrave Macmillan, 2002). Papers in James Kelly and M.A. Lyons (eds), *Death and dying in Ireland, Britain and Europe: historical perspectives* (Dublin: Irish Academic Press, 2013) look at death and dying from thematic and historical perspectives.

[11] Koji Mizoguchi, 'Time in the reproduction of mortuary practices', *World Archaeology* 25 (2) (1993), 223–35; Richard Bradley, *The past in prehistoric societies* (London: Routledge, 2002); Gavin Lucas, *The archaeology of time* (London: Routledge, 2005).

[12] Thomas Bartlett, *Ireland: a history* (Cambridge: Cambridge University Press, 2010), 2. For a statement of the significance of the written word and religion as a basis for Irish history, see T.M. Charles-Edwards, 'Introduction: prehistoric and early Ireland', in Dáibhí Ó Cróinín (ed.), *A new history of Ireland* vol. 1 (Oxford: Oxford University Press, 2005), pp lvii–lxxxii: lvii.

[13] Andrew Shyrock and Daniel Lord Smail (eds), *Deep history: the architecture of past and present* (Berkeley: University of California Press, 2012); Clive Gamble, *Settling the Earth: the archaeology of deep human history* (Cambridge: Cambridge University Press, 2013); P.R. Schmidt and S.A. Mrozowski, 'The death of prehistory: reforming the past, looking to the future', in Schmidt and Mrozowski (eds), *The death of prehistory* (Oxford: Oxford University Press, 2013), pp 1–28; Ann Macdonald and Aron Mazel, 'Challenging "Prehistory" in South African archaeology', *South African Archaeological Bulletin* 76 (215) (2021), 91–2. John Moreland, *Archaeology and text* (London: Duckworth, 2001) and 'Archaeology and texts: subservience or enlightenment', *Annual Review of Anthropology* 35 (2006), 135–51, provides an important discussion of the need to challenge traditional assumptions about the relationship between artefacts and documents as a basis for understanding the past.

[14] For the impact of prehistoric people on the Irish landscape, see Michael Stanley *et al.* (eds), *Stories of Ireland's past* (Dublin: Transport Infrastructure Ireland, 2017); F.H.A. Aalen *et al.* (eds), *Atlas of the Irish rural landscape* (2nd edn; Cork: Cork University Press, 2012); Kelly and Ó Carragáin (eds), *Climate and society* (2021). Danny Miller, *Stuff* (Cambridge: Polity Press, 2010), argues that things make us as much as we make things. Ian Hodder, *Entangled: an archaeology of the relationships between humans and things* (Oxford: Wiley and Blackwell, 2012), considers the entangled relationships between humans and things.

[15] Bjørnar Olsen *et al.*, *Archaeology: the discipline of things* (Berkeley: University of California Press, 2012), 191.

[16] See, for example, Eavan Boland, *Object lessons* (London: Carcanet, 1995); Moya Cannon, *Hands* (London: Carcanet, 2011); Seamus Heaney, *North* (London: Faber and Faber, 1975). Christine Finn, *Past poetic: archaeology in the poetry of W.B. Yeats and Seamus Heaney* (London: Duckworth, 2004), considers how Heaney (and W.B. Yeats) used archaeology as inspiration.

[17] Dan Hicks, 'The material-cultural turn: event and effect', in D. Hicks and M.C. Beaudry (eds), *The Oxford handbool of material culture studies* (Oxford: Oxford University Press, 2010), pp 25–98; Gabriel Cooney, 'Material culture', in A. Gardner *et al.* (eds), *The Oxford handbook of archaeological theory* (Oxford: Oxford University Press, 2016), (doi.org/10.1093/oxfordhb/9780199567942.013.019).

[18] Eavan Boland, *In a time of violence* (London: Carcanet, 1994), 35.

[19] Bernard O'Donoghue, *Outliving* (London: Chatto and Windus, 2003), 28.

[20] Period-based reviews are provided by P.C. Woodman, *Ireland's first settlers: time and the Mesolithic* (Oxford: Oxbow, 2015) and Graeme Warren, *Hunter-Gatherer Ireland: making connections in an island world* (Oxford; Oxbow, 2022) (Mesolithic); Gabriel Cooney, *Landscapes of Neolithic Ireland* (London: Routledge, 2000) (Neolithic); Neil Carlin, *The Beaker phenomenon: understanding the character and context of social practices in Ireland 2500–2000 BC* (Leiden: Sidestone Press, 2018); Joanna Brück, *Personifying prehistory: relational ontologies in Bronze Age Britain and Ireland* (Oxford: Oxford University Press, 2019) (Chalcolithic and Bronze Age); and Barry Raftery, *Pagan Celtic Ireland: the enigma of the Irish Iron Age* (London: Thames and Hudson, 1994) (Iron Age). The papers in Stanley *et al.*, *Stories* (2017), consider the role of 'roads archaeology' on the understanding of Ireland's past and demonstrate the transformative impact on data and knowledge that development-led archaeology in Ireland has had since the 1990s.

[21] For Killuragh cave, see P.C. Woodman *et al.*, 'Archaeological excavations at Killuragh Cave, Co. Limerick: a persistent place in the landscape from the Early Mesolithic to the Late Bronze Age', *Journal of Irish Archaeology* 26 (2017), 1–32. For Kilmahuddrick, see I.W. Doyle, 'Excavation of a prehistoric ring-barrow at Kilmahuddrick, Clondalkin, Dublin 22', *Journal of Irish Archaeology* 14 (2005), 43–5.
[22] Tim Robinson brilliantly conveys the centrality of a sense of place in Irish life and landscape for the Aran Islands (*Stones of Aran: pilgrimage* Mullingar: Lilliput in association with Wolfhound Press, 1986; *Stones of Aran*: *labyrinth* Dublin: Lilliput, 1995) and Connemara (*Connemara: listening to the wind* Dublin: Penguin Ireland, 2006; *Connemara: the last pool of darkness* Dublin: Penguin Ireland, 2008; *Connemara: a little Gaelic kingdom* Dublin: Penguin Ireland, 2011). As one comparison, Keith Basso, *Wisdom sits in places* (Albuquerque: University Press of New Mexico Press, 1996), similarly narrates the centrality of place in the world of the Western Apache in Arizona.
[23] Maurice Bloch, 'The past and the present in the present', *Man* 12 (1977), 278–92; Richard Bradley, *The significance of monuments* (London: Routledge, 1998), 88–91. See also Lucas, *Archaeology of time* (2005).
[24] John McGahern, *That they may face the rising sun* (London: Faber and Faber, 2002).
[25] Elizabeth O'Brien 'Burial practices in Ireland: first to seventh centuries', in J. Downes and A. Ritchie (eds), *Sea change: Orkney and Northern Europe in the later Iron Age, A.D. 300–800* (Angus: Pinkfoot Press, 2003) pp 63–72; 'Pagan or Christian? Burial in Ireland during the 5th to 8th centuries A.D.', in N. Edwards (ed.), *The archaeology of early medieval Celtic churches* (Leeds: Maney. Society for Medieval Archaeology Monograph 29, 2009), pp 135–54; *Mapping death* (2020). See also Lorcan Harney, 'Christianising pagan worlds in conversion-era Ireland: archaeological evidence for the origins of Irish ecclesiastical sites', *Proceedings of the Royal Irish Academy* 117C (2017), 103–30.
[26] For example, Thomas Hylland Eriksen, *Small places, large issues: an introduction to social and cultural anthropology* (London: Pluto, 1995), 196–213.
[27] R.N. Bellah, *Religion in human evolution: from the Paleolithic to the Axial Age* (Cambridge, Mass: Belknap Harvard, 2011), chapter 2. One definition of a distinction between different modes of religion ('imagistic' and doctrinal) is set out by Harvey Whitehouse, 'Theorizing religions past', in H. Whitehouse and L.H. Martin (eds), *Theorizing religions past: archaeology, history, and cognition* (Walnut Creek, CA: Altimira Press, 2004), pp 215–32.
[28] Ronald Hutton, *Pagan Britain* (New Haven, CT: Yale University Press, 2013). This covers the history of religion in Britain from the Palaeolithic to the coming of Christianity and beyond, including a balanced discussion of the reception of prehistoric sites by different audiences—professional and religious—in British society today.
[29] Daithí Ó hÓgáin, *The sacred isle: belief and religion in pre-Christian Ireland* (Cork: Collins Press, 1999).
[30] Timothy Insoll, *Archaeology, ritual and religion* (London: Routledge, 2004), 22.
[31] Insoll (2004), 78–80. There is an extensive anthropological and related literature on religion. See for example Clifford Geertz, *The interpretation of cultures: selected essays* (New York: Basic Books, 1973); R.A. Rappaport, *Ritual and religion in the making of humanity* (Cambridge: Cambridge University Press, 1999); Fiona Bowie, *The anthropology of religion: an introduction* (Oxford: Blackwell, 2000); Bellah, *Religion in human evolution* (2011); Neil McGregor, *Living with the Gods: on beliefs and people* (London:

Allen Lane, 2018); Robin Dunbar, *How religion evolved and why it endures* (London: Penguin Random House, 2022). All argue from different perspectives that religion is central to people. As Bellah put it, 'religion is a system of beliefs and practices relative to the sacred that unite those who adhere to them in a moral community', (2011), 1.
[32] Cooney, *Landscapes* (2000), 87–8. For broader discussion of Neolithic religion, see David Lewis-Williams and David Pearce, *Inside the Neolithic mind* (London: Thames and Hudson, 2005).
[33] Hutton, *Pagan Britain*, for example 134–43.
[34] Geertz, *The interpretation of cultures* (1973), chapter 4. See Catherine Bell, *Ritual: perspectives and dimensions* (Oxford: Oxford University Press, 1997), chapter 4; David S. Whitley, 'Hunter-Gatherer religion and ritual', in V. Cummings *et al.* (eds), *The Oxford handbook of the archaeology and anthropology of Hunter-Gatherers* (Oxford: Oxford UniversityPress, 2014), pp 1221–42.
[35] See Bruce Trigger, *A history of archaeological thought* (2nd edn; Cambridge: Cambridge University Press, 2006); R.W. Chapman and Klaus Randsborg, 'Perspectives on the archaeology of death', in R.W. Chapman, *et al.* (eds), *The archaeology of death* (Cambridge: Cambridge University Press, 1981), pp 1–24; Parker Pearson, *Archaeology of death* (1996). John Waddell, *Foundation myths: the beginnings of Irish archaeology* (Dublin: Wordwell, 2005), covers the development of the study of Irish archaeology from medieval times to the early twentieth century; see also Cooney, 'Theory and practice in Irish archaeology', in P. Ucko (ed.), *Theory in archaeology: a world perspective* (London: Routledge, 1995), pp 263–77.
[36] Eugene Conwell, *Discovery of the tomb of Ollamh Fodhla, Ireland's famous monarch and law-maker upwards of three thousand years ago* (Dublin: McGlashen, 1873); Chapman *et al.*, *Archaeology of death* (1981).
[37] Liam de Paor, *Archaeology: an illustrated introduction* (Harmondsworth: Penguin, 1967). For an accessible introduction to archaeological theory, see Matthew Johnson, *Archaeological theory: an introduction* (2nd edn; Chichester, West Sussex: Wiley-Blackwell, 2010).
[38] Catherine Nash, *Of Irish descent: origin stories, genealogy and the politics of belonging* (Syracuse, New York: Syracuse University Press, 2008), 189–90. See also Barra Ó Donnabháin and Eileen Murphy, 'The development of the contextual analysis of human remains in Ireland', in B. Ó Donnabháin and M.C. Lozada (eds), *Archaeological human remains: global perspectives* (New York: Springer, 2014), pp 165–77; Mairéad Carew, *The quest for the Irish Celt: the Harvard Archaeological Mission to Ireland 1932–1936* (Newbridge: Irish Academic Press, 2018).
[39] See, for example, Herity and Eogan, *Ireland in prehistory* (1977); see discussion in Cooney, 'Theory and practice' (2005).
[40] Johnson, *Archaeological theory* (2010), chapters 2 and 3.
[41] L.R. Binford, 'Mortuary practices: their study and their potential', in J. Brown (ed.), *Approaches to the social dimensions of mortuary practices* (Washington, DC: Memoir of the Society for American Archaeology 25, 1971), pp 6–25. For an accessible introduction to Binford's work and approach, see Binford, *In pursuit of the past* (London: Thames and Hudson, 1983). See Cormac McSparron, *Burials and society in Late Chalcolithic and Early Bronze Age Ireland* (Oxford: Archaeopress. Irish Archaeological Monographs QUB 1, 2021), for an application of the processual approach in an Irish context.

[42] See Johnson, *Archaeological theory* (2010), chapter 7 in particular. As examples, see Hodder, *The archaeological process* (Oxford: Blackwell, 1999); *Entangled* (2012).
[43] On material culture, see, for example, Cooney, 'Material culture' (2016). Innovative interpretative approaches to death include Sarah Tarlow, *Bereavement and commemoration: an archaeology of mortality* (Oxford: Blackwell, 1999); Tim Taylor, *The buried soul: how humans invented death* (London: Fourth Estate, 2002); J.E. Robb and O.J.T. Harris (eds), *The body in history. Europe from the Palaeolithic to the future* (Cambridge: Cambridge University Press, 2013); Ian Kuijt *et al.* (eds), *Transformation by fire: the archaeology of cremation in cultural context* (Tucson: University of Arizona Press, 2014); Melanie Giles, *Bog bodies: face to face with the past* (Manchester: Manchester University Press, 2020).
[44] See J.C. Barrett, 'The living, the dead and the ancestors: Neolithic and Early Bronze Age mortuary practice', in J.C. Barrett and I. Kinnes (eds), *The archaeology of context in the Neolithic and Bronze Age: recent trends* (Sheffield: Department of Archaeology and Prehistory, University of Sheffield, 1988), pp 30–41; Kuijt, 'The regeneration of life: Neolithic structures of symbolic remembering and forgetting', *Current Anthropology* 49 (2008), 171–97; Robb, 'Burial treatment as transformation of bodily ideology', in N. Laneri (ed), *Performing death: social analyses of funerary traditions in the Ancient Near east and Mediterranean* (Chicago: Oriental Institute, University of Chicago, 2007), pp 287–97.
[45] See discussion of the remains of St Oliver Plunkett in Tarlow, 'Cromwell and Plunkett: two Early Modern heads called Oliver', in Kelly and Lyons (eds), *Death and dying in Ireland, Britain and Europe* (2013), pp 59–76.
[46] See, for example, Carlin, *Beaker phenomenon* (2018); Brück, *Personifying prehistory* (2019) in relation to Bronze Age burial practices.
[47] See Stanley *et al.*, *Stories* (2017).

Chapter 2

[1] Mary Cahill and Maeve Sikora, *Breaking ground, finding graves—reports on the excavations of burials by the National Museum of Ireland, 1927–2006* (vol. 1; Dublin: Wordwell/ National Museum of Ireland. National Museum of Ireland Monograph Series 4, 2011). This publication reports on excavations carried out by National Museum of Ireland during the period 1927–2006 and is a good starting point for looking at the contexts of discovery of prehistoric burials.
[2] Eileen Murphy *et al.*, 'INSTAR—The people of prehistoric Ireland: Phase 1', *Archaeology Ireland* 24 (1) (2010), 23–5.
[3] See discussion of different periods in Cooney and Grogan, *Irish prehistory* (1999).
[4] Christopher Meiklejohn and P.C. Woodman, 'Radiocarbon dating of Mesolithic human remains in Ireland', *Mesolithic Miscellany* 22 (1) (2012), 22–41; Warren, *Hunter-Gatherer Ireland* (2022).
[5] Charles Mount, 'Early Bronze Age burial in south-east Ireland in the light of recent research', *Proceedings of the Royal Irish Academy* 97C (1997), 101–93, provides a very

useful discussion of the factors influencing the discovery of Early Bronze Age burials in Ireland. On cremated deposits, see, for example, Jacqueline McKinley, 'Cremation: excavation, analysis and interpretation of material from cremation-related contexts', in S. Tarlow and L. Nilsson Stutz (eds), *The Oxford handbook of the archaeology of death and burial* (Oxford: Oxford University Press, 2013), pp 147–71. On commingled deposits, see A.J. Osterholtz, 'Advances in documentation of commingled and fragmentary remains', *Advances in Archaeological Practice* 7 (1) (2019), 77–86. Murphy *et al.*, 'INSTAR' (2010), found that over 70% of all prehistoric burial deposits in Ireland are cremations.

[6] On the visible dead, see Jennie Bradbury and Chris Scarre (eds), *Engaging with the dead: exploring changing human beliefs about death, mortality and the human body* (Oxford: Oxbow, 2017); Bradbury and Scarre, 'Introduction: engaging with the dead' (2017), pp 1–6. On demography and children, see Andrew Chamberlain, 'Minor concerns: a demographic perspective on children in past societies', in J. Sofaer Derevenski (ed.), *Children and material culture* (London: Routledge, 2000), pp 206–12; Siân Halcrow and Nancy Tayles, 'The bioarchaeology of children and childhood', in S. Agarwal and B. Glencross (eds), *Social bioarchaeology* (Oxford: Wiley-Blackwell, 2011), pp 333–60. It has been argued that one demographic consequence of the transition to farming was a dramatic increase in the number of children in the population; see J.-P. Bocquet-Appel, 'When the world's population took off: the springboard of the Neolithic demographic transition', *Science* 333 (2011), 10–27.

[7] M.E. Lewis, *The bioarchaeology of children: perspectives from biological and forensic anthropology* (Cambridge: Cambridge University Press, 2007); Sofaer, *The body as material culture* (2006), chapters 5 and 6; E.M. Murphy and Melié Le Roy (eds), *Children, death and burial: archaeological discourses* (Oxford: Oxbow, 2017). On children's burial grounds (*cillini*) in Ireland, see C.J. Donnelly and E.M. Murphy, 'The origins of *cillini* in Ireland', in E.M. Murphy (ed.), *Deviant burial in the archaeological record* (Oxford: Oxbow, 2008), pp 191–223.

[8] Allison James and Alan Prout (eds), *Constructing and reconstructing childhood: contemporary issues in the sociological study of children* (3rd edn; London: Routledge, 2015); Sofaer Derevenski, *Children and material culture* (2000).

[9] R.A. Joyce, *Ancient bodies, ancient lives: sex, gender and archaeology* (London: Thames and Hudson, 2008), looks at the complex relationship of sex and gender in the archaeological record. There is an extensive literature on gender archaeology, for example, J.M. Gero and M.W. Conkey, *Engendering archaeology: women and prehistory* (Oxford: Blackwell, 1991); M.L.S. Sørensen, *Gender archaeology* (Oxford: Polity Press, 2000); S.M. Nelson (ed.), *Handbook of gender in archaeology* (Walnut Creek, CA: Altamira Press, 2006); Laura Coltofean-Arizancu *et al.* (eds), *Gender stereotypes in archaeology* (Leiden: Sidestone Press, 2021), with select bibliography. For discussion of gender and death, see Bettina Arnold and N.L. Wicker (eds), *Gender and the archaeology of death* (Walnut Creek, CA: Altamira Press, 2001); J.R. Sofaer and M.L.S. Sørenson, 'Death and gender', in Tarlow and Nilsson Stutz (eds), *Oxford handbook: archaeology of death and burial* (2013), pp 527–41; Alice Roberts, *Ancestors: a prehistory of Britain in seven burials* (London: Simon and Schuster, 2021), 329–49.

[10] Martin Smith and Megan Brickley, *People of the long barrow: life, death and burial in the Earlier Neolithic* (Stroud: The History Press, 2009), focus on the Neolithic long

barrows in Britain, but the discussion is more broadly relevant to the critical assessment of the archaeo-osteological record, including the determination of sex. See also Roberts, *Ancestors* (2021), 331.

[11] J.E. Robb, 'What can we really say about skeletal part representation, MNI and funerary ritual: a simulation approach', *Journal of Archaeological Science: Reports* 10 (2016), 684–92; J.F. Beckett, 'Interactions with the dead: a taphonomic analysis of burial practices in three megalithic tombs in County Clare, Ireland', *European Journal of Archaeology* 17 (2011), 394–418; R.J. Schulting *et al.*, 'New dates from the north, and a proposed chronology for Irish court tombs', *Proceedings of the Royal Irish Academy* 112C (2012), 1–60; Flanagan, *Ancient Ireland* (1998), 145–7. For wider discussion, see Chris Fowler, 'Social arrangements. Kinship, descent and affinity in the mortuary architecture of Early Neolithic Britain and Ireland', *Archaeological Dialogues* 29 (2022), 67–88.

[12] For example, Eriksen, *Small places* (1995), chapter 8.

[13] Ralph Linton, *The study of man: an introduction* (New York: Appleton, 1936); R.K. Merton, *Social theory and social structure* (New York: Free Press, 1968).

[14] For different cultural views of childhood in the Neolithic, see Penny Bickle and Linda Fibiger, 'Ageing, childhood, and social identity in the Early Neolithic of Central Europe', *European Journal of Archaeology* 17 (2014), 208–28; Fibiger, 'Misplaced childhood? Interpersonal violence and children in Neolithic Europe', in C. Knüsel and M. Smith (eds), *The Routledge handbook of the bioarchaeology of human conflict* (London: Routledge, 2014), pp 127–45. On the importance of the social treatment of the dead, see M.W. Helms, *Access to origins: affines, ancestors and aristocrats* (Austin: University of Texas Press, 1998).

[15] Tim Ingold, *The perception of the environment* (London: Routledge, 2000); Helms, *Access to origins* (1998), 23–54; Fowler, *The archaeology of personhood: an anthropological approach* (London: Routledge, 2004); Cooney, 'Parallel worlds or multi-stranded identities? Considering the process of "going over" in Ireland and the Irish Sea zone', in A. Whittle and V. Cummings (eds), *Going over: the Mesolithic–Neolithic Transition in North-West Europe* Proceedings of the British Academy 144 (Oxford: Oxford University Press, 2007), pp 543–66: 544–5.

[16] For example, Joanna Brück, 'Material metaphors: the relational construction of identity in Early Bronze Age burials in Ireland and Britain', *Journal of Social Archaeology* 4 (3) (2004), 307–33, and *Personifying prehistory* (2019).

[17] For example, Smith and Brickley, *People of the long barrow* (2009), 92–4; Fowler, 'Social arrangements' (2022). For Eulau, see Wolfgang Haak *et al.*, 'Ancient DNA, strontium isotopes and osteological analyses shed light on social and kinship organization of the Later Stone Age', *Proceedings of the National Academy of Sciences* 105 (47) (2008), 18226–31.

[18] Peter Ucko, 'Ethnography and archaeological interpretation of funerary remains', *World Archaeology* 1 (1969), 262–90. For the unburied dead, see Estella Weiss-Krejci, 'The unburied dead', in Tarlow and Nilsson Stutz (eds), *Oxford handbook: archaeology of death and burial* (2013), pp 281–301.

[19] See T.R. McLaughlin, 'An archaeology of Ireland for the Information Age', *Emania* 25 (2020), 7–29, followed by comments from different disciplines, and 'An archaeology of Ireland for the Information Age: a reply to Baillie, Cassidy, Plunkett and Waddell',

Emania 25 (2020), 61–5. For one earlier population guestimate for Irish prehistory, see Cooney and Grogan, *Irish prehistory* (1999), 216–18.

[20] T.R. McLaughlin, 'An archaeology of Ireland for the Information Age' (2020), 10. Emma Hannah and T.R. McLaughlin, 'Long-term archaeological perspectives on new genomic and environmental evidence from Early Medieval Ireland', *Journal of Archaeological Sence* 106 (2019), 23–8.

[21] For relevant discussion, see papers in Kelly and Ó Carragáin (eds), *Climate and society* (2021). For discussion of population in later prehistoric Ireland and the challenges of comparing trends in different datasets, see Ian Armit *et al.*, 'From dates to demography in later prehistoric Ireland? Experimental approaches to the meta-analysis of large ^{14}C data-sets', *Journal of Archaeological Science* 40 (1) (2013), 433–8; Armit *et al.*, 'Rapid climate change did not cause population collapse at the end of the European Bronze Age', *Proceedings of the National Academy of Science USA* 111 (48) (2014), 17045–9; Katharina Becker *et al.* 'New perspectives on the Irish Iron Age: the impact of NRA development on our understanding of later prehistory', in Stanley *et al.* (eds), *Stories of Ireland's past* (2017), pp 85–100.

[22] For boom and bust in the European Neolithic, see Stephen Shennan *et al.*, 'Regional population collapse followed initial agriculture booms in mid-Holocene Europe', *Nature Communications* 4 (2013), 2486, and Shennan, *The first farmers of Europe: an evolutionary perspective* (Cambridge: Cambridge University Press, 2018), for the wider evolutionary context. For Ireland, see Nicki Whitehouse *et al.*, 'Neolithic agriculture on the European western frontier: the boom and bust of early farming in Ireland', *Journal of Archaeological Science* 51 (2014), 181–205; T.R. McLaughlin *et al.*, The changing face of Neolithic and Bronze Age Ireland: a big data approach to the settlement and burial records', *Journal of World Prehistory* 29 (2016), 117–53. On the dating of Knowth and Newgrange, see R.J. Schulting *et al.*, 'Dating the human remains at Knowth', in G. Eogan and K. Cleary, *Excavations at Knowth 6. The passage tomb archaeology of the Great Mound at Knowth* (Dublin: Royal Irish Academy, 2017), pp 331–79. See also, Meriel McClatchie and Aaron Potito, 'Tracing environmental, climatic and social change in Neolithic Ireland, in Kelly and Ó Carragain (eds), *Climate and society* (2021), pp 23–50.

[23] See Alasdair Whittle, *The archaeology of people: dimensions of Neolithic life* (London: Routledge, 2003); Clive Gamble, *Origins and revolutions: human identity in earliest prehistory* (Cambridge: Cambridge University Press, 2007).

[24] Shuichi Matsumura and Peter Forster, 'Generation time and effective population size in Polar Eskimos', *Proceedings of Biological Science* 275 (1642) (2008), 1501–08.

[25] See Catryn Power, 'Reconstructing patterns of health and dietary change in Irish prehistoric populations', *Ulster Journal of Archaeology* 56 (1993), 9–17. For people of prehistoric Ireland, see Murphy *et al.*, 'INSTAR' (2010). For wider context, see Ó Donnabháin and Murphy, 'Development of the contextual analysis of human remains' (2014).

[26] Power, 'Human remains', in P.C. Woodman *et al.*, *Excavations at Ferriter's Cove, 1983–95* (Bray, Wicklow: Wordwell, 1999), pp 102–3. For stable isotope analysis, see, for example, Gunilla Eriksson, 'Staple isotope analysis of humans', in Tarlow and Nilsson Stutz (eds), *Oxford handbook: archaeology of death and burial* (2013), pp 123–46.

[27] On cross-sectional geometry and entheseal changes, see, for example, V.S. Sparacello *et al.*, 'Inferences on Sicilian Mesolithic subsistence patterns from cross-sectional

geometry and entheseal changes', *Archaeological and Anthropological Sciences* 12 (2020), 1–21. Tim Robinson, *Aran: pilgrimage* (1986), 107–8, gives an evocative description of how the shape of the human body is related to the daily routines it undertakes. See Power, 'Reconstructing patterns' (1993), for stature figures.

[28] Christopher Meiklejohn and Jeff Babb, 'Long bone length, stature and time in the European Late Pleistocene and Early Holocene', in Ron Pinhasi and J.T. Stock (eds), *Human bioarchaeology of the transition to agriculture* (Oxford: Wiley-Blackwell, 2011), pp 153–75; C.S. Larsen *et al.*, 'Bioarchaeology of Neolithic Catalhoyuk reveals fundamental transitions in health, mobility and lifestyle in early farmers', *Proceedings of the National Academy of Sciences* 116 (26) (2019), 12615–23. See C.A. Roberts, 'What did agriculture do for us? The bioarchaeology of health and diet', in G. Barker and C. Goucher (eds), *The Cambridge world history* (Cambridge: Cambridge University Press, 2015), pp 93–123; and George Milner, 'Early agriculture's toll on human health', *Proceedings of the National Academy of Sciences* 116 (28) (2019), 13721–23, on the bioarchaeological impact of agriculture. For combination of osteological, isotopic and archaeological analysis to address the lifeways of thc first farmers of central Europe, 5500 BC—5000 BC, see papers in Penny Bickle and Alasdair Whittle (eds), *The first farmers of Central Europe: diversity in LBK lifeways* (Oxford: Oxbow, 2013).

[29] M.P. Richards *et al.*, 'Sharp shift in diet at the onset of the Neolithic', *Nature* 425 (2003), 366; Schulting, 'Dietary shifts at the Mesolithic–Neolithic transition in Europe: an overview of the stable isotope data', in J. Lee-Thorp and M.A. Katzenberg (eds), *The Oxford handbook of the archaeology of diet* (Oxford: Oxford University Press, 2018), 1–32; Jessica Smyth and R.P. Evershed, 'The molecules of meals: new insight into Neolithic foodways', *Proceedings of the Royal Irish Academy* 115C (2015), 27–46. For discussion and comparison of Mesolithic and Neolithic foodways in Ireland and Britain, see Vicki Cummings, *The Neolithic of Britain and Ireland* (London: Routledge, 2017), 15–19, 68–75.

[30] C.A. Roberts and Margaret Cox, *Health and disease in Britain: prehistory to the present day* (Gloucester: Sutton Publishing, 2003), chapter 3.

[31] Power, 'Reconstructing patterns of health' (1993). For wider discussion of disease, see C.A. Roberts and Keith Manchester, *The archaeology of disease* (3rd edn; Stroud: Sutton Publishing, 2010).

[32] See J.W. Wood *et al.*, 'The osteological paradox: problems of inferring prehistoric health from skeletal samples', *Current Anthropology* 33 (4) (1992), 343–70; S.N. DeWitte and C.W. Stojanowski, 'The osteological paradox 20 years later: past perspectives, future directions', *Journal of Archaeological Research* 23 (2015), 397–450 for the osteological paradox. A.L. Grauer (ed.), *A companion to paleopathology* (Chichester: Wiley-Blackwell, 2012), provides a comprehensive overview of research in palaeopathology.

[33] Statistics available at: https://www.cso.ie/en/statistics/birthsdeathsandmarriages/. Note, as recently as 1926, average life expectancy for men and women in Ireland was 57.

[34] On estimating age of older adults, see C.G. Falys and D. Prangle, 'Estimating age of mature adults from the degeneration of the sternal end of the clavicle', *American Journal of Physical Anthropology* 156 (2015), 203–14: 203. For Ashley Park, see Con Manning, 'A Neolithic burial mound at Ashleypark, Co. Tipperary', *Proceedings of the Royal Irish Academy* 85C (1985), 61–100. For Ballymacaward, see Elizabeth O'Brien,

'Excavation of a multi-period burial site at Ballymacaward, Ballyshannon, Co. Donegal', *Journal of the Co. Donegal Historical Society* 51 (1999), 56–61; Elizabeth O'Brien and Edel Bhreathnach, 'Burial in early medieval Ireland: politics and religion', in Kelly and Lyons (eds), *Death and dying in Ireland, Britain and Europe* (2013), pp 37–58: 44.
[35] See discussion in Whittle *et al.* (eds), *Gathering time: dating the early Neolithic enclosures of southern Britain and Ireland* (Oxford: Oxbow, 2011), 911–14. On mortality patterns, see Kristen Hawkes and James F. O'Connell, 'How old is human longevity?', *Journal of Human Evolution* 49 (2005), 650–53; Erik Trinkaus, 'Late Pleistocene adult mortality patterns and modern human establishment', *Proceedings of the National Academy of Sciences* 108 (4) (2010), 1267–71.
[36] Jean Guilaine and Jean Zammit (eds), *The origins of war: violence in prehistory* (Oxford: Blackwell, 2005), ix; also John Carmen and Anthony Harding (eds), *Ancient warfare: archaeological perspectives* (Stroud: Sutton Publishing, 1999); Schulting and Fibiger (eds), *Sticks, stones and broken bones: Neolithic violence in a European perspective* (Oxford: Oxford University Press, 2012); I.J.N. Thorpe, 'Fighting and feuding in Neolithic and Bronze Age Britain and Ireland', in T. Otto *et al.* (eds), *Warfare and society: archaeological and social anthropological perspectives* (Åarhus: Åarhus University Press, 2006) , pp 141–65; Jared Diamond, *The world until yesterday* (London: Allen Lane, 2012), chapters 3 and 4; J.M. Heath, *Warfare in Neolithic Europe: an archaeological and anthropological analysis* (Barnsley, UK: Pen and Sword Archaeology, 2017).
[37] Detlef Jantzen *et al.*, 'A Bronze Age battlefield: weapons and trauma in the Tollense valley, north-eastern Germany', *Antiquity* 85 (2011), 417–33.
[38] For the Irish Mesolithic, see Woodman, *Ireland's first settlers* (2015). Woodman *et al.*, *The archaeology of a collection: the Keiller–Knowles collection of the National Museum of Ireland* (Dublin: Wordwell, 2006), 127–55, discusses Neolithic projectile points. As one example, see A.E.P. Collins 'The flint javelin heads of Ireland', in D. Ó Corráin (ed), *Irish antiquity: essays and studies presented to Professor M.J. O'Kelly* (Cork: Tower Books 1981), pp 111–33. For stone axes, see Cooney and Stephen Mandal, *The Irish stone axe project* Monograph 1 (Bray: Wordwell, 1998). For an overview of enclosure, with particular focus on prehistoric hillfort traditions in Ireland, see William O'Brien 'The development of the hillfort in prehistoric Ireland', *Proceedings of the Royal Irish Academy* 117C (2017), 3–61. On experimental work, see M.J. Smith *et al.*, 'Experimental evidence for lithic projectile injuries: improving identification of an under-recognised phenomenon', *Journal of Archaeological Science* 34 (2007), 540–53; Meaghan Dyer and Linda Fibiger, 'Understanding blunt-force trauma and violence in Neolithic Europe: the first experiments using a skin-skull-brain model and the Thames Beater', *Antiquity* 91 (360) (2017), 1515–28; Barry Molloy, 'Hunting warriors: the transformation of weapons, combat practices and society during the Bronze Age in Ireland', *European Journal of Archaeology* 20 (2) (2017), 280–316.
[39] Christopher Knüsel, 'The physical evidence of warfare: subtle stigmata?', in M. Parker Pearson and I.J.N. Thorpe (eds), *Warfare, violence and slavery in prehistory* (Oxford: Archaeopress. BAR International Series 1374, 2005), pp 49–65: 50.
[40] For Linkardstown, see Joseph Raftery, 'A Neolithic burial in Co. Carlow', *Journal of the Royal Society of Antiquaries of Ireland* 74 (1944), 61–2; for Kilgreany, see Marion Dowd, 'Kilgreany, Co. Waterford: biography of a cave', *Journal of Irish Archaeology* 11

(2002), 77–97, and *The archaeology of caves in Ireland* (Oxford: Oxbow, 2015), 103; Fibiger, 'Osteological analysis of human skeletal remains from 23 Irish caves', in Dowd (ed.), *Underground archaeology: studies on human bones and artefacts from Ireland's caves* (Oxford: Oxbow, 2016), pp 3–37: 12. On Drumman More, see Waddell, 'Bronzes and bones', *Journal of Irish Archaeology* 2 (1984), 71–2.

[41] Helle Vandkilde, 'Commemorative tales: archaeological responses to modern myth, politics, and war', *World Archaeology* 35 (1) (2003), 126–44: 127.

[42] See Fibiger, 'The past is a foreign country: bioarchaeological perspectives on Pinker's "prehistoric analogy"', *Historical Reflections* 44 (1) 2018), 6–16; Diamond, *The world until yesterday* (2012), 157–70.

[43] For Talheim, see Joachim Wahl and Iris Trautmann, 'The Neolithic massacre at Talheim: a pivotal find in conflict archaeology', in Schulting and Fibiger (eds), *Sticks, stones and broken bones* (2012), pp 77–100. For Schöneck-Kilianstadten, see Christian Meyer *et al.*, 'The massacre mass grave of Schöneck-Kilianstadten reveals new insights into collective violence in Early Neolithic Central Europe', *Proceedings of the National Academy of Sciences* 112 (36) (2015), 11217–22; for Asparn/Schletz, see Maria Teschler-Nicola, 'The Early Neolithic site Asparn/Schletz (Lower Austria); anthropological studies of interpersonal violence', in Schulting and Fibiger (eds), *Sticks, stones and broken bones* (2012), 101–20. See Bickle and Whittle, *The first farmers* (2013), for wider LBK (*Linearbandkeramik*) context and lifeways. The papers in Schulting and Fibiger, *Sticks, stones and broken bones* (2012) discuss violence in European Neolithic societies. For Wassenaar, see L.P. Louwe Kooijmans, 'An Early/Middle Bronze Age multiple burial at Wassenaar, the Netherlands', *Analecta Praehistorica Leidensia* 26 (1993), 1–20.

[44] On the character of LBK warfare, see, for example, E.M. Wild *et al.*, 'Neolithic massacres: local skirmishes or general warfare in Europe?', *Radiocarbon* 46 (2004), 377–85; Meyer *et al.*, 'The massacre mass grave of Schöneck-Kilianstadten' (2015). For the Bronze Age, see Barry Cunliffe, *Europe between the oceans 9000 BC–AD 1000* (Oxford: Oxford University Press, 2008), 232; Kristian Kristiansen, *Europe before history* (Cambridge: Cambridge University Press, 1998), 410–11. On Late Bronze Age hillforts in Ireland, see James O'Driscoll, 'A multi-layered model for Bronze Age hillforts in Ireland and Europe', *Journal of Irish Archaeology* 26 (2017), 77–100. See also William O'Brien and James O'Driscoll, *Hillforts, warfare and society in Bronze Age Ireland* (Oxford: Archaeopress, 2017).

[45] George Eogan, *Hoards of the Irish Later Bronze Age* (Dublin: University College, Dublin, 1983); Mallory, *Origins of the Irish* (2013), 140–54; Molloy, 'Hunting warriors' (2017); W. O'Brien 'Development of the hillfort' (2017), 55. On the wider social context of Bronze Age hoards, see discussion in David Fontijn, 'Everything in its right place? On selective deposition, landscape and the construction of identity in Later Prehistory', in A. Jones, (ed), *Prehistoric Europe: theory and practice* (Chichester: Wiley-Blackwell 2008), pp 86–106; and Fontijn, *Economies of destruction: how the systematic destruction of valuables created value in Bronze Age Europe, c. 2300–500 BC* (London: Routledge, 2020).

[46] Mallory, *Origins of the Irish* (2013), 290. See critique in Tomás Ó Carragáin, *Churches in the Irish landscape AD 400–1100* (Cork: Cork University Press, 2021), 12.

[47] See M.N. Zendeno and B.J. Bowser, 'The archaeology of meaningful places', in Bowser and Zendeno (eds), *The archaeology of meaningful places* (Salt Lake City: The University of Utah Press, 2009), pp 1–14, on the need to think about the importance of place and local experience in understanding the world. Movement and interaction are themes emphasised in Cunliffe, *Britain begins* (Oxford: Oxford University Press, 2012), for example in discussion of the Beaker and Early Bronze Age period, pp 196–219, and the Middle and Late Bronze Age, pp 276–88.

[48] For background, see, for example, L.L. Cavalli-Sforza, *Genes, peoples and languages* (London: Allen Lane / Penguin Press, 2000); Colin Renfrew and Katherine V. Boyle (eds), *Archaeogenetics: DNA and the population prehistory of Europe* (Cambridge: McDonald Institute for Archaeological Research, 2000); Mallory, *Origins of the Irish* (2013). On the impact of aDNA, see David Reich, *Who we are and how we got here: ancient DNA and the new science of the human past* (Oxford: Oxford University Press, 2018). On aDNA and Irish prehistory, see L.M. Cassidy and D.G. Bradley, 'Ancient DNA and Irish human prehistory: uncovering the past through palaeogenomics', *Journal of Irish Archaeology* 24 (2015), 1–18 (published 2017; hereafter cited as Cassidy and Bradley 2017).

[49] Carleton Jones, 'Coasts, mountains, rivers and bogs. Using the landscape to explore regionality in Neolithic Ireland', in K. Brophy, and G. Barclay (eds), *Defining a regional Neolithic: the evidence from Britain and Ireland* (Oxford: Oxbow, 2009), pp 119–28.

[50] See Herity and Eogan, *Ireland in prehistory* (1977), for classic presentation of Irish prehistory in cultural historical terms.

[51] Elizabeth DeMarrais, 'The materialization of culture', in E. DeMarrais *et al.* (eds), *Rethinking materiality: the engagement of mind with the material world* (Cambridge: McDonald Institute Monographs, 2004), pp 11–22; Cooney, 'Material culture' (2016).

[52] See discussion in B. Raftery, *Pagan Celtic Ireland* (1994); Waddell, 'Celts, Celticisation and the Irish Bronze Age', in Waddell and E. Shee Twohig (eds), *Ireland in the Bronze Age* (Dublin: Stationery Office, 1995), pp 158–69; Simon James, *The Atlantic Celts: ancient people or modern invention?* (London: British Museum Press, 1999); Cunliffe, *Facing the ocean: the Atlantic and its peoples 8000 BC–AD 1500* (Oxford: Oxford University Press, 2001); Mallory, *Origins of the Irish* (2013), chapter 9.

[53] Cunliffe and John T. Koch (eds), *Celtic from the west: alternative perspectives from archaeology, genetics, languages and the literature* (Oxford: Oxford University Press, 2010); Koch and Cunliffe (eds), *Celtic from the west 2: rethinking the Bronze Age and the arrival of Indo-European in Atlantic Europe* (Oxford: Oxbow, 2013); Koch and Cunliffe (eds), *Celtic from the west 3: Atlantic Europe in the Metal Ages: questions of shared language* (Oxford: Oxbow, 2016); Cunliffe, *Britain begins* (2012), chapter 7, fig. 7.5.

[54] See discussion in Patrick Sims-Williams, 'Bronze- and Iron-Age Celtic speakers. What we don't know, what can't we know, what could we know? Language, genetics and archaeology in the twenty-first century', *Antiquaries Journal* 92 (2012), 427–49, and 'An alternative to "Celtic from the East" and "Celtic from the West"', *Cambridge Archaeological Journal* 30 (3)(2020), 511–29. It should be noted also that there is some divergence of opinion among the contributors to the Cunliffe and Koch (2010) and Koch and Cunliffe (2012) volumes.

[55] Colin Renfrew, *Archaeology and language: the puzzle of Indo-European origins* (London: Jonathan Cape, 1987).
[56] Mallory, *Origins* (2013), chapter 9; Sims-Williams, 'An alternative' (2020), 24.
[57] A.J. Ammerman and L.L. Cavalli-Sforza, *The Neolithic transition and the genetics of populations in Europe* (Princeton: Princeton University Press, 1984). See also Cavalli-Sforza, *Genes, peoples and languages* (2000) and Sims-Williams, 'Genetics, linguistics and prehistory: thinking big and thinking straight', *Antiquity* 72 (277) (1998), 505–27.
[58] Stephen Oppenheimer, *The origins of the British: a genetic detective story* (London: Robinson, 2006). Bryan Sykes, *The seven daughters of Eve* (London: Bantam Books, 2001) and *Blood of the Isles* (London: Corgi, 2006).
[59] Emmeline Hill *et al.*, 'Y chromosome variation and Irish origins: a pre-Neolithic gene gradient starts in the Near East and culminates in Western Ireland', *Nature* 204 (2000), 351–2; Brian McEvoy *et al.*, 'The *longue durée* of genetic ancestry: multiple genetic marker systems and Celtic origins on the Atlantic façade of Europe', *American Journal of Human Genetics* 75 (2004), 693–702.
[60] Mallory, *Origins* (2013), 226–42.
[61] Mallory, *Origins* (2013), chapter 8; Nash, *Of Irish descent* (2008), chapters 6 and 7; Mallory and Ó Donnabháin, 'The origins of the population of Ireland: a survey of putative immigrations in Irish prehistory and history', *Emania* 17 (1998), 47–81.
[62] David Brett, *A book around the Irish Sea* (Dublin: Wordwell, 2009); Norman Davies, *The isles: a history* (Oxford: Oxford University Press, 1999).
[63] See, for example, Haak *et al.*, 'Massive migration from the steppe was source for Indo-European languages in Europe', *Nature* 522 (2015), 207–11; Qiaomei Fu *et al.*, 'The genetic history of Ice Age Europe', *Nature* 534 (2016), 200–05; Kristiansen *et al.*, 'Re-theorising mobility and the formation of culture and language among the Corded Ware culture in Europe', *Antiquity* 91 (2017), 334–47; Iñigo Olalde *et al.*, 'The Beaker phenomenon and the genomic transformation of northwest Europe', *Nature* 555 (7695) (2018), 190–96.
[64] Cassidy and Bradley, 'Ancient DNA and Irish human prehistory' (2017); Cassidy *et al.*, 'Neolithic and Bronze Age migration to Ireland and establishment of the insular Atlantic genome', *Proceedings of the National Academy of Sciences* 113 (2) (2016), 368–73; Cassidy *et al.*, 'A dynastic elite in monumental Neolithic society', *Nature* 582, 384–88 (2020); Cassidy, 'Ancient DNA in Ireland: isolation, immigration and elite incest', *British Archaeology* (September–October 2020), 32–41.
[65] See, for example, Volker Heyd, 'Kossinna's smile', *Antiquity* 91 (356) (2017), 348–59; Carlin, *Beaker phenomenon* (2018; 198–202); Martin Furholt, 'Massive migrations? The impact of recent aDNA studies on our view of third millennium Europe', *European Journal of Archaeology* 21 (2) (2018), 159–91; Catherine Frieman and Daniela Hofmann, 'Present pasts in the archaeology of genetics, identity and migration in Europe: a critical essay', *World Archaeology* 52 (2019), 528–45; R.J. Crellin and O.J.T. Harris, 'Beyond binaries. Interrogating ancient DNA', *Archaeological Dialogues* 27 (2020), 37–56; Omer Gokcumen and Michael D. Frachetti, 'The impact of ancient genome studies in archaeology', *Annual Review of Anthropology* 49 (2020), 277–98; Brück, 'Ancient DNA, kinship and relational identities in Bronze Age Britain', *Antiquity* 95 (379) (2021), 228–37 and responses.

[66] For discussion of aDNA and kinship, see Brück, 'Ancient DNA, kinship and relational identities' (2021); T.J. Booth *et al.*, 'Tales from the supplementary information: ancestry change in Chalcolithic-Early Bronze Age Britain was gradual with varied kinship organization', *Cambridge Archaeological Journal* 31 (2021), 379–400.
[67] On the cultural context of human lives, see, for example, Michael Carrithers, *Why humans have cultures* (Oxford: Oxford University Press, 1992).
[68] See Carlin and Cooney, 'Early prehistoric societies in Ireland: the contribution of aDNA', *Archaeology Ireland* 134 (2020), 19–23, for a critical response to aDNA 'big picture' work in Ireland. On the value of integrated bioarchaeological studies of particular lives and communities, see Haak *et al.*, 'Ancient DNA' (2008); Larsen *et al.*, 'Bioarchaeology of ancient Catalhoyuk' (2019); Fowler *et al.*, 'A high-resolution picture of kinship practices in an Early Neolithic tomb', *Nature* 601 (2021), 584–7. On local knowledge and the interpretation of human lives, see Geertz, *Interpretation of cultures* (1973); *Local knowledge* (New York: Basic Books, 1983).

Chapter 3

[1] G.F. Mitchell, 'An early kitchen midden in Co. Louth', *Journal of the County Louth Archaeological and Historical Society* 11 (1947), 169–74; 'Further early kitchen middens in Co. Louth', *Journal of the County Louth Archaeological and Historical Society* 12 (1949), 14–20.
[2] P.C. Woodman *et al.*, *Excavations at Ferriter's Cove, 1983–95: last foragers, first farmers in the Dingle Peninsula* (Bray: Wordwell, 1999), table 8.1; see also Warren, *Hunter-Gatherer Ireland* (2022), table 2 (noting that all calibrations compensate for marine reservoir effects where appropriate).
[3] Woodman, *Ireland's first settlers* (2015) and Warren, *Hunter-Gatherer Ireland* (2022) are major syntheses of the Irish Mesolithic, with Woodman, *The Mesolithic in Ireland: Hunter-Gatherers in an insular environment* (Oxford: Archaeopress. BAR British Series 58, 1978), as the first major modern account. Warren, 'The human colonization of Ireland in northwest European context', in P. Coxon *et al.* (eds), *Advances in Irish Quaternary Studies* (New York: Springer, 2017), pp 293–316; *Hunter-Gatherer Ireland* (2022), provides a review of the colonisation of Ireland. Marion Dowd and Ruth Carden, 'First evidence of a late Upper Palaeolithic human presence in Ireland', *Quaternary Science Review* 139 (2016), 158–63, present the evidence of the earliest human presence. Chantal Conneller, *The Mesolithic in Britain: landscape and society in times of change* (London: Routledge, 2021), provides a comprehensive synthesis of the Mesolitic in Britain.
[4] Warren, '"Mere food gatherers they, parasites upon nature …": food and drink in the Mesolithic of Ireland', *Proceedings of the Royal Irish Academy* 115C (2015), 1–26; and 'Britain and Ireland inside Mesolithic Europe', in H. Anderson-Whymark *et al.* (eds), *Continental connections: exploring cross-Channel relationships from the Mesolithic to the Iron Age* (Oxford: Oxbow, 2015), pp 43–58; Warren *et al.*, 'The potential of humans in structuring the wooded landscapes of Mesolithic Ireland: a review of data and

discussion of approaches', *Vegetation History and Archaeobotany* 23 (5) (2014), 629–46; Woodman, 'Making yourself at home on an island: the first 1000 years (+?) of the Irish Mesolithic', *Proceedings of the Prehistoric Society* 78 (2012), 1–34. For detailed discussion of population and lifestyle, see Warren, *Hunter-Gatherer Ireland* (2022). For changes over time, see R.M. Chapple *et al.*, '"…where they pass their unenterprising existence…": change over time in the Mesolithic of Ireland as shown in radiocarbon-dated activity', *Proceedings of the Royal Irish Academy* 122C (2022), 1–38.

[5] Cassidy *et al.*, 'A dynastic elite' (2020); Cassidy, 'Ancient DNA in Ireland' (2020). For earlier discussion, see McEvoy *et al.*, 'The *longue durée* of genetic ancestry' (2004); Cunliffe, *Britain begins* (2012), 128–30; Mallory, *Origins of the Irish* (2013), chapter 2.

[6] Meiklejohn *et al.*, 'From single graves to cemeteries: an initial look at chronology in Mesolithic burial practice', in S.B. McCartan *et al.* (eds), *Mesolithic horizons: papers presented at the Seventh International Conference on the Mesolithic in Europe, Belfast 2005* (Oxford: Oxbow, 2009), pp 639–45, and 'A chrono-geographic look at Mesolithic burials: an initial study', in J.M. Grünberg *et al.* (eds), *Mesolithic burials—rites, symbols and social organisation of early postglacial communities* (Halle: Tagungen des Landesmuseums für Vorgeschichte Halle, 2016), pp 25–46; Paul Pettitt, *The Palaeolithic origins of human burial* (London: Routledge, 2011), 249–51; Jörg Orschiedt, 'The Late Upper Palaeolithic and earliest Mesolithic evidence of burials in Europe', *Philosophical Transactions of the Royal Society of London* B 373 (264) (2018); available online: doi.org/10.1098/rstb.2017.0264.

[7] Pettitt, *Palaeolithic origins* (2011), 251; see also Nilsson Stutz, 'Mortuary practices', in Cummings *et al.* (eds), *Oxford handbook: archaeology and anthropology of Hunter-Gatherers* (2014), pp 712–28: 714; Julien Riel-Salvatore and Claudine Gravel-Miguel, 'Upper Palaeolithic mortuary practices in Eurasia', in Tarlow and Nilsson Stutz (eds), *Oxford handbook of the archaeology of death and burial* (2013), pp 303–46.

[8] See J.M. Grünberg, 'Mesolithic burials—rites, symbols and social organisation of early postglacial communities', in Grünberg *et al.* (eds), *Mesolithic burials* (2016), pp 13–24, for review of European Mesolithic burials. For southern Scandinavia, see, for example, S.E. Albrethsen and E. Brinch Petersen, 'Excavation of a Mesolithic cemetery at Vedbaek, Denmark', *Acta Archaeologica* 47 (1977), 1–28; Lars Larsson, *The Skateholm Project I. Man and environment* (Lund: Regiae Societatis Humaniorum Litterarum Lundensis 79, 1988), 'Man and the sea in southern Scandinavia during the Late Mesolithic: the role of cemeteries in the view of society', in A. Fisher (ed.), *Man and the sea in the Mesolithic: coastal settlement above and below present sea level* (Oxford: Oxbow, 1995), pp 95–104, and 'Some aspects of mortuary practices at the Late Mesolithic cemeteries at Skateholm, southernmost Sweden', in Grünberg *et al.* (eds), *Mesolithic burials* (2016), pp 175–84; Liv Nilsson Stutz, *Embodied rituals and ritualized bodies: tracing ritual practices in late Mesolithic burials* (Stockholm: Almqvist and Wiksell, 2003); Sara Gummesson and Fredrik Molin, 'The Mesolithic cemetery at Strandvagen, Motala, in eastern central Sweden', in Grünberg *et al.* (eds), *Mesolithic burials* (2016), pp 145–60; Gummesson *et al.*, 'Keep your head high: skulls on stakes and cranial trauma in Mesolithic Sweden', *Antiquity* 92 (2018), 74–90. For Brittany: see, for example, Catherine Dupont *et al.*, 'Harvesting the seashores in the Late Mesolithic of northwestern Europe: a view from Brittany', *Journal of World Prehistory* 22 (2009), 93–111; Schulting, 'Antlers, bone pins and flint blades: the Mesolithic

cemeteries of Téviec and Hoedic, Brittany', *Antiquity* 70 (1996), 335–50; Schulting and M.P. Richards, 'Dating women and becoming farmers: new palaeodietary and AMS dating evidence from the Breton Mesolithic cemeteries of Téviec and Hoedic', *Journal of Anthropological Archaeology* 20 (2001), 314–44. For Iberia: see, for example, Pablo Arias Cabal and E. Álvarez-Fernandez, 'Iberian foragers and funerary ritual—a review of Palaeolithic and Mesolithic evidence on the Peninsula', in M.R. González Morales and G.A. Clark (eds), *The Mesolithic of the Atlantic façade: proceedings of the Santander Symposium* (Tempe: Arizona State University (Anthropological Research Papers 55), 2004), pp 225–48; Arias Cabal *et al.*, 'Burials in the cave: new evidence on mortuary practices during the Mesolithic of Cantabrian Spain', in S.B. McCartan *et al.* (eds), *Mesolithic horizons* (2009), pp 650–56; and Mary Jackes and David Lubell, 'Muge Mesolithic burials, a synthesis on mortuary archaeology', in Grünberg *et al.* (eds), *Mesolithic burials* (2016), pp 645–72.

[9] For example, Nicolas Cauwe, 'Skeletons in motion, ancestors in action: early Mesolithic collective tombs in southern Belgium', *Cambridge Archaeological Journal* 11 (2001), pp 147–63; John O'Shea and Marek Zvelebil, 'Oleneostrovski mogilnik: reconstructing the social and economic organization of prehistoric foragers in Northern Russia', *Journal of Anthropological Archaeology* 3 (1) (1984), 1–40; Ken Jacobs, 'Returning to Oleni'ostrov: social, economic and skeletal dimensions of a boreal forest Mesolithic cemetery', *Journal of Anthropological Archaeology* 14 (1995), 359–403; and Ilga Zagorska, 'Mesolithic burial traditions in Latvia: a case study from Zvejnieki burial ground', in Grünberg *et al.* (eds), *Mesolithic burials* (2016), pp 225–40; Dušan Borić *et al.* 'Late Mesolithic lifeways and deathways at Vlasac (Serbia)', *Journal of Field Archaeology* 39 (1) (2014), 4–31.

[10] Relevant discussion in R.W. Chapman, 'The emergence of formal disposal areas and the "problem" of megalithic tombs in prehistoric Europe', in R.W. Chapman *et al.* (eds), *Archaeology of death* (1981), pp 71–81 and 'Death, burial and social representation', in Tarlow and Nilsson Stutz (eds), *Oxford handbook: archaeology of death and burial* (2013), pp 47–57; Cooney, 'The place of megalithic tomb cemeteries in Ireland', *Antiquity* 64 (1990), 741–53; Judith Littleton and Harry Allen, 'Hunter-Gatherer burials and the creation of persistent places in southeastern Australia', *Journal of Anthropological Archaeology* 26 (2) (2007), 282–98; Nilsson Stutz, 'Mortuary practices' (2014), 720–1.

[11] For reviews, see Grünberg, 'Mesolithic burials' (2016); Conneller, 'Power and society: Mesolithic Europe', in Tarlow and Nilsson Stutz (eds), *Oxford handbook: archaeology of death and burial* (2013), pp 347–58; Nilsson Stutz, 'Mortuary practices' (2014); Amy Gray Jones, 'Cremation and the use of fire in Mesolithic mortuary practices in northwest Europe', in J.I. Cerezo-Román *et al.* (eds), *Cremation and the archaeology of death* (Oxford: Oxford University Press, 2017), pp 27–51. On skulls, see Schulting, 'Mesolithic skull cults?', in K. von Hackwitz and R. Peyroteo-Stjerna (eds), *Ancient death ways* (Uppsala: Uppsala University Occasional Papers in Archaeology 59, 2015), pp 19–46. Nilsson Stutz, *Embodied rituals and ritualized bodies* (2003), 310, for removal of human bones; see Meiklejohn *et al.*, 'Spatial relationships, dating and taphonomy of the human bone for the Mesolithic site of Cnoc Coig, Oronsay, Argyll, Scotland', *Proceedings of the Prehistoric Society* 71 (2005), 85–105, and Erik Brinch Petersen, 'Afterlife in the Danish

Mesolithic: the creation, use and discarding of "Loose Human Bones"', in Grünberg *et al.* (eds), *Mesolithic burials* (2016), pp 47–62, on loose human bone.
[12] See Grünberg, 'Mesolithic burials' (2016); Lars Larsson, 'Dogs in fraction—symbols in action', in P. Vermeersch and P. Van Peer (eds), *Contributions to the Mesolithic in Europe* (Leuven: Leuven University Press, 1990), pp 153–60, on dogs; Schulting, 'Creativity's coffin: innovation in the burial record of Mesolithic Europe', in S. Mithen (ed.), *Creativity in human evolution and prehistory* (London: Routledge, 1998), pp 203–26, for a discussion of diversity and innovation in the burial record of Mesolithic Europe; and Zagorska, 'The use of ochre in Stone Age burials of the east Baltic', in F. Fahlander and Terje Østigård (eds), *The materiality of death: bodies, burials, beliefs* (Oxford: Archaeopress. BAR International Series 1768, 2008), pp 115–24, on use of ochre.
[13] L.J. Costa *et al.*, 'Microlith to macrolith: the reasons behind the transformation in production in the Irish Mesolithic', *Antiquity* 79 (2005), 19–33; Woodman, 'Making yourself at home', (2012); Woodman, *Ireland's first settlers* (2015), 232–3; Warren, *Hunter-Gatherer Ireland* (2022); Chapple *et al.*, '"…where they pass…"' (2022).
[14] For Britain, see Conneller, *Mesolithic in Britain* (2021). For Mount Sandel: Woodman, *Excavations at Mount Sandel 1973–1977* (Belfast: HMSO. Northern Ireland Archaeological Monographs 2, 1985); Alex Bayliss and Woodman, 'A new Bayesian chronology for Mesolithic occupation at Mount Sandel, Northern Ireland', *Proceedings of the Prehistoric Society* 75 (2009), 101–24.
[15] Woodman, 'Ireland's place in the European Mesolithic: why it's okay to be different', in McCartan *et al.* (eds), *Mesolithic horizons* vol. 1. (2009), xxxvi–xlvi, and 'Making yourself at home' (2012); Warren, 'Human colonization of Ireland' (2017). On mammalian fauna, see W.I. Montgomery *et al.*, 'Origin of British and Irish mammals: disparate post-glacial colonisation and species introductions', *Quaternary Science Review* 98 (2014), 144–65; Warren, *Hunter-Gatherer Ireland* (2022); and, on red deer, Ruth F. Carden *et al.*, 'Phylogeographic, ancient DNA, fossil and morphometric analyses reveal ancient and modern human introductions of a large mammal: the complex case of red deer (*Cervus elaphus*) in Ireland', *Quaternary Science Reviews* 42 (2012), 74–84.
[16] Warren *et al.*, 'The potential of humans (2014); Warren, 'Human colonization of Ireland' (2017), 308.
[17] See Meiklejohn and Woodman, 'Radiocarbon dating of Mesolithic human remains' (2012), for an overview of Mesolithic human remains in Ireland. For Rockmarshall: Mitchell, 'An early kitchen midden' (1947), and 'Further early kitchen middens' (1949). For Ferriter's Cove: Woodman *et al.*, *Excavations at Ferriter's Cove 1983–95* (1999). For Killuragh Cave: Woodman *et al.*, 'Archaeological excavations at Killuragh Cave, Co. Limerick' (2017). For Hermitage: Tracy Collins and Frank Coyne, 'Fire and water … Early Mesolithic cremations at Castleconnell, Co. Limerick', *Archaeology Ireland* 17 (2) (2003), 24–7; Collins and Coyne, 'As old as we thought', *Archaeology Ireland* 20 (4) (2006), 21; Collins, 'Hermitage, Ireland: life and death on the western edge of Europe', in McCartan *et al.* (eds), *Mesolithic horizons* (2009), pp 876–9; Aimée Little *et al.*, 'Stone dead: uncovering Early Mesolithic mortuary rites, Hermitage, Ireland', *Cambridge Archaeological Journal* 27 (2) (2017), 223–43.

[18] For Port of Larne: Meiklejohn and Woodman, 'Radiocarbon dating of Mesolithic human remains' (2012), 31. For Sramore: Marion Dowd, 'The use of caves for funerary and ritual practices in Neolithic Ireland', *Antiquity* 82 (2008), 305–17: 307; and 'Archaeology of caves' (2015), 85–6; Thomas Kador *et al.*, 'Movement and diet in early Irish prehistory: first evidence from multi-isotope analysis', *Journal of Irish Archaeology* 23 (2014), 83–96. For Stoneyisland: A.L. Brindley and J.N. Lanting, 'Irish bog bodies: the radiocarbon dates', in R.C. Turner and R.G. Scaife (eds), *Bog bodies: new discoveries and new perspectives* (London: British Museum, 1995), pp 133–6; Raghnall Ó Floinn, 'Recent research into Irish bog bodies', in Turner and Scaife (eds), *Bog bodies* (1995), pp 137–45: 140; Kador *et al.*, 'Movement and diet' (2014). For Ballynaclogh: Meiklejohn and Woodman, 'Radiocarbon dating of Mesolithic human remains' (2012), 33.
[19] Meiklejohn and Woodman, 'Radiocarbon dating of Mesolithic human remains' (2012), 27; Woodman, *Ireland's first settlers* (2015), 159–64; Warren, *Hunter-Gatherer Ireland* (2022), tables 1 and 2.
[20] Collins and Coyne, 'Fire and water … Early Mesolithic cremations' (2003), 'As old as we thought' (2006); Collins, 'Hermitage, Ireland' (2009); Little *et al.*, 'Stone dead' (2017).
[21] On weight of cremated remains, see J.I. McKinley, 'Bone fragment size and weights of bone from modern British cremations and its implications for the interpretation of archaeological cremations', *International Journal of Osteoarchaeology* 3 (1993), 283–7; on the objects, see Little *et al.*, 'Stone dead' (2017), 3.
[22] Collins, 'Hermitage, Ireland' (2009), 877.
[23] Gray Jones, 'Cremation and the use of fire' (2017); Grünberg, 'Mesolithic burials' (2016), 14–15; Little *et al.*, 'Stone dead' (2017), table 2 for details of the range of European Mesolithic cremation burials. For Langford, Essex, the only British Mesolithic cremation burial, see Nick Gilmour and Louise Loe, 'A Mesolithic cremation-related deposit from Langford, Essex, England; a first for the British Mesolithic', *Mesolithic Miscellany* 23 (2) (2015), 55–7.
[24] Little *et al.*, 'Stone dead' (2017), 225; Edward Blinkhorn and Aimée Little, 'Being ritual in Mesolithic Britain and Ireland: identifying ritual behaviour within an ephermeral material record', *Journal of World Prehistory* 31 (2018), 403–20: 408.
[25] Discussion and references in Little *et al.*, 'Stone dead' (2017), 232–3. For wider context in Ireland, see Cooney and Mandal, *Irish stone axe project* (1998); Woodman, *Ireland's first settlers* (2015), 146–8. For Scandinavia, see Astrid Nyland, *Humans in motion and places of esscence: variations in rock procurement strategies in the Stone, Bronze and Early Iron Ages in southern Norway* (Oslo: University of Oslo, 2016).
[26] Cooney, 'Stone and flint axes in Neolithic Europe', in C. Fowler *et al.* (eds), *The Oxford handbook of Neolithic Europe* (Oxford: Oxford University Press, 2015), pp 513–34; for example, see R.A. Bentley *et al.*, 'Community differentiation and kinship among Europe's first farmers', *Proceedings of the National Academy of the Sciences of the United States of America* 109 (June 2012), 9326–30.
[27] R. Chatterton, 'Ritual', in C. Conneller, and G. Warren (eds), *Mesolithic Britain and Ireland: new approaches* (Stroud: Tempus, 2006), pp 101–20: 110. For the Hammelev, Denmark cremation burial of an adult, probably female, see B.V. Eriksen and H.C.H. Andersen, 'Hammelev: an Early Mesolithic cremation grave from Southern Jutland,

Denmark', in Grünberg *et al.* (eds), *Mesolithic burials* (2016), pp 73–80; Little *et al.*, 'Stone dead' (2017), 227.

[28] David Sanger and M.A.P. Renouf, *The archaic of the far northeast* (Orono: Maine University Press, 2006); for the Port au Choix cemetery, see James Tuck, *Ancient people of Port au Choix, Newfoundland* (St John's: Memorial University of Newfoundland. Newfoundland Social and Economic Studies 17, 1976), 91.

[29] Little *et al.*, 'Stone dead' (2017), 233–8.

[30] See Warren, 'Roads to affluence: NRA roads archaeology and the Mesolithic in Ireland', in Stanley *et al.* (eds), *Stories of Ireland's past* (2017), pp 7–22: 15–19; Warren, *Hunter-Gatherer Ireland* (2022) for location of Mesolithic sites; see Woodman, *Ireland's first settlers* (2015), 146–8 on stone axe deposition. For the extraordinary site of Kanaljorden, Motala, Sweden, see Gummesson *et al.*, 'Keep your head high' (2018). See Chatterton, 'Ritual' (2006), 103–12, for discussion of deposition in water.

[31] For the Port of Larne site, see Woodman, *Ireland's first settlers* (2015), 68, 212–15. Note Warren, *Hunter-Gatherer Ireland* (2022), table 1 caution.

[32] For British Mesolithic mortuary practice, see Conneller, 'Death', in Conneller and Warren (eds), *Mesolithic Britain and Ireland* (2006), pp 139–64; see Conneller, 'Power and society' (2013), 354, on location of cemeteries. On the Greylake cemetery, see Brunning and Firth, 'An early Mesolithic cemetery at Greylake, Somerset, UK', *Mesolithic Miscellany* 22 (1) (2012), 19–21; Conneller, *Mesolithic in Britain* (2021), 158.

[33] See Schulting *et al.*, 'Aveline's Hole: an unexpected twist in the tale', *Proceedings of the University of Bristol Spelaeological Society* 28 (1) (2019), 9–63, for discussion of Aveline's Hole. For wider discussion, see Conneller, *Mesolithic in Britain* (2021), 150–59.

[34] On placement of the dead in relation to the living, see Conneller, *Mesolithic in Britain* (2021), 158; and 'Death' (2006), 154–7; Larsson, 'Dogs in fraction' (1990), 154; Grünberg, 'Mesolithic burials' (2016), 13–14; Nilsson Stutz, 'Mortuary practices' (2014), 721.

[35] Woodman *et al.*, 'Archaeological excavations at Killuragh Cave' (2017); Cassidy *et al.*, 'A dynastic elite' (2020); Cassidy, 'Ancient DNA in Ireland' (2020). For eels and lampreys at Killuragh, see Woodman, *Ireland's first settlers* (2015), 282.

[36] Dowd, *Archaeology of caves* (2015), 85–6; Kador *et al.*, 'Movement and diet' (2014), 89, 92; Cassidy *et al.*, 'A dynastic elite' (2020); Cassidy, 'Ancient DNA in Ireland' (2020).

[37] Chapple *et al.*, '"…where they pass…"' (2022); Kador *et al.*, 'Movement and diet' (2014), 88, 89, 92. Note Warren, *Hunter-Gatherer Ireland* (2022), table 1 caution. For the Stoneyisland remains as a bog body, see Brindley and Lanting, 'Irish bog bodies' (1995); Ó Floinn, 'Recent research into Irish bog bodies' (1995), 140. For discussion of the deposition of human and animal remains at Kanaljorden, see Gummesson *et al.*, 'Keep your head high' (2018).

[38] Mitchell, 'Early kitchen midden in Co. Louth' (1947); and 'Further early kitchen middens' (1949); Woodman *et al.*, *Excavations at Ferriter's Cove* (1999), table 8.1, 142; Warren, *Hunter-gatherer Ireland* (2022), table 2.

[39] Woodman *et al.*, *Excavations at Ferriter's Cove* (1999). There is an earlier fifth millennium BC date for a cattle metatarsal; see Woodman and Margaret McCarthy, 'Contemplating some awful(ly interesting) vistas: importing cattle and red deer into prehistoric Ireland', in I. Armit, *et al.*, *Neolithic settlement in Ireland and Western Britain* (Oxford: Oxbow, 2003), pp 31–9: 33; Warren, *Hunter-Gatherer Ireland* (2022), 158.

On human bone, see Power, 'Human remains' (1999); for stable isotope analysis, see Woodman *et al.*, *Excavations at Ferriter's Cove* (1999), 143; and for cache of stone axes, pp 43–5.

[40] Woodman, *Ireland's first settlers* (2015), 239–54; Conneller, 'Death' (2006), 162. For Oronsay, see, for example, Paul Mellars, *Excavations on Oronsay* (Edinburgh: Edinburgh University Press, 1987); Meiklejohn *et al.*, 'Spatial relationships, dating and taphonomy' (2005).

[41] P.J. Lane, 'Hunter-Gatherer-Fishers, ethnoarchaeology and analogical reasoning', in Cummings *et al.* (eds), *Oxford handbook: archaeology and anthropology of Hunter-Gatherers* (2014), pp 104–50; Whitley, 'Hunter-gatherer religion and ritual' (2014), 1221–25; Peter Jordan, *Material culture and sacred landscape: the anthropology of the Siberian Khanty* (New York: Rowman and Littlefield, 2003); Marek Zvelebil, 'Enculturation of Mesolithic landscapes', in L. Larsson *et al.* (eds), *Mesolithic on the move: papers presented at the Sixth International Conference on the Mesolithic in Europe: Stockholm* (Oxford: Oxford University Press, 2003), pp 65–73, and 'Innovating hunter-gatherers: the Mesolithic in the Baltic', in G. Bailey and P. Spikins (eds), *Mesolithic Europe* (Cambridge: Cambridge University Press, 2008), pp 18–59; Nilsson Stutz, 'Mortuary practices' (2014), 717.

[42] Blinkhorn and Little, 'Being ritual' (2018), 416; Richard Bradley, *The archaeology of natural places* (London: Routledge 2000), 12; Todd Whitelaw, 'Order without architecture: functional, social and symbolic dimensions in hunter-gatherer settlement organization', in M. Parker Pearson and C. Richards (eds), *Architecture and order* (London: Routledge, 1994), pp 217–43: 229–34; Mircea Eliade, *Shamanism, archaic techniques of ectasy* (Princeton: Princeton University Press, 1972), 451–53.

[43] Eliade, *Shamanism* (1972); Guenther, 'From totemism to shamanism: hunter-gatherer contributions to world mythology and spirituality', in R. Lee and R. Daly (eds), *The Cambridge encyclopaedia of hunters and gatherers* (Cambridge: Cambridge University Press, 1999), pp 426–33; Bowie, *Archaeology of religion* (2000), 190–208; Bellah, *Religion in human evolution* (2011), 138–74; Damm, 'Enfolded by the long winter's night', in M. Dowd and R. Hensey (eds), *The archaeology of darkness* (Oxford: Oxbow, 2016), pp 107–16: 113. See Martin Porr and K.W. Alt, 'The burial of Bad Dürrenberg, Central Germany: osteopathology and osteoarchaeology of a Late Mesolithic shaman's grave', *International Journal of Osteoarchaeology* 16 (2006), 395–406, for discussion of what appears to be a Mesolithic shaman's grave.

[44] Bradley, *Archaeology of natural places* (2000), especially chapters 1–3 and 10; Lane, 'Hunter-Gatherer-Fishers' (2014).

[45] Meiklejohn *et al.*, 'From single graves to cemeteries' (2009); and 'A Chrono-geographic look at Mesolithic burials' (2016); Conneller, 'Power and society' (2013), 347–9; Nilsson Stutz, 'Mortuary practices' (2014), 720–1.

[46] Schulting, 'Creativity's coffin' (1998), 219; Nilsson Stutz, 'Mortuary practices' (2014), 721.

[47] For Hermitage as an exceptional site at European level, see Grünberg, 'Mesolithic burials' (2016), 15; Gray Jones, 'Cremation and the use of fire' (2017), 50. See also Hutton, *Pagan Britain*, (2013), 29, 31.

[48] Conneller, 'Death' (2006), 154–7.
[49] Schulting and Richards, 'Finding the coastal Mesolithic in Southwest Britain: AMS dates and staple isotope results on human remains from Caldey Island, South Wales', *Antiquity* 76 (2002), 1011–25; Conneller 'Death' (2006), 156; and *Mesolithic in Britain* (2021), 240–43.
[50] Grünberg, 'Mesolithic burials' (2016); B.S. Robinson, 'Burial ritual, technology and cultural landscape in the far northeast: 8600–3700 BP', in Sanger and Renouf (eds), *The archaic of the far northeast* (2006), pp 341–81; M.A.P. Renouf and Trevor Bell, 'Across the Tickle: the Gould site, Port au Choix 3 and the Maritime Archaic Indian mortuary landscape', in Renouf (ed.), *The cultural landscapes of Port au Choix; precontact Hunter-Gatherers of Northwestern Newfoundland* (New York: Springer, 2011), pp 43–64: 46; Zvelebil, 'Innovating hunter-gatherers' (2008).
[51] I.J. McNiven, 'Saltwater people: spiritscapes, maritime rituals and the archaeology of Australian indigenous seascapes', *World Archaeology* 35 (3) (2003), 329–49: 333.
[52] Meiklejohn *et al.*, 'Spatial relationships, dating and taphonomy' (2005).
[53] Schulting, 'Creativity's coffin' (1998), 211; Jörg Orschiedt, 'The head burials from Ofnet Cave: an example of warlike conflict in the Mesolithic', in Parker Pearson and Thorpe (eds), *Warfare, violence and slavery in prehistory* (2005), pp 67–73.
[54] For wider context of Mesolithic cemeteries, see Conneller, 'Power and society' (2013), 352–5; Nilsson Stutz, 'Mortuary practices' (2014), 719–23; also Chris Scarre, *Landscapes of Neolithic Brittany* (Oxford: Oxford University Press, 2011), 42–6.
[55] Conneller, 'Death' (2006), 162; and 'Power and society' (2013), 352–3; see also Lesley McFadyen, 'Landscape', in Conneller and Warren (eds), *Mesolithic Britain and Ireland: new approaches* (2006), pp 121–38: 137; Martin King, *Unparalleled behaviour: Britain and Ireland during the 'Mesolithic' and the 'Neolithic'* (Oxford: Archaeopress. BAR British Series 355, 2003), 142; Joshua Pollard, 'Ancestral places in the Mesolithic landscape', *Archaeological Review from Cambridge* 17 (1) (2000), 123–38; Aidan O'Sullivan, 'Living with the dead amongst hunter gatherers', *Archaeology Ireland* 16 (2) (2002), 10–12.
[56] Marshall Sahlins, *Stone Age economics* (London: Routledge, 1974); Christopher Tilley, *An ethnography of the Neolithic: early prehistoric societies in Southern Scandinavia* (Cambridge: Cambridge University Press, 1996), 68–9.
[57] For Ofnet, see David Frayer, 'Ofnet: evidence of a Mesolithic massacre', in D.L. Martin and D. Frayer (eds), *Troubled times: violence and warfare in the past* (Amsterdam: Gordon and Breach, 1997), pp 181–216; and Orschiedt, 'Head burials from Ofnet Cave' (2005). Slavomil Vencl, 'Stone Age warfare', in Carman and Harding (eds), *Ancient warfare* (1999), pp 57–72: 58–60, puts Ofnet in the wider context of Mesolithic violence and warfare. Gummesson *et al.*, 'Keep you head high' (2018), 83–7, discuss the causes of the trauma to the head seen on the human crania from Kanaljorden.
[58] For example, see Alasdair Whittle and Vicki Cummings (eds), *Going over: the Mesolithic-Neolithic transition in North-West Europe* (Oxford: Oxford University Press/British Academy. Proceedings of the British Academy 144, 2007); J.E. Robb, 'Material culture, landscapes of action, and emergent causation', *Current Anthropology* 54 (2013), 657–83; Cummings, 'Hunting and gathering in a farmers' world', in Cummings *et al.* (eds), *Oxford handbook: archaeology and anthropology of Hunter-Gatherers* (2014), pp 767–86; N. Thorpe,

'The Atlantic Mesolithic–Neolithic transition', in Fowler, *et al.* (eds), *Oxford handbook of Neolithic Europe* (2015), pp 215–29. For a critical view, see Bill Finlayson, 'The end of hunting and gathering', in Finlayson and Warren (eds), *The diversity of Hunter-Gatherer pasts* (Oxford: Oxbow, 2017), pp 52–67; Warren, *Hunter-Gatherer Ireland* (2022).

[59] Dušan Borić *et al.*, 'The limits of the body', in J. Robb, and O.J.T. Harris (eds), *The body in history: Europe from the Palaeolithic to the future* (Cambridge: Cambridge University Press, 2013), pp 32–63: 49; O.J.T. Harris *et al.*, 'The body in its social context', in Robb and Harris (eds), *The body in history* (2013), pp 64–97, for discussion see table 4; A. Whittle, *The times of their lives: hunting history in the archaeology of Neolithic Europe* (Oxford: Oxbow, 2018), 113–25.

[60] Julian Thomas, *The birth of neolithic Britain* (Oxford: Oxford University Press, 2013), 424. See relevant discussion in Ben Elliott *et al.*, 'No pottery at the western periphery of Europe: why was the Final Mesolithic of Britain and Ireland aceramic?', *Antiquity* 94 (377) (2020), 1152–67; Conneller, *Mesolithic in Britain* (2021), chapter 6.

[61] Cooney, 'Parallel worlds or multi-stranded identities?' (2007); J.A. Sheridan, 'The neolithization of Britain and Ireland: the Big Picture', in Finlayson and Warren (eds), *Landscapes in transition* (Oxford: Oxbow/Council for British Archaeology in the Levant, 2010), pp 89–105.

[62] David Miles, *The tale of the axe: how the Neolithic revolution transformed Britain* (London: Thames and Hudson, 2016), 234. For a continuity versus colonisation summary, see Cummings and Harris, 'The continuity of hunting and gathering in the Neolithic and beyond in Britain and Ireland', in Cummings *et al.* (eds), *Oxford handbook: archaeology and anthropology of Hunter-Gatherers* (2014), pp 824–37: 828–9, and see Cummings, 'Hunting and gathering in a farmer's world' (2014), 773–4 for the processes behind the transition to farming. On aDNA, see Selina Brace *et al.*, 'Ancient genomes indicate population replacement in Early Neolithic Britain', *Nature Ecology and Evolution* 3 (2019), 765–71; Cassidy *et al.*, 'A dynastic elite' (2020).

[63] Whittle *et al.* (eds), *Gathering time: dating the early Neolithic enclosures* (2011). For detailed discussion and review, see Whittle *et al.*, 'Gathering time: the social dynamics of change', in Whittle *et al.* (eds), *Gathering time* (2011), pp 848–914; Thomas, *Birth of Neolithic Britain* (2013); Hugo Anderson-Whymark and Duncan Garrow, 'Seaways and shared ways: imaging and imagining the movement of people, objects and ideas over the course of the Mesolithic–Neolithic transition, *c.* 5000–3500 BC', in Anderson-Whymark *et al.* (eds), *Continental connections* (Oxford: Oxbow, 2015), pp 59–77; Richard Bradley, *The prehistory of Britain and Ireland* (2nd edn. Cambridge: Cambridge University Press, 2019), chapter 2; Jessica Smyth *et al.*, 'Exploring the "somewhere" and "someone" else: an integrated approach to Ireland's earliest farming practice', in K.J. Grons *et al.* (eds), *Farmers at the frontier: a pan-European perspective on Neolithisation* (Oxford: Oxbow 2020), pp 425–41.

[64] Cooney and Grogan, *Irish prehistory* (1999), 105–14; McSparron, *Burials and society* (2021).

[65] A.E.P. Collins and D.M. Waterman, *Millin Bay, a Late Neolithic cairn in Co. Down* (Belfast: HMSO, 1955); Cooney, *Landscapes of Neolithic Ireland* (2000); Schulting *et al.*, 'New dates from the north' (2012).

[66] Collins and Coyne, 'As old as we thought' (2006).

[67] Schulting *et al.*, 'Aveline's Hole' (2019), 38–49; Schulting, 'Holes in the world: the use of caves for burial in the Mesolithic', in Grünberg *et al.* (eds), *Mesolithic burials* (2016), pp 555–68: 563–4; Dowd, *Archaeology of caves in Ireland* (2015), 9–12; Warren, 'Transformations? The Mesolithic of north-west Europe', in Cummings *et al.* (eds), *Oxford handbook: archaeology and anthropology of Hunter-Gatherers* (2014), pp 537–55: 543.
[68] G.D. Liversage, 'Excavations at Dalkey Island, Co. Dublin, 1956–1959', *Proceedings of the Royal Irish Academy* 66C (1968), 53–233: 103–4, 176; Barbara Leon, 'Mesolithic and Neolithic activity on Dalkey Island—a reassessment', *Journal of Irish Archaeology* 14 (2005), 1–21; Meiklejohn and Woodman, 'Radiocarbon dating of Mesolithic human remains' (2012), 34.
[69] Göran Burenhult, *The Carrowmore excavations: excavation season 1981* (Stockholm: Institute of Archaeology, University of Stockholm (Stockholm Archaeological Reports 8), 1981), 11–23; Burenhult, *The archaeology of Carrowmore: environmental archaeology and the megalithic tradition at Carrowmore, Co. Sligo, Ireland* (Stockholm: Göran Burenhult. Theses and Papers in North-European Archaeology 14, 1984), 338–40.
[70] Sheila Paine, *Amulets: a world of secret powers, charms and magic* (London: Thames and Hudson, 2004), 18.
[71] Bradley, *The passage of arms* (London: Routledge, 1990); Lorraine Bourke, *Crossing the Rubicon: Bronze Age metalwork from Irish rivers* (Galway: Department of Archaeology, National University of Ireland. Bronze Age Studies 5, 2001); Fontijn, *Economies of destruction* (2020).
[72] See Gummesson *et al.*, 'Keep your head high' (2018), for discussion.
[73] Aidan O'Sullivan, *Foragers, farmers and fishers in a coastal landscape: an intertidal archaeological survey of the Shannon estuary* (Dublin: Discovery Programme/Royal Irish Academy. Discovery Programme Monographs 5, 2001), 69–86.
[74] For example, Bradley, *Prehistory of Britain and Ireland* (2019), 236–8. Discussion in Cooney and Grogan, *Irish prehistory* (1999), chapters 7–10. See Christina Fredengren, *Crannogs: a study of people's interaction with lakes* (Dublin: Wordwell, 2002); Maire Delaney and Peter Woodman, 'Searching the Irish Mesolithic for the humans behind the hatchets', in Helen Roche *et al.* (eds), *From megaliths to metals: essays in honour of George Eogan* (Oxford: Oxbow, 2004), pp 6–11; and Meiklejohn and Woodman, 'Radiocarbon dating of Mesolithic human remains' (2012), 36–8, for human skulls in Irish wetlands dating to the Bronze Age, medieval and modern periods.
[75] Malcolm Fry, *Coití: logboats from Northern Ireland* (Belfast: Environment and Heritage Service, 2000), 116; Warren, *Hunter-Gatherer Ireland* (2022), 43-45, noting possible toy logboat from Clowanstown, Co. Meath.
[76] Ole Crumlin-Pedersen and Birgitte Munch Thye, *The ship as symbol in prehistoric and medieval Scandinavia* (Copenhagen: The National Museum of Denmark, 1995). For the Møllegabet Mesolithic boat burial, see Ole Grøn and Jørgen Skaarup, 'Møllegabet II: a submerged Mesolithic site and "boat burial" from Ærø', *Journal of Danish Archaeology* 10 (1994), 38–50.
[77] Vicki Cummings *et al.*, 'Chambered tombs and passage graves of Western and Northern Europe', in Fowler *et al.* (eds), *Oxford handbook of Neolithic Europe* (2015), pp 813–35.

[78] For example, Cummings and O.J.T. Harris, 'Animals, people and and places: the continuity of hunting and gathering practices across the Mesolithic Neolithic transition in Britain', *European Journal of Archaeology* 14 (3) (2011), 361–82; more broadly, see the chapters in Part V of Cummings *et al. Oxford handbook: archaeology and anthropology of Hunter-Gatherers* (2013).

Chapter 4

[1] For the Ballyglass tombs, see Ruaidhrí de Valera and Seán Ó Nualláin, *Survey of the megalithic tombs of Ireland* (vol. 2. Dublin: The Stationery Office, 1964); Ó Nualláin, 'Excavation of the smaller court-tomb and associated hut sites at Ballyglass, County Mayo', *Proceedings of the Royal Irish Academy* 98C (1998), 125–75. On the Neolithic house, see Ó Nualláin, 'A Neolithic house at Ballyglass near Ballycastle, Co. Mayo', *Journal of the Royal Society of Antiquaries of Ireland* 98 (1972), 1–29. For discussion of house and tomb, see Jessica Smyth, 'House of the living, house of the dead: an open and shut case from Ballyglass, Co. Mayo?', in A. Barclay *et al.* (eds), *Houses of the dead?* (Oxford: Oxbow, 2020), pp 145–57; Smyth *et al.*, *The Neolithic house and tomb, Ballyglass, Co. Mayo, Ireland: excavations by Seán Ó Nualláin 1969–71* (Leiden: Sidestone Press, forthcoming). Andrew Powell, 'The language of lineage: reading Irish court tomb design', *European Journal of Archaeology* 8 (1) 2005, 9–28: 15, suggests a social context for the tomb structure. An overview of and wider context on the Céide Fields is given in Patrizia Boschiero *et al.*, *The Céide Fields Ireland: International Carlo Scarpa Prize for Gardens 2018* (Treviso: Fondazione Benetton Studi Ricerche, 2018).
[2] On dietary change, see Schulting, 'On the northwestern fringes: earlier Neolithic subsistence in Britain and Ireland as seen through faunal remains and stable isotopes', in S. Shennan *et al.* (eds), *The origins and spread of stock-keeping in the Near East and Europe* (Walnut Creek CA: Left Coast Press, 2013), pp 313–38; and 'Stable isotopes and Neolithic subsistence: pattern and variation', in Fowler *et al.* (eds), *Oxford handbook of Neolithic Europe* (2015), pp 361–83; Meriel McClatchie *et al.*, 'Food production, processing and foodways in Neolithic Ireland: an archaeobotanical perspective', *Environmental Archaeology* DOI: doi.org/10.1080/14614103.2019.1615215 2019. See also Shennan, *First farmers of Europe* (2018), on a cultural evolutionary perspective; D. Hofmann, 'What have genetics ever done for us? The implications of aDNA data for interpreting identity in Early Neolithic Central Europe', *European Journal of Archaeology* 18 (3) (2015), 454–76, on aDNA; Whittle *et al.*, *Gathering time* (2011), for regional change; and Duncan Garrow and Fraser Sturt, *Neolithic stepping stones: excavation and survey within the western seaways of Britain 2008–2014* (Oxford: Oxbow, 2017), on islands in this process. See Maïté Rivollat *et al.*, 'Ancient genome-wide DNA from France highlights the complexity of interactions between Mesolithic hunter-gatherers and Neolithic farmers', *Science Advances* 6 (22) (2020), eaaz5344. DOI: 10.1126/sciadv.aaz5344, on complexity of aDNA evidence from France.
[3] For a range of perspectives on the character of the transition from a hunter-gatherer to a famer lifestyle, see Peter Rowley-Conwy, 'How the West was lost: a reconsideration of

agricultural origins in Britain, Ireland, and southern Scandinavia', *Current Anthropology* 45 (2004), 83–113; Cooney, 'Parallel worlds or multi-stranded identities?' (2007); Thomas, 'Birth of Neolithic Britain' (2013); Sheridan, 'Neolithization of Britain and Ireland' (2010); Whittle *et al.*, 'Gathering time: the social dynamics of change' (2011); Cummings and Harris, 'Animals, people and places' (2011); Robb, 'Material culture' (2013); Anderson-Whymark and Garrow, 'Seaways and shared ways' (2015); Garrow and Sturt, *Neolithic stepping stones* (2017); Elliott *et al.*, 'No pottery at the western periphery of Europe' (2020); Smyth *et al.*, 'Exploring the "somewhere" and "someone" else' (2020). Overviews of the Neolithic in Ireland and Britain can be found in Cooney, *Landscapes of Neolithic Ireland* (2000); Malone, *Neolithic Britain and Ireland* (Stroud: Sutton, 2001); Cummings, *Neolithic of Britain and Ireland* (2017); Keith Ray and Julian Thomas, *Neolithic Britain: the transformation of social worlds* (Oxford: Oxford University Press, 2018).

[4] Hofmann and Whittle, 'Neolithic bodies', in A.M. Jones (ed.), *Prehistoric Europe: theory and practice* (Oxford: Wiley-Blackwell, 2008), pp 285–311; Robb and Harris, *The body in history* (2013); Bradbury and Scarre, *Engaging with the dead* (2017); Penny Bickle and Emilie Sibbesson, *Neolithic bodies* (Oxford: Oxbow. Neolithic Studies Group Papers 15, 2018). See King, *Unparalleled behaviour* (2003) on circulation of bone. For megalithic monuments as a feature of Atlantic Europe in the Neolithic, see, for example, M.S. Midgley, *The megaliths of northern Europe* (London: Routledge, 2008); Cummings *et al.*, 'Chambered tombs and passage graves' (2015); Luc Laporte and Chris Scarre, *The megalithic architectures of Europe* (Oxford: Oxbow, 2016); Johannes Müller *et al.* (eds), *Megaliths—societies—landscapes: early monumentality and social differentiation in Neolithic Europe*, volume 2 (Bonn: Habelt, 2019); as a global phenomenon, see Roger Joussaume, *Dolmens for the dead: megalithic building throughout the world* (London: Batsford, 1985); K.W. Beinhauer *et al.*, *The megalithic phenomenon: recent research and ethnoarchaeological approaches* (Weissbach: Beier and Beran, 1999). Scarre, *The megalithic monuments of Britain and Ireland* (London: Thames and Hudson, 2007), puts the monuments in Britain and Ireland in their European setting. See Sheridan and Schulting, 'Making sense of Scottish Neolithic funerary monuments: tracing trajectories and understanding their rationale', in A.B. Gebauer *et al.* (eds), *Monumentalising life in the Neolithic: narratives of change and continuity* (Oxford: Oxbow, 2020), pp 195–215, on Scotland.
On mortuary practice, see K.-G. Sjogren, 'Mortuary practices, bodies and persons in northern Europe', in Fowler *et al.* (eds), *Oxford handbook of Neolithic Europe* (2015), pp 1005–22; Fowler and Scarre, 'Mortuary practices and bodily representations in north-west Europe', in Fowler *et al.* (eds), *Oxford handbook of Neolithic Europe* (2015), pp 1023–47.

[5] Cooney and Grogan, *Irish prehistory* (1999), fig. 4.14; Carlin and Cooney, 'Transforming our understanding of Neolithic and Chalcolithic society (4000–2200 BC) in Ireland', in Stanley *et al.* (eds), *Stories of Ireland's past* (2017), pp 23–56, on wider evidence. Laureen Buckley *et al.*, 'The human remains', in Eogan and Cleary, *The passage tomb archaeology of the Great Mound at Knowth* (Excavations at Knowth 6, 2017), pp 277–329, table 3.28, demonstrate that there are over 200 individuals in the deposits of human remains just from the passage tomb complex at Knowth.

[6] For discussion of the length of Neolithic generations, see Whittle, *Times of their lives* (2018), 28. On population, see T.R. McLaughlin, 'An archaeology of Ireland for the Information Age' (2020); and see Cooney and Grogan, *Irish prehistory* (1999), 217, for lower population guestimate.
[7] See Jay and Scarre, 'Tracking the dead in the Neolithic: the "Invisible Dead" in Britain', in Bradbury and Scarre (eds), *Engaging with the dead* (2017), pp 7–23, on the invisible dead in Neolithic Britain.
[8] The volumes of the Megalithic Survey provide the detail: de Valera and Ó Nualláin, *Survey of the megalithic tombs of Ireland* vol. 1 (1961); vol. 2 (1964); vol. 3 (1972); vol. 4 (1982); Ó Nualláin, *Survey of the megalithic tombs of Ireland* vol. 5 (1989); and Eamon Cody, *Survey of the megalithic tombs of Ireland* vol. 6 (2002). See also Herity, *Irish passage graves: Neolithic tomb-builders in Ireland and Britain 2500 B.C.* (Dublin: Irish University Press, 1974), on passage tombs. Elizabeth Shee Twohig, *Irish megalithic tombs* (Princes Risborough: Shire Books, 1990), is a valuable brief overview; Carleton Jones, *Temples of stone: exploring the megalithic tombs of Ireland* (Cork: Collins Press, 2007), provides an accessible and detailed discussion.
[9] For example, see Ed Danaher, *Monumental beginnings: the archaeology of the N4 Sligo Inner Relief Road* (Dublin: National Roads Authority. NRA Scheme Monographs 1, 2007); Rose M. Cleary and Hilary Kelleher, *Archaeological excavations at Tullahedy, County Tipperary: Neolithic settlement in north Munster* (Cork: Collins Press, 2011); Smyth, *Settlement in the Irish Neolithic: new discoveries at the edge of Europe* (Oxford: Oxbow/Prehistoric Society. Prehistoric Society Research Paper 6, 2014). See Bettina Schulz Paulsson, 'Radiocarbon dates and Bayesian modelling support maritime diffusion model for megaliths in Europe' *Proceedings of the National Academy of Sciences* 116 (2019), 3460–65, on the dating and maritime diffusion of megalithic tombs in Atlantic Europe. Robinson, *Stones of Aran* (1995), 226–35, discusses the enduring fascination of megalithic monuments.
[10] Schulting *et al.*, 'New dates from the north' (2012). See Robb, 'What can we really say' (2016), on possible under-estimates of remains and clearing out.
[11] Smith and Brickley, *People of the Long Barrow* (2009), 89; see also Lewis, *Bioarchaeology of children* (2007).
[12] C. Jones, *The Burren and the Aran Islands: exploring the archaeology* (Cork: Collins Press, 2004), 46–51; Beckett, 'Interactions with the dead' (2011); Schulting *et al.*, 'New dates from the north' (2012). Cassidy *et al.* (2020) dated 11 inhumations from Parknabinnia, all dating before 3100 BC, with seven individuals falling between 3647 and 3353 BC.
[13] Ann Lynch, *Poulnabrone: an Early Neolithic portal tomb in Ireland* (Dublin: The Stationery Office. Archaeological Monograph Series 9, 2014); Beckett, 'A taphonomic assessment of the human bone assemblage', in Lynch, *Poulnabrone* (2014), pp 56–61; Ó Donnabháin and Mara Tesorieri, 'Bioarchaeology', in Lynch, *Poulnabrone* (2014), pp 61–86.
[14] Ó Donnabháin and Tesorieri, 'Bioarchaeology' (2014), 84. On the dating and duration of use of Poulnabrone, see Schulting, 'The dating of Poulnabrone, Co. Clare', in Lynch, *Poulnabrone* (2014), pp 93–113, table 5.3.
[15] Muiris O'Sullivan, *Duma na nGiall. The Mound of the Hostages, Tara* (Bray: Wordwell/UCD School of Archaeology, 2005), 123; Brindley *et al.*, 'Radiocarbon-dated samples

from the Mound of the Hostages, Tara', in O'Sullivan, *Duma na nGiall* (2005), pp 282–96; Alex Bayliss and O'Sullivan, 'Interpreting chronologies for the Mound of the Hostages, Tara, and its contemporary contexts in Neolithic and Bronze Age Ireland', in M. O'Sullivan *et al.* (eds), *Tara: from the past to the future. Towards a new research agenda* (Dublin: Wordwell/UCD School of Archaeology, 2013), pp 26–104.

[16] Smith and Brickley, *People of the Long Barrow* (2009), chapter 3.

[17] Mike Parker Pearson, 'Dead and (un)buried: reconstructing attitudes to death in long-term perspective', in Bradbury and Scarre (eds), *Engaging with the dead* (2017), pp 129–37: 130; William O'Brien, *Sacred ground: megalithic tombs in coastal south-west Ireland* (Galway: Department of Archaeology, NUI Galway; Bronze Age Studies 4, 1999); Carlin, *The Beaker phenomenon* (2018).

[18] Cummings and Whittle, *Places of special virtue: megaliths in the Neolithic landscapes of Wales* (Oxford: Oxbow, 2004), 69; Tatjana Kytmannow, *Portal tombs in the landscape: the chronology, morphology and landscape setting of the portal tombs of Ireland, Wales and Cornwell* (Oxford: Archaeopress. BAR British Series 455, 2008); Phyllis Mercer, *Irish portal tombs: a ritual perspective* (Oxford: Archaeopress. BAR British Series 616, 2015). Michael Connolly, *Stone, bone and belonging: the Early Neolithic portal tombs at Killaclohane, Co. Kerry* (Tralee: Kerry County Council, 2021), 171–82 on Killaclohane 1; Cummings and Colin Richards, *Monuments in the making: raising the great dolmens in early Neolithic northern Europe* (Oxford: Windgather Press, 2021).

[19] de Valera, 'The court cairns of Ireland', *Proceedings of the Royal Irish Academy* 60C (1960), 9–140; and 'Transeptal court cairns', *Journal of the Royal Society of Antiquaries of Ireland* 95 (1965), 5–37; Powell, 'Language of lineage' (2005); Schulting *et al.*, 'New dates from the north' (2012).

[20] Waterman, 'The excavation of a court tomb at Tully, Co. Fermanagh', *Ulster Journal of Archaeology* 41 (1978), 3–14.

[21] Cooney *et al.*, 'Ireland', in Whittle *et al.* (eds), *Gathering time* (2011) pp 562–669; Stefan Bergh and Robert Hensey, 'Unpicking the chronology of Carrowmore', *Oxford Journal of Archaeology* 32 (4) (2013), 343–66; Schulting *et al.*, 'Dating the human remains at Knowth' (2017); Schulting *et al.*, 'Radiocarbon dates for a multi-phase passage tomb on Baltinglass Hill, Co. Wicklow', *Proceedings of the Prehistoric Society* 83 (2017), 1–19; Kador *et al.*, Rites of passage: mortuary practice, population dynamics and chronology at the Carrowkeel Passage Tomb Complex, Co. Sligo, Ireland', *Proceedings of the Prehistoric Society* 84 (2018), 225–55. For the new large tomb at Dowth Hall in Brú na Bóinne, see Clíodhna Ní Lionáin, 'Remembering a long-lost monument: a whistle-stop tour through the life of the Dowth Hall passage tomb', *Archaeology Ireland* 36 (3) (2022), 36–40; Ní Lionáin *et al.*, 'Spirals, lozenges and a "Christmas tree": an introduction to the megalithic art of the Dowth Hall passage tomb', *Archaeology Ireland* 36 (4) (2022), 14–19.

[22] For the Mound of the Hostages: O'Sullivan, *Duma na nGiall* (2005); for Knowth: Buckley *et al.*, 'The human remains' (2017). For passage tomb mortuary practice: Cooney, 'The role of cremation in mortuary practice in the Irish Neolithic', in Kuijt *et al.* (eds), *Transformation by fire* (2014), pp 198–206; and 'The Knowth mortuary practices in context', in Eogan and Cleary, *Passage tomb archaeology of the Great Mound at Knowth* (2017), pp 387–410.

[23] Cooney, *Landscapes of Neolithic Ireland* (2000), 97–9. Ashley Park: Manning, 'A Neolithic burial ground at Ashley Park, Co. Tipperary' (1985). Poulawack: Hugh O'Neill Hencken, 'A cairn at Poulawack, Co. Clare', *Journal of the Royal Society of Antiquaries of Ireland* 65 (1935), 191–222; M.F. Ryan, 'Poulawack, Co. Clare: the affinities of the central burial structure', in D. Ó Corráin (ed.), *Irish antiquity* (1981), pp 134–46; Beckett, 'Interactions with the dead: a taphonomic analysis' (2011). Jerpoint West: M.F. Ryan, 'The excavation of a Neolithic burial mound at Jerpoint West, Co. Kilkenny', *Proceedings of the Royal Irish Academy* 73C (1973), 107–27.
[24] Dowd, 'Use of caves' (2008); *Archaeology of caves in Ireland* (2015), chapter 5; and *Underground archaeology: studies on human bones and artefacts from Ireland's caves* (Oxford: Oxbow, 2016), specifically Fibiger, 'Osteological analysis', pp 3–37. Dowd *et al.*, 'The role of caves in complex Neolithic funerary rituals on Knocknarea Mountain, Co. Sligo, Ireland', *Journal of Irish Archaeology* 28 (2019), 1–15; and Dowd *et al.*, 'Neolithic engagements with the dead: mortuary processing on Bengorm Mountain in the north-west of Ireland', *Oxford Journal of Archaeology* 39 (4) (2020), 368–94.
[25] Dowd, *Archaeology of caves in Ireland* (2015), 109–12. Ballycarty: Michael Connolly, *Discovering the Neolithic in County Kerry: a passage tomb at Ballycarty* (Bray: Wordwell, 1999).
[26] Carlin, 'Getting into the groove: exploring the relationship between Grooved Ware and developed Passage Tombs in Ireland *c.* 3000–2700 cal BC', *Proceedings of the Prehistoric Society* 83 (2017), 155–88; Sheridan, 'Little and large: the miniature "carved stone ball" beads from the eastern tomb at Knowth, Ireland, and their broader significance', in R.M. Arbogast and A. Greffier-Richard (eds), *Entre archéologie et écologie: une préhistoire de tous les milieux. Mélanges offerts à Pierre Pétrequin* (Besançon: Presses Universitaires de Franche-Comté, 2014), pp 303–14; M. O'Sullivan *et al.*, 'Henges in Ireland: new discoveries and emerging issues', in A. Gibson (ed.), *Enclosing the Neolithic: recent studies in Britain and Europe* (Oxford: Archaeopress. BAR International Series 2440, 2012), pp 37–53; Steve Davis and Knut Rassmann, 'Beyond Newgrange: Brú na Bóinne in the later Neolithic', *Proceedings of the Prehistoric Society* 87 (2021), 189–218.
[27] Sheridan, 'A non-megalithic funerary tradition in early Neolithic Ireland', in M. Meek (ed.), *The modern traveller to our past: festschrift in honour of Ann Hamlin* (Rathfriland: DPK, 2006), pp 24–31; Cummings, *Neolithic of Britain and Ireland* (2017), 118–23; Sheridan and Schulting, 'Making sense of Scottish Neolithic funerary monuments' (2020), 198. Dooey's Cairn: see E. Estyn Evans, 'Dooey's Cairn, Dunloy, County Antrim', *Ulster Journal of Archaeology* 1 (1938), 59–78; A.E.P. Collins, 'Dooey's Cairn, Ballymacaldrick, Co. Antrim', *Ulster Journal of Archaeology* 39 (1976), 1–7; Cooney, *Landscapes of Neolithic Ireland* (2000), 99–103. It is possible that there was a similar pre-megalithic phase at the Tirnony, Co. Derry portal tomb; Cormac McSparron, 'Tirnony portal tomb, Co. Derry', *Archaeology Ireland* 25 (4) (2011), 26-30; McSparron *et al.*, *Excavations at Tirnony, Co. Derry/Londonderry. Data Structure Report 82, AE/10/172* (Belfast: Centre for Archaeological Fieldwork, School of Archaeology and Palaeoecology, Queen's University Belfast, 2013).
[28] Ó Ríordáin, 'Lough Gur excavations' (1954), 321–84; Smyth, *Settlement in the Irish Neolithic* (2014), 126–30, on human remains in pits.

[29] For discussion of mortuary practice in different cultural and religious contexts, see papers in Robben, *Death, mourning and burial* (2004); Parkes *et al.*, *Death and bereavement across cultures* (1997); Tarlow and Nilsson Stutz (eds), *Oxford handbook: archaeology of death and burial* (2013). For comparison with Britain, see Cummings, *Neolithic of Britain and Ireland* (2017), 91–4.
[30] For example, Ó Donnabháin and Tesorieri, 'Bioarchaeology' (2014); Buckley *et al.*, 'The human remains' (2017). For review of relevant British evidence, see Smith and Brickley, *People of the Long Barrow* (2009).
[31] Fowler, 'Patterns and diversity in the Early Neolithic mortuary practices of Britain and Ireland: contextualizing the treatment of the dead', *Documenta Praehistorica* 37 (2010), 1–22: 15; Cummings, *Neolithic of Britain and Ireland* (2017), 108. On Hazleton North, see Fowler *et al.*, 'High resolution picture of kinship practices' (2021).
[32] On the 'too many ancestors' argument, see James Whitley, 'Too many ancestors', *Antiquity* 76 (2002), 119–26; see Barrett, 'The living, the dead' (1988), on ancestral rites, and A.M. Jones, 'How the dead live: mortuary practices, memory and the ancestors in Neolithic and Early Bronze Age Britain and Ireland', in J. Pollard (ed), *Prehistoric Britain* (Oxford: Blackwell, 2008), pp 177–201: 193 for discussion.
[33] Helms, *Access to origins* (1998), 35. On house societies: Claude Lévi-Strauss, *The way of the masks* (London: Jonathan Cape, 1982); Carsten and Hugh-Jones, *About the house: Lévi-Strauss and beyond* (Cambridge: Cambridge University Press, 1995); Thomas, 'Birth of Neolithic Britain' (2013), 290–96; Smyth, *Settlement in the Irish Neolithic* (2014); Colin Richards and Richard Jones, *The development of Neolithic house societies in Orkney* (Oxford: Oxbow, 2016); Fowler, 'Social arrangements' (2022), 69–70.
[34] Helms, *Access to origins* (1998), chapter 4; Whittle, *Archaeology of people* (2003), 107–32.
[35] Kuijt, 'Regeneration of life' (2008).
[36] Helms, *Access to origins* (1998), 24–9.
[37] Connerton, *How societies remember* (Cambridge: Cambridge University Press, 1989).
[38] Helms, *Access to origins* (1998), 51; Parker Pearson, 'Dead and un-buried' (2017), 133.
[39] For example, Hodder, *The domestication of Europe* (Oxford: Blackwell, 1990), 245–6; Robb, 'Creating death: an archaeology of dying', in Tarlow and Nilsson Stutz (eds), *Oxford handbook of death and burial* (2013), 441–57: 452.
[40] On body worlds, see Robb and Harris, *The body in history* (2013); Harris *et al.*, 'The body in its social context' (2013); Harris, 'Both permeable and partible: exploring the body world of Early Neolithic southern Britain', in P. Bickle and E. Sibbesson (eds), *Neolithic bodies* (Oxford: Oxbow, 2018), pp 7–24. See Smith and Brickley, *People of the Long Barrow* (2009), on mortuary rituals in the earlier British Neolithic, 41 and 64; on cremation and inhumation as complementary rites, 62. See also Williams, 'A well-urned rest: cremation and inhumation in early Anglo-Saxon England', in Kuijt *et al.* (eds), *Transformation by fire* (2014), pp 93–118. On the cultural contexts of cremation, see Colin Quinn *et al.*, 'Introduction: contextualizing cremations', in Kuijt *et al.* (eds), *Transformation by fire* (2014), pp 3–21; Quinn *et al.*, 'Perspectives—complexities of terminologies and intellectual frameworks in cremation studies', in Kuijt *et al.* (eds), *Transformation by fire* (2014), pp 25–32. See also Jessica Cerezo-Román *et al.* (eds), *Cremation and the archaeology of death* (2017). For general discussion, see McKinley, 'Cremation: excavation, analysis and interpretation' (2013).

[41] Robert Hertz, *Death and the right hand* (London: Cohen and West, 1960); see extracts published as Hertz, 'A contribution to the study of the collective representation of death', in A.C.G.M. Robben (ed.), *Death, mourning, and burial* (Oxford: Blackwell, 2004), pp 197–222.
[42] Bocquet-Appel, 'Palaeoanthropological traces of a Neolithic demographic transition', *Current Anthropology* 43 (2002), 637–50, suggests that in Neolithic communities about 50% of the dead would be children and infants. Lewis, *Bioarchaeology of children* (2007), 22, argues for an estimate of 30–40% of people in prehistoric societies dying before they reached adulthood.
[43] Beckett, 'Interactions with the dead' (2011). For Knowth, see Buckley *et al.*, 'The human remains' (2017); Cooney, 'Knowth mortuary practices in context' (2017), 400.
[44] Seán P. Ó Ríordáin, 'Lough Gur excavations: Neolithic and Bronze Age houses on Knockadoon', *Proceedings of the Royal Irish Academy* 56C (1954), 297–459; Eoin Grogan and George Eogan, 'Lough Gur excavations by Séan P. Ó Ríordáin: further Neolithic and Beaker habitations on Knockadoon', *Proceedings of the Royal Irish Academy* 87C (1987), 299–506; Rose M. Cleary, 'Later Bronze Age settlement and prehistoric burials, Lough Gur, Co. Limerick', *Proceedings of the Royal Irish Academy* 95C (1995), 1–93.
[45] R. Hedges *et al.*, 'The supra-regional perspective', in Bickle and Whittle (eds), *First farmers* (2013), 373–4; Bickle and Fibiger, 'Aging, childhood and social identity' (2014), 215; see Mélie Le Roy, 'How were infants considered at death during the Neolithic period in France?', in Murphy and Le Roy (eds), *Children, death and burial* (2017), pp 19–34, on the treatment of infants at death in Neolithic France.
[46] For relevant archaeological discussion in different cultural contexts, see Riel-Salvatore and Gravel-Miguel, 'Upper Palaeolithic mortuary practices' (2013), 328; A.J. Waterman and J.T. Jones, 'When the bough breaks: childhood mortality and burial practice in Late Neolithic Atlantic Europe', *Oxford Journal of Archaeology* 30 (2) (2011), 165–83: 171; Aline Thomas *et al.*, 'Unpacking burial and rank: the role of children in the first monumental cemeteries of Western Europe (4600–4300 BC)', *Antiquity* 85 (2011), 772–86. For broader discussion, Murphy and Le Roy, *Children, death and burial* (2017).
[47] Jones, *The Burren and the Aran Islands* (2004), 50. Noting that aDNA suggests lack of close biological kin in tomb, Cassidy *et al.*, 'A dynastic elite' (2020).
[48] The Mound of the Hostages, Tara: M. O'Sullivan, *Duma na nGiall* (2005), 119–23; Kuijt and Quinn, 'Biography of the Neolithic body: tracing pathways to cist II, Mound of the Hostages, Tara', in M. O'Sullivan *et al.* (eds), *Tara—from the past to the future* (2013), pp 170–83: 173. Fourknocks: Cooney, 'Body politics and grave messages: Irish Neolithic mortuary practices', in N. Sharples and A. Sheridan (eds), *Vessels for the ancestors* (Edinburgh: Edinburgh University Press 1992), pp 128–42, and *Landscapes of the Neolithic* (2000), 103–12; Finlay, 'Outside of life: traditions of infant burial in Ireland from cillín to cist', *World Archaeology* 31 (3) (2000), 407–22. Knowth: Buckley *et al.*, 'The human remains' (2017); Cooney, 'Knowth mortuary practices in context' (2017), 401. Robb, 'Burial treatment as transformation' (2007), argues that the pathways of the post-mortem treatment of children tended to be simpler because they were not central to society.

[49] Fowler, 'Identities in transformation: identities, funerary rites, and the mortuary process', in Tarlow and Nilsson Stutz (eds), *Oxford handbook of the archaeology of death and* (2013), pp 511–26: 518–9. For Creggandevesky: Claire Foley, 'The excavation of a court tomb at Creggandevesky, County Tyrone', *Ulster Journal of Archaeology* 73 (2015/6), 68–147; Annaghmare: D.M. Waterman, 'The court cairn at Annaghmare, Co. Armagh', *Ulster Journal of Archaeology* 28 (1965), 3–46. Cummings and Richards, *Monuments in the making* (2021) focus on the elevation and display of a substantial roof stone as a distinctive feature of portal tombs, employing the term 'dolmen'.
[50] For Killaclohane, see Connolly, *Stone, bone and belonging* (2021); Carrowkeel: Jonny Geber *et al.*, 'Facilitating transitions: postmortem treatment of the dead at the Carrowkeel Passage Tomb Complex, Ireland (3500-3000 cal BC)', *Bioarchaeology International* 1 (2017), 35–51; and Kador *et al.*, 'Rites of passage' (2018). Millin Bay: Murphy, 'Funerary processing of the dead in prehistoric Ireland', *Archaeology Ireland* 17 (2003), 13–15.
[51] For Poulawack: Beckett, 'Interactions with the dead' (2011). On selective removal of skulls and long bones at Poulnabrone, see Ó Donnabháin and Tesorieri, 'Bioarchaeology' (2014), 67.
[52] For Ashley Park, Manning, 'Neolithic burial ground at Ashley Park' (1985); Cooney, *Landscapes of Neolithic Ireland* (2000), 97–9.
[53] Elizabeth Rega, 'Age, gender and biological reality in the Early Bronze Age cemetery at Mokrin', in J. Moore and E. Scott (eds), *Invisible people and processes: writing gender and childhood into European archaeology* (Leicester: Leicester University Press, 1997), pp 229–47: 237–8; Eleanor Scott, *The archaeology of infancy and infant death* (Oxford: Archaeopress. BAR International Series 819, 1999); Lewis, *Bioarchaeology of children* (2007), 90.
[54] Fowler, 'Identities in transformation' (2013), 518.
[55] Cooney, 'Icons of antiquity: remaking megalithic monuments in Ireland', in M. Díaz-Guardamino *et al.* (eds), *The lives of prehistoric monuments: in Iron Age, Roman and Medieval Europe* (Oxford: Oxford University Press, 2015), pp 55–76.
[56] See discussion in Bergh, *Landscape of the monuments: a study of the passage tombs in the Cúil Irra region, Co. Sligo, Ireland* (Stockholm: Riksantikvarieämbetet Arkeologiska undersöknigar, 1995); Powell 'Language of lineage' (2005); Guillaume Robin, 'Spatial structures and symbolic systems in Irish and British passage tombs: the organization of architectural elements, parietal carved signs and funerary deposits', *Cambridge Archaeological Journal* 20 (3) (2010), 373–418; Rob Hensey, *First light: the origins of Newgrange* (Oxford: Oxbow, 2015).
[57] Whittle, *Times of their lives* (2018), chapter 2.
[58] Robb, 'Tradition and agency: human body representation in later prehistoric Europe', *World Archaeology* 40 (2008), 332–53; Robb and Harris, *The body in history* (2013), 2–3; Cooney, 'Knowth mortuary practices in context' (2017), 406.
[59] Robb and Harris, 'Becoming gendered in European prehistory: was Neolithic gender fundamentally different?', *American Antiquity* 83 (2018), 128–47: 136, see also Bickle, 'Thinking gender differently: new approaches to identity difference in the Central European Neolithic', *Cambridge Archaeological Journal* 30 (2) (2019), 201–18, looking at gender in the Linearbandkeramik.

[60] Jones, *Temples of stone* (2007), 78–80; Cassidy *et al.*, 'A dynastic elite', (2020); Federico Sánchez-Quinto *et al.*, 'Megalithic tombs in western and northern Europe were linked to a kindred society', *Proceedings of the National Academy of Sciences* 116 (2019), 9469–74.
[61] T.C. Darvill, 'Court cairns, passage graves and social change in Ireland', *Man* 14 (1979), 311–27; discussion in Powell, 'Language of lineage' (2005).
[62] Bradley, *The past in prehistoric societies* (2002).
[63] Cassidy *et al.*, 'A dynastic elite' (2020); Cassidy, 'Ancient DNA in Ireland', (2020); Sánchez-Quinto, 'Megalithic tombs in western and northern Europe' (2019); Powell, 'Language of lineage' (2005); Frank Prendergast, Linked landscapes: spatial, archaeoastronomcal and social network analysis of the Irish passage tomb tradition (Unpublished PhD thesis; University College Dublin, 2011); Prendergast *et al.*, 'Facing the sun', *Archaeology Ireland* 31 (122) (2017), 10-17.
[64] Whittle, *The archaeology of people* (2003), 67–8; Evžen Neustupný, 'Structures and events: the theoretical basis of spatial archaeology', in Neustupný (ed.), *Space in prehistoric Bohemia* (Praha: Institute of Archaeology, Academy of Sciences of the Czech Republic, 1998), pp 9–44: 10–21; Gamble, *The Palaeolithic societies of Europe* (Cambridge: Cambridge University Press, 1999), tables 2.8 and 2.9.
[65] Dunbar, *Human evolution* (London: Penguin, 2014), 67–72.
[66] Dunbar, *Human evolution* (2014), 276.
[67] O'Sullivan, *Duma na nGiall* (2005); Kuijt and Quinn, 'Biography of the Neolithic body' (2013); Cooney, 'Role of cremation in mortuary practice' (2014).
[68] Robin, 'Spatial structures and symbolic systems' (2010). The observation on mortuary practice can be traced back to P.J. Hartnett, 'Excavation of a passage grave at Fourknocks, Co. Meath', *Proceedings of the Royal Irish Academy* 58C (1957), 197–277, 269; see also the discussion of Fourknocks II in Hartnett, 'The excavation of two tumuli at Fourknocks (sites II and III), Co. Meath', *Proceedings of the Royal Irish Academy* 71C (1971), 35–89; see also Cooney, 'Knowth mortuary practices in context' (2017); Geber *et al.*, 'Facilitating transitions' (2017); Kador *et al.* 'Rites of passage' (2018); Dowd *et al.* 'The role of caves' (2019); Linda G. Lynch, 'The human remains', in E. Cody, *Magheracar, Co. Donegal: excavation of a passage tomb on Ireland's north-west coast* (Dublin: Stationery Office. Archaeological Monograph Series 12, 2019), 74–86.
[69] Schulting *et al.*, 'Radiocarbon dates for a multi-phase passage tomb' (2017); Carlin and Cooney, 'Transforming our understanding' (2017), 35–40; T.R. McLaughlin *et al.*, 'Changing face of Neolithic and Bronze Age Ireland' (2016); T.R. McLaughlin, 'An archaeology of Ireland for the Information Age' (2020). For comparison of large and small complex sites, see M. O'Sullivan, 'Little and large: comparing Knockroe with Knowth', in Roche *et al.*, *From megaliths to metals* (2004), 44–55.
[70] Kador *et al.*, 'Rites of passage' (2018); Hensey, *First light* (2015); for settlement at Mullaghfarna, see Bergh, 'Where worlds meet: two Irish prehistoric mountain-top "villages"', in U. Moscatelli and A. Stagno (eds), 'Archaeology of Europe's mountain areas: methods, problems and case studies', *Il Capitale Culturale. Studies on the Value of Cultural Heritage* 12 (2015), 21–44. http://riviste.unimc.it/index.php/cap-cult/issue/view/54/showToc; Prendergast, 'Linked landscapes' (2011); and 'Facing the sun' (2017).
[71] Bergh, 'Knocknarea—the ultimate monument: megaliths and mountains in Neolithic Cúil Irra, north-west Ireland', in Scarre (ed.), *Monuments and landscape in Atlantic Europe: perception and society during the Neolithic and Early Bronze Age* (London:

Routledge 2002), pp 139–5. For discussion of the Great Palisade at Newgrange, see Davis and Rassmann, 'Beyond Newgrange' (2021), 206–07; Prendergast *et al.*, 'Facing the sun' (2017); Prendergast, *Solar alignment and the Irish passage tomb tradition* (Dublin: Archaeology Ireland. Heritage Guide 82, 2018). For a broader landscape perspective, see M. O'Sullivan, 'Megalithic tombs and storied landscapes in Neolithic Ireland', in Martin Furholt *et al.* (eds), *Megaliths and identities* (Bonn: Habelt, 2011), pp 53–66.

[72] On Knowth, see George Eogan and Kerri Cleary, *Passage tomb archaeology of the Great Mound at Knowth* (2017), 65–77; on mortuary practice in Orcadian passage tombs, see David Laurence, 'Neolithic mortuary practice in Orkney', *Proceedings of the Society of Antiquaries of Scotland* 136 (2006), 47–59; Schulting *et al.*, Revisiting Quanterness: new AMS dates and stable isotope data from an Orcadian chamber tomb', *Proceedings of the Society of Antiquaries of Scotland* 140 (2010), 1–50; Crozier, 'Fragments of death: a taphonomic study of human remains from Orkney', *Journal of Archaeological Science: Reports* 10 (2016), 725–34. On wrapping, see Cummings and Richards, 'Passage graves as material technologies of wrapping', in Bickle, *et al. The Neolithic of Europe* (Oxford: Oxbow, 2017), pp 235–48. On Irish/Orcadian links, see Carlin and Cooney, 'On the sea roads: the ebb and flow of links with a wider world', in N. Card *et al.* (eds), *The Ness of Brodgar: as it stands* (Kirkwall: The Orcadian. Kirkwall Press, 2020), pp 320–32. On passage tombs as special places for important people, see Eogan and Shee Twohig, *The megalithic art of the passage tombs at Knowth, County Meath* (Dublin: Royal Irish Academy. Excavations at Knowth 7, 2022), 305–07.

[73] See, for example, Williams, 'Death, memory and material culture: catalytic commemoration and the cremated dead', in Tarlow and Nilsson Stutz (eds), *Oxford handbook of the archaeology of death and burial* (2013), pp 195–208.

[74] Barrie Hartwell, 'The Ballynahatty complex', in A. Gibson and D.D.A. Simpson (eds), *Prehistoric ritual and religion* (Sutton: Stroud, 1998), pp 32–44; Schulting *et al.*, 'New dates from the north' (2012); Carlin, 'Getting into the Groove' (2017).

[75] Cassidy *et al.*, 'Neolithic and Bronze Age migration to Ireland' (2016); Cassidy and Bradley, 'Ancient DNA and Irish human prehistory' (2017); Dowd *et al.*, 'Neolithic engagements with the dead' (2020).

[76] Ó Donnabháin, 'Human remains, Annagh, Co. Limerick', in Cahill and Sikora (eds), *Breaking ground: finding graves* (vol. 1, 2011), pp 34–47; Cassidy, 'Ancient DNA in Ireland' (2020).

[77] See discussion in Jones, 'How the dead live' (2008), 190–96.

[78] On violence in the Neolithic, see Schulting and Michael Wysocki, '"In this chambered tomb were found cleft skulls…". An assessment of the evidence for cranial trauma in the British Neolithic', *Proceedings of the Prehistoric Society* 71 (2005), 107–38; Schulting and Fibiger, *Sticks, stones and broken bones* (2012) and 'Skeletal evidence for interpersonal violence in the Neolithic', in *Sticks, stones and broken bones*, pp 1–16.; Fibiger *et al.*, 'Patterns of violence-related skull trauma in Neolithic Southern Scandinavia', *American Journal of Physical Anthropology* 150 (2013), 190–202; Dyer and Fibiger, 'Understanding blunt-force trauma and violence' (2017); Buckley *et al.*, 'The human remains' (2017), 322.

[79] Reich, *Who we are and how we got here* (2018), 117–21; Haak *et al.*, 'Massive migration from the Steppe' (2015); Renfrew, *Archaeology and language* (1987). For broader discussion, see Mallory, 'Language in prehistoric Ireland', *Ulster Folklore* 45 (1999), 3–16.

[80] Reich, *Who we are* (2018); Cassidy and Bradley, 'Ancient DNA and Irish human prehistory' (2017).
[81] Carlin, *Beaker phenomenon* (2018); Furholt, 'Massive migrations?' (2018); N.N. Johannsen *et al.*, 'A composite window into human history', *Science* 356 (6343) (2017), 1118–20; see also reviews of Reich, *Who we are* (2018) in *Current Anthropology* 59 (2018), 655–62.
[82] On Mesolithic hunter-gatherer and Neolithic farmer genetic admixture, see Sánchez-Quinto *et al.*, 'Megalithic tombs in western and northern Europe' (2019); Cassidy *et al.*, 'A dynastic elite' (2020); Rivollat *et al.*, 'Ancient genome-wide DNA from France' (2020).
[83] Cassidy *et al.*, 'A dynastic elite' (2020); Cassidy, 'Ancient DNA in Ireland' (2020); Sánchez-Quinto *et al.*, 'Megalithic tombs in western and northern Europe' (2019). For a critical perspective, see Carlin and Cooney, 'Early prehistoric societies in Ireland' (2020). For wider discussion, see Brück, 'Ancient DNA, kinship and relational identities' (2021).
[84] Cassidy, 'Ancient DNA in Ireland' (2020), 39.
[85] Carlin and Cooney, 'Early prehistoric societies in Ireland' (2020). For Late Neolithic cremated bone at Magheracar passage tomb, see Cody, *Magheracar* (2019), 146.
[86] Cassidy *et al.*, 'A dynastic elite' (2020), 385; Carlin and Cooney, 'Early prehistoric societies in Ireland' (2020), 22. Eogan and Shee Twohig, *Megalithic art of the passage tombs at Knowth* (2022), 306–07, place aDNA evidence in the wider passage-tomb context.
[87] Cooney, 'The role of cremation' (2014); and 'Pathways to ancestral worlds: mortuary practice in the Irish Neolithic', in K. Brophy *et al.* (eds), *The Neolithic of mainland Scotland* (Edinburgh: Edinburgh University Press (2016), pp 74–94.
[88] Ó hÓgáin, *The sacred isle* (1999); M. O'Sullivan, 'Megalithic tombs and storied landscapes' (2011).
[89] See William O'Brien, 'Megaliths in a mythologized landscape: south-west Ireland in the Iron Age', in Scarre (ed.), *Monuments and landscape in Atlantic Europe* (2002), pp 152–76; Cooney, 'Icons of antiquity' (2015).
[90] For example, see discussion of Emain Macha, the late prehistoric royal site of Ulster, in C.J. Lynn, *Navan Fort archaeology and myth* (Bray: Wordwell, 2003), chapter 9.
[91] Cummings, *Neolithic of Britain and Ireland* (2017), 193–221.
[92] Davis and Rassmann, 'Beyond Newgrange' (2021); Carlin, 'Getting into the groove' (2017); Hutton, *Pagan Britain* (2013), 82.
[93] A.J. MacSween *et al.*, 'Refining the chronology of the Neolithic settlement at Pool, Sanday, Orkney', *Proceedings of the Prehistoric Society* 81 (2015), 283–310; Richards and Jones, *Development of Neolithic house societies* (2016); Bayliss *et al.*, 'Islands of history: the Late Neolithic timescape of Orkney', *Antiquity* 91 (359) (2017), 1171–88.
[94] Parker Pearson and Ramilisonina, 'Stonehenge for the ancestors: the stones pass on the message', *Antiquity* 72 (1998), 308–26; and 'Stonehenge for the ancestors: part two', *Antiquity* 72 (1998), 855–6; Parker Pearson, *Stonehenge: exploring the greatest Stone Age mystery* (London: Simon and Schuster, 2012), 342–3.
[95] Bayliss *et al.*, 'Islands of history' (2017), figure 5.
[96] M. O'Sullivan *et al.*, 'Henges in Ireland' (2012); Sheridan, 'Little and large' (2014); Carlin, 'Getting into the groove' (2017).

Chapter 5

[1] For the excavation of the Bronze Age cemetery at Grange, see B.A. Ó Ríordáin, 'A Bronze Age cemetery mound at Grange, Co. Roscommon', *Journal of Irish Archaeology* 8 (1997), 43–72.

[2] See Ó Donnabháin, 'The human remains', in Ó Ríordáin, 'Bronze Age cemetery mound at Grange,' (1997), 57–71.

[3] Brindley, *The dating of Food Vessels and Urns in Ireland* (Galway: Department of Archaeology, National University of Ireland, Galway. Bronze Age Studies 7, 2007), provides a detailed study of the chronology and development of the pottery found in Early Bronze Age Ireland. Other important studies of the funerary evidence that is central to our understanding of the period include Waddell, *The Bronze Age burials of Ireland* (Galway: Galway University Press, 1990); B. Ó Ríordáin and Waddell, *The funerary bowls and vases of the Irish Bronze Age* (Galway: Galway University Press, 1993); Mount, 'Early Bronze Age burial' (1997); and McSparron, *Burials and society* (2021). Overviews of the Chalcolithic and the Early Bronze Age can be found in Cooney and Grogan, *Irish prehistory: a social perspective* (1999); Carlin and Brück, 'Searching for the Chalcolithic: continuity and change in the Irish Final Neolithic/Early Bronze Age', in M.J. Allen *et al.* (eds), *Is there a British Chalcolithic? People, place and polity in the later 3rd millennium* (Oxford: Oxbow/Prehistoric Society. Prehistoric Society Research Paper 4, 2012), pp 191–208; W. O'Brien, 'The Chalcolithic in Ireland: a chronological and cultural framework', in Allen *et al.* (eds), *Is there a British Chalcolithic?* (2012), pp 211–25; Carlin and Cooney, 'Transforming our understanding' (2017); Grogan, 'The Bronze Age: a surfeit of data?', in Stanley *et al.* (eds), *Stories of Ireland's past* (2017), pp 57–84; Carlin, *Beaker phenomenon* (2018); Waddell, *Prehistoric archaeology of Ireland* (2022), chapters 4–9. Brück, *Personifying prehistory* (2019) and Robert Johnston, *Bronze Age worlds: a social prehistory of Britain and Ireland* (London: Routledge, 2021) are important additions to the literature, taking innovative, relational perspectives on Bronze Age Britain and Ireland. M.K. Holst, 'Burials', in H. Fokkens and A.F. Harding (eds), *Oxford handbook of the European Bronze Age* (Oxford: Oxford University Press, 2013), pp 102–20, provides an overview of European Bronze Age burial.

[4] See discussion in Harris *et al.*, 'The body in its social context' (2013); Sørensen, 'Identity, gender, and dress in the European Bronze Age', in Fokkens and Harding (eds), *Oxford handbook of the European Bronze Age* (2013), pp 216–33: 216–17; Brück, *Personifying prehistory* (2019), chapter 2.

[5] Harris *et al.*, 'The body in its social context' (2013), 82.

[6] Robb and Harris, 'Becoming gendered' (2018), 132–3.

[7] Timothy Earle, *Bronze Age economics: the beginnings of political economies* (Oxford: Westview Press, 2002); Kristian Kristiansen and Thomas Larsson, *The rise of Bronze Age society: travels, transmissions and transformations* (Cambridge: Cambridge University Press, 2005); Kristiansen and Earle, 'Neolithic versus Bronze Age social formations: a political economy approach', in Kristiansen *et al.* (eds), *Paradigm found. Archaeological theory: past, present and future* (Oxford: Oxbow, 2015), pp 234–47. For critiques, see Brück and Fontijn, 'The myth of the chief: prestige goods, power, and personhood in the European Bronze Age', in Fokkens and Harding (eds), *Oxford handbook of the European Bronze Age* (2013), pp 197–215; Carlin, *Beaker phenomenon* (2018), 34–6; Brück, *Personifying prehistory* (2019), 2–6.

[8] For example, see Haak *et al.*, 'Massive migration from the Steppe' (2015); Olalde *et al.*, 'Beaker phenomenon and the genomic transformation of northwest Europe' (2018).
[9] Carlin, *Beaker phenomenon* (2018), provides an up-to-date and innovative review of the Beaker phenomenon in Ireland against the wider European background.
[10] For Beaker, see Carlin, *Beaker phenomenon* (2018), 16. For Early Bronze Age, see Grogan, 'Bronze Age cemetery at Carrig, Co. Wicklow', *Archaeology Ireland* 4 (4) (1990), 12–14; Mount, 'Early Bronze Age burial in south-east Ireland' (1997); James Eogan, 'The construction of funerary monuments in the Irish Early Bronze Age', in Roche *et al.* (eds), *From megaliths to metals* (2004), pp 56-60; Cahill and Sikora (eds), *Breaking ground: finding graves* (2011); Sikora *et al.*, 'Recent discoveries of Early Bronze Age burials in Ireland', *Journal of Irish Archaeology* 27 (2018), 1–32; Brück, *Personifying prehistory* (2019), 19–20.
[11] See contrasting perspectives in Carlin and Brück, 'Searching for the Chalcolithic' (2012); W. O'Brien, 'The Chalcolithic in Ireland' (2012). For European links at this time, see Humphrey Case, 'Irish Beakers in their European context', in Waddell and Shee Twohig (eds), *Ireland in the Bronze Age* (Dublin: Stationery Office, 1995), pp 14–29; and 'The Beaker culture in Britain and Ireland: groups, European contacts and chronology', in F. Nicolis (ed.), *Bell Beakers today: pottery, people, culture, symbols in prehistoric Europe* (Trento: Servizio Beni Culturli, Ufficio Beni Archeologici, 2004), pp 361–77; Bradley, *Prehistory of Britain and Ireland* (2019), 150–63.
[12] Mount, 'New research on Irish Early Bronze Age cemeteries', in Waddell and Shee Twohig, (eds), *Ireland in the Bronze Age* (Dublin: The Stationery Office, 1995), pp 97–112; 'Early Bronze Age burial in south-east Ireland' (1997); Brindley *Dating of Food Vessels and Urns* (2007); Grogan, 'Bronze Age: a surfeit of data?' (2017), 60; McSparron, *Burials and society* (2021); Johnston, *Bronze Age worlds* (2021), 44–6. For European links, see Bradley, *Prehistory of Britain and Ireland* (2019), 163–70; Waddell, *Prehistoric archaeology of Ireland* (2022), chapter 5.
[13] Melanie McQuade 'Archaeological excavation of a multi-period prehistoric settlement at Waterunder, Mell, Co. Louth', *County Louth Archaeological and Historical Journal* 26 (2005), 31–66; Alexandra Shepherd, 'Stepping out together: men, women and their beakers in time and space', in M.J. Allen *et al.* (eds), *Is there a British Chalcolithic* (2012), pp 257–80; Carlin, *Beaker phenomenon* (2018), 121–2.
[14] On Beaker burials in Atlantic Europe, see Laure Salanova, 'Behind the warriors: Bell Beakers and identities in Atlantic Europe (third millennium B.C.)', in Koch and Cunliffe (eds), *Celtic from the west 3* (2016), pp 13–34.
[15] Brindley, *Dating of Food Vessels and Urns* (2007); Kerri Cleary, 'Burial practices in Ireland during the late third millennium BC connecting new ideologies with local expressions', in Koch and Cunliffe (eds), *Celtic from the West 3* (2016), pp 139–79.
[16] Humphrey Case, 'Beaker burial in Britain and Ireland. A role for the dead', in M. Besse and J. Desideri (eds), *Graves and funerary rituals during the Late Neolithic and the Early Bronze Age in Europe* (Oxford: Archaeopress, 2004), 195–201: 195–7; Stuart Needham, 'Transforming Beaker culture in north-west Europe; processes of fusion and fission', *Proceedings of the Prehistoric Society* 71 (2005), 171–217: 205; Brindley, *Dating of Food Vessels and Urns* (2007), 249; Carlin and Brück, 'Searching for the Chalcolithic (2012), 198–9; Carlin, *Beaker phenomenon* (2018).
[17] H.E. Kilbride-Jones, 'The excavation of an unrecorded megalithic tomb on Kilmashogue Mountain, Co. Dublin', *Proceedings of the Royal Irish Academy* 56C (1954), 461–79.

[18] William O'Brien, *Sacred ground: megalithic tombs in coastal south-west Ireland* (Galway: Department of Archaeology, NUIG. Bronze Age Studies 4, 1999), 203–10; Carlin, *Beaker phenomenon* (2018), 96–106.
[19] See de Valera and Ó Nualláin, *Survey of the megalithic tombs* (vol. 1, 1961); P. Walsh, 'Structure and deposition in Irish wedge tombs: an open and shut case?', in Waddell and Shee Twohig (eds), *Ireland in the Bronze Age* (1995), pp 113–27; W. O'Brien, *Sacred ground* (1999); C. Jones *et al.*, 'Monuments, landscape and identity in Chalcolithic Ireland', in K.D. Springs (ed.), *Landscape and identity: archaeology and human geography* (Oxford: Archaeopress. BAR International Series 2709, 2015), pp 3–25; Carlin, *Beaker phenomenon* (2018); Connolly, *Stone, bone and belonging* (2021), 53–4.
[20] W. O'Brien, *Sacred ground* (1999), 192–3; Carlin, *Beaker phenomenon* (2018), 210–11.
[21] Ros Ó Maoldúin, *Preliminary report on the excavation of wedge tomb CL017_009 Parknabinnia, Co. Clare* (Galway: Irish Field School of Prehistoric Archaeology, University of Galway, 2022).
[22] Carlin, *Beaker phenomenon* (2018), 100.
[23] I.J. Herring, 'The cairn excavation at Well Glass Spring, Largantea, Co. Londonderry', *Ulster Journal of Archaeology* 1 (1938), 164–88; Schulting *et al.*, 'Largantea and the dating of Irish wedge tombs', *Journal of Irish Archaeology* 17 (2008), 1–18.
[24] W. O'Brien, *Sacred ground* 1999, 223–9.
[25] D.P. Hurl, 'Excavation of a wedge tomb in Ballybriest townland, Co. Londonderry', *Ulster Journal of Archaeology* 60 (2001), 9–31; Murphy, 'Appendix: cremated human bone from Ballybriest wedge tomb', in Hurl, 'Excavation of a wedge tomb in Ballybriest' (2001), 27–31.
[26] E. Estyn Evans, 'Excavations at Carnanbane, Co. Londonderry: a double horned cairn', *Proceedings of the Royal Irish Academy* 45C (1939), 1–12; Herity, 'The finds from Irish court tombs', *Proceedings of the Royal Irish Academy* 87C (1987), 103–281; Carlin, *Beaker phenomenon* (2018), 109; Hurl, 'Excavation of a wedge tomb in Ballybriest (2001), 10.
[27] H.G. Leask and Liam Price, 'The Labbacallee Megalith, Co. Cork', *Proceedings of the Royal Irish Academy* 43C (1936), 77–101.
[28] Brindley *et al.*, 'Radiocarbon dates from Moneen and Labbacallee, County Cork', *Journal of Irish Archaeology* 4 (1987/8), 13–19. There are also later cremated deposits at Labbacallee.
[29] Brindley and Lanting, 'Radiocarbon dates from wedge tombs', *Journal of Irish Archaeology* 6 (1991/2), 19–26: 21.
[30] Leask and Price, 'Labbacallee megalith' (1936); Brindley *et al.*, 'Radiocarbon dates from Moneen and Labbacallee' (1987/8). For relevant discussion of post-mortem manipulation of bodies in Early Bronze Age graves in Britain, see Brück, *Personifying prehistory* (2019), 24–7.
[31] The Lough Gur wedge tomb provides another interesting case study—S.P. Ó Ríordáin and G. Ó h-Iceadha, 'Lough Gur excavations: the megalithic tomb', *Journal of the Royal Society of Antiquaries of Ireland* 87 (1955), 34–50; Brindley and Lanting, 'Radiocarbon dates from wedge tombs' (1991/2), 24–5. Carlin, *Beaker phenomenon* (2018), 204. For wider European context, see, for example, papers in Janusz Czebreszuk (ed.), *Similar but different: Bell Beakers in Europe* (Poznan: Adam Mickiewicz University, 2004).
[32] Herring and A. McL. May, 'The Giants Grave, Kilhoyle, Co. Londonderry', *Proceedings of the Belfast Natural History and Philosophical Society* 1 (3) (1937), 34–48: 45–6.
[33] W. O'Brien, *Sacred ground* (1999), chapters 5 and 6.

[34] W. O'Brien, *Sacred ground* (1999), 261–2; see also W. O'Brien, 'The Chalcolithic in Ireland' (2012), 221–2.
[35] Carlin, *Beaker phenomenon* (2018), 124–33.
[36] Carlin, *Beaker phenomenon* (2018), chapter 9.
[37] K. Cleary, 'Burial practices in Ireland' (2016), 168. Salanova, 'The frontiers inside the western Bell Beaker block', in J. Czerbreszuk (ed.), *Similar but different: Bell Beakers in Europe* (Poznan: Adam Mickiewicz University, 2004), pp 63–75: 73, referring to Bell Beaker graves in western Europe, makes the point that single graves and individualised deposits in collective graves produce the same assemblages.
[38] W. O'Brien, *Sacred ground* 1999, 133–40.
[39] See discussion in W. O'Brien, 'Megaliths in a mythologized landscape' (2002).
[40] Carlin, *Beaker phenomenon* (2018), 193–6.
[41] Carlin, *Beaker phenomenon* (2018), 129. Looking at cultural interaction in Britain during the Chalcolithic, Needham, 'Case and place for the British Chalcolithic', in Allen *et al.* (eds), *Is there a British Chalcolithic* (2012), pp 1–26: 17–22, argues that initially the Grooved Ware and Beaker traditions were very separate, with interaction increasing over time.
[42] Schulting *et al.*, 'New dates from the north' (2012); K. Cleary, 'Burial practices in Ireland' (2016), 148–51; Carlin, *Beaker phenomenon* (2018), 107–13. For the patterns of deposition of Beaker pottery at Neolithic monuments in Scotland, see N.C.A. Wilkin, 'Pursuing the penumbral: the deposition of Beaker pottery at Neolithic monuments in Chalcolithic and early Bronze Age Scotland', in K. Brophy *et al.* (eds), *The Neolithic of mainland Scotland* (Edinburgh: Edinburgh University Press, 2016), pp 261–318. On caves, see Dowd, *Archaeology of caves in Ireland* (2015), chapter 6; Cleary 'Burial practices in Ireland' (2016), 161–2.
[43] S.P. Ó Ríordáin, 'Discovery of an ancient burial in a cairn near Ballyconnell, Co. Cavan', *Journal of the Royal Society of Antiquaries of Ireland* 63 (1933), 167–71; Cleary, 'Burial practices in Ireland' (2016), 162.
[44] John Lehane *et al.*, 'Ballynacarriga 3: Multi-period prehistoric ceremonial site', in P. Johnston and J. Kiely (eds), *Hidden voices: the archaeology of the M8 Fermoy-Mitchelstown motorway* (Dublin: Transport Infrastructure Ireland. TII Heritage 7, 2019), pp 40–51: 45–50; Lynch and Magee, 'Cremated human remains', in Johnston and Kiely (eds), *Hidden voices* (2019), pp 171–7: 171–5; Grogan and Helen Roche, 'Prehistoric pottery', in Johnston and Kiely (eds), *Hidden voices* (2019), pp 177–93: 185–9; Carlin, *Beaker phenomenon* (2018), 113–14.
[45] J. Eogan, 'Excavations at a cairn at Coolnatullagh townland, County Clare', *North Munster Antiquarian Journal* 42 (2002), 113–50; K. Cleary, 'Burial practices in Ireland' (2016), 157; Carlin, *Beaker phenomenon* (2018), 114.
[46] Hencken, 'A cairn at Poulawack' (1935); Brindley and Lanting, 'Radiocarbon dates for the cemetery at Poulawack' (1991/2); see also Ryan, 'Poulawack, Co. Clare: the affinities of the central burial structure' (1981); Cleary, 'Burial practices in Ireland' (2016), 151.
[47] For Moneen, see M.J. O'Kelly, 'Excavation of a cairn at Moneen, Co. Cork', *Proceedings of the Royal Academy* 54C (1952), 121–59; Waddell, 'The antique order of the dead: cemeteries and continuity in Bronze Age Ireland', in Ó Corráin (ed.), *Irish antiquity* (1981), pp 163–72; Brindley *et al.* 'Radiocarbon dates from Moneen and

Labbacallee' (1987/8); Cleary, 'Burial practices in Ireland' (2016), 156–8; Carlin, *Beaker phenomenon* (2018), 118–19. See Christina O'Regan *et al.*, 'A unique burial monument at Brackagh, County Londonderry', *Ulster Journal of Archaeology* 68 (2009), 27–39 on the intriguing site at Brackagh, Co. Derry.

[48] Ruairí Ó Baoill, 'The excavation of a segmented Bronze Age cist at Newtownstewart Castle, County Tyrone', *Ulster Journal of Archaeology* 64 (2005), 26–42; Murphy, 'The cremated bone', in Ó Baoill, 'Excavation of a segmented Bronze Age cist at Newtownstewart Castle (2005), 36–40; Cleary, 'Burial practices in Ireland' (2016), 169.

[49] Parker Pearson *et al.*, 'Evidence for mummification in Bronze Age Britain', *Antiquity* 79 (2005), 529–46; Booth *et al.*, 'Mummification in Bronze Age Britain', *Antiquity* 89 (347) (2015), 111–19; Brück, *Personifying prehistory* (2019), 29–30; Booth and Brück, 'Death is not the end: radiocarbon and histo-taphonomic evidence for the curation and excarnation of human remains in Bronze Age Britain', *Antiquity* 94 (2020), 1186–203.

[50] Lehane *et al.*, 'Ballynacarriga 3: multi-period prehistoric ceremonial site' (2019), 47; Lynch and Magee, 'Cremated human remains' (2019), 174–5; Grogan and Roche, 'Prehistoric pottery' (2019), 187; Carlin, *Beaker phenomenon* (2018), 113–14.

[51] Carlin, *Beaker phenomenon* (2018), 128.

[52] Needham, 'Transforming Beaker culture' (2005); and 'Case and place for the British Chalcolithic' (2012); Carlin, *Beaker phenomenon* (2018), 128.

[53] See Cahill and Sikora, *Breaking ground: finding graves* (2011), 4. On multiple burials, see Lynch and Magee, 'Cremated human remains' (2019), 174–5. For historical context, see Waddell, 'Irish Bronze Age cists: a survey', *Journal of the Royal Society of Antiquaries of Ireland* 100 (1970), 91–139, and compare Waddell, 'Antique order of the dead' (1981), 166, with Mount, 'New research on Irish Early Bronze Age cemeteries' (1995); and 'Early Bronze Age burial in south-east Ireland' (1997); Cooney and Grogan, *Irish prehistory: a social perspective* (1999), 105–14. See Kenneth Wiggins, 'A rescue excavation on Rathlin Island, County Antrim', *Ulster Journal of Archaeology* 59 (2000), 47–70, and Brian Sloan *et al.*, 'A Bronze Age cist burial at Glebe, Rathlin Island, County Antrim', *Ulster Journal of Archaeology* 67 (2008), 60–83, for a good example of where our understanding of the extent of Bronze Age cemetery activity has changed as more burials were uncovered with modern changes in land use.

[54] See Grogan, 'Bronze Age: a surfeit of data?' (2017), 68–9 for discussion of the Bronze Age landscape of the Crusheen area, east Co. Clare. For background activity from the Early Neolithic on, see, for example, Ballynacarriga, Co. Cork, in Lehane *et al.*, 'Ballynacarriga 3: multi-period prehistoric ceremonial site' (2019).

[55] See N.C.A. Wilkin, 'Grave-goods, contexts and interpretation: towards regional narratives of early Bronze Age Scotland', *Scottish Archaeological Journal* 33 (1–2) (2011), 21–37, DOI: 10.3366/saj.2011.0022; Fowler, *The emergent past: a relational realist archaeology of Early Bronze Age mortuary practices* (Oxford: Oxford University Press, 2013); Holst, 'Burials' (2013), 106; Mark Haughton, 'Social relations and the local: revisiting our approaches to finding gender and age in prehistory. A case study from Bronze Age Scotland', *Norwegian Archaeological Review* (2018), DOI: 10.1080/00293652.2018.1517821.

[56] See Binford, 'Mortuary practices' (1971), as a key reference for identifying variables in mortuary practices as the basis for looking at cultural and social patterns. See Tarlow

and Nilsson Stutz, *Oxford handbook: archaeology of death and burial* (2013), for coverage of mortuary practice across a wide range of time and global location. McSparron, *Burials and society* (2021), analyses these variables in an Irish Early Bronze Age context.

[57] Compare C.A. Roberts, The bioarchaeology of health and well-being: its contribution to understanding the past', in Tarlow and Nilsson Stutz (eds), *Oxford handbook of the archaeology of death and burial* (2013), pp 79–98; Barbara Bramanti, 'The use of DNA analysis in the archaeology of death and burial', in Tarlow and Nilsson Stutz (eds), *Oxford handbook of the archaeology of death and burial* (2013), pp 99–122; G. Eriksson, 'Stable isotope analysis of humans' (2013).

[58] Brindley, *Dating of Food Vessels and Urns* (2007).

[59] See Brindley, *Dating of Food Vessels and Urns* (2007); R.M. Kavanagh, 'The encrusted urn in Ireland', *Proceedings of the Royal Irish Academy* 73C (1973), 507–617; 'Collared and cordoned urns in Ireland', *Proceedings of the Royal Irish Academy* 76C (1976), 293–403; and 'A reconsideration of razors in the Irish Earlier Bronze Age', *Journal of the Royal Society of Antiquaries of Ireland* 121 (1991), 77–104; Waddell, *Prehistoric archaeology of Ireland* (2022), chapter 5.

[60] Mount, 'Five Early Bronze Age cemeteries at Brownstown, Graney West, Oldtown and Ploopluck, County Kildare, and Strawhall, County Carlow', *Proceedings of the Royal Irish Academy* 98C (1998), 25–99, 42–4; Buckley, 'Human skeletal report', in Mount, 'Five Early Bronze Age cemeteries' (1998), 69–97: 83–8.

[61] Ó Floinn, 'Baggotstown, Co. Limerick, E1109', in Cahill and Sikora (eds), *Breaking ground, finding graves* (2011) vol. 1, pp 225–59; Ó Donnabháin, 'Human remains, Baggotstown, Co. Limerick', in Cahill and Sikora (eds), *Breaking ground: finding graves* (2011), 259–62; Brindley, *Dating of Food Vessels and Urns* (2007), 248.

[62] P.J. Hartnett and Ellen Prendergast, 'Ballybrennan, Co. Westmeath, E1162', in Cahill and Sikora (eds), *Breaking ground, finding graves* (2011), vol. 1, pp 484–90; L. Buckley, 'Human remains, Ballybrennan, Co. Westmeath, E1162', in Cahill and Sikora (eds), *Breaking ground, finding graves* (2011), vol. 1, pp 490–501; Sikora and Fiona Reilly, 'Tomfarney, Co. Wexford, E1190', in Cahill and Sikora (eds), *Breaking ground: finding graves* (2011), vol. 1, pp 259–62; Buckley, 'Human remains, Tomfarney Co. Wexford, E1190', in Cahill and Sikora (eds), *Breaking ground: finding graves* (2011), vol. 1, pp 602–45. While Tomfarney is exceptional, other cists such as that at Altaghaderry, Co. Donegal, with a cremation deposit containing 9–11 individuals, suggest a more widespread occurrence of commingled deposits of multiple individuals; see Halpin and Roche, 'Altaghaderry, Co. Donegal', in Cahill and Sikora (eds), *Breaking ground: finding graves* (2011), vol. 1, pp 98–103; Buckley, 'Human remains, Altaghaderry, Co. Donegal, 02E1474', in Cahill and Sikora (eds), *Breaking ground: finding graves* (2011), vol. 1, pp 104–11.

[63] See discussion in McSparron, *Burials and society* (2021).

[64] Williams, *Death and memory in Early Medieval Britain* (Cambridge: Cambridge University Press, 2006); and 'A well-urned rest' (2014), 100, 102; A.M. Jones, 'Layers of meaning: concealment, memory and secrecy in the British Early Bronze Age', in D. Boric (ed.), *Archaeology and memory* (Oxford: Oxbow 2010), pp 105–20; Brück, *Personifying prehistory* (2019), 72. Rob Wiseman *et al.*, 'The inverted dead of Britain's Bronze Age barrows: a perspective from Conceptual Metaphor Theory', *Antiquity* 95

(381) (2021), 720–34, argue that the inversion of urns is the strongest evidence that people in Bronze Age Britain saw their dead as inhabiting an inverted underworld.
[65] Cooney and Grogan, *Irish prehistory* (1999), 105–13. For case studies, see Mount, 'The context of the Early Bronze Age cemetery in the Mound of the Hostages, Tara', in M. O'Sullivan, *et al.* (eds), *Tara: from the past to the future* (2013), pp 184–95; Quinn and Kuijt, 'The tempo of life and death during the Early Bronze Age at the Mound of the Hostages, Tara', in M. O'Sullivan *et al.* (eds), *Tara: from the past to the future* (2013), pp 154–64; Quinn, 'Returning and resuse: diachronic perspectives on multi-component cemeteries and mortuary politics at Middle Neolithic and Bronze Age Tara, Ireland', *Journal of Anthropological Archaeology* 37 (2015), 1–18; Haughton, 'Social relations and the local' (2018).
[66] Mount, 'Early Bronze Age burial in south-east Ireland' (1997), 169; McSparron, *Burials and society* (2021), 154.
[67] See Fowler, 'Identities in transformation' (2013), 516–22; and *The emergent past* (2013). See discussion in Holst, 'Burials' (2013), 104–06; Brück, *Personifying prehistory* (2019), 235–6.
[68] J. Wren and J. Price, 'Newrath 37—Neolithic building and Early Bronze Age cemetery', in J. Eogan and Shee Twohig (eds), *Cois tSiúire—nine thousand years of human activity in the Lower Suir Valley: archaeological excavations on the N25 Waterford City Bypass* (vol. 1. Dublin: National Roads Authority. NRA Scheme Monographs 8, 2011), pp 135–46: 139–44.
[69] B.A. Ó Ríordáin, 'Bronze Age cemetery mound at Grange' (1997); Brindley, 'The radiocarbon dates', in Ó Ríordáin, 'Bronze Age cemetery mound at Grange', *Journal of Irish Archaeology* 8 (1997), 43–72: 56–7; Ó Donnabháin, 'Human remains' (1997); Brindley, *Dating of Food Vessels and Urns* (2007), 64–5, 125.
[70] Mount and P.J. Hartnett, 'Early Bronze Age cemetery at Edmondstown, County Dublin', *Proceedings of the Royal Irish Academy* 93C (1993), 21–79; Mount, 'Adolf Mahr's excavations of an Early Bronze Age cemetery at Keenoge, County Meath', *Proceedings of the Royal Irish Academy* 97C (1997), 1–68.
[71] For Carn More, see D. Bayley and Shane Delaney, 'Chalcolithic and Bronze Age settlement and burials', in S. Delaney *et al.*, *Around the Bay of Dundalk: archaeological investigations along the route of the M1 Dundalk Western Bypass* (Dublin: Transport Infrastructure Ireland. TII Heritage 10, 2020), pp 42–72. On adult with juvenile burials, see Lynch and Magee, 'Cremated human remains' (2019), 174–75. On Fourknocks, see Hartnett, 'Excavation of a passage grave at Fourknocks' (1957), 254–62; and 'The excavation of two tumuli at Fourknocks (sites II and III), Co. Meath', (1971), 64–74; Waddell, *Bronze Age burials of Ireland* (1990), 123–6; Finlay, 'Outside of life: traditions of infant burial' (2000). K. Cleary, 'Burial practices in Ireland' (2016), 150.
[72] For the Mound of the Hostages, see M. O'Sullivan, *Duma na nGiall* (2005). For Knockast, see Hencken and H.L. Movius, 'The cemetery cairn at Knockast', *Proceedings of the Royal Irish Academy* 41C (1934), 232–84.
[73] Bayliss and M. O'Sullivan, 'Interpreting chronologies for the Mound of the Hostages' (2013); Mount, 'Context of the Early Bronze Age cemetery in the Mound of the Hostages' (2013); Quinn and Kuijt, 'The tempo of life and death' (2013); Quinn, 'Returning and resuse' (2015).

[74] M. O'Sullivan, *Duma na nGiall* (2005), 231; see also S.P. Ó Ríordáin, 'A burial with faience beads at Tara', *Proceedings of the Prehistoric Society* 21 (1955), 163–73; Sheridan *et al.*, '"Tara Boy": local hero or international man of mystery', in M. O' Sullivan *et al.* (eds), *Tara: from the past to the future* (2013), pp 207–32. Quinn 'Returning and resuse' (2015), suggests two phases of burial between 2050 BC and 1850 BC, with 'Tara Boy' as a later, isolated deposition.

[75] Olalde *et al.*, 'Beaker phenomenon and the genomic transformation of northwest Europe' (2018); Reich, *Who we are* (2018), 114–7. For more nuanced views of the relationship between genetics, mobility and cultural change, see Van der Linden, 'Population history in third millennium BC Europe: assessing the contribution of genetics', *World Archaeology* 48 (5) (2016), 714–28; Furholt, 'Massive migrations?' (2018); Johannsen, *et al.*, 'Composite window into human history' (2017); Callaway, 'Divided by DNA: the uneasy relationship between archaeology and ancient genomics', *Nature* 555 (7698) (2018), pp 573–57; Carlin, *Beaker phenomenon* (2018), 198–200.

[76] Olalde *et al.*, 'Beaker phenomenon and the genomic transformation of northwest Europe' (2018), 193–4; Ian Armit and Reich, 'The return of the Beaker folk? Rethinking migration and population change in British prehistory', *Antiquity* 95 (384) (2021), 1464–77; Parker Pearson *et al.*, *The Beaker People: isotopes, mobility and diet in prehistoric Britain* (Oxford: Oxbow/Prehistoric Society. Prehistoric Society Research Paper 7, 2019); see also Parker Pearson *et al.*, 'Bell Beaker people in Britain: migration, mobility and diet', *Antiquity* 90 (2016), 620–37. See Booth *et al.*, 'Tales from the supplementary information: ancestry change in Chalcolithic–Early Bronze Age Britain' (2021), for a nuanced discussion showing that ancestry change in Britain took up to 16 generations and that there was persistence of groups descended from Neolithic populations. Carlin, *Beaker phenomenon* (2018), 198–200 presents the Beaker complex as a regionally divergent, socially constructed phenomenon, not a biological condition.

[77] Cassidy *et al.*, 'Neolithic and Bronze Age migration to Ireland' (2016), 372; Cassidy and Bradley, 'Ancient DNA and Irish human prehistory' (2017), 14.

[78] Reich, *Who we are* (2018), 114–21; see also Morten Allentoft *et al.*, 'Population genomics of Bronze Age Eurasia', *Nature* 522 (2015), 167–72; Haak *et al.*, 'Massive migration from the Steppe' (2015); Kristiansen *et al.*, 'Re-theorising mobility and the formation of culture and language' (2017).

[79] Kristiansen *et al.*, 'Re-theorising mobility' (2017), 336.

[80] Case, 'Beaker culture in Britain and Ireland' (2004), 361; W. O'Brien, *Ross Island: mining, metal and society in early Ireland* (Galway: Department of Archaeology, NUIG. Bronze Age Studies 6, 2004), 557–69; Cunliffe, *Europe between the oceans* (2008), 203–13; and *Britain begins* (2012), 196–33; B.W. Roberts, 'Britain and Ireland in the Bronze Age: farmers in the landscape or heroes on the high seas?', in Fokkens and Harding (eds), *Oxford handbook of the European Bronze Age* (2013), pp 531–49.

[81] Needham, 'Transforming Beaker culture' (2005); and 'Case and place for the British Chalcolithic' (2012). Also Booth *et al.*, 'Tales from the supplementary information: ancestry change in Chalcolithic-Early Bronze Age Britain' (2021): on continuity, 2; on incomers forming enclaves, 8; Fokkens, 'Dutchmen on the move? A discussion of the adoption of the Beaker package', in Allen *et al.* (eds), *Is there a British Chalcolithic?* (2012), 123; Johnston, *Bronze Age worlds* (2021), 65.

[82] See discussion in Furholt, 'Massive migrations?' (2018). See Matthew Engelke, *Think like an anthropologist* (London: Penguin Random House, 2017), 301–4, and wider discussion, for a critique of the 'genes as the key to everything' approach. See also Brück, 'Ancient DNA, kinship and relational identities' (2021); Booth *et al.*, 'Tales from the supplementary information: ancestry change in Chalcolithic–Early Bronze Age Britain' (2021), 8. On the 'face cup' from Mitchelstown, see B. Sutton, 'Mitchelstown 2—the "Mitchelstown Face Cup" deposit and nearby burnt mound', in K. Hanley and M.F. Hurley (eds), *Generations: the archaeology of five national road schemes in County Cork* (Dublin: National Roads Authority; NRA Scheme Monographs 13, 2013) vol. 1: *prehistoric sites*, pp 80–4; Grogan and Roche, 'Prehistoric pottery and the development of the prehistoric landscape in the Cork region', in Hanley and Hurley (eds), *Generations: the archaeology of five road schemes in County Cork* (2013), vol. 2, pp 305–22: 315–16. On the ceramic ear-plugs from Ballinchalla, see Sikora *et al.*, 'Recent discoveries of Early Bronze Age burials' (2018).

[83] Michael Morris, 'Megalithic exegesis. Megalithic monuments as sources of sociocultural meanings: the Irish case', *Irish Archaeological Research Forum* 1 (2) (1974), 10–25; W. O'Brien, *Sacred ground* (1999), 207.

[84] W. O'Brien, *Sacred ground* 1999), 210.

[85] Gearóid Ó Crualaoich, *The Book of the Cailleach: stories of the wise-woman healer* (Cork: Cork University Press 2003).

[86] Ó Crualaoich, *Book of the Cailleach* (2003), 81–93; see also Daithí Ó hÓgáin, *Myth, legend and romance: an encyclopaedia of the Irish folk tradition* (London: Ryan Publishing, 1991), 67–8.

[87] McMann, *Loughcrew: the cairns* (Oldcastle: After Hours Books, 1993), 19–21.

[88] W. O'Brien, 'Megaliths in a mythologized landscape' (2002), 169–70.

[89] E. O'Brien, 'Excavation of a multi-period burial site at Ballymacaward' (1999).

[90] Mount and Hartnett, 'Early Bronze Age cemetery at Edmondstown' (1993), 24–30; Mount, 'Adolf Mahr's excavations' (1997), 13–17; B.A. Ó Ríordáin, 'Bronze Age cemetery mound at Grange' (1997), 49.

[91] Buckley, 'Skeletal report', in Mount and Hartnett, 'Early Bronze Age cemetery at Edmondstown' (1993), pp 64–79: 64; Buckley, 'Skeletal report', in Mount, 'Adolf Mahr's excavations' (1997), 44–57: 49–50; Bradley, *Prehistory of Britain and Ireland* (2019), 176–7.

[92] Booth *et al.* 'Tales from the supplementary information: ancestry change in Chalcolithic–Early Bronze Age Britain' (2021), 16; Johnston, *Bronze Age worlds* (2021), 44–52.

[93] Mount, 'Adolf Mahr's excavations' (1997), 23–4; Sheridan *et al.*, '"Tara Boy": local hero or international man of mystery' (2013); Frieman, 'Going to pieces at the funeral: completeness and complexity in Early Bronze Age jet "necklace" assemblages', *Journal of Social Archaeology* 12 (3) (2012), 334–55; Brück, 'Material metaphors' (2004), 314; Johnston, *Bronze Age worlds* (2021), 60.

[94] For Poulawack, see Brindley and Lanting, 'Radiocarbon dates from the cemetery at Poulawack' (1991/92), and for Baunogenasraid, see Barry Raftery, 'A prehistoric burial mound at Baunogenasraid, Co. Carlow', *Proceedings of the Prehistoric Society* 74C (1974), 277–312. For the Mound of the Hostages, see M. O'Sullivan, *Duma na nGiall* (2005).

Chapter 6

[1] For the excavation report of the Ballintaggart barrow cemetery, see R.M Chapple *et al.*, *Archaeological investigations along the A1 Dualling Scheme, Loughbrickland to Beach Hill, Co. Down, N. Ireland* (Oxford: Archaeopress. BAR British Series 479, 2009), 50–97; on dating, see Chapple, 'The absolute dating of archaeological excavations in Ulster carried out by Northern Ireland Archaeological Consultancy 1998–2007', *Ulster Journal of Archaeology* 67 (2008), 153–81; for details of the cremated bone from ring barrow 6, see E.M. Murphy, 'Appendix 3: Report on the cremated remains recovered from Archaeological Licences AE/04/077, AE/05/014 and AE/04/055', in Chapple et al., Archaeological investigations *along the A1 Dualling Scheme* (2009), pp 214–41: 223–4; for discussion, see Colin Dunlop, *Down the road: the archaeology of the A1 road scheme between Lisburn and Newry* (Belfast: Northern Archaeological Consultancy, 2015).

[2] See discussion in Cooney and Grogan, *Irish prehistory* (1999), 126–33; J. Eogan 'The later prehistory of the Lower Suir Valley (2400 BC–AD 400), in J. Eogan and E. Shee Twohig (eds), *Cois tSiúire—nine thousand years of human activity in the Lower Suir Valley* (2011), pp 253–83: 274. Specifically on the Middle Bronze Age, see Grogan, 'Middle Bronze Age burial traditions in Ireland', in Roche *et al.* (eds), *From megaliths to metals* (2004), pp 61–71. For general coverage of the period, see Cooney and Grogan, *Irish prehistory* (1999), chapters 7 and 8; Bradley, *Prehistory of Britain and Ireland* (2019), chapter 5; Grogan, 'The Bronze Age: a surfeit of data?' (2017); Brück, *Personifying prehistory* (2019); Johnston, *Bronze Age worlds* (2021); Waddell, *Prehistoric archaeology of Ireland* (2022), chapter 7.

[3] Linda Lynch and Lorna O'Donnell, 'Cremation in the Bronze Age: practice, process and belief', in Grogan *et al.* (eds), *The Bronze Age landscape of the Pipeline to the West: an integrated and environmental assessment* (Bray: Wordwell, 2007), 105–24; see also Cooney, 'Pathways for the dead in the Middle and Late Bronze Age in Ireland', in J.I. Cerezo-Román, *et al.* (eds), *Cremation and the archaeology of death* (2017), pp 117–29; Brück, *Personifying prehistory* (2019), 42–68; Johnston, *Bronze Age worlds* (2021), 92–98, 105–17.

[4] Lynch and O'Donnell, 'Cremation in the Bronze Age' (2007), 109; Murphy, 'Appendix 3: Report on the cremated remains recovered from Archaeological Licences AE/04/077, AE/05/014 and AE/04/055' (2009), 232. See also discussion of related issues in McKinley, 'Bone fragment size and weights of bone' (1993); 'Bronze Age "barrows", funerary rites and rituals of cremation' *Proceedings of the Prehistoric Society* 63 (1997), 129–45; 'The analysis of cremated bone', in M. Cox and S. Mays (eds), *Human osteology in archaeology and forensic science* (London: Greenwich Medical Media, 2000), pp 403–21; and 'Cremation, excavation, analysis and interpretation' (2013). Note that figures are based on cremations of single individuals in modern crematoria.

[5] See, for example, Lynch and O'Donnell, 'Cremation in the Bronze Age' (2007),116–24; Jonny Geber, 'The Bronze Age burials', in M. McQuade *et al.* (eds), *In the shadow of the Galtees: archaeological excavations along the N8 Cashel to Mitchelstown Road Scheme* (Dublin: National Roads Authority. NRA Scheme Monographs 4, 2009), pp 209–35; Siân Anthony, 'Cremated remains', in N. Bermingham *et al.* (eds), *Beneath the banner:*

archaeology of the M18 Ennis Bypass and N85 Western Relief Road, Co. Clare (Dublin: National Roads Authority. NRA Scheme Monographs 10, 2012), pp 103–8.
[6] Lynch and O'Donnell, 'Cremation in the Bronze Age' (2007), 123. For comparable situation in Britain, see Edward Caswell and B.W. Roberts, 'Reassessing community cemeteries: cremation burials in Britain during the Middle Bronze Age (*c.* 1600–1150 BC)', *Proceedings of the Prehistoric Society* 84 (2018), 329–57.
[7] Brindley, *Dating of Food Vessels and Urns* (2007), 328; see also Grogan, 'Middle Bronze Age burial traditions in Ireland' (2004).
[8] Grogan and Roche, 'Clay and fire: the development and distribution of pottery traditions in prehistoric Ireland', in Stanley *et al.* (eds), *Creative minds* (2010), pp 27–45.
[9] Grogan, 'Bronze Age cemetery at Carrig' (1990); Cooney and Grogan, *Irish prehistory* (1999), 128.
[10] Important overviews of cremation practices are provided by Lynch and O'Donnell, 'Cremation in the Bronze Age' (2007); Geber, 'The Bronze Age burials' (2009); Carmelita Troy, 'Contextualising cremations: evidence from prehistoric burials', in T. Bolger *et al.* (eds), *A journey along the Carlow corridor: the archaeology of the M9 Carlow Bypass* (Dublin: National Roads Authority. NRA Scheme Monographs 16, 2015), pp 131–44. See also Lorna O'Donnell, 'The power of the pyre—a holistic study of cremation focusing on charcoal remains', *Journal of Archaeological Science* 65 (2016), 161–71; Cooney, 'Pathways for the dead' (2017). For Britain, see Caswell and Roberts, 'Reassessing community cemeteries' (2018); Brück, *Personifying prehistory* (2019), 32–50; Johnston, *Bronze Age worlds* (2021), chapter 3. For review of European burial practice, see A.F. Harding, *European societies in the Bronze Age* (Cambridge: Cambridge University Press, 2000), chapter 3; Holst, 'Burials' (2013); regional papers in H. Fokkens and A.F. Harding, *Oxford handbook of the European Bronze Age* (Oxford: Oxford University Press, 2013).
[11] For Bronze Age settlement, see Victoria Ginn, 'The fusion of settlement and identity in dispersed and nucleated settlements in Bronze Age Ireland', *Journal of Irish Archaeology* 20 (2011), 27–44; and *Mapping society: settlement structure in Later Bronze Age Ireland* (Oxford: Archaeopress, 2016); Ginn and Gill Plunkett, 'Filling the gaps: a chronology of Bronze Age settlement in Ireland', *Journal of Irish Archaeology* 29 (2020), 41–61, with discussion of phases of activity. K. Cleary, 'Broken bones and broken stones: exploring fragmentation in Middle and Late Bronze Age settlement contexts in Ireland', *European Journal of Archaeology* 21 (3) (2017), 1–25, looks at the occurrence and fragmentation of human bone in Irish Middle and Late Bronze Age settlement contexts. See also Cleary, 'Skeletons in the closet: the deposition of human remains on Irish Bronze Age Settlements', *Journal of Irish Archaeology* 14 (2006), 23–42. For Britain, see Brück, 'Houses, lifecycles and deposition' (1999); 'Body metaphors and technologies of transformation in the English Middle and Late Bronze Age', in Brück (ed.), *Bronze Age landscapes: tradition and transformation* (Oxford: Oxbow, 2001), pp 149–60; and *Personifying prehistory* (2019), chapter 4; Johnston, *Bronze Age worlds* (2021), chapters 4 and 5.
[12] For Inchagreenoge, see Kate Taylor, 'Inchagreenoge. *Fulachta fiadh*, ritual deposit of a human skull, wooden artefacts, post-medieval trackway', in Grogan *et al.* (eds), *Bronze Age landscapes of the Pipeline to the West* (2007), pp 281–4. Other examples are Cragbrien, Co. Limerick, see Graham Hull, 'Cragbrien, burnt mound and human skull

parts', in Grogan *et al.* (eds), *Bronze Age landscapes* (2007), pp 202–3; and Belan, Co. Kildare, see Lyndsey Clark, Final report on archaeological investigations at site E2953 in the townland of Belan, Co. Kildare. Unpublished report. (Headland Archaeology, 2010). For the Leshemstown burial, see Lawrence McGowan and Donal Fallon, Archaeological excavation: Leshemstown (05E0398). (Unpublished excavation report for CRDS Ltd, 2008); Fibiger, Report on the human skeletal remains, Leshemstown, Co. Meath. (Unpublished report for CRDS Ltd, 2008).

[13] On wet places, see Cooney and Grogan *Irish prehistory* (1999), 144–8; Fredengren, *Crannogs* (2002), 178–82. For deposition of partial remains of an adolescent or young adult dated from between 1543 BC to 1411 BC at Lisbeg, Co. Tyrone, see Colin Dunlop and Jonathan Barkley, *Road to the west, a road to the past* vol. 2: *The archaeology of the A4/A5 road improvement scheme from Dungannon* (Belfast: Northern Archaeological Consultancy, 2015), pp 81–2. On caves, see Dowd, *Archaeology of caves* (2015), chapter 6; Glencurran, 148–54.

[14] Ó Nualláin, 'The stone circle complex of Cork and Kerry', *Journal of the Royal Society of Antiquaries of Ireland* 105 (1975), 83–131; W. O'Brien, 'Boulder burials: a later Bronze Age megalith tradition in south-west Ireland', *Journal of the Cork Historical and Archaeological Society* 97 (1992), 11–35; E.M. Fahy, 'A recumbent stone circle at Drombeg, Co. Cork', *Journal of the Cork Historical and Archaeological Society* 64 (1959), 1–27. Brück, *Personifying prehistory* (2019), 55–6; Johnston, *Bronze Age worlds* (2021), 106. For combination of circles, alignments and cairns with cremation deposits at Beaghmore, Co. Tyrone, see J.R. Pilcher, 'Archaeology, palaeoecology and ^{14}C dating of the Beaghmore stone circle site', *Ulster Journal of Archaeology* 32 (1969), 73–91.

[15] See Brück, *Personifying prehistory* (2019), 62; see also Cleary, 'Broken bones and broken stones' (2017).

[16] A relational view of identity is taken here, but for alternative perspectives see O'Driscoll, 'A multi-layered model for Bronze Age hillforts' (2017), 89–90, for a presentation of later Bronze Age society as a prestige goods economy, and Molloy, 'Hunting warriors' (2017), 307–09, for recognition of expert warriors and their wider social impact. The enduring image of the Bronze Age warrior is discussed in Paul Treherne, 'The warrior's beauty: the masculine body and self-identity in Bronze Age Europe', *European Journal of Archaeology* 3 (1995), 105–44, and twenty years on by C.J. Frieman *et al.*, 'Aging well: Treherne's "Warrior beauty" two decades later', *European Journal of Archaeology* 20 (1) (2017), 36–73. On the relationship of fragments of people and querns, see Cleary, 'Broken bones and broken stones' (2017), 14–18; Brück, 'Ancient DNA, kinship and relational identities' (2001), 153, comments that both were broken down upon death.

[17] Brück, *Personifying prehistory* (2019), 62; for discussion of Middle Bronze Age mortuary practice, see 42–50.

[18] Johnston, *Bronze Age worlds* (2021), 98. For discussion of the range of activities in a Bronze Age landscape at Crusheen, east Clare, see Grogan, 'Bronze Age: a surfeit of data?' (2017), 68–9.

[19] Brück, *Personifying prehistory* (2019), 61–8.

[20] For discussion of later prehistoric cemeteries discovered on development-led projects, see for example L. Lynch and L. O'Donnell, 'Cremation in the Bronze Age' (2007), 105–14; McQuade *et al.* (eds), *In the shadow of the Galtees* (2009), 123–48; Bermingham *et al.* (eds), *Beneath the Banner* (2012), 44–55; Troy, 'Contextualising cremations' (2015).

[21] For Templenoe, see McQuade *et al.* (eds), *In the shadow of the Galtees* (2009), 130–3; Geber, 'The Bronze Age burials' (2009). For Killoran 10 Lisheen, see Paul Stevens, 'Killoran 10', in Margaret Gowen *et al.* (eds), *The Lisheen Mine archaeological project 1996–8* (Bray: Wordwell, 2005), pp 292–4; Buckley, 'Human Remains', in Gowen *et al.* (eds), *The Lisheen Mine archaeological project 1996–8* (2005), pp 326–8.
[22] For Manusmore, see Bermingham *et al.* (eds), *Beneath the Banner* (2012), 44–7, 48–50. The Manusmore cemeteries provide a good example of multi-period cremation cemeteries. For Gransha, see Chapple, *The excavation of an enclosed Middle Bronze Age cemetery at Gransha, Co. Londonderry, Northern Ireland* (Oxford: Archaeopress. BAR British Series 521, 2010).
[23] C. Jones, 'Prehistory in the Fergus Valley', in N. Bermingham *et al.* (eds), *Beneath the Banner* (2012), pp 55–8.
[24] For example, Geber, 'The Bronze Age burials' (2009).
[25] For Dalystown, see Bernice Molloy, 'Dalystown: Ring-barrow complex', in Grogan *et al.* (eds), *Bronze Age landscapes of the Pipeline to the West* (2007), pp 337–9. For Ballybannon 5, see Louise Baker *et al.*, 'Site summaries', in Bolger *et al.* (eds), *A journey along the Carlow corrider* (2015), pp 11–76: 72–4. For Ask, see Paul Stevens, 'Burial and ritual in late prehistory in north Wexford: excavation of a ring-ditch cemetery in Ask townland', in J. O'Sullivan and M. Stanley (eds), *New Routes to the past* (Dublin: National Roads Authority. NRA Monograph Series 4, 2007), pp 35–46; and 'Burial and ritual in early medieval north Wexford: new evidence from Ask townland', in B. Kelly (eds), *Encounters between people* (Dublin: National Roads Authority. NRA Monograph Series 9, 2012), pp 49–60. For discussion of round barrow distribution and patterning in Ireland, see Grogan, *The North Munster project,* vol. 2*: The prehistoric landscape of north Munster* (Bray: Wordwell. Discovery Programme Monograph 6, 2005), 174–86; for ring-ditches, see Tiernan McGarry, 'Irish late prehistoric burial ring-ditches', in Cooney *et al.* (eds), *Relics of old decency: archaeological studies in Later Prehistory: a Festschrift for Barry Raftery* (Dublin: Wordwell, 2009), pp 413–23.
[26] See discussion in Cooney and Grogan, *Irish prehistory* (1999), 126–32; Cooney, 'Tracing lines across landscapes' (2009); Corlett and Potterton, *Life and death in Iron Age Ireland in the light of recent archaeological excavations* (Dublin: Wordwell, 2012).
[27] For discussion, see Lynch and O'Donnell, 'Cremation in the Bronze Age' (2007); Geber, 'The Bronze Age burials' (2009); Anthony, 'Cremated remains' (2012); Troy, 'Contextualising cremations' (2015); O'Donnell, 'The power of the pyre' (2016); Cooney, 'Pathways for the dead' (2017); Johnston, *Bronze Age worlds* (2021), 87–93.
[28] For discussion of modern crematoria and pyre cremation, see McKinley, 'Cremation, excavation, analysis and interpretation' (2013), 157–61.
[29] On Buddhist practice, see Kate Crosby and Alice Collett, 'Buddhism', in D.J. Davies with L.H. Mates (eds), *Encylopedia of cremation* (Ashgate: Aldershot, 2005), pp 96–100. On traditional Hindu cremation, see Mariana Caixeiro, 'Antiesthi: traditional Hindu cremation', in Davies, with Mates (eds), *Encylopedia of cremation* (2005), pp 234–5. As an example, Anders Kaliff and Terje Østigård, 'Cultivating corpses: a comparative approach to disembodied mortuary remains', *Current Swedish Archaeology* 12 (2004), 83–104, draw on comparison with Hindu tradition to interpret ritual practice during the Bronze Age and Iron Age in Scandinavia.

[30] For contextual discussion of cremation, see Davies with Mates (eds), *Encyclopedia of cremation* (2005); Williams, 'Death, memory and material culture' (2013); Østigård, 'Cremations in culture and cosmology', in Tarlow and Nilsson Stutz (eds), *Oxford handbook of the archaeology of death and burial* (2013), pp 497–509; Kuijt *et al.*, *Transformation by fire* (2014); Tim Thompson, *The archaeology of cremation: burned human remains in funerary studies* (Oxford: Oxbow, 2015); Cerezo-Román *et al.*, *Cremation and the archaeology of death* (2017).
[31] For Dalystown, see Lynch and O'Donnell, 'Cremation in the Bronze Age' (2007), 117. On circulation of unburnt human bone, see K. Cleary, 'Broken bones and broken stones' (2017); Fredengren, *Crannogs* (2002), 191–2.
[32] See discussion in Becker, 'Token explanations: Rathgall and the interpretation of cremation deposits in later prehistoric Ireland', *Archaeology Ireland* 107 (2014), pp 13–15. Brück, *Personifying prehistory* (2019), 40, comments that careful deposition of pyre material indicates that it may have been considered a symbolically powerful material. For pyres at Rathgall, Co. Wicklow and wider discussion, see B. Raftery and Katharina Becker, *A Bronze Age hillfort through time. Barry Raftery's excavation at Rathgall hillfort, Rath East, Co. Wicklow 1969–75; 1978* (Dublin: Wordwell, forthcoming).
[33] On use of wood in funeral pyres, see O'Donnell, 'Environmental archaeology: identifying patterns of exploitation in the Bronze Age', in Grogan *et al.* (eds), *Bronze Age landscapes of the Pipeline to the West* (2007) pp 27–79, and 'The power of the pyre' (2016). O'Donnell, 'Environmental archaeology' (2007), 50, comments on heat levels achieved. See also O'Donnell, 'Charcoal results', in McQuade *et al.* (eds), *In the shadow of the Galtees* (2009), pp 243–61: 251–2; Murphy, 'Appendix 3: Report on the cremated remains recovered from Archaeological Licences AE/04/077, AE/05/014 and AE/04/055' (2009), 230, 238; Troy, 'Contextualising cremations' (2015), 138–9. Lynch and O'Donnell, 'Cremation in the Bronze Age' (2007), 112, comment on the inclusion of apple and cherry wood to mask the smell of burning flesh.
[34] For Manusmore, see Bermingham *et al.* (eds), *Beneath the Banner* (2012), 46–50. See also wider discussion in P. Johnston, 'Analysis of carbonized plant remains', in Grogan *et al.* (eds), *Bronze Age landscapes of the pipeline to the west* (2007), 70–79; S.J. Halwas, 'Macro-plant remains', in McQuade *et al.* (eds), *In the shadow of the Galtees* (2009), pp. 262–74: 269–70.
[35] For Templenoe, see McQuade *et al.* (eds), *In the shadow of the Galtees* (2009), 133. The Newford pyre is discussed by Brendon Wilkins, 'Excavating death in Galway: Newford, Ballygarraun and Carrowkeel', *Current Archaeology* 246 (2010), 36–43. An example of a barrow covering a cremation pyre is Carrowbeg North, Co. Galway; see G.F. Wilmot, 'Two Bronze Age burials at Carrowbeg North, Belclare, Co. Galway', *Journal of the Galway Archaeological and Historical Society* 18 (1939), 121–40; B. Raftery, *Pagan Celtic Ireland* (1994), 193–4.
[36] Geber, 'The Bronze Age burials' (2009), 215–18.
[37] For Killoran 10 and evidence for crushing, see Buckley, 'Human Remains', in Gowen *et al.* (eds), *Lisheen Mine* (2005), 328. On Dalystown, see Lynch and O'Donnell, 'Cremation in the Bronze Age' (2007), 117. For Mitchelstowndown, see Gowen, *Three Irish gas pipelines: new archaeological evidence from Munster* (Dublin: Wordwell, 1988), 98–102. For Grey Abbey, see L. Lynch, Osteoarchaeological report on cremated bones excavated at Grey Abbey Friary, Nurney Road, Kildare. Licence 04E0233. (Unpublished report for Aegis Archaeology Ltd, 2005).

[38] For Killemly, see McQuade *et al.* (eds), *In the shadow of the Galtees* (2009), 140–41. For Kiltenan South and Rathcannon, see Grogan *et al.*, *Bronze Age landscapes of the Pipeline to the West* (2007), 292–3, 302–04; For Ballybar Lower 1–3, see L. Baker *et al.*, 'Site summaries' (2015), 58–63; Colm Moloney, 'Sacred places, *fulachtai fia* and settlements', in Bolger *et al.* (eds) *A journey along the Carlow Corridor* (2015), pp 109–30: 123–9. Note that a stone upright marked a Late Bronze Age burial at Carrig, and an outlying Late Bronze Age cremation pit at Kiltenan South was marked with a timber post. For Carrig, see Grogan, 'Bronze Age cemetery at Carrig' (1990).
[39] For the Gas Pipeline to the West, see Lynch and O'Donnell, 'Cremation in the Bronze Age' (2007), 109. For discussion of the Templenoe cemetery, see Geber, 'The Bronze Age burials' (2009), 213–19.
[40] Caswell and Roberts, 'Reassessing community cemeteries' (2018), 332, see discussion of deposit weights, 339 and table 5, figs 6-7; see also Johnston, *Bronze Age worlds* (2021), 93.
[41] Brück, 'Death, exchange and reproduction' (2006); Cooney, 'Pathways for the dead' (2017), 125; Johnston, *Bronze Age worlds* (2021), 92; T. Lynch, *Apparition and late fictions* (London: Jonathan Cape, 2010), 16.
[42] Molloy, 'Dalystown: ring-barrow complex' (2007); L. Lynch, Osteological report on cremated skeletal remains excavated from thirteen sites along the gas pipeline to the west. Unpublished report. (Aegis Archaeology Ltd for Margaret Gowen and Co. Ltd, 2003); Lynch and O'Donnell, 'Cremation in the Bronze Age' (2007), 117; Cooney, 'Pathways for the dead' (2017), 126–8.
[43] Ann Woodward, *British barrows: a matter of life and death* (Stroud: Tempus, 2000). The central role of barrows in the burial record of the European Bronze Age is outlined by Holst, 'Burials' (2013); see also Harding, *European societies in the Bronze Age* (2000), 73–123.
[44] Cooney, *Landscapes of Neolithic Ireland* (2000), chapter 4.
[45] For Keenoge, see Mount, 'Adolf Mahr's excavations' (1997). For Corrower, see J. Raftery, 'A Bronze Age tumulus at Corrower, Co. Mayo', *Proceedings of the Royal Irish Academy* 61C (1960), 79–93; Waddell, *Bronze Age burials of Ireland* (1990), 118.
[46] For relevant wider discussion of Britain and Ireland, see Bradley, *Prehistory of Britain and Ireland* (2019), 183–68. For Newrath, see Wren and Price, 'Newrath 37—Neolithic cemetery and Bronze Age cemetery' (2011). For wider discussion, see J. Eogan, 'Later prehistory of the Lower Suir Valley' (2011), 274–80. On containment and covering of burials with range of materials, see Anwen Cooper *et al.*, 'Covering the dead in later prehistoric Britain: elusive objects and powerful technologies of funerary performance', *Proceedings of the Prehistoric Society* 85 (2019), 223–50.
[47] Doyle, 'Excavation of a prehistoric ring-barrow at Kilmahuddrick' (2005).
[48] See discussion in Doyle, 'Excavation of a prehistoric ring-barrow at Kilmahuddrick' (2005), 62; Cooney and Grogan, *Irish prehistory* (1999), 146–8.
[49] Doyle, 'Excavation of a prehistoric ring-barrow at Kilmahuddrick' (2005), 65–6; Brück, *Personifying prehistory* (2019), 24. For relevant discussion, see Paul Garwood, 'Ritual tradition and the reconstitution of society', in Garwood *et al.* (eds), *Sacred and profane* (Oxford: Oxford University Committee for Archaeology, 1991), pp 10–32; 'Before the hills in order stood: chronology, time and history in the interpretation of Early Bronze Age round barrows', in J. Last (ed), *Beyond the grave: new perspectives on round barrows* (Oxford: Oxbow, 2007), pp 30–52; and 'The present dead: the making

of past and future landscapes in the British Chalcolithic', in Allen *et al.* (eds), *Is there a British Chalcolithic?* (2012), pp 298–316; Johnston, *Bronze Age worlds* (2021), 86.
[50] Woodward, *British barrows* (2000), chapter 4. For relevant discussion, see Andrew Fleming, 'Territorial patterns in Bronze Age Wessex', *Proceedings of the Prehistoric Society* 37 (1971), 138–66; David Field, 'Round barrows and the harmonious landscape: placing Early Bronze Age burial monuments in south-east England', *Oxford Journal of Archaeology* 17 (3) (1998), 309–26; Frances Lynch *et al.*, *Prehistoric Wales* (Stroud, Gloucs: Sutton, 2000), 121–8; Johnston, *Bronze Age worlds* (2021), 83–7.
[51] For Tara, see Conor Newman, *Tara: an archaeological survey* (Dublin: Royal Irish Academy/Discovery Programme. Discovery Programme Monographs 2, 1997). For Rathcroghan, see Waddell *et al.*, *Rathcroghan: archaeological survey and geophysical survey in a ritual landscape* (Dublin: Wordwell, 2009). For North Munster and wider discussion of barrows, see Grogan, *North Munster project* vol. 2 (2005); Bradley, *Prehistory of Britain and Ireland* (2019), 234.
[52] Chapple, 'Absolute dating of archaeological excavations in Ulster' (2008); Chapple *et al.*, *Archaeological investigations along the A1 Dualling Scheme* (2009): Derrycraw, pp 101–27, Ballintaggart, pp 50–97. See also Dunlop, *Down the road: the archaeology of the A1 Road Scheme* (2015), 78–83.
[53] Dunlop, *Down the road: the archaeology of the A1 Road Scheme* (2015), 81; see Murphy, 'Appendix 3: Report on the cremated remains recovered from Archaeological Licences AE/04/077, AE/05/014 and AE/04/055' (2009), 238–9, for discussion of the cremated human remains from Derrycraw.
[54] Chapple *et al.*, *Archaeological investigations along the A1 Dualling Scheme* (2009), 123.
[55] Chapple *et al. Archaeological investigations along the A1 Dualling Scheme* (2009), 4–50.
[56] Chapple, 'Absolute dating of archaeological excavations in Ulster' (2008); Dunlop, *Down the road: the archaeology of the A1 Road Scheme* (2015), 74–7. For the analysis of cremated bone from Ballintaggart, see Murphy, 'Appendix 3: Report on the cremated remains recovered from Archaeological Licences AE/04/077, AE/05/014 and AE/04/055' (2009), 214–33, summarised in table 7.
[57] Chapple *et al.*, *Archaeological investigations along the A1 Dualling Scheme* (2009), 55–60, 67–72.
[58] Murphy, 'Appendix 3: Report on the cremated remains recovered from Archaeological Licences AE/04/077, AE/05/014 and AE/04/055' (2009), 224–6.
[59] See Chapple *et al. Archaeological investigations along the A1 Dualling Scheme* (2009), 74–97 for discussion. For the reference to maintenance of differences in burial practice, see Duncan Garrow *et al.*, 'Dating the dead: a high-resolution radiocarbon chronology within an Early Bronze Age barrow cemetery at Over, Cambridgeshire', *Proceedings of the Prehistoric Society* 80 (2014), 207–36: 232.
[60] Newman, *Tara: an archaeological survey* (1997), 153–70, on barrow types at Tara; on the development of the Tara complex, 225–30; Newman, 'Reflections on the making of a "royal site" in early Ireland', *World Archaeology* 30 (1) (1998), 13–22; Aidan O'Connell, *Harvesting the stars: a pagan temple at Lismullin, Co. Meath* (Dublin: National Roads Authority. NRA Scheme Monographs 11, 2013), 43–50. For other cemeteries, see Mount, 'Created and appropriated continuity at Rathdooney Beg, Co. Sligo', in Corlett, and Potterton (eds), *Life and death in Iron Age Ireland* (2012), pp 189–98.

[61] On the Banqueting Hall (*Tech Mid Chúarta*) at Tara, see Newman, 'Procession and symbolism at Tara: analysis of Tech Midchúarta (the "Banqueting Hall") in the context of the sacral campus', *Oxford Journal of Archaeology* 26 (4) (2007), 415–38. On the Ditched Pit Circle, see Joseph Fenwick and Newman, 'Geomagnetic survey on the Hill of Tara, Co. Meath, 1988–9', *Discovery Programme Report* 6 (Dublin: Royal Irish Academy/Discovery Programme, 2002), pp 1–17. Extensive geophysical prospection, LIDAR and aerial photographic surveys have been undertaken at Tara by the Discovery Programme and its research partners.
[62] Newman, *Tara: an archaeological survey* (1997), 169; Cooney, 'Tracing lines across landscapes' (2009), 379; for discussion of Late Bronze Age parallels for the Ráith Gráinne sequence, see Grogan, 'Bronze Age: a surfeit of data?' (2017), 76.
[63] Mizoguchi, 'Time in the reproduction of mortuary practices (1993); Lynch *et al.*, *Prehistoric Wales* (2000), 122–6; Bradley, *The past in prehistoric societies* (2002), 111; Garrow *et al.*, 'Dating the dead' (2014). Brück, *Personifying prehistory* (2019), 66, comments that the placement of cremation deposits on the south side of earlier barrows linked the remains to concepts of light, life, fertility and rebirth.
[64] For discussion of the emergence of Tara as a place of kingship and inauguration in the early medieval period, set in a landscape context of prehistoric activity and memorialisation, see Newman, 'The sacral landscape of Tara: a preliminary exploration', in R. Schot *et al.* (eds), *Landscapes of cult and kingship* (Dublin: Four Courts Press, 2011), pp 22–43; see also essays in M. O'Sullivan *et al.* (eds), *Tara: from the past to the future* (2013); David Rollason, *The power of place: rulers and their palaces, landscapes, cities and holy places* (Princeton: Princeton University Press, 2016), 331–5; Waddell, *Prehistoric archaeology of Ireland* (2022), 294–300. On a barrow south-east of the Mound of the Hostages, see Bayliss and M. O'Sullivan, 'Interpreting chronologies for the Mound of the Hostages' (2013), 54.
[65] Liam de Paor and Marcus Ó h-Eochaidhe, 'Unusual group of earthworks at Slieve Breagh, Co. Meath', *Journal of the Royal Society of Antiquaries of Ireland* 86 (1956), 97–101; Michael J. Moore, *Archaeological inventory of County Meath* (Dublin: The Stationery Office, 1987); Victor Buckley and P.D. Sweetman, *Archaeological survey of County Louth* (Dublin: The Stationery Office, 1991).
[66] G.J. Mulrooney, An analysis of the spatial distribution of barrow cemeteries with a focus on the barrow landscape of the Plains of Boyle, Co. Roscommon. Unpublished MA thesis. (University College Dublin, 2008), 107–26; Cooney, 'Tracing lines across landscapes: corporality and history in later prehistoric Ireland', in Cooney *et al.* (eds), *Relics of old decency* (2009), pp 375–88.
[67] Cooney and Grogan, *Irish prehistory: a social perspective* (1999), 129–33; Grogan, *North Munster project* vol. 2 (2005), 67–76. For the application of a similar territorial argument to Bronze Age hillforts, see O'Driscoll, 'A multi-layered model for Bronze Age hillforts' (2017), 92.
[68] Joseph Raftery, 'The tumulus cemetery of Carrowjames, Co. Mayo; Part I—Carrowjames I', *Journal of the Galway Archaeological and Historical Society* 18 (1938–9), 157–67; and 'The tumulus cemetery of Carrowjames, Co. Mayo; Part II—Carrowjames II', *Journal of the Galway Archaeological and Historical Society* 19 (1940–41), 16–85. See also discussion in Barry Raftery, 'Iron Age burials in Ireland', in Ó Corráin (ed.), *Irish antiquity* (1981),

pp 173–204; Waddell, *Bronze Age burials of Ireland* (1990); Mount, 'Created and appropriated continuity at Rathdooney Beg' (2012).

[69] For Site 8 at Carrowjames, see E. O'Brien, *Mapping death* (2020), 22, 24.

[70] For southern Britain, see Garwood, 'Ritual tradition and the reconstitution of society' (1991), 26; Garwood, 'Before the hills in order stood' (2007); and 'The present dead' (2012). For southern Netherlands, see Fontijn, 'Everything in its right place?' (2008), 89–94; Fontijn *et al.*, 'Bronze Age ancestral communities. New research of Middle Bronze Age burials in the barrow landscapes of Apeldoorn-Wieselseweg', in C.C. Bakels *et al.* (eds), *Local communities in the big world of prehistoric northwest Europe* (Leiden: Sidestone Press. Analecta Praehistorica Leidensia, 2018), pp 77–104.

[71] Brück, *Personifying prehistory* (2019), chapter 5 on social landscapes, 163–223; Johnston, *Bronze Age worlds* (2021), chapter 3 on dispersed lives, 75–130. On the importance of curated human remains in the relationships between the living and the dead, see Booth and Brück, 'Death is not the end' (2020). On the spectrum of depositional practice, see Cooper *et al.*, 'Spectrums of depositional practice in later prehistoric Britain and beyond: grave goods, hoards and deposits in between', *Archaeological Dialogues* 27 (2020), pp 135–57.

[72] See, for example, Ginn and Plunkett, 'Filling the gaps: a chronology' (2020); For core areas or micro-landscapes, see K. Cleary, *Archaeological networks: excavations on six gas pipelines in County Cork* (Cork: Collins Press, 2015), 38–63; Grogan, 'Bronze Age: a surfeit of data?' (2017), 68–9; W. O'Brien, 'Late prehistoric settlement in mid and north Cork', in Hanley and Hurley (eds), *Generations: the archaeology of five national road schemes* (vol. 1, 2013), pp 178–99: 194–6.

[73] See, for example, Cooney and Grogan, *Irish prehistory* (1999), chapters 7 and 8; Mallory, *Origins of the Irish* (2013), chapter 5. Becker, 'Transforming identities—new approaches to Bronze Age deposition in Ireland', *Proceedings of the Prehistoric Society* 79 (2013), 137–65, provides a new perspective on Bronze Age deposition; Molloy, 'Hunting warriors' (2017); Waddell, *Prehistoric archaeology of Ireland* (2022), chapters 7 and 8.

[74] W. O'Brien, 'Late prehistoric settlement' (2013), 194; Mallory, *Origins of the Irish* (2013), 154.

[75] For example, the suggested shift in focus to metalwork deposition. As 'graveless grave goods', see G. Eogan, 'The Later Bronze Age in Ireland in the light of recent research', *Proceedings of the Prehistoric Society* 30 (1964), 268–351: 285; and *Hoards of the Irish Later Bronze Age* (1983). As an expression of wealth, see Cooney and Grogan, *Irish prehistory* (1999), 158–67; L. Bourke, *Crossing the Rubicon* (2001).

[76] As a regional example, see the development of Bronze Age society in mid and north Cork suggested by W. O'Brien, 'Late prehistoric settlement' (2013), 178–96. On metalwork, see Becker, 'Transforming identities' (2013); Molloy, 'Hunting warriors' (2017). On hillforts, see W. O'Brien, 'Development of the hillfort' (2017); W. O'Brien and James O'Driscoll, *Hillforts, warfare and society in Bronze Age Ireland* (Oxford: Archaeopress, 2017); O'Driscoll, 'A multi-layered model for Bronze Age hillforts' (2017).

[77] Ingold, *Perception of the environment* (2000), chapter 8. See relevant discussion on landscape and construction of identity in Fontijn, 'Everything in its right place?' (2008); and *Economies of destruction* (2020), chapter 7.

[78] For North Munster, see Grogan, *North Munster project* vol. 2 (2005), pp 133–44. For east Cork, see K. Cleary, *Archaeological networks* (2015), 168–70. For Crusheen area, see Grogan, 'Bronze Age: a surfeit of data?' (2017), 68–9.
[79] K. Cleary, 'Broken bones and broken stones' (2017), 13; Brück, 'A place for the dead; the role of human remains in Late Bronze Age Britain', *Proceedings of the Prehistoric Society* 61 (1995), 245–77; 'Houses, lifecyles and deposition on Middle Bronze Age settlements in southern England', *Proceedings of the Prehistoric Society* 65 (1999), 145–66; 'Death, exchange and reproduction in the British Bronze Age', *European Journal of Archaeology* 9 (1) (2006), 73–101: 86; and *Personifying prehistory* (2019), 65.
[80] K. Cleary, 'Broken bones and broken stones' (2017), 14–18; Matthew Seaver, Draft report on the archaeological excavation of an archaeological complex at Laughanstown townland, Co. Dublin. Unpublished report (Valerie J. Keeley Ltd, n.d.). For querns at Ballybrowney Lower and Mitchelstown 1, Co. Cork houses, see Eamonn Cotter, 'Ballybrowney Lower 1—nucleated settlement', in Hanley and Hurley (eds), *Generations: the archaeology of five national road schemes in County Cork* (vol. 1, 2013), pp 93–104, 101; and 'Mitchelstown 1—settlement', in Hanley and Hurley (eds), *Generations* (vol. 1, 2013), pp 110–113: 113.
[81] Cleary, 'Broken bones and broken stones' (2017), 18–19; Brück, *Personifying prehistory* (2019), 148–9.
[82] Cooney and Grogan, *Irish prehistory* (1999), 146; Lynn, 'Trial excavations at the King's Stables, Tray Townland, County Armagh', *Ulster Journal of Archaeology* 40 (1977), 40–62: 48; Newman, *Tara: an archaeological survey* (1997), 46; Fredengren, *Crannogs* (2002), 191–2; M. Delaney and Woodman, 'Searching the Irish Mesolithic (2004); Grogan *et al.*, *Bronze Age landscapes of the Pipeline to the West* (2007), 94. On curation, see Booth and Brück, 'Death is not the end' (2020), 1200; Brück and Booth, 'The power of relics: the curation of human bone in British Bronze Age burials', *European Journal of Archaeology* 25 (4) (2022), 440–62.
[83] Garwood, 'The present dead' (2012), 301.
[84] Brück, *Personifying prehistory* (2019), 61–8. Albeit referring to the earlier part of the Bronze Age regarding cemeteries, see relevant discussion in Bradley, *Prehistory of Britain and Ireland* (2019), 178–83.
[85] G. Eogan, *Hoards of the Irish Later Bronze Age* (1983); see discussion in Brück, *Personifying prehistory* (2019), chapter 3; Ingold, *Making: anthropology, archaeology, art and architecture* (London: Routledge, 2013), 21. Molloy, 'Hunting warriors' (2017), 306–7, notes how changes in weaponry would have impacted on the body and conduct of combat in later Bronze Age society.
[86] Fontijn, 'Everything in its right place?' (2008); Brück, *Personifying prehistory* (2019), 102; Becker, 'Left but not lost', *Archaeology Ireland* 22 (1) (2008), 12–15; and 'Transforming identities' (2013).
[87] On metalwork deposition as kinwork, see Johnston, *Bronze Age worlds* (2021), 4–13. On landscapes of deposition, see Fontijn, *Economies of destruction* (2020), 144–9. On depositional practices, see Cooper *et al.*, 'Spectrums of depositional practice' (2020), 139. On Tara torcs, see G. Eogan, *Hoards of the Irish Later Bronze Age* (1983), 40–41. On Rathgall, see B. Raftery, 'Rathgall: a Late Bronze Age burial in Ireland', *Antiquity*

47 (1973), 293–95; and 'Iron Age burials in Ireland' (1981), 173–7. See also B. Raftery and Becker, *Bronze Age hillfort through time* (forthcoming).

[88] On the North Munster settlement model, see Grogan *et al.*, 'Tracing the late prehistoric landscape in North Munster', *Discovery Programme Reports* 4 (1996), 26–46; Grogan, *The North Munster Project*, vol. 1*: The later prehistoric landscape of south-east Clare* (Bray: Wordwell. Discovery Programme Monograph 6, 2005), 79–101 and Grogan, *North Munster Project*, vol. 2 (2005), 145–67, placing the model in wider contexts. On the role of hillforts, see W. O'Brien, 'Development of the hillfort' (2017), 54–5; W. O'Brien and James O'Driscoll, *Hillforts, warfare and society* (2017), chapters 9 and 10; O'Driscoll, 'A multi-layered model for Bronze Age hillforts' (2017), 91–2.

[89] Ginn, 'Fusion of settlement and identity' (2011); and *Mapping society* (2016); Ginn and Plunkett, 'Filling the gaps: a chronology' (2020). On Corrstown, see Ginn and Stuart Rathbone (eds), *Corrstown: a coastal community. Excavations of a Bronze Age village in Northern Ireland* (Oxford: Oxbow, 2012). On hillforts as gathering places for dispersed communities, see Niall Sharples, *Social relations in later prehistory: Wessex in the first millennium BC* (Oxford: Oxford University Press, 2010), 116–24; Gary Lock, 'Hillforts, emotional metaphors, and the good life: a response to Armit', *Proceedings of the Prehistoric Society* 77 (2011), 355–62 (359); Brück, *Personifying prehistory* (2019), 155–8; Johnston, *Bronze Age worlds* (2021), 210–12. On metalwork as reflecting kin, networks and relations, see Johnston, *Bronze Age worlds* (2021), 104–05.

[90] As a notable exception, see Grogan, *North Munster project* vol. 2 (2005), pp 135–7. Ginn and Punkett, 'Filling the gaps: a chronology' (2020), 54. The authors note that while the settlement record implies a considerable increase in population during the Bronze Age, the population estimates in T.R. McLaughlin, 'An archaeology of Ireland for the Information Age' (2020) appear to be overstated.

Chapter 7

[1] Holger Schweitzer, 'Iron Age toe-rings from Rath, Co. Meath on the N2 Finglas-Ashbourne Road Scheme', in J. O'Sullivan and M. Stanley (eds), *Recent archaeological discoveries on National Road Schemes 2004* (Dublin: National Roads Authority, 2005), pp 93–8; J. Montgomery *et al.*, Report on the lead, strontium and oxygen isotopes of the Iron Age burial from Rath, Ireland. Unpublished report. (Prepared for CRDS, Dublin, 2006); Finola O'Carroll *et al.*, 'Rath, Co. Meath: of beads and burials', in Corlett and Potterton (eds), *Life and death in Iron Age Ireland* (Dublin: Wordwell 2012), pp 223–32: 225–6; E. O'Brien, *Mapping death* (2020), 39–40; for earlier work to the north, see Emmet Byrnes, 'Rath. Bronze Age enclosures', in Grogan *et al.*, *Bronze Age landscapes of the Pipeline to the West* (2007), pp 329–30; see also Giles, *A forged glamour: landscape, identity and material culture in the Iron Age* (Oxford: Oxbow, 2012), 150 for evidence from Yorkshire.

[2] The classic text with which all recent discussions begin is B. Raftery, *Pagan Celtic Ireland* (1994). For Britain, see Cunliffe, *Britain begins* (2012), chapters 9–12; Bradley, *Prehistory of Britain and Ireland* (2019), chapter 5. Recent important discussions of the Iron Age include Becker, 'Redefining the Irish Iron Age', in Corlett and Potterton (eds), *Life and death in Iron Age Ireland* (2012), pp 1–14; and 'Iron Age Ireland: continuity,

change and identity', in T. Moore and X.-L. Armada, *Atlantic Europe in the first millennium BC: crossing the divide* (Oxford: Oxbow, 2012), pp 449–67; Jacqueline Cahill Wilson, 'Lost in transcription: rethinking our approach to the archaeology of the later Iron Age', in Corlett and Potterton (eds), *Life and death in Iron Age Ireland* (2012), pp 15–33; and 'Romans and Roman material in Ireland: a wider social perspective', in 'Late Iron Age and "Roman" Ireland', *Discovery Programme Reports* 8 (2014), 11–58; Cahill Wilson *et al.*, 'Investigating mobility and migration in the Later Iron Age', in 'Late Iron Age and "Roman" Ireland' (2014), 127–49; Brian Dolan, 'Beyond elites: reassessing Iron Age society', *Oxford Journal of Archaeology* 33 (4) (2014), 361–77; Becker, 'Irish Iron Age settlement and society: reframing royal sites', *Proceedings of the Prehistoric Society* 85 (2019), 273–306; Waddell, *Prehistoric archaeology of Ireland* (2022), chapters 10 and 11. On climatic deterioration at the end of the Bronze Age, see Armit *et al.*, 'Rapid climate change did not cause population collapse' (2014); Becker *et al.*, 'New perspectives on the Irish Iron Age' (2017), 98–9; Benjamin Gearey *et al.*, 'On the brink of Armageddon? Climate change, the archaeological record and human activity across the Bronze Age–Iron Age transition in Ireland', in Kelly and Ó Caragáin (eds), *Climate and society in Ireland* (2020), 105–28. On the impact of development-led archaeology, see Becker *et al.*, 'New perspectives on the Irish Iron Age' (2017), 85.

[3] E. O' Brien, *Mapping death* (2020) is the key text for burial in Late Iron Age and early medieval Ireland, with coverage of the earlier Iron Age also. This builds on a number of influential earlier papers, for example E. O'Brien, 'Pagan and Christian burial in Ireland during the first millennium AD: continuity and change', in N. Edwards and A. Lane, (eds), *The eary church in Wales and the West: recent work in early Christian archaeology, history and place-names* (Oxford: Oxbow, 1992), pp 130–37; *Post-Roman Britain to Anglo-Saxon England* (1999); 'Burial practices in Ireland (2003); 'Pagan or Christian?' (2009); and 'From burial among the ancestors to burial among the saints: an assessment of some burial rites in Ireland from the fifth to the eighth centuries AD', in Edwards *et al.* (eds), *Transforming landscapes of belief in the Early Medieval Insular world and beyond* (Turnhout: CELEMA 23, 2017), pp 259–86; O'Brien and Bhreathnach, 'Irish boundary *ferta*, their physical manifestation and historical context', in F. Edmonds and P. Russell (eds), *Tome: studies in Medieval Celtic history and law in honour of Thomas Charles-Edwards* (Woodbridge: Boydell and Brewer, 2011), pp 53–64; and 'Burial in Early Medieval Ireland' (2013). For key overviews of death in the Iron Age and continuity into the early medieval period, see T. McGarry, Irish late prehistoric burials. Unpublished PhD thesis. (University College Dublin, 2008); 'Irish late prehistoric burial ring-ditches' (2009); and 'Late pagan and Early Christian burials in Ireland: some issues and potential explanations', in Corlett and Potterton (eds), *Death and burial in Early Medieval Ireland* (2010), pp 173–85; Corlett and Potterton, *Death and burial in Early Medieval Ireland* (2010); *Life and death in Iron Age Ireland* (2012); Cahill Wilson, 'Lost in transcription' (2012); Patrick Gleeson and Rowan McLaughlin, 'Ways of death: cremation and belief in first-millennium AD Ireland', *Antiquity* 95 (380) (2021), 382–99 (cremation); Gleeson, 'Reframing the first millennium AD in Ireland: archaeology, history, landscape', *Proceedings of the Royal Irish Academy* 122C (2022), 87–122. Ó Carragáin, 'Trends in mortuary practices to 800', in *Churches in the Irish landscape* (2021), pp 14–29.

[4] Elva Johnston, 'Ireland in Late Antiquity: a forgotten frontier', *Studies in Late Antiquity* 1 (2) (2017), 107–23. For detailed coverage of the archaeology of the early medieval

period in Ireland, see A. O'Sullivan *et al.*, *Early Medieval Ireland AD 400–1100* (2014). For more historically based approaches, see Edel Bhreathnach, *Ireland in the medieval world AD 400–1000: landscape, kingship and religion* (Dublin: Four Courts Press, 2014); Charles-Edwards, *Early Christian Ireland* (Cambridge: Cambridge University Press, 2000); Dáibhí Ó Cróinín, *Early Medieval Ireland, 400–1200* (London: Longman, 1995); Matthew Stout, *Early Medieval Ireland 431–1169* (Dublin: Wordwell, 2017). See also Gleeson, 'Reframing the first millennium AD in Ireland' (2022), calling for a reframing of approaches to the first millennium AD.

[5] For secular cemeteries, see M. Stout and Geraldine Stout, *Excavation of an Early Medieval secular cemetery at Knowth Site M, Co. Meath* (Dublin: Wordwell, 2008); for cemetery settlements, see Tomás Ó Carragáin, 'Cemetery settlements and local churches in pre-Viking Ireland in light of comparisons with England and Wales', in J. Graham-Campbell and M. Ryan (eds), *Anglo-Saxon/Irish relations before the Vikings* (Oxford: Oxford University Press. Proceedings of the British Academy 157, 2009), pp 329–65; 'From family cemeteries to community cemeteries in Viking Age Ireland?', in Corlett and Potterton (eds), *Death and burial in Early Medieval Ireland* (2010), pp 217–26: 217; note that Ó Carragáin in *Churches in the Irish landscape* (2021), 14, 24, uses the term burial ground rather than cemetery. For settlement-cemeteries see A. O'Sullivan *et al.*, *Early Medieval Ireland AD 400–1100* (2014), 285 with references; E. O'Brien, *Mapping death* (2020), 98. On continuity of cremation, see Gleeson and R. McLaughlin, 'Ways of death' (2021).

[6] For discussion of types of cemeteries, see J. Eogan, 'Excavation of an unenclosed early medieval cemetery at Bettystown, Co. Meath', in Corlett and Potterton (eds), *Death and Burial in early medieval Ireland* (2010), pp 103–16; Ó Carragáin, *Churches in the Irish landscape* (2021), 22, on the relative inclusivity of some settlement-cemeteries; E. O'Brien *Mapping death* (2020), chapters 4 and 9.

[7] For relevant discussion, see Carlin *et al.*, 'Ironworking and production', in Carlin *et al.* (eds), *Archaeology of life and death in the Boyne Floodplain: the linear landscape of the M4* (Dublin: National Roads Authority. NRA Scheme Monographs 2, 2008), pp 87–112; Dolan, 'Beyond elites' (2014); Ger Dowling, 'Landscape and settlement in Late Iron Age Ireland: some emerging trends', in 'Late Iron Age and "Roman" Ireland', *Discovery Programme Reports* 8 (2014), 151–74; Becker, 'Iron Age Ireland—finding an invisible people', in Cooney *et al.* (eds), *Relics of old decency* (2009), pp 353–61; 'Redefining the Irish Iron Age (2012); 'Iron Age Ireland' (2012); and 'Iron Age settlement and society' (2019); Becker *et al.*, 'New perspectives on the Irish Iron Age' (2017); Mallory, *Origins of the Irish* (2013); Ó Drisceóil and Devine 'Invisible people or invisible archaeology? Carrickmines Great, Co. Dublin and the problem of Irish Iron Age settlements', in Corlett and Potterton (eds), *Life and death in Iron Age Ireland* (2012), pp 249–65.

[8] B. Raftery, 'Rathgall: a Late Bronze Age burial' (1973); and 'Iron Age burials in Ireland' (1981); Becker, *Rathgall, Co. Wicklow.* (Dublin: Archaeology Ireland. Heritage Guide 51, 2010); Johnston, *Bronze Age worlds* (2021), 106; B. Raftery and Becker, *Bronze Age hillfort through time* (forthcoming).

[9] For Reask, see Tom Fanning, 'Excavation of an Early Christian cemetery and settlement at Reask, County Kerry', *Proceedings of the Royal Irish Academy* 81C (1981),

67–172: 79–81, 151; see E. O'Brien, *Mapping death* (2020), 207–09, for discussion of Reask and other early community church cemeteries. Ó Carragáin, *Churches in the Irish landscape* (2021), 25.

[10] For contacts with the Celtic world, see; B. Raftery, *A catalogue of Irish Iron Age antiquities* (Marburg: Veröffentlichungen des Vorgeschichtlichen Seminars Marburg, Sonderband 1, 1983), *La Tène in Ireland: problems of origin and chronology* (Marburg: Veröffentlichungen des Vorgeschichtlichen Seminars Marburg, Sonderband 1, 1984); and *Pagan Celtic Ireland* (1994). For contacts with the Roman world, see John Soderberg, '"Between Britain and Hispania": Ireland in Roman-period Europe', in P. Wells (ed.), Rome beyond its frontiers: imports, attitudes and practices', *Journal of Roman Archaeology Supplementary Series* 94, (2013), 71–86; Cahill Wilson, 'Romans and Roman material in Ireland' (2014); and '*Et tu Hibernia*—Frontier zones and cultural contact: Ireland in a Roman World', in S. Gonzaléz Sánchez and A. Guglielmi (eds), *Romans and Barbarians beyond the frontiers: archaeology, ideologies and identities in the north* (Oxford: Oxbow, 2017), pp 48-69; Alex Guglielmi, Roman personal ornaments in Iron Age Ireland and Southern Scandinavia 100 BC–AD 500. Unpublished PhD thesis. (University College Dublin, 2018).

[11] For the ambiguous context of settlement-cemeteries, see, for example, Christine Baker, 'Occam's Duck: three early medieval settlement cemeteries or ecclesiastical sites?', in Corlett and Potterton (eds), *Death and burial in early medieval Ireland* (2010), pp 1–21. Lehane *et al.*, 'Three cemetery-settlement excavations at Carrowkeel, Treanbaun and Owenbristy', in Corlett and Potterton (eds), *Death and burial in early medieval Ireland* (2010), pp 139–56. For unenclosed cemeteries, see, for example, J. Eogan, 'Excavation of an unenclosed early medieval cemetery at Bettystown, Co. Meath' (2010). For cremation, see Gleeson and McLaughlin, 'Ways of death' (2021).

[12] Kevin Whelan, *Religion, landscape and settlement in Ireland: from Patrick to the present* (2018), 1. Whelan, 2, also provides a useful definition of syncretism in religion as the combination of different beliefs through the blending of originally distinct traditions.

[13] B. Raftery, *Pagan Celtic Ireland* (1994), 178.

[14] See discussion in Cooney, 'Icons of antiquity' (2015).

[15] For detailed overview of cremation in the Iron Age, see E. O'Brien, *Mapping death* (2020), chapter 1, and discussion in Gleeson and McLaughlin 'Ways of death' (2021), especially 388. Troy, What the bones tell us', in James Hession, 'The Iron Age: grain, ore and death', in P. Long *et al.*, *In the Vale of Tralee: the archaeology of the N22 Tralee Bypass* (Dublin: Transport Infrastructure Ireland. TII Heritage 9, 2020), 142–4: 142, comments on the occurrence of whole cremation burials and token deposits at Ballinorig West, Co. Kerry. For Manusmore AR100, see Bermingham *et al.* (eds), *Beneath the Banner* (2012), 44–50. For Carrowjames, see J. Raftery, 'Tumulus cemetery of Carrowjames, Part I (1938–9); and 'Tumulus cemetery of Carrowjames, Part II (1940–1). For Cush, see S.P. Ó Ríordáin, 'Excavations at Cush, Co. Limerick', *Proceedings of the Royal Irish Academy* 45C (1940), 83–181. For Tara, see Newman, *Tara: an archaeological survey* (1997), 225–30.

[16] For Ballynakelly, see Ciara McCarthy, 'An Iron Age ring-ditch at Ballynakelly, Co. Dublin', in Corlett and Potterton(eds), *Life and death in Iron Age Ireland* (2012), pp 157–59. On the link between Iron Age monuments and earlier activity, see Mount, 'Created and appropriated continuity at Rathdooney Beg' (2012), 194–7, E. O'Brien, *Mapping death* (2020), 14.

[17] For Knockcommane, Knockgraffon and Marlhill, see Molloy, 'Knockcommane, Co. Limerick. Embanked ring-ditch Site 4700.1a', in McQuade *et al.* (eds), *In the shadow of the Galtees* (2009), pp 163–5; and 'Marlhill, Co. Tipperary. Ring-barrow. Site 141.1', in McQuade *et al.* (eds), *In the shadow of the Galtees* (2009), pp 166–9; Colm Moriarty, 'Knockgraffon, Co. Tipperary. Ring-barrow Site 143.3', in McQuade *et al.* (eds), *In the shadow of the Galtees* (2009), pp 170–8; McQuade and Molloy, 'Recent Iron Age discoveries in south County Tipperary and County Limerick', in Corlett and Potterton (eds), *Life and death in Iron Age Ireland* (2012), pp 175–87. For Ballyboy 1 and 2, see Siobhán McNamara and Shane Delaney, 'Iron Age ring-ditches and cremation burials at Ballyboy', in Delaney *et al.* (eds), *Borderlands: archaeological investigations on the route of the M18 Gort to Crusheen road scheme* (Dublin: National Roads Authority. NRA Scheme Monographs 9, 2012), pp 123–37. On pennannular ring-ditches, see J. Eogan and Buckley, 'An Iron Age penannular ring-ditch at Ballybronoge South, Co. Limerick', in Corlett and Potterton (eds), *Life and death in Iron Age Ireland* (2012), pp 105–20. On Ballinorig West 4, Co. Kerry pennular ring-ditch, see Hession and Troy, 'The Iron Age: grain, ore and death', in Long *et al.*, *In the Vale of Tralee* (2020), pp 131–44.
[18] For Ballydavis, see Valerie Keeley, 'Iron Age discoveries at Ballydavis', in P.G. Lane and W. Nolan (eds), *Laois history and society* (Dublin: Geography Publications, 1999), pp 25–34. For Holdenstown, see Yvonne Whitty and Jennie Coughlan, 'An Iron Age ring-ditch complex at Holdenstown 1, Co. Kilkenny', in Corlett and Potterton (eds), *Life and death in Iron Age Ireland* (2012), pp 313–26.
[19] For Ferns Lower, see F. Ryan and L. Buckley, 'Excavation of a late Iron Age ring-ditch at Ferns, Co. Wexford', in Corlett and Potterton (eds), *Life and death in Iron Age Ireland* (2012), pp 273–89. Eogan and Buckley, 'An Iron Age penannular ring-ditch at Ballybronoge' (2012), 111.
[20] Giles, *A forged glamour* (2012), 36–8 and chapter 5.
[21] Giles, 'Making metal and forging relations: ironworking in the British Iron Age', *Oxford Journal of Archaeology* 26 (4) (2007), 394–413. For Ballydavis, see Keeley, 'Iron Age discoveries at Ballydavis' (1999), 30; E. O'Brien, *Mapping death* (2020), 26. For Wetwang, Yorkshire, see John Dent, 'Three cart burials from Wetwang, Yorkshire', *Antiquity* 59 (1985), 85–92: 88–90. For wider discussion of Yorkshire cart or chariot burials, see I.M. Stead, *Iron Age cemeteries in East Yorkshire* (London: English Heritage, 1991); Giles, *A forged glamour* (2012).
[22] On Yorkshire cart burials, see Bradley, *Prehistory of Britain and Ireland* (2019), 315–18; Cunliffe, *Britain begins* (2012), 316–19. On interpreting objects placed with the dead, see Giles, *A forged glamour* (2012), 124–6.
[23] Eamonn P. Kelly, 'The Iron Age', in P.F. Wallace and R. Ó Floinn (eds), *Treasures of the National Museum of Ireland: Irish antiquities* (Dublin: Gill and Macmillan, 2002), p. 137; B. Raftery, *Pagan Celtic Ireland* (1994), 188–99; E. O'Brien, *Mapping death* (2020), 19–28.
[24] Leonora O'Brien, 'Decayed, consumed, dried, cut up, drowned or burnt? An overview of burial practices in Iron Age Britain', *Archaeologia Mosellana* 9 (2014), 25–51; Rowan Whimster, *Burial practices in Iron Age Britain c. 700 BC–AD 43* (Oxford: Archaeopress. BAR British Series 191 (2 vols), 1981), 147, 194; E. O'Brien, *Post-Roman Britain to Anglo-Saxon Englnd* (1999), 1–11; see Cunliffe, *Britain begins* (2012), figs 11.4 (p. 365), 11.6 (p. 367) and 11.7 (p. 369).

[25] See discussion of the Stoneyford burial and context in B. Raftery, *Pagan Celtic Ireland* (1994), 206–7; Edward Bourke, 'A first century Roman burial from Ireland', *Archaeology Ireland* 3 (2) (1989), 56–7; Aideen Ireland, 'The Stoneyford burial: fact or fiction (part I)', *Journal of the Royal Society of Antiquaries of Ireland* 142 (3) (2013), 8–27; and 'The Stoneyford burial: fact or fiction (part II)', *Journal of the Royal Society of Antiquaries of Ireland* 144 (5) (2015), 27-44; E. O'Brien, *Mapping death* (2020), 8.

[26] For Kiltierney, see Claire Foley and Ronan McHugh, *An archaeological survey of County Fermanagh*. Vol. 1, Part 1, *The prehistoric period* (Belfast: Northern Ireland Environment Agency, 2014), 125–38, 175–8. For Carrowmore Grave 26, see G. Burenhult, *The archaeological excavation at Carrowmore Co. Sligo, Ireland: excavation seasons 1977–79* (Stockholm: Institute of Archaeology, University of Stockholm. Theses and Papers in North-European Archaeology 9, 1980), 40–9; also Burenhult, *Archaeology of Carrowmore: environmental archaeology and the megalithic tradition* (1984), 60. There was also Iron Age activity at Carrowmore Grave 27. For Rathdooney Beg, see Mount, 'Excavation and environmental analysis of a Neolithic mound and Iron Age barrow cemetery at Rathdooney Beg, County Sligo, Ireland', *Proceedings of the Prehistoric Society* 65 (1999), 337–71; and 'Created and appropriated continuity at Rathdooney Beg' (2012), 192.

[27] B. Raftery, *Pagan Celtic Ireland* (1994), fig. 134; Robert Janiszewski, 'A fragment of a gold bracelet from Newgrange, Co. Meath and its Late Roman context', *Journal of Irish Archaeology* 20 (2011), 53–63; Cahill Wilson, 'Romans and Roman material in Ireland' (2014), 43–4.

[28] For Ardsallagh 1 and 2, see Linda Clarke and Neil Carlin, 'From focus to locus: a window upon the development of a funerary landscape', in M.B. Deevy and D. Murphy (eds), *Places along the way: first findings on the M3* (Dublin: National Roads Authority. NRA Scheme Monographs 5, 2009), pp 1–20. For Ardsallagh 2, see Clarke and Carlin, 'From focus to locus' (2009), 3–8.

[29] Clarke and Carlin, 'From focus to locus (2009), 8.

[30] For pyres and cremation deposits at Cush, see S.P. Ó Ríordáin, 'Excavations at Cush' (1940), 133–9, 154–6; B. Raftery, 'Iron Age burials in Ireland' (1981), 181. For Rockfield, see Tracy Collins and Linda Lynch, 'Prehistoric burial and ritual in south-west Ireland', *Antiquity* 75 (289) (2001), 493–4. For Ballyvelly, see Laurence Dunne, 'Late Iron Age crematoria at Ballyvelly, Tralee', *Archaeology Ireland* 13 (2) (1999), 10–11. For discussion of pyre sites, see E. O'Brien, *Mapping death* (2020), 14, 28–30. Lorna O'Donnell, 'Into the woods, revealing Ireland's Iron Age woodlands through archaeological charcoal analysis', *Environmental Archaeology* 23, 3 (2015), 240–53.

[31] L. O'Brien, 'Decayed, consumed, dried' (2014), on burial practices in Iron Age Britain. McGarry, 'Late pagan and Early Christian burials in Ireland' (2010), 177; E. O'Brien, *Mapping death* (2020), 34–45, for detailed discussion. On isotopic evidence, see Cahill Wilson *et al.*, 'Strontium and oxygen isotope analysis on Iron Age and Early Historic burials around the great mound at Knowth', in G. Eogan and K. Cleary, *The archaeology of Knowth in the first and second millennia AD* (2012), pp 775–88; Cahill Wilson *et al.*, 'Investigating mobility and migration' (2014); Cahill Wilson and Standish, 'Mobility and migration in Late Iron Age and Early Medieval Ireland', *Journal of Archaeological Science: Reports* 6 (2016), 230–41.

[32] E. O'Brien, 'Burial practices in Ireland' (2003), 65; 'Pagan or Christian?' (2009), 136–8; 'From burial among the ancestors' (2017), 261; and *Mapping death* (2020), 34. Gleeson, 'Reframing the first millennium AD in Ireland' (2022), 95–9.
[33] See discussion in Cahill Wilson, 'Lost in transcription' (2012); relevant discussion also in Maeve Tobin *et al.* 'Punishment in the Iron Age? A case study from Carroweighter, Co. Roscommon', *Journal of Irish Archaeology* 31 (2022), 7–26.
[34] E. O'Brien, *Mapping death* (2020), 19–28.
[35] E. O'Brien, *Mapping death* (2020), 41, table 2.1.
[36] One relevant issue here is the question of periodisation. Here, the Iron Age is defined as beginning at 800 BC, with the Early Iron Age dating from 800 BC to 400 BC. In the literature, however, this period can still be regarded as the Late Bronze Age, with the Iron Age seen as beginning at 600 BC to 400 BC. See, for example, Dowd, *Archaeology of caves* (2015), 161; E. O'Brien, *Mapping death* (2020), 7.
[37] For Dún Aonghasa, see Claire Cotter, *The western stone forts project: excavations at Dún Aonghasa and Dún Eoghanachta* (vol. 2., Dublin: Wordwell. Discovery Programme Monograph, 2012), 196; Ó Donnabháin, 'Human remains', in Cotter, *The western stone forts project* (2012), pp 189–96. For Culleenamore, see Burenhult, *Carrowmore excavations: excavation season 1981* (1981), 21. Katharina Becker and Barra Ó Donnabháin are leading a multidisciplinary project investigating later prehistoric infant burials.
[38] E. O'Brien, *Mapping death* (2020), 46–7.
[39] For Mullamast, see L. Hackett and J. Twomey, N9–N10 Kilcullen to Waterford scheme: phase 3, Kilcullen to Carlow. Archaeological Services Contract No. 5—Resolution, Kilcullen to Moone and Athy Link Road. Final report on archaeological investigations at Site E272, in the townland of Mullamast, Co. Kildare. Unpublished report. (Headland Archaeology for Kildare County Council and the NRA, 2010); E. O'Brien, *Mapping death* (2020), 34. For Parknabinnia, O'Brien, *Mapping death* (2020), 34.
[40] For Robber's Den, see Dowd, *Archaeology of caves* (2015), 127, 143–5.
[41] For Derrymaguirk, see Ó Floinn, 'Recent research into Irish bog bodies' (1995), 140–1; Brindley and Lanting, 'Irish bog bodies' (1995), 134; Wijnand Van der Sanden, *Through nature to eternity: the bog bodies of north west Europe* (Amsterdam: Batavian Lion International, 1996), 96; Giles, *Bog bodies* (2020), 173–4.
[42] J. Eogan, 'Excavation of an unenclosed early medieval cemetery' (2010), 106, 110–11; E. O'Brien, *Mapping death* (2020), 39.
[43] Cahill Wilson *et al.*, 'Investigating mobility and migration' (2014), 139; Cahill Wilson, 'Lost in transcription' (2012), 27.
[44] Cahill Wilson *et al.*, 'Strontium and oxygen isotope analysis' (2012), 782; E. O'Brien, *Mapping death* (2020), 3, 37–40; Giles, *Bog bodies* (2020), 174. See also Cahill and Sikora, *Breaking ground, finding graves* vol. 2 (2011), 113–20, for Late Iron Age inhumation of a young/middle adult woman and an infant, at Rossnaree, Co. Meath.
[45] Giles, *Bog bodies* (2020), 1–11. For different approaches to bog bodies, see Karin Sanders, *Bodies in the bog and the archaeological imagination* (Chicago: University of Chicago Press, 2009); Giles, 'Preserving the body', in Tarlow and Nilsson Stutz (eds), *Oxford handbook of the archaeology of death and burial* (2013), pp 475–96; M.J. Aldhouse-Green, *Bog Bodies uncovered: solving Europe's ancient mystery* (London: Thames and Hudson, 2015); Dolan, 'Beyond elites (2014), 365.

[46] Ó Floinn, 'Recent research into Irish bog bodies' (1995), 140; Brindley and Lanting, 'Irish bog bodies' (1995), 135; Van der Sanden, *Through nature to eternity* (1996), 73; E.P. Kelly, 'An archaeological interpretation of Irish Iron Age bog bodies', in S. Ralph (ed), *The archaeology of violence: interdisciplinary approaches* (New York: State University of New York Press, 2013), pp 232–40, Giles, *Bog bodies* (2020), 184.
[47] M.J. Green, 'The gods and the supernatural', in Green (ed.), *The Celtic world* (London: Routledge, 1995), pp 465–88; G.A. Wait, 'Burial and the otherworld', in Green (ed.), *The Celtic world* (1995), pp 489–511: 495; Aldhouse-Green, *Dying for the Gods. Human sacrifice in Iron Age and Roman Europe* (Stroud: Tempus, 2001); Aldhouse-Green, *Bog Bodies uncovered: solving Europe's ancient mystery* (2015), 180–97. Giles, *Bog bodies* (2020), 210.
[48] The name of the townland is actually Moydrum or Boestown. Giles, *Bog bodies* (2020), 189–92. Isabella Mulhall, pers. comm., for ongoing research on bog bodies.
[49] E.P. Kelly, *Kingship and sacrifice: Iron Age bog bodies and boundaries* (Bray: Wordwell. Archaeology Ireland Heritage Guide 35, 2006); E.P. Kelly, 'An archaeological interpretation of Irish Iron Age bog bodies' (2013); Fintan O'Toole, *A history of Ireland in 100 objects* (Dublin: Royal Irish Academy, 2013), 30; Giles, *Bog bodies* (2020), 192.
[50] E.P. Kelly, *Kingship and sacrifice* (2006); E.P. Kelly, 'An archaeological interpretation of Irish Iron Age bog bodies' (2013); Giles, *Bog bodies* (2020), 189–92. On Suebian knot, see Van der Sanden, *Through nature to eternity* (1996), 91.
[51] E.P. Kelly, *Kingship and sacrifice* (2006); Giles, *Bog bodies* (2020), 107.
[52] Giles, *Bog bodies* (2020), 193.
[53] Tobin *et al.*, 'Punishment in the Iron Age?' (2022), 7–26.
[54] Bryony Coles, 'Anthropomorphic wooden figurines from Britain and Ireland', *Proceedings of the Prehistoric Society* 56 (1990), 315–33; Van der Sanden and Torsten Capelle, *Mosens Guder/Immortal images* (Silkeborg: Silkeborg Museum, 2001).
[55] For Ralaghan, see Adolf Mahr, 'A wooden idol from Ireland', *Antiquity* 4 (1930), 487; Coles, 'Anthropomorphic wooden figurines' (1990), 320–26; Van der Sanden and Capelle, *Mosens Guder/Immortal images* (2001), 57.
[56] For Ballachulish, see Robert Christison, 'On the ancient wooden image, found in November last at Ballachulish Peat Moss', *Proceedings of the Society of Antiquaries of Scotland* 15 (1881), 158–78; Coles, 'Anthropomorphic wooden figurines' (1990), 320; Van der Sanden and Capelle, *Mosens Guder/Immortal images* (2001), 57.
[57] For Corlea figure and wider discussion, see B. Raftery, *Pagan Celtic Ireland* (1994), 186–7; Van der Sanden and Capelle, *Mosens Guder/Immortal images* (2001), 82–3.
[58] For Ballykean and Cloncreen, see Conor McDermott *et al.*, 'Bog standard', *Archaeology Ireland* 17 (4) (2003), 20–23; Michael Stanley, 'Anthropomorphic wooden figures: some recent Irish discoveries', in J. Barber *et al.* (eds), *Archaeology from the wetlands: recent perspectives* (Edinburgh: Society of Antiquaries of Scotland, 2007), pp 183–90; and '"Red Man" of war and death?', *Archaeology Ireland* 26 (2) (2012), 34–7.
[59] For Gortnacrannagh, see E. Campbell and R. Ó Maoldúin, 'Idols, ards and severed heads', *Archaeology Ireland* 139 (2022), pp 14–19.
[60] Helen Roche, 'Excavations at Ráith na Ríg, Tara, Co. Meath, 1997', *Discovery Programme Reports* 6 (2002), 19–82: 45; E. O'Brien, *Mapping death* (2020), 40–1; Cahill Wilson and Standish, 'Mobility and migration' (2016), 233.
[61] Dowling, 'The liminal boundary: an analysis of the sacral potency of the ditch at Ráith na Ríg, Tara, Co. Meath', *Journal of Irish Archaeology* 15 (2006), 15–37: 29–30.

[62] See Grogan, *The Rath of the Synods, Tara, Co. Meath: excavations by Seán P. Ó Ríordáin* (Dublin: Wordwell/UCD School of Archaeology, 2008); Grogan and M. O'Sullivan, 'Radiocarbon dates from the Rath of the Synods', in Grogan, *Rath of the Synods* (2008) pp 141–8; Dowling, 'The architecture of power: an exploration of the origins of closely-spaced multivallate monuments in Ireland', in R. Schot *et al.* (eds), *Landscapes of cult and identity* (Dublin: Four Courts Press, 2011), pp 213–32: 220–2; Cahill Wilson, 'Lost in transcription' (2012), 21–7. For shrines in Iron Age Ireland, see A. O'Connell, *Harvesting the stars* (2013), 57–60, and wider discussion of Lismullin; Richard Clutterbuck, 'Iron Age ritual and settlement at Cookstown, Co. Meath', in Corlett and Potterton (eds), *Life and death in Iron Age Ireland* (2012), pp 35–51; Fintan Walsh, 'Kilmainham 1C sanctuary and burials', in F. Walsh, *The road to Kells: prehistoric archaeology of the M3 Navan to Kells and N52 Kells Bypass road project* (Dublin: TII. TII Heritage 12, 2021), pp 157–61, on sanctuary and associated burials at Kilmainham, Co. Meath; and Gleeson, 'Reframing the first millennium AD in Ireland' (2022), 104–10.
[63] G. Eogan, *The archaeology of Knowth in the first and second millennia AD* (2012), 43.
[64] For discussion of the Knowth cemetery, see Eogan and B. Weekes, 'Late Iron Age burials', in *Archaeology of Knowth in the first and second millennia AD* (2012), pp 13–44; see also Eogan, 'Prehistoric and early historic culture change at Brugh na Bóinne', *Proceedings of the Royal Irish Academy* 91C (1991), 105–32: 118–20; Cooney, 'Icons of antiquity' (2015), 66–8; E. O'Brien, *Mapping death* (2020), 36–9.
[65] B. Raftery, *Pagan Celtic Ireland* (1994), 195–6; Eogan and Weekes, 'Late Iron Age burials' (2012), 23–6; E. O'Brien, *Mapping death* (2020), 37–8; Giles, *Bog bodies* (2020), 212. On skulls and decapitation, see discussion in Giles, *Bog bodies* (2020), 188–95, referring to Armit, *Headhunting and the body in Iron Age Europe* (Cambrige: Cambridge University Press, 2012) and 'Headhunting and social power in Iron Age Europe', in Moore and Armada (eds), *Atlantic Europe in the first millennium BC* (Oxford: Oxford University Press, 2012), pp 590–607, with particular reference to Armit's point in 'Headhunting and social power', 591, that decapitation almost always concerns social power.
[66] Cahill Wilson *et al.*, 'Strontium and oxygen isotope analysis' (2012).
[67] See O'Brien and Bhreathnach, 'Burial in Early Medieval Ireland' (2013), 42–4, on social context of Knowth burials. On Romanisation, see Cahill Wilson, 'Romans and Roman material in Ireland' (2014), 43–4; Cooney, 'Icons of antiquity' (2015), 68–70.
[68] R.A.S. Macalister, 'On some antiquities discovered on Lambay', *Proceedings of the Royal Irish Academy* 38C (1929), 240–46; Etienne Rynne, 'The La Tène and Roman finds from Lambay, County Dublin: a reassessment', in Colloquium on Hiberno-Roman relations and material remains, *Proceedings of the Royal Irish Irish Academy* 76C (1976), 231–44; B. Raftery, *Pagan Celtic Ireland* (1994), 200–03; Cahill Wilson *et al.*, 'Investigations on Lambay, Co. Dublin', in 'Late Iron Age and "Roman" Ireland', *Discovery Programme Reports* 8 (2014), 91–112. Linda Fibiger, pers. comm. on Lambay paleodemography.
[69] Cahill Wilson *et al.*, 'Investigations on Lambay' (2014), 110. For ongoing research at Drumanagh, see C. Baker, 'Digging Drumanagh', *Archaeology Ireland* 33 (1) (2019), 26–9.
[70] Bartlett, *Ireland: a history* (2010), 1, states that the first authentic date in Irish history is AD 431, when it is recorded that Palladius was sent as the first bishop to Ireland. But see Ó Carragáin, *Churches in the Irish landscape* (2021), 12, that the idea of a stark cultural or religious divide at AD 400 is no longer tenable.

[71] See discussion in Ó Carragáin, 'From family cemeteries to community cemeteries' (2010); A. O'Sullivan *et al.*, *Early Medieval Ireland AD 400–1100* (2014), chapter 8; E. O'Brien, *Mapping death* (2020). For the relevance of the comparative complexity of burial in early medieval Scotland, see Adrián Maldonado, 'Burial in early medieval Scotland: new questions', *Medieval Archaeology* 57 (2013), 1–34. For explicit call for recognition of the agency of the living and the dead in these processes, see Gleeson, 'Reframing the first millennium AD in Ireland' (2022).
[72] Gleeson and McLaughlin, 'Ways of death' (2021), fig. 3.
[73] On isotopic evidence, see Cahill Wilson *et al.*, 'Investigating mobility and migration' (2014); Cahill Wilson and Standish, 'Mobility and migration in Later Iron Age and Early Medieval Ireland' (2016). On pottery, see Doyle, 'Mediterranean and Frankish pottery imports in early medieval Ireland', *Journal of Irish Archaeology* 18 (2009), 17–62; A.M. Kelly, 'The discovery of Phocaean Red slip-ware (PRSW) form 3 and Bii ware (LR1 amphorae) on sites in Ireland: an analysis within a broader framework', *Proceedings of the Royal Irish Academy* 110C (2010), 35–88. See discussion in A. O'Sullivan *et al.*, *Early Medieval Ireland AD 400–1100* (2014), 320–5.
[74] Gleeson and McLaughlin, 'Ways of death' (2021), 387. Ó Carragáin, *Churches in the Irish landscape* (2021), 15–16.
[75] Moriarty, 'Knockgraffon, Co. Tipperary. Ring-barrow Site 143.3' (2009), 170–2, 176–7; McQuade and Molloy, 'Recent Iron Age discoveries' (2012), 180. For Ballinorig West, see Hession and Troy, 'The Iron Age: grain, ore and death' (2020), 140.
[76] E. O'Brien, *Mapping death* (2020), 45–6.
[77] E. O'Brien, *Mapping death* (2020), 49.
[78] Wilmot, 'Three burial sites at Carbury, Co. Kildare', *Journal of the Royal Society of Antiquaries of Ireland* 68 (1938), 130–42; Cahill Wilson and Standish, 'Mobility and migration in Later Iron Age and Early Medieval Ireland' (2016), 237–8; E. O'Brien, *Mapping death* (2020), 77–9.
[79] E. O'Brien, *Mapping death* (2020), chapter 4; Gleeson, 'Reframing the first millennium AD in Ireland' (2022), 94–9. Ó Carragáin, *Churches in the Irish landscape* (2021), 17–29.
[80] Gerry Mullins, 'Pagan or Christian? Excavation of a hilltop cemetery at Cross, Co. Galway', in O'Sullivan and Stanley (eds), *New routes to the past* (2007), pp 101–10; Mullins and Bermingham, 'Ring-ditches with cremations and inhumations at Cross', in J. McKeon and J. O'Sullivan (eds), *The quiet landscape: archaeological investigations on the M6 Galway to Ballinasloe national road scheme* (Dublin: National Roads Authority. NRA Monographs 15, 2014), pp 100–05; E. O'Brien, *Mapping death* (2020), 87–8, on *ferta*, 64–82.
[81] Ian Russell, 'The excavation of an Iron Age site at Claristown, Co. Meath', in Corlett and Potterton (eds), *Life and death in Iron Age Ireland* (2012), 267–72; E. O'Brien, *Mapping death* (2020), 41–2.
[82] Clarke and Carlin, 'From focus to locus' (2009), 8–20; E. O'Brien, *Mapping death* (2020), 90–1, 148–9.
[83] Ó Carragáin, 'From family cemeteries to community cemeteries' (2010), 217–18. In *Churches in the Irish landscape* (2021), 25, Ó Carragáin argues that the relative inclusivity of these sites represents an important expansion in ideas about who could be accorded formal burial. See detail and discussion of Ranelagh, Co. Roscommon in S. Delaney and

E. Murphy, *The forgotten cemetery: excavations at Ranelagh, Co. Roscommon* (Dublin: TII. TII Heritage 13, 2022).

[84] Lehane *et al.*, 'Three cemetery-settlement excavations at Carrowkeel, Treanbaun and Owenbristy' (2010).

[85] Lehane *et al.*, 'Three cemetery-settlement excavations at Carrowkeel, Treanbaun and Owenbristy' (2010), 143–7; Marta Muñiz Pérez, 'A Bronze Age lead-mine, cist burials and a ditched cemetery-settlement enclosure at Treanbaun', in McKeon and J. O'Sullivan (eds), *The quiet landscape* (2014) 130–4.

[86] Brendon Wilkins and Susan Lalonde, 'An early medieval settlement/cemetery at Carrowkeel, Co. Galway', *Journal of Irish Archaeology* 17 (2009), 57–83; Lehane *et al.*, 'Three cemetery-settlement excavations at Carrowkeel, Treanbaun and Owenbristy' (2010), 139–43.

[87] Lehane *et al.*, 'Three cemetery-settlement excavations at Carrowkeel, Treanbaun and Owenbristy' (2010), 147–52; Finn Delaney and Zachary Silke, 'Owenbristy: towards an understanding', in F. Delaney and J. Tierney, *In the lowlands of south Galway: archaeological excavations on the N18 Oranmore to Gort national road scheme* (Dublin: National Roads Authority. NRA Scheme Monographs 7, 2011), pp 98–109.

[88] Seaver (ed.), *Meitheal: the archaeology of lives, labours and beliefs at Raystown, Co. Meath* (Dublin: Transport Infrastructure Ireland. TII Heritage 4, 2016).

[89] Seaver (ed.), *Meitheal* (2016); Fibiger *et al.*, 'Population, death and burial', in Seaver (ed.), *Meitheal* (2016), pp 61–85: 77–85; Seaver, The significance of Raystown', in Seaver (ed.), *Meitheal* (2016), pp 161–71: 168.

[90] Ó Carragáin, 'From family cemeteries to community cemeteries' (2010), 218–19; Gleeson, 'Reframing the first millennium AD in Ireland' (2022), 99.

[91] Roy Flechner, *Saint Patrick retold: the legend and history of Ireland's patron saint* (Princeton: Princeton University Press, 2019), chapter 5.

[92] Cahill Wilson, 'Romans and Roman material in Ireland' (2014), 45–50; Bhreathnach, *Ireland in the medieval world AD 400–1000* (2014), 152–62.

[93] A. O'Sullivan *et al.*, *Early Medieval Ireland AD 400–1100* (2014), 320–2; Sheehan, 'A peacock's tale: excavations at Caherlehillan, Iveragh, Ireland', in N. Edwards (ed.), *The archaeology of the early medieval Celtic churches* (2009), pp 191–206; Bhreathnach, *Ireland in the medieval world AD 400–1000* (2014), 162–7.

[94] Ó Carragáin, *Churches in the Irish landscape* (2021), 14. Ó hÓgáin, *Myth, legend and romance* (1999), 201–7, 210–16.

[95] E. O'Brien, *Mapping death* (2020), 49–50, 54–7.

[96] A.L. Meaney, 'Anglo-Saxon pagan and early Christian attitudes to the dead', in M. Carver (ed), *The cross goes north* (Woodbridge; Boydell, 2003), pp 229–41: 238.

[97] Gleeson and McLaughlin, 'Ways of death' (2021). For Ask, see Stevens, 'Burial and ritual in late prehistory in north Wexford' (2007); and 'Burial and ritual in early medieval north Wexford' (2012).

[98] Dunlop and Barkley, *Road to the west: the archaeology of the A4/A5 road improvement scheme from Dungannon to Ballygawley* (Belfast: Northern Archaeological Consultancy, 2016), 103–5, 127–31.

[99] Gleeson and McLaughlin, 'Ways of death' (2021), 390–6; Ó Carragáin, *Churches in the Irish landscape* (2021), 16–17

[100] On excarnation, see Michael Connolly *et al.*, *Underworld? Death and burial in Cloghermore cave. Co. Kerry* (Bray: Wordwell, 2005), 166–76; Dowd, *Archaeology of caves* (2015), 204–5. See E. O'Brien, *Mapping death* (2020), chapter 4 on cemeteries.
[101] Ó Carragáin, 'The architectural setting of the cult of relics in early medieval Ireland', *Journal of the Royal Society of Antiquaries of Ireland* 133 (2003), 130–76; and 'From family cemeteries to community cemeteries' (2010), 222–3.
[102] E. O'Brien, *Mapping death* (2020), 196–200.
[103] E. O'Brien, 'Burial practices in Ireland' (2003), 69; *Mapping Death* (2020), 14.
[104] Ó Carragáin, 'From family cemeteries to community cemeteries' (2010), 218–21.
[105] Clarke and Carlin, 'Living with the dead at Johnstown 1: an enclosed burial, settlement and industrial site', in Carlin *et al.*, *The archaeology of life and death in the Boyne Floodplain* (2008), pp 55–86: 59–70; L. Clarke, 'Johnstown 1, Co. Meath: a multi-period burial, settlement and industrial site', in Corlett and Potterton (eds), *Death and burial in early medieval Ireland* (2010), pp 61–75; Fibiger *et al.*, 'The social and economic context of the enclosures', in Carlin, *et al.* (eds), *Archaeology of life and death in the Boyne Floodplain* (2008), pp 113–28.
[106] McGahern, 'Saving Grace', *The Guardian* 8 April 2006.

Chapter 8

[1] Valeria Luiselli, *Lost children archive* (London: 4th Estate, 2019), 215.
[2] With thanks to AMS, particulary Paddy Walsh, and to Transport Infrastructure Ireland for details of Ballaghcullia; see Walsh *et al.*, N5 Ballaghaderreen to Scramoge Road Project Stage (iii). Post-excavation assessment report: Ballaghcullia 3. (Archaeological Management Solutions (AMS) Ltd, prepared for TII and Roscommon County Council, 2022).
[3] Nuala Johnson, *Ireland, the Great War and the geography of remembrance* (Cambridge: Cambridge University Press, 2003); Shane Mac Thomáis, *Glasnevin: Ireland's Necropolis* (Dublin: Glasnevin Trust, 2010); John Horne and Edward Madigan (eds), *Towards commemoration: Ireland in war and revolution 1912–1923* (Dublin: Royal Irish Academy, 2013); Euan O'Halpin and Daithí Ó Corráin, *The dead of the Irish revolution* (London: Yale University Press, 2020).
[4] For fictional accounts, see, for example, Anne Griffin, *Listening still* (London: Sceptre, 2021); Damon Galgut, *The promise* (London: Chatto and Windus, 2021); Elif Shafak, *10 Minutes 38 Seconds in this strange world* (London: Penguin/Viking, 2019). On traditional funerary rites, see Anne Ridge, *Death customs in rural Ireland* (Dublin: Arlen House, 2009). On the modern Irish way of death, see Ann Marie Hourihane, *Sorry for your trouble: the Irish way of death* (Dublin: Penguin/Sandycove, 2021).
[5] Khaled Khalifa, *Death is hard work* (London: Faber and Faber, 2019); Gillian O'Brien, *The darkness echoing: exploring Ireland's places of famine, death and rebellion* (London: Doubleday Ireland, 2020); Mark O'Connell, *To be a machine* (London: Granta, 2017).
[6] Department of Children, Equality, Disability, Integration and Youth, *Final Report of the Commission of Investigation into Mother and Babies Homes* (Dublin: Government

Publications, 2021). Also, Catherine Corless, *Belonging: one woman's search for truth and justice for the Tuam Babies* (Dublin: Hachette Ireland, 2021).

[7] Karina Croucher *et al.*, 'Archaeology and contemporary death: using the past to provoke, challenge and engage', *PloS One* 15 (12): e0244058 (2020): doi.org/10.1371/journal.pone.0244058; Buster *et al.*, 'From plastered skulls to palliative care: what can the past teach us about dealing with death?' *AP: Online Journal in Public Archaeology* special volume 3 (2018), 249–76.

[8] A. McGrath and M. Shortall, 'Has pandemic changed how we conduct funerals?', *The Irish Times*, 2 November 2021.

[9] Ó Carragáin, 'From family cemeteries to community cemeteries' (2010).

[10] Cooper *et al.*, *Grave goods* (2022).

[11] Louise Erdrich, *The painted drum* (New York: Harper Perennial, 2005), 28.

[12] Thomas Lynch, from the poem, 'At the opening of Oak Grove Cemetery Bridge', in *The undertaking: life studies from the dismal trade* (London: Jonathan Cape, 1997), 138. As an example of a long-term use of place from Galloway, Scotland, see Warren Baillie *et al.*, *Dunragit—the prehistoric heart of Galloway* (Glasgow: Guard Archaeology Ltd, 2021), 266–72.

[13] M. O'Sullivan, 'Megalithic tombs and storied landscapes' (2011); Morris, 'Megalithic exegesis' (1974); W. O'Brien, *Sacred ground* (1999), 207–10; Ó Crualaoich, *Book of the Cailleach* (2003).

[14] Brück and Booth, 'The power of relics' (2022), 457. On dying when our name is spoken for the last time, see, for example, David Eagleman, *Sum: forty tales from the afterlives* (Edinburgh: Canongate, 2009), 23.

[15] George Orwell, *Nineteen Eighty-Four* (originally published 1949, London: Secker and Warburg; London: Penguin pocket edition, 1954), 34–5.

[16] For example Cooney, 'Icons of antiquity' (2015).

[17] On the significance of the head, see B. Raftery, *Pagan Celtic Ireland* (1994), 185.

[18] On the Maori phrase, see Janet Davidson, *The prehistory of New Zealand* (Auckland: Longman Paul, 1984).

[19] P.C. Rosenblatt, 'Grief in small-scale societies', in C.M. Parkes *et al.* (eds), *Death and bereavement across cultures* (London: Routledge, 1997), pp 27–51: 31–3.

[20] E. O'Brien, *Mapping death* (2020).

[21] As examples of integrated research projects, see S. Delaney and E. Murphy, *The forgotten cemetery* (2022) on the Ranelagh, Co. Roscommon settlement-cemetery; and The Passage Tomb People project led by Dr Jessica Smyth (UCD). On the value of theoretically informed approaches, see Gleeson, 'Reframing the first millennium AD in Ireland' (2022).

[22] ICOMOS, Climate Change and Cultural Heritage Working Group, *The future of our pasts: engaging cultural heritage in climate action* (Paris: ICOMOS, 2019); Rachel Clarke, *Dear life: a doctor's story of love and loss* (2020), 101.

[23] Tarlow and Nilsson Stutz, *Oxford handbook of the archaeology of death and burial* (2013), 2–3.

LIST OF ILLUSTRATIONS AND PLATES

FIGURES

Chapter 1

Chapter 2

Chapter 3

Chapter 4

Chapter 5

Chapter 6

Chapter 7

PLATES

Chapter 1

Pl. 1.A. Archaeologists excavating an Early Bronze Age cist burial at Tevrin, Co. Westmeath in 2019 (photo: Colm Flynn Archaeology Ltd, courtesy of Transport Infrastructure Ireland).

Pl. 1.B. Zen Buddhist cemetery, the temple of Ryosokuin, Kyoto, Japan (photo: Gabriel Cooney).

Pl. 1.C. The Erico Production coffin-making workshop in Accra, Ghana (photo: Sally Hayden).

Pl. 1.D. Newgrange passage tomb, Brú na Bóinne, Co. Meath, with satellite passage tombs, pit enclosure and Great Stone Circle, from the south-east (photo: © Photographic Archive, National Monuments Service, Government of Ireland).

Pl. 1.E. The ring-barrow at Kilmahuddrick, Dublin after excavation, viewed from the west (from Ian W. Doyle, 'A prehistoric ring-barrow in Kilmahuddrick, Co. Dublin, *Archaeology Ireland* 15 (4) (2001), 16–19; photo: Ian Doyle).

Pl. 1.F. Cairn T, Loughcrew, Co. Meath, and the cluster of passage tombs on Carnbane East, at the centre of the Loughcrew cemetery, from the north-east (© Photographic Archive, National Monuments Service, Government of Ireland).

Pl. 1.G. The ring-ditch cemetery at Ask, Co. Wexford under excavation, looking south-east towards Ask Hill (from Paul Stevens (2007), illus. 3; photo: Valerie J. Keeley Ltd, courtesy of Transport Infrastructure Ireland).

Chapter 2

Pl. 2.A. Annaghmare, Co. Armagh court tomb (photo: Ken Williams).

Pl. 2. B. A Balinese Hindu ceremonial placement of cremated bone in the sea, near Goa Lawah, Bali, Indonesia (photo: Gabriel Cooney).

Pl. 2.C. Palaeopathologies in the skeletal assemblage from Poulnabrone, Co. Clare portal tomb. I– dental enamel hypoplasia, II– adult left talus (ankle) bone with sheen (eburnation) as a result of abrasion of cartilage, III– depressed fracture to cranium of an younger or middle-aged adult, IV– dorsal view of right hip bone of an adult with embedded tip of projectile point (from Barra Ó Donnabháin and Mara Tesorieri, in Ann Lynch (2014), pls 4.4, 4.9, 4.15 and 4.16; photos: © Photographic Archive, National Monuments Service, Government of Ireland).

Pl. 2.D. A well-healed, perforating traumatic injury on the left side of the lower mandible of a Neolithic adult female probably over 25 years old, from Kilgreany Cave, Co. Waterford. Likely to have been caused by horizontal penetration with a sharp object (from Linda Fibiger, in Marion Dowd (2016), pl. 9; photo: Linda Fibiger).

Chapter 3

Chapter 4

Chapter 5

Chapter 6

Chapter 7

Chapter 8

INDEX

Pages in italics refer to *figures*, pages in bold to **plates**